Royals of England

Royals of England

◆

A Guide for
Readers, Travelers, and Genealogists

Kathleen Spaltro and Noeline Bridge

To Bob,

Very best wishes & regards,

Noeline.

iUniverse, Inc.
New York Lincoln Shanghai

Royals of England
A Guide for Readers, Travelers, and Genealogists

iUniverse books may be ordered through booksellers or by contacting:

iUniverse
2021 Pine Lake Road, Suite 100
Lincoln, NE 68512
www.iuniverse.com
1-800-Authors (1-800-288-4677)

An earlier version of the chapter on Lady Margaret Beaufort (© 1997 by Kathleen Spaltro) appeared in *Ricardian Register* (Winter 1997), the publication of the Richard III Society, American Branch, which also featured it on its website (www.r3.org).

ISBN-13: 978-0-595-37312-3 (pbk)
ISBN-13: 978-0-595-81711-5 (ebk)
ISBN-10: 0-595-37312-7 (pbk)
ISBN-10: 0-595-81711-4 (ebk)

Printed in the United States of America

To my parents, and to my husband

—Kathleen Spaltro

To my mother and my husband

—Noeline Bridge

Contents

Authors' Preface

Most books for travelers that discuss sites of historical significance scatter the information, making it difficult for the traveler to integrate material presented out of context. The books do this because their organization stresses geographic locales. However, a travel reference book organized by persons rather than places would integrate the biographical and historical information for the user, especially if the book sorts the persons chronologically. A detailed geographic index (in addition to a personal name index) would allow the traveler to plan visits to neighboring sites with ease. In other words, the chapters group together the places associated with a particular person, whereas the geographic index groups together the people associated with a particular place.

This book presents 42 profiles of members of royal houses that ruled England from William the Conqueror through Victoria and Albert. Each profile includes a readable, lively, yet well-informed account of one or more royal personages. In each section, following the profile, appears an account of sites associated with the person(s) in England, Scotland, Ireland, France, Germany, Italy, and elsewhere. This account also includes websites from which the user could gain detailed and up-to-date information as well as notes about statuary and portraits.

Following each of the 42 profiles, travel information presented for both the actual and the virtual traveler includes URLs for online visiting. **Sites** comprises information regarding places associated with each personage. Noeline would like to hear of others she may have missed; contact her by e-mail at nbridge@nb.sympatico.ca. All information in these sections was current as of time of writing; every effort was made to ensure this, along with accuracy of information, and the authors can assume no responsibility for missing or inaccurate information. Websites tend to come and go, and only those that seemed likely to stay were included, which, alas, necessitated the exclusion of some personal websites containing beautiful photographs. Readers of this book are encouraged to pursue their own interests further by searching the Web themselves as well as exploring the list of suggested reading inserted before the indexes.

In addition, each chapter features one or more genealogical trees, all of them intended to explicate the chapters in which they appear. (Please note that dates may vary among sources, for many dates—especially those most remote in time—derive from inference, not from explicit documentation.) The 42 profiles include some people who never ruled England but whose lives remain part of the history of the English monarchy from 1066 to 1901. These include Maud the Empress and her daughter-in-law Eleanor of Aquitaine; Edward III's sons Edward the Black Prince and John of Gaunt; Henry V's widow Catherine of Valois and her Tudor progeny; Edmund Tudor's wife Margaret Beaufort, mother of Henry VII; Henry VIII's six Queens; Mary Queen of Scots; and the Old Pretender and his sons. (Chapters originally included on Elizabeth Woodville, Elizabeth of Bohemia, and the children of George III were dropped because of space limitations.) A 43th chapter explains the genealogical bases for the intermittent civil war later named the Wars of the Roses.

The focus on the monarchs who have ruled England from 1066 to 1901 provides a narrative stream from which flow many tributaries. The reader may select any chapter to read out of order, for each profile tells its story in a self-contained way. If the profile mentions a topic but does not dwell upon it, a glance at the personal names index may uncover a lengthier discussion in another profile. (For example, the chapter on Edward III mentions the Hundred Years War, but the profile of his sons Edward the Black Prince and John of Gaunt narrates the progress of the conflict with much greater specificity.) Please note that, despite the wide scope of this book, it does *not* include sovereigns of England before 1066, Kings of Scotland before Mary Queen of Scots, or any native rulers of Wales or Ireland. In addition, when referring to the royal titles of James I, Charles I, Charles II, James II, William III and Mary II, it uses "Great Britain" to refer to the separate Kingdoms of England and Scotland ruled by a single sovereign. While this "Union of Crowns" began with the accession of James VI of Scotland to the throne of England in 1603, the "Union of Parliaments" that unified Scotland and England into a single Kingdom of Great Britain took place in 1707 during the reign of Queen Anne. After Edward I conquered Wales, it lost its status as a separate Principality in 1284. During the reign of Henry II of England, his son Prince (later King) John became Lord of Ireland in 1185, and John's successors bore that title until Henry VIII changed it to King of Ireland.

Besides providing a flow of narrative, the focus on the royals of England also displays an infinite variety of human personality in all its perfidy and valor. The profiles' opinionated interpretation of character intends to provide a starting point for discussion, discovery, and cordial disagreement about these fascinating people. Whether or not, as Ralph Waldo Emerson wrote, "An institution is the lengthened shadow of one man;…and all history resolves itself very easily into the biography of a few stout and earnest persons," the lengthened shadow of England's royal family comes very near to being a history of England itself.

◆   ◆   ◆

The writer of the profiles as well as the compiler of the family trees, Kathleen Spaltro came up with the concept for this book after recent travel to Italy prompted her to realize that the travel books she consulted scattered biographical and historical information too widely to allow her to achieve much clarity. A writer, editor, indexer, proofreader, and teacher of professional writing for a quarter-century, Kathleen Spaltro most recently edited *Genealogy and Indexing* for Information Today, Inc. (ISBN 1-57387-163-X). She earned a doctorate in English literature in 1981. Immersion in English literature naturally familiarized her with British history and biography. She has published short biographical analyses of Flannery O'Connor and Etty Hillesum. You may reach her at kathleen.spaltro@gmail.com.

The writer of the Sites sections and compiler of the indexes, Noeline Bridge wrote a pivotal chapter about names indexing for *Genealogy and Indexing* and an appendix, "Using the Internet," to the 3rd edition of Hazel Bell's *Indexing Biographies*. A librarian and professional indexer, she has presented workshops and published articles on the indexing of names, including royal and geographical names. As an armchair traveler, she has collected travel brochures, maps, and guidebooks, and she has devoured library books on travel. Besides her actual journeys, the Internet has enabled her to become a keen virtual traveler. The several nonfiction pieces she has published include an account of her visit to the Dead Sea, the First Prize winner in the 2000 competition of the Writers' Federation of New Brunswick. You may reach her at nbridge@nb.sympatico.ca.

Acknowledgments

Kathleen Spaltro

Richard Hugunine provided advice from his knowledge of computers, as well as offsite backup for files and artistry for the necessary manipulation of images. His constant interest in the project heartened me, as did the ready support of Susan Bosanko. Sue offered much help and counsel with great generosity. Ian Watt's incisive editorial opinions improved the book's quality. The librarians at the Woodstock [Illinois] Public Library displayed much resourcefulness and patience as they secured for me the many books I requested on interlibrary loan.

Wendy Moorhen helped me to track down John Ashdown-Hill, whose scholarly opinions about the Lancastrian claims to the throne illuminate chapter 15. Laura Blanchard listed for me what she considered the most dispassionate discussions of Richard III. Earlier, Laura had asked me to research and write an article on Lady Margaret Beaufort; the resulting biographical sketch engendered this book. So did an online article I wrote for Illya D'Addezio on "royal genes." Cheryl Rothwell checked some genealogical data for me and read a draft of the chapter on Edward V and Richard III.

Reverend Paul Milarvie, Vice Rector of the Pontifical Scots College in Rome, allowed my husband to photograph the three original tombstones of the Jacobite Kings that once graced their graves in St. Peter's but now hang in the College crypt. He also secured permission for us to use those photographs and told us how to get to other sites in Frascati associated with "Henry IX."

Other valued friends and associates who answered questions and provided support as well as advice include Linda Aaavang, John Bryans, Rachel Corneilia Dixon, Lindsey Halpern-Givens, Donald Hoffman, Richard Kieckhefer, Stacey Kirsch, Steve Krause, Cyndy Letteri, Deborah McCormick, Nell Logan, Joel Schorn, Howard Voeks, and Carolyn Young. The interest displayed by my sisters, Karen Earley and Kristina Spaltro, and by my niece, Janine Earley, also encouraged me. Benefactors more remote in time include my history teacher in high school, Joan McCracken of Villa Maria Academy in Malvern, Pennsylvania; a college mentor and English literature professor, Sister Marie Eugenie, I.H.M., of Immaculata College in Immaculata, Pennsylvania; and an 18th-century scholar and graduate school professor, Jean Hagstrum of Northwestern University in Evanston, Illinois. All three fostered my love of learning, my scholarship, and my writing, as well as served as models for excellence in teaching.

My dear husband, John Daab, read the book in various drafts and encouraged me throughout its development. I could not imagine any better collaborator than Noeline Bridge, whose emails and computer files constantly delighted me.

Noeline Bridge

I thank my mother for having aroused my interest in royal history and British and European architecture at an early age. Also, thanks go to Auntie Rene and her daughter, my cousin Rosalie Menzies, for having encouraged my interest in writing, also at an early age. Many thanks go to Ian Watt, a supportive cousin in all ways, but one who took a special interest in this book, providing needed encouragement. Jeanne-Marie Lawrence, in Leicester, provided splendid hospitality, along with valuable help in finding locales and taking photographs I was otherwise unable to obtain, and following up with some research I needed. Jonathan Booth, in Cardiff, also provided hospitality and took follow-up photographs for this book. John McArthur, in Epsom, generously hosted me as I used his house as a hotel. Finally, I wish to thank my husband Dave Alston, who chauffeured me around Britain and helped lug cameras up steep flights of stone steps, as well as locating some venues I'd otherwise missed. His advice and encouragement are always welcome, and his expertise with computer-related matters has been invaluable.

Normans

William the Conqueror and William Rufus

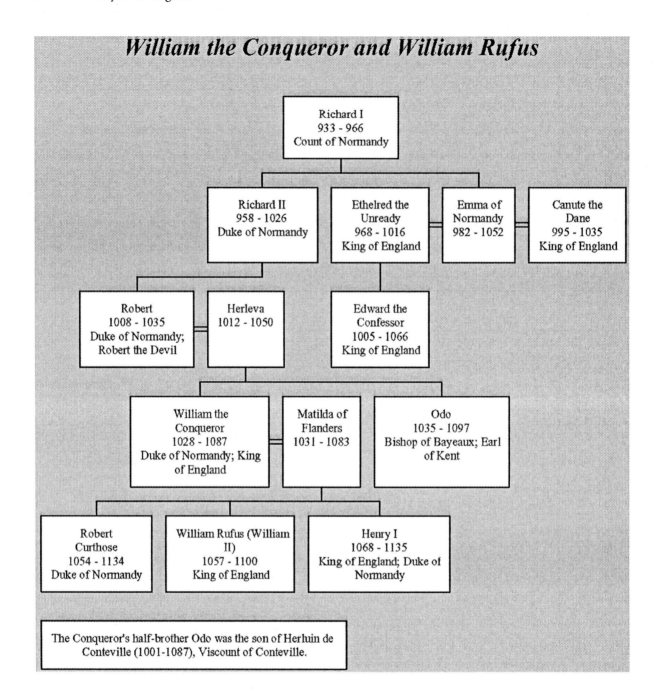

Richard I
933 - 966
Count of Normandy

Richard II
958 - 1026
Duke of Normandy

Ethelred the
Unready
968 - 1016
King of England

Emma of
Normandy
982 - 1052

Canute the
Dane
995 - 1035
King of England

Robert
1008 - 1035
Duke of Normandy;
Robert the Devil

Herleva
1012 - 1050

Edward the
Confessor
1005 - 1066
King of England

William the
Conqueror
1028 - 1087
Duke of Normandy; King
of England

Matilda of
Flanders
1031 - 1083

Odo
1035 - 1097
Bishop of Bayeaux; Earl
of Kent

Robert
Curthose
1054 - 1134
Duke of Normandy

William Rufus (William
II)
1057 - 1100
King of England

Henry I
1068 - 1135
King of England; Duke of
Normandy

The Conqueror's half-brother Odo was the son of Herluin de
Conteville (1001-1087), Viscount of Conteville.

William the Conqueror (1028–1087; reigned as Duke of Normandy, 1035–1087 and as King of England, 1066–1087)

Famous to posterity as William the Conqueror, he was known to his contemporaries as William the Bastard because of his illegitimate birth to Herleve of Falaise and Robert I, Duke of Normandy. His father secured the Duchy of Normandy for William, despite his illegitimacy, and he succeeded as Duke in 1035 at the age of seven. Having surmounted the many dangers and difficulties that threatened him both within and from without Normandy, William in 1051 won the hand of Matilda of Flanders, daughter of Count Baldwin V and granddaughter of the French King Robert the Pious. Successful in his domination both of Normandy and of his neighbors, William eventually invaded England in 1066 to press his claim upon the English crown. He defeated the much-respected English sovereign, Harold II, whom the witan or King's council had elected King. William the Bastard thereby by right of conquest inaugurated an hereditary monarchy that displaced the Anglo-Saxon elective monarchy. This royal line (which excludes bastards from the succession) has continued to reign to this day—despite the periodic hiccup of an usurpation like William's own.

The English had elected Harold Godwineson, not the foreigner William of Normandy, as their King. The dying King Edward the Confessor had indicated Harold as his chosen successor. In addition, William had no shadow of any valid hereditary claim. Nevertheless, he carefully cast himself as the rightful successor to King Edward, named Harold as the usurper, and gained papal support for his invasion and subjugation of England to his will.

The background to William's claim to the English crown includes the history of Viking intrusions shared by Normandy and England. The Vikings had conquered much of England in the 9th century, resisted successfully only by Wessex, from which Alfred the Great and his successors eventually subjugated the Scandinavian holdings in the 10th century. Also in the early 10th century, the Viking Rollo (William's ancestor) settled in Rouen. A hundred years later, Rollo's descendant and William's grandfather, Richard II, ruled as Duke of Normandy. The Duke's sister Emma married the English King Ethelred the Unready. In 1013, Ethelred and Emma fled from a Danish invasion of England to Normandy, bringing their children with them—among them their son Edward (later King Edward the Confessor). Edward would remain in Normandy until 1041. After Ethelred and Emma returned to England without their children, Ethelred resumed his rule, only to face defeat by the Dane Canute. The widowed Emma married Canute in 1017.

William of Normandy based his claim to succeed Edward the Confessor partly on his blood relationship to his great-aunt Queen Emma and partly on a promise Edward the Confessor supposedly made to William in 1051. Ten years earlier, Edward had returned to England as King. Godwine, Earl of Wessex, however, ruled in Edward's name, and Edward even married Godwine's daughter, Edith. After exiling Godwine and his family in 1051, Edward may have promised the succession to his first cousin once removed, William of Normandy, but he had no right to do so. Godwine returned to power in 1052, and in the next year Harold Godwineson became Earl of Wessex. Harold, like his father before him, actually ruled during Edward's reign. The dying Edward indicated that he preferred Harold as his successor, and the witan later elected Harold as King.

Being a mere Queen Consort, Emma of Normandy could not convey any hereditary claim to the throne. Nor could Edward the Confessor do more than indicate a preference to the witan, much less actually promise the crown. William's rage when he learned of Harold Godwineson's succession as Harold II really had no sound basis, as he perhaps discovered when he consulted Lanfranc, whom he had appointed abbot of St. Stephen's Abbey in Caen in 1063 and who had advised William since the late 1040s. Lanfranc may have suggested that William seek papal support for his invasion on the grounds that William sought to protect the interests of the English Church. Not only had the current Pope, Alexander II, formerly studied under Lanfranc at Bec, but they also gained support from a powerful force at the papal court, Hildebrand (later Pope Gregory VII). No one argued Harold's case there.

With the papal blessing strengthening his weak claim and overpowering Harold's valid one, William prepared to invade England. He chafed at the delays created by the weather. Harold, on his side of the Channel, waited for three months with an army that he eventually disbanded so that the men could return to their domestic responsibilities after William's crossing seemed unlikely. Harold then discovered that Harald Hardrada of Norway had invaded in the North of England. Having defeated the English at the Battle of Gate Fulford, Harald Hardrada was surprised to encounter Harold of England, who then won the Battle of Stamford Bridge against the Norsemen. Meanwhile, the south wind blew for William of Normandy, allowing his crossing. A few days after his victory in the North, Harold learned of this second invasion.

Harold raced back with his exhausted men to meet William at Hastings. William, who claimed that Harold had actually sworn in 1064 to advocate William's right to the witan, now had a papal blessing for his invasion as well as the threat of excommunication for those who fought for Harold. Although advised to wait for reinforcements, Harold took his stand against William at the Battle of Senlac (near Hastings) on 14 October. The Norman invaders eventually overwhelmed the Anglo-Saxon defenders. Harold's lover and the mother of his children, Edith Swan's Neck, identified his butchered remains.

Stunned by the loss of their King, the English soon succumbed—with Canterbury, Winchester, and London surrendering and the English bishops interpreting the defeat as God's punishment. William took the crown on Christmas Day 1066 at his coronation in Westminster Abbey. Revolts soon began, however, and continued intermittently for six years. Subduing his English rebels, William also fought off a Danish invasion in 1069–70, devastating the North to discourage English support for the Danes.

William solidified his hold on England by confiscating from the Anglo-Saxon aristocracy most of their estates, which he then awarded to his Norman magnates. More than 80 Norman castles protected them from the natives. Control of the English Church also passed to Norman churchmen, among them Lanfranc, appointed Archbishop of Canterbury in 1070. The Domesday Book of 1086 itemized the wealth of England so that William might more efficiently exploit its riches through taxation. The English also resented William's making the New Forest in Hampshire a royal hunting preserve.

While the new Norman ruling class built its English castles, William in 1078 ordered the building of the White Tower, or central keep of the Tower of London. Continually on the move, William when in England resided at the Anglo-Saxon palaces of Winchester, Westminster, and Gloucester; in Normandy, he lived at Fécamp, Rouen, Caen, Bayeux, and Bonneville-sur-Touques. His many enemies forced him constantly to reassert his dominance in both England and Normandy. While William spent the six years after the Conquest in England, from 1072 until his death in 1087 he lived mostly in Normandy. Almost completely absent from England from 1072 to 1080, after 1072 he made four journeys to England that amounted to about 40 months there.

Family quarrels preoccupied him. His oldest son, Robert Curthose, rebelled against William's control and even allowed himself to become a pawn in the power of William's enemies. Besides fighting with his son, William in 1082 imprisoned his half-brother, Odo, whom he had appointed Bishop of Bayeux, Earl of Kent, and Regent of England, for seeking to buy the papal office for himself during the tumultuous reign of Pope Gregory VII.

His quarrel with Robert Curthose preoccupied William as he lay dying in 1087 at the priory of St-Gervais outside Rouen. Herself dying in 1083, William's Queen Matilda had annoyed her husband by her maternal loyalty to their wayward eldest. Despite this irritation, Matilda's death left William distraught for days. She had founded a convent, Abbaye-aux-Dames, at the church of La Trinité in Caen in 1063; in 1059, William had founded a monastery, Abbaye-aux-Hommes, at the church of St-Etienne in Caen. Both were buried in the churches they had founded.

At his deathbed, William also may have pondered his long career of conquest and domination. In the two decades after William's conquest, while 200,000 Norman or French settlers came, 300,000 English—one-fifth of the population—were killed or starved; French and Latin supplanted Anglo-Saxon as the language of the governing classes; English women lost the near-equality that they had enjoyed; both English peasants and the English aristocracy felt the Norman heel ground into their faces. The indomitable leader William, who had spent a lifetime fighting for control, feared no man, but William did fear the wrath of his God. Well might William have uttered these words, recorded as his: "I persecuted the native inhabitants of England beyond all reason…. I cruelly oppressed them; many I unjustly disinherited; innumerable multitudes…perished through me by famine and sword…I am stained with the rivers of blood that I have shed."

William the Conqueror Sites

In central Normandy, the many-towered château of **Falaise** stands on a high rock overlooking the town and the surrounding countryside, and from this height William's father noticed Herleve (or Arlette), the tanner's daughter, far below, bent over the family laundry in a natural spring in the gorge of the river Ante, on which Falaise is sited. Today the site of her labors, called the Fontaine d'Arlette, sports a plaque recording the conception of William the Bastard in March 1027.

The château known to William's father and himself has long ceased to exist. Its present appearance is owing to William's youngest son Henry Beauclerc (later Henry I) who built the encircling wall (enceinte), fortified with 15 towers and surrounding three connecting keep towers, the latter unique to this château. In 1944, the retreating German army used the Talbot tower in the château as an observation post, then battered by the advancing Canadians. The château withstood the fire, but the town of Falaise took a bad beating, losing 85 percent of its buildings.

Recently, the château, now known as Château Guillaume le Conquérant, has been extensively renovated, and controversially, with the use of new materials like steel, concrete, and glass. Read its history at http://www.chateau-guillaume-leconquerant.fr/web/visite_virtuelle/avant_corps.php, along with paying a virtual visit (in French). See more photographs at http://www.falaise.fr/tourisme/chateau.htm (in French). Falaise is a straight run south of Caen, 34 km on the N158.

When William was seven years old, Duke Robert announced his intention at La Trinité, **Fécamp** to undertake a pilgrimage to the Holy Land, designating William as his heir. The church was destroyed by fire in 1168 and rebuilt from 1175 to 1225, and today's buildings date from that period. View the abbey at http://freespace.virgin.net/doug.thompson/normandy/fecamp.htm. Fécamp was temporarily a primary residence of the Dukes of Normandy; the ruins of the ducal palace are situated opposite the church. For tourist information regarding Fécamp, see http://www.normandy-tourism.org/gb/02ville/F/Fecamp.html.

William was married at **Eu** to Matilda of Flanders in 1053. Eu is inland from Le Tréport, at the junction of Normandy and Picardy, on the river Bresle. It can be visited at http://www.ville-eu.fr/ (in French; by clicking on links "La Ville" and "Culture et Tourisme," you can get past the scrolling images to more tranquil pictures and information).

Before he set out to take what he considered his rightful place on the throne of England, William wrestled for control of Normandy. A column at **Vimont**, just southeast of Caen, commemorates his conquest of rebelling barons at Val-ès-Dunes in 1047. **Brionne**, on the river Risle, was under siege for three years, 1047–50. He destroyed and he built: the châteaux at **Domfront** and **Arques-la-Bataille**, for example, were begun by him. View Domfront and its château at http://freespace.virgin.net/doug.thompson/normandy/domfront.htm, along with an attractive street scene at http://www.frenchwayoflife.net/int/ville.asp?v=Domfront, and

Arques-la-Bataille at http://persocite.francite.com/dompilon/arques%20castle1.html, and http://www.casteland.com/puk/castle/hnormand/seinem/arques/arques_diapo.htm.

Caen is a city of some 115,000, standing on the Orne river 15 km from the sea. Most of the town was destroyed in the summer of 1944, and it has been rebuilt in a traditional style, using the local Caen stone. The château is still the "hub," flanked by the Abbaye-aux-Hommes and the Abbaye-aux-Dames, roughly speaking at each end of Rue St-Pierre, which runs past the château. All three buildings owe their origins to William, who transformed what was a small village into the capital of Basse-Normandie. By 1060 he had established the château; as is so often the case, the present shape was due to Henry I, who erected the donjon (reduced to its foundations in 1793) and began the enceinte walls. The website http://www.normandy-tourism.org/gb/02ville/C/Caen.html contains tourist information; click on the symbols across the screen.

William's greatest achievement at Caen was accomplished with his Queen, Matilda. In order to have the excommunication imposed on them since their marriage as cousins lifted, they founded two monasteries at what was then each end of Caen. His, St-Etienne, or Abbaye-aux-Hommes, is one of the great Romanesque buildings of Europe, and its recent restoration was sensitive and scholarly. Matilda's La Trinité (Abbaye-aux-Dames) was subject to the over-restoration that occurred too often in the 19th century, most of its original masonry having been replaced. Visit St-Etienne at its official website, http://abbaye-aux-hommes.cef.fr/. You can view Abbaye-aux-Dames at http://www.ville-caen.fr/mdn/Emeute/abbaye.htm.

By contrast, there's very little left of William's once-great château at **Bonneville-sur-Touques**, virtually just a ditch and fragments of enceinte wall, the latter enclosed within a later manor. It's open to the public on Saturdays, Sundays, and the mornings of public holidays only, but the views from the top of the hill are worth the climb. See it at http://www.norman-world.com/angleterre/Patrimoine_architectural/Normandie/Pays_Auge/pontEveque/Bonneville/.

William assembled his invasion fleet, reputedly 250,000 but probably closer to 7,000, in **Dives-sur-Mer.** Dives-sur-Mer is the medieval port of Houlgate, on the mouth of the river Dives. It was an important port until the river silted up, placing it inland, no longer on the sea. However, the river was dredged in preparation for the construction of a new harbor and marina, Port Guillaume. Houlgate became fashionable as a resort during the latter half of the 19th century, with its neighbor Cabourg being constructed as a model resort at the same time, further isolating Dives-sur-Mer. Read about Cabourg and Dives at http://www.jack-travel.com/Normandy/Cabourg_Dives_sur_mer.htm.

Dives' main attraction is its medieval market hall, Les Halles, one of the largest medieval timber halls in Europe. Along with Les Halles, Dives has managed to preserve most of its medieval center. Another notable building is, of course, the church of Notre-Dame, built in 1067 with money provided by William in thanksgiving, although very little remains of William's construction: it was added to over the centuries, and has been in a state of disrepair for some time.

William's landing-place on the south coast of England was **Pevensey Bay**, today a town of modest size with a long, shingle beach. The Romans established the fortress Anderida here. William granted the site to his half-brother Robert de Mortain, who constructed the Norman castle on the foundations of the Roman fortress; part of the Roman wall still exists. Visit the castle at http://www.theheritagetrail.co.uk/castles/pevensey%20castle.htm. Information about the town and beach may be gleaned from http://www.villagenet.co.uk/pevenseylevels/villages/pevenseybay.php.

Some 10 miles northeast of Pevensey Bay and inland from Hastings, William met Harold in battle. The town of **Battle** takes its name from that event. Founded by William, Battle Abbey is now a school for children of all ages, and naturally has limited visiting times—read about the school at http://www.battleabbeyschool.com/welcome.html, and read and view photographs of the old parts of the abbey at http://www.castles-abbeys.co.uk/Battle-Abbey.html, which also provides visiting details.

After securing the southeast, William went on to London, crossing the Thames from the northwest. At **Berkhamsted**, the leading men came out and surrendered the city to William, offering him the crown at the castle. See a sketch of how this castle may have looked at http://www.berkhamsted.gov.uk/about_berkhamsted.htm. William was then crowned at **Westminster Abbey** on Christmas Day, the first in the long series of monarchs to receive their crowns there.

St. Dunstan established a Benedictine abbey at Westminster in 960, but Edward the Confessor built the abbey. The chapel of Edward the Confessor is named after him. The abbey's official website is http://www.westminster-abbey.org/. There's a wealth of information provided via the menu. Another website providing good photographs is http://www.castles-abbeys.co.uk/Westminster-Abbey.html.

Visiting hours need to be heeded: the abbey closes perhaps earlier than one may think, especially on Saturdays (the last admissions are at 1:45 p.m.), and it is not open on Sundays at all except for visitors wishing to attend services. At such times, only the part of the church used in the service is open, the rest being roped off.

Edward the Confessor also built the **Palace of Westminster** nearby, and close to the river Thames. It would have been William's residence in London, but he spent his few years in Britain (1066–70, and only intermittently after that) consolidating his control by building castles all over the country. These were rudimentary, hastily constructed wood and earth fortifications, consisting of a motte and bailey: the motte was a mound of earth on which a keep (tower) was built, and the bailey a fence or wall around the motte. Essentially, they looked more like stockades built in North America than the stone castles we imagine; these latter were built either later in his reign or by his descendants.

Edward had been crowned in the old minster of **Winchester** in 1043, and William was also crowned here. The present cathedral was begun in 1079. William made Winchester a joint capital with London and began the castle. Only the excavated foundations of the castle can be seen today, although the beautiful Great Hall remains intact. In spite of the lack of more substantial remnants of the castle, Winchester has preserved many medieval buildings, and is a lively and pleasant town of 33,000 inhabitants. Like any medieval city, it's not easy to drive in but rewards walking. Take a virtual walk through Winchester at http://www.britannia.com/tours/winchester/city.html, with links to history and more walking and photographic tours. The cathedral's informative website is at http://www.winchester-cathedral.org.uk/.

Winchester is located in the south of England, near the **New Forest**, which William established as a hunting preserve in 1079 and named as such. At that time, "forest" meant an area not subject to common law but safeguarded for the King's hunting. Today, the New Forest is a large area mixing various ecological spaces, heaths contrasting with woodland, and housing a rich wildlife, especially the New Forest ponies, easily seen by the visitor. Rural roads and lanes cut through it, with car parks, picnic grounds, and camping facilities; and there are also marked tracks and trails for walkers and cyclists, a precious facility where trees and plants, people, animals, and commercial places (there are villages and restaurants) coexist, and where the hectic tourist can find refreshment for body and soul. Its informative website is http://www.thenewforest.co.uk/. Various main highways from all directions lead to the New Forest; it's best to simply get off them as soon as possible, and then make one's way to the Visitor Information Center (also a museum) in the High Street of **Lyndhurst**. There is also an information center at **Ringwood**, at the southwestern edge of the New Forest.

Once crowned King, William set out to establish and consolidate his control over the kingdom. Thus he began the **Tower of London**. The **White Tower** was begun by William in 1078 and completed later. Built both to impress Londoners and keep them away, the White Tower is still the dominant building in the complex that is now the Tower of London. (It became known as the White Tower only in the reign of Henry III, when the exterior was whitewashed). Take a virtual tour of the Tower at http://www.camelotintl.com/tower_site/index.html. If this is too irritating, go to the quieter stuff at http://www.hrp.org.uk/webcode/tower_home.asp.

The Tower is by the river; the Tower Hill Underground station is nearest, as its name would suggest. Once inside the walls of the Tower, you have the option of taking a tour with a Yeoman Warder (Beefeater) guide or doing your own. The guides assume an anecdotal style, laced with a broad humor, that doesn't suit everyone, but they are well-informed, and taking the tour is the only way to get into the Chapel of St. Peter ad Vincula, for example.

Windsor Castle, quite apart from its reputation as a premier royal residence, forms one of the most striking castle complexes in the world for the approaching visitor. Standing high on its hill above the Thames valley, it was begun by William in the usual wood, then continued in stone by Henry II and added to by many others as it became less important as a defense and more important as a royal residence. To the east of London, it makes an easy day trip by bus or train from the capital. The surrounding town, of over 28,000 inhabitants, includes many restaurants and high-end shops, and visitors can picnic in **Windsor Great Park**, extending for many acres down a gentle slope from the castle, and with splendid views of it. Off the park is **Frogmore House** (see *George III*), and contiguous to the town in another direction is **Eton College** (see *Henry VI*) where Charles Prince of Wales's sons Prince William and Prince Harry were educated. A good introduction to Windsor Castle can be read at http://www.royal.gov.uk/output/Page557.asp. Note the lengthy list of opening dates (after several screens) to avoid disappointment, especially if you wish to visit the royal apartments: Windsor Castle is a royal home and, like the others, is sometimes closed, in whole or in part.

Of William's other, many castles, some, like **Baynard's** and **Mountfichet** castles in London, do not survive at all; others, added to by his descendants, remain as fragments. **Colchester** has retained more of its castle than many others, perhaps not surprising in a city that has preserved nearly two miles of its Roman walls! Its keep is the largest in Europe, half the size again of the White Tower. A museum within the keep displays Celtic and Roman antiquities. The building was sold in 1629 to a local businessman who wished to sell its stone to builders; fortunately for posterity, this quickly proved unprofitable, and restoration begun in the 1700s continued for 200 years. See the castle at http://www.castlexplorer.co.uk/england/colchester/colchester.php.

Colchester goes back to Bronze Age times and was the first Roman colonia in Britain. After it was threatened by Boudicca, it became a garrison and later a Saxon stronghold. Known as Britain's oldest recorded town, it boasts seven medieval churches and the remains of three abbeys. Visit it at http://www.colchesterguide.co.uk/. The commercialism of the site is a bit annoying, and historical information is lacking, but there are lots of photographs and information for the visitor, including maps and travel. Note also the website for its museums at http://www.colchestermuseums.org.uk/.

At **York**, William established two castles. **York Castle** is a stone motte and bailey, notable for **Clifford's Tower**, a mid-13th century keep with a square forebuilding, on top of the motte with a long, steep flight of steps to it. Today, the castle is occupied by York Castle Museum and Assize Courts; the 1773 cells of the latter are still used today. **York Motte**, or **Baile Hill Castle**, was one of two castles established by William. Located in the city center off Skeldergate, it is an earthwork motte and bailey castle which once sported timber buildings on the motte. Part of the bailey ramparts are incorporated into York's city walls. The motte was raised during the Civil War to serve as a gun emplacement.

The castles stand each side of the river Ouse. Visit York Castle at http://www.castleuk.net/castle_lists_north/105/yorkcastle.htm and York Motte at http://www.castleuk.net/castle_lists_north/105/yorkmotte.htm.

Lincoln Castle was started in 1068. Unusually, the bailey wall incorporates two mottes: one of these is topped by a shell (round) keep called the Lucy Tower, constructed in the 12th century, and the other by a tower used as an observatory, built in the 19th century. Entry to the castle is gained through the Eastern Gate, which consists of 14th century building on top of a Norman tunnel vault. The curtain walls of the castle remain, and visitors can walk on most of these. The castle was later used as a court and prison, the court still used today. The prison building possesses a copy of Magna Carta, on display in an exhibition area. Visit the castle at http://www.castlexplorer.co.uk/england/lincoln/lincoln_photos.php#main. The castle is located almost next door to the cathedral, so both can be visited easily in tandem.

Another of William's castles was at **Cambridge**, but this has since been demolished, the stone being used to construct college buildings—the last to be pulled down was the gatehouse, in 1842. Only the artificial mound of Castle Hill, located predictably along Castle Street, remains. Visitors can climb the hill; the view of Cambridge itself isn't worth the climb, but the strategic importance of the site can be appreciated from the top with views over the flat countryside. Visit Castle Hill at http://www.castleuk.net/castle_lists_east_anglia/ 154/cambridgecastle.htm and read about the castle there.

In July 1087 William injured himself in a fall from his horse and was taken to **Rouen** (see *Henry V*), where he died on September 9. His end was inglorious as his corpse was stripped by servants and left while local barons fought over his effects. Worse was to come, however: when he was taken to **Caen** for burial at St-Etienne, as he wished, a fire broke out, causing panic. As his body was being lowered into the grave under the lantern tower of the church, his bloated corpse burst, releasing a foul odor, which caused the congregation to flee before the final obsequies. Even in death, he didn't remain untouched: his remains were twice disturbed, the first time in 1562 during the wars of religion, and then during the French Revolution in 1793.

Matilda had died on November 2, 1083 and is buried at La Trinité (Abbaye-aux-Dames), in **Caen**. A black marble slab at the entrance to the chancel marks her resting place.

William Rufus (William II) (1057–1100; reigned as King of England, 1087–1100)

The Anglo-Saxon Chronicler thundered in his denunciation of William Rufus ("The Red"): "everything that was hateful to God and to righteous men was the daily practice in this land during his reign. Therefore he was hated by almost all his people and abhorrent to God. This his end testified, for he died in the midst of his sins without repentance or any atonement for his evil deeds." In contrast, Geoffrey Gaimar compared William Rufus to the legendary King Arthur. Gaimar noted his popularity amongst his people, as well as the fear in which his barons held him. Although the monkish denigration of William Rufus has affected his status in history, his modern biographer Frank Barlow stresses that this soldier-King deserves better. He got along with most of his bishops and abbots and with most of his barons. His evil repute derived mostly from the monks' anger over some of his dealings with the Church and over his possible homosexuality. They treated his unexpected death while hunting as God's judgment upon the Church's enemy but did not celebrate his courage, valor, chivalry, generosity, or success in governing England.

In the usual course of events, William Rufus would never have ruled England at all. His father, William the Conqueror, would have left everything to William Rufus's elder brother, Robert Curthose. If we apply the Biblical formula, Robert was the prodigal son, whereas William Rufus devotedly served their father. Indeed, in 1079, Robert unhorsed William the Conqueror in battle and wounded his arm. On his deathbed in 1087, pressured by the Norman barons with whom Robert was popular, the Conqueror struggled against his preference to disinherit Robert completely. Instead, he left Robert the patrimony of Normandy, and he gave William Rufus his acquired territory of England. The father's unhealed anger at Robert motivated him to divide his empire rather than transmit it as an intact whole.

This dismayed many Norman barons who held land in both Normandy and England. Their two lords would be quarrelling brothers, and they would be caught in between. Led by William the Conqueror's half-brother Odo of Bayeux, who was close to Robert, many rose against William Rufus in 1088, but he quickly squelched their rebellion. In his turn, William Rufus revenged himself by seeking to undermine Robert's unsure hold on Normandy. By 1096, Robert had decided to finance his expedition in support of the First Crusade by pawning Normandy to William Rufus for 10,000 marks. Robert would not return from the Holy Land until 1100, the year William Rufus died. Not only did William Rufus rule Normandy for several years as well as ruled England, but he also reconquered Maine for Robert.

He had shown himself to be a successful ruler as well as a courageous and skillful military commander. The sodomy common in his court flourished also in the all-male armies and monasteries, though the Church sought to suppress it. His tolerance for sodomy alienated William from his most important churchman, Anselm (later canonized and recognized as a Doctor of the Church), as did the King's use of Church offices and Church revenues to raise money for the royal coffers. This tempestuous relationship probably most influenced the monks' later condemnation of William Rufus.

Originally from Tuscany, Anselm had served as prior and abbot at Bec in Normandy. His predecessor in both of those posts, the Italian Lanfranc, had become William the Conqueror's Archbishop of Canterbury. Anselm would eventually succeed Lanfranc at Canterbury as well, much to his own dismay and to the chagrin of William Rufus.

William Rufus liked to leave vacant sees unfilled, so that he could use the revenues for his own purposes. After Lanfranc died in 1089, the King left the see of Canterbury vacant for four years. When William Rufus himself fell ill in 1093, he feared death and, wanting to make a conventional repentent end, pressured Anselm to take the position. Anselm's political skills were as scanty as his personal probity and sanctity were unquestionable. He rightly suspected his unfitness for the position and refused; the English bishops then forced him to accept it. A recovered William Rufus, angry with God for (as he saw it) tricking him into godly behavior and angry with Anselm over assorted quarrels, later failed to persuade the Pope to depose Anselm. This failure, as well as Anselm's proposal to hold a synod on sodomy, motivated repeated attempts by the King to rid himself of this Archbishop. Eventually, Anselm exiled himself in 1097.

Anselm aside, William Rufus ruled successfully and in 1100 seemed at the height of his powers. He had mastered the barons, restored the border with Scotland and restored control over the North of England, reconquered Maine, and resolved his quarrel with his brother Robert over dominion of England and Normandy. A King on horseback, William Rufus always was on the move—travelling, making war, hunting. (His more sedentary pursuits included building Westminster Hall.) The hunting accident that ended his rule in 1100 seemed to the monks to reveal the judgment of God and to more modern commentators to conceal a nefarious assassination plot by his younger brother Henry, who succeeded him. More likely, William Rufus died, not at the hand of God or of Henry, but simply as the result of a hideous accident—a misaimed arrow shot by a hunting companion in the New Forest. The magnanimous Anselm, to his credit, wept when he heard of his enemy's untimely and unshriven end.

While William Rufus still lived, Anselm had not cared for the King's notorious liveliness of expression, famous among their contemporaries, as was what Barlow calls William Rufus's "slightly diabolical charisma." The King had once announced to some monks, "I grant you this my kinsman as your Abbot and if you do not accept him on the spot, I will come and burn your monastery down." To his barons who resisted a plan to expel Anselm, William Rufus exploded, "If you don't like this, what do you like? I'm not going to have someone equal to me in my kingdom while I'm alive. And if you knew he had such a good case why did you let me start the suit against him? Come on! Give me some advice! Because, by God's face, if you don't do as I want and condemn him, I will condemn you." At one point, Anselm asked leave to go to Rome. Refusing permission, William Rufus parried, "No way! I can't believe he has committed such a dreadful sin that he has to go and get special absolution from the Pope, or that he is so short of counsellors that he needs to get the Pope's advice. I would have thought he could give the Pope some advice." Clearly, William Rufus deserves to be remembered as more than the mere victim of a hunting accident.

William Rufus (William II) Sites

Born in France, William departed from **Touques** to take up the English throne. Touques is inland from the famous resort of Deauville on the Normandy coast, and, as its name implies, near William the Conqueror's château of Bonneville-sur-Touques (see *William the Conqueror*). Wooden medieval houses remain in the center; its port has been in disuse for centuries. Its website is http://touques.free.fr/, in French only, but, even so, it provides little to entice the visitor. Better go to Deauville, another planned resort of the 19th century, or nearby Trouville, known to arts lovers as a magnet for artists and writers, and later a resort, as both are today, and make a sidetrip to Touques. Deauville at http://www.deauville.org/en/ (in English) and Trouville at http://www.trouvillesurmer.org/fr/bienvenue/frameset_hp_bien.htm (in French) provide some temptation.

William's great architectural achievement was **Westminster Hall**, which almost alone survived the fire that destroyed the rest of the great Westminster Palace in 1834. The fire led to the construction of the beautiful Houses of Parliament by Charles Barry and A.W.N. Pugin in a Gothic style sympathetic to both Westminster Abbey and Westminster Hall. At the time of its building, the hall was perhaps the largest in Europe. The exterior can be easily seen, being the building furthest from the Thames and on the street side of the Houses of Parliament, between New and Old Palace Yards, and opposite St. Margaret's Church and the east end of Westminster Abbey; as well, St. Stephen's Porch, where visitors enter the Houses of Parliament, is at its southern end. However, quite apart from its situation, it just looks like a hall!

The hall can be toured in conjunction with the Houses of Parliament; for details, and a detailed history, see http://www.parliament.uk/works/palace.cfm. A clear link leads to information about Westminster Hall. Visiting the Houses of Parliament is included in this website; note the days and hours suggested, and the word "usually." The hall, used for ceremonial functions and Parliament, is a working building, and inquiries ahead of time can avert frustration.

An English castle William Rufus was responsible for beginning is **Carlisle Castle**, of great strategic importance, as it's on the eastern border of England with Scotland. He founded the castle in wood, later Kings having constructed the castle we see today. Both city and castle passed back and forth between the English and Scots, up to 1745 when Bonnie Prince Charlie's Jacobite army occupied it briefly. For photographs and visiting details, go to http://www.castlexplorer.co.uk/england/carlisle/carlisle.php. A much more detailed history can be read at http://www.heritage.me.uk/castles/carlisle.htm. Carlisle today is a city of 72,000, which grew through industry in the 19th century, demonstrated in its architecture, and as an important center within the region.

One of the earliest stone castles in England, **Rochester Castle**, was originally built at the time of the Conquest. It was rebuilt for William Rufus from 1087 to 1089, but the dramatic, five-story stone keep we see today was built after 1127 for William de Corbeil, Archbishop of Canterbury. Quite a lot of the curtain wall remains intact, together with remnants of other towers. Visitors can climb to the battlements and will be rewarded by splendid views of Rochester Cathedral, the city, and the river Medway. There is a display on the second floor of the keep, including a reconstruction. A detailed account, along with illustrations, can be read at http://www.castles-abbeys.co.uk/Rochester-Castle.html. The castle belongs to English Heritage, which has supplied visiting details at http://www.english-heritage.org.uk/server.php?show=ConProperty.211. It's only a short walk from **Rochester**, which is an attractive old city in its own right. Rochester is associated with several of Charles Dickens's works, including Restoration House, the model for Miss Havisham's Satis House in *Great Expectations* (http://www.lang.nagoya-u.ac.jp/~matsuoka/CD-Kent-Rochester.html for description and photographs). At time of writing, the city of Rochester's website was undergoing reconstruction, but information can be found at http://www.historic-uk.com/DestinationsUK/Rochester.htm.

In France, William Rufus was responsible for the château of **Gisors**, also of strategic importance for his purposes. In 1097 he constructed an artificial motte, 20 metres high, with a wall around the top, and built a donjon (keep) within the wall. Its height remains striking, and it is the focus of the town of Gisors. Pay a virtual visit to the château at http://www.casteland.com/puk/castle/hnormand/eure/gisors/gisors.htm for history and photographs. Gisors suffered badly during 1940, when many buildings were destroyed. A small city of 12,000 inhabitants, it's situated between Rouen and Beauvais, to the northwest of Paris. Its cheerful website can be found at http://www.ville-gisors.fr/ (in French).

William Rufus's untimely death in 1100 from an arrow whilst hunting in the **New Forest** is commemorated in the Rufus Stone, in the Forest near the village of Minstead. Supposedly marking the spot where he was killed, the stone stands in a clearing that's also a picnic area, with a car park, which makes it easy to visit but isn't conducive to atmosphere. Information regarding the Stone, including a photograph and directions, can be viewed at http://www.new-forest-uk.co.uk/history.htm. Information on Minstead appears at http://www.hants.gov.uk/localpages/south_west/lyndhurst/minstead/. For background material regarding the New Forest, see *William the Conqueror*.

The Verderers' Hall in Lyndhurst contains a stirrup-iron supposedly belonging to William Rufus, but probably dating from the 17th century. Stirrups of this size were used to judge which dogs could be allowed to run in the forest without danger of competing with the hunters for game: any that were too big to get through the stirrup were then maimed. The verderers are guardians of the forest with responsibilities for balancing conservation and grazing with visitors, and also for rounding up the New Forest ponies each fall and monitoring the herds and their grazing sites. The verderers date back from the 12th century and meet five times a year in their hall in the Queen's House. Their website is http://www.verderers.org.uk/home.htm.

A marble tomb traditionally considered William Rufus's but more likely to be that of Henry of Winchester (brother to King Stephen) stands in the choir of **Winchester Cathedral**. That he was buried in the cathedral seems not to be in dispute, but his bones are more likely to be contained in one of six mortuary chests which stand on top of the screen on the side side of the Presbytery, among those of early monarchs of Wessex and bishops of Winchester. The names are listed on a plaque below, including the name of William Rufus. When Cromwell's troops seized the cathedral, they opened the chests and scattered the bones, allegedly using some of them to smash windows. To view the mortuary chests, see http://britannia.com/tours/winchester/mortuary.html. William's supposed tomb can be seen at http://britannia.com/tours/winchester/william2.html. Seven years after his burial, the tower above collapsed. Although it was theorized that his burial occasioned the disaster, more knowledgeable minds blamed the collapse on deficient workmanship. For basic information about Winchester Cathedral, see *William the Conqueror*.

Henry I

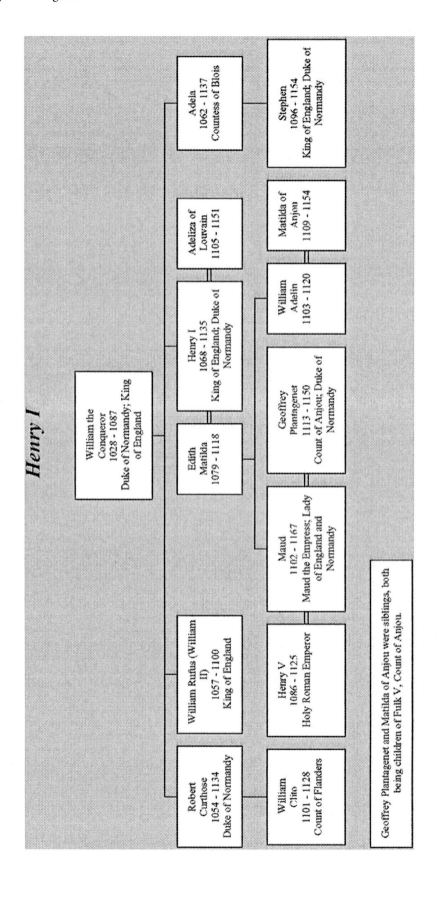

Geoffrey Plantagenet and Matilda of Anjou were siblings, both being children of Fulk V, Count of Anjou

Henry I (1068–1135; reigned as King of England, 1100–1135 and as Duke of Normandy, 1106–1135)

When William the Conqueror's son Henry was about eight years old, he and his 20-year-old brother William Rufus allegedly embarrassed their elder sibling Robert Curthose by pouring urine on him from an upper gallery. If true, this anecdote pithily characterizes the always tumultuous and often treacherous relations among the Conqueror's sons. Two of them often banded together against the third—which two varied from time to time, until the death of William Rufus and the perpetual imprisonment of Robert Curthose left Henry I the surviving victor. Not merely his brothers' survivor, Henry I also surpassed them in the quality of his governance of England and Normandy. Henry I's successful administration of his realms, however, did not avert a recurrence after his own death of the succession problem that had set the Conqueror's sons against one another.

At his death, William the Conqueror had bequeathed Normandy to Robert Curthose, England to William Rufus, and 5,000 pounds of silver or 3,000 silver marks to Henry. As William Rufus took possession of England, the landless Henry became an adviser to Robert Curthose in Normandy. Preparing in 1088 to invade England to reclaim it from William Rufus, Robert Curthose asked Henry for a loan. Refusing to lend money to his thriftless brother, Henry instead bought most of western Normandy from him and thereby became a Count. The rising in England against William Rufus failed to dislodge him, and in his turn he soon invaded Normandy. During this 1090 conflict, Henry supported Robert Curthose. This did not prevent Robert Curthose and William Rufus from allying themselves against Henry in 1091, beseiging Henry at Mont-Saint-Michel, and finally exiling him. However, the two older brothers soon repudiated the Treaty of Rouen that had allied them against a disinherited Henry, who regained control of his base in western Normandy between 1092 and 1094. William Rufus threw his support to Henry to undermine Robert Curthose. A respite followed after Robert Curthose in 1096 financed his expedition to the Holy Land during the First Crusade by pawning Normandy to William Rufus. Five years later, William Rufus died in England in a hunting accident, and Robert Curthose returned to Normandy.

Henry quickly seized control of the royal treasury at Winchester and secured the assent of the barons to his own accession as King of England. Despite this assent, most of the Anglo-Norman barons soon supported Robert Curthose's challenge to Henry's rule in England. Eventually, Robert Curthose renounced his claim to England in 1101 in the Treaty of Alton; in return, Henry surrendered almost all of his territory in western Normandy and agreed to pay Robert an annuity. Four years later, Henry—this time with the barons' support—invaded Normandy. Henry I won his final fraternal victory in 1106 at Tinchebray in western Normandy. The captured Robert Curthose would spend his last 28 years in prison.

Henry I had won over the barons by his skillful use of both punishment and patronage. Besides demonstrating sound political skills, Henry I established a centralized and powerful administrative structure that included the court, the treasury and the exchequer, as well as a judicial system that won him renown as "the Lion of Justice." His councils and feasts often took place at Winchester and Westminster, though later in his reign he favored his hunting park at Woodstock as well as Windsor. The court gathered for the first time at the newly built New Windsor in 1110 and returned there more often than anywhere else. England prospered during Henry I's long reign—not least because he won lasting peace: 33 years of peace in England and (after 1106) 27 years of peace in Normandy.

Like his predecessor William Rufus, however, Henry I found it somewhat difficult to live in peace with his Archbishop of Canterbury, the saintly Anselm. Having recalled Anselm from exile, Henry I was surprised that Anselm then made an issue out of lay investiture, which concerned the King's royal authority over ecclesiastical appointments. Threatened with excommunication, Henry eventually compromised on this issue, and Anselm (who returned from yet another exile) may even have served as Regent during the King's absences.

For a long time, it seemed that Henry could number among his many successes various solutions to the succession problem. The sire of more than 20 acknowledged bastards, Henry fathered children by his able wife, Edith Matilda, who also served as Regent when necessary. A daughter of Scottish royals Malcolm Canmore and his Queen St. Margaret, Edith Matilda descended (through her mother) from the Anglo-Saxon Kings of England, including the 9th-century King Alfred the Great. She bore two legitimate children to Henry: Maud (or Matilda) in 1102 and William Adelin in 1103. Two years after the death of Queen Edith Matilda in 1118, Henry's male heir William Adelin drowned in the foundering of the *White Ship* upon a hidden rock.

Henry's hopes of siring another male heir by his subsequent marriage to Adeliza of Louvain in 1121 also foundered. The King wanted to discourage the hopes of his nephew, Robert Curthose's son William Clito, whose popularity threatened Henry's own hold on his realms until William Clito died in 1128. When his son-in-law, the Holy Roman Emperor Henry V, died in 1125, Henry I brought his daughter, Maud the Empress, back to his court. He sought to make Maud his female heir, to replace William Adelin, and to marry her to Geoffrey of Anjou, to replace the diplomatic alliance once sealed by William Adelin's wedding to Matilda of Anjou. Most unenthusiastically did the barons swear allegiance to Maud, but Henry's solution might have worked, except for a rift in 1135 between the King and his daughter and son-in-law. In the end, Henry's best-laid plans failed to secure the peace that had been his life's achievement, and Maud would struggle for supremacy with her first cousin Stephen during a prolonged civil war.

Henry I Sites

According to tradition, Henry was born in **Selby**, North Yorkshire. The large, beautiful Abbey Church is the dominant feature of Selby today, although it formed only a part of the rich Benedictine monastery founded in the late 11th century by a monk, Benedict, the first abbot. The church is owing to Benedict's successor, Abbot Hugh. It survived Henry VIII's Dissolution of the Monasteries by becoming the parish church for Selby, only to become badly damaged during the Civil War. To add to its woes, in 1690 part of the central tower collapsed, destroying the south transept and part of the choir. Although services were still held in the choir, the nave was used as a store for market stalls, and essentially the building was allowed to lapse. However, in 1871 Gilbert Scott was commissioned to oversee the restoration of the nave, and the choir was fully restored by the end of the century. In spite of a fire in the roof timbers of the nave in 1906, the church has been restored beautifully to its Norman appearance. Note the deep diamond-shaped carving on the pillars, and the Norman geometric patterns in the carving in the arches, especially in the West doorway. Among other attractions, the arms of the Washington family, ancestors of George Washington, appear in a clerestory window in the south choir transept.

Read about the Abbey Church at http://www.heritage.me.uk/religiou/selby.htm and http://www.theheritagetrail.co.uk/abbeys/selby%20abbey.htm. The town of Selby lies in Yorkshire, southwest of York, on the A63.

Henry's first wife, Edith Matilda, was born in **Dunfermline.** Her parents, Malcolm Canmore and Margaret, a Saxon princess, lived at the palace. The devout Margaret founded the abbey to introduce the Benedictine rule to Scotland. After the destruction of the monastic buildings by Edward I, the abbey was rebuilt on a much grander scale, but fell into disuse after the Reformation. Relatively extensive remains of the palace survive, which can be seen very clearly in the many pictures at http://www.undiscoveredscotland.co.uk/dunfermline/abbeypalace/.

Today, Dunfermline is the main center for the "Kingdom" of Fife, separated from Edinburgh and environs by the Firth of Forth, and accessed over the elegant Forth Road Bridge.

When she married, Edith Matilda had been living in **Romsey Abbey**, of which the abbey church survives and is in current use. Romsey Abbey Church boasts an extensive website at http://www.romseyabbey.org.uk/, along with a history and photographs. Of interest is its proximity to Broadlands, the home of the late Lord Mountbatten (a floor slab in the south transept marks his memory), still lived in by his heirs, where both Queen Elizabeth II and Charles Prince of Wales spent part of their honeymoons. Romsey, at the junction of several highways, is southeast of Winchester and a few miles north of Southampton.

Henry's second wife Adeliza was born in **Leuven** (Louvain in French), Belgium. This old university town, which had flourished due to the cloth trade in the 13th century, was almost destroyed in 1914 and then bombed in 1944. Since then it was been slowly reconstructed. With a population of 87,000, Leuven is situated a few miles northeast of Brussels. Visit it online at http://www.trabel.com/leuven/leuven.htm, and also for details regarding an actual visit.

The enchanting **Mont-Saint-Michel** appears to float in its bay, although it's linked to the mainland by a causeway. The hill of the island is doubled in height by its crown, the steep-walled Benedictine monastery, with the buildings of the small town tucked into the hillside below. It's an amazing sight and a national monument, attracting crowds of visitors; avoid coming in summer, if possible. Also avoid walking on the sands of the bay without a guide; there are areas of quicksand, and the tide comes in fast. Founded after an apparition of St. Michael the Archangel to St. Aubert in 708, an oratory was first built, followed by a church and then the Romanesque basilica, and became a center of monastic learning; a small Benedectine community still lives there. Its geography helped spurn assaults and attempts at conquest. During the French Revolution, it became a prison, and kept that status until 1863. The Bay of Mont-Saint-Michel divides Normandy and Brittany, with the island off the coast of the southern shore; the nearest city is Avranches. Mont-Saint-Michel has been a Unesco World Heritage site since 1979. Visit it at http://www.mont-saint-michel.net/, and for visiting details.

Henry was also out hunting in the **New Forest** on the day his brother William II was struck by an arrow and killed. See *William Rufus*. Upon his brother's death, Henry moved swiftly to claim the throne: he rode to **Winchester**, where he took possession of the treasury, and then on to **Westminster**, where he was crowned on August 5.

Arundel Castle was besieged by Henry in 1102, surrendering after three months, and was thereafter willed to his second wife, Adeliza. Three years later, she married William d'Albini II who built the keep on the motte. In 1155 he was confirmed as Earl of Arundel by Henry II, who built most of the oldest part of the castle. Since that time, the castle has been in the ownership of the same family, whether d'Albinis, Fitzalans, or Howards, and the seat of the Dukes of Norfolk for over 850 years. In history, the name of Howard is interwoven with those of royals, especially from the 15th to 17th centuries. The Dukes of Norfolk are premier dukes, and Earls Marshal of England, which involves being in charge of state ceremonial, among other responsibilities. The castle's website appears at http://www.castles-abbeys.co.uk/Arundel-Castle.html.

The park and palace of **Woodstock** owed their origins to Henry, who enclosed a hunting area within a seven-mile stone fence and built a lodge. He also kept a menagerie of exotic animals in the enclosure. Read an account of Woodstock at http://www.smithsonianmag.si.edu/journeys/01/feb01/woodstock.html, and view what is probably a fanciful image of what it looked like.

The massive Norman keep of **Carlisle Castle** was begun by Henry in 1122. The castle had been begun by William Rufus in wood; Henry built the earliest surviving parts, the base of the keep and some of the perimeter walls. For basic information about the castle, see *William Rufus*.

Domfront became Henry's power base in southern Normandy. This was the earliest of Henry's great stone keeps, built while his brother Robert Curthose was on crusade and he was ruling Normandy. Only two walls of the keep survive, but the setting is spectacular, and the ruins can be seen for miles, on their perch above the river. View Domfront and its château at http://freespace.virgin.net/doug.thompson/normandy/ domfront.htm. Domfront is located directly north of Mayenne and east of Avranches.

Tinchebray, where Henry prevailed against his brother Robert Curthose, is located on the D524 between Vire and Flers, in Normandy. The church of St-Rémy was the chapel of the castle; all that remains today are the choir, transepts, and Romanesque tower. Tinchebray is a hardware-manufacturing center, and also hosts a chocolate factory. See the church and visit the town very briefly at http://www.normandy-tourism.org/gb/ 02ville/T/Tinchbray.html.

At the Conqueror's château at **Caen**, Henry constructed the square donjon (or keep) to the north of the bailey in 1120, and the Great Hall, which became known as the Salle de l'Echiquier in the 19th century. The donjon was completed with corner towers by Philip Augustus; alas, nothing remains today but the foundations. However, the Salle de l'Echiquier still stands, along with several later buildings and the 1960s Musée des Beaux-Arts. View the château at http://www.chateau.caen.fr/ (in French). Click on "histoire" and "projet" for diagrams of the château: "projet" provides not only history but details of the forthcoming renovations. A photo gallery with several screens of images begins at http://www.casteland.com/puk/castle/ bnormand/calvados/caen/caen_diapo.htm.

The château at **Arques-la-Bataille** had been begun in 1038 by William, Count of Arques and uncle to William the Conqueror, but became a ducal possession and was extensively rebuilt by Henry in 1123, who added the keep and much of the outer wall. The walls sport 14 towers, and are themselves surrounded by a deep moat, although the château is on top of a hill. Although the huge double towers at the west end were added in the 16th century, the château was abandoned to the point where it was used as a quarry 200 years later. View the château and read its history, in that extraordinarily convoluted English produced by instant translation software, at http://www.casteland.com/puk/castle/hnormand/seinem/arques/arques.htm. Arques-la-Bataille is attractively sited 6 km southeast of Dieppe, on the river Arques and the edge of the Forest of Arques.

At **Gisors** in 1125, Henry surrounded the large bailey with an enceinte wall. (See *William Rufus* for details regarding Gisors.) He fortified the site of the château at **Creully**, about 15 km northwest of Caens on the D22, then giving this to his son Robert of Gloucester. The 12th century enceinte wall and square central block forming the keep remain, along with two other towers, but, unusually and gracefully, a pleasant mansion attached to the château in the 16th century now houses the "*mairie*" of Creully. It's open only during July and August, on Tuesdays, Thursdays, and Fridays. The arrangement can be best seen at http:// www.mondes-normands.caen.fr/france/Patrimoine_architectural/Normandie/Bessin/creully/0241Creully/. He also fortified the town of **Verneuil-sur-Avre** by constructing a series of outer ramparts and built a canal to connect the town with the river Iton. Verneuil provided strategic importance in being located where Normandy yields to the spacious wheatfields of Beauce. It retains many old half-timbered houses, as well as its walls. View the château at http://www.casteland.com/puk/castle/hnormand/eure/verneuil/verneuil.htm.

Two churches benefiting from Henry's largesse were the Cistercian abbey of **Mortemer** and the cathedral at Evreux, but in different ways. Mortemer stands in the Forest of Lyons on a small lake, about 5 km from **Lyons-la-Forêt** via lanes through the woods. Typically, it was sold after the Revolution and stripped of its stone, so only fragments remain. However, the remnants do provide an idea of the scale and relative grandeur of the abbey. Pageants are held there during the summer, and there is a small museum devoted to information on the monastic life. For information regarding the pageants, see http://www.whatsonwhen.com/events/ ~73564.jml.

In 1119 Henry set fire to the town of **Evreux**, one of several such bellicose acts of destruction experienced by Evreux over the centuries, the latest having occurred during German air raids in June 1940 and again during the Allied advance in 1944. Each time the town has rebuilt itself. When threatened with excommunication, Henry rebuilt the Cathedral of Notre-Dame in the contemporary style. The present style indicates the range over the centuries: each episode of destruction resulted in a contemporary rebuilding, all major periods now incorporated. One of the largest in France, the church is famous for the quality and range of its stained glass which dates from the 13th through 17th centuries, especially in the choir, and which has, happily, survived. Basic tourist information about Evreux may be found at http://www.normandy-tourism.org/gb/02ville/E/Evreux.html. Stained-glass aficionados may wish to study the glass at http://ica.princeton.edu/metcalf/browse.php?p=4500&s=.

From **Barfleur**, Henry's son and heir William Adelin set out on his fatal voyage in 1120. His ship was wrecked, and he drowned along with many of the royal court. Barfleur hosts its own attractive website at http://www.ville-barfleur.fr/. In French only; but readers who don't know French can still enjoy the enticing pictures. For all its attractiveness, Barfleur isn't large; its population of 3,000 is about one-third that of its medieval population. Most of the town dates from the mid-19th century when it was remodelled; nothing remains of the medieval town.

In Wales, Henry planted Flemish colonies in the Pembroke and Gower peninsulas, where their descendants still remain, speaking English. Among these was **Haverfordwest**, since associated with the visits of various Kings. Henry's Flemings built the castle, seen along with Haverfordwest's other attractions at http://www.haverfordwest-wales.info/vis_landmarks.asp. At the conjunction of several roads, Haverfordwest makes an excellent center for touring Pembrokeshire.

Henry died in **Lyons-la-Forêt**, supposedly from eating "a surfeit of lampreys." Lyons-la-Forêt is picturesquely situated between Rouen and Gisors, northwest of Paris, in the middle of the Forest of Lyons, once a favorite hunting ground of the Dukes of Normandy. Today, this beech forest is a haven for walkers, with many paths leading through the beautiful woods to destinations like nearby villages and the abbey of Mortemer (see above). Considered one of the most beautiful villages in France, Lyons displays medieval wooden houses and a 17th century covered market on the river Lieure. Its population of 800 swells considerably during the summer as visitors descend to enjoy its beauty and peace. The website http://www.normandy-tourism.org/gb/02ville/L/Lyons.html provides scanty information in English; at http://lyonslaforet.free.fr/ you will find photos and much more information, but in French.

His body was taken to **Rouen** (see *William the Conqueror*). In the cathedral, his bowels, brain, and eyes were removed, and these parts were then buried in the monastery of **Notre-Dame-des-Prés**, near Rouen (see *Stephen*), while his body was taken to **Caen** (see *William the Conqueror*). It remained there for a month until taken to England, and Reading.

He was interred in **Reading** Abbey, which he had founded in 1121. Very little is left of what was once the third-ranking abbey; the remnants are at the end of Forbury Walk in Reading. An imaginative sketch and a history can be viewed at http://www.berkshirehistory.com/churches/reading_abbey.html. In Forbury Gardens, adjacent to the abbey ruins, an early 20th century monument stands, commemorating his death.

Edith Matilda died at Westminster and was buried in **Westminster Abbey**. Adeliza died and was buried at **Affligem** (or **Afflighem**) **Abbey**, Belgium. Her father was also buried there. The abbey is to the north of the small town of **Hekelgem**, a few miles west of Brussels, exit 19a off the A10-E40. Of the original abbey, all that remains from the expulsion of the community and the destruction of the abbey in 1796 is one wall of the church nave and some 17th century buildings. The Benedictines returned in 1869 and have since been reconstructing their abbey; the present church dates from 1971. For online information, start at http://www.affligem.be/servlet/page?_pageid=1838&_dad=portal30&_schema=PORTAL30. Click on "Tourism en historiek" and then "Historiek." Choose "Abdij Affligem," which leads you to links such as "Korte historiek" and "Bezienswaardigheden" ("sights"). Clicking on "Ruïnes" will give you a photograph of what's left of the abbey. For the interior of the modern abbey church and its service times, see "Abdijkerk."

Stephen and Maud the Empress

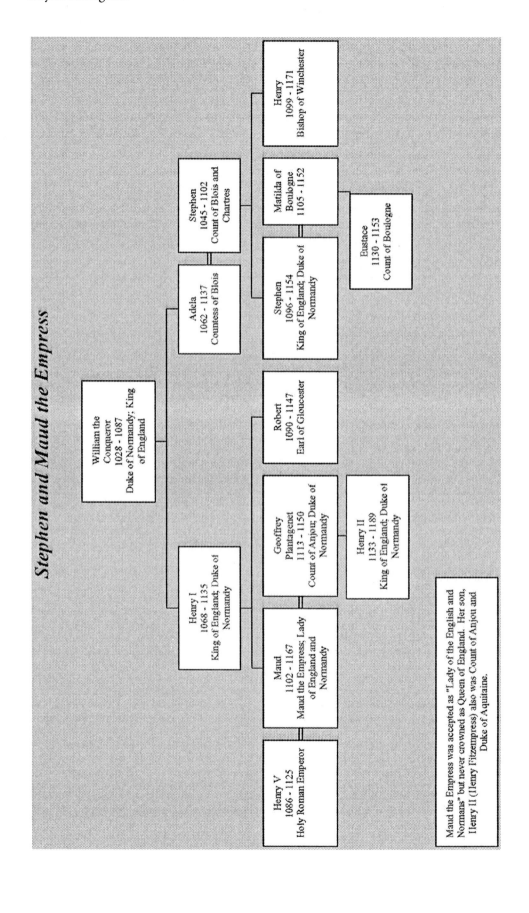

Maud the Empress was accepted as "Lady of the English and Normans" but never crowned as Queen of England. Her son, Henry II (Henry Fitzempress) also was Count of Anjou and Duke of Aquitaine.

William the Conqueror
1028 - 1087
Duke of Normandy; King of England

Adela
1062 - 1137
Countess of Blois

Stephen
1045 - 1102
Count of Blois and Chartres

Henry
1099 - 1171
Bishop of Winchester

Stephen
1096 - 1154
King of England; Duke of Normandy

Matilda of Boulogne
1105 - 1152

Eustace
1130 - 1153
Count of Boulogne

Robert
1090 - 1147
Earl of Gloucester

Henry I
1068 - 1135
King of England; Duke of Normandy

Maud
1102 - 1167
Maud the Empress; Lady of England and Normandy

Geoffrey Plantagenet
1113 - 1150
Count of Anjou; Duke of Normandy

Henry II
1133 - 1189
King of England; Duke of Normandy

Henry V
1086 - 1125
Holy Roman Emperor

Stephen (1096–1154; reigned as Duke of Normandy, 1135–1145 and as King of England, 1135–1154)
Maud the Empress (Matilda)(1102–1167; recognized as Lady of England and Normandy, 1141)

Exactly one century after William the Bastard succeeded his father, Robert the Devil, as Duke of Normandy, William's grandson Stephen succeeded Henry I as Duke of Normandy and King of England. In a recurring and prolonged squabble over their inheritance, the Conqueror's sons, then his grandchildren, and then his great-grandsons fought for his lands. Henry I had triumphed over his brothers William Rufus and Robert Curthose. Having lost his son William Adelin in 1120, Henry I finally chose his daughter Maud (or Matilda) as his own successor. When Henry I died in 1135, however, his nephew Stephen seized power in both England and Normandy. A few years later, Maud's determined challenge to her first cousin Stephen's rule brought over a decade of civil war to England. Maud's son Henry Fitzempress later sought to undermine Stephen's grip on the crown and Stephen's determination to pass it on to his own son Eustace, Henry's second cousin. In each of three generations, these Norman kin clawed one another in their fratricidal struggle for the throne.

A few years older than Maud, Stephen lost his father Stephen, Count of Blois and Chartres, in the year Maud was born, 1102. Stephen's mother, the Conqueror's remarkable daughter Adela, ruled Blois after her husband died and by 1113 had sent Stephen to live at the court of her brother Henry I. The King made his nephew a rich landowner. He also betrothed his daughter Maud to the Holy Roman Emperor, Henry V. Having left for Germany when she was eight years old, Maud married her 32-year-old bridegroom in 1114 when she was 12. Her husband the Emperor died in 1125.

Maud's widowhood made her available for another purpose. Since Maud's brother William Adelin had drowned in the sinking of the *White Ship* five years before, their royal father had been trying to beget new legitimate male offspring by his second wife. Failing in this, Henry I now brought Maud back to his court and compelled his nobles to swear to accept her as his successor in England and Normandy. They swore this oath three times: at the Christmas court of 1126–27, at Easter in 1128, and in September 1131. Among many others, Maud's first cousin Stephen swore this oath at his uncle's bidding.

Maud's usefulness did not end there. Wanting to secure Fulk V, Count of Anjou as an ally, in 1128 Henry I married Maud to Fulk's son Geoffrey. While the Emperor had been 20 years older than his bride, her new bridegroom was a decade younger than she and of lower rank. Maud's displeasure over the match may have triggered the turmoil that soon separated these newlyweds. After Maud returned to Geoffrey, she bore him sons, among them Henry Fitzempress, the future Henry II, in 1133. The old King her father adored his grandson.

Geoffrey of Anjou resented the fact that Henry I retained control of some Norman châteaux included in Maud's dowry. He was fighting a border war with Henry I in Normandy in 1135 when the King died suddenly. Stephen quickly crossed the Channel from Boulogne, gained the allegiance of London, at Winchester won support from such a powerful figure as Henry I's administrator Roger of Salisbury, and was anointed as King by the Archbishop of Canterbury. Stephen's clever and influential younger brother Henry, Bishop of Winchester, guided and aided his usurpation.

Seeking legitimacy, Stephen sought papal approval by claiming that the dying Henry I had changed his mind about the succession and named Stephen as his preference. Maud appealed against Pope Innocent II's 1136 acceptance of this rationale, but the Pope again upheld Stephen as King at the Lateran Council of

1139. Most of the barons had swung their support to Stephen because they did not want to be ruled by a woman and possibly because, as Normans, they did not want to be ruled by Maud's Angevin husband.

Maud's half-brother, Henry I's bastard Robert, Earl of Gloucester, had seemed to accept Stephen's rule until he openly allied himself with Maud in 1138. Stephen possibly had tried to ambush Robert of Gloucester. If so, trying and then failing to kill Robert both proved to be deadly errors. Maud invaded England with Robert's aid in 1139. From their base in western England, they instigated a full-scale rebellion in 1141.

Besides alienating Robert of Gloucester, Stephen's weak and treacherous rule had been earning the disrespect of other magnates and the distrust of the Church, especially when in 1139 he ordered the sudden arrest of three bishops who had adminstered England for Henry I—among them Roger of Salisbury. Both David I of Scotland, Maud's maternal uncle, and Maud's husband, Geoffrey of Anjou, were invading Stephen's realms. The King actually lost the loyalty of his brother, Henry of Winchester, in 1138 when Stephen disregarded Henry's views and even named another churchman to the post of Archbishop of Canterbury. Maud's supporter Brian Fitzcount tartly noted that Henry of Winchester "had a remarkable gift of discovering that duty pointed in the same direction as expediency." Whether out of duty or out of expediency, Henry of Winchester tried to negotiate terms of a settlement between Stephen and Maud. Maud agreed, but Stephen would not, so Henry of Winchester's negotiations failed in 1140. He would try again, at the end of the civil war, 13 years later.

In the fateful year of 1141, Stephen fought bravely at the Battle of Lincoln, only to fall into the hands of his enemies after defeat. Henry of Winchester changed his allegiance to Maud, while Stephen's Queen, Matilda of Boulogne, a descendant of Charlemagne, organized resistance to the victorious Empress. The nobles violated the oaths they had sworn to Stephen as they scrambled to ally themselves with Maud, herself forsworn by them in 1135. Although recognized as "Lady of England and Normandy" and taken to London for her coronation, Maud reacted to her victory by displaying a tactlessness and arrogance that angered her new supporters—including Henry of Winchester, whose advice she ignored. Maud was never crowned as Queen. Alarmed by Matilda of Boulogne's attacks on their city, disenchanted with the Empress, rioting Londoners drove Maud from their city. Then, at the Rout of Winchester, the King's forces captured Robert of Gloucester. This necessitated the exchange of Stephen, held at Bristol, for Robert. A revitalized Stephen eventually beseiged Maud at Oxford, from where the Empress and a few companions made a spectacular escape, dressed in white clothing that blurred their forms against a heavy snowfall.

Stephen regained his ascendancy and his allies (including Henry of Winchester) after a few more years, Robert of Gloucester died in 1147, and Maud departed forever from England to Normandy in 1148. Although declining to aid Maud's English expeditions, her husband had occupied himself by conquering Normandy. After 10 years, by 1145, Geoffrey had made himself Duke of Normandy in place of Stephen. In 1150, he gave it to his son Henry Fitzempress to rule. Stephen's loss of Normandy kept the succession question alive.

The Empress retired to Normandy, where she would live in the palace built by her father in Rouen next to Notre-Dame-des-Prés. Her son Henry became the new standard-bearer. As a 14-year-old invader in 1147, Henry had led a faltering expedition. Failing in his pleas for funds to his mother and uncle Robert of Gloucester, Henry asked his kinsman and opponent King Stephen for money, and Stephen, in an endearing gesture, sent Henry the funds. Henry invaded England again in 1149 and finally in 1153.

A new generation descended from the Conqueror now sought to control his legacy. Stephen had tried to settle the succession problem by asking the Archbishop of Canterbury to crown Stephen's son Eustace during Stephen's lifetime. Pope Celestine II, however, in 1143 had reversed the previous papal opinion about the legitimacy of Stephen's rule, and the Archbishop consequently refused to crown Eustace in 1152. Indeed, the reformer St. Bernard of Clairvaux had soured the papacy on Stephen and his brother Henry, to whom the plainspoken St. Bernard referred as "that old whore of Winchester." With Maud's claim quiescent after a decade's struggle, Henry Fitzempress seemed to be the obvious alternative to his second cousin Eustace.

In 1153, at Malmesbury and then at Wallingford, Stephen and Henry met to fight, but their armies, rather sensibly, refused. The Church also pressured them for a settlement. Although Stephen and Henry complained to each other about their followers' recalcitrance, in the Treaty of Winchester that followed they agreed that Stephen would retain his throne until he died, and that Henry would succeed him. Eustace's 1153 death had simplified matters and probably disheartened Stephen, already grieved by his wife's death the year before. He did not survive Eustace and Matilda for very long.

Stephen lost followers because they perceived him as weak and untrustworthy; Maud lost hers because they perceived her as overly strong and arrogant. Both certainly had their good points. Stephen, a brave fighter, often acted with generosity. Maud, whom her German subjects had admired, devoted herself to her son, ruled Normandy as his Regent, and gave him the advice he sought—as when she urged Henry II not to name Becket Archbishop of Canterbury. Each unfortunately instigated and prolonged the great misery of a decade of civil war, epitomized by the memorable phrase from the Anglo-Saxon Chronicle, "Men said openly that Christ and his saints slept."

Stephen and Maud the Empress Sites

Stephen was born in **Blois**. The château, one of the legendary group in the Loire river valley, became his seat as Count of Blois. It was rebuilt and added to over the centuries, in various styles, and has been recently restored, with very little remaining from Stephen's time. It's best seen online at http://www.marie-stuart.co.uk/France/Blois.htm. The town of Blois lines the river Loire, and the Quartier Vieux (Old Quarter) still contains beautiful old buildings.

Stephen was at **Boulogne** when he heard of the death of Henry I. An old Normandy city on the Channel, Boulogne suffered much bomb damage during the Second World War, although the 13th century ramparts dividing the Basse-Ville (Lower Town) from the Haute-Ville (Upper Town) remain. Predictably, it has been an important port over the years, and a terminus of ferries crossing the Channel. See Boulogne at http://www.theotherside.co.uk/tm-heritage/towns/boulogne.htm for tourist information.

Maud was born in 1101, possibly at the old manor of **Sutton Courtenay**. Sutton Courtenay is a pretty village just south of Abingdon and Oxford, on the B4016. Visit it and read its history at http://www.berkshirehistory.com/villages/suttoncourtenay.html. She was betrothed to Henry V at **Utrecht**, crowned Queen at **Mainz**, and lived at **Speyer** with Henry when she had married him, at the age of 12. **Utrecht** is an old university city in the Netherlands, home to not only students but painters over the years, which still contains medieval buildings along its central canal, the Oude Gracht. Its website can be found at http://www2.holland.com/utrechtstad/gb/. Utrecht is located pretty well in the center of the Netherlands, east of the Hague and southeast of Amsterdam. **Mainz**, at the confluence of the Rhine and the river Main, southwest of Frankfurt-am-Main, is also an old university city and the capital of the Rhineland-Palatinate, maintaining many old buildings although its center suffered much bomb damage during the Second World War. For tourist information and photographs, see http://www.info-mainz.de/verkehrsverein/index_e.htm.

Speyer, also on the left bank of the Rhine and between Karlsruhe and Ludwigshafen, is noted for its cathedral, which was made a Unesco World Heritage site in 1980. A number of emperors are buried within its walls, including Maud's husband and his father. For information and pictures, see http://www.info-mainz.de/verkehrsverein/index_e.htm.

She was married to Geoffrey of Anjou in **Le Mans Cathedral**. Le Mans is a busy market town and industrial center, with, nevertheless, an old town (Vieux Mans) containing old houses and the magnificent Cathedral of St-Julien. See photographs of the old town and walls of Le Mans, and the cathedral, at http://www.nissan.co.jp/Lemans/environ/oldmans.html. Le Mans is probably best-known outside France for the annual car race, which receives its start at the cathedral. Get the best of both worlds at http://www.c5registry.com/Special/LeMans2k1/prelemans.htm.

Stephen was proclaimed King at Pentecost, 1138 at **Hereford Cathedral**, and in the sanctuary a wooden chair said to have been used by him bears his name. The cathedral's website is http://www.herefordcathedral.org/. Hereford, a city of 48,000 population, is on the river Wye and near the Welsh border, and its location has involved it in a lot of military activity. It was badly damaged during the troubles of Stephen's reign, for example, but the cathedral and several other old buildings, along with the medieval street pattern, survive. The most informative website for the city of Hereford is http://www.herefordwebpages.co.uk/herefor2.shtml.

On the east side of the A167, two miles north of **Northallerton**, North Yorkshire, a stone obelisk marks the site where Stephen defeated the Scots under King David at the **Battle of the Standard** in 1138. Northallerton, the county town of North Yorkshire with a population of 9600, is located between Darlington and York. Its website is at http://www.northallertonweb.co.uk.

In his battles with Maud, Stephen besieged **Arundel Castle** in 1139, where Maud was being harbored by William d'Albini and his wife, her stepmother Adeliza of Louvain. For details regarding Arundel, see *Henry I*.

The battle at **Lincoln Castle** was the only substantial one in the long conflict between Stephen and Maud. Finally, on February 2, 1141, Stephen was defeated and taken to Bristol, where he was held prisoner in **Bristol Castle**. For Lincoln Castle, see *William the Conqueror*. Bristol Castle was demolished in 1650, and only a few fragments remain in Castle Park; view them at http://www.about-bristol.co.uk/old-02.asp. Bristol is a city of 400,000 population, unabashedly commercial with its history of trade and manufacturing, and architecturally of the 18th and 19th centuries. Tourism is covered at http://www.visitbristol.co.uk/; visit http://www.about-bristol.co.uk for more photographs and general information about the city.

After her rout of Stephen, Maud entered **Winchester** in triumph and in a bid for the throne, but where she was acknowledged only as "Lady of the English." She took up residence in the castle. For information regarding Winchester, see *William the Conqueror*. From there she was forced to flee, and went first to **Devizes**. Devizes, in Wiltshire, standing at the confluence of several A roads, is a busy market town of 11,000 inhabitants. It can be visited at http://www.devizes.co.uk/, and http://www.yourguide.org.uk/devizes/. The present castle is a 19th century creation; see it at http://www.geocities.com/TheTropics/3670/.

Maud then retreated to **Oxford Castle**, where she was besieged by Stephen's forces. Her daring escape on a cold December night in 1142 has become the stuff of legend. With Stephen's army around the castle, she and four companions, all dressed in white, slipped out through a gate, making their way over the frozen Thames to Abingdon, where they took refuge in the abbey. The more fanciful version of their escape from the castle has them being let down over the side walls by rope. Nothing is lost of the audacity of the escape in the likelier version.

The castle, built in 1071 by Robert d'Oilly, a follower of the Conqueror, survives in its mound and the impressive St. George's Tower. The hexagonal well-chamber is still to be seen on the mound; permission to climb the mound needs to be obtained from the Museum of Oxford. Later, the castle housed a prison, which closed in 1996. The complex is now intended for development for both commercial and heritage purposes. The castle mound, located at New Road and Tidmarsh Lane, is opposite Nuffield College. At http://www.oxfordshire.gov.uk/index/libraries_heritage_countryside/oxfordshire_museums_service/oxfordcastleprison.htm, the Oxford County presents two historical images of Oxford Castle; and at http://www.oxfordshire.gov.uk/index/libraries_heritage_countryside/oxfordshire_museums_service/oxfordcastleprison/castlemillviews.htm, two images of the Castle Mill, demolished in 1930.

Abingdon is a pleasant old town a few miles south of Oxford. It grew around its Benedictine abbey, founded in 675. The remains of the abbey are on the north bank of the Thams, but difficult to distinguish from later buildings. The beautiful (restored) 15th century gatehouse, next to the old church of St. Nicholas, provides the entry to the abbey. The remains of the abbey consist of a large 14th century hall known as the Checker (Exchequer), now the Unicorn Theatre, and of the Long Gallery and Guildhall, all constructed well after Maud's stay there; the abbey church has gone. Abingdon's website is http://abingdonpages.co.uk/history.htm. However, the best photos for the abbey are at http://www.berkshirehistory.com/churches/abingdon_abbey.html, with visiting details at http://www.information-britain.co.uk/showPlace.cfm?Place_ID=5159.

From Abingdon she went to the safe stronghold of **Wallingford Castle**, where she was supported by Brian Fitzcount. Wallingford is south of Oxford, on the A4130, tucked beside the river Thames. It's an old town of 6300 population that preserves its medieval plan, although not a lot is left of the once-royal castle, whose site is now public gardens. Read about Wallingford at http://www.oxtowns.co.uk/wallingford/home.html. The best website for the castle appears to be http://www.northmoortrust.co.uk/home/countryside/ wallingford. After Brian Fitzcount died, Stephen took Wallingford Castle.

Stephen died at **Dover** and was buried at the Cluniac **Faversham Abbey** in 1154, which he had founded in 1147, at the side of his wife Matilda and son Eustace. The site, and the base of Stephen's tomb, were located in 1965. The former abbey guesthouse (c.1520) is now Arden's House, the site of the murder of Thomas Arden by his wife in 1551. Faversham itself is an old port and town east of London, on the way to Canterbury; its attractive website is http://www.faversham.org. Visit the abbey by clicking on Historic Buildings—Faversham Abbey, or go to http://www.faversham.org/history/favabbey.asp directly. Matilda had died at **Hedingham Castle**. The tall keep of the castle survives in the village of Castle Hedingham, in Essex, southwest of Cambridge; turn off the A1017 at the village of Sible Hedingham. Owned for centuries by the de Vere family, the castle was demolished to make way for the family's Tudor mansion, but the keep, surrounded by lawns and woodland, is open to the public and hosts a variety of activities, including jousting tournaments. Read about them, and the castle, at http://www.hedinghamcastle.co.uk/, along with more details of the castle at http://www.theheritagetrail.co.uk/castles/hedingham%20castle.htm.

Maud retired to the abbey of **Bec-Hellouin**. Bec-Hellouin, renowned since medieval times so that it's usually just called Bec, is still a working Benedictine convent, although little remains of the original buildings. The Benedictine Order bought the ruins in 1948 and carried out restoration. The buildings belong to the state and may be visited, although not those parts where the community of nuns lives and works. It's located about 30 km southwest of Rouen, on the Risle river, north of Brionne. Visit the abbey of Bec-Hellouin at http://www.abbayedubec.com/.

Maud died at the priory of **Notre-Dame-des-Prés**, **Rouen**, and is buried in Rouen's Notre-Dame cathedral. The **Cathedral of Rouen**, one of the most beautiful in France, consists almost entirely of the rebuilding from 1201, following a fire in 1200; its west front is well-known to art lovers, being the subject of several paintings by Monet, for example. It was extensively damaged during the Second World War, with subsequent restoration. For images of Rouen Cathedral, see http://www.beloit.edu/~arthist/historyofart/gothic/rouencath.htm.

Plantagenets

Wives and Children of Louis VII of France

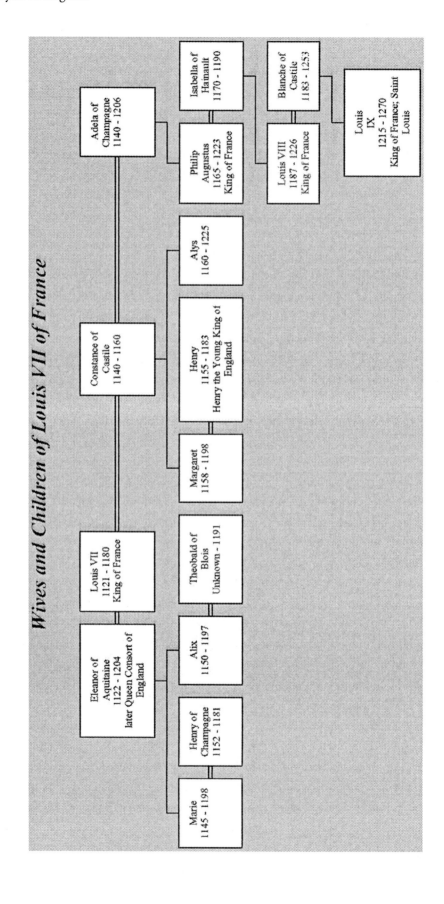

Some Descendants of Eleanor of Aquitaine

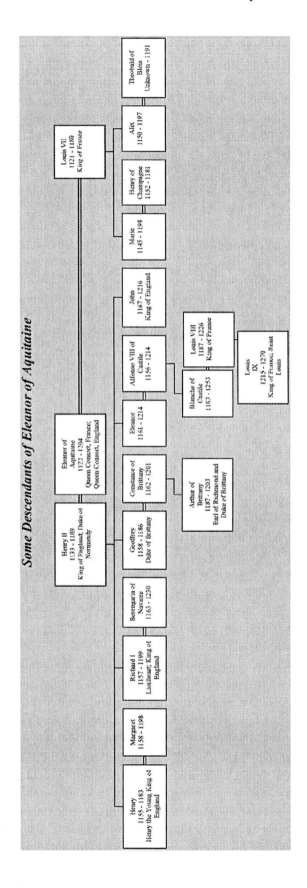

Eleanor of Aquitaine (1122–1204; Queen Consort of France, 1137–1152, Queen Consort of England, 1154–1189)

Eleven years older than her second husband, the Angevin Henry II, King of England, Eleanor of Aquitaine outlived him by about fifteen years. The very remarkable consort of a remarkable English monarch, Eleanor had already reigned as Queen Consort of France from the time her second husband was four years old. The annulment of her marriage to Louis VII of France in 1152 made possible Eleanor's marrying Henry of Anjou a few short weeks later. It also set the stage for the strange history of unstable friendship, marital alliances both realized and deferred, and deadly emnity that for decades would characterize the relationship between the Plantagenets and the Capets. Indeed, as her Plantagenet husband and sons themselves attacked and betrayed one another, or eventually sought reconciliation and forgiveness, Eleanor very often played a crucial part in whatever patricidal or fratricidal drama had begun. So did her first husband, Louis VII, and his son by his third wife, Philip Augustus.

Marriages undertaken for both dynastic and diplomatic purposes underpinned these untidy relationships between members of the French dynasty that had conquered England and the French dynasty that reigned in Paris. During the marriage of Eleanor to Louis VII, she produced two daughters, Marie and Alix. Both of Eleanor's daughters married nephews of Stephen, King of England—Henry of Anjou's predecessor and antagonist. Louis's second wife, Constance of Castile, also bore him two daughters. Margaret married the Lord Henry, son of Eleanor and Henry II of England. Alys's intended union with their son the Lord Richard, although promised for many years, never occurred—creating much friction between the Plantagenets and Capets as well as among the Plantagenets themselves. Louis's third wife, Adela of Champagne, finally bore him the long-deferred male heir, Philip Augustus. He would quarrel with Richard of England about Richard's not marrying Philip's half-sister Alys. Despite this and many other rifts, a granddaughter of Henry II and Eleanor would eventually wed Philip Augustus's son Louis and bear him a boy who would become Louis IX of France (later canonized as St. Louis). Doubtless, Eleanor's having married both Louis VII and Henry II complicated and intensified these interrelationships—when it did not actually envenom them.

Eleanor's father, as he lay dying in 1137, had advocated the marriage of the son of the King of France to his great heiress to Poitou, Aquitaine, and Gascony. Shortly after their 1137 wedding, her husband succeeded to the throne as Louis VII, and Eleanor became his Queen Consort. Although Louis loved Eleanor passionately, his Queen found their essential incompatibility more and more irksome. The preaching of the Second Crusade in 1146 provided a distraction, and Eleanor departed for the Holy Land with Louis in the following year. They would not return until 1149. Scurrilous gossip about Eleanor's closeness to her decade-older paternal uncle, Raymond of Antioch, put a further strain on an already unstable marriage, and Eleanor told Louis that she agreed with those who believed they were too closely related by blood to have a valid union. Eventually, their lack of a male heir after 15 years persuaded Louis to pursue an annulment, granted three years after their return.

In the meantime, Henry of Anjou had become Duke of Normandy in 1150. Louis—threatened by Henry's growing power in France—and his brother-in-law Eustace (the son of Stephen of England, formerly Duke of Normandy)—threatened by Henry's claim on England—invaded Normandy in 1151. A truce preceded peace talks arbitrated by Bernard of Clairvaux in Paris. There Henry of Anjou met Eleanor of Aquitaine, Queen Consort of France.

A few weeks after the annulment of Eleanor's marriage to Louis in 1152, in the Cathedral of Saint-Pierre in Poitiers, she married Louis's vassal and antagonist, Henry of Anjou—without Henry's notifying Louis or seeking his permission. (Eleanor and Henry also were related by blood to a degree that prohibited marriage by Church law.) The annulment had cost Louis Aquitaine as well as Eleanor; Henry's control of Aquitaine now added greatly to his power. In response, Eustace and Louis harried Henry in Normandy, while Stephen threatened Henry's allies in England. The indomitable Henry fought off all attacks, not neglecting to invade England as well in 1153. Having reached a political settlement with Stephen, Henry succeeded Stephen as King of England in 1154. He and his wife waited for their coronation in the Saxon palace at Bermondsey opposite the Tower of London. For many years, Eleanor would from time to time act as Henry's Regent either in England or on the Continent. In 1161, a peace agreement arranged at Fréteval solidified a truce with Louis.

As Eleanor bore Henry son after son, while Louis waited in vain for a male heir, they negotiated a marriage between Henry's oldest surviving son, the Lord Henry, and Louis's daughter Margaret. If Louis begot no sons, Henry stood to benefit from his heir's claim on Margaret's inheritance. Louis frustrated that scheme in 1165 when his third Queen gave birth to Philip Augustus. As Henry, who invaded Brittany in 1166 and planned to add it to his domains, became even more of a threat to Louis's royal prestige, Louis encouraged Henry to divide his lands among his sons. In 1169, during peace talks at Montmirail, Henry announced his intentions. The Lord Henry would get England, Normandy, and Anjou; the Lord Richard would inherit Aquitaine (Eleanor had been living there with Richard, her favorite) and would marry Louis's daughter Alys; the Lord Geoffrey would receive Brittany. In the following year, the crowning of the Lord Henry as Henry the Young King seemingly solidified this division of spoils.

So far, Louis had sought to check the success of the marital alliance of his former wife and her second husband. At this point, however, Eleanor seems to have become estranged from Henry as she reigned splendidly in her court in Poitiers at the ducal palace, including the Maubergeon Tower. This estrangement may—or may not—have had to do with Henry's love affair with Rosamund Clifford, who would die in 1176. Unaware of or impervious to mounting tensions among the Plantagenets, preoccupied with the aftermath of the murder of Thomas Becket, Henry left England for Ireland in 1171. In order to prevent a Norman baron of Wales, Richard de Clare (called "Strongbow") from establishing himself in Ireland, Henry became overlord of three-quarters of the island. In 1172, he also reconciled himself with the Church. Louis, who had given asylum to Becket during his exile from England, now allied himself with Eleanor and with Henry's sons against Louis's old enemy.

As Henry discovered in 1173 the intricacies of this conspiracy between his wife, his sons, and his wife's first husband, he captured Eleanor and began an imprisonment of her (mostly at Winchester and Sarum [Salisbury]) that would last for over 15 years, until Henry's own death. He also considered annuling their marriage but did not act upon this purpose. Outfoxing Louis as well as his own sons Henry, Geoffrey, and Richard, the victorious Henry in the 1174 Treaty of Montlouis offered additional revenues to his sons in place of the increased authority and power they had vainly sought. From 1174 to 1177, other treaties established Henry as overlord of Scotland, Wales, and Ireland.

With Philip Augustus being crowned as King of France by Henry the Young King in 1179 in the presence of Geoffrey and Richard and with Louis VII succumbing to mortal illness in 1180, a new actor enlivened the drama. Far more effectively than his father, Philip Augustus would for decades manipulate the Plantagenets. Setting the sons against each other or the sons against their father, he schemed to destroy the Plantagenet threat to Capetian power and prestige.

Helped by Philip and Geoffrey, Henry the Young King in 1183 feuded with his brother Richard and his father. The Young King's sudden death made the Lord Richard the eldest surviving Plantagenet heir. In spite of his new prospects, Richard resented Henry II's suggestion that he give Aquitaine to his youngest brother, John, Henry's favorite "Lackland." (Henry's attempts to grant land and property to John often enraged John's older brothers.) During this 1184 quarrel, Geoffrey and John attacked Poitou, while Richard attacked

Brittany, which Geoffrey had taken over upon his marriage to the heiress Constance of Brittany in 1181. Philip supported Geoffrey.

Further events muddied the outcome of this family conflict. Given Ireland as a responsibility, John in 1185 failed miserably in his expedition there. Richard gave Aquitaine back to Eleanor. Plotting further with Philip Augustus, Geoffrey died in a tournament in 1186. Geoffrey's posthumous son, Arthur of Brittany, was born in the next year.

Now Henry II's only remaining male heirs, Richard and John, both conspired with Philip against their father in 1189. Richard suspected that Henry might supplant him with John. In addition, both Richard and Philip resented Henry's failure to marry Alys of France to Richard. Ill and defeated, Henry accepted their peace terms. When he discovered that his favorite, John, had joined the conspiracy against him, Henry died in despair and grief. He had just watched his birthplace burn, and now he had lost the family for which he had assembled an empire. His wife and his sons all had betrayed him; only his bastard son Geoffrey had remained loyal and had comforted the King in his last desolate hours.

Henry's 1189 death released him from despair; it also released Eleanor from the confinement she had endured since 1173. The new King both gave orders for her liberty and made her Regent of England. As her beloved Richard eagerly left in 1190 to fight in the Third Crusade, Eleanor escorted Berengaria of Navarre to Sicily so that she might marry Richard. Richard's choosing not to marry Alys angered his fellow Crusader Philip Augustus, who soon returned to France and began conspiring with the Lord John against King Richard. On Richard's way back from the Holy Land in 1192, he fell into the hands of another enemy, Leopold V of Austria, who imprisoned him and then handed him over to the Holy Roman Emperor to hold for ransom. While Eleanor sought to raise the enormous amount demanded and actually delivered the ransom, John and Philip tried to bribe the Emperor Henry VI to break his word and not release Richard. When the ransomed Richard did return in 1194, Eleanor reconciled him with his brother John. After years more of fighting Philip, Richard died of a mangled wound in 1199. In Eleanor's presence, he had named John his heir. Nevertheless, Philip would support her grandson Arthur of Brittany against her son King John and would seek every opening he could use to erode the Plantagenets' hold on their French territories.

In the year of Eleanor's death at the age of 82 in 1204, John lost hold of the Plantagenets' Continental empire. Normandy, Anjou, Maine, Touraine, and Poitou would acknowledge Philip Augustus as their lord, and Gascony would bow to John's brother-in-law Alfonso VIII of Castile. Eleanor would not live to see the consequent transformation of the Plantagenets from French potentates with an English Kingdom into an English dynasty. The notorious consort and the revered ruler was now a very old woman. Both of her husbands and all of her children had died before her, except John and Alfonso's wife Eleanor. Although approaching 80, fostering yet another dynastic and diplomatic marriage between a Plantagenet offshoot and the royal house of Capet, in 1200 the intrepid Eleanor had escorted her granddaughter Blanche from Castile to France so that Blanche might marry Philip Augustus's son Louis.

Eleanor of Aquitaine Sites

Eleanor was probably born at either the ducal palace at **Poitiers** or in **Bordeaux**, at either the Ombrière Palace or the château of Belin. All these were favorite residences of her family's, especially the ancient palace at **Poitiers**, dating from Merovingian times. The ducal palace is now incorporated within the Palais de Justice. Notable is the splendid great hall called the Salle des Pas-Perdus (hall of lost footsteps), 48 m long and 16 m wide. See the hall at http://www.ca-poitiers.justice.fr/capoib/juri/ca-hist.php?rank=7 (in French), displaying arcaded sides (round arches one side, the other pointed) leading to the south gable end, which features beautiful mullioned windows above a set of fireplaces. Another building of note is the Tour Maubergeon, in which Eleanor's grandfather William X had installed his mistress, the Viscountess of Châtellerault, nicknamed Dangerosa. Known as La Maubergeonne because of her residence there. she later became Eleanor's grandmother after her daughter wed William's son and heir.

Poitiers, with 83,000 population, is the ancient capital of Poitou. On Eleanor's marriage to Henry II, it passed to the English crown. On a hill overlooking a bend in the river Clain, it has seen industrial growth and subsequent sprawl. The best information and photograhs are presented at http://www.francebalade.com/poitou/poitiers.htm. There's a photograph of the ducal palace itself, along with a fine photograph of the fireplace and window end of the Salle des Pas-Perdus. The English translation is quite comprehensible, with only minimal howlers.

The château of Ombrière at **Bordeaux** consisted of a high tower set in courtyards with tiled fountains and gardens, towering at the mouth of the Peugue river. It no longer exists, although the Porte Cailhau stands on the site of the former gate leading to the palace. Another proposed birthplace is the château of Belin. The village of **Belin-Béliet** is located in the Landes area, south of Bordeaux on the N10. No trace of the château remains.

Eleanor married Louis VII at **St-André Cathedral, Bordeaux**. Only the plain, aisleless nave would have existed then; the huge, elaborate, Rayonnant Gothic choir, which contrasts so notably with the nave, was not begun until later. The city of Bordeaux, with about 215,000 inhabitants, is not one of the most elegant in France, lacking the great buildings one would expect, but is noted, of course, for its food and the wines of the region. There's an array of attractive photographs of Bordeaux at http://www.eurotravelling.net/france/bordeaux/bordeaux_gallery.htm.

At http://www.virtourist.com/europe/bordeaux/09.htm you will see what the site calls the "back view" of the cathedral, with the Pey Berland campanile in the distance at right.

The website http://www.bordeaux.com/j_city.html is refreshingly uncluttered and clearly expressed, providing a walking tour of the city with brief but clear tourist information in the section titled "Define." Otherwise, the site emphasizes the wines of the eminent Bordeaux region along with food, and has intriguingly titled section headings, especially one called "Seduction."

The ducal family owned a number of other keeps and châteaux that Eleanor would have been visited, at Limoges, Niort, Saint-Jean d'Angély, Blaye, Melle, and Bayonne. The hunting lodge of **Talmont**, on the coast north of La Rochelle, is shown at http://www.casteland.com/puk/castle/ploire/vendee/talmont/talmont.htm.

Eleanor joined her uncle in **Antioch**. At one time called the Queen of the East because of its strategic trading position, and famous for its early Christian community, Antioch is today's **Antakya**, with a population of over 100,000. It is located on the Orontes river, in southernmost Turkey, on a spur of land running down the coast beside Syria. The ancient city is mostly buried, but important archeological finds are housed in the archeological museum and at Daphne, a coastal suburb. For tourist information, see http://www.turkeytravelplanner.com/WhereToGo/Mediterranean/Antakya-Hatay/Antakya.html

The years in which Eleanor was kept constrained by Henry are not documented thoroughly; her whereabouts were kept fairly quiet. Among the places documented is **Ludgershall Castle**. Earthworks and part of one wall remain of this previous royal castle and hunting lodge. Owned by British Heritage, the site is northwest of the village of Ludgershall, Wiltshire (not the village of the same name in Buckinghamshire), a few miles northwest of Andover. See this at http://www.btinternet.com/~timeref/hpl806.htm.

Mainly she stayed in Winchester and Sarum (Salisbury). For **Winchester**, see *William I*. Graciously situated in a valley where the Avon, Bourne, and Nadder rivers meet, **Salisbury** is today a popular market town of 36,000 population, with a notably beautiful cathedral complex. However, the town was developed there when its precursor, **Sarum**, was abandoned by the see. Sarum, in which Eleanor stayed, was in a bleak location on the nearby uplands, lacking sources of water and apt to be battered by gales. Old Sarum traces its past to an Iron Age hill fort, occupied by the Romans followed by the Saxons, then the Normans with their castle and cathedral. The excavated remains are mostly Norman, the earthworks of the castle and the foundations of the cathedral; the cathedral was stripped of its materials for the new one in Salisbury. See images of the site at http://www.britannia.com/travel/magical/magic13.html.

She died either at Fontevraud or Poitiers, but probably at **Fontevraud**, where she had been consecrated a nun. Her tomb in the abbey depicts her reading a book, rare in effigies, which don't usually show the person living, let alone engaged in any activity. Like those of Henry II and Richard I, also in Fontevraud, her tomb was vandalised during the French Revolution. The tombs, along with that of King John's second wife, Isabella of Angoulême, are ranged in the south transept of the abbey. For more details, see *Henry II*.

Henry II

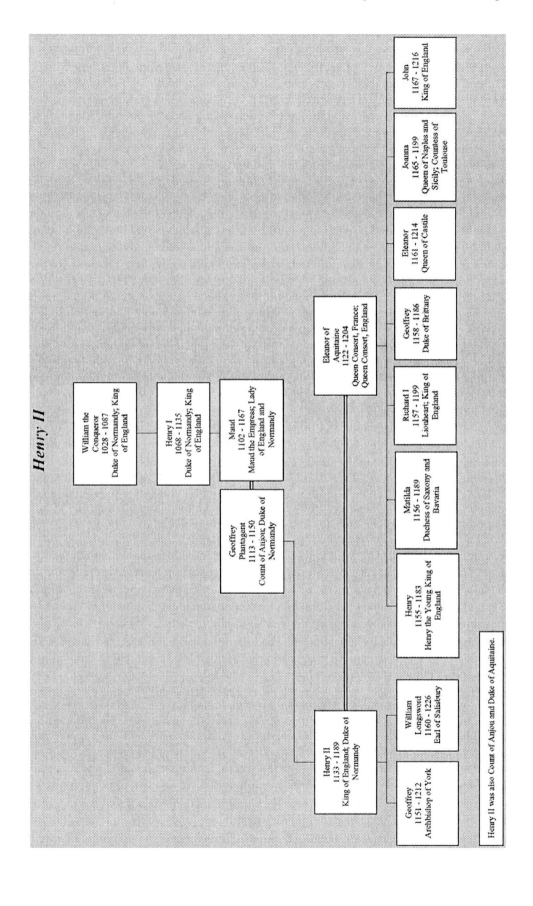

Henry II was also Count of Anjou and Duke of Aquitaine.

Henry II (1133–1189; Duke of Normandy, 1150–1189; Count of Anjou, 1151–1189; Duke of Aquitaine, 1152–1189; King of England, 1154–1189)

The young Henry of Anjou who added England to his vast French holdings grew into an aggressor who expanded an empire to bequeath to his sons. With lands that stretched from northern England to the Pyrenees, Henry II also made himself overlord of Scotland, Wales, and Ireland. A man who embodied many contradictions, Henry hated war and sought to impose order and lawful authority by his regal will. Both his territorial aggression and his imposition of his authority, of course, heightened his control of men and events. Henry's inability to cede control and relinquish power inflicted on him the most grievous crises of his reign: the rupture of his friendship with Thomas Becket and the rebellions of his sons against him. Although Henry's need to dominate alienated both Becket and Henry's sons, the King perceived only their betrayal of his love. The rage and hatred with which he reacted to these many betrayals masked—perhaps even from Henry himself—wounded affection, desire for reconciliation, and profound grief over loss.

In one manifestation of his regal authority, Henry sought to extend his control over civil and criminal law in England. He asserted his jurisdiction over freemen and freehold property in civil cases. In criminal cases, he wanted authority over everyone, including serfs, given only to royal officers like sheriffs and judges. (Norman lords were freemen, whereas most English natives were serfs.) There being no police force, prominent local figures serving as jurors decided the fate of criminals and the outcome of property cases. Royal assizes ordered trials by jury of property disputes. Jury trials replaced trials by battle or ordeal. Royal writs to the King's itinerant justices and to other royal officers standardized procedures in both civil and criminal cases. This improved the efficiency of the judicial system, as well as made it more consistent.

In thus bringing many judicial matters under royal control, Henry claimed he was merely reimposing customs from the reign of his maternal grandfather, Henry I. (This rationale respected the value given to tradition in an extremely conservative society.) A charter issued in the last years of Henry II's reign noted, "When by God's favour I attained the kingdom of England, I resumed many things which had been dispersed and alienated from the royal demesne in the time of Stephen my usurper." When Henry attempted to extend his control to clerical lawbreakers, he used this same argument that he simply sought to reinstate the venerable customs of Henry I.

In response to Henry's pressure, his barons had surrendered castles and the authority stolen from the crown during Stephen's time. Thomas Becket, an archdeacon of Canterbury whom Henry made Chancellor in 1155 at the suggestion of Archbishop Theobald, had helped Henry challenge baronial and ecclesiastical privileges. After Henry made his Chancellor Archbishop of Canterbury in 1162, the King expected Becket's continuing support in the struggle to impose royal control. To everyone's surprise, and especially to Henry's, his close friend Becket instead immediately resigned his post as Chancellor and cast himself as the King's antagonist.

King and Archbishop fell out over the issue of criminous clerks. The many lay clergy of England claimed the same right as ordained priests to trial only in an ecclesiastical court. Doubting that Church courts inflicted penalties adequate to serious crimes, Henry wanted to reinstate a past custom whereby a secular court would punish a clerk already convicted in an ecclesiastical court. The Church court punished an offender by degradation from his clerical status. Becket argued that such degradation was punishment enough. Henry contended that the secular court should inflict a sentence on an already degraded clerk. Becket denied the validity of secular jurisdiction even over degraded clerks.

In upholding the Church's freedom from secular control, Becket followed Pope Gregory VII's lead. When Gregory battled with the Holy Roman Emperor Henry IV in 1081, he asserted, "Who does not know that kings and dukes originated from those who, being ignorant of God, strove with blind greed and insufferable presumption to dominate their equals...by pride, violence, treachery, and murder? And when they try to force the priests of the Lord to follow them, can kings not best be compared to him who is the head over all the children of pride? The Devil." (Henry II's contemporary Bernard of Clairvaux himself had noted of the Plantagenets, "From the Devil they came, and to the Devil they will return.") Gregory had invoked a separate status for the clergy that amounted to privilege. Becket upheld this special privilege even for criminous clerks.

What Becket saw as a royal and secular encroachment, Henry saw as an attempt to deter crime. The King's 1164 Constitutions of Clarendon attempted to force Becket and the English bishops to agree to a reinstatement of earlier customs subjecting clerical offenders to secular punishment. Becket resisted the Constitutions of Clarendon. An enraged Henry then sought to badger and harass the Archbishop, who eventually fled into exile in November 1164. Louis VII of France offered Becket asylum.

Once Becket had left England, Henry remained preoccupied with many other concerns until 1170, when he wanted to crown his eldest son during his own lifetime. Although the prerogative to crown belonged to the Archbishop of Canterbury, Henry II had the Archbishop of York perform the coronation of Henry the Young King. Two months later, at Fréteval, Henry and Becket reconciled and agreed to a second coronation by Becket. After his return as Archbishop of Canterbury, news of Becket's excommunication of the Archbishop of York infuriated Henry into his famous, ill-considered outburst that unintentionally incited four knights to leave his Christmas court at Bures in Normandy and murder Becket in his cathedral.

Henry reacted to the death of Becket with intense, even extravagant grief. Arnulf, Bishop of Lisieux, noted, "the king burst into loud lamentations and exchanged his royal robes for sackcloth and ashes, behaving more like the friend than the sovereign of the dead man. At times he fell into a stupor, after which he would again utter groans and cries louder and more bitter than before.... it seemed from the excess of his grief that he had determined to contrive his own death.... First we had to bewail the death of the archbishop; now, in consequence, we began to despair of the life of the king...." When Henry and Becket had reconciled at Fréteval, the King had pleaded with tears in his eyes, "My lord archbishop, let us return to our old friendship, and each show the other what good he can; and let us forget our hatred completely." Clearly, whatever bitterness Henry felt about Becket's betrayal had never destroyed the King's affection or his longing for his friend.

Although deeply shocked by the murder of the Archbishop, whom he had tried to restrain, Pope Alexander III authorized the Compromise of Avranches in 1172 that provided a means of reconciliation. The Church yielded some jurisdiction over clerical offenders but only at its own initiative and discretion. The Compromise created a framework within which the secular and religious powers could negotiate continually and successfully about jurisdictional questions—something Becket's dramatic and extreme posturing had prevented by alienating Henry. The more diplomatic Alexander III nevertheless recognized Becket's heroism by canonizing him in 1173.

Henry II had had to negotiate a compromise with the Church that negated his unilateral attempts to extend his royal authority over criminous clerks. Becket had gained his point in death. His resistance to Henry produced other notable results. Instead of merely referring to traditions, the Constitutions of Clarendon of 1164 had specified the applicable customs of Henry I in order to counter Becket's reliance on a system of canon law. Royal writs continued this response of writing down the customs, as did the assize of Clarendon, 1166; the inquest of Sheriffs, 1170; the assize of Northampton, 1176; the assize of Arms, 1181; and the assize of Woodstock, 1184. The consequent establishment of a legal bureaucracy promulgating written customs and procedures made it practical to assert and extend the King's authority, standardized and replicated by writing.

With the creation of a permanent governmental bureaucracy that included much more than a system of justice and could operate in the King's absence, Henry could travel throughout his farflung lands in order to defend his possessions and keep an eye on his officials. Henry's energetic dedication during these constant travels usually exhausted his companions. The King rarely settled anywhere for more than a few weeks. During his 34-year reign in England, Henry celebrated Christmas in 24 different places and crossed the Channel 28 times. Normandy and Anjou (rather than England) being central to his realm, he spent 176 months in Normandy; 154 months in England, Ireland, and Wales; and 84 months elsewhere in his French lands. His chief residence in England, as well as the site of the court and the exchequer, was Westminster; Winchester held the treasury; the King favored his former hunting lodges at Clarendon and Woodstock, where legend says his lover Rosamund Clifford lived. Henry II also added to the reworking of William the Conqueror's wooden castle at Windsor in stone.

Well might Henry II recall the memory of his great-grandfather, as many themes recurred from the life of the Conqueror—England being part of a Continental empire; sons quarrelling over their inheritance and even fighting their father—with this difference: Henry II possessed a larger empire and more sons. Resentful of his reluctance to cede any real authority to them, his elder sons conspired with their mother and Louis VII of France to rebel against Henry. Faced with this 1173–74 uprising, Henry allowed the monks and clergy of Canterbury to flog him as a penitent at Becket's shrine and felt rewarded by the immediate capture of another antagonist, William the Lion of Scotland. Henry's victory over this insurrection did not prevent later trouble culminating in the King's defeat by his son Richard and Philip Augustus of France. Already very ill, Henry learned that his favorite son, John, had joined this rebellion and then despairingly welcomed his own death. As the dying King acknowledged, only his bastard son Geoffrey had remained loyal to the end. The pathos of his grief and sorrow over his family's betrayal, coupled with Henry II's immense administrative achievements and vivid personality, render him a fascinating figure—especially when viewed from the safe distance of over eight centuries.

Henry II Sites

Henry was born at Le Mans, on March 5, 1133. For detail regarding Le Mans, see the chapter on ***Stephen and Maud***. A useful website appears at http://www.francebalade.com/maine/lemans.htm. Amongst all the clutter are attractive photographs and information (in French). Tortured but better-than-nothing English is available to clicking on "anglais" in the top left corner.

In 1154, Henry landed in **Lymington** on his way to his coronation. Lymington, positioned on the estuary where the Lymington river flows into the Solent, is an old port and boating center. It's also a pleasant town of 39,000 inhabitants, a Georgian High Street and posh shops selling nautical wear and gear. Situated down on the coast just south of the New Forest, the site includes the attractions of Hurst Castle on a sandspit stretching out into the Solent, and the Isle of Wight beyond. Visit http://www.lymington.biz/lymington/visiting.asp for photographs and information.

The town of **Fréteval** is tucked into a curve of the river Loir (a tributary of the Loire) just before the intersection of the N157 with the N10, between Châteaudun and Vendôme; the remnants of its château, where Henry met Becket, rear up above. Visit Fréteval at http://www.cc-haut-vendomois.com/cchv.html (in French), by clicking on the name on the local map provided. There is a website in English, giving the visiting hours along with one photograph and not much else; the URL is impossibly long, so go to http://www.western-loire.com/ and enter Freteval in the Search box. On the next screen, click on Cultural sites and historic monuments, and then on "Château féodal." Also famous, for having served as a hiding place for Allied airmen during the Second World War, the nearby Forest of Fréteval is located beside the N10, south of Châteaudun.

The murder of Thomas Becket in **Canterbury Cathedral** led to Becket's prompt canonization and the development of pilgrimages to the cathedral, which still take place. Apart from that, the cathedral is, of course, one of the major ecclesiastical attractions in Europe, being the seat of the Archbishop of Canterbury. Under Lanfranc, the first Norman archbishop, the cathedral was begun on the site of St. Augustine's church (he was the first archbishop of Canterbury). This was replaced from 1096–1130 and again beginning from 1391. Architecturally, the exterior, of Caen stone, is grander than the interior; the value of the latter lies in the many tombs and the beautiful stained glass. Canterbury Cathedral's website is at http://www.canterbury-cathedral.org/histbuild.html. Further down the screen, you will see the statue of Becket. At http://www.sacredsites.com/europe/england/canterbury_cathedral.html, there is a photograph of the stained glass window in the cathedral depicting the murder of Becket, along with an account of pilgrimages to Canterbury.

Henry did penance for the murder of Becket at various times for the rest of his life. Among the places he visited was the cathedral at **Avranches**, where, barefoot and dressed only in a shirt, he abased himself before the cathedral and asked forgiveness. This event is memorialized in a paving stone by the west portal. Nothing remains of the cathedral but excavated fragments on a square called La Plate-Forme, including the paving stone (chained down). Avranches is better known for its outlook over the major tourist and pilgrimage attraction of the striking Mont-Saint-Michel. The website for Avranches can be found at http://www.ville-avranches.fr/english/histoire/histoire_abrincates.htm.

By the time Henry ascended the throne, private castles had grown like mushrooms in the anarchy of Stephen's reign. Henry's aim was to take control of all castles for the sake of law and order within the Kingdom. In the process, he destroyed ("slighted") far more than he built as he got rid of privately-owned ones.

Orford is situated in Suffolk, up the coast from Felixstowe, in a relatively isolated position on the river Ore which provides it with a port, sheltered from the North Sea by Orford Ness. Henry drained the local marshes and had the castle constructed 1165–67 to defend himself against the powerful Bigod family. The castle is uniquely shaped as an irregular polygon, comprising 21 sides to a keep with three projecting towers. It was also the first castle for which the entire building accounts survive, now held in the Public Record Office. Orford Castle stands on an elevation overlooking the village. A full account, with illustrations, appears at http://www.castles-abbeys.co.uk/Orford-Castle.html, including a depiction of the castle c.1600, showing the curtain wall, which has since disappeared.

At **Windsor Castle**, Henry's work was extensive. He is traditionally considered to be responsible for rebuilding the Conqueror's wooden fortress in stone, notably the Round Tower. However, it seems more likely that he worked with an existing stone shell, building essentially a new keep inside the old one. In addition, he added a curtain wall and fortified the lower ward, as well as improving accommodations for the court. For background information on Windsor Castle, see *William the Conqueror*.

At **Dover Castle**, Henry undertook a massive construction program: the cubical keep, a curtain wall with 14 towers, and two gatehouses were built from 1181–87. The work cost over £6,000. Although the rectangular keep was now being superseded by more complex shapes, as at Orford Castle, the plumbing at Dover was advanced: a well runs from the top of the keep down through the walls and 289 feet into the cliff below. Dover Castle dates from an Iron Age fortification and includes the Pharos, which, dating from about AD 50, may be the oldest standing building in Britain, and a Saxon church, St. Mary-in-Castro, restored in 1860. Visit it at http://www.theheritagetrail.co.uk/castles/dover%20castle.htm.

At **Newcastle** (Newcastle-upon-Tyne), the plumbing system became complex, with pipes conveying water all over the keep. The well, lined with stone all the way down, is 99 feet deep. The keep is of sandstone and 85 feet high, prominent on Newcastle's skyline, and is one of the few surviving buildings of what was once a vast complex, one of the most important castles in northern England. Spiral staircases lead up to the restored 19th century battlements and down to the chapel. The Black Gate dates from 1247, the only surviving tower;

the only other substantial building remaining is the heavily restored chapel. Unhappily, the site of the castle is bisected by a railway line. View the castle at http://www.touruk.co.uk/castles/castle_Newcastle.htm. (Note that there is also a castle at Newcastle in Wales; it's easy to confuse the two when searching the Internet.)

Henry founded the château at **Niort**, a town of 16,000 on the edge of the Marais area of France, northeast of La Rochelle. Apart from this situation as a tourist venue, Niort's main attraction is its château. There's a lovely photograph at the appropriately titled http://www.alovelyworld.com/webfranc/htmgb/fra081.htm.

An archeological and history museum with an extensive pottery collection, pieces dating from 2000 BC, is housed within the towers, and the view from the battlements is superb. Tourist information can be found at http://www.letsgo.com/FRA/08-PoitouCharentes-247.

At **Gisors** Castle, Henry reinforced and buttressed the walls. In 1184 he inserted a chapel dedicated to Thomas Becket, fitting it into a space between the inner walls and the donjon. For Gisors, see chapter on *William Rufus*.

Henry's incursions into **Wales** were for purposes of teaching the Welsh about his overlordship, but after the failed campaign of 1165, Henry left Wales and thus no legacy of his building survives there. Nevertheless, King Street in the town of **Laugharne**, on Carmarthen Bay on the south coast, is named thus in memory of his visit, and he is known to have visited **Haverfordwest** (see *Henry I*). Nearby **Milford Haven** is a long, beautiful harbor in southwestern Wales, its tidal inlets extending long fingers inland, one reaching as far as Haverfordwest. Not surprisingly, it has often served as a departure point for monarchs bound for **Ireland**. The town of Milford Haven perches on the north side of the harbor, at the foot of the A4076, the main highway from the north. See the website for harbor and town at http://www.milfordhaven.info/.

In 1171, with a fleet of several hundred ships, Henry departed from Milford Haven to receive the submission from many of the Irish chiefs. At the same time, he declared himself Lord of Ireland, a claim later affirmed by Pope. At **Selskar Abbey**, Wexford, Henry did penance for the murder of Becket. See the abbey, with historical information about the abbey and town of Wexford, at http://www.wexfordweb.com/WexHistory.htm#top. Selskar was an Augustinian monastery, founded in 1190 and later laid waste by Cromwell's troops in 1649.

On the Thames (here called the Isis) at Wolvercote, northwest of Oxford, is **Godstow Lock.** The famous Trout Inn (a favorite of Inspector Morse) is here, and also the remains of the Benedictine abbey where Henry's mistress, the Fair Rosamund (sometimes spelled Rosamond), was educated and buried (c.1176). Detailed information about Godstow Abbey (or Nunnery) may be read at http://www.british-history.ac.uk/report.asp?compid=1485, and pictures seen at two walking-tour sites, http://www.waterscape.com/River_Thames/walking/Thames Path 5: Eynsham to Oxford and http://thames.joncombe.org/thames_oxford_northmoor.html.

Her death at Woodstock, according to dubious legend, resulted from a poisoned chalice given her by Eleanor. Henry built a secluded bower for Rosamund at **Woodstock manor.** The old manor was destroyed when Blenheim Palace was built (see the chapter on *Anne*.) In the grounds of Blenheim Palace, there is a pool called Rosamund's Well, supposedly constructed by Henry from a natural spring, and water from it is sold in the palace gift shop (Blenheim Water). For more about Woodstock manor, see *Henry I*.

During Henry's reign, **Clarendon** was extended from a hunting lodge to a palace. The remains of Clarendon stand in the Clarendon Forest, which was a deer park for hunting. Clarendon fell into disuse during the 16th century; over the centuries since, it was rediscovered from time to time, and most notably in the 1980s, when the site was excavated and studied in light of previous excavations, and woodland cleared discreetly to show the remains in its original setting: Clarendon is unique in that it is the only English medieval royal palace in its original landscape setting. Clarendon is located in Clarendon Park, on the east edge of Salisbury. The palace remains are a feature of a walk from Salisbury to Winchester called the Clarendon Way; read the description of the walk at http://www.hants.gov.uk/walking/clarendon/. A photograph of what's left of the palace can be seen at http://www.bbc.co.uk/southampton/features/joesjaunts/clarendonway.shtml.

Henry died at **Chinon**, where he had built Fort St-Georges. One of the great sights of the châteaux of the Loire is that of Chinon, a long complex consisting of three châteaux within its walls, the whole stretching along the hills overlooking the river Vienne. As well as Henry's St-Georges, the Tour de l'Horloge leading to the middle château contains a display on the life of Joan of Arc: in its Great Hall, Joan picked out her Dauphin from amongst his courtiers. The town of Chinon is itself elderly and picturesque, with narrow streets and old houses. Visit Chinon at http://www.francebalade.com/valvienne/chinon.htm. It's in French, but the English translation is so bad the information is either incomprehensible or deceptive (stating that the château is "overhanging Vienna," for example). Like all these sites, it contains a lot of colorful "noise," but the information is there. For basic tourist information in English and an illustration of each site, see http://tourisme.chinon.com/gb/visites/chinon.php.

A few kilometres west of Chinon is the burial place of Henry, along with Eleanor and their son Richard, **Fontevraud** (or Fontevrault) abbey. This large and remarkably intact abbey was founded by Robert d'Arbrissel for both women's and men's communities in 1101 and usually ruled by abbesses. In 1793, the monks' quarters were mostly destroyed; in 1804, the whole was transformed into a penitentiary, which lasted until 1963. Since then, prisoners have worked on the continuing restoration of the abbey, a process that began in 1910, and there is much to see: the Great Cloister (Grand-Moûter), the Chapter House and its paintings, the refectory and hospital, quite apart from the major attraction for our purposes, the Angevin tombs.

These lie in the south transept, on plinths, side by side, as if sleeping in a dormitory, Henry and Eleanor, their son Richard, and (possibly) John's second wife, Isabella of Angoulême. Henry's is the oldest effigy of any English King. At one time, the effigies were painted, and some of the color remains today. Visit the abbey at http://www.abbaye-fontevraud.com/index2.html (in French), or, more easily, at http://www.francebalade.com/anjou/fontevraud.htm. The English is mostly comprehensible here, although the "religieuses" have metamorphized into "chocolate eclairs."

Richard I and the Angevin Kings of Jerusalem

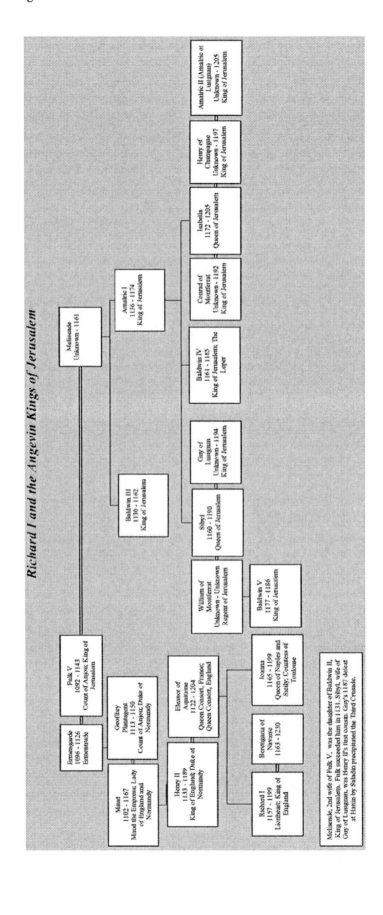

Melisende, 2nd wife of Fulk V, was the daughter of Baldwin II, King of Jerusalem. Fulk succeeded him in 1131. Sibyl, wife of Guy of Lusignan, was Henry II's first cousin. Guy's 1187 defeat at Hattin by Saladin precipitated the Third Crusade.

Richard I (Lionheart) (1157–1199; Duke of Normandy, Count of Anjou, Duke of Aquitaine, and King of England, 1189–1199)

Determining Richard's contemporary and posthumous reputation, the Third Crusade proved to be the central event of his life. The fervor with which Richard "took the cross" in 1187 derived in part from the intense religious emotions that he shared with many other European Christians but also from family concerns. The Latin Kingdom of Jerusalem that the Crusaders sought to wrest from Muslim control had Angevin rulers descended from Richard's great-grandfather, Fulk V, Count of Anjou, who had embarked on a second career as King of Jerusalem. Richard had spent his earlier manhood fighting his brothers and his father for possession of the Angevin empire in France. After Henry II's death in 1189 made Richard King, he would spend his last decade fighting for the Angevin Kingdom of Jerusalem (against Saladin) and then for his own Angevin empire (against his brother John and Philip Augustus of France).

In 1131, Fulk had succeeded his father-in-law, Baldwin II, as King of Jerusalem. With the failure of the male line of succession in 1186 after the death of Baldwin V, the Patriarch of Jerusalem had asked Henry II of England to take the crown, but Richard's father had declined to rule the Latin Kingdom to which he had given much financial support. The heiress, Henry II's first cousin Sibyl, had married Guy of Lusignan, familiar to the Plantagenets as a member of a baronial family from Poitou. His marriage to Sibyl made Guy King of Jerusalem. In July 1187, Salah ad-Din (Saladin)—a Kurd born in Tikrut who ruled Egypt and Syria—defeated Guy at the Battle of Hattin and captured the True Cross. In October, Jerusalem fell to Saladin, who treated both Jews and Christians with tolerance. Soon afterwards, Richard pledged that he would embark on a crusade to reconquer the Holy Land for Christianity.

A quarrel with Henry II pursued in partnership with Philip Augustus, while it ended with Henry's defeat and death and led to Richard's accession, also delayed Richard's departure on Crusade. Upon becoming King, he ensured the his deputies could govern in his absence, raised money for expenses, and prepared to leave. He would be gone for more than four years. The new King of England and the King of France met to set a date for embarking, to underscore that Richard would at last marry Philip's half-sister Alys, and to promise that neither would invade the other's domains.

On the way to the Holy Land, Richard and Philip met again in Norman Sicily, at Messina, where Richard revealed to Philip that he had decided not to marry Alys, perhaps because Henry II had seduced and impregnated his son's betrothed. Releasing Richard from his pledge in return for 10,000 marks, Philip contained his anger—for the moment. He left Sicily before Eleanor of Aquitaine arrived with Richard's newly chosen bride, Berengaria of Navarre. This prospective marriage secured an alliance with Berengaria's father, Sancho VI, that protected Richard's southernmost lands. Berengaria became close to Richard's sister Joanna, the recently widowed Queen of Sicily, whom Richard had released from prison upon his arrival. (He also conquered Messina and spent Christmas 1190 at a wooden castle he had erected there, called Mategriffon.) Joanna would spend most of the Third Crusade in Berengaria's company at Acre. During Richard's negotiations with Saladin, he would offer to marry Joanna to Saladin's brother el Melek el-Adel and have them rule jointly in Jerusalem. No one knows how seriously Richard meant this somewhat impractical offer.

Still making his way to Jerusalem, Richard conquered Cyprus as well—a strategic gain for the security of the Latin Kingdom. He married Berengaria there. When Richard arrived in the Holy Land, Philip and Guy were beseiging Acre, the largest town and chief port, won by Saladin in July 1187. Richard aided the Crusaders to victory at Acre in July 1191. Perceiving Saladin as failing to honor the surrender terms, Richard ordered the massacre of nearly 3,000 prisoners. Other victories at Arsuf and Jaffa did not bring with them the longed-for Christian control of Jerusalem. As a seasoned commander and strategist, Richard knew that Jerusalem, even if captured, would remain indefensible. The terms of peace he eventually negotiated with Saladin in 1192 left Jerusalem in Muslim hands but provided for access by unarmed Christian pilgrims. The Christians retained Jaffa, Caesarea, Haifa, Arsuf, Tyre, and Acre.

Philip had plotted with Conrad of Montferrat to displace Guy as King of Jerusalem. Philip and Richard eventually decreed that Guy could retain the throne for life, but that it would pass after Guy's death to his sister-in-law, Isabella, now forcibly and illegally married to Conrad. (She had a living husband.) Recurrent pressure to displace the little-respected King Guy with Conrad caused Richard to sell Cyprus to Guy, who founded a line that ruled Cyprus for three centuries. A few days before Conrad's coronation as King of Jerusalem, his murder spread rumors of Richard's involvement. (Actually, Rashid al-Din Sinan, "the Old Man of the Mountains" in Syria, had sent assassins to settle a score with Conrad.) Isabella, pregnant with Conrad's child, now married Richard's and Philip's nephew, Henry of Champagne, grandson of Eleanor of Aquitaine and Louis VII of France. Henry would rule with her over the Kingdom of Jerusalem.

Richard's negotiations with Saladin and failure to conquer Jerusalem created suspicion among some European Christians. The murder of Conrad, attributed to Richard, heightened their hostility. Enraged by Richard's repudiation of Alys, Philip Augustus had left the Crusade after Acre, determined to drive Richard from his Angevin holdings in France. Aware of her son John's plots with Philip against Richard, Eleanor of Aquitaine attempted to block them. Richard learned of these threats while still in the Holy Land. Feeling pressured to return to protect his realm, he nevertheless proceeded cautiously to avoid capture by his many Christian enemies.

When Richard left for Europe in October 1192, he may have intended to arrive in Saxony, where his brother-in-law Henry the Lion defied the Holy Roman Emperor, Henry VI. After a possible shipwreck in the Adriatic and even an encounter with pirates, Richard fell into the hands of Leopold, Duke of Austria, who had felt insulted by Richard at Acre and who (as Conrad's cousin) suspected Richard's complicity in his murder. Holding Richard at Dürnstein on the Danube, Leopold arranged to hand over his prisoner in December to Leopold's nephew Henry VI. The Emperor, who had his own claim to the Sicilian throne and therefore bore Richard a grudge, notified Philip Augustus of this prize captive, emphasizing "the treason, treachery, and mischief of which he had been guilty in the Holy Land."

At Easter 1193, at Speyer, Henry VI put Richard on trial concerning allegations that he had betrayed the Crusade and that he had arranged for Conrad's murder. The Emperor withdrew these charges after Richard defended himself with dignity and force. He then ordered Richard's removal to Trifels. Until February 1194, he would remain the Emperor's prisoner. Eleanor of Aquitaine and Richard's deputies strove to raise the two-thirds down payment of a ransom amounting to 150,000 silver marks. Philip tried to bribe the Emperor to keep Richard in prison in spite of being offered a King's ransom. Because the Emperor surmounted this temptation and also forced Richard to receive England from him as a fief of the Holy Roman Empire, Henry VI eventually released Richard in return for the down payment and noble hostages. In March 1194, Richard arrived in England at last.

He left again almost at once. In what remained of his life after his release, Richard spent three years in Normandy, one year in Anjou, and eight months in Aquitaine, but less than two months in England. (During his decade-long reign, he spent about six months in England—being crowned, preparing for the Crusade, or preparing to fight Philip Augustus.) He had to counter the results of Philip's conspiracies with John and invasions of Angevin territory. At one point in 1195, Philip offered trial by combat to settle their disputes: five knights would fight for each side. After Richard modified the suggestion to include himself and Philip as two of the 10 knights, Philip lost interest in his own proposal. During their recurrent fighting, Richard built his château Château-Gaillard in 1196. There he spent his last two years.

Richard died, not while battling with Philip, but while suppressing rebels in Aquitaine, the domain closest to his heart. While the King was beseiging the château of the Viscount of Limoges in March 1199, a crossbowman shot him from the ramparts. Gangrene poisoned his mangled wound. To his brother John, Lionheart left his empire; to the world, he left his legend—pervaded by military greatness, physical courage, and constant violence.

Richard I Sites

Richard was born at **Beaumont Palace** in Oxford. At the time, this was a substantial home; later it became a church of the White Friars, then a workhouse. By the 19th century, the birthplace of the Lionheart was roofless, a crumbling ruin with the remains of a fireplace.

In a reign lasting 10 years, Richard spent six months in Britain. In 1189, he was crowned Duke of Normandy in **Rouen Cathedral**. After his death in 1199, his heart was interred in the cathedral; an effigy on the south side of the ambulatory marks the spot. The cathedral is one of the great cathedrals of Europe, its façade often painted by Monet. It dates almost entirely from its rebuilding in 1201. For more information, see *Stephen and Maud.*

A flourishing port city of 260,000 population, **Messina** is tucked beside the northeastern tip of Sicily, facing the toe of mainland Italy. It is frequently troubled by earthquakes, spectacularly so in 1908 when over 90 percent of the city was devastated. The best website for tourist and historical information regarding Messina is http://sicilia.indettaglio.it/eng/comuni/me/messina/messina.html.

After he had conquered **Cyprus**, Richard married Berengaria of Navarre in the town of **Limassol**. An ancient civilization, Cyprus has been settled and conquered by many others. After the fall of the Ottoman Empire, it was under British rule and, since independence, has been plagued by the division between Turkish and Greek Cypriots (by far the majority). Nevertheless, tourism has been important for years, only occasionally affected by political unrest. **Limassol**, with a population of 87,000, is a port and resort, a well-known tourist center located on the western part of the south coast.

Visit Limassol at http://www.limassolmunicipal.com.cy/. Tourist information for Cyprus appears at http://www.visitcyprus.org.cy/.

Berengaria's birthplace is unknown, but she was the daughter of Sancho VI of Navarre. The old Kingdom of **Navarre** (now a province) was and is centered on the city of **Pamplona** (Iruña to the Basques) on the slopes of the foothills of the western Pyrenees. Pamplona is probably best-known for the annual running of the bulls through the narrow streets on the Feast of San Fermin (July 7), made famous outside Spain by Ernest Hemingway. Surrounded by its old walls and fortifications, it is nevertheless a relatively prosperous agricultural, communications, and industrial center with a population of 190,000. Pay a virtual visit and read tourist information at http://www.red2000.com/spain/pamplona/. Instructions (and warnings) for running with the bulls are posted at http://www.spanish-fiestas.com/spanish-festivals/pamplona-bull-running-san-fermin.htm, with a link to photographs or seen separately at http://www.sanfermin.com/2005/portada_new.php?lang=cas.

Acre has been an important sea port from ancient times. The present-day name is Akko, although Acre is still widely used for the Old City. An abundance of monuments in its densely populated, lively Old City attest to its varied occupation and citizens, including the Crusader city, now underground, a large complex of buildings built by the Knights of St. John during the 200 years of Crusader occupation. There are photographs of Acre, along with historical information, at http://www.jewishvirtuallibrary.org/jsource/vie/Acco.html. The Old City of Acre is now a Unesco World Heritage Site.

On the northern outskirts of the modern city of Herzliya lie the ruins of **Arsuf**, the ancient port of Rishpon where Richard defeated Saladin in 1191. Arsuf was destroyed by the Mamelukes in 1265. With its long, sandy beach, Herzliya is a favorite destination for excusions from the larger cities, and bus and train service is frequent. View the ruins at http://archnet.org/library/images/thumbnails.tcl?location_id=10105.

Jaffa (present name Yafo) now forms the southern part of the city of Tel Aviv, and its ancient half—Tel Aviv being a modern city. Although it began life as a suburb of Jaffa, Tel Aviv has 360,000 in population and is the commercial and financial center of Israel. Jaffa (or Yafo) hosts the old port, around which has grown an artists' colony and the usual associated shops and restaurants; during summer, outdoor events and festivals are popular here. Excavations at Jaffa have unearthed traces of settlement going back millennia; more recently, Jaffa was populated by the Hyksos, Egyptians, and Philistines. King David took the city, and Solomon's cedars of Lebanon were transported through the port of Jaffa. Tourist information for Tel Aviv-Yafo can be found at http://www.tel-aviv.gov.il/English/Tourism/Sites/Index.htm.

After being taken captive by Leopold, Duke of Austria, Richard was held at **Dürnstein** Castle in Austria. Dürnstein is located on the south bank of the Danube, 8 km west of Krems; it's a picturesque wine town, the castle on a hill high above. There's a fine photograph at http://www.cycletourist.com/Scenes/Austria/Durnstein.html. Other photographs of the town can be viewed at http://www.hominids.com/donsmaps/durnstein.html.

Richard was put on trial in **Speyer** (see *Stephen and Maud*). The imperial castle at **Trifels** saw him as an incumbent at the same time. Trifels consists of three mountains above the town of Annweiler, each about 500 m high and each with a castle on top. The imperial castle stood on the highest, Sonnenburg, and was the most formal of the three castles. The castle today is a 20th century re-creation; the original 12th century schloss was destroyed in 1602. See the castle at http://www.caltim.com/rheinland/trifels_castle.htm; a detailed history and photographs are provided at http://stronghold.heavengames.com/history/cw/cw45/.

Château-Gaillard was constructed by Richard in 1196, when the loss of Gisors left Rouen undefended, and eventually destroyed in 1603. The ruins are nevertheless grand, and its perch on sheer cliffs towering above the Seine is remarkable. The château is located near the town of Les Andelys, southeast of Rouen. Legend has it that it was constructed in one year, but it was more likely two. Richard's experience with warfare in the Holy Land shows itself in this château, which he described as "my beloved daughter." There are two parts, the main château atop the cliffs, and a redoubt below, called the Châtelet, separated from the main château by a moat and itself ringed with a moat and five towers, of which one survives. For photographs of Château-Gaillard, see the website for Les Andelys at http://www.giverny-art.com/andelys/indexen.htm.

Richard died at **Châlus** in 1199. Châlus is located on the N21, 35 km south of Limoges, and has been important strategically for its position on a main north-south route. Its château dates back to the 11th century, and underwent a number of sieges in its history, which have altered the appearance considerably. The most distinctive remaining feature is its cylindrical, 12th century donjon. The remains of the ancient chapel house Richard's entrails. Châlus is one of several châteaux associated with Richard that are on the Richard the Lionheart Route (Route Richard Coeur de Lion) in Limousin; read about the route at http://www.chateauribagnac.com/en/limousin_chateaux.php. The château recently passed into private hands and is no longer open to the public, and its previously informative website (http://www.chateaudechalus.com) is "under construction" at time of writing. A photograph can be seen at http://www.limousingite.com/area.html.

Richard's widow Berengaria of Navarre founded the **Abbaye de l'Epau** (l'Espan at the time) on the eastern outskirts of **Le Mans** and on the eastern side of the river Sarthe in 1230. Nothing of this building remains as it was burned down in 1365; the present building dates mostly from the late 14th century, and rebuilding was only partial. A picture of this can be seen at http://www.cister.net/viewabbey/122/. (At time of writing, any attempts to get into the abbey's website appear to be blocked.) The abbey now hosts an annual music festival, Festival de l'Epau. For Le Mans, see http://www.francebalade.com/maine/lemans.htm. Amongst all the clutter are attractive photographs and information (in French). Tortured but better-than-nothing English is available. (More information also appears in *Stephen and Maud*.)

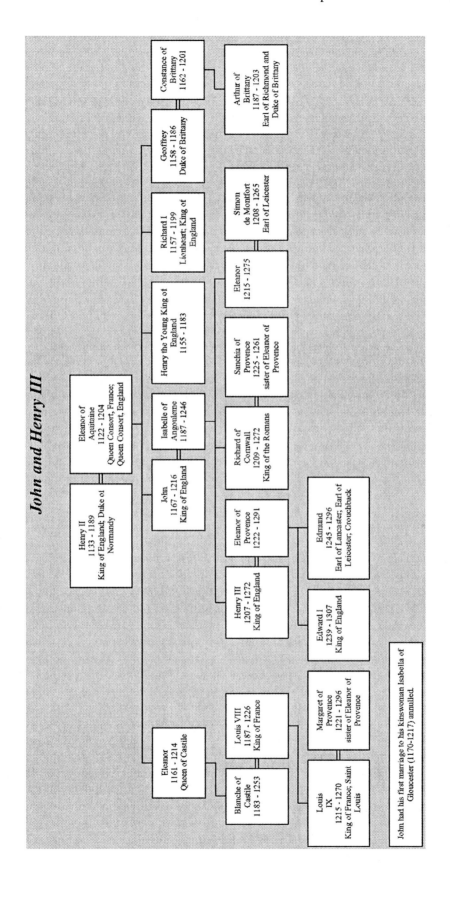

John and Henry III

Henry II
1133 - 1189
King of England; Duke of Normandy

Eleanor of Aquitaine
1122 - 1204
Queen Consort, France;
Queen Consort, England

Eleanor
1161 - 1214
Queen of Castile

Henry the Young King of England
1155 - 1183

Richard I
1157 - 1199
Lionheart; King of England

Geoffrey
1158 - 1186
Duke of Brittany

Constance of Brittany
1162 - 1201

Arthur of Brittany
1187 - 1203
Earl of Richmond and Duke of Brittany

Isabelle of Angoulême
1187 - 1246

John
1167 - 1216
King of England

Richard of Cornwall
1209 - 1272
King of the Romans

Sanchia of Provence
1225 - 1261
sister of Eleanor of Provence

Eleanor
1215 - 1275

Simon de Montfort
1208 - 1265
Earl of Leicester

Eleanor of Provence
1222 - 1291

Henry III
1207 - 1272
King of England

Edmund
1245 - 1296
Earl of Lancaster; Earl of Leicester; Crouchback

Edward I
1239 - 1307
King of England

Louis VIII
1187 - 1226
King of France

Blanche of Castile
1188 - 1253

Margaret of Provence
1221 - 1296
sister of Eleanor of Provence

Louis IX
1215 - 1270
King of France; Saint Louis

John had his first marriage to his kinswoman Isabella of Gloucester (1170-1217) annulled

John (1167–1216; Lord of Ireland, 1185–1216; Duke of Normandy, 1199–1204; Duke of Aquitaine, 1199–1216; King of England, 1199–1216)

Henry II's youngest son and least likely successor, John schemed against both his father and his elder brother Richard I in hopes of attaining the crown. After John finally became King in 1199, over the next seven years he lost most of the Angevin possessions in France to his family's clever antagonist Philip Augustus. A quarrel begun in 1206 with Pope Innocent III over the Pope's naming of Stephen Langton as Archbishop of Canterbury extended until John's submission in 1213. In the meantime, Innocent III punished England with a papal interdict and John with excommunication. Then the barons revolted against John's rule, with his 1215 signing of Magna Carta at Runnymede the culmination of one episode of their revolt. With the barons seeking French aid against John and John relying on the Pope, civil war plagued England at John's death in 1216. This tumultuous history of quarrels explains John's traditionally bad repute, but it also fails to depict his lasting achievements as a great administrator.

Like a Plantagenet successor in the 15th century, Richard III, John acquired a sulphurous reputation as a barely human devil. Many generations have shuddered enjoyably over the atrocities of which each stands accused. These include John's alleged murder of his nephew Arthur in 1203 and Richard's alleged complicity in the deaths of his nephews Edward V and Richard Duke of York. Although Richard III has suffered from the most diabolical depictions, these accusations picture his ordering his nephews' deaths. In contrast, some suspected that John himself killed Arthur rather than have him killed. The probable truth about both Richard and John is both less and more interesting than the lurid legends propagated by their enemies and popularized by Shakespeare. Each bears some guilt for crimes, though the scope of their crimes was no greater than that of many better-regarded contemporaries. Moreover, each deserves some honor for attempting to rule England well.

In John's case, his position in his family as the lastborn son determined much of his fate. Because his father, Henry II, had already portioned out his domains to John's elder brothers (Henry the Young King, Richard, and Geoffrey), he had nothing left to give his favorite son, John, whom he dubbed "Lackland." When Henry proposed to shift some of their properties to John, the older sons became enraged and rebelled. While this particular crisis eventually passed, John had insecure prospects during much of his young manhood as well as unclear prospects of succeeding to the throne. Henry II's passing, after the premature deaths of John's brothers Henry the Young King and Geoffrey, left Richard and John, as well as Geoffrey's son Arthur, as potential successors.

In the 19th century, Victoria succeeded her uncle William IV because her dead father was the next male sibling and she inherited his right. In the 12th century, however, this rule was not yet fast. If Richard I died, should the son of his next male sibling, his nephew Arthur of Brittany, succeed, or should Richard's own brother, John? The eminent statesman William Marshal contended for John, arguing "Undoubtedly, a son has a better claim to his father's land than a grandson; it is right that he should have it."

So, after much travail and uncertainty, Lackland finally inherited the domains ruled by Henry II and Richard I. The lastborn also inherited with these domains much accumulated anger at perceived injustices perpetrated by his father and brother. John himself alienated French magnates by pursuing Isabella of Angoulême, the betrothed of Hugh de Lusignan, and marrying her in 1200. All this anger culminated in the loss of John's French possessions as well as in the rebellion against John of his English barons. Believing that he must preserve his family's Angevin empire, John thereby alienated magnates in England who later resisted his rule. Magna Carta checked the strong rule of the Angevin Kings as embodied in Henry II and currently practiced by his last son. Hence, John's struggles within his French domains and his English Kingdom, though undoubtedly worsened by his own mistakes, also paid for the misdeeds of his predecessors. But his own actions were merely the last scenes in a long play in which he entered late.

One surprising ally John did retain in his struggle with the English barons—his former antagonist, Pope Innocent III, who had placed England under interdict in 1208, excommunicated John in 1209, and threatened to depose him. They had clashed over prerogatives concerning the appointment of the next Archbishop of Canterbury. So far from hurting John, what Englishmen saw as papal interference gathered support for him, and he solved his chronic financial problems for several years by diverting Church revenue to the Crown. Eventually, however, the quarrel with Innocent III—especially the threat of papally authorized deposition—seemed to cost John too much. By 1213, he submitted himself to Innocent as the Pope's vassal. Innocent thereafter protected John, not only from the English barons, but even from the Archbishop of Canterbury, Stephen Langton, whose disputed accession had sparked the initial quarrel.

Therefore, many of John's problems had roots in the bad behavior of others, and he had a reasonable case to make in his disputes over French territory, baronial prerogatives, and papal interference in English ecclesiastical appointments. Moreover, John's proposal that he become the Pope's vassal showed his cleverness in resolving a diplomatic impasse.

Regarding more tractable problems, John showed great ability as an administrator and serious interest in governing England well. W.L. Warren described in great detail "John's indefatigable attention to the business of government. It is probable that there had never been a King who devoted himself so keenly to the job of ruling…. John's government was alive and enterprising, and it owed much of its vigor to the zealous activity of the king himself."

Constantly on the move, John visited his Continental and English domains so assiduously that, according to Alan Lloyd, he "attained a personal knowledge of his vast and varied realm unprecedented in the history of his royal predecessors." A contemporary noted, "there was now no one in Ireland, Scotland, or Wales, who did not bow to his nod, a situation which, as is well known, none of his predecessors had achieved." He heard lawsuits, oversaw the workings of the exchequer, expanded the system of public records, reformed the currency, and authorized the formation of the first full-time Royal Navy. Moreover, unlike his English barons, he showed interest in the plight of the English masses and consistently demonstrated compassion and liberality toward them.

Doing his best with the problems begotten by others (even if worsened by his own mistakes), ruling effectively, John did, however, deserve blame for some crimes. He may have slain Arthur himself or had Arthur slain. However, Arthur, so far from being an innocent victim, struck other contemporaries, such as William Marshal and Innocent III, as a treacherous villain. John seems to have been responsible for the destruction of the Briouse family, including the deaths in exile of the baron William of Briouse and by starvation in prison of Matilda of Briouse and her son, atrocities that angered the English barons. He intrigued against his brother Richard I and against their father, Henry II. Given that Richard himself had warred against Henry and that Henry's Queen, Eleanor of Aquitaine, had encouraged her sons to rebel against their father, one can hardly single John out as being uniquely evil for seeking his own in a highly contentious family.

The portrait painted by modern biographers stands in stark contrast with the legendary bad repute created by hostile early chroniclers and perpetuated in the popular mind by tales of Robin Hood's aversion to the evil Prince John. One can only call upon Shakespeare to rectify the damage done by his own portrayal of King John. John, like Shakespeare's Lear, could justly cry, "I am a man / More sinn'd against than sinning."

John Sites

John was born at **Beaumont Palace**, Oxford. For more detail regarding Beaumont, see *Richard I*.

John was crowned Duke of Normandy in **Rouen Cathedral**. For information regarding the cathedral, see *Stephen and Maud*.

John married his cousin Isabella of Gloucester, at **Marlborough**, which netted him her vast estates. The childless marriage, which Baldwin, Archbishop of Canterbury, had declared null and void, was annulled in 1199. Isabella remarried twice after that, and died in 1217; she is buried in **Canterbury Cathedral**.

Marlborough Castle was one of the many homes of his parents, and after Richard I gave it to him, John often stayed there. The site is now within the grounds of Marlborough College, the famous school. The castle was probably first built as a motte and bailey, but is known to have been a castle during the reign of Stephen. It was in ruins by 1403, but recent excavation has revealed parts of the keep and curtain wall. Marlborough, a town of about 6,000, is notable primarily for its school. It's located west of Reading and north of Salisbury, and is close to the famous Avebury Stone Circles. Read about Marlborough and see photographs at http://www.castleandball.com/aboutmarlborough.htm (the website for the Castle and Ball Hotel).

John and Isabella of Angoulême married in **Bordeaux Cathedral**, on August 24, 1200. See *Eleanor of Aquitaine* for information regarding Bordeaux and the cathedral. **Angoulême**, a city of around 45,000 inhabitants, overlooks the river Charente, and is situated about equidistant from Bordeaux (to the south) and Poitiers (to the north). In spite of its being ancient, with an old city, its architecture isn't interesting. The city's website, http://www.angouleme.fr/portail/, is dull and uninformative, and in French only, including its link to its old city at http://www.vieil-angouleme.org/. A photograph of the one remaining wall of the Taillefer Palace, Isabella's family home, can be seen at http://www.vieil-angouleme.org/taillefer/plus.html, along with historical information in French. Angoulême may well be best known today for its annual International Comics Festival; see http://www.bdangouleme.com/index.ideal?langue=gb for details.

In 1204, John established the Cistercian house of **Beaulieu Abbey**. The most important remnants are the refectory, now the parish church, and the gatehouse, the home of Lord Montagu. The latter has maintained the remains of the abbey and the rest of the estate, as a home and as an important tourist site. Motoring buffs should visit the National Motor Museum there, with its large collection of vintage cars and motorcycles. Beaulieu is beautifully situated in the New Forest (take the B3056 from Lyndhurst). Its friendly website can be found at http://www.beaulieu.co.uk/.

At nearby Corfe Castle, a favorite residence of his, King John built the outer curtain wall, domestic ranges, great hall, and chapel. One-thousand-year-old **Corfe Castle** is now a ruin, towering spectacularly above the village of the same name, both harmoniously built from the local Purbeck stone. Corfe Castle is located in Dorset, on the Isle of Purbeck on the south coast near the popular seaside resorts of Swanage, Bournemouth, and Weymouth. It is owned by the National Trust, so visiting information, with a link to a useful local map, is available at http://www.nationaltrust.org.uk/scripts/nthandbook. dll?ACTION=PROPERTY&PROPERTYID=295, or through NT's home page. Some detail regarding John's contributions to Corfe Castle can be found at http://www.britainexpress.com/counties/dorset/castles/corfe.htm and more photographs at http://www.thedorsetpage.com/locations/place/C350.htm.

Liverpool was first recognized as a town when granted a charter by John in 1207, to serve as a departure point for Ireland. He founded a market and built a castle there. An account, along with a translation of the charter, can be read at http://www.fortunecity.com/meltingpot/park/346/history.html. Nothing remains of the castle except the name in the nearby parts of the city; the Civil War saw its destruction, and the remnants were moved in the early 1700s. Some illustrations of how it may have looked can be seen at http://www.mersey-gateway.org/server.php?show=ConGallery.54.

Like so many monarchs, John had a connection with **Dover**, when he met with the papal legate Pandulf in 1213 to surrender his Kingdom. This meeting seems to have taken place either in the round church of the Templars on the Western Heights or in the Templar Preceptory at Temple Ewell. Clear photographs of the exposed footings of the Templar church can be viewed at http://www.thecyberfarm.com/templars/templarbritain/dover/doverhome.htm. The Templar preceptory, now the parish church of St. Peter and St. Paul, appears at http://www.thecyberfarm.com/templars/templarbritain/dover/ewellhome.htm.

At the door of **Winchester Cathedral** in 1213, Stephen Langton, Archbishop of Canterbury, absolved John from excommunication. For Winchester Cathedral, see *William Rufus*.

In 1215 John recaptured **Rochester Castle** from rebellious barons. See *William Rufus* for basic information.

Magna Carta is on display in the British Library, London (http://www.bl.uk/index.shtml), 96 Euston Road, next door to St. Pancras Station. You can view Magna Carta and read a translation at http://www.bl.uk/collections/treasures/magna.html. Those with a nostalgia for the famous and beautiful **British Library Reading Room**, former home of Magna Carta, can see it at the **British Museum**, Russell Street, or view its splendid interior online at http://www.mcgalliard.org/content/Pictures/readingroom/. See also the Great Court, which has enclosed it, at http://www.bondpix.com/The_British_Museum_and_The_Great_Court.htm Hours, etc., are posted at http://www.thebritishmuseum.ac.uk/greatcourt/read.html.

Runnymede is run by the National Trust. Although Runnymede also hosts a lively adventure and picnic ground, the site of the Magna Carta memorial is located at a small distance from the adventure ground, at the back of long, tranquil meadows, reached by a rustic footpath leading from the A308 east of Windsor. Details for visiting can be found at http://www.nationaltrust.org.uk/scripts/nthandbook.dll?ACTION=PROPERTY&PROPERTYID=244, with full instructions about getting there and a link to one of the NT's detailed maps. At Runnymede, you will also find the John F. Kennedy Memorial. View both the Magna Carta and John F. Kennedy Memorials at www.egham.co.uk/info/jfk.html.

During his final struggles to maintain control of England, John supposedly lost his belongings, including his treasure, upon being overtaken by the tide when attempting to march across the shores of **the Wash**, near the present town of **Sutton Bridge**, on the Lincolnshire-Norfolk border of the river Nene. Read about Sutton Bridge at http://suttonbridge.mysite.wanadoo-members.co.uk/page1.html. The Lincolnshire Fens are a center of outdoor activity; read about the possibilities at http://www.fenlandactivities.co.uk/Activities.html.

Swineshead Abbey is where John stayed in 1216 after crossing the Wash. The abbey lay about a mile away from the present village of Swineshead, which can be visited at http://www.any-town.co.uk/S/Swineshead/Texts/AVirtualTourOfSwineshead.asp. The few remains of the abbey are now incorporated in a farmhouse. After leaving the abbey, John is reputed to have stayed at an inn. The Three Kings Inn, at Threekingham, suggests it may have had the honor of his presence: see http://www.threekingham.org.uk/html/places_of_interest.html for a photograph of the inn's present incarnation and its history, thought to date from 871.

John died at **Newark Castle** in 1216, although he may not have died in the tower called King John's Tower. Note that this is Newark-on-Trent, in Nottinghamshire, not the smaller Newark near Peterborough. Newark, a town of 24,000 population, is halfway along the A46 between Leicester and Lincoln, and can also be accessed from the A1. Its history and details for visiting can be found at http://www.touruk.co.uk/castles/castle_Newark.htm; a longer, more detailed account of its history is related at http://www.newarkadvertiser.co.uk/notts/tourism/castle.htm.

Henry III (1207–1272; King of England, Lord of Ireland, and Duke of Aquitaine, 1216–1272)

With the loss of most of the Angevin holdings in France by John, the status of England changed. Once an important but peripheral focus for its Norman and Plantagenet Kings, it now became central. With the passage of decades since the Norman Conquest of 1066, even the Norman-descended nobility increasingly identified itself as English. Henry III bore an uneasy relationship to this rise of nationalistic feeling. His devotion to the cult of the Anglo-Saxon King St. Edward the Confessor emphasized his own descent from Edward's great-grandniece Edith Matilda, Queen of the Norman Henry I. Yet Henry III also maintained an Angevin outlook that transcended English nationalism as it revealed a hope of reclaiming parts of the Angevin empire. The King's patronage of relatives and favorites from Provence and Poitou—one manifestation of this transnational outlook—bred great hostility among English potentates. Their rebellion, coupled with Henry III's weakness and naiveté, culminated in a fundamental loss of royal power to representative assemblies, or Parliaments. Their most significant leader, Henry's brother-in-law Simon de Montfort, actually ruled England in Henry's stead for over a year. Simon contemptuously characterized Henry as simpleminded and unworthy to reign.

Henry's reign actually began in the midst of another rebellion against royal authority—that of the barons against his father King John. Although John had in 1215 agreed to the provisions of Magna Carta, he then (with papal support) repudiated it. The dying John in 1216 asked the Pope to protect the rule of his young heir. The rebel barons elected as King of England the son of Philip Augustus and husband of Henry's first cousin Blanche of Castile, Prince Louis of France (later Louis VIII). After his 1216 landing, Louis eventually held London and eastern England. While Louis secured support from the Welsh and the Scots, the Church upheld the right of the boy Henry. Thirty-six barons stayed loyal to Henry, but 97 barons rebelled. Of the 27 most important barons, Henry retained the allegiance of only eight.

In these desperate hours, Henry's supporters crowned the boy in 1216 in Gloucester and agreed to abide by a version of Magna Carta. They reissued Magna Carta in 1217 (and then in definitive form in 1225). With papal and Church support, their resistance to Louis succeeded in crushing his hopes of an English throne. After his 1217 defeats in the Battle of Lincoln and in a sea battle off Sandwich, Louis withdrew, and the Peace of Kingston ended his pretensions to rule England.

The civil war won, Henry's supporters established a regency until he came of age. The great William Marshal, 1st Earl of Pembroke, ruled with the advice and consent of great councils. The first regent, William Marshal resigned in 1219, the year of his death. From 1219 onward, the justiciar Hubert de Burgh dominated. In order to underscore the legitimacy of Henry's rule, in 1220 the Archbishop of Canterbury crowned him during a second coronation in Westminster Abbey. The greater degree of power and responsibility assigned to great councils during Henry III's minority appealed to the English nobles. When the adult King Henry later tried to dispense with consulting them about appointments, policy, or patronage, their anger grew. Besides their having become used to more influence, the King needed the great councils to meet more regularly in order to grant him revenue. The councils would use their ability to deny money to the King to force him to concede power.

However, despite Henry's growing involvement in governance from 1223 to 1226, the King did not assume his full powers until 1227. His expedition to Gascony and Brittany in 1230 failed. The 1232 dismissal of Hubert de Burgh led to the two-year dominance of two Poitevin civil servants, the King's former guardian Peter des Roches, Bishop of Winchester and former justiciar, and his nephew, Peter des Rivaux.

Resentment of their tyranny fed a revolt by the barons that caused the dismissal of their government. The King then assumed the direct control that he would maintain until 1258.

The ouster of these Poitevin rulers did not end the King's reliance on foreign favorites, motivated in part by Henry's desire to reclaim parts of the old Angevin empire. His happy marriage to Eleanor of Provence had begun in 1236. Thereafter, and throughout the 1240s, Henry extended favor to Eleanor's relatives, especially her Savoyard maternal uncles. While the Savoyards won some acceptance for themselves, they united with the Queen and many native Englishmen in detesting Henry's Poitevin half-brothers. Four years after King John's death in 1216, his widow Isabella married a Poitevin noble, Hugh de Lusignan. In 1242, Henry III failed to dislodge Louis IX from Poitou. The King's 1247 welcome of his Lusignan half-brothers to England began his practice of favoring them that extended throughout the 1250s. Not only did the Lusignans gobble excessive amounts of royal patronage, but they acted as if they were above the law. The peaceloving Henry acted too leniently. He possessed neither the sophistication nor the political skills required to create harmony between his English nobles and these hotly resented foreign upstarts.

Another relative eventually would consolidate the opposition to Henry's government—Simon de Montfort, Earl of Leicester. Montfort in 1238 secretly married Henry's sister Eleanor. Eleanor and Montfort felt displeased by Henry's failure to help Eleanor reclaim a dowry held by the survivors of her first husband. In addition, Henry sent Montfort to Gascony to restore order in 1248 but recalled him in 1252. Henry would pay dearly for arousing Montfort's emnity. The common dislike of the Lusignans and resentment of Henry's personal rule culminated in rebellion in the late 1250s. Montfort went from being one of the rebel leaders to being the steadfast champion who displaced even the King himself for a time.

The "Sicilian business" put the fat in the fire. Henry's Continental aspirations included having his relatives assume foreign crowns. In the late 1250s, Henry wanted his younger brother, Richard, Earl of Cornwall, to become Holy Roman Emperor, and Richard actually was crowned King of the Romans at Aachen. A few years before, in 1254, Henry contracted with Pope Alexander IV to accept the Kingdom of Sicily and Apulia for his younger son, Edmund, Earl of Lancaster, in exchange for money and troops for the Pope. The contract specified a time limit beyond which it threatened excommunication and a papal interdict. Not as enamored as Henry of the papacy, dubious about the project itself, and angry about not being consulted regarding this expensive commitment, the barons (Montfort among them) rebelled.

Henry wanted to impose a tax to pay for this Sicilian crown for Edmund. In reply, an armed band told the King, "Let the wretched and intolerable Poitevins and all aliens flee from your face." The barons wanted control of this weak King's ministers, policy, and patronage—demands encapsulated in the Provisions of Oxford (1258) and the Provisions of Westminster (1259). Although Henry III succumbed to pressure to agree to these demands, by 1261 (with papal support) he had repudiated them. Despite an expulsion that had purged England of the Lusignans, the Queen and her Savoyard uncles felt threatened by still-rising hatred of foreigners and supported the King's repudiation. Almost all of the barons then accepted the failure of the Provisions. Montfort, in France, did not.

Montfort's return to England and the Barons' War of 1263 forced Henry to reaffirm the Provisions. In yet another twist of the story, in 1264 Louis IX acted as arbitrator and ruled entirely in Henry's favor against the Provisions. Continuing to lead the resistance, Montfort actually took the King prisoner after the Battle of Lewes. Ruling England from May 1264 to August 1265, Montfort summoned a representative Parliament. At the Battle of Evesham in 1265, however, Henry's son the Lord Edward prevailed, and Montfort died. After a few more years, Edward had vanquished the barons and ruled in his father's name.

Henry III won no glory as a strong and capable ruler—indeed, his enemy Montfort outshone him there. Good intentions did not suffice to secure peace, especially in the absence of good sense. Yet Henry's devotion to his Anglo-Saxon predecessor, St. Edward the Confessor, led him to build Westminster Abbey and Westminster Palace in the Confessor's honor. (The King also rebuilt Clarendon and Winchester Castle.) Henry had his own body buried near the Confessor's shrine in the new Westminster Abbey. He wanted his heart buried at Fontevrault—near his mother and his Angevin relatives. This sepulchral division preserved the divided identity of Henry III—both Continental and English—that had so bedeviled his long reign.

Henry III Sites

Henry was born in 1207 at **Winchester Castle**, where he later built the Great Hall. In 1216, he was hastily crowned at **Gloucester Cathedral** when he was nine years old. His coronation is depicted in an 1860 stained-glass window in the cathedral, in the nave to the right of the main entrance. The cathedral began as an abbey church and became a cathedral only after Henry VIII's Dissolution of the Monasteries, in 1541. It's noted for its exceptionally fine fan and lierne vaulting, depicted, along with other images and a history of the architecture at http://www.britannia.com/church/studies/glosarch.html. Also, two of the Harry Potter movies were filmed there. For a more general history, see http://www.theheritagetrail.co.uk/cathedrals/gloucester%20cathedral.htm. The cathedral's own website is at http://www.gloucestercathedral.org.uk.

In 1236, Henry married Eleanor Berenger, daughter of the Count of Provence, in Canterbury Cathedral. Eleanor was one of four daughters, all Queens Consort, of Raymond Berenger V, Count of Provence, and his wife Beatrice of Savoy. Their reconstructed tombs are in the church of St-Jean-Malte, **Aix-en-Provence**, also Eleanor's probable birthplace. Read about Aix-en-Provence at http://www.aixenprovencetourism.com/.

The castle of **Hen Domen**, just to the north, was demolished to make way for **Montgomery Castle**, built by Henry after 1223. On a steep rocky ridge overlooking the town of Montgomery are the remains: portions of the gatehouse, the lower courses of wards, outer ditches. View these at http://www.castlewales.com/montgom.html. The Georgian town of Montgomery (Trefaldwyn) is located southwest of Shrewsbury, directly west of Birmingham (and a world away!); see it at http://www.montgomery-powys.co.uk/mont1.html for a personal tour. Montgomery is well located for a visit to Offa's Dyke; a length of it is preserved in Lymore Park, east of the town.

View the site of Hen Domen Castle at http://www.castlewales.com/hen_d.html. The remains of the castle lie to the west of Hendomen, just north of the town of Montgomery, in Powys. It stands on private land, so can be visited only by arrangement; however, the site is visible from the road.

White Castle, with Grosmont and Skenfrith Castles, is one in a triangle of castles, called the Welsh Trilateral, in southeast Wales, in the steep triangle formed by Abergavenny, Monmouth, and Hereford. Henry refortified White Castle about 1263, which included moving the main entrance from the south to the north and erecting a twin-towered gatehouse there, the enclosure of an earlier earthwork beyond that within a curtain wall with circular towers, and its own gatehouse in turn. A deep water-filled moat surrounded the castle. All this was preparation for an event that did not happen: the castle was never attacked. By the 16th century, all three castles were becoming ruined. The name White Castle refers to white rendering on the walls; originally it was called Llantilio Castle, from the nearby village called Llantilio Crossenny. Visit White Castle at http://www.castlewales.com/white.html and, with links to directions and information, http://www.castlexplorer.co.uk/wales/white/white.php.

During a revolt by the barons, Henry's army was routed at **Grosmont Castle** in 1233—the owner of Grosmont, Hubert de Burgh, being among the routed and fleeing. Hubert de Burgh returned to his castle. In 1267 Henry granted it to his second son Edmund ("Crouchback"), who converted the fortress into a residence suitable for a Lancaster household. The ruins are relatively well-preserved: Edmund's new, tall keep with a two-story false entrance and an elegant Gothic chimney which faces the visitor proceeding over the bridge to the castle. Pay a virtual visit to Grosmont at http://www.castlewales.com/grosmnt.html.

In 1259, Henry ceded Normandy to France at **Abbeville**. An historic textile town of 25,000 inhabitants, Abbeville lies on the river Somme in northwest France, near the coast and north of Dieppe. Like so many towns in Normandy, its old center was almost completely destroyed by bombing in 1940. Visit Abbeville at http://www.ville-abbeville.fr/ (in French).

Henry built the town walls of **Lewes**. In 1264 he and his son, Prince Edward (later Edward I), were defeated and taken captive by Simon de Montfort in the battle fought on the downs to the west of the town. Lewes, a pleasant town of about 16,000 population, lies inland on the Sussex Downs, northeast of Brighton. The town's rather unattractive website is http://www.lewes-town.co.uk/index.asp.

Henry and Edward were held prisoner by Simon de Montfort in **Hereford Castle**, in 1264. Nothing is left but the site called Castle Green, on the southeast of the town and on the river Wye, and the surrounding earthworks and part of the moat. One of only four known castles in England prior to the Conquest, the castle was sold after the Civil War and demolished. However, during its lifetime, it saw action involving royals at several times. It passed back and forth between Stephen's and Maud's armies, and witnessed the retreat of Prince Rupert of the Rhine in 1645, as well as hosting Henry and Edward. Read about the castle and see diagrams at http://www.smr.herefordshire.gov.uk/castles/castlesdata_az/hereford.htm. At http://www. ecastles.co.uk/hereford.html you can see a house considered to have been the governor's residence.

Prince Edward defeated Simon de Montfort in 1265 at the battle of **Evesham**, less a battle than a massacre. Montfort and his son were both killed, along with the rest of their men. Simon's body was dismembered, and the remains were taken to the Abbey of Evesham, later to become a place of pilgrimage. An obelisk from 1845 marks the site of the battle, which took place about one mile north of the town. Evesham, with 15,000 inhabitants, is pleasantly situated on the river Avon, northeast of Cheltenham and southwest of Stratford-on-Avon. The Vale of Evesham is noted for its orchards and market gardens. The remains of the ancient Benedictine abbey consist of the gateway and the ornate bell tower. The town's website is http://www. evesham.uk.com/, for visiting details. It's a bit short on images; the remains of the abbey may be viewed at http://www.worcestershire.gov.uk/home/cs-museum/cs-museum-royal-tales-evesham.htm, where there's an account of the battle.

At **Windsor Castle** he constructed a chapel on the site of what is now the Albert Memorial Chapel, in the lower ward. He built that part of the curtain wall around the lower ward that faces the High Street of Windsor, with three half-round towers, the Curfew, Garter, and Salisbury towers. Also, he rebuilt Henry II's apartments in the lower ward and improved those in the upper ward. For visiting details, go to http:// www.royal.gov.uk/output/Page557.asp.

At the **Tower of London** Henry built the inner curtain wall on three sides, with a series of nine D-shaped towers. The **Wall Walk** takes visitors along the west part of this, from the **Salt Tower**, where the walk is accessed, on the southwest side to the Martin Tower on the northwest side. The **Martin Tower** houses an exhibition on the making of the Crown Jewels (the jewels themselves are kept in Waterloo Barracks). He constructed a private watergate which would have led directly from the river Thames into the ground floor of the **Wakefield Tower**. The latter, not one of the towers on the curtain wall, is the second largest in the Tower of London, after the White Tower. The Wakefield Tower provided accommodation, and has now been furnished to the appearance it would have had in the time of his son, Edward I. For visiting details, see *William the Conqueror.*

Among his other accomplishments, Henry built the **Great Hall** at **Winchester Castle**, the only part of the castle remaining today in any state of wholeness. The hall was built as a "double cube," its height and width exactly half the width. At the time of its building, it reflected a new design in halls, lighter and more accommodating, with its tracery windows and fine Purbeck stone columns. In Henry's time, the walls would have been colorfully decorated. An attraction not of Henry's time is the round tabletop on an end wall, supposedly King Arthur's Round Table but probably made in the 13th century. Another is the large statue of Queen Victoria at the same end, which detracts from the historicity of the hall. Visit the castle at http://www.cityofwinchester.co.uk/history/html/castle.html, and see more of the Great Hall at http://www.hants.gov.uk/discover/places/great-hall1.html.

Behind the Great Hall is **Queen Eleanor's Garden**, named after two Queen Eleanors, Eleanor of Provence and Eleanor of Castile (see *Edward I*). It's a small, gentle space, fragrant with herbs, narrow and walled. Surviving records of the gardens of royal palaces aided the design of this garden to incorporate plants that would have been present in medieval gardens. See part of the garden at http://www.britainexpress.com/counties/hampshire/winchester/eleanors-garden.htm, and read about it—a link leads you to information about medieval gardens in general.

The present appearance of **Westminster Abbey** is thanks to Henry, who envisioned the transformation of the solid Norman abbey into the lighter and more graceful, new Gothic being developed in France. Edward the Confessor's abbey was taken down to be replaced by today's building, financed by Henry, who eventually had to sell gold plate, and, in 1267, to retrieve and pawn the jewels he had given for Edward the Confessor's new shrine. The money was gone by mid-1269: the central part of the church was built (the apse with its radiating chapels, the transepts, and choir), but most of the nave was still in Norman style, the roof much lower than that of the new Gothic building. Neverthess, the church was opened on October 13, the feast day of St. Edward. Building resumed only after another century, under Richard II first, then Henry V. Henry VII was to add the exquisite finishing touch, the Lady Chapel, known as Henry VII Chapel. For more details, see *Henry VII*.

The shrine of Edward the Confessor, in the chapel of the same name, was finished in 1269. It comprised a stone base decorated in cosmati-style mosaic work, a gold feretory (a portable bier) containing the saint's coffin, and a canopy which could be raised to reveal the coffin. A following grew up around his name, resulting in pilgrimages to the shrine. Votive offerings of gold and jewels enriched the feretory. After the Dissolution of the Monasteries during the reign of Henry VIII, the feretory was taken from the abbey, although the monks were permitted to bury the Confessor's body elsewhere in the abbey, and the shrine dismantled. Mary I had the shrine reassembled. Without the feretory, the coffin was now placed in the top part of the marble base, within the canopy. See the shrine at http://www.westminster-abbey.org/tour/edw_confess.htm; to read more about Edward the Confessor and see the shrine in its setting, turn to http://www.westminster-abbey.org/library/burial/confessor.htm.

Henry III died in Westminster, and is buried in the abbey. Queen Eleanor died at **Amesbury Abbey**, Wiltshire, in 1291, where she had become a nun in 1284, and is buried there. Amesbury, a small town, is located a few miles north of Salisbury and a shorter distance east of Stonehenge. The abbey, reputedly where Queen Guinevere fled after the death of King Arthur, is now a nursing home and not open to the public. Read the history of Amesbury at http://www.thisiswiltshire.co.uk/wiltshire/tourism/towns/amesbury.html.

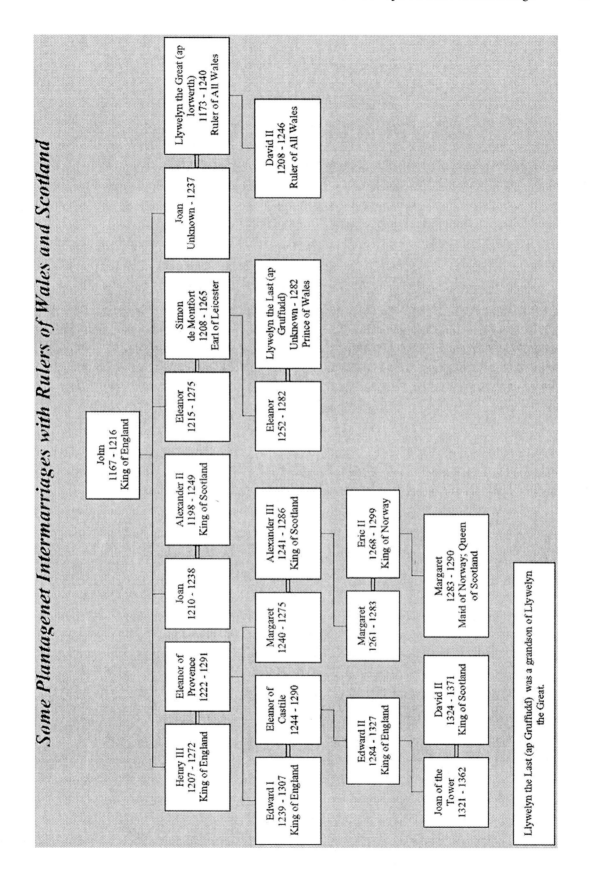

Some Plantagenet Intermarriages with Rulers of Wales and Scotland

Llywelyn the Last (ap Gruffudd) was a grandson of Llywelyn the Great.

Edward I (1239–1307; King of England, Lord of Ireland, and Duke of Aquitaine, 1272–1307)

Renowned both as "Longshanks" and "the Hammer of the Scots," the formidable Edward I, born at Westminster, won both glory and shame for his many decisive and determined actions. His legal reforms made for greater efficiency. His wars sped the evolution of Parliament as a representative body to which the King turned for consent to the necessary taxation. On the other hand, resistance to the expense of the King's wars in Scotland, Wales, and France precipitated a constitutional crisis in 1297. Later, the unpopularity of taxation caused Edward to run up an immense indebtedness to Italian financiers and to avoid paying bills, leaving his successor with disturbed finances. In addition, although Edward had profited by taxing the Jews of England heavily on their transactions, and they had paid large fines for release after their mass arrest in 1287, Edward expelled them from England in 1290. (They would not return as a group for almost 400 years.) Assuming the debts owed to them, the King also appropriated their property. Like the Jews, the Welsh and the Scots—as victims of his aggression—remembered Edward with bitterness.

The King who perpetrated these horrors also devoted himself to his first Queen, Eleanor of Castile, and her death in 1290 devastated him. Their 1254 diplomatic marriage had secured for Edward the possession of Gascony. (In the middle 1250s, he also administered Ireland, the Channel Islands, Wales, and the County Palatine of Chester.) Where her funeral procession between Harby (near Lincoln) and Westminster had paused overnight, Edward ordered the erection of the 12 Eleanor Crosses. Those at Waltham, Northampton, and Geddington still stand. Monuments that had marked the journey of St. Louis's body from Paris to St. Denis possibly inspired this famous testament to marital tenderness. Edward had greatly admired St. Louis (Louis IX of France), his uncle by marriage, and had joined St. Louis on the Eighth Crusade.

Undeterred by the failure of his first crusade in 1249–1254, in 1267 St. Louis "took the cross" again. In the following year, Edward pledged to join his crusade. After leaving England in 1270, Edward found that his uncle had died in Tunis, but Edward went on to Sicily and finally arrived at Acre in 1271. During his 16 months' stay in the Holy Land, Edward survived an assassination attempt with a poisoned dagger. Recovering from his wound, Edward in 1272 learned in Sicily of his father's death and his own accession to the throne. His prolonged return journey to England did not end until 1274, the year of his coronation. Despite the failure of his crusade, Edward never lost his desire to mount another one and in fact took the cross again in 1287. Possessing much prestige among Europeans because of both his crusade and his survival of assassination, Edward engaged in diplomacy to settle European disputes precisely because he viewed European unity as a necessity precondition for the next crusade. Many conflicts and crises closer to home would prevent his ever going—among them his recurring wars in Wales and Scotland. Determined to secure and preserve what he deemed his rights as feudal overlord of Wales and Scotland, Edward crushed Welsh resistance but ultimately failed to repeat this success in Scotland.

In 1267, Henry III in the Treaty of Montgomery had confirmed Llywelyn the Last (ap Gruffudd) in the title of Prince of Wales that Llywelyn ap Gruffudd had assumed in 1258. Not long after Edward I's coronation in 1274, his first cousin Eleanor de Montfort journeyed from France to marry Llywelyn. Captured in the Bristol Channel, Eleanor de Montfort would remain imprisoned by Edward at Windsor until Llywelyn paid homage to Edward as his overlord. His refusal to do homage precipitated Edward's 1276 invasion of Wales. Hampered by his brother Dafydd's support of Edward, Llywelyn agreed to peace terms in 1278, and Edward even paid for his wedding to Eleanor de Montfort. Edward, however, failed to reward Dafydd sufficiently for his support. Llywelyn became drawn into the 1282 rebellion by Dafydd, in which Llywelyn met his death. Capture and execution soon disposed of Dafydd as well. Having broken this revolt, Edward sought to maintain his mastery of Wales by building castles such as Caernarfon and several others, all constructed between 1277 and 1295. In addition, the Statute of Rhuddlan in 1284 abolished Wales as a separate principality. Edward put down another revolt in 1287, as well as Madog's rebellion in 1294–1295. English dominance meant oppression and severe taxation. Edward focused on his own prerogatives as overlord, lacking both the ability to understand the grievances of the Welsh and the practical wisdom to reward those who had supported him. In addition, his singleminded and resolute pursuit of his goals could trap him into inflexible policies and methods that only added to his difficulties. He would repeat all of these mistakes in Scotland.

After defeating Dafydd and Llywelyn in Wales, Edward went to Gascony from 1286 to 1289. Madog's rebellion in 1294–1295 coincided with Edward's war with Philip IV of France (1294–1298) over Philip's confiscation of Gascony. (Part of the peace settlement with France included Edward's marriage in 1299 to Philip's sister Margaret.) In 1295, the Scots would seek to take advantage of France's hostility to Edward by creating the "Auld Alliance" between France and Scotland against England.

Edward had angered the Scots by meddling in their affairs in his self-proclaimed role as feudal overlord. The death of his brother-in-law Alexander III of Scotland in 1286 had offered him one opportunity to influence Scottish policies. Edward had wanted to marry Alexander III's successor, Alexander's little grandaughter Margaret (the "Maid of Norway"), to his own son, the future Edward II. Margaret's death in 1290 during her journey to Scotland frustrated Edward I's plan. Her passing, however, also created a second opportunity for the determined King.

Asked to choose Margaret's successor as ruler of Scotland from among 13 claimants (a proceeding called "the Great Cause"), Edward in 1291 persuaded the "Competitors" to recognize his authority as Scotland's overlord. The Competitors with the most compelling claims included John Balliol and Robert Bruce. Choosing John Balliol in 1292, Edward made it clear that he expected homage and the other rights of an overlord. Resentful of Edward's overbearing meddlesomeness, the Scots by treaty in 1295 created the "Auld Alliance" between France and Scotland against England, and Balliol rebelled in the following year.

Edward's occupation of Scotland included the deposition of Balliol as well as the removal of the Stone of Destiny associated with Scottish coronations from Scone to Westminster Abbey. The Scottish rebels of 1297 included Robert Bruce (grandson of Robert Bruce the Competitor), as well as William Wallace, who fought for Balliol. Wallace's victory at Stirling Bridge stunned and united the English, who defeated Wallace in 1298 at Falkirk. Robert Bruce and Balliol's nephew John Comyn replaced Wallace as Guardians of Scotland. However, in 1302, Robert Bruce allied himself with Edward I after seeking pardon. After Edward's 1304 campaign in Scotland, which included the successful siege of Stirling Castle, most Scottish nobles accepted Edward's terms for peace. The next year would see Wallace's capture near Glasgow, his trial in Westminster Hall, and his horrific execution at Smithfield. Edward's oppression and failure to reward his supporters, as in Wales, then began to cripple English control of Scotland. Edward's unrewarded ally Robert Bruce, after murdering John Comyn, had himself crowned at Scone in 1306 as Robert I of Scotland. Edward's infamous retaliation included imprisoning for many months Bruce's mistress, Isabel, Countess of Buchan (who had assisted in Robert I's crowning), and Bruce's sister Mary in open-air cages hung on the walls of Berwick and Roxburgh castles. Determined to regain mastery over the Scots, Edward I died in present-day Cumbria in 1307 on his way to war, leaving his much less formidable successor with massive debts and looming rebellion.

Edward I Sites

Edward was born at **Westminster** on June 17, 1239. In 1254, the year of his marriage to Eleanor of Castile, Edward kept vigil in the rich and powerful **Monasterio de Las Huelgas**, near Burgos, Spain, as did many Castilian Kings, and he was knighted there. We can visit the Cistercian sisters at Las Huelgas via http://www3.planalfa.es/lashuelgas/introduccion_i.htm (in Spanish). He and Eleanor were married in the **Castillo,**

Burgos. See the Castillo, along with links to other attractions in Burgos, at http://www.burgoscard.com/en/Contenido.aspx?id=3; note that the castle is closed between 2 and 4 p.m., and longer on Saturdays.

For information regarding Edward's involvement at **Lewes**, **Hereford**, and **Evesham**, see *Henry III*. Edward made his crusade in 1270–74, arriving in Acre in 1271 and spending 16 months there. For **Acre (Akko)** see *Richard I*.

Edward and Eleanor added much to **Leeds Castle**, the gloriette, the revetment wall, and additions to the gatehouse. The castle, situated near Maidstone, Kent, is, however, mostly a product of the 19th and 20th centuries. Its website is http://www.leeds-castle.com/.

At **Rockingham Castle**, Edward transformed the square towers of the gatehouse to curved ones. This gatehouse still stands; see it at http://www.touruk.co.uk/castles/castle_Rockingham.htm. Rockingham and its castle are situated southeast of Leicester, a few miles to the north of Corby.

Edward I and Eleanor were present at **Glastonbury Abbey** in 1276, when the remains of Arthur and Guinevere, reputedly unearthed in 1191, were reinterred in a marble tomb in front of the high altar. During the Dissolution of the Monasteries during the reign of Henry VIII, the remains disappeared and have never been found since. Visit Glastonbury Abbey at http://www.glastonburyabbey.com/, and read about the remains under Myths and Legends.

At the **Tower of London**, Edward continued his father's wall down the west side and constructed the lower curtain wall outside Henry III's wall, and added the surrounding moat. This transformed the Tower into a concentric fortress, two walls running parallel to each other around all sides but the river side. This outer curtain wall provided two more entrances to the Tower. Edward also created new royal lodgings in the **Thomas Tower**.

For the evolution of the Tower and Edward's role in it, see http://www.castles.org/castles/Europe/Western_Europe/United_Kingdom/England/england12.htm.

Edward used **Shrewsbury** as the seat of his government during his subjugation of North Wales, rebuilding the castle. Shrewsbury's official website is http://www.shrewsbury-guide.co.uk/, which doesn't do justice to the grace of this beautifully-situated old city built within a loop of the Severn river; more attractive is http://www.shrewsbury.info/. Shrewsbury's very position has given it historical importance, along with its proximity to Wales. In spite of often being in the thick of action over the centuries, Shrewsbury retains many quaint old half-timbered buildings on narrow, winding streets.

Wales

Edward and his master mason James of St. George not only constructed a stunning array of fortresses in a relatively few years, but often erected the town (bastide) and its walls to go with them. For example, over half the expenditure on Caernarfon went toward the fortified town. Some of the castles (Cardigan, Carmarthen, Aberystwyth, Builth, and Montgomery) already existed and were merely strengthened; some he replaced (Dyserth and Deganwy were replaced by Rhuddlan and Conwy). The four greatest, however, were built from scratch: Conwy, Harlech, Caernarfon, and Beaumaris.

For each of the Welsh castles in turn, and collectively, the website http://www.castlewales.com/ is the best. The information is comprehensive and scholarly, written by experts who are real enthusiasts, illustrated profusely by photographs, diagrams, and layouts. Detailed information and lots of pictures are given for all the major castles, along with the history and evolution of the castle, warfare, and Welsh-English relations generally, people associated, etc. Actual visiting details are best accessed through http://www.cadw.wales.gov.uk/default.asp?id=3&lang=en, the website for Cadw, Welsh Historic Monuments.

Flint, near Chester and thus the border with England, was the site of Edward's first Welsh castle (constructed from 1277–81) and was also the site of a bastide. The remains overlook the estuary of the river Dee; Flint isn't as spectacularly situated as many other castles are, but there's a charm about its harmony with its rocky seat and scale in the landscape, so that entering the remains seems like the continuation of a walk in the surrounding area. Flint Castle is open at all times, and is free: http://www.greatcastlesofwales.co.uk/flint.htm.

There was a motte-and-bailey to the north of **Rhuddlan Castle**, constructed by Robert of Rhuddlan in 1073, with a small settlement around it. Edward's castle at Rhuddlan was begun after Flint, later that summer, and, with it, he established a bastide: the town of Rhuddlan today still preserves its 13th century layout. His daughter Elizabeth was born in the castle in 1282. From Rhuddlan, in 1284 Edward issued his Statute providing for the English government of Wales. The supposed site is the present-day Parliament House on the corner of Parliament Street. In 1648, the castle fell to the Parliament troops who partly demolished it to prevent its further use. See Rhuddlan Castle at http://www.theheritagetrail.co.uk/castles/rhuddlan%20castle.htm.

At nearby **St. Asaph**, the cathedral had been destroyed by the English in 1282. Edward tried and failed to have the episcopal seat moved to Rhuddlan, and the new cathedral built there. But not even Edward could prevail against the Church, and the King backed down when the bishop insisted upon remaining in St. Asaph. Visit St. Asaph at http://www.stasaph.co.uk/; clicking on History takes you to the cathedral.

One of the most beautiful castles anywhere is **Conwy**, originally Aberconwy. Edward simply removed the abbey to Maenan, thus discarding the "Aber" part of the name. Conwy Castle has a compactness of appearance belying its massiveness. It rears up above and right out of the streets of its town, a startling, almost theatrical sight as you cross the bridge from Llandudno Junction. The castle is very well-preserved; the curtain walls can be walked and the towers climbed. The bridges of the 19th century, Thomas Telford's road bridge and James Stevenson's tubular railway bridge, add only elegance to the scene; the plain, modern road bridge does not. Conwy Castle is situated on Conway Bay, a few miles west of the popular resort, Colwyn Bay. For striking views, see http://www.greatcastlesofwales.co.uk/conwy.htm, especially the one showing the 19th century bridges.

On the opposite side of the Menai Strait lies **Beaumaris Castle**, the last of the great four to be constructed, in 1295. It's also the largest and most symmetrical, a concentric castle with two parallel circuits of walls and massive, regularly placed D-shaped towers surrounding a square ward. The moat, filled in on the eastern side, was once tidal—the castle was built on the marshland bordering the Menai Street (hence the derivation of the castle's name, "beau marais"). The castle is an attractive place to visit, with a park and picnic tables for people and the moat for ducks and swans. For a striking aerial view, see http://www.greatcastlesofwales.co.uk/beaumaris.htm.

In order to build Beaumaris, Edward had to move the Welsh inhabitants of Llanfaes. He sent them down to the other end of the Menai Strait, to an area he called **Newborough**, and he used the stonework for the building of Beaumaris Castle. Newborough Warren and Llanddwyn Island is a national nature reserve of dunes and beaches, with views over the sea to the mountains of Snowdonia; nearby Newborough Forest is also an attraction. Llanddwyn Island can be walked to at low tide. During the 1990s the site of a court used by the powerful medieval Princes of Gwynned was uncovered and excavated, Llys (court) Rhosyr; the field in which it lies was always called Cae Llys, and the discovery of the foundations of the palace suddenly gave a meaning to the name. The site is near St. Pedr's Church, which would also have been connected to the court. Read an account and see photographs at http://www.anglesey.info/Rhosyr.htm. The juiciest photographs appear at http://www.awelfryn.co.uk/information.asp.

Located at the southern end of the Menai Street, with access to the agriculturally rich Anglesey and to both the northern and the western coasts of Wales, **Caernarfon Castle** is probably the best known from its association with the first English Prince of Wales (see *Edward II*). Here, Edward destroyed the original Welsh settlement, using the site of the Norman motte and bailey—which had, in its turn, replaced the Roman fort of Segontium. Both castle and city walls were built quickly, in about two years. The outward appearance of Caernarfon is different: The towers are multiangular, not round, and horizontal bands of different-colored stone in the walls give the castle an exotic appearance, perhaps reminiscent of those of Constantinople. Read about the castle and the attractions of Caernarfon at http://www.britainexpress.com/ Where_to_go_in_Britain/Destination_Library/caernarfon.htm. For exterior views of the castle, see http:// www.greatcastlesofwales.co.uk/caernarfon.htm. Caernarfon is a Unesco World Heritage Site.

Harlech Castle, the southernmost of the great four, is dramatically sited on a rock platform 200 ft above the marshes of Morfa Harlech; at one time, the sea would have come to the foot of the rock. It was the last castle taken by Parliamentary forces during the Civil War, and, like others in the same circumstances, was "slighted." In addition to http://www.castlewales.com, see http://www.greatcastlesofwales.co.uk/harlech.htm for views of the castle. The website for the town of Harlech is http://www.harlech.com/.

Scotland

Only traces remain of Edward's wall at **Berwick-upon-Tweed**. The Castle where Edward judged in favor of John Balliol's claim to the Scottish crown in 1292 was largely demolished to make way for the railway station in the 19th century, but a few fragments stand nearby. Until it became English in 1482, Berwick suffered many transferrals from English to Scottish and back again. After 1482, it was made into a bastion against the Scots with an extra-territorial autonomy that lasted until the 19th century. Visit the now-peaceful Berwick-upon-Tweed and its neighboring attractions at http://www.northumberland.gov.uk/vg/berwick.html.

In the church at **Norham**, Edward arbitrated between the rival claims of Bruce and Balliol to the Scottish throne. See the church at http://www.ejayar.ndo.co.uk/cuthbertnorham.html. Norham's history can be read at http://www.berwick.org.uk/norham/norham.htm, along with a description and photograph of its castle. Norham is several miles down the winding Tweed river from Berwick.

Standing high on volcanic rock, Stirling Castle can be seen for miles around and, in its turn, commanded all movement throughout the surrounding countryside: it has been witness to some of the most important battles in Scotland's history and changed hands several times between the English and the Scots. Evidence of the presence of a royal castle dates from the 12th century, of the present castle from the 15th century.

The castle has seen recent renovations of the chapel and the Great Hall. The latter is notable for its beautiful hammerbeam ceiling. Of interest also are the kitchens, with a display of use in the 16th century, including lifesize models and foodstuffs. Stirling Castle is situated roughly at the apex of a northeast/northwest triangle from Glasgow and Edinburgh. Visiting details from Historic Scotland at http://www.historic-scotland.gov.uk/ index/properties_sites_detail?propertyID=PL_275. The Marie Stuart Society website offers a reconstruction of the castle as it would have appeared before the 15th century; see http://www.marie-stuart.co.uk/index.htm, then click on links down the left side of the screen.

When Edward captured **Perth** in 1296, he had the Stone of Destiny, the seat on which Kings of Scotland were traditionally crowned, moved to London. For centuries, it remained under the Coronation Chair in Westminster Abbey: in fact, the chair was designed especially to accommodate the Stone! It was officially returned to Scotland in 1996 and is now on display with the Scottish crown jewels in the royal palace of Edinburgh Castle. See the Stone illustrated at http://www.aboutscotland.com/stone/destiny.html. The Coronation Chair may be viewed at http://www.westminster-abbey.org/tour/coronation_chair/, along with a detailed account. Visiting details for Edinburgh Castle are best accessed through Historic Scotland, http:// www.historic-scotland.gov.uk/properties_sites_detail.htm?propertyID=PL_121.

The Stone of Destiny had been on Moot Hill, facing **Scone Palace**. The Palace is a few miles north of Perth. The 3rd Earl of Mansfield transformed it in 1803 from a medieval house to a Gothic palace. There's a copy of the Stone outside the chapel on Moot Hill. The home page for Scone Palace can be entered at http://www.scone-palace.net/; it's a handsome residence with extensive gardens, and hospitable to visitors.

Information about Perth, along with attractive photographs, appears at http://www.undiscoveredscotland.co.uk/ perth/perth/.

Both Edward and Eleanor had attended the consecration of the beautiful Angel Choir of **Lincoln Cathedral**. Edward had also declared his son and heir Prince of Wales at the 1301 Parliament held in the cathedral's Chapter House.

Look around the Angel Choir (360 degrees) at http://www.bbc.co.uk/lincolnshire/360/cathedral_angel.shtml. Links below the image will give you similar views of other parts of the cathedral and Lincoln itself, including the castle. Edward's and Eleanor's association with Lincoln Cathedral can be viewed and read about at http://homepage.ntlworld.com/peter.fairweather/docs/Lincoln_cathedral.htm#edward&eleanor. Note their statues on the outer south wall, the tomb containing Eleanor's viscera, and the Chapter House in which Edward declared his son Prince of Wales.

Eleanor died in 1290 near Lincoln, at the town of **Harby**. Edward had crosses erected at the various stages of the funeral procession that bore her body to Westminster Abbey, probably 12 in all, although the list varies. There is a fragment on the lawn of Lincoln Castle gardens. The apparent list after that is Grantham, Stamford, Geddington, Northampton, Stony Stratford, Woburn, Dunstable, St Albans, and Waltham, as well as Cheapside and Charing Cross in London. The only remaining ones can be seen at Geddington, Hardingstone (just out of Northampton, and sometimes referred to as the Northampton cross), and Waltham Cross.

The website for **Geddington** is http://www.geddington.net/history.htm, with a portion of the Eleanor Cross depicted, along with information about this charming stone village. The Eleanor Cross stands in the local square, its steps forming a launching pad for local boys on skateboards on the evening I last saw it! The best online depiction of the cross at **Hardingstone** is at http://www.northampton.org.uk/art/local_artists/stephens.htm. The Hardingstone cross can be viewed actually beside the A506 after the junction with the A45, just south of Northampton. **Waltham Cross**, north of London and just to the west of Waltham Abbey east of St Albans and Potters Bar, is on the A10, just after it crosses London's ring road, the M25. See the cross in the center of **Waltham Cross** at http://www.broxbourne.gov.uk/Living_in_Broxbourne/walthamcross.htm.

Eleanor is also memorialized in **Queen Eleanor's Garden** behind the Great Hall at Winchester Castle. See *Henry III* for details. The Queen Eleanor Primary School in **Harby** is, needless to say, named after her.

Edward's second wife Margaret, daughter of Philip III, King of France, died at **Marlborough Castle** (see *John*) on February 14, 1317. She was buried at the **Grey Friars Church, London**, whose rebuilding she had largely financed. The Grey Friars monastery stood on the north side of Newgate Street, at the end of Greyfriars Passage, to the east of St. Paul's Cathedral. The site, just south of St. Bartholomew's Hospital, is now a ruin; see a photograph at http://homepage.mac.com/crowns/gb/avgal.html. Read an exhaustive history of the Grey Friars in London at http://www.british-history.ac.uk/report.asp?compid=35364.

The place of Edward's death at **Burgh-by-Sands** (pronounced "Bruff"), in present-day Cumbria, is marked by a monument. Burgh-by-Sands is five miles northwest of Carlisle and a mile inland from the Solway Firth, dividing England from Scotland. The monument stands isolated in a farmer's field. From the rustic car park, a footpath leads down to the fence with a gate, padlocked on the day I visited; hop over the stile near the gate, and walk to the monument overlooking the field and marshes of the Firth. The monument can be visited online at http://www.visitcumbria.com/car/edmon.htm. Links are provided to other features of the neighborhood.

But the plainness and rather bleak location of the monument are more than made up for by the splendor of Edward's tomb in **Westminster Abbey**. He and Eleanor lie side by side in the Chapel and Shrine of Edward the Confessor. Their effigies, the work of William Torel, are of great beauty, lending a grace and tenderness to their features; Eleanor's is especially fine. Westminster Abbey's website describes the tombs at http://www.westminster-abbey.org/library/monarchs/edward_i.htm, and Eleanor's effigy can be vaguely seen at http://www.westminsterabbey.org/library/monarchs/edward_i.htm.

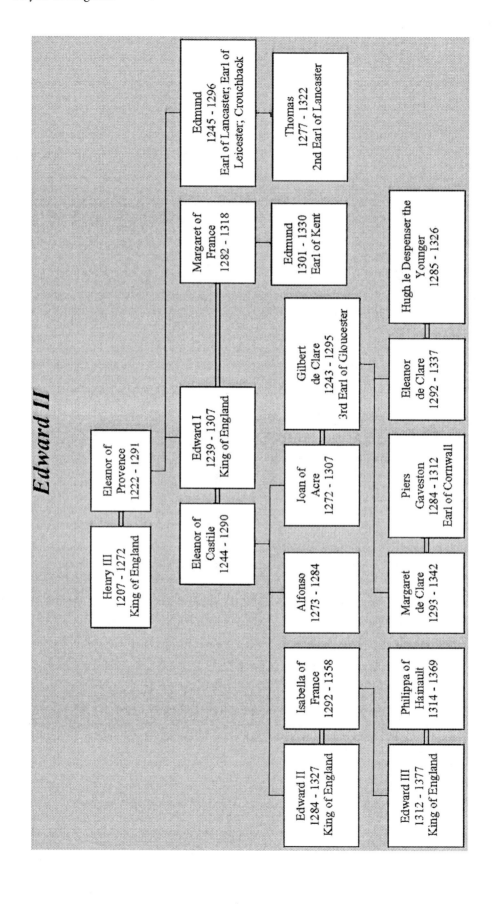

Edward II (1284–1327; Duke of Aquitaine, 1306–1327; King of England and Lord of Ireland, 1307–1327)

The hatred inspired by Edward II's homosexuality led to his hideous murder by the vicious means of penetrating his anus with a red-hot poker. It also gravely damaged his posthumous reputation. As with James I, who reigned over Great Britain 300 years later, history has luridly remembered Edward's besotted favoritism towards male lovers. This emphasis has done each of them scant justice. James I was a great King, Edward merely an adequate one. Although usually portrayed as an inept and foolish King ripe for deposition, Edward certainly did not deserve posterity's automatic contempt any more than he deserved his miserable death.

Born in 1284 to Edward I and Eleanor of Castile at Caernarfon Castle in Wales, baby Edward became heir apparent to the throne of England when his older brother Alfonso died. Named the first English Prince of Wales in 1301, Edward gained all the royal lands in Wales as well as the earldom of Chester. Five years later, Prince Edward received the title of Duke of Aquitaine (of which Gascony formed a part). From 1297 onward, a Gascon knight, Piers Gaveston, had served as a squire of the royal household and a official companion to the Prince. Edward loved Piers passionately. His disapproving father, Edward I, sent Gaveston into exile in 1307, but the King's death that year rendered his disapproval impotent, and the new King, Edward II, immediately recalled Gaveston to England.

Not only did Edward II bring Gaveston back, but he also made his lover Earl of Cornwall and married him to a very eligible heiress, Margaret de Clare, daughter of Edward's sister Joan. Regent of England while Edward II journeyed to France in 1308 to wed his own bride, the French King's sister Isabella, Gaveston also organized and played a very prominent role in the coronation ceremonies that followed Edward II's and Queen Isabella's return. All of this enraged other nobles, who pressed for Gaveston's exile in 1308 and then again in 1311 after Edward had recalled him.

Gaveston's being a brave soldier, an accomplished jouster, and an excellent ruler of Ireland during his exile did not sidetrack the nobles from their goal of destroying him. Edward doubtless compounded his friend's peril by unwisely showing him excessive favor, but neither Edward, Gaveston, nor their relationship merited the intense loathing that precipitated Gaveston's murder. Thomas, Earl of Lancaster, the King's first cousin, breaking a pledge of safety given to Gaveston upon his surrender to his enemies in 1312, ordered his slaughter. Overwhelmed with grief, Edward also suffered from severe restrictions upon his royal powers imposed by his rebellious barons. Isabella bore him his son Edward (later Edward III) a few months after Gaveston's death. Edward II eventually would lay Gaveston to rest in the King's beloved Hertfordshire residence of Langley.

English disunion lent force to Scottish insurrection against English domination, and Robert Bruce's successes caused Edward II to invade Scotland and to endure devastating defeat at Bannockburn. The King fought bravely, displaying resolute courage if not military greatness, but it all went for naught. Moreover, the disaster of Bannockburn weakened further Edward's grasp on royal power. Thomas of Lancaster remained a threat, checked somewhat by Aymer of Valence, Earl of Pembroke, who hated Lancaster because of his betrayal of the promises Pembroke made to Gaveston after his surrender. Pembroke worked with Hugh le Despenser, who had supported Edward in his defense of Gaveston. Despenser's son, Hugh the Younger, attracted the King's affection, and he married the King's niece, the heiress Eleanor de Clare. The rise of the Despensers stoked the hatred of other nobles, who in 1321 demanded their exile. As he had with Gaveston, Edward recalled them. War with his nobles included his victory at Boroughbridge in 1322 and the execution of Lancaster.

Although their greed and arrogance corrupted their rule, the Despensers in many ways governed well, and Hugh le Despenser the Younger in particular showed his gifts as an administrator and reformer. Their virtues impressed their enemies no more than Gaveston's had impressed his. Somehow, they fatally alienated the Queen. Isabella left England with Prince Edward in 1325 on a mission to her brother, Charles IV of France. Not only did she refuse to return as long as the Despensers remained, but she also began an affair with Roger Mortimer of Wigmore. After arranging in the summer of 1326 a marriage between her son and Philippa of Hainault, Isabella invaded England with Mortimer in September. Londoners supported Isabella's invasion, and Edward's advocates could not protect him. Mortimer executed the elder Despenser for treason in October, and the younger Despenser also died the horrible death of a traitor. After the King's capture in November and his imprisonment in Kenilworth Castle, Parliament in January 1327 deposed him in favor of his son. Threats compelled the reluctant Edward II to abdicate as well. Moved to Berkeley Castle in Gloucestershire, Edward continued his inconvenient existence. A successful rescue attempt led only to his recapture. Isabella and Mortimer allegedly had the King murdered in September but announced his death from natural causes and attended his burial at St. Peter's Abbey in Gloucester.

In 1330, the arrest of Edmund, Earl of Kent, Edward II's half-brother, focused attention on rumors that Edward II had not actually died in prison but had escaped, for Edmund stood accused of plotting to rescue Edward II from Corfe Castle on the Dorset coast. The consequent execution of the Earl of Kent eventually provoked a coup against the continued rule in the name of Edward III of Roger Mortimer and Queen Isabella. Created the 1st Earl of March in 1328, Roger Mortimer died at the command of Edward III after this coup at Nottingham. Confined by her son at Berkhamsted and then at Windsor for a few years, Isabella escaped any real punishment because Edward III blamed Mortimer for all that had happened. After living at Castle Rising in Norfolk for many years, Isabella died in 1358. She went to her grave in her wedding dress and with a silver casket holding the heart of Edward II. Had her husband died at her and Mortimer's order at Berkeley in 1327, or did Isabella and Mortimer stage a funeral to cover up Edward II's escape from prison and to discredit any future attempts by him to regain power?

Edward II Sites

The first English Prince of Wales, Edward was born at **Caernarfon Castle** (see *Edward I*) in 1284. Tradition has it that he was born on the first floor of the Eagle Tower, but the castle was under construction at that time, so this is far from certain.

Edward II was never to return to Caernarfon, and by the 14th century it was maintained and garrisoned, but never the great royal residence and seat of power Edward I envisioned for it. After being taken by Parliamentary forces during the Civil War, it fell further into neglect until the late 19th century. It splendidly resumed a royal role in the 20th century, seeing first Prince Edward (later Edward VIII, then Duke of Windsor) and Prince Charles invested as Princes of Wales in 1911 and 1969, respectively. The first Prince of Wales was given the title in **Lincoln**. For information about Lincoln Castle and its Great Hall, see *William I*; read about the Princes of Wales at http://www.princeofwales.gov.uk/about/rol_prevprinces.html.

Anthony Bek, Bishop of Durham, who had built **Eltham Palace**, gave it to Edward in 1305 when he was Prince of Wales. Edward and the monarchs following him carried out extensions to it until the reign of Henry VIII, who added a chapel but then preferred Greenwich. The palace was left to decay and, apart from the Great Hall, didn't survive the Commonwealth period. The Great Hall was then used as a farm and an indoor tennis court until the Courtauld family leased it in 1931. They restored the Great Hall and built an adjoining new house in the contemporary art deco style, finished in 1937. Although this move has had its detractors, essentially the Courtaulds preserved Eltham and provided the facility of the hall and their own property for public visiting. A virtual tour of Eltham Palace, hosted by English Heritage, can be made at http://www.elthampalace.org.uk/, which also provides details regarding visiting: note that the property is open on Wednesday-Friday and Sundays only, and other limitations.

Edward's efforts at battle saw the vast English loss at **Bannockburn**, against the Scots, when he was trounced by Robert Bruce with a numerically inferior force, and had to flee with a few companions, leaving English dead all over the battlefield and all his baggage train, worth a vast sum of money. With Bannockburn, England had lost its claim to Scotland. Run by the National Trust for Scotland, the Bannockburn Heritage Center stands near the old battlefield, with an equestrian statue of Robert Bruce (see http://www.rampantscotland.com/visit/blvisitbannockburn.htm for a photograph). The rotunda of the Center surrounds the Borestone, supposed to be Robert Bruce's command post during the battle. Otherwise, you can see displays of the period and an audiovisual presentation of the battle. Visiting details at http://www.stirling.co.uk/attractions/heritage.htm. A detailed description of the battle, with a link to a map, can be read at http://www.braveheart.co.uk/macbrave/history/bruce/banseq.htm. The actual site of the battle may now lie under the town of Bannockburn.

In 1322, Edward had more success when he defeated the Earl of Lancaster's forces at **Boroughbridge**. Boroughbridge is in Yorkshire, southeast of Ripon, sandwiched between the B6265 and the M168 and A1. At one time it was on the Great North Road from Edinburgh to London and was an important coach stop. Now the motorway runs a mile west. Read about the town at http://www.dalesview.fsnet.co.uk/aldborough/, including an account of the battle.

Oriel College, Oxford University was founded as St. Mary's College in 1324 by Adam de Brome, Edward's almoner and rector of St. Mary the Virgin Church, used as the college chapel. In 1326 Edward refounded the college, then known officially as the King's College; its name was later changed to **Oriel College**, after La Oriole, a building on the site acquired in 1329. Read the history, and see the college at http://www.oriel.ox.ac.uk/library/collbuildings.htm. The buildings mostly date from the 1600s and 1700s, with St. Mary's Quad and the Rhodes Building from the early 1900s. The home page for Oriel College, with details for prospective students, is http://www.oriel.ox.ac.uk/.

Edward was imprisoned at **Kenilworth Castle** (see *John of Gaunt*) before his deposition at **Westminster Hall** in 1327, and then at **Corfe Castle** (see *John*), before being taken to Berkeley. **Berkeley Castle** is entered by a bridge over the moat. There is a medieval kitchen, Great Hall with original timber roof, and chapel, later made into a living room. To add to the other strong attractions, the Berkeley family still reside there today. The website for the castle, predictably http://www.berkeley-castle.com/, is attractive, professional, and informative.

After Bristol, Kingswood, and Malmesbury Abbeys had turned away his body for burial, **Gloucester Cathedral** (then Abbey) received it. His son, Edward III, had his tomb built, the most beautiful in the cathedral: the peaceful expression on the face of the effigy and the exquisite tracery of the cage surrounding the tomb belie the brutishness of his passing. The abbey's charity was rewarded. Pilgrims began to crowd to the tomb, and the resultant income financed the commencement of the rebuilding of both church and abbey. His shrine quickly began to attract pilgrims, and, from the vast income which resulted, the monks rebuilt both church and abbey. The tomb is located under the north arcade of the presbytery. See the tracery on part of the canopy in the first part of http://www.britannia.com/church/studies/gloscath.html, and the head of the effigy in the second part, the next screen. For basic information about the cathedral, see *Henry III*.

After Edward II's death, Edward III sent his mother, Queen Isabella, to live in **Castle Rising**, about halfway between King's Lynn and Sandringham House, in Norfolk, where she spent the remaining 30 years of her life. The remains of the castle show that it must have been very large, with earthworks covering more than 12 acres. Only the square keep and the earthworks survive. Read about it and see photographs at http://www.castles-abbeys.co.uk/Castle-Rising-Castle.html. She was buried in the **Grey Friars Church, London** (see *Edward I*).

Some Descendants of Edward III

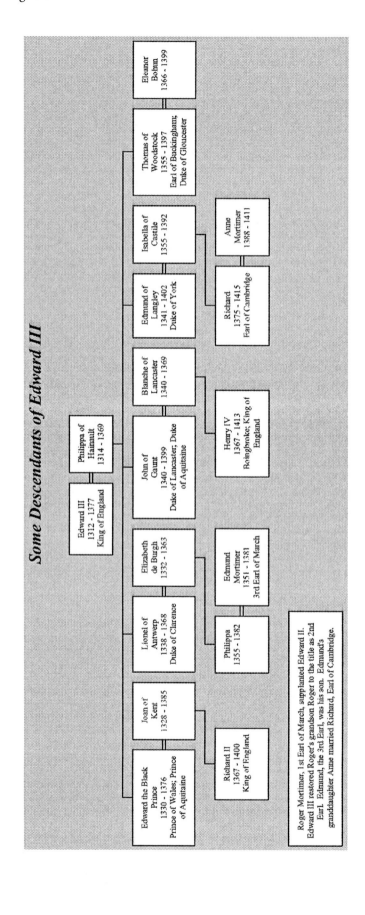

Roger Mortimer, 1st Earl of March, supplanted Edward II. Edward III restored Roger's grandson Roger to the title as 2nd Earl. Edmund, the 3rd Earl, was his son. Edmund's granddaughter Anne married Richard, Earl of Cambridge.

Edward III (1312–1377; Duke of Aquitaine, 1327–1362; King of England and Lord of Ireland, 1327–1377)

The very long reign of Edward III reached its apex in the decade following the middle 1340s, with the victories of Crécy, Calais, and Poitiers in France and of Neville's Cross in Scotland. The reign had suffered a shaky beginning with the deposition and murder of the King's father, the detested control of the King by his mother Queen Isabella and her lover Roger Mortimer, the coup by which the King overthrew and executed Mortimer, and a parliamentary crisis in 1340–1341. Thereafter, the nobles and Edward III sought to sustain their shared interests. The emerging Commons representing minor landowners and merchants adopted the nobility's former role of opposition and used its financing of the King's wars to wring concessions. Far less heavyhanded than his grandfather Edward I, the King employed diplomacy and negotiation. Adept at delegating and consulting, Edward III became highly successful at building cooperative relationships with important Church leaders and nobles. His negotiations with Parliament financed his wars, which the nobility supported partly because of the glory and honor won in the King's service and embodied in his newly created Order of the Garter. The English victories over the French and the Scots, however stunning, did not, in the end, achieve the King's goals of overlordship in Scotland and full sovereignty in his French lands. First striking England in the year in which Edward established the Order of the Garter, the recurring Black Death limited or prevented military expeditions. Ultimately, the aging King lost both interest and control, while the Scots and the French successfully fought off English interference.

The struggle with Scotland often intertwined with England's conflicts with the French because Scotland and France preserved their "Auld Alliance" against England. (For a discussion of the beginnings of England's Hundred Years War against France, see the chapter on Edward III's sons ***Edward the Black Prince and John of Gaunt.***) In the Declaration of Arbroath sent to Pope John XXII in 1320, the Scots declared, "we will never on any conditions be subjected to the lordship of the English. For we fight not for glory, nor riches, nor honours, but for freedom alone, which no good man gives up except with his life." Then, in 1326, the Franco-Scottish Treaty of Corbeil solidified their alliance versus England. In the year of Edward III's accession, 1327, English forces suffered defeat at Stanhope Park, and in 1328 the consequent Treaty of Northampton renounced England's claims of feudal overlordship. It also arranged the marriage of Edward's sister Joan to Robert I's young son, who became David II in 1329. Refusing to attend his sister's wedding, Edward resented this ignominious capitulation and instead supported the claims of Edward Balliol, son to John Balliol, against those of his new brother-in-law.

In the early 1330s, Edward Balliol's and David II's wheels of Fortune spun giddily. Edward Balliol invaded Scotland, vanquished David II's army at Dupplin Moor, and, after further exile from Scotland, gained from Edward III's 1333 victory in his behalf, in the Battle of Halidon Hill. In 1334, Edward Balliol paid homage to Edward III. Supporting the exiled David II, Philip VI of France emphasized that no Anglo-French peace settlement could scant the interests of France's ally Scotland. (In this period, the gallant womanizer Edward III rode from Perth to the beseiged castle of Lochindorb to rescue the Countess of Atholl.) In 1341, David II returned to Scotland, and, in the following year, the Scots took Stirling Castle from the English. However, the English victory at Neville's Cross in 1346 included the capture of David II. During his prolonged stay in England while his captors and subjects disputed the terms of his ransom, David II stayed at Nottingham Castle. In the decade of the King's absence (1346–1357), his kinsman Robert Stewart ruled as Guardian of Scotland. In 1356, Edward Balliol surrendered his rights to the Scottish throne to Edward III, and the 1357 Treaty of Berwick arranged for a truce as well as the ransom for David II, who then departed for Scotland with his wife, Edward III's sister Joan. Won over by Edward III, David II asked the indignant Scottish nobility to accept the Black Prince as his own successor. Instead, Robert Stewart, himself a grandson of Robert I, became King Robert II in 1371 after the death of David II. This founder of the Scottish Stewart (Stuart) dynasty that would one day rule both Scotland and England revived the alliance with France against England. Edward III had not succeeded in his objective of subjugating Scotland to his will.

His English nobles' support of Edward III's wars in Scotland and France in part derived from the good fellowship they felt with this King, accentuated by his fostering of chivalric honors. Edward III shared an intense interest in the legendary King Arthur of Britain and his Knights of the Round Table with his grandfather Edward I and even more distant predecessors. Henry II apparently had urged the Benedictine monks at Glastonbury Abbey in Somerset to search for the rumored resting places of Arthur and Guinevere, and, in 1191, the monks of Glastonbury claimed to have unearthed them near the Lady Chapel of the Abbey church. They also discovered an accompanying leaden cross inscribed *Hic iacet inclitus rex Arturius in insula Avallonis sepultus* ("Here lies the famous king Arthur in the isle of Avalon buried"). A tomb built in 1192–1193 housed the remains. Edward I and Queen Eleanor witnessed in 1278 the excavation and reburial of these remains in a marble tomb positioned before the high altar in the main Abbey church. (Henry VIII closed the Abbey at Glastonbury in 1539 during his Dissolution of the Monasteries, during which the remains vanished. The leaden cross—still seen as late as the 18th century in Wells—has since disappeared.) During Edward I's subjugation of Wales, he also received what the Welsh venerated as Arthur's crown.

His grandson Edward III visited Glastonbury in 1331 and 14 years later decreed a search there for the bones of Joseph of Arimathea, by legend bearer of the Grail to Britain as well as Arthur's ancestor. Edward III's knightly interests included tournaments, which he both advocated and enjoyed as a participant, as did his sons. In a 1344 joust at his birthplace of Windsor, the King announced his design to revive the Arthurian Round Table. He envisoned a circular building at Windsor that would house his Order of the Round Table. The King's carpenter created a Round Table—perhaps the one that survives at Winchester College—and construction began on the circular building, but war with France permanently interrupted the work.

In 1348, Edward revived his scheme. He would renovate Henry III's Chapel of St. Edward the Confessor at Windsor in which his own christening had occurred and rededicate his new St. George's Chapel to St. Edward the Confessor, the Virgin, and St. George. (Not the present St. George's Chapel, which dates from the mid-15th century, Edward III's St. George's Chapel stood on the site of the present Albert Memorial Chapel.) The renovation of the chapel occurred as part of a larger building project to create a College of St. George at Windsor. Originally called the Order of St. George, the Order of the Garter was integrated from the start with Edward III's College of St. George.

The priestly community of College of St. George at Windsor included a Dean and 12 secular priests or canons, 13 vicars, clerks (professional singers), boy choristers, a verger, and bell ringers. The Dean, canons, and vicars numbered 26—a total mirrored by the 26 Companions of the Garter, who included the King himself. Twenty-six poor veterans, called the Poor Knights, received room and board from the college in exchange for their prayers for the King and the other Companions. Each Companion received his own stall in the chapel and had to perform certain duties. The first annual Garter celebration occurred at Windsor on St. George's Day, 23 April 1348. From conquered Wales in 1284, Edward I had taken a piece of the True Cross (the Croes Naid) belonging to Llywelyn the Last; Edward III presented it to St. George's Chapel at the founding of his Order of the Garter.

Home of the Order of the Garter, St. George's Chapel stands foremost among Edward's architectural achievements at Windsor, Sheen, Hadleigh, Westminster, and Rotherhithe. Both religious and political in inspiration, with a motto that probably referred to Edward III's aspiration to the French throne (*Honi soit qui mal y pense:* "Evil to him who thinks evil of it"), the Order itself stood as a embodiment of the fellowship that Edward III created with his nobility. It enshrined contemporary strivings and purposes by entwining them with a mythic chivalric past saturated with both military glory and the lure of the sacred. Edward succeeded so well in reviving Arthurian glamor that the chronicler Jean Froissart repeatedly reached back to Arthur in describing the royal family. Exalting the Black Prince as "the Flower of Chivalry of all the world," Froissart noted about Edward III's passing that "His like had not been seen since the days of King Arthur" and commemorated Edward's Queen Philippa thus: "since the days of Queen Guinevere…, so good a Queen never came to that land."

In 1348, the year of the founding of the Order of the Garter, the very antithesis of its glamor and romance first devastated England. Called the Black Death in the 16th century and "The Great Pestilence" by Edward III's contemporaries, it struck again in 1361–1362, 1368–1369, and 1374–1375. Its chronicler in 1348, Henry Knighton, noted, "After the pestilence many buildings both great and small in all cities, towns, and boroughs fell into total ruin for lack of inhabitants; similarly many small villages and hamlets became desolate and no houses were left in them, for all those who had dwelt in them were dead, and it seemed likely that many such little villages would never again be inhabited." Probably, though not certainly, bubonic plague as well as pneumonic plague concurrent with outbreaks of influenza and typhoid, the pestilence killed from one-third to one-half of the population over its four visitations. An eminent physician observed at the time, "The plague was shameful for the physicians, who could give no help at all, especially as, out of fear of infection, they hesitated to visit the sick." Widespread death created economic upheaval consequent to the loss of tenants and workers; more lasting effects included pervasive bitterness towards the powerful in the land and in the Church that would culminate in the Peasants' Revolt of 1381. The pestilence also saved many lives and much property because its occurrences forced breaks in military campaigning.

Resentment grew in the Commons and among the people of the expense of Edward III's foreign wars expecially when expeditions failed and England's purposes went for naught. After John of Gaunt's failed expedition from Calais to Bordeaux in 1373, the English now held in Aquitaine only Bordeaux and Bayonne and contingent areas as well as garrisons in Calais, Boulogne, and Normandy. Despite a general truce agreed to in 1375, England and France still wrangled over questions of full sovereignty, and Scotland continued to resist English encroachments. The King spent his last years at Havering, Woodstock, Windsor, Sheen, Eltham, and Queenborough—all country residences near the capital—and came to Westminster to conduct business. After Queen Philippa ended their 40-year marriage by dying in 1369, Edward noticeably declined. The King's mistress since 1364 and maid of Philippa's bedchamber since 1366, Alice Perrers easily dominated the old man in his dotage. Strokes possibly accelerated Edward's cognitive deterioration. Alice and her allies alienated the nobles by their constriction of access to the King and by their greedy monopolization of patronage. The Good Parliament of 1376 expelled Alice Perrers from court and sought to impeach some of Gaunt's supporters, but Alice soon returned at the distressed King's request, and Gaunt undid the Good Parliament's other actions. Honoring the tradition of holding an annual tournament on the feast of St. George, Edward III in 1377 on St. George's Day at Windsor knighted both the Black Prince's son Richard and Gaunt's son Henry and admitted them to the Order of the Garter. The mere shadow of his former glorious self died two months later at Sheen.

Edward III Sites

Edward was born at **Windsor Castle** on November 13, 1312. He was proclaimed King on January 25, 1327 and crowned on February 2. On January 24, a year later, he married Philippa, 3rd daughter of William, Count of Holland and Hainault. For background information on Windsor Castle, see *William the Conqueror*.

Edward and Philippa of Hainault were married in **York Minster** in 1328. York Minster is the largest English medieval cathedral, with the second-highest nave (Westminster Abbey has the highest), and it ranks second to Canterbury in ecclesiastical importance. The interior is outstanding with its abundance of beautiful stained glass, fine tracery, and carved decoration. York Minster's official website appears at http://www.yorkminster.org/index1.html. York is an attractive old city and manages to remain so despite the hordes of tourists; the street pattern mostly follows the medieval, narrow and winding, so leave the car outside the walls and walk. The city's website URL is http://www.york-tourism.co.uk/, opening with a magnificent aerial photograph of the Minster.

Mortimer's Hole is a secret passage to the keep of **Nottingham Castle**, through which a young Edward and his companions broke into Nottingham Castle where his mother, Queen Isabella, was resident with her lover Roger Mortimer. They seized Mortimer and rushed him to London to execution and packed Isabella off to live in **Castle Rising**. (For Castle Rising, see *Edward II*). Conducted tours of passages in the rock beneath the castle, including Mortimer Hole, are available, advertised in various places on the Web and in the tourist information office in Nottingham. A city of 271,000 population, Nottingham displays dual medieval and 19th century industrial development. The only remnant of the castle atop its sandstone mound is the heavily restored 13th century gatehouse. The castle was dismantled during the Civil War, in 1651. An Italianate mansion built on the site is now the municipal museum and art gallery—in fact, the first such in England outside London. See http://www.itsnottingham.info/ for visiting information about Nottingham.

In Pursuit of Scotland

The 1333 Battle of **Halidon Hill** took place just outside **Berwick-upon-Tweed**; the site is on the north side of the A6105, 2 miles northwest of Berwick. Read about the battle at http://members.tripod.com/~midgley/halidon.html. For basic information about Berwick, see *Edward I*. For the duration of the battle, Philippa stayed at **Bamburgh Castle**. This dramatically situated castle has a Norman keep and curtain wall, but most of the remainder dates from the 19th century. Bamburgh is on the North Sea coast south of Berwick and the Holy Island (Lindisfarne), the castle perched on a crag by the shore. Its friendly website is http://www.bamburghcastle.com/.

Lochindorb is in the Scottish Highlands, a loch south and east of the A939, reached by country roads. The best photograph appears on the website for Lochindorb Lodge at http://www.lhhscotland.co /House123.asp. The castle is behind the lodge, on an island in the lake. The clearest map, at http://www.higharch.demon.co.uk/leaflets/badenoch/sites_a.html, also gives a history of the castle, describing how James II of Scotland demolished it.

In Europe

Until the end of the 15th century, **Sluis** (modern spelling) was on the estuary of Het Zwin and served as a foreport for Bruges, to the south. In 1340 the French fleet was assembled in the estuary in preparation for invasion of England. Edward forestalled them and, with Flemish allies, almost totally destroyed the French fleet. The Battle of Sluys is depicted in Froissart's *Chronicles* and reproduced on the Internet at http://www.bnf.fr/enluminures/manuscrits/aman1/i3_0012.htm.

No longer a port, today's Sluis remains a fortified town in spite of war damage, and is a busy tourist center for daytrippers. It's tucked into a southwestern corner of the Netherlands, close to the border with Belgium. The reclaimed land of Het (The) Zwin estuary has been cultivated or, in the case of dunes and marshes near the sea, preserved as a nature reserve and bird sanctuary. See Het Zwin at http://www.trabel.com/knokke/knokke-zwin.htm, the same site also presents information about Knokke, one of several popular North Sea resorts nearby.

Edward's siege of Tournai following his victory in the Battle of Sluys was unsuccessful. **Tournai** was damaged in both World Wars. In November 1918, the retreating German army blew up the bridges over the Scheldt, but much more damaging was the heavy bombing by the Luftwaffe in 1940, that destroyed most of the old houses of the Grand-Place, the center of Tournai. It was the first Belgian town liberated in 1944 by the advancing British troops. The damage has been mostly repaired by careful reconstruction. Many styles of architecture are represented in this busy and attractive city which dates from before the 4th century. Tournai's official website is http://www.tournai.be/.

In 1342, Edward was back in Europe, this time in Brittany. **Vannes**, the subject of his unsuccessful siege, is strategically placed on the huge natural harbor of the Gulf of Morbihan in southeastern Brittany. Just as the city was the gateway to the conquest of Brittany at that time, it now serves the same purpose, peacefully, for the excursioner. Vannes has a population of 55,000 and still contains attractive old houses and well-preserved city walls. The official website for Vannes is informative, with an English version; the URL is http://www.mairie-vannes.fr/indexdiscoveringvannes.html.

Northeast of the village of **Crécy-en-Ponthieu,** Edward defeated the threefold strong French army of Philip VI in 1346 at the Battle of Crécy. Crécy-en-Ponthieu lies north of Abbeville and beside the Forêt de Crécy. The Moulin Edouard III is where Edward watched the progress of the battle in 1346; it's located between Crécy-en-Ponthieu and the neighboring village of Wadicourt. See background regarding the battle, along with photographs of the terrain, at http://www.smg-authie.co.uk/france/crecy_01.htm, with more about the town at http://www.smg-authie.co.uk/france/crecy_02.htm, including the Crécy memorial and instructions for reaching the battle site.

The seaside towns of **Honfleur** and **Caen** were also taken by Edward in 1346. Before Le Havre was founded in 1517, the twin ports flanking the Seine estuary, Harfleur on the right bank and Honfleur on the left, flourished. The rise of Le Havre reduced Harfleur, but Honfleur prospered as a center for expeditions to the New World. It was from here that Samuel de Champlain sailed for Canada in 1603. As an old port with picturesque houses, it has been a magnet for artists and, without a bathing beach, a foil for the neighboring cosmopolitan resorts running down the coast from Trouville and Deauville. The website for Honfleur presents only the Museums and Accommodation sections in English, but see attractive photographs of the "quartiers pittoresques" at http://www.ville-honfleur.fr/Honfleur/Lieux/index.htm.

For **Caen**, pillaged by Edward in 1346, see *William the Conqueror*.

Edward took **Calais** in 1347 after a siege lasting 11 months. Six burghers offered their lives as a ransom to save the town and were spared only when Queen Philippa intervened. In 1885, Rodin was commissioned to create a monument to their heroism; his moving bronze sculpture of these gaunt, despairing men stands in front of the Hôtel de Ville in the southern part of the town. It also can be seen in the Musée de Rodin in Paris, along with versions in the gardens of the Hirschhorn Museum in Washington, DC, the Rodin Museum in Philadelphia, and in the gardens next to the Houses of Parliament in London. Read about the sculpture at http://www.musee-rodin.fr/smonu-e.htm. Today, Calais, a town of 79,000 inhabitants, is the nearest to England, an important ferry and hovercraft port; the Channel Tunnel (Chunnel) to England is nearby. The old town was razed during World War II and has been rebuilt.

Back in England

Edward built the **Cradle Tower** at the **Tower of London**, as a private watergate to his own lodgings in and around the **Lanthorn Tower**. For Edward's role in the evolution of the Tower, along with a photograph of the Cradle Tower, see http://www.castles.org/castles/Europe/Western_Europe/United_Kingdom/England/england12.htm.

At **Windsor Castle**, his contribution was momentous, amounting to the transformation of the castle into a Gothic palace and the seat of the new Order of the Garter. In the Lower Ward, the **College of St George** was built on the site of the present Albert Memorial Chapel. The **Upper Ward** saw reconstruction under the direction of William of Wykeham, Bishop of Winchester. An inner gatehouse, now incorrectly called the **Norman Gate**, was built as the principal entrance to the Upper Ward, and extensive royal apartments surrounded inner courtyards, supported by stone-vaulted undercrofts. Edward's state apartments survived until the 17th century; the undercrofts are still there. The **Great Hall** and **Royal Chapel** were built along south side of the Upper Ward, facing the Quadrangle.

Each year in June, the Knights of the **Order of the Garter** gather at Windsor Castle, where new Knights take the oath and are invested in the 12th century Garter Throne Room. They then take lunch in the Waterloo Chamber, after which they process through the castle precincts to St. George's Chapel, for the Garter service. On Garter Day, the castle is closed to all visitors except those with invitations to attend the service and watch the procession to St. George's Chapel. There's a wealth of useful information, along with many detailed photographs at http://www.heraldicsculptor.com/Garters.html.

At **Cambridge**, Edward founded King's Hall, later one of the colleges forming **Trinity College**. **King Edward's Tower**, built in 1428, stands in Great Court on the north side. Formerly part of King's Hall, it bears a statue of Edward wearing Elizabethan armor and impaling three crowns on his sword. Trinity College's website is at http://www.trin.cam.ac.uk/. See King Edward's Tower at http://www.cambridge2000.com/cambridge2000/html/0001/P1010020.html; a closer view of Edward's statue appears at http://viewfinder.english-heritage.org.uk/search/detail.asp?calledFrom=oai&imageUID=73008.

Hadleigh, home to a ruined castle, repaired and rebuilt in 1359–70 for Edward, is situated on the Essex marshes of the north shore of the Thames, between Southend-on-Sea and Basildon. See Hadleigh at http://www.hadleigh.org.uk/.

In **Rotherhithe**, on the south bank of the Thames and east of Bermondsey, lie the remains of a medieval moated manor house identified as belonging to Edward. The remains, discovered in 1903, are just past the Angel Pub, with storyboards to guide the visitor. The manor originally contained a hall, kitchen, chamber, gatehouse, and garden. Rotherhithe's shipping past is captured in its old name, Redriff, from two Saxon words meaning mariner and haven. For Americans, it's important because the *Mayflower* departed from here in 1620 (there's the Mayflower pub along Rotherhithe Street, dating from 1553, but the present building is much newer). Although the docks were closed in the 1970s and built over, reminders of its past exist in its seamen's churches, and, along Rotherhithe Street by the river, the old warehouses and some stairs to the river, and the river itself, once a hive of activity here. There's a very comprehensive visitors' guide at http://www.btinternet.com/~se16/. See a photograph of the Angel pub and other historical images of Rotherhithe at http://www.ideal-homes.org.uk/southwark/rotherhithe/angel.htm.

Edward died at **Sheen Palace**, Surrey on June 21, 1377, and is buried in **Westminster Abbey**. Philippa had died at Windsor Castle on August 14, 1369; she is buried in Westminster Abbey.

The royal manor of **Sheen** once embraced all of the area that is now Kew and Richmond, a site beloved of monarchs over the centuries (the word Sheen is derived from an Anglo-Saxon word meaning a spot of beauty). For a history and photographs of Sheen Palace, see http://www.plus44.com/royal/richmond/richmopal.html.

Edward's and Philippa's tombs are among those surrounding the shrine of St Edward the Confessor, in **Westminster Abbey**. Their faces on their effigies are less idealized and more representative of character and probable physical appearance than those of Edward I and Eleanor of Castile, reflecting the contemporary trend in portraiture. Their effigies can be seen at http://www.westminster-abbey.org/library/monarchs/edward_iii.htm.

Queenborough was named by Edward in honor of Queen Philippa, after he built a castle there. The castle was demolished during the Commonwealth years. Queenborough is located on the Medway estuary, about three miles from Sheerness, which stands where the Medway empties into the Thames. At one time prosperous, Queenborough has declined over the centuries, which is candidly admitted on its website at http://queenborough.freeservers.com/.

Interrelationships between Houses of Valois and Plantagenet

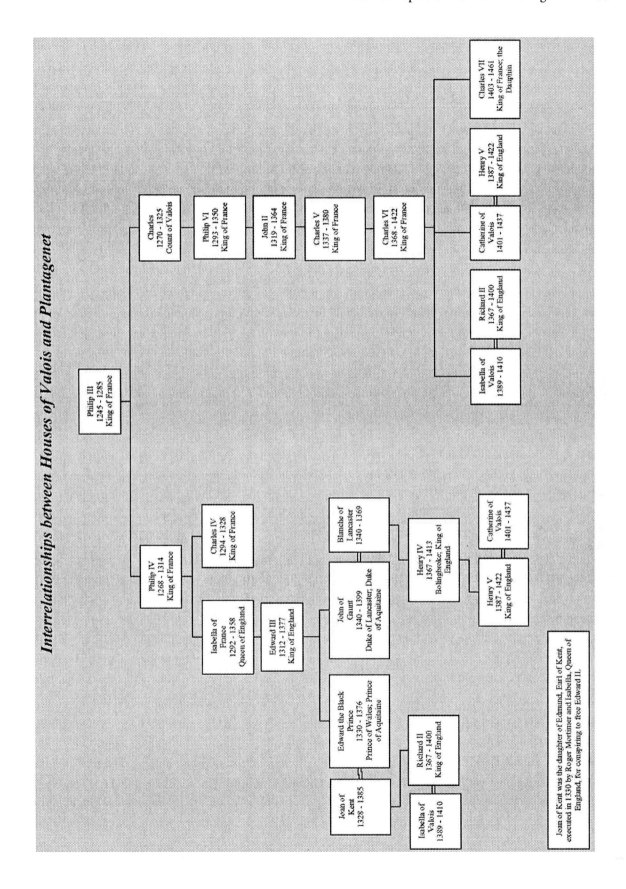

Joan of Kent was the daughter of Edmund, Earl of Kent, executed in 1330 by Roger Mortimer and Isabella, Queen of England, for conspiring to free Edward II.

Edward the Black Prince (1330–1376), John of Gaunt (1340–1399), and the Beginnings of the Hundred Years War

Sons and fathers of Kings of England rather than Kings of England themselves, these two sons of Edward III served the royal interests as warriors and diplomats. Their lives intertwined from the birth of the younger brother at the Abbey of St. Bavo in Ghent in 1340 until the death of the elder brother at Westminster in 1376. Born at Woodstock in 1330, Prince Edward became Earl of Chester at the age of three, Duke of Cornwall (the first English Duke) at the age of seven, and Prince of Wales at the age of 13. As Prince Edward grew older, he acquired many residences and properties, among them Berkhamsted, Kennington, Restormel, his London town house of Pulteney House, Castle Rising, and Cheylesmore. He also acquired a reputation for gambling and extravagance. Famous for physical courage, excellent as an inspirational leader of soldiers, the Black Prince displayed less competence or interest in goverance and diplomacy. John, named Earl of Richmond in 1342, formed a very close relationship with his elder brother Edward, in whose household he lived from 1350 onward. Gaunt's varied service in military, diplomatic, and governance matters demonstrated consistent and intense loyalty towards Edward III and Prince Edward during their lifetimes, and he transferred this code of service to his new sovereign, his brother's son Richard II. Ironically, these very close brothers begat antipathetic sons in Richard II and Henry Bolingbroke, later Henry IV, who usurped Richard II's crown and had his cousin murdered.

These quarrels about the English succession lay six decades in the far future when the absorbing interest of these brothers' lives began: the Hundred Years War between England and France. An old grievance—the loss of the Angevin empire in France—gave rise to a new claim—to the French throne.

The 1259 Treaty of Paris negotiated between Henry III of England and Louis IX of France recognized the loss of the Plantagenet dynasty's French lands and established that Henry III would hold Gascony (part of Aquitaine) as a fief of the French crown. In the early 14th century, Philip IV of France had questioned Edward I of England's right to Aquitaine until Edward I rendered liege homage, and in 1324 Charles IV of France had actually confiscated Gascony from Edward II of England. In 1329, Edward III of England performed simple homage to Philip VI of France for Aquitaine but refused to do liege homage, precipitating French attempts to undermine English rule there, until, in 1331, Edward III acknowledged that he held Aquitaine by liege homage. After such further irritants as Edward III's embargo on the export of English wool to Flanders (an anti-French move) and his refusal to surrender the fugitive Robert, Count of Artois, Philip IV declared in 1337 that Edward III had forfeited his French fiefs.

This ongoing struggle to retain part of the Angevin lands in France metamorphosized into a new contest for the French succession in 1328 when the death of Charles IV ended succession in the direct male line for the House of Capet. His pregnant widow eventually produced a daughter; Salic Law forbade accession by or through a female; thus, the Regent, Philip of Valois, became Philip VI of France. Despite Salic Law, ten years later, Edward III declared his claim to Philip VI's crown through Edward III's mother, Isabella of France, sister to Charles IV and first cousin to Philip VI. In 1340, Edward actually assumed the French royal arms. Rising tensions between the sovereigns had at last led to an attempt to disrupt the French succession.

The Hundred Years War naturally featured many truces and pauses. Action in the early 1340s included the defeat by the English of a French-Castilian fleet at Sluys and Edward III's invasion of France. Defeating Philip VI, Edward III and the Black Prince in 1346 won the Battle of Crécy. Mourning the death of a great warrior, the French ally John, King of Bohemia, Prince Edward assumed the Bohemian King's badge of ostrich feathers and motto *Ich dien* ("I serve"). The English commanders at Crécy made up the original members of the Order of the Garter formed in 1348, with the 36-year-old Edward III being one of its oldest members. In 1347, Calais had fallen to the English. Almost a decade later, Prince Edward led an expedition to Aquitaine, while Gaunt campaigned with their father. At the 1356 Battle of Poitiers, Prince Edward captured John II of France. While his captors negotiated his ransom, they lodged the French King for a time in Gaunt's Savoy Palace near London. At the end of the decade, an expedition to Rheims to crown Edward III King of France failed. The Treaty of Brétigny gave Edward III full sovereignty over Aquitaine, as well as other French lands, and secured a lesser ransom for John II. In return, Edward III renounced his claim to French throne and to Normandy, Maine, and Anjou. However, this treaty's provisions were never enacted.

Honors and marriage came to the brothers in these years as well. Gaunt married his kinswoman, the great heiress Blanche of Lancaster, and he soon afterwards received Hertford Castle from Edward III. Already Earl of Richmond, Gaunt would become Earl of Lancaster, Earl of Derby, and eventually Duke of Lancaster. David II of Scotland even considered making Gaunt his successor. Edward III in 1362 also named Prince Edward Prince of Aquitaine, where local resentment of direct English rule and heavy taxation for the Prince's Spanish wars would fester. Edward married his beautiful kinswoman, Joan of Kent, and took her to Bordeaux. Gaunt advised his father in his brother's absence.

An alliance formed in 1362 by Edward III with Peter the Cruel of Castile sought to protect the interests of Aquitaine as well as disrupt the alliance between Castile and France. Four years later, the French dethroned Peter and restored his half-brother Henry of Trastamara; Peter put himself under the protection of the Black Prince in Aquitaine. In 1367, the year in which Joan of Kent gave birth to the future Richard II and Blanche of Lancaster bore the future Henry IV, the Black Prince and John of Gaunt defeated Henry at Nájera and restored Peter. Soon, however, with the help of Charles V of France, Henry supplanted Peter and assassinated him. When, in 1369, Charles V confiscated Aquitaine, Edward III reassumed his claim to French crown, but the resumption of hostilities posed great difficulties for the English. Suppressing rebellion in Aquitaine, the ailing Black Prince directed the siege, massacre, and destruction of Limoges from a litter. Gaunt assumed command because of Prince Edward's illness and Edward III's decline. In the middle 1370s, after the failure of an expedition from Calais to Bordeaux, Gaunt involved himself in peace negotiations.

Blanche of Lancaster had died not long after the birth of Gaunt's son Henry, and in 1371 John married Constance of Castile, Peter's daughter and heiress. Gaunt's new diplomatic marriage did not prevent his concurrent adultery with Catherine Swynford, a female servant of Blanche and governess of Blanche's daughters. (Patron of John Wycliffe, Gaunt also patronized Geoffrey Chaucer, whose wife Philippa served Constance but was also Catherine's sister.) Edward III recognized Gaunt's claim to the throne of Castile.

In 1376, the Black Prince died after years of suffering from dysentery and was buried at Canterbury Cathedral. His young son Richard, the Prince of Wales, succeeded to the throne after the 1377 death of Edward III. In these years, Gaunt dominated Parliament and strove to protect royal authority and interests for his nephew just as he had for his father. Gaunt became the focus of much resentment. During the 1381 Peasants' Revolt in England, rebels destroyed by fire Gaunt's Savoy Palace (located near Charing Cross between London and Westminister). (His many other residences included a favorite manor—Kingston Lacy in Dorset, Richmond, Hertford, Leicester, Lancaster, Kenilworth, Tutbury, Pontefract, and Knaresborough.) Gaunt's tense relationships with Londoners, the Commons, ecclesiastics, his nephew the King, and courtiers caused him to go to Scotland until recalled by Richard; Gaunt also fled to Pontefract to escape an assassination plot possibly approved by Richard II.

Eventually, Richard II sent Gaunt to negotiate with the Scots and the French, and Gaunt's 1386 expedition to Castile in pursuit of his own claim to the throne also absented him from England. This failed expedition led Gaunt in 1388 to turn over his claim to his and Constance's daughter Catherine, who married her second cousin, the future Henry III of Castile. Besides Gaunt's Castilian descendants, the progeny of his daughter by Blanche, Philippa of Lancaster, who married John I of Portugal, also honored him as their ancestor. Future generations boasting Lancastrian descent included Catharine of Aragon and Philip II of Spain.

Returning to England in 1389, Gaunt reconciled with Richard II and resumed his high position in the King's councils for several years. Named Duke of Aquitaine in 1390, Gaunt became heavily involved in the peace negotiations that Richard favored with the French. A 1396 truce specified that Richard II would marry Isabella of Valois, daughter of Charles VI, and would retain the lands specified in Treaty of Brétigny as well as his claim to the French throne. Warfare would cease until 1426. However, domestic problems in both France and England threatened this truce.

In these last years of the 1390s, after Constance's death in 1394, Gaunt finally married his longtime mistress Catherine Swynford and legitimized their bastards retroactively. In 1398, Richard II darkened Gaunt's last years by banishing Gaunt's heir, Henry Bolingbroke. When, in the following year, John of Gaunt died at Leicester Castle, Richard II declared his estates forfeited to the crown. Gaunt had asked for burial in St. Paul's Cathedral near his long-deceased first wife, Blanche of Lancaster. After 60 years of quarreling over the French succession, the next chapter would concern a rivalry for the English succession. Death spared Gaunt from witnessing it.

Edward the Black Prince Sites

The Black Prince's birthplace, **Woodstock Palace**, north of Oxford, was originally a royal hunting ground which became a favorite residence. See *Henry II* for details. It was pulled down when Blenheim Palace was built (see *Anne*).

Cheylesmore Manor House, in **Coventry**, now serves as the Register Office, where marriages are conducted. It has been altered, but doesn't look it; only the old gatehouse remains today after it fell into disrepair; it was restored during the 1960s, and can be reached from New Union Street. See it at http://www.thecoventrypages.net/hstoric-cov/manor-house.asp.

Restormel Castle stands just to the north of **Lostwithiel**, Cornwall, between Bodmin and Fowey. There's a circular keep dating from 1200, and the remains of a great hall added c.1300, within a moat. See http://www.english-heritage.org.uk/server.php?show=conProperty.300 for photos and a description and visiting details. More historical detail can be read at http://www.theheritagetrail.co.uk/castles/restormel%20castle.htm.

Wallingford Castle was a favorite home (see *Stephen and Maud* for details). Among his many other homes was the manor at **Byfleet** (Surrey)—later granted to Catherine of Aragon upon the annulment of her marriage to Henry VIII, and over two and a half centuries later bought by Frederick, Duke of York. The manor house was completely rebuilt during 17th century. Byfleet is southwest of London, near the intersection of the M25 and the A3; with West Byfleet, which is on the other side of the M25, it's part of the Woking urban area. For **Berkhamsted Castle**, see *William I* and *Richard II*; for **Castle Rising**, see *Edward II*.

In London, Edward bought **Pulteney House** from Sir John Pulteney. Later known as **Cold Harbour Palace** and long since destroyed, the house was situated on the north bank of the Thames, in the east end, near Candlewick Street. On the other side of the Thames, he owned a palace at **Kennington**. Nothing remains but the name Black Prince Road. Read a comprehensive history of Kennington and its royal manor at http://www.vauxhallsociety.org.uk/Kennington.html.

Joan inherited the manor of **Deeping** through her family, the Wakes, Earls of Kent; this manor then passed to the crown when she married Edward, inherited ultimately by Lady Margaret Beaufort (the Lady of the Deepings). The villages with Deeping in their names are clustered north of Peterborough, around the intersection of the A15 and A16. See http://www.deepings.com/about/history.htm for a history with a photograph of the town center, and links.

At **Crécy**, Edward "won his spurs." For information about this battle and the village of **Crécy-en-Ponthieu**, see *Edward III*. For **Poitiers**, scene of the Black Prince's victory in 1356, and also for **Bordeaux**, where Edward held his court from 1356–71, see *Eleanor of Aquitaine*. An account of the Battle of Poitiers, with a diagram of the armies, appears at http://home.eckerd.edu/~oberhot/poitiers.htm.

Libourne, where Edward signed a treaty in 1366 with Peter the Cruel of Castile and Charles II of Navarre, is situated east of Bordeaux, on the confluence of the Dordogne river with that of the Isle. You can read about it at http://www.libourne-tourisme.com/office.html (in French); there are some relevant photos to be seen by clicking on Bastide to the left of the screen.

Nájera lies to the west of Logroño, on the banks of the Najerilla river. Edward had led his army over the **Roncesvalles pass** from France, a well-known route at that time for being on the pilgrims' route to Santiago, as it still is today. On the pass, Charlemagne's army was cut off by Roland in 778. The village of Roncesvalles surrounds an Augustinian abbey founded by Sancho the Strong, the Real Colegiata, which still houses today's pilgrims. The website for Roncesvalles is http://www.roncesvalles.es/indice.asp?sec=1&lg=eng, with photographs and information. For the Colegiata, click on "First Hospitals." Nájera is a small town of under 10,000 population. For a description of the battle, along with diagrams, see http://es.geocities.com/endovelico2001/med/najera.html.

In 1370, **Limoges** experienced Edward's atrocity, when 3,000 citizens were slain and the city sacked. Limoges is a city of about 140,000 population, famous for its porcelain and enamels. It stands above the river Vienne, and although it has been subject to urban sprawl, still has many old streets. In medieval times, it was famous for its goldsmithing and coin minting. Limoges is located northeast of Bordeaux, and south of Poitiers; its website appears at http://www.ville-limoges.fr/, with an English version. The Musée National Adrien-Dubouché contains a large collection of porcelain and chinaware.

Edward's tomb and moving effigy are in the Trinity Chapel of **Canterbury Cathedral**, along with modern reproductions of his armor. Canterbury Cathedral's website is http://www.canterbury-cathedral.org/.

His wife Joan of Kent was buried at the Greyfriars monastery in **Stamford**. A plaque commemorates the site of the monastery; it's by the fork where St. Paul's Street becomes Ryall Road, opposite the gateway of Whitefriars, where the hospital now stands. Stamford's website is http://www.stamford.co.uk/. Its claim to be the finest stone town in England is only a slight exaggeration, if at all: it retains many fine later buildings, along with its medieval street plan when it was an important town, as well as its situation on the Welland river. In Lincolnshire, south of Grantham and east of Leicester, it makes a pretty center for touring many attractions around.

John of Gaunt Sites

St. Bavo's Abbey (Abdij Sint Baaf) in Ghent, where John of Gaunt was born, stands at Gandastraat 7. The Museum voor Stenen Voorwerpen (monumental carving) now occupies the site, housing materials in the former great hall of the abbey, which has been, in turn, refectory, abbey chapel, and parish church, and displaying others in the grounds. Remains of the abbey comprise the lavatorium, chapter house, and old refectory, which was used as a store. The website for the charming old city of Ghent is http://www.gent.be/gent/english/.

John married Blanche of Lancaster in **Reading Abbey**. For information about the abbey, see *Henry I*. He married Constance of Castile in **Roquefort** (not the Roquefort of the cheese, which is Roquefort-sur-Soulzon). Roquefort, a relatively small town, is located in the Landes area of France, off the D932, about 22 km north of Mont-de-Marsan, and south of Bordeaux. There is a 13th century church; no informative website could be located at time of writing.

Lancaster Castle has been transformed into a prison, so it can be visited only in a limited way. The chief medieval remains are the gatehouse, which dates from c.1400—one of the turrets is called John of Gaunt's Chair; the Norman keep, restored around 1585; the Well or Witches' Tower (1325); and Hadrian's Tower, possibly used as a bakery in John's days. Hadrian's Tower now displays ankle and neck irons. In its capacity as a court and prison, other buildings were added during the 18th century, including the Shire Hall and Crown Court. For comprehensive information about the castle, see http://www.lancastercastle.com/ newhome.htm, including photographs and plans, along with location and visiting information. Lancaster is near the west coast of England, to the south of the Lake District.

John received **Hertford Castle** from his father. The remains now comprise parts of the curtain wall enclosing the Norman motte and a gatehouse dating from after John's time, the 1460s, and gothicized in 1787. Hertford is an old county (Hertfordshire) town on the river Lea. It's north of London, and near the much-larger Welwyn Garden City. See the rebuilt gatehouse at http://www.hertford.net/history/castle/ index.asp.

In Lincolnshire, east of the city of Lincoln and four miles west of Spilsby, at Mavis Enderby, turn left onto the country road that leads to **Old Bolingbroke**. Only the ground floors of the towers and lower parts of the walls remain of John of Gaunt's castle, where his son Henry, to become Henry IV, was born. See and read about Bolingbroke Castle at http://www.lincsheritage.org/sites/bolingbroke/castle.html.

John added the Strong Tower, the Great Hall, and the southern rooms in the 1390s to **Kenilworth Castle**, whose keep had been built in 1170–80, followed 20 years later by the outer wall and towers. Kenilworth Castle is maintained by English Heritage; see the castle at http://www.english-heritage.org.uk/server/show/ conProperty.341, along with visiting details. More information, along with a photo gallery, is at http:// tudorhistory.org/castles/kenilworth/. Kenilworth and its castle are tucked away on the A452 between Warwick and Birmingham, but can be reached in any number of ways from the spaghetti of roads in a surrounding half-circle, from Warwick, through Royal Leamington Spa, to Coventry and Birmingham.

Another residence was **Kingston Lacy**, in Dorset. The present house dates from the 17th century, and stands on about one-quarter of the land that belonged to the early royal manor. Over the past 20 years, a combination of accidents (a gale that tore up tree roots and exposed remains) and refurbishment and upgrading have revealed traces of John's substantial home there, including old records. An account appears at http://www.britarch.ac.uk/ba/ba46/ba46regs.html. Kingston Lacy is owned by the National Trust; visiting details appear at http://www.nationaltrust.org.uk/scripts/nthandbook. dll?ACTION=PROPERTY& PropertyId=297.

The **Savoy Palace** was John's huge London residence. No traces of it exist, but the name endures in the Savoy Hotel and the Savoy Theatre next door. The land was originally given to Peter, Count of Savoy, by his niece, Queen Eleanor, wife of Henry III. He built the palace but left England, so Eleanor gave it to her son Edmund, 1st Earl of Lancaster. John then received the palace through his first wife Blanche of Lancaster. During the Peasants' Revolt, the palace was burned down and its contents destroyed. A hospital was later built on the site, and then the Examination Hall of the Royal College of Physicians and Surgeons. From 1923 to 1932, the British Broadcasting Corporation was housed here; the Institution of Electrical Engineers (IEE) bought it in 1984, and uses it for events and meetings. Its website includes historical information, along with a contemporary photograph of Savoy Place, as it is called now, and old prints, at http://www.r-and-d-efficiency.com/TheIEE/Research/Archives/IEEMembers/SavoyPlace.cfm.

The Savoy Hotel remains one of London's grandest. Both were built in the 1880s by Richard D'Oyly Carte, who built the theatre specifically to produce Gilbert and Sullivan operas (his company still perform them there), and then the hotel. The Savoy Hotel was the first public building in London to be lit by electricity. The Savoy Hotel and Savoy Theatre stand back from The Strand, to the west of Waterloo Bridge. Read about the hotel, and if you're feeling rich, reserve a room at http://www.fairmont.com/Savoy/. The history of the Savoy Theatre can be read at http://www.thisistheatre.com/londontheatre/savoytheatre.html, along with information about shows, etc.

For **Pontefract Castle** and **Knaresborough**, see *Richard   II*. By the time Mary Queen of Scots was a prisoner in **Tutbury Castle**, John's castle had mostly deteriorated, and she suffered bitterly. John's experiences were much happier, of course. In our own time, the castle has been undergoing renovation; see it, and read its history at http://www.tutburycastle.com. The small remnant can be clearly seen at http://www.castlexplorer.co.uk/england/tutbury/tutbury.php. Tutbury stands off the A511 northwest of Burton Upon Trent.

In Spain

During John's 1386 expedition to Castile, he landed in **La Coruña**, now a sizeable city and commercial port on a fine harbor in northwest Spain. This ancient port, possibly founded by the Phoenicians and captured by the Romans in 60 BC, later was in Moorish hands. The old city (Ciudad Vieja) has been preserved on the north spur of the harbor, walled, with narrow streets and old houses. See http://www.aytolacoruna.es/en/4turismo/indextur.htm for tourist information in English.

In pursuit of John's claim to the throne of Castile, he was crowned in **Santiago de Compostela**, south of La Coruña. A Unesco World Heritage Site, it's a picturesque city of 70,000, its many towers visible from the green plain around. The legend has it that the body of St. James the Great (Santiago) was discovered in 813 by Theodomir, bishop of Iria Flavia, directed by a miraculous star which appeared above a wood on the site where Santiago now stands (hence the name Compostela). A chapel was built, which was enlarged into a cathedral in 874–99, around which a town grew. The cathedral is one of the great Christian monuments of Europe, remaining almost as it was after the rebuilding from 1075 to the 12th century. The interior is spacious, to accommodate many pilgrims. Inside the west door is the Pórtico de la Gloria, richly carved in 1168 by Master Mateo, whose kneeling figure appears at the foot of the central shaft. The large figure of Christ in glory forms the centerpiece, encircled by elders with musical instruments and the other usual dramatis personae. A tourism site is http://www.santiagoturismo.com/; a probably more compatible site appears at http://www.cyberspain.com/ciudades-patrimonio/isanti.htm.

The centuries-old pilgrimage, which may begin from one of several points in France or over the border in Roncesvalles and which ends in Santiago, is still made today by both devout and secular travelers. See the "camino" to Santiago at http://www.caminosantiago.com/web_ingles/index.htm. The *Telegraph* newspaper in Britain has set up a guide for making the pilgrimage; see this at http://dspace.dial.pipex.com/telegraph/040001d1.htm.

Orense, where John held court during the few months of his "reign" as King of Castile, lies inland and southeast of Santiago. A city of 100,000 population, it takes its name from its hot springs, the Roman Aquae Urentes. At time of writing, the best site in English is http://www.world66.com/europe/spain/galicia/ourense.

Back in England

Leicester Castle, where John died, no longer exists in any recognizable form. A half-timbered gateway of 1445 leads to the few remains. The original late Norman Great Hall, with a 1698 façade, was converted into a county court in the 19th century. A fragment of the castle wall is in the Castle Gardens; the Turret Gateway is in a ruined state. The so-called John of Gaunt's Cellar dates from the 15th century and runs under a courtyard adjacent to the hall. The most comprehensive information can be read at http://www.leicester.gov.uk/index.asp?pgid=2668&mtype=print; there's nothing in the way of helpful illustration here or elsewhere. At his request, John was buried before the high altar of the old **St. Paul's Cathedral**, London, next to Blanche, his first wife. This Wren masterpiece was a rebuilding of the original building destroyed in the Great Fire of London. The official website is http://www.stpauls.co.uk/; useful information and photographs can also be seen at http://www.aboutbritain.com/StPaulsCathedral.htm. A memorial plaque in the crypt of St. Paul's Cathedral contains the names of John and Blanche among those whose memorials were lost in the Great Fire

of London; it's online at http://homepage.mac.com/crowns/gb/avgal.html. St. Paul's was the site of the marriage of Charles and the late Diana, Prince and Princess of Wales.

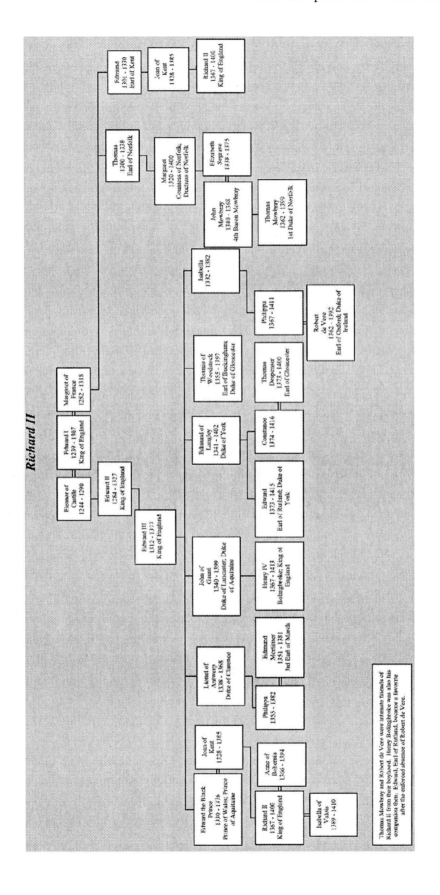

Richard II

Eleanor of Castile 1244 - 1290

Edward I 1239 - 1307 King of England

Margaret of France 1282 - 1318

Edmund 1301 - 1330 Earl of Kent

Joan of Kent 1328 - 1385

Richard II 1367 - 1400 King of England

Edward II 1284 - 1327 King of England

Edward III 1312 - 1377 King of England

Thomas 1300 - 1338 Earl of Norfolk

Margaret 1320 - 1400 Countess of Norfolk, Duchess of Norfolk

Elizabeth Segrave 1338 - 1375

John Mowbray 1340 - 1368 4th Baron Mowbray

Thomas Mowbray 1362 - 1399 1st Duke of Norfolk

Edward the Black Prince 1330 - 1376 Prince of Wales; Prince of Aquitaine

Joan of Kent 1328 - 1385

Lionel of Antwerp 1338 - 1368 Duke of Clarence

John of Gaunt 1340 - 1399 Duke of Lancaster; Duke of Aquitaine

Edmund of Langley 1341 - 1402 Duke of York

Thomas of Woodstock 1355 - 1397 Earl of Buckingham; Duke of Gloucester

Isabella 1332 - 1382

Richard II 1367 - 1400 King of England

Anne of Bohemia 1366 - 1394

Isabella of Valois 1389 - 1410

Philippa 1355 - 1382

Edmund Mortimer 1351 - 1381 3rd Earl of March

Henry IV 1367 - 1413 Bolingbroke; King of England

Edward 1373 - 1415 Earl of Rutland; Duke of York

Constance 1374 - 1416

Thomas Despencer 1373 - 1400 Earl of Gloucester

Philippa 1367 - 1411

Robert de Vere 1362 - 1392 Earl of Oxford; Duke of Ireland

Thomas Mowbray and Robert de Vere were intimate friends of Richard II from their boyhood. Henry Bolingbroke was also his companion; then Edward, Earl of Rutland, became a favorite after the enforced absence of Robert de Vere.

Richard II (1367–1400; King of England and Lord of Ireland, 1377–1399)

The deposition and murder of Richard II influenced English history well into the 16th century. Did this son of Edward the Black Prince and successor to Edward III indeed rule so badly as to warrant deposition? His near-complete loss of support in 1399 certainly indicates that by the end he had alienated almost every English magnate. However, Richard II's courageous leadership during the Peasants' Revolt of 1381, as well as his persistent efforts to secure more peaceful relations with France and Ireland, mark him as an imaginative and intelligent leader willing to reach out to opponents. Why, then, could the King not conciliate his own English nobles? Never as comfortable with the nobles as his father and grandfather had been, Richard II nevertheless finally established a relationship with them that worked fairly well for several years. It broke down in his final months of rule because the King had transgressed against common sense and prudence in asserting his royal supremacy and finally the nobility had had enough.

Born in Bordeaux at the Abbey of St-André in 1367 while his father ruled Aquitaine, Richard eventually returned with the ailing Black Prince and his mother, Joan of Kent, to England, where they lived at Berkhamsted or Kennington. When Edward the Black Prince died in 1376, the young Richard became heir apparent to the aged Edward III, who himself died in 1377. The new King Richard II reigned, but his uncle John of Gaunt ruled in his name. Close to her brother-in-law John of Gaunt, the influential Joan of Kent reconciled Gaunt with angry Londoners as she would later reconcile Gaunt with her son. The companions of Richard's youth included Gaunt's heir Henry Bolingbroke, as well as Richard's close friends Robert de Vere, 9th Earl of Oxford, and Thomas Mowbray, later Earl of Nottingham, Earl Marshal of England, and Duke of Norfolk—both brought up in the royal household. De Vere and Mowbray also belonged to the royal family: de Vere by his marriage to Richard's first cousin Philippa and Mowbray by descent from Edward I and his second wife, Margaret of France.

During the Peasants' Revolt of 1381, the young King first displayed his regality and courage. In 1380, a formerly graduated poll tax was made level and also increased, causing widespread tax evasion. Attempts to enforce collection of the tax sparked increasing anger. Not the dregs of the peasantry, but many of its more enterprising members, many with leadership experience, rebelled in Essex and Kent, then united and advanced toward London. Wat Tyler, a former soldier or criminal, led them; John Ball, a priest preaching in Kent, advised them. Ball had asserted, "We are all descended equally from Adam and Eve: why then should some hold others in subjection? They wear ermine; we wear rags; they drink wine; we drink water. They are comfortable in their big houses, while we are out in the fields. It is our sweat which keeps them in luxury." The peasants appealed to the King against the rule of his advisers.

Fourteen-year-old Richard agreed to meet them at Blackheath and sailed on a barge from the Tower of London to a location between Rotherhithe and Greenwich that would allow for easy escape. This unsuccessful parley preceded two days of rioting in London including the destruction of Gaunt's Savoy Palace (built by Peter of Savoy, uncle to Henry III's Queen Eleanor of Provence). Although the King and his council in the Tower decided to conciliate the rebels in order to get them out of the city, and Richard made promises to the peasants at Mile End, rioting continued. Another meeting at Smithfield with Wat Tyler ended with Tyler's death, after which the King rode out to the rebel masses and told them to meet him at Clerkenwell. There he discussed terms with them and offered mercy. He intended to diminish the threat to London and perhaps to better the peasants' condition, but after the threat had passed, his ministers decided to crush the rebels. Disagreeing with the council's severity, the country gentry focused on needed reforms and brought pressure from within the Commons for change. The Peasants' Revolt also caused the government to abandon its attempts to collect the hated poll tax.

Richard's meetings with the rebels in 1381 showed him in a good light, as did his marriage to Anne of Bohemia, with whom he enjoyed an extremely close and affectionate relationship. Neither their failure to produce progeny nor the failure of the diplomatic alliance purportedly secured by the marriage soured Richard's devotion to his wife. Daughter of Charles IV, King of Bohemia and Holy Roman Emperor, and thus granddaughter of John, the blind King of Bohemia who had died at Crécy, Anne was also a sister to Wenceslas of Bohemia. Anne and Richard's 1382 wedding in St. Stephen's Chapel in Westminster Palace had supported an Anglo-Imperial alliance that wilted because Wenceslas did not act upon his promises to the English to ally himself with them against the French. Richard gave to Anne the royal residences of Leeds in Kent, Woodstock in Oxfordshire, and Havering in Essex.

Richard confined his affections and loyalty to Anne and such close friends as de Vere and Mowbray, lavishing patronage on them and a few others. Nobles excluded from the King's largesse resented his neglect. They also complained that the King ignored their advice. Mowbray and de Vere plotted against John of Gaunt, with whom the King had an uneasy relationship, and these attacks on Gaunt angered his son Henry Bolingbroke. Eventually, Mowbray himself felt that Richard favored de Vere too greatly. The King named de Vere Duke of Ireland, as well as Marquess of Dublin, and because de Vere fell in love with Agnes Lancecrona, a lady-in-waiting of Queen Anne, Richard helped de Vere divorce Richard's own cousin Philippa. When, in 1386, Gaunt left England for Spain and Portugal, Richard may have felt relieved, but the absence of Gaunt's firm support for his nephew left the King vulnerable to attack by the disgruntled.

Over the next few years, Parliament impeached Richard's chancellor, Michael de la Pole, Earl of Suffolk, called for the exile of de Vere, and restricted Richard's royal authority, which led to rule by council in his name. The Lords Appellant who challenged the King included his uncle Thomas of Woodstock, Duke of Gloucester; Richard Fitzalan, 9th Earl of Arundel; and Thomas Beauchamp, 12th Earl of Warwick. Supporting these senior Appellants, the two junior Appellants, Henry Bolingbroke and Thomas Mowbray, Earl of Nottingham, joined in their opposition to the King a little later. Following the lead of the Lords Appellant, Parliament charged five of the King's officials and favorites of treason. These included de Vere, de la Pole, and Richard's former tutor (later vice-chamberlain), Sir Simon Burley. Despite the King's determined resistance, his friends either died or went into permanent exile. He never forgave London's support for these attacks on his favorites.

Hamstrung by these events, Richard suddenly burst from confinement in 1389, when he declared himself of age to rule. Gaunt's return that year to England strengthened his nephew's position. In addition, realizing that the previous lack of a power base had left him vulnerable to the Appellants, Richard distributed patronage more widely and fairly, allied himself with the Commons against the senior Appellants when discord developed, and sought to detach the junior and more moderate Appellants Bolingbroke and Mowbray from their alliance against him. For several years into the 1390s, Richard solidified his hold on many members of the nobility. Bereft of his friends, he formed a new intimacy with his first cousin Edward, son of Duke of York, who soon became Earl of Rutland.

With the inception of Richard II's personal rule came a resumption of his pacific policy towards France, reversed by Gloucester and Arundel when they had held power. Supporting his nephew's pacific intentions, Gaunt conducted the peace negotiations that spanned the first half of the 1390s. Anne of Bohemia's 1394 death at Sheen prompted her distraught widower to destroy the manor house in which she died and never again to return to Sheen. For state reasons, Richard began to negotiate for a second bride, but his consideration of Yolande of Aragon galvanized the French into resuming peace negotiations that included the offer of Charles VI's daughter Isabella of Valois. The 28-Year Truce agreed to in 1396 specified that Richard would marry Isabella of Valois and that he would retain all French lands specified in Treaty of Brétigny in full sovereignty, as well as his claim to the French throne. The King treated his little bride with paternal indulgence and affection, for she was only a small child at the time of their marriage. Besides creating a breakthrough in the peace negotiations with France, Anne of Bohemia's death also preceded Richard's very successful expedition to Ireland in 1394. The only sovereign of England to visit Ireland from the early 13th century through the late 17th century, Richard II pursued an imaginative and conciliatory policy towards Irish rebels that noted, in his words, "the grievances and wrongs done unto them." He sought to extend and solidify royal authority over Ireland.

In England, Richard II's insistence on the new forms of address "Your Majesty" and "Your Highness" underlined his determination to emphasize the regality thrown into question by the Lords Appellant and by Parliament when they had made him a mere puppet King. Always a lavish spender, Richard bought the appearance of royalty in order to indicate its substance. He enlarged Eltham in the 1380s, as well as Sheen with its island lodge, La Neyt, while in the 1390s work proceeded on Edward III's hunting lodge Windsor Manor. Richard II also rebuilt Westminster Hall. Then, in the late 1390s, after years of getting along with the nobility, the King suddenly attacked the Lords Appellant—a move that set into motion the avalanche that eventually crushed him. Did belated revenge for the death and exile of his friends and for his own humiliation motivate him? Or did some new plot by Gloucester cause him to overreact to a new threat?

In 1397–98, the King revoked the pardons issued a decade earlier, for he kept a secret list of 50 unpardoned traitors. New Lords Appellant accused the senior Lords Appellant of treason. Richard had Gloucester murdered, Arundel executed, and Warwick banished. New honors named Mowbray Duke of Norfolk, Rutland Duke of Aumerle (Albemarle), and Bolingbroke Duke of Hereford. Richard again narrowed the scope of his patronage, which also displaced some long-established magnates. The consequent estrangement only increased as the King forced the rich to loan him money and fined shires that had supported his enemies.

Mowbray, the friend of the King's youth who had turned against Richard out of jealousy of de Vere, apparently feared that the King's seeming benevolence hid more sinister intentions. His confiding this perception to his fellow junior Appellant, Bolingbroke, caused Bolingbroke to reveal Mowbray's thoughts to John of Gaunt and thereby to the King. If Richard indeed sought an opportunity to rid himself of both the junior Lords Appellant, this betrayal by Bolingbroke offered him his opportunity. Bolingbroke went on to accuse Mowbray of murdering Gloucester and of embezzling public funds. When, in 1398, Richard banished both Mowbray and Bolingbroke, he confirmed Bolingbroke's rights of inheritance but broke that pledge upon the death in 1399 of John of Gaunt. Motivated by suspicion of Bolingbroke and the perpetual royal need of money, the King's confiscation of the vast Lancastrian estates greatly alarmed owners of property.

When Bolingbroke invaded England during Richard's second expedition to Ireland in 1399, most of Richard's supporters were with him in Ireland. He had left England in the care of his uncle Edmund, Duke of York, who soon went over to the invader. York's son, Richard's favorite Rutland, advised the King in Ireland to delay his return. That perhaps treacherous advice doomed Richard's survival as King of England. Once he had finally arrived, he found himself largely deserted, by Rutland among many others. At Conwy Castle in Wales, the Earl of Northumberland persuaded Richard to leave Conwy Castle to meet Henry Bolingbroke at Flint Castle, where he became Henry's prisoner. Eventually imprisoned in the Tower and forced to abdicate, Richard was deposed because of his alleged "perjuries, sacrileges, unnatural crimes, exactions from his subjects, reductions of his people to slavery, cowardice and weakness of rule." Thomas Merke, Bishop of Carlisle registered a lonely and courageous objection as Parliament proceeded to depose Richard II in order to make way for Bolingbroke as Henry IV.

His captors moved Richard from the Tower to Leeds Castle in Kent, then north to Pickering and Knaresborough, and finally to Pontefract in Yorkshire—where he remained in the custody of Sir Thomas Swynford, Henry IV's step-brother. A plot to reinstate Richard after the murder of Henry IV and his heir involved Thomas Despenser, son-in-law to the Duke of York, and his brother-in-law Rutland, who betrayed the conspiracy to the Duke of York and then to Henry IV. This discovery, in the new King's mind, necessitated Richard's own death. After his probable murder by starvation in Pontefract Castle in 1400, Richard was transported to London for a service in St. Paul's attended by Henry IV, then buried near King's Langley. Eventually, Henry V, whom Richard II had knighted in Ireland in 1399, ordered the remains moved to Westminster Abbey, where they lie with those of Richard's beloved Anne of Bohemia. Richard's grieving widow, his pampered little bride Isabella of Valois, indignantly refused proposals that she marry Henry IV's heir. Isabella herself died a decade later, her second marriage having led to a disastrous childbed. Henry V eventually wed her younger sister Catherine.

Richard II Sites

Richard was born at the Abbey of St-André, **Bordeaux**, where his father, the Black Prince, held court in 1356–71. For information about Bordeaux and the cathedral of St-André, see *Eleanor of Aquitaine*.

Richard's meeting with Wat Tyler took place in the Smithfield area of London. **Smithfield**, now the home of Smithfield Market (meat), was once a "smooth field." First a horse market, then a cattle market, it was also the place of execution of criminals, witches, and heretics. Smithfield is located northwest of St. Paul's Cathedral, between Aldersgate Street, Holborn Viaduct, and Farringdon Street. Read an account and see photographs at http://www.urban75.org/london/smithfield.html.

Among his building achievements, Richard's renovation of **Westminster Hall** in the 1390s is momentous, especially the construction of the splendid hammerbeam roof. Designed by Henry Yevele, it replaced the old supports with the new technology that enabled the full span to be covered. See this roof at http://www.bbc.co.uk/history/society_culture/architecture/great_hall_02.shtml. Details regarding the Hall and visiting appear in the chapter *William Rufus*.

At **Westminster Abbey**, building resumed after a century of inaction, under Richard's patronage. During the short time of his reign, the nave, under Henry Yevele, was largely finished. See the magnificent nave at http://www.westminster-abbey.org/tour/index.html.

Richard also undertook extensions and rebuilding at **Eltham Palace**, with Geoffrey Chaucer supervising the work. Richard built part of the stone bridge over the moat, which still remains. For Eltham Palace, see *Edward II*. **Sheen Palace** was a favorite home of Richard's and Anne's until she died there. He then ordered the building razed: the dead Queen's apartments were pulled down, but the rest was left for Henry V's building program there. For basic information regarding Sheen, see *Edward III*. The manor at **Old Windsor** was a hunting lodge for **Windsor Great Park**, often preferred by the Plantagenets to the castle, and a favorite residence of Richard's. He pulled down Wychemere Lodge, the "new manor," and used its materials to renovate the "old manor." Read the history at http://www.berkshirehistory.com/castles/old_windsor_manor.html, and a briefer and more racy account at http://oldwindsor.freewebspace.com/custom3.html, along with an account of the current village. Old Windsor is situated south of the town and castle, and to the north of Windsor Great Park, on the A358. For **Leeds Castle**, see *Edward I*; for **Woodstock**, see *Henry I*; and for **Havering**, see *Henry IV*—all homes he gave to Anne.

At **Portchester Castle**, Richard added battlements and constructed a palace, which came to be known as Richard's Palace. This formed the south and west ranges of the inner bailey, the Great Hall to the south and a range of apartments to the west. The impressive complex of Portchester, comprising Roman, Norman, and Plantagenet construction, is maintained by English Heritage; go to http://www.english-heritage.org.uk/server/show/conProperty.207. Portchester is on the north side of Portsmouth Harbor, and the whole of the harbor can be seen from the top of the keep.

When Richard went to Ireland on his first trip in 1394, he landed in **Waterford**. Ireland's oldest city was founded by Vikings in 914 on a strategic position by the estuary of the river Suir. The well-preserved city walls contain sections dating from Viking times, as in that part containing Reginald's Tower (which dates from 1185). For information about Waterford, see http://www.waterfordtourism.org/, but note that this is the website for the entire county: access the city of Waterford through "Towns & Villages." The famous Waterford crystal can be viewed (and ordered!) at http://www.waterford.ie/default_flash.asp, along with other Waterford products. The Waterford Crystal Factory is open to visitors.

On his return from his second visit to Ireland, Richard landed in **Wales**. In his endeavors to seek support, he visited several castles, Caernarfon, Conwy, Rhuddlan, and Flint. For details of these castles, see *Edward I*.

At **Knaresborough**, Richard spent one night as a prisoner in the castle, one given to John of Gaunt by his mother. The castle is perched high above the town, overlooking the river Nidd. The King's Tower and the twin towers of the East Gate are the best-preserved remnants. Knaresborough lies on the northeastern edge of Harrogate, on the river Nidd. For comprehensive information about Knaresborough Castle, go to http://www.knaresborough.co.uk/castle/.

Isabella was confined in the Bishop's Palace at **Sonning**. Sonning-on-Thames is west of London, off the A4 between Henley and Reading. A pretty village, its website appears at http://www.sonning.net/index.html, including a picture gallery. Read its history at http://www.berkshirehistory.com/villages/sonning.html.

Tucked on the eastern edge of the conurbation of Bradford and Leeds, is **Pontefract Castle** in the town of the same name. A history of the castle can be read at http://www.castleuk.net/castle_lists_north/105/pontefractcastle.htm, and an enlightening virtual tour, illustrated with sketches, can be taken at http://www.wildyorkshire.co.uk/naturediary/docs/pomfmap.html.

Anne of Bohemia died at **Sheen Palace**, and is buried in Westminster Abbey, where Richard is also buried. Isabella of Valois remarried, died at **Blois**, was buried at Abbey of St Saumer, and finally was reburied in Paris about 1624. For more information about Blois, see *Stephen and Maud*.

Lancastrians and Yorkists:

Plantagenets at War

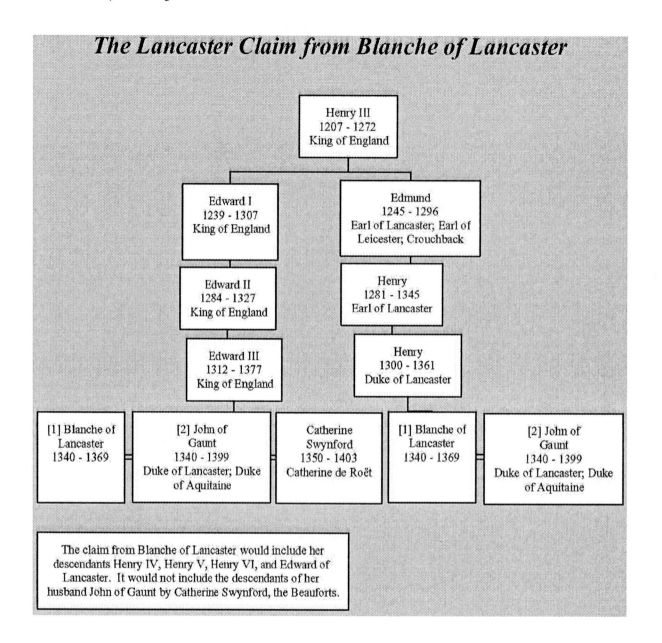

The Lancaster Claim from Blanche of Lancaster

The claim from Blanche of Lancaster would include her descendants Henry IV, Henry V, Henry VI, and Edward of Lancaster. It would not include the descendants of her husband John of Gaunt by Catherine Swynford, the Beauforts.

The Lancaster Claim from John of Gaunt

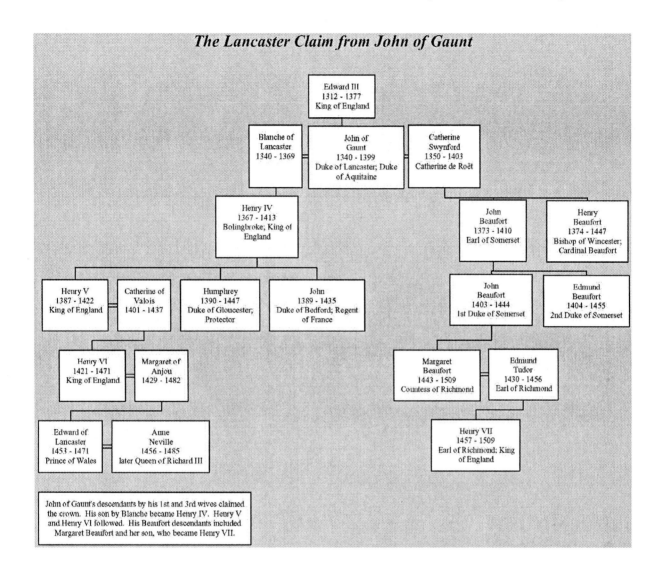

John of Gaunt's descendants by his 1st and 3rd wives claimed the crown. His son by Blanche became Henry IV. Henry V and Henry VI followed. His Beaufort descendants included Margaret Beaufort and her son, who became Henry VII.

The York Claim

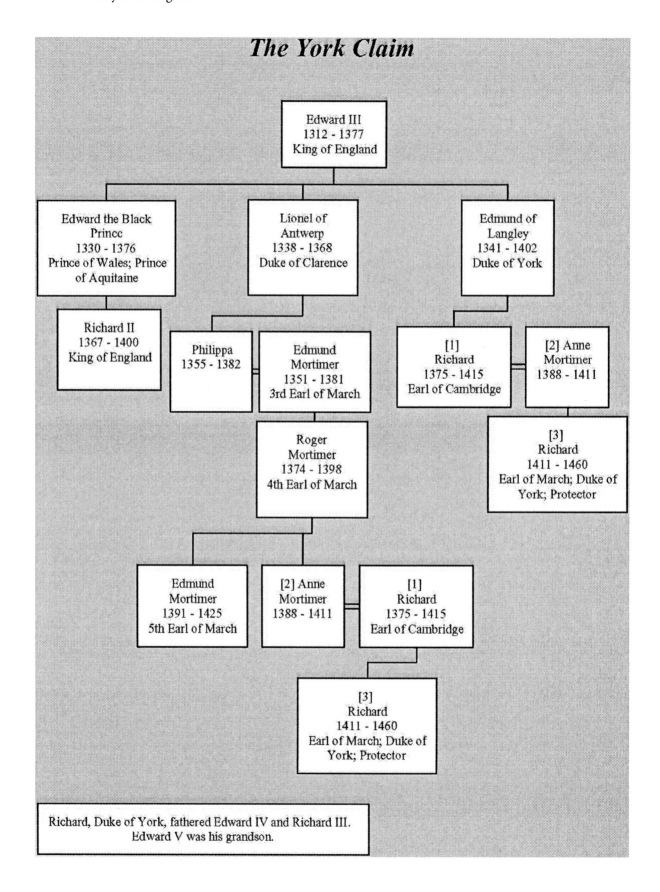

The Genealogical Bases for the Quarrel between Lancaster and York

Overview

Edward III had five sons who survived infancy. They included (in order of birth) Edward the Black Prince, Prince of Wales; Lionel of Antwerp, Duke of Clarence; John of Gaunt, Duke of Lancaster; Edmund of Langley, Duke of York; and Thomas of Woodstock, Duke of Gloucester.

The eldest son and heir presumptive, Edward the Black Prince, predeceased Edward III, whose crown later passed to the son of Edward the Black Prince, Richard II.

The controversial rule of Richard II eventually led to usurpation of his throne by his first cousin, who became Henry IV. The son of John of Gaunt, Duke of Lancaster, Henry IV began the line of **Lancastrian Kings**. These included his son Henry V and grandson Henry VI.

Dissatisfaction with the rule of Henry VI led to the assertion of a claim to the throne by his cousin, Richard, Duke of York, a descendant of both Lionel of Antwerp and Edmund of Langley. Although the Duke of York failed to attain the throne, his sons and grandson all reigned as **Yorkist Kings** after the deposition of the Lancastrian Henry VI. They included Edward IV, Edward V, and Richard III.

Rebellion against Richard III caused the raising of the Lancastrian standard again, this time by a descendant of John of Gaunt who became Henry VII. Marrying the daughter of the Yorkist King Edward IV, Henry VII began the Tudor dynasty.

The Lancastrian claims

The claims through John of Gaunt, Duke of Lancaster. The son of John of Gaunt by his first wife, Blanche of Lancaster, Henry IV usurped the crown of his first cousin Richard II. Many explanations of his claim to the throne point to his paternal descent. Richard II had no children, and the next son of Edward III, Lionel, Duke of Clarence, had a daughter but no son. According to this version of the Lancastrian claim, the Salic Law would not allow for a female to transmit a claim to the throne, and so the claim passed to the line of John of Gaunt. **This would include Henry IV, Henry V, Henry VI, and Edward of Lancaster.**

This commonly advanced explanation of the Lancastrian claim, however, actually *contradicts* the original rationale for Henry IV's usurpation. Instead of being the original rationale for that usurpation, it is a rationalization concocted at a later date. In addition, it also contradicts Henry V's claim to the French throne, which itself depended on descent in the female line.

Another claim through John of Gaunt highlighted the rights of his descendants from his third wife, Catherine Swynford or Catherine de Roët. Originally Gaunt's bastards by Catherine, the Beauforts received retroactive legitimization from Pope Boniface IX in 1396 and then from Richard II in 1397. Henry IV relegitimized the Beauforts in 1407 but barred them from the succession. However, Parliament never sanctioned this exclusion. **This claim would include Margaret Beaufort and her son, who became Henry VII.** Of course, this claim through a woman would make nonsensical any later rationalization that a Lancastrian claim depended on the Salic Law.

Although Henry VII won his throne as the Lancastrian champion, other descendants of John of Gaunt actually possessed genealogical credentials superior to his. For example, Philippa of Lancaster, Queen of Portugal (a daughter of Gaunt by his first wife and a sister to Henry IV), transmitted a Lancastrian claim advocated to Parliament by her daughter the Infanta Isabella in 1471. Henry VII seems to have been well aware of the poverty of his claim by inheritance. During his French exile, he misrepresented himself as a son of Henry

VI; in England, he noted that his father and Henry VI were half-brothers (although the Valois blood they shared conveyed no rights to the English crown).

The claim through Blanche of Lancaster. John Ashdown-Hill asserted in an article about the Lancastrian claim that the usual explanation of descent from John of Gaunt is incorrect. Noting that John of Gaunt in 1394 argued in Parliament for his son's right to the crown, Ashdown-Hill pointed out that John of Gaunt traced the claim through his wife, Blanche of Lancaster, not through himself. This argument posited that Edward I had wrongly become King in place of his sickly older brother Edmund of Lancaster. Blanche, as a descendant of Edmund of Lancaster, therefore transmitted the right to her and Gaunt's son. Henry IV actually used this argument in 1399 to justify his accession to Parliament. (No evidence supports the contention that Edmund of Lancaster was born before Edward I.) **This interpretation would underscore the claims of Henry IV, Henry V, Henry VI, and Edward of Lancaster, but the Beauforts and their Tudor offspring—not being descended from Blanche of Lancaster—would have no standing.** Of course, transmission of the right through Blanche would also violate the Salic Law. Thus, the later rationalization of Lancastrian rule that relied on the Salic Law is utterly inconsistent with the actual rationalization used by Henry IV.

The Yorkist claim

The claim through Lionel, Duke of Clarence. Because Richard II had no issue, the claim would pass to the descendants of his uncle, the next son of Edward III, Lionel, Duke of Clarence. Lionel himself died in 1368. In 1385, Richard II acknowledged as his own heir Lionel's grandson Roger Mortimer (the son of Lionel's daughter Philippa). Roger Mortimer died in 1398, Henry IV supplanted Richard II in 1399, and Richard II himself died in 1400. Roger Mortimer's son Edmund died without issue, thereby transmitting his right to his sister, Anne. Roger Mortimer's daughter Anne and her husband, Richard, Earl of Cambridge, in 1411 had a son named Richard, who became Duke of York.

A later son of Edward III, Edmund, Duke of York, himself had a son, Richard, Earl of Cambridge, who married Anne Mortimer and begat Richard, Duke of York. Because Richard, Duke of York, challenged the Lancastrian hold on the throne, he and his descendants are known as the House of York, but his and their claim really derived from the Mortimers.

The Mortimer claim provided the rationale for the rights of Richard, Duke of York; his sons Edward IV and Richard III; and his grandson Edward V. In addition, the 1460 Act of Accord made Richard, Duke of York, the heir of Henry VI, displacing the Prince of Wales, Edward of Lancaster.

All of the original arguments for Yorkist and Lancastrian claims asserted by Henry IV and by Richard, Duke of York, assumed primogeniture and depended on descent through a female. The explanation for the Lancastrian claim through John of Gaunt that argued that the Salic Law forbade transmission of the claim through a female and invalidated primogeniture is a later invention. As Ashdown-Hill clarified, "There is no mention of the Salic Law in 15th century sources as far as I am aware, and any notion that the Salic Law operated in England directly contradicts the documented claims actually advanced by both Lancaster and York. All of the 15th century claimants—Lancaster, York, Tudor—based their claims *explicitly* on descent in the female line."

Henry IV, the Mortimers, and the Percies

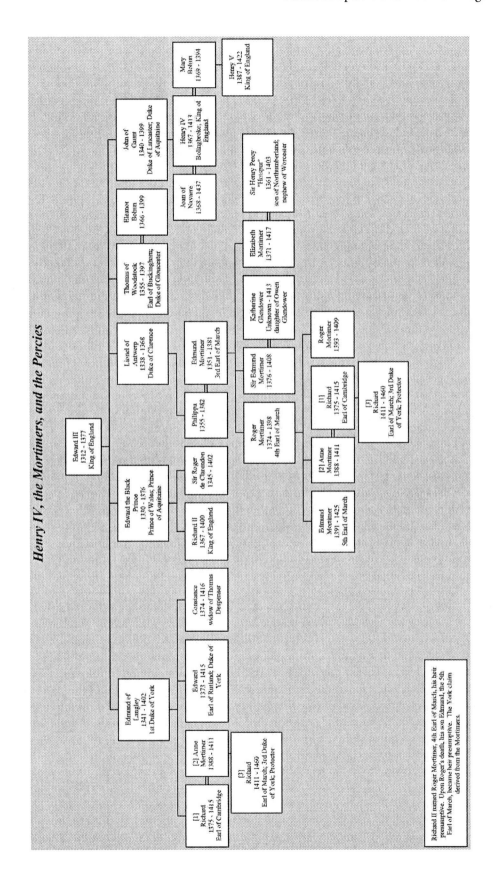

Richard II named Roger Mortimer, 4th Earl of March, his heir presumptive. Upon Roger's death, his son Edmund, the 5th Earl of March, became heir presumptive. The York claim derived from the Mortimers.

Henry IV (1367–1413; King of England and Lord of Ireland, 1399–1413)

Having decided to depose and then kill a reigning King, his first cousin Richard II, Henry Bolingbroke (now Henry IV) until his own death remained bedeviled by this decision. Bolingbroke's being a highly conventional nobleman, soldier, and skilled jouster had made him a far more sympathetic figure than Richard II to many other Englishmen. Unconventional enough to contemplate usurpation of the crown, Henry IV nevertheless suffered from a deeply conventional conscience that reproached him for his crime. His unresolved guilt undermined the King's ability to rule and dominate England. Others repeatedly questioned his title to the throne. Recurrent rebellions sought to replace Henry IV with a candidate with a hereditary claim superior to his: the child Edmund Mortimer, 5th Earl of March. The Mortimers' supporters included the powerful northern magnates the Percies as well as descendants of Edmund, 1st Duke of York, uncle to Henry IV. Although the King surmounted all of these challenges and died still possessed of his royal title, the Mortimer claim would resurface during the reign of his Lancastrian grandson, Henry VI, eventually precipitating Henry VI's two depositions and his murder, as well as the destruction of the House of Lancaster by the rival House of York, which had inherited the Mortimer claim.

Henry, the son of John of Gaunt, Duke of Lancaster, born at Bolingbroke Castle in Lincolnshire, grew up at the nearby Bourne Castle and later lived at Kenilworth, Leicester, Lincoln, or Hertford Castles. Henry Bolingbroke especially favored Hertford Castle. Named Earl of Derby in 1377, Bolingbroke eventually became Earl of Hereford and Earl of Northampton as a result of his 1380 marriage to Mary Bohun, co-heiress of Earl of Hereford with her sister Eleanor. Henry's uncle Thomas of Woodstock, Eleanor's husband, wanted to secure all of the inheritance for himself and so tried to block Bolingbroke's marriage to Mary by sending Mary to a convent, but he did not succeed. Despite this quarrel, in 1387 Bolingbroke joined Thomas of Woodstock, Duke of Gloucester, in his resistance to the rule of Richard II. The Lords Appellant who challenged the King included Gloucester; Bolingbroke; Richard Fitzalan, 9th Earl of Arundel; Thomas Beauchamp, 12th Earl of Warwick; and Thomas Mowbray, Earl of Nottingham (later Duke of Norfolk). After Bolingbroke defeated Richard II's favorite, Robert de Vere, Earl of Oxford, at Radcot Bridge in Oxfordshire, de Vere fled abroad. During 1388–1389, although Bolingbroke ruled England with the other Lords Appellant, he supported Richard versus some of the Lords Appellant, and the King eventually recovered his power. During the next few years, Bolingbroke went on crusade with the Teutonic Knights in Lithuania and on pilgrimage to Jerusalem. While in Italy during these travels, he became friends with Gian Galeazzo Visconti, Duke of Milan. Bolingbroke's uncle Lionel of Antwerp had married Visconti's sister and died in Milan, and Henry visited Lionel's tomb there.

Lionel's brother and Bolingbroke's uncle Thomas, Duke of Gloucester, continued to conspire against Richard II. Thomas Mowbray, Earl of Nottingham, in 1397 betrayed to the King the particulars of a conspiracy hatched by Gloucester at Arundel Castle. Bolingbroke also accused the conspirators. After these accusations precipitated the arrest and murder of Gloucester, Richard II created Bolingbroke Duke of Hereford and Mowbray Duke of Norfolk. Then a quarrel divided Bolingbroke from Mowbray. In a private conversation, Mowbray allegedly had speculated to Bolingbroke that Richard, now just biding his time, would eventually destroy them both because of their former opposition to him as Lords Appellant. Bolingbroke betrayed Mowbray's words to his father, John of Gaunt, who told Richard II. Mowbray asked for a trial by battle between himself and Bolingbroke to determine which of them spoke truly.

Just before the trial by battle began in 1398 at Gosford Green outside Coventry, Richard II aborted it, decreeing instead the banishment of both contenders. After John of Gaunt persuaded the King to reduce Bolingbroke's sentence from 10 years to six, Bolingbroke said farewell to his father and to the King at Eltham. John of Gaunt died in 1399. The King then sentenced Bolingbroke to perpetual banishment and confiscated his Lancastrian estates. While Richard led an expedition to Ireland and left England in the care of their inept uncle Edmund of Langley, Duke of York, Bolingbroke invaded England, landing at Ravenspur in Yorkshire. The returning King, deserted by most (including Edmund of Langley) eventually surrendered to his triumphant cousin, who forced his abdication. Bolingbroke made a show of legality by claiming a right to the crown superior to Richard's, but others regarded this as bogus. He also claimed the throne by right of conquest and as a result of Parliamentary election. The deposed Richard II died at Pontefract Castle in 1400, possibly by starvation, probably murdered at the order of Henry IV.

Besides deposing the rightful King and authorizing his murder, Henry IV had supplanted the rightful heir, the child Edmund Mortimer, 5th Earl of March. The 3rd Earl of March had married Philippa, daughter of Lionel of Antwerp, after Edward the Black Prince the next son in birth order of Edward III. In 1385, Richard II had declared the 4th Earl of March his heir presumptive. The death in 1398 of the 4th Earl of March in the Irish Battle of Kells prompted Richard II's Irish expedition in 1399 during which Bolingbroke invaded England. This death of the 4th Earl made his son Edmund (born in 1391) the 5th Earl of March and Richard II's new heir presumptive. The new Henry IV acknowledged the power of this claim by imprisoning the 5th Earl, regarded by many as the rightful King of England after the death of Richard II.

The 4th Earl had a brother named Sir Edmund and a sister named Elizabeth, uncle and aunt to the child heir presumptive. Elizabeth had married Sir Henry Percy ("Hotspur"), son of the Earl of Northumberland and nephew to the Earl of Worcester. Northumberland, Worcester, and Hotspur all had aided Bolingbroke in his deposition of Richard II. Henry IV's imprisonment of the 5th Earl of March angered Hotspur, as did the King's refusal to ransom Hotspur's brother-in-law Sir Edmund Mortimer, fallen captive to the Welsh rebel Owen Glendower. (He married Glendower's daughter Katherine and took the side of the Welsh, dying of starvation during the English siege of Harlech that ended in 1409.) The Percies claimed that, at Doncaster, Henry Bolingbroke had sworn that he intended only to reclaim his own Lancastrian inheritance and that Richard II would remain King (or the eight-year-old 5th Earl of March would become King), guided by a council. Yet another grievance flowered after Hotspur's 1402 victory over the Scots at Homildon Hill, when he captured Archibald Douglas, 4th Earl of Douglas. Enraged that Henry IV forbade ransoming or liberating any of the prisoners, Hotspur refused to surrender Douglas to Henry IV. In 1403, Hotspur openly rebelled against Henry IV. Conspiring with Northumberland, Worcester, Douglas, Glendower, and his brother-in-law Sir Edmund Mortimer, Hotspur intended to crown Edmund Mortimer, 5th Earl of March. Instead, Hotspur died at the Battle of Shrewsbury, Worcester was captured and executed, and Northumberland submitted to Henry IV.

This setback for the opponents of Henry IV did not end Northumberland's conspiracies, for he soon resumed plotting with Glendower and Sir Edmund Mortimer. Others besides the Percies conspired against the King. In 1402, Richard II's half brother Sir Roger de Clarendon and some Franciscan friars had alleged that Richard II still lived. Henry IV had executed them for treason. Three years later, Edward, Duke of York (the son of Edmund of Langley who had become Richard II's favorite, the Earl of Rutland), helped the 5th Earl of March and his brother Roger to escape from custody at Windsor. Intending to flee to Wales and meet with Glendower and their uncle Sir Edmund Mortimer, the 5th Earl and his brother instead endured recapture. The Duke of York's sister and co-conspirator Constance (widow of the Thomas Despenser who had tried to restore Richard II) alleged that her brother had also intended to assassinate Henry IV at Eltham. (Henry V released the 5th Earl in 1413, the year of his accession.) Northumberland became involved with a new rising in 1405, aided by the followers of Richard Scrope, Archbishop of York (who along with the Archbishop of Canterbury had crowned Henry IV). The King crushed this rising and, to his eternal remorse, executed the Archbishop of York. Northumberland escaped the King's wrath. After more journeys to Wales,

Scotland, Flanders, and France, Northumberland invaded England in 1408 but died in battle at Branham Moor in Yorkshire.

Northumberland's passing ended the threat from the Percies, as well as major uprisings against Henry IV, but others continued to intrigue against the Lancastrian dynasty in the name of the 5th Earl of March. Two years after the accession of Henry V, Richard, Earl of Cambridge—the brother of Edward, Duke of York and the husband of Anne Mortimer—planned to assassinate Henry V and replace him with Cambridge's brother-in-law, the 5th Earl of March. Other conspirators included Henry Lord Scrope of Masham, a relative of the Archbishop whom Henry IV had executed, and Sir Thomas Grey of Heton. Released from prison by Henry V in 1413, the 5th Earl perhaps had wearied of plots conducted in his name or felt gratitude to the King. In any event, he informed Henry V of this Southampton conspiracy in July 1415, as Henry prepared to embark for France. The executions that followed disposed of Richard, Earl of Cambridge, but not of the York support of the Mortimer right to the crown. When the 5th Earl died in Ireland of the plague a decade later, his earldom and hereditary claim passed to Cambridge's son by Anne Mortimer, Richard, who would as Duke of York challenge Henry VI's hold on the throne. His sons included the Yorkist Kings Edward IV (who came to the throne as Earl of March and Duke of York) and Richard III.

Troubled not only by incessant rebellions but also by a bad conscience about Richard II and Archbishop Scrope, Henry IV developed a mysterious illness that both disfigured and debilitated him. His increasing disability left him ill-equipped to prevail in his struggles with Parliament, his council, and his heir. For much of the latter part of the reign, others ruled in his name, while he spent these last years at Rotherhithe and Eltham. After fainting before the shrine of St. Edward the Confessor in 1413, Henry IV died in the Jerusalem Chamber of Westminster Abbey, supposedly fulfilling a prophecy that he would die in Jerusalem. He had desired burial in Canterbury Cathedral and was interred in Becket's Chapel (Trinity Chapel) opposite the Black Prince. After his second wife Joan of Navarre (the widow of Duke John of Brittany whom Henry IV married in 1402) herself died in 1437, she would lie there with him. Before then, however, Henry V in 1419 accused his stepmother of attempting his death by sorcery and confined her in Leeds Castle. On his own deathbed three years later, Henry V ordered her release because of her innocence. Possibly, he had concocted the charge of witchcraft because he wanted to control her revenues.

Henry IV Sites

Of Henry's birthplace, **Bolingbroke Castle**, very little remains. For information, see *John of Gaunt*. Henry married Mary Bohun in **Arundel Castle** in 1380; for information regarding Arundel Castle, see *Henry I*. In 1402, he married Joan of Navarre in **Winchester Cathedral** (see *William Rufus*).

Henry's residences were the castles at Hertford, Kenilworth, Leicester, and Lincoln. For **Hertford, Kenilworth**, and **Leicester** Castles, see *John of Gaunt*. For **Lincoln Castle**, see *William the Conqueror*. No traces of **Bourne Castle** survive except the flattened motte. Bourne is located on the edge of the Lincolnshire fens northeast of Stamford, on the A15. See http://homepages.which.net/~rex/bourne/bournecastle.htm for an account of evidence and theories regarding the castle.

Bolingbroke defeated Richard II's favorite Robert de Vere at Radcot Bridge. The village of **Radcot** is just south of Clanfield, Oxfordshire, on the A4095 to Faringdon. Of the sequence of three bridges at Radcot, Radcot Bridge is not only the oldest, but the oldest bridge over the Thames: it's the low, triple-arched one. See it at http://www.faringdon.org/hyradcot.htm. A depiction of the battle from Froissart's *Chronicles* can be seen at http://www.bnf.fr/enluminures/manuscrits/aman3/i3_0064.htm. There's a better view of the latter, along with a description of the battle and the bridge, at http://www.berkshirehistory.com/articles/radcot_bridge_bat.html.

Gosford Green lies to the east of the city of **Coventry**, and is reached via Far Gosford Road. It's now a park with courts for tennis and bowls, not the country heath on which Henry set foot. A monument marks the site of the combat that didn't take place. Read about this anticlimax at http://www.thecoventrypages.net/hstoric-Cov/far-gosford.asp, and see photographs of Gosford Green, including the inscription on the monument; also at http://iccoventry.icnetwork.co.uk/, by clicking on "City History," then "1251–1500," then "Combat on Gosford Green."

The night before his anticipated ordeal at Gosford Green, Henry stayed at **Baginton Castle**, home of Sir William Bagot. To the south of Coventry, near the airport, the site of the castle is mostly overgrown, with some masonry fragments which can be read about and viewed at http://www.castleuk.net/castle_lists_midlands/140/bagintoncastle.htm.

No trace remains of the port of **Ravenspur**, located at Spurn Head on the north bank of the mouth of the Humber river when Bolingbroke landed there during his 1399 invasion. Spurn Head is now a nature reserve and trail. See a photograph and read a detailed description, along with visiting details, at http://www.english-nature.org.uk/special/nnr/nnr_details.asp?NNR_ID=192.

Site of Hotspur's 1402 victory over the Scots, **Homildon Hill** is now called **Humbleton Hill**, rising above the village of Humbleton. The village is located 1 and ½ miles west of Wooler, and on the A697 where this skirts Northumberland National Park. See http://www.northumberland-national-park.org.uk/VisitorGuide/Visiting/Publications/HumbletonHillpdf.htm to find the National Park leaflet with instructions and map for Humbleton Hill.

To the north of **Shrewsbury**, by the Whitchurch road, lies the heritage area of **Battlefield**, marking the site of the Battle of Shrewsbury where Hotspur died rebelling against Henry IV. The church, St. Mary Magdalene, founded in 1409 to commemorate the battle, houses pertinent items and displays. Visit the battlefield at http://www.shrewsburyguide.co.uk/tourist_visit_bhpark.html, and the church at http://www.shrewsburyguide.co.uk/tourist_visit_bchurch.html. The High Cross in Shrewsbury itself commemorates the executions that have taken place in Shrewsbury at this place, including that of Hotspur, whose dead body was decapitated there. The present cross is a replacement; a plaque on the wall of Barclays Bank opposite lists the executions.

Henry IV stayed at **Haughmond Abbey** before the Battle of Shrewsbury. Three miles east of Shrewsbury, on the B5062, overlooking the river Severn, are the remnants of the abbey buildings, especially notable for the abbot's lodgings, entrance to the chapter house, and some rich medieval decoration. There's plenty of information at http://www.theheritagetrail.co.uk/abbeys/Haughmond%20abbey.htm and http://www.shrewsburyguide.co.uk/tourist_visit_habbey.html.

Mary Bohun died at **Peterborough Castle** in 1394; see what's left of the castle—only the motte—and visiting details at http://www.castleuk.net/castle_lists_midlands/142/peterboroughcastle.htm. Some sources place her burial at St. Mary's Church, **Leicester**, which would be the church of St. Mary de Castro. Its name indicates its location within the bailey of **Leicester Castle**; see the church at http://www.users.surfaid.org/~tdoughty/welcome.htm. However, a tomb in the chapel of the former Hospital of the Holy Trinity is also thought to be hers, other sources stating that she was buried there; the chapel is now part of De Montfort University (previously Leicester Polytechnic), and is called Trinity House Chapel, a venue for concerts and university events. Read about the old hospital, an almshouse for the elderly, at http://www.duchyoflancaster.org.uk/output/page64.asp.

For Leeds Castle, where her stepson Henry V confined Joan of Navarre, see *Edward I*. She died at **Havering-atte-Bower** in 1437. Havering-atte-Bower is a village in Essex, east of London on the B175, north of Romford. The royal manor of Havering occupied extensive lands, used by royals for hunting and summer visits: high up in the Forest of Essex, there were views down to the Thames. The royal palace was falling into ruin by the time of the Restoration and was gone by 1800. Its chapel was used as the village church, but replaced in 1878. The village green now occupies the site of the palace; a reconstruction of the latter can be seen at http://www.romford.org/manors/havering/havering01.htm.

The **Jerusalem Chamber, Westminster Abbey** is one of two meeting rooms (the other is the Jericho Parlour) that are part of the Deanery and not open to the public. See and read about this room, also an account of Henry's death there, at http://www.westminster-abbey.org/tour/jerusalem_chamber.htm.

Both Henry and Joan are buried in **Canterbury Cathedral**. They lie in the Trinity Chapel, behind the High Altar, on the north side of the shrine of Becket, with the Black Prince's tomb on the south side. Read about their tombs at http://www.digiserve.com/peter/henry4.htm, and see the face of Henry's effigy.

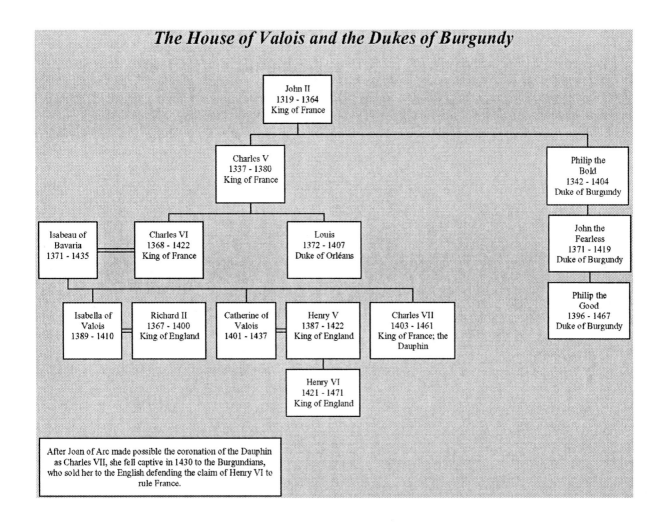

The House of Valois and the Dukes of Burgundy

John II
1319 - 1364
King of France

Charles V
1337 - 1380
King of France

Philip the
Bold
1342 - 1404
Duke of Burgundy

Isabeau of
Bavaria
1371 - 1435

Charles VI
1368 - 1422
King of France

Louis
1372 - 1407
Duke of Orléans

John the
Fearless
1371 - 1419
Duke of Burgundy

Isabella of
Valois
1389 - 1410

Richard II
1367 - 1400
King of England

Catherine of
Valois
1401 - 1437

Henry V
1387 - 1422
King of England

Charles VII
1403 - 1461
King of France; the
Dauphin

Philip the
Good
1396 - 1467
Duke of Burgundy

Henry VI
1421 - 1471
King of England

After Joan of Arc made possible the coronation of the Dauphin
as Charles VII, she fell captive in 1430 to the Burgundians,
who sold her to the English defending the claim of Henry VI to
rule France.

Henry V (1387–1422; King of England and Lord of Ireland, 1413–1422)

The masterful personality of Henry V allowed him to dominate and control men and events as he took advantage of chaotic political situations in both England and France. His resolute and cool leadership, careful planning, and strict discipline won Henry V the glory of the victorious hour, suddenly lost by his early death. The King's deputies strove to maintain his gains, but England's unstable hold on France gradually weakened, and the baby successor Henry V had left to rule both France and England probably inherited the mental illness that had caused his French grandfather Charles VI to lose control of France. The madness of Charles VI had permitted the growth of fratricidal strife among members of the House of Valois—strife that had given Henry V his opportunity to conquer France. Yet, the French eventually united against English rule in the name of his son, and that son's incapacity to govern England created a power vacuum in which members of the House of Plantagenet fought to succeed him. Irony could not design a more devastating nemesis.

The chaos that Henry V surmounted in England had resulted from the uneasy reign of Richard II and the usurpation of Richard's crown by his first cousin, Henry Bolingbroke, who thereby became Henry IV in 1399. In the previous year, Richard II had banished Bolingbroke. Leaving England for a campaign in Ireland, Richard II took Bolingbroke's eldest son Henry with him as a hostage. News of Bolingbroke's return to England in the King's absence had prompted Richard II to leave the young Henry at Trim Castle in County Meath as he journeyed back to defend his throne. The forced abdication of Richard II created a new sovereign, Henry IV, who subsequently knighted his heir and named him Prince of Wales, Duke of Cornwall, Earl of Chester, Duke of Aquitaine, and Duke of Lancaster. Discontent with the Lancastrian usurpation of Richard's crown motivated several English conspiracies to dethrone Henry IV, as well as resistance to English domination in Wales. For most of the decade after the accession of Henry IV, his Prince of Wales fought in campaigns both in Scotland and against Owen Glendower, who called himself Prince of Wales. By 1408, the Lancastrians had squelched domestic insurrection as well as Scottish and Welsh opposition.

Not only had Prince Henry helped to suppress the Welsh, but he began to attend meetings of Henry IV's council in 1406, and by 1410–1411 he dominated it with the help of the Chancellor, Henry Beaufort, Bishop of Winchester, his father's half-brother. The question of how best to meddle in French affairs divided the Prince from his father the King. In 1392, Charles VI of France had begun to endure episodes of insanity. With the development of this power vacuum, conflict between members of the House of Valois pitted the Armagnacs against the Burgundians. Charles VI's brother Louis, Duke of Orléans, strove against his first cousin John the Fearless, Duke of Burgundy. Their personal feud ended in 1407 when John of Burgundy succeeded in assassinating Louis of Orléans in Paris. Prince Henry favored the Burgundians. When Henry IV had recovered from illness in 1411, he dismissed his heir from the council and instead allied himself with the Armagnacs.

The Prince's firm leadership had caused his irresolute and unsuccessful father to resent and fear him, especially because he apparently advocated that his father should abdicate in his own favor. When Henry IV finally died in 1413, the new King, Henry V, came to the throne with a record of having suppressed Welsh revolt, as well as having worked well with the council and with Parliament. He established a sound basis for troubled royal finances. The disorder of his father's reign gave way to good government much appreciated by his English subjects. As he put England in good order, he developed ambitions for military victories in France—ambitions consistent with his subjects' expectations of their King.

Like his great-grandfather, Edward III, Henry V found a French war useful in uniting his nobility behind him. In addition, Henry V resurrected English claims to French territory unresolved since the failure to implement the Treaty of Brétigny of 1360. The proposed renunciation by Edward III of his claim to the French throne and by the French of their sovereignty over Aquitaine had never actually occurred. Despite this fact, the Treaty of Brétigny had remained for decades the framework within which discussions took place between France and England. Henry V aggressively changed that framework. Not limiting his territorial demands to Aquitaine, he reasserted claims to French lands deriving from William the Conqueror, Henry II, and Henry III's Queen Eleanor of Provence. Henry V also wanted the unpaid balance of the ransom promised for the release of the hostage John II of France.

As negotiations spun on, the French in 1414–1415 indignantly rejected these demands. A French representative countered Henry's proposals with this unpalatable rebuke: "the King of France our sovereign lord is true King of France, and regarding those things to which you say you have a right you have no lordship, not even to the Kingdom of England which belongs to the true heirs of King Richard." Nevertheless, strife between the Armagnacs and the Burgundians weakened the House of Valois. In 1413, the year of Henry V's accession, John of Burgundy was banished from Paris. Now, in 1415, with Burgundian support, Henry V invaded France. He had the support of his brothers as well as his Beaufort uncles, including Henry Beaufort, Chancellor again since 1413, and he left England well-governed.

This first of three expeditions to France included the seige of Harfleur that led to its surrender. On the way to Calais, Henry V against tremendous odds won the famous battle of Agincourt, a remarkable feat besmirched by his massacre of French prisoners. Alliances with the Holy Roman Emperor Sigismund and with the Burgundians strengthened Henry's ability to launch his second invasion in 1417, which encompassed Normandy and the capture of Caen. In 1418–1419, Falaise fell, as did Rouen after a prolonged seige; Henry V dominated Normandy; John of Burgundy seized control of Paris and of the person of Charles VI while Charles the Dauphin fled; and Queen Isabeau made common cause with the Burgundians and the English against her son the Dauphin.

Then an apparent setback for Henry V metamorphosized into his triumph. Fearing French revulsion against their support of the English, John of Burgundy and Queen Isabeau allied themselves with the Armagnacs and Charles the Dauphin against Henry V. When Duke John and his new ally Charles the Dauphin met at Montereau, the Dauphin, in apparent retaliation for the 1407 murder of his uncle Louis, Duke of Orléans, had Duke John slain. The new head of the Burgundians, Duke Philip, naturally joined Henry V's party against his father's murderer. With his unsteady allies the Burgundians and Queen Isabeau (who controlled her husband Charles VI), Henry V now set the terms for resolution of the conflict.

No longer content with his previous claims derived from William the Conqueror, Henry II, and Eleanor of Provence, Henry V for now asserted his non-negotiable right to all French territory he had won in battle. More shockingly, he shifted his ground in his quest for the ultimate solution. He no longer wanted English sovereignty over French territory. Instead, he created a new framework in 1420 to replace the 60-year-old Treaty of Brétigny. Henry V demanded that Charles VI disinherit the Dauphin, allow Henry to marry his daughter Catherine of Valois, and recognize Henry V as Regent of France during Charles VI's fits of madness as well as the heir to the French crown. The 1420 Treaty of Troyes established the concept that Henry V and his issue by Catherine of Valois would reign in the two separate Kingdoms of France and England. In return, Henry V abandoned his own claim to the French throne as a descendant of Edward III (and of his mother Isabella of France, Queen to Edward II) and acknowledged Normandy as belonging to the French crown.

Given the disunion among members of the House of Valois, Henry V naturally prevailed. At the ceremony ratifying the Treaty of Troyes, Henry V used the same seal that Edward III had used for the Treaty of Brétigny. He soon married Catherine of Valois, whom he brought with him to England in 1421 after his absence of more than three years. Opposition in England both to the Treaty of Troyes and to continuance of his war of conquest failed to prevent Henry V's third invasion of France later that year. Despite his diplomatic and military successes, much of France still lay outside of his control. As he conducted his ultimately successful seige of Meaux, the King learned of the birth of his son Henry at Windsor.

The foe of all human accomplishment, death, soon undercut the successes of Henry V. On 31 August, 1422, he died from dysentery at Vincennes, a favorite residence near Paris. Not only did Henry V leave much of France unconquered, but he died leaving only an infant successor to rule after him in England and after Charles VI in France. A few weeks after the death of Henry V, his father-in-law, Charles VI, also died. Many in France naturally preferred their adult Dauphin to a baby King from England, and the Burgundian alliance with England remained unstable. Eventually, Joan of Arc would energize the Dauphin's fight against the English and Burgundians—a fight that would drive the English from French soil now ruled by Charles VII. Catherine of Valois's son and Charles VII's nephew, Henry VI of England, exhibiting mental illness perhaps inherited from his grandfather Charles VI of France, would rule England weakly. His misrule would precipitate the fratricidal struggles among members of the House of Plantagenet later named the Wars of the Roses, his own deposition, his brief restoration, and his murder.

Henry V Sites

Henry's birthplace, **Monmouth**, with about 7500 inhabitants, is a market center and county town for the attractive surrounding area in the rolling countryside of the Welsh borders. Its street plan is essentially unchanged since the 15th century, adding to its charm, and it's located at the confluence of the Wye, Monnow, and Trothy rivers. In Agincourt Square, the market square, a statue of Henry stands in front of the Shire Hall. Monmouth's attractive and informative website is http://www.monmouth.org.uk/. There's very little left of the castle; see it at at http://www.castlewales.com/monmouth.html, and read its history. The castle is occupied by the Royal Monmouthshire Royal Engineers and can be seen only from the nearby parade ground.

Henry married Catherine of Valois at **Troyes**. This charming old city of about 60,000 population is located on a loop in the Seine, southeast of Paris. Its old center contains restored half-timbered houses, 16th century courtyards, and several fine Gothic churches. Visit it at http://www.ville-troyes.fr/; alas, the website is somewhat short on information and is in French only, but http://vieuxtroyes.free.fr/t/ provides photographs and much more information. Begun in 1208 but still unfinished at its consecration in 1429, the cathedral exhibits every period of Gothic architecture. See the cathedral at http://vieuxtroyes.free.fr/t/engcath.htm.

Trim Castle in Ireland, where Richard II took Henry of Monmouth in 1399, is one of those idyllically sited places more often seen in paintings than in life. Beside the river Boyne, it's one of the largest medieval castles in Europe. For visiting details, see http://www.heritageireland.ie/en/HistoricSites/East/TrimCastleMeath/; and http://www.heritageisland.com/Trim.asp, the latter including information about other available activities in the neighborhood.

In Wales

Edward I's castles withstood the efforts of Welsh forces during the reign of Henry IV, and only two fell, Aberystwyth and Harlech, used by Owen Glendower as his capital. Henry Prince of Wales seized them both for the English. Later, Harlech was to fall during the War of the Roses but withstood a seven years' siege. For background information about Harlech Castle, see *Edward I.*

The Iron Age fortress atop the hill called Pen Dinas attests to Aberystwyth's age as a settlement. **Aberystwyth** Castle began as a Norman castle, to be rebuilt by Llywelyn the Great. The third phase came when Edmund of Lancaster rebuilt the castle again, this time as a concentric fortress according to Edward I's plan (see *Edward I*). At its completion, it was one of the greatest castles in Wales; now, of all Edward I's castles, it's the most ruined. See the castle at http://www.castlewales.com/aberystw.html. Today, Aberystwyth is a pleasant seaside town, with one of those elegant 19th century "fronts" facing a curve of sandy beach and the usual rowdy entertainment center on the pier. Aberystwyth's website appears at http://www.aberystwyth.com/.

Before he went to France for the first time, Henry V made a pilgrimage to **Holywell**, in north Wales. Holywell is the shrine of St. Winefride. In Celtic hagiography, when her unwanted suitor Caradoc cut off her head, a well sprang up from where her severed head lay. Her grieving father then placed her head back on her body, praying for her life. She went on to live and become a nun, with a white scar around her neck. Caradoc sank into the ground and was never seen again. This gave rise to the shrine around the well, to which many pilgrims—royal, religious, and secular—have traveled ever since. Her relics were taken to **Shrewsbury Abbey** in 1138. After the battle of Agincourt, Henry V made another pilgrimage to Holywell in thanksgiving, this time allegedly travelling on foot from St. Winefride's tomb in Shrewsbury Abbey. Read and see photographs of the well at http://www.britainexpress.com/wales/north/churches/st-winefrides.htm. With the more modern church behind the shrine, the two provide a fine, contrasting yet sympathetic image. Holywell (Treffynnon) is just inland from the estuary of the river Dee; its website is http://www.holywell-town.co.uk/.

To France

Henry V put together his troops for his first expedition to France at **Portchester**; see *Richard II* for information about this great castle.

He landed in **Harfleur**, at this time an important port at the mouth of the Seine and not the industrial suburb of Le Havre it has since become. Le Havre was developed in 1517 because Harfleur was becoming silted up and unusable, growing into the massive port it has become today while Harfleur stagnated. Today it has a population of about 8600; the best website for Harfleur is http://perso.club-internet.fr/glecornu/. It's in French only, but there are photographs to be seen, if one persists, also plenty of information for those who can read French.

The village of **Azincourt** (Agincourt) lies just off the D928 between Abbeville and St-Omer, north of Hesdin. The new Medieval History Center (Centre Historique Médiéval) in Azincourt opened in 2001; its website is at http://www.azincourt-medieval.com/. Note that the building was designed to be reminiscent of a medieval barn. More information can be found at http://www.theotherside.co.uk/tm-heritage/visit/visit-azincourt-battle.htm. The Azincourt Alliance claims to be a consortium of groups fostering the memory of the battle by hosting events that re-enact it; for the aficionados, their webpage is http://www.azincourt-alliance.org.uk/welcome.htm.

On Henry's next foray into France, in 1517, **Caen** was his first captive territory (for information about Caen, see *William the Conqueror*), followed by **Falaise** (see *William the Conqueror*) and **Rouen**, which fell after a long siege. Rouen, a city of about 106,000 population, is the ancient capital of the Duchy of Normandy and a flourishing city and port in spite of being badly damaged during the Second World War. It contains many buildings of interest, and the old have been restored well. The cathedral and the old quarter nearby with a large number of half-timbered houses are of special interest. For images of Rouen, see http://home.earthlink.net/~parisinjune/rouen.htm.

During Henry V's long six-months' siege of **Meaux**, he contracted his fatal illness. Meaux, with a population of about 50,000, nestles in a loop of the river Marne, just to the east of Paris on the N3. The website for Meaux is http://www.ville-meaux.fr/.

The place of his death, **Vincennes**, is a vast property at the eastern edge of Paris, at the end of Line 1 on the Métro. Until Versailles was built, the château of Vincennes was its equivalent as a grand royal residence outside Paris. Originally built as a fortress with a donjon (keep) and ramparts, and later as a palace, Vincennes has led a chequered history, serving various purposes as a porcelain factory, arsenal, and prison, with a number of people dying or being executed there as late as the Second World War. Today, it's a splendid excursion place for

Parisians and tourists, supplying not only the château, but, within the surrounding Bois-de-Vincennes, the 31-hectare Parc Floral of gardens, sculpture, and restaurants; and also Paris's zoo along with a cycle track and racecourse. It's also a city of about 43,000, an industrial and residential suburb of Paris. Alas, its only websites seem to deal with entirely practical matters regarding the city. The best option for views is http://www.casteland.com/pfr/chateau/idf/valmarne/vincennes/vincennes.htm, in French, with photographs of the château. The site for Bois-de-Vincennes, http://www.boisdevincennes.com/site/ chateau.php3, is also in French but gives visiting information.

Henry's body lay in state in the **Basilica of St-Denis** in Paris, on its way from Vincennes to Westminster. The basilica, originally an abbey, was replaced by Abbot Suger in what has generally been regarded the first instance of the Gothic cathedral, then widely copied elsewhere. To this day, it's one of the major churches in Europe, containing many French royal tombs in addition to its trail-blazing architecture. The best site for history and photographs is http://architecture.relig.free.fr/denis.htm (in French). The city of St-Denis has been important commercially since the Middle Ages. Today it is still an industrial city of about 91,000 inhabitants in the north of Paris, but with redevelopment of its core and museums (art and history, silverware) that makes a trip worthwhile, even apart from the cathedral. It's easily reached on the Métro. The city's website, including the basilica, is at http://www.ville-saint-denis.fr/jsp/site/Portal.jsp?page_id=131, in French only.

Information about his tomb in **Westminster Abbey**, along with artefacts in the **Abbey Museum**, may be read and seen at http://www.westminster-abbey.org/library/monarchs/henry_v.htm.

Henry's building achievements in England were, notably, at **Westminster Abbey** and **Sheen Palace**. At the former, his provision of 1,000 marks a year marked the recommencement of the rebuilding of the abbey (see *Henry III* for more details).

At **Sheen Palace**, he rebuilt extensively, beginning by clearing away the rubble left by Richard II after the latter had burned down the Queen's apartments in his grief when Anne of Bohemia died. Then, like so many other royals, he endowed a monastery, the House of Jesus of Bethlehem of Sheen, and, on the opposite bank of the river Thames, he established a nunnery for Bridgettine nuns, **Syon House**, at Isleworth. The abbey has since moved to Ivybridge, near Plymouth. Syon House suffered during Henry VIII's Dissolution of the Monasteries, but was taken over by the Earl of Somerset, who built the present, beautiful house, now owned by the Duke of Northumberland and called Syon Park. There are several features for the visitor: the splendid Robert Adam interiors and the artworks within the house, and, outside, the beautiful gardens originally designed by Capability Brown, which now come with a children's playground, garden center, aviary, and butterfly collection. See Syon Park at its website, http://www.syonpark.co.uk/, along with the history and photographs.

Henry VI

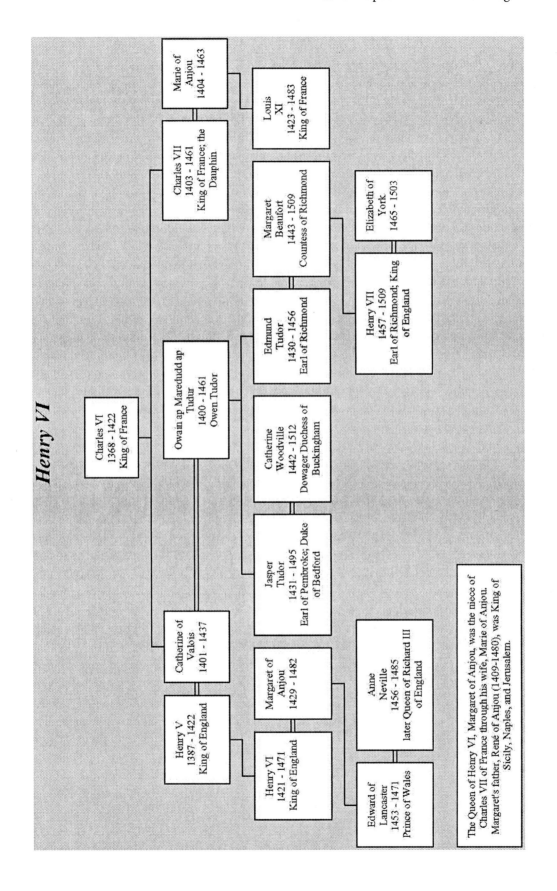

Charles VI
1368 - 1422
King of France

Charles VII
1403 - 1461
King of France; the
Dauphin

Marie of
Anjou
1404 - 1463

Louis
XI
1423 - 1483
King of France

Owain ap Maredudd ap
Tudur
1400 - 1461
Owen Tudor

Edmund
Tudor
1430 - 1456
Earl of Richmond

Margaret
Beaufort
1443 - 1509
Countess of Richmond

Henry VII
1457 - 1509
Earl of Richmond; King
of England

Elizabeth of
York
1465 - 1503

Catherine
Woodville
1442 -1512
Dowager Duchess of
Buckingham

Jasper
Tudor
1431 - 1495
Earl of Pembroke; Duke
of Bedford

Catherine of
Valois
1401 - 1437

Henry V
1387 - 1422
King of England

Margaret of
Anjou
1429 - 1482

Henry VI
1421 - 1471
King of England

Anne
Neville
1456 - 1485
later Queen of Richard III
of England

Edward of
Lancaster
1453 - 1471
Prince of Wales

The Queen of Henry VI, Margaret of Anjou, was the niece of
Charles VII of France through his wife, Marie of Anjou.
Margaret's father, René of Anjou (1409-1480), was King of
Sicily, Naples, and Jerusalem.

Henry VI (1421–1471; reigned as King of England and Lord of Ireland, 1422–1461 and 1470–1471; contended with Charles VII for title of King of France, 1422–1461)

In the story of Henry VI's fifty-year journey from being a baby King to being a twice-deposed and finally murdered King, Henry VI himself is extraordinarily absent. Many vivid personalities populate his story: his parents, the warrior King Henry V and the French princess Catherine of Valois; his uncles, John, Duke of Bedford, and Humphrey, Duke of Gloucester, and his great-uncle, Henry Cardinal Beaufort; his advisors and ministers, the Dukes of Suffolk and Somerset; his antagonists, Richard, Duke of York, and Richard Neville, Earl of Warwick; his wife, Margaret of Anjou; and his supplanter, Edward IV. The faint image of Henry VI, in contrast, dissolves into greater indistinctness the more closely we look at it, as if all these planets remained in thrall to a dead sun.

Of necessity, others ruled for Henry VI during his minority. Even after he came of age to rule in 1437, others consistently compensated for his incompetence. Then his mental health succumbed to psychosis in 1453, and he never completely recovered, forcing an overt recognition of an incapacity to govern that had always characterized his reign. Whether his chronic incapacity resulted at various times from extreme youth, inexperience, emotional problems, intellectual deficits, or active psychosis, these causes all had the same result: inability to exercise his regal powers and unfitness to rule. Because the system had no remedy for such radical weakness in its sovereign, the center did not hold, loosing the anarchy of the civil war later named the Wars of the Roses.

Henry VI's rule faltered in its handling of the long struggle for control of France. In 1420, the Treaty of Troyes had bound the French King Charles VI to marry his daughter Catherine of Valois to the English aggressor Henry V. In addition, Charles VI disinherited his son Charles the Dauphin and named Henry V his heir. After the death of Charles VI, Henry V was to rule the totally separate Kingdom of France as well as his Kingdom of England.

Complicating matters, Henry V unexpectedly died in 1422, a few weeks before his father-in-law; the Dauphin disputed the English claim to the French throne; and Joan of Arc came from nowhere to crown the Dauphin as Charles VII at Rheims in July 1429. This prompted an English coronation for Henry VI at Westminster in November 1429, a journey to France that began in 1430, and his 1431 coronation in Paris as "Henry II" of France.

Henry VI's paternal uncle, John, Duke of Bedford, ruled France for him as Regent and sought to preserve his claims against the challenge presented by Henry VI's maternal uncle, Charles VII. Bedford's death in 1435 loosened Henry VI's precarious hold both on the French crown and on French territories claimed by England. The 1444 Treaty of Tours that arranged for Henry VI to marry Margaret of Anjou, the niece of Charles VII's Queen, strengthened Charles VII's hold on France. By 1453, Henry VI had lost England's French territories and any viable claim to the French crown.

Concurrently, domestic troubles mounted. The rule by council necessitated by Henry VI's weakness fostered power struggles such as that between Humphrey, Duke of Gloucester, Protector of England, and Henry Beaufort, Bishop of Winchester, later Cardinal Beaufort. The 1435 death of Bedford, who had supported the council versus Gloucester and Beaufort, removed a moderating force. Another major power struggle in the 1450s featured Gloucester's former ward Richard, Duke of York, against Edmund Beaufort, Duke of Somerset, and Queen Margaret of Anjou, who previously had allied herself with Cardinal Beaufort.

Charging bad advice to Henry VI, corruption, injustice, and the unfair distribution of patronage, both common people and nobles expressed their discontent. Cade's Rebellion, a peasant uprising, followed, as did the impeachment and murder of William de la Pole, Duke of Suffolk, in 1450. Richard, Duke of York, found support among members of the powerful Neville family, among them Richard Neville, Earl of Warwick.

Dissatisfaction with both domestic and French policies pushed the Duke of York to the fore, and he became Protector after Henry VI's collapse into psychosis in 1453 extended into 1454. Henry's unfortunate recovery in 1455 of that slender reed, his reason, pushed the Duke of York out of power. Then began a dizzying series of military struggles that centered upon attempts to secure the King's person and thereby assume his authority to rule. After seizing Henry VI in the First Battle of St. Albans (1455), the Duke of York resumed the role of Protector. Through 1461, in pitched battle, Lancastrians and Yorkists repeatedly won and lost custody of Henry VI, that battered rag doll of a monarch.

Concurrent with possession of the King's person and exercise of his authority, Lancastrians and Yorkists fought to establish the succession, to determine who would succeed Henry VI as King of England. So long as Henry VI begat no living son, his paternal uncles and, after their deaths, his other male relatives were his presumed successors. In 1450, the Duke of York attempted to gain acceptance as heir presumptive. The birth of Edward of Lancaster to Henry VI and Margaret of Anjou in 1453 seemed to herald another long royal minority after the death of Henry VI—an unsatisfying prospect of more of the same. In addition, some doubted whether Henry VI had actually begotten the child.

Seizing the King's person and seeking recognition as his heir presumptive gave way, finally, to attempting to supplant Henry VI altogether, especially after Parliament attainted the Duke of York in 1459. After Yorkist victory in the field at Northampton, the Duke of York in 1460 presented to Parliament his claim—not to succeed Henry VI—but actually to displace him as King. Deriding the Lancastrian dynasty as usurpers, the Duke of York pointed to his own descent from Lionel of Antwerp, Duke of Clarence, an older brother of John of Gaunt, Duke of Lancaster. (In 1415, Richard, Earl of Cambridge—the Duke of York's father—had plotted to replace Henry V with another descendant of Lionel, Duke of Clarence, a plot that ended in his execution.) This 1460 effort by the Duke of York to replace Henry VI as King also failed. Parliament gave him the consolation prize of the Act of Accord, which made him Protector for the third time and named him as the successor of Henry VI. This Act disinherited Edward of Lancaster and enraged his mother, Margaret of Anjou.

The Lancastrians killed the Duke of York at the 1460 Battle of Wakefield and dishonored his severed head with a mocking paper crown, but Henry VI's—and their own—hold on the throne remained tenuous. London spurned the Lancastrians even after military victory in the Second Battle of St. Albans (1461) but welcomed Edward, Earl of March, the oldest son of the Duke of York. A Yorkist victory at Towton in March 1461 made secure the Earl of March's accession as Edward IV.

Fleeing into exile and hiding in the North of England and in Scotland, Henry VI eventually fell into his captors' net in 1465 at Waddington Hall near Clitheroe. After being paraded in London, he was put in the Tower, where he remained until his bizarre and brief restoration as King in 1470. Having fallen out with Edward IV, the Earl of Warwick allied himself with Margaret of Anjou to effect this "re-adoption" of her imprisoned husband. But Edward IV defeated Warwick and Margaret and restored himself as King in 1471, and Henry VI died in the Tower. His murdered corpse was buried in the Lady Chapel of Chertsey Abbey; Richard III later transferred it to St. George's Chapel, Windsor.

In the ten years between the first and second depositions of Henry VI, his wife vigorously resisted his ouster and the exclusion from the succession of their son, Edward of Lancaster. From her base at Bamburgh Castle in Northumberland, Margaret sought French and Scottish aid to foment trouble for Edward IV in the North of England. After the Lancastrian defeat at Hexham in 1464, Margaret and Edward of Lancaster reportedly sought refuge in the Queen's Cave, where legend insists robbers hid and protected them. She then settled for a while in the Duchy of Bar, permitted by her father, René of Anjou, to live in the château of Koeur. Warwick (and her first cousin Louis XI of France) in 1470 persuaded Margaret into an alliance against Edward IV, but their armed revolt finally failed, and her son died at Tewkesbury in 1471. The Yorkist victors eventually imprisoned her in Wallingford Castle. René of Anjou, following her ransom, gave her a home at Reculée, near Angers; after his death in 1480, she lived for her final two years at Dampierre, near Saumur.

Henry VI enjoyed a posthumous vogue as miracle worker that prompted canonization attempts that crested in 1484 and 1923 but never captured Rome's permanent attention. (Apparently, his case is still pending!) His gaining a perhaps undeserved repute for sanctity and his founding Eton and King's College, Cambridge have preserved a smidgen of Henry VI's good repute from the opprobrium caused by his manifest unfitness for his regal role. Why did he fail so completely? To borrow a phrase from Winston Churchill, Henry VI's character remains "a riddle wrapped in a mystery inside an enigma."

Henry VI Sites

Henry was born at **Windsor Castle** 1421. In 1431, his French coronation took place at **Notre-Dame Cathedral** in Paris. Constructed from 1163 to 1345, Notre-Dame is not only one of the greatest of Gothic cathedrals but a familiar landmark that has witnessed many important historical events, including being turned into a Temple of Reason during the French Revolution. Notre-Dame is situated on the Île-de-la-Cité, the boat-shaped island on the river Seine. See http://www.paris.org/Monuments/NDame/ for a basic account of the cathedral, along with a couple of exterior views. At http://www.elore.com/Gothic/History/Overview/paris.htm, eight views of the cathedral are listed, to be opened in separate windows. The photograph of the north transept rose window is especially beautiful. When paying an actual visit, don't miss the exquisite little **Sainte-Chapelle**, at the other end of the island: also Gothic, it represents a quite different facet with its 15 vivid stained glass windows, separated by tall, fine columns, pointing up to the star-studded roof. See http://www.paris.org/Monuments/Sainte.Chapelle/ for practical information and some small idea of the church.

Margaret of Anjou's birthplace, **Pont-à-Mousson**, is an industrial town of about 15,000 inhabitants. It lies beside the river Moselle, between Nancy and Metz. Its website, at http://www.ville-pont-a-mousson.fr/ (in French), is refreshingly simple and uncluttered.

Henry and Margaret were married at **Titchfield Abbey**, near Southampton where Margaret had landed. After Henry VIII's Dissolution of the Monasteries, the 1st Earl of Southampton replaced the abbey church with the tall, fortified manor house whose splendid ruins are visible today. The nave of the abbey church became the Tudor gatehouse, and there are some scattered remains of the original abbey buildings. Titchfield is reached off the M27, where the A27 meets the B3334, and is a short distance west of Fareham. The history of the abbey can be read at http://www.theheritagetrail.co.uk/abbeys/titchfield%20abbey.htm.

Henry's major achievements were architectural, the founding of **Eton College** and **King's College, Cambridge**. **Eton College** was founded in 1440 to provide an education for 70 poor boys, who would then go on to Henry's other creation, King's College, Cambridge. It now educates well over 1,000 boys, including Princes William and Harry during the 1990s. The college is open to visitors, but read the websites below for visiting details: the hours are limited, and access other than by foot can be tricky. The town of Eton forms a long street, Eton High Street, over Windsor Bridge (pedestrians only; and otherwise parking is very limited on the street) from the castle down to the college and beyond. It's about half a mile from Windsor Castle to the college. At the main entrance to the college, an archway leads into School Yard (the larger of two quadrangles) with a statue of Henry in the center. The Lower School building is the oldest; it's been in business for over 550 years (the Upper School was built in the 17th century when the Lower School became too small for the number of pupils). The Chapel was begun in 1441 and finished in 1483; it was to have been much larger, but Henry's deposition curtailed its building. Basic visiting details are at http://www.windsor.gov.uk/attractions/eton.htm, along with information about the town and its vicinity. Eton College's official website, where you can find out what it's like to be a pupil and other such practical matters, including taking virtual tours, is http://www.etoncollege.com/default.asp.

As envisaged by Henry, **King's College, Cambridge University**, was originally to contain a Rector and 12 scholars. By 1445 plans had expanded to include 70 scholars, the number at his Eton College, and the projected site had also grown so that substantial clearing away of other buildings, and even streets, was undertaken for it. However, only the chapel was started during Henry's life. The chapel was completed by the Tudors and the rest during the 18th and 19th centuries. Only Eton graduates were admitted up to the 1870s. The following expansion of students included women, in 1972, the first of the men's colleges to admit them. The official King's College website is http://www.kings.cam.ac.uk/. Note visiting times, which change according to the demands of the academic year; like all the colleges, it's a working institution, and visitors are asked to respect that. The website includes King's College Chapel, the glory of King's College and notable in church architecture generally. The elegant building with its theme of tall, slim towers flanking large windows has a simplicity extended by its setting: from the river walk behind (part of the Backs, meaning the backs of the colleges), the chapel rises up from a sweep of grass. The interior forms a long, high rectangle, with no side aisles. Overhead, the soaring stone vaulting features the finest and most delicate of fan vaulting; the walls are almost non-existent in the great expanses of stained glass. A visit to one of the services is recommended; the choir is world-famous and, in that setting, makes for a superb experience for all but the tone-deaf. Get there early, follow the signs, and join the queue. The chapel can be approached either from the Backs or from King's Parade, the street in front of the college. Information about the chapel and its choir is given in the website above.

Queens' College was first established as St. Bernard's College by Andrew Dokett, rector of St. Botolph's Church, in 1447. The next year, Margaret of Anjou took up patronage, and the college was renamed Queen's, in her honor. The plural, Queens', came into effect when, in 1465, Edward IV's Queen, Elizabeth Woodville, became the new patron. The college is divided by the river Cam: access is over the Chippendale-like wooden bridge (popularly called the Mathematical Bridge) leading to the 20th century buildings on the other side of the Cam. Queens' College website is http://www.quns.cam.ac.uk/, with photographs reached through its Image Gallery, and much detailed information.

St. Albans saw two battles. The first, in 1455, took place between St. Peter's Church and the abbey, the area called Holywell Hill. The site of the second (1461) seems less certain, but the battle apparently took place over Barnard's Heath, Sandridge, and Nomansland Common. Barnard's Heath is now a built-up area of the city; Sandridge is a town to the north, on the B651; and Nomansland Common lies between Sandridge and Wheathampstead.

St. Albans is the successor of the Roman Verulamium. One of the two museums includes finds from the Roman excavation site. See it, along with another museum, at a combined website at http://www.stalbansmuseums.org.uk/. The city today has a population of about 75,000 and lies north of London in Hertfordshire, between Hemel Hempstead and Hatfield. Read about St. Albans generally at http://www.aboutbritain.com/towns/StAlbans.asp. For St. Albans Cathedral and abbey church, see http://www.stalbanscathedral.org.uk/index1.htm.

Henry and Margaret based Parliament in the **Guildhall, Coventry**, from 1456–59. St. Mary's Guildhall is one of the old buildings to survive the Second World War bombing of Coventry, a beautiful medieval relic of decoration, stained glass, and tapestries. The Coventry Tapestry on the north wall commemorates their visit, and the large stained glass window above it memorializes Henry's ancestors. Read about the Guildhall at http://www.historiccoventry.co.uk/tour/tour3.html.

Margaret's army won the Battle of **Wakefield**, near **Sandal Castle**, in December 1460. At http://www.castleuk.net/castle_lists_north/111/sandalcastle.htm, see an aerial photograph of Sandal Castle along with a detailed map indicating the location of the castle and the battle site, which is about 1 and ½ miles south of the town of Wakefield. A city of about 60,000 population, Wakefield overlooks the river Calder in West Yorkshire. On the edge of the Leeds/Bradford/Huddersfield conurbation, Wakefield has never become as industrialised.

Towton is in North Yorkshire, on the A162 between Pontefract and Tadcaster. From Towton, take the B1217 to see the cross marking the death of the Lancastrian Lord Dacre during the battle. Most of the battlefield is visible from this point. In 1996, workers came upon a mass grave at Towton Hall, discovering a number of skeletons piled in one place. Subsequently, the 40 skeletons were examined by archaeologists and found to be of an age and to have suffered trauma consistent with the 1461 battle. The Battle of Towton Landscape Project is described at http://www.brad.ac.uk/acad/archsci/depart/resgrp/archpros/Towton_Landscape/, with links to the Towton Battle Archaeological Survey and the Towton Mass Grave Project, where detailed information regarding the findings is described.

From her base at **Bamburgh Castle**, Margaret gathered forces to fight again, this time at **Hexham**. The battlefield of Hexham can be found in a field known as Hexham Levels. The town of Hexham is on the A695 about 20 miles west of Newcastle-upon-Tyne, the battlefield on the B6306 two miles southeast of the town. Visit this attractive town of about 10,000 population at http://communities.northumberland.gov.uk/hexham.htm, read the history and facts, then click on Photographs for a number of views. **Koeur**, in France, where she was then permitted to live for a time, is located on the river Meuse, east of Bar-le-Duc.

Waddington Hall, where Henry was captured, is in the village of Waddington, on the B6478 just north of Clitheroe, in Lancashire. The hall is privately owned and not open to the public; no contemporary photographs could be located at time of writing. Accounts of Henry's capture there may be read at http://www.ormerod.uk.net/Places/Waddington/waddington_hall.htm, along with sketches from an 1842 publication; a 1903 photograph of the hall appears at http://www.frithphotos.com/pageloader.asp?partner=ca&page=/search/viewphotos.asp&cid=10&location=lancashire/waddington. The village of Waddington is called "picture postcard," and regularly wins the prize of the best-kept village in Lancashire. See pictures at http://www.lancashireparishcouncils.gov.uk/parishes/parish_display.asp?parishid=23,

After landing at Weymouth in 1471 with a force of French troops, Margaret encountered the Yorkists at **Tewkesbury**. Tewkesbury is located on the A38 north of Gloucester, an old town of about 10,000 inhabitants, on the river Avon. It's an attractive town with riverside scenery, half-timbered houses, and an astonishingly large and splendid abbey church. A brass in the pavement of the chancel marks what is considered to be the burial site of Prince Edward of Lancaster, Henry's and Margaret's son, killed in the battle. The church's website is at http://www.tewkesburyabbey.org.uk/. For visiting information for Tewkesbury and the charming Cotswolds neighborhood, see http://www.visitcotswoldsandsevernvale.gov.uk/.

Henry died, a prisoner, in the Wakefield Tower at the **Tower of London** in 1471. See the Wakefield Tower, and read about his death at http://www.toweroflondontour.com/gatewake.html. He was buried at **Chertsey Abbey** initially, then re-buried in St. George's Chapel, Windsor Castle. **Chertsey** is located southwest of London, just off the junction between the M3 and the M25. Of the once-famous Benedictine abbey, originally founded in the 7th century and then again in 1110, almost nothing remains but some stonework and tiles, and the curfew bell, now forming part of the set in the nearby St. Peter's Shared Church, Chertsey. Read the history of the abbey, along with photographs, at http://www.whisker.f2s.com/StPeters/history/abbey_index.htm. Henry VI's tomb in **St. George's Chapel, Windsor Castle** is to be found on the south chancel aisle, marked by a simple slab. View it at http://homepage.mac.com/crowns/gb/avgal.html.

After Tewkesbury, Margaret was imprisoned in various English castles until 1475, when Louis XI of France secured her release. One of these was **Wallingford Castle**; for information regarding the castle, see

Stephen and Maud. The town of Wallingford is south of Oxford, on the A4130, tucked beside the river Thames. It's an old town of 6300 population that preserves its medieval plan, although not a lot is left of the once-royal castle, whose site is now public gardens. Read about Wallingford at http://www.oxtowns.co.uk/wallingford/home.html.

Back in France, she lived in poverty until her death at the château of **Dampierre-sur-Loire** at Souzay-Champigny, near Saumur, in 1482. See the village and château at http://www.villagesdefrance.free.fr/dept/page49_saumurois.htm (in French). Saumur is upriver from **Angers**, the nearest city, where Margaret is buried in the **cathedral**. The ancient capital of the Duchy of Anjou, Angers, with about 146,000 inhabitants, is located on the first stretch of the Loire, at its confluence with the river Maine. The cathedral dates from the 12th and 13th centuries. Its website is at http://catholique-angers.cef.fr/site/102.html; for more photographs, see http://www.culture.gouv.fr/culture/inventai/itiinv/cathedrale/docimage/angers/cat_angers.html.

Edward IV

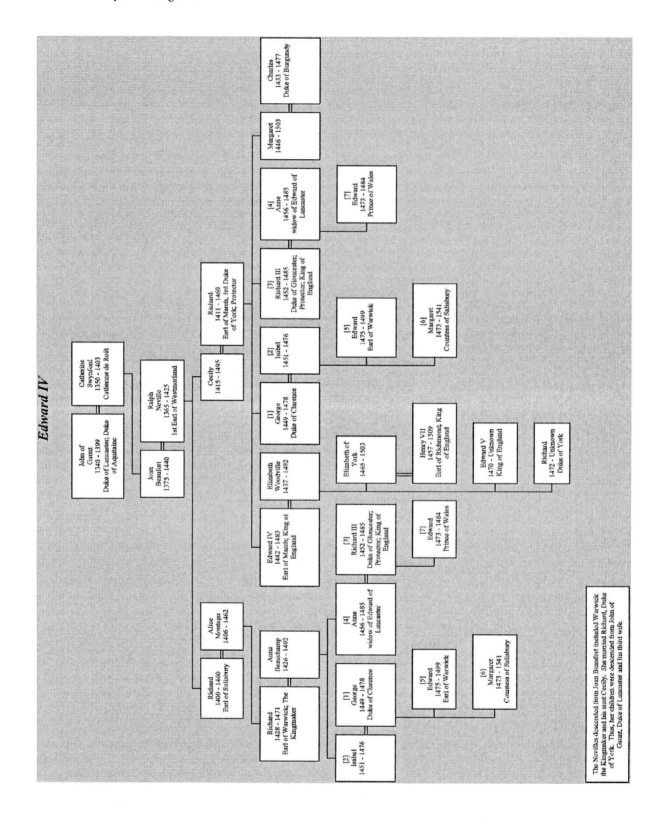

The Nevilles descended from Joan Beaufort included Warwick the Kingmaker and his aunt Cecily. She married Richard, Duke of York. Thus, her children were descended from John of Gaunt, Duke of Lancaster and his third wife.

Edward IV (1442–1483; reigned as King of England and Lord of Ireland, 1461–1470 and 1471–1483)

A Shakespearean playwright seems to have designed Edward IV's regal career for dramatic effect, so neatly does his reign fall into bisected portions of roughly equal duration. Intriguingly, the same pattern of events unfolds in the second half of his reign as in the first. Crucial deaths clear the cluttered stage; Yorkist military victories establish Edward as King; growing tension between Yorkists gives Lancastrians a chance to strike; Edward or, after his death, his son loses the crown.

Defeat in the battle of Wakefield in December, 1460 caused the death of Edward's father, Richard, Duke of York, whom the 1460 Act of Accord had named heir presumptive to the Lancastrian Henry VI. Edward's generalship then won the Yorkist victories of Mortimer's Cross (February, 1461) and Towton (March, 1461), and London welcomed him while it spurned Margaret of Anjou and Henry VI, who fled northward. Thus the 18-year-old Earl of March supplanted Henry VI and began the first half of his reign, which stretched to 1470. Unhappy with Edward's rule, his cousin Richard Neville, Earl of Warwick, and his brother and heir presumptive, George, Duke of Clarence, revolted against Edward. Warwick's eventual alliance with Margaret of Anjou caused the flight of Edward IV to the Continent and the restoration of Henry VI.

After his deposition in 1470, Edward invaded England in 1471, and the subsequent Yorkist victories of Barnet and Tewkesbury resulted in the deaths of Warwick and of Henry VI's heir presumptive, Edward of Lancaster. Soon afterward, Henry VI himself died in the Tower of London. His passing and Yorkist military success effected the restoration of Edward IV. Again, the Duke of Clarence plotted against his brother the King but this time was executed before his plans succeeded. Edward then enjoyed some years of apparent security from sedition, but the King's unexpected and early death in 1483 let loose tensions and conflicts that he had managed to submerge. These dissensions within Yorkist ranks led to the deposition of Edward IV's heir, Edward V; to the reign of Edward IV's brother, Richard, Duke of Gloucester—now Richard III; and to rebellions against Richard III that elevated a new Lancastrian standard-bearer to the throne. Ending the Yorkist dynasty, Henry Tudor, Earl of Richmond, became Henry VII and established the House of Tudor in its stead.

Such a short life for the Yorkist dynasty must have seemed improbable at the peaks of both of Edward IV's reigns. If Yorkist dissidents had not sought to supplant the Yorkist monarchs, Henry VI would never have enjoyed the dubious honor of his "re-adeption," nor would Henry VII ever have ascended to the throne of England.

After his 1461 victory at Towton, Edward IV rewarded his cousin Warwick lavishly but also angered Warwick by favoring others and by charting his own course. The apparently final defeats of the Lancastrians at Hedgeley Moor and Hexham in 1464 and the capture of the deposed Henry VI in 1465 doubtless enhanced Edward's confidence. Warwick advocated a pro-French foreign policy, while Edward leaned towards an alliance with Burgundy. While Warwick negotiated for a royal marriage to Bona of Savoy, sister to the French Queen, Edward in 1464 secretly married an unsuitable if alluring English subject, Elizabeth Woodville, and revealed this marriage only after much delay. (Complicating matters, in earlier years, Edward seems also to have precontracted himself to another woman, Lady Eleanor Talbot, later Butler—a precontract that supposedly invalidated the Woodville marriage. Edward's boundless lechery caused him to seduce and then discard many women. Breaking his precontract to Lady Eleanor and deceiving Elizabeth Woodville would have continued his well-established pattern of ruthless seduction.) Adding to Warwick's irritation, Edward fostered the 1468 wedding of his sister Margaret to Charles, Duke of Burgundy.

Frustrated in his promotion of a pro-French policy, Warwick also resented being frustrated in his ambitions for his daughters, Isabel and Anne Neville. The Queen's Woodville sisters made some brilliant marriages that severely depleted the pool of available husbands for Isabel and Anne. In addition, Edward had opposed a match between Isabel Neville and his own brother Clarence.

Intriguing against Edward with his new son-in-law Clarence's help, Warwick first rebelled by capturing the King in July, 1469 and imprisoning Edward for a few months, first in Warwick Castle, then in Middleham. Forced by necessity to release the King, Warwick was expelled from England in April, 1470, but by the following October had invaded England, restored Henry VI, and caused Edward to flee to Burgundy with his brother Gloucester. During this "re-adeption" (the fruit of Warwick's alliance with Margaret of Anjou and their agreement to marry Margaret and Henry's son Edward of Lancaster to Warwick's daughter Anne Neville), Henry VI lived in the palace of the Bishop of London. A French attack on Burgundy supported by Warwick motivated the otherwise indifferent Charles of Burgundy to support in secret his brother-in-law Edward IV's invasion of England in March, 1471. Warwick died at the battle of Barnet in April, while Edward of Lancaster died at Tewkesbury in May. Someone murdered Henry VI in the Tower soon afterward.

In Edward IV's second reign, the pattern of destructive Yorkist infighting recurred. After betraying Edward by intriguing with Warwick, Clarence had then betrayed Warwick and allied himself with the King. With his father-in-law Warwick now dead, Clarence resumed his career as a narcissistic and heedless troublemaker. Wanting all of the vast Warwick inheritance of his wife Isabel for himself, Clarence bitterly opposed his brother Gloucester's 1472 marriage to Anne Neville, the widow of Edward of Lancaster and the sister of Isabel. After Isabel herself died in 1476, Clarence resented Edward's opposition to his own plans to woo Mary of Burgundy. By 1477, Edward had finally had enough of Clarence's sequential betrayals and had him tried for high treason and executed in 1478. However, Clarence's death (tradition says, by submersion in a butt of malmsey wine) did not permanently submerge Yorkist discontent, which resurfaced after Edward's death and destroyed his sons, the "Princes in the Tower" (Edward V and Richard, Duke of York).

Edward IV's own accomplishments survived the destruction of his short-lived dynasty. An effective and attractive King, Edward established economic policies that rescued the monarchy from insolvency and made him the first solvent King of England in 300 years. Edward's great building projects included the Great Hall at Eltham Palace, his favorite residence, and the Chapel of St George at Windsor Castle associated with the Order of the Garter. His Queen, Elizabeth Woodville, in 1465 refounded Queens' College, Cambridge—first founded by Margaret of Anjou in 1448. (Margaret had befriended Elizabeth's parents, and Elizabeth had served Queen Margaret as lady-in-waiting.) Twice, Edward IV created political stability after a period of civil war. A merciful victor, he extended clemency many times to his political enemies, who often betrayed him as soon as they could do so with impunity. At last, Edward recognized that his often-forgiven brother Clarence would never cease to undermine him, and Edward's execution of Clarence demonstrated the King's determination to impose order. Yet Edward's own death released the torrential disorder he had held in check for a time.

Edward IV Sites

Edward was born at **Rouen** in 1442 and baptized in **Rouen Cathedral**. For the city of Rouen, see *Henry V*; for Rouen Cathedral, see *Stephen and Maud*.

He married Elizabeth Woodville probably at her birthplace, **Grafton Regis**, Northamptonshire. Grafton Regis (Regis was bestowed by Henry VIII during a visit) is a village on the A508, northwest of Milton Keynes. The Woodvilles had first settled there in the 13th century. Grafton was small, the church and manor house being the two largest buildings. The town's website is http://www.grafton-regis.co.uk/. It's an attractive site which gives very little away: to read Grafton's history, you have to buy a two-CD set. Elizabeth's grandfather is represented by a brass in the church, viewed online at http://www.mbs-brasses.co.uk/pic_lib/ Grafton_Regis_Brass.htm.

The battle of **Wakefield**, where Edward's father Richard, Duke of York, died, took place near **Sandal Castle**, about 1-½ miles south of the town of Wakefield. See *Henry VI* for information about both Wakefield and Sandal Castle.

Edward led his troops at the winning Battle of **Mortimer's Cross** in 1461. This was one of his victories; it's sometimes called the Battle of the Three Suns because Edward saw a "sun dog" in the sky, which he took to be a good omen, and so it proved—he added "the sun in splendour" to his banner. The probable site of the battlefield is in Herefordshire, northwest of Leominster, to the left of the A4110 and just after its junction with the B4300. See http://www.richard111.com/mortimer1.htm for a description of the battle and diagrams of the possible positions of the armies, and http://www.battlefieldstrust.com/resource-centre/ warsoftheroses/battleview.asp?BattleFieldId=25 for photographs and illustrations, and visitor information.

For **Towton** and **Hexham**, see *Henry VI*.

The battle of **Hedgeley Moor** took place in 1464; the site is to the left of the A697 after the village of Powburn. Read a description at http://www.richard111.com/hedgeley1.htm. Hedgeley Moor is marked on a map including the other battlefields of the northeast, useful for planning a tour, along with indications of the terrain. Hedgeley Moor, along with Homildon Hill and Bamburgh Castle (see *Henry VI*), is incorporated in a suggested round trip from Alnwick Castle, at http://www.northumbrian-coast.co.uk/alnwick.htm.

Warwick Castle, where Edward was imprisoned by the Earl of Warwick, has all the aspects enjoyed by visitors: a well-preserved 14th century castle along with later conversion of the living quarters into a palace, set idyllically in lawns and gardens on a bed in the river Avon. Beginning as a Norman motte, the wooden structure was rebuilt in stone in the 12th century and rebuilt again in the 14th century, this time with the addition of the gateways, spectacular towers, and outer walls. The Great Hall contains a display of arms and armor among other items; the state rooms were refurbished mostly during the elegant 1770–90 period; in the private apartments is a reconstruction of a royal weekend party of 1898, with lifesized wax figures. Similar figures used in other parts illustrate past life in the castle: Madame Tussauds has owned the castle since 1978. Capability Brown contributed the basic layout of the gardens. The castle hosts medieval festivals and jousting tournaments—see a list at http://www.warwick-uk.co.uk/places-of-interest/warwick-castle.asp. At this same website, you can make a virtual, 360-degree tour of the Great Hall. Warwick Castle's showy website at http://www.warwick-castle.co.uk/warwick2004/includes fine images of the castle once you get past the flashy parts.

Middleham Castle, another stronghold of Warwick's, also hosted Edward. It's situated in North Yorkshire, on the A6108 north of Ripon, on the edge of the Yorkshire Dales. Unlike Warwick, this castle is in ruins, but there's a lot left, and it's an impressive sight. For more information regarding Middleham, see *Richard III*.

No trace has survived of the port of **Ravenspur** where Edward arrived on his return from exile in 1471. See *Henry IV* for details regarding Ravenspur.

The Battle of **Barnet** in April 1471 was fought by Edward against the troops of Richard Neville, Earl of Warwick—Warwick died in this battle. The battle took place on the northern end of today's Barnet (now a city of Greater London). Read a description of the battle, along with a plan, at http://www.richard111.com/ barnet1.htm. More is to be found at http://www.btlse.co.uk/barnet.html, with photographs of the terrain and information regarding location. A monument, Hadley High Stone, erected in 1740, stands at the junction of the A1000 and Kitts End Road.

Tewkesbury, site of the decisive 1471 battle, is located on the A38 north of Gloucester, an old town of about 10,000 inhabitants, on the river Avon. For more information, see *Henry VI*.

On the domestic front, Edward gave **Sheen Palace** to Elizabeth, who made it her principal home. Sheen, much improved by Henry V, was still a favorite royal residence in what is now Richmond, London, until it burned down in December 1498, to be replaced by Richmond Palace. See *Edward III* for the origins of Sheen, and *Henry VII* for the building of Richmond Palace.

At **Eltham Palace**, Edward had the Great Hall built. This is the only part of the palace surviving the Commonwealth period. The Great Hall was then used as a farm and an indoor tennis court until the Courtauld family leased it in 1931. They restored the Great Hall and built an adjoining new house in the contemporary art deco style, finished in 1937. Although this move has had its detractors, essentially the Courtaulds preserved Eltham and provided the facility of the hall and their own property for public visiting. A virtual tour of Eltham Palace, hosted by English Heritage, can be made at http://www.elthampalace.org.uk/, which also provides details regarding visiting: note that there are some limitations on areas and opening hours.

At **Windsor Castle**, Edward was responsible for the Horseshoe Cloister and, more spectacularly, the commencement of St. George's Chapel. He began **St. George's Chapel** in 1475, with plans for a cathedral-sized chapel and, within it, a chantry chapel to accommodate his own burial place. Under master mason Henry Janyns, construction began to the west of Edward III's Chapel of St. George, absorbing its façade and necessitating the rearrangement of the buildings in the lower bailey—the Horseshoe Cloister was one of the results. Edward's chantry chapel was never accomplished: the gate made for it, in elaborate and intricate ironwork with flanking turrets by John Tresilian, now stands to the left of the high altar, and Edward's and Elizabeth's tombs are located in the north choir aisle. By the time Edward's body was placed in St. George's Chapel, the choir was roofed but not vaulted, and the walls of the nave were still under construction. Henry VII and Henry VIII continued the work. See http://www.stgeorges-windsor.org/welcome.asp for an incredibly informative website. There's a forest of information, diagrams, and photographs concealed behind the list of links.

The **Horseshoe Cloister** is a horseshoe-shaped, timber-framed building, using the fashionable brick. Intended to accommodate the vicars of Edward III's College of St. George, it basically remains today, although with changes by Sir George Gilbert Scott in the 1870s and with copper roofs added in the 1950s. The Horseshoe Cloister is still inhabited: today, boys of the Chapel choir school and lay clerks of the choir live there. See it at http://www.stgeorges-windsor.org/tour/tour_horseshoe.asp.

Edward died at **Westminster Palace**. For information regarding the Palace, see *William the Conqueror*. He and Elizabeth Woodville are buried side-by-side in the north choir aisle of **St. George's Chapel, Windsor**, behind an ironwork grille probably made by John Tresilian. Their tomb can be seen online at http://homepage.mac.com/crowns/gb/avgal.html.

Henry Stafford, 2nd Duke of Buckingham

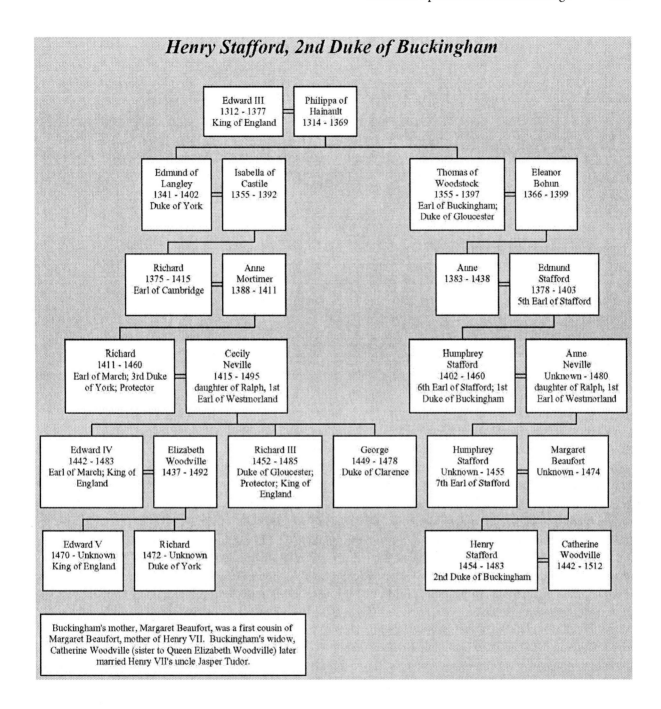

Buckingham's mother, Margaret Beaufort, was a first cousin of Margaret Beaufort, mother of Henry VII. Buckingham's widow, Catherine Woodville (sister to Queen Elizabeth Woodville) later married Henry VII's uncle Jasper Tudor.

Edward V (1470–Unknown; King of England and Lord of Ireland, 1483) Richard III (1452–1485; King of England and Lord of Ireland, 1483–1485)

Edward V had only a walk-on part on history's stage. He was born in 1470 while his mother, Edward IV's consort Elizabeth Woodville, protected herself in sanctuary provided by Westminster Abbey and his father waited in Holland for the opportunity to win back the English throne after the Lancastrians had deposed him. After Edward IV's death, Prince Edward became King on 9 April 1483 but gave way to his paternal uncle who became Richard III on 26 June 1483 after alleging the illegitimacy of Edward IV's children by Elizabeth Woodville. Housed in the Tower of London (then a royal residence), Edward V and his brother Richard, Duke of York, hereafter known to history as "the Princes in the Tower," eventually disappeared from public view. They were possibly—though not certainly—murdered, possibly—though not certainly—by their uncle Richard III.

Thus Edward V entered and exited history merely as a victim. Nevertheless, the question of whether his uncle really did murder him and his brother has dominated all attempts to evaluate the character and career of Richard III. As with King John, the contamination of the historical record by biased contemporary accounts has led to endless repetitions, as if by rote, of the certainty of the sovereign's almost diabolical guilt. In reaction, some fervent defenders of Richard's reputation often have indulged in what Keats in another context called "a wild surmise," in effect mirroring their opponents. More judicious presentations by Ricardians in mock trials—one involving former Lord Chancellor Elwyn Jones in 1984 and two involving United States Supreme Court Chief Justice William Rehnquist in 1996 and 1997—all won acquittal for Richard. It is possible not only to argue that Richard III did not order the murders of the Princes but also to argue that no one murdered them. Spirited out of the Tower, they may have remained alive and then surfaced years later when Yorkist Pretenders threatened the throne of Henry VII.

Any consideration of these possibilities must first acknowledge the fascinating portrayal by Shakespeare of his character "Richard III," enjoying the characterization's undoubted power but disputing the confusion in the public mind of the "bottled spider" "Richard III" with his living namesake. "Richard III," the Devil's imp, confides to the audience his plots to rid himself of all obstacles to the throne: his older brothers George, Duke of Clarence and Edward IV; the male Woodville relations of Edward V; and his nephews Edward V and Richard, Duke of York. In effect, "Richard III" with crafty premeditation and complete lack of scruple aims at the destruction of each and all of these human obstacles to his sovereignty.

A very different account emerges after reading two of the most dispassionate accounts of the controversy: A.J. Pollard's *Richard III and the Princes in the Tower*, which found Richard guilty of their deaths, and Bertram Fields's *Royal Blood: Richard III and the Mystery of the Princes*, which found his guilt improbable. Just as the more fervent condemnations and praises of Richard constitute odd mirror images of improbability, these two dispassionate accounts mirror each other. While Pollard and Fields disagreed about Richard's complicity in the deaths of the Princes, each presented a far more nuanced, human, and believable portrait of the man. Their portraits resembled each other far more than either resembled the popular image of a human devil.

In some ways, the comparison with a humanized King John is constructive. Like John, Richard was the youngest and least privileged son. As with John, anxiety about his position and holdings may have motivated much of Richard's behavior. As husband of Anne Neville, daughter of the late Earl of Warwick, for example, Richard won only conditional possession of some of the Neville lands. Richard's power and status depended on his remaining a northern magnate, as Pollard explained, but on 4 May 1483, a few weeks after the death of Edward IV, Richard's enemies changed his title to the Neville estates to only a life interest. He may have taken power initially with the motive of self-protection.

While Pollard considered that Richard, so far from plotting Clarence's death, may have merely gone through the motions of supporting Edward IV in trying and condemning the often-treacherous Clarence, Fields contended that Richard deeply mourned Clarence's death, which he blamed on Woodville influence. If Richard feared Woodville power during Edward IV's life, how much more he had to fear from Woodville ascendancy after the accession of the young Prince Edward. He moved against the Woodvilles quickly, claiming a conspiracy against himself as Protector. He then deposed the Woodville sovereign by alleging his bastardy because Edward IV's marriage to Elizabeth Woodville had ignored a precontract to another woman. Clarence may have invited his death at the hands of Edward IV and the Woodvilles by first revealing proof of this precontract that invalidated the Woodville marriage.

It is possible to see all of Richard's actions to this point as reasonable, if one considers valid Richard's concerns about his position, fears of Woodville conspiracy, and beliefs about the illegitimacy of Elizabeth Woodville's children by Edward IV. In addition, the Princes in the Tower, although they disappeared from public sight, may have not fallen victim to Richard or any other murderer at all but have been smuggled out of the Tower to more obscure lives elsewhere. Fields detailed their possible involvement with uprisings against Henry VII by Yorkist Pretenders supported by their mother, Elizabeth Woodville, and their paternal aunt, Margaret, Duchess of Burgundy. If so, this would obviously absolve Richard of any responsibility for their deaths.

If the Princes did indeed die in the Tower, they may not have been murdered by anyone but instead died of disease or illness. Even if they died by the hand of a murderer, he may not have been Richard but instead Richard's supplanter, Henry VII, or Henry Stafford, Duke of Buckingham, first the ally and then the enemy of Richard III. (Buckingham's own descent from Edward III may have fostered ambitions to gain the crown.) Then, again, Richard III may indeed have ordered their deaths.

Pollard argued that the probabilities point to Richard as his nephews' murderer; Fields contended for the probability of Richard's innocence. (Most historians now dismiss the possibility of his being guilty of the other crimes tradition attributes to him.) Whether Richard was indeed guilty or innocent of this main charge against him, Pollard and Fields concurred that he was not the moral monster of legend. Fields quoted Elizabeth Jenkins as believing "The story is not the sensational one of the crime of a habitual murderer, but the awe-inspiring one of a capable, strong minded, dedicated King driven to a dreadful act from which he chose to think there was no escape." Believing Richard guilty, Pollard nevertheless pointed out, "He was neither a hateful child-murderer, nor a paragon of contemporary virtue. He was a man who lived up to several of the ideals of contemporary nobility, yet one who when tested was found wanting. It is possible that he himself came to understand this and that the realization was the cause of great anguish."

Edward V Sites

After Edward IV had fled to France, in the **Sanctuary at Westminster Abbey** Elizabeth gave birth to their fourth child, Edward, later to become Edward V, in 1470. She was to go to the Sanctuary again, in 1483, after Edward IV died. The Sanctuary building stood at the end of St. Margaret's churchyard; it was demolished in 1750.

When Edward's father, Edward IV, became King in 1461, **Ludlow Castle** became a royal property. The King sent Edward to Ludlow when he was two or three years old, where he and his younger brother Richard spent the next ten years, almost all the years of their tragically short lives (if indeed they were murdered in

1483). They were there when they learned of the death of their father, and it was from Ludlow Castle that they set out for London.

Ludlow Castle was constructed probably in the late 11th century by the de Lacy family. Then added to by later owners, the de Genevilles and Mortimers, the castle eventually passed into the ownership of the Plantagenets. More construction followed in the latter half of the 1500s, when Ludlow was an important administrative center for control over Wales. However, the castle was abandoned after 1689, and by the 1700s was a ruin, becoming well known for its romantic nature. Since 1811, the Earls of Powis have owned and maintained it. Substantial amounts of the castle remain; take a virtual tour and study the history of Ludlow Castle at http://www.ludlowcastle.com/home.htm?http://www.ludlowcastle.com/tour.htm, including an account of life within the castle during earlier times. Edward and Richard are rumored to have lived in the Tudor Lodging (once called the Pendover Tower), the splendid North Range. The town of Ludlow is also worth the time spent, with its winding streets still in their medieval pattern, and half-timbered and carved buildings, some of them spectacularly so.

Stony Stratford ("the jewel of Milton Keynes") is where Richard of Gloucester (later Richard III) intercepted Edward V and the Woodvilles. Stony Stratford's home page is http://www.stonystratford.co.uk/index.html, with links to its history, enticements to visit (including a "virtual weekend"), and maps. Stony Stratford, now on the outskirts of one of England's fastest-growing cities, Milton Keynes, grew on the site of a ford on the Roman highway Watling Street over the river Ouse, developing into a coaching center especially when the Ouse flooded. A clear diagram/map can be found at http://clutch.open.ac.uk/schools/stmarystgiles99/Thelong.html.

Once known as the Garden Tower, the **Bloody Tower** is considered to have got its name from the alleged murder of Edward and Richard while they were living there. However, it's highly possible that the Princes were held in the **White Tower**. Lodged in the **Tower of London** under the protection of their uncle for a short time, they were not seen again there. The bones of two children of the same ages were found buried close to the White Tower in 1674 and officially reburied in **Westminster Abbey** as those of the Princes, but uncertainty regarding their true origin remains. Take a virtual tour of the Bloody Tower at http://www.toweroflondontour.com/bloodytw.html, and the White Tower at http://www.toweroflondontour.com/whitetow.html. Their bones now lie in the so-called Innocents' Corner of **Westminster Abbey**, in a marble urn in the Henry VII (or Lady) Chapel. Read about some challenges to the traditional assumption that the children's bones are those of the Princes at http://www.r3.org/basics/basic1.html#princes.

Richard III Sites

Richard's fan club, the **Richard III Society**, American Branch, hosts a travel page, "Ricardian Travel," at http://www.r3.org/travel/index.html. (The home page of its British parent Society itself can be found at http://www.richardiii.net/begin.htm.) The home page of another fan club, the **Richard III Foundation**, can be viewed at http://www.richard111.com/. The Foundation provides a wealth of information regarding properties owned by or associated with Richard at http://www.richard111.com/Lord%20of%20the%20North.htm. See also The Society of Friends of King Richard III at http://www.silverboar.org/.

Richard was born at **Fotheringhay Castle** in 1452. Alas, nothing but a mound of the once-mighty keep remains of the castle, first built in the time of William the Conqueror and then rebuilt in the reign of Edward III. Visit what remains at http://www.castleuk.net/castle_lists_midlands/142/fotheringhaycastle.htm, and also through http://www.marie-stuart.co.uk/index.htm: for the latter, you need to click on Places to Visit, then scroll down to the bottom of the screen to "In England," which will provide a list, with Fotheringhay included. Note that a reconstruction can be accessed, among the information and photographs about Fotheringhay.

Richard married Anne Neville at **Westminster Abbey**. Anne had been born at **Warwick Castle**; see *Edward IV* for information regarding the castle.

Richard's sites in Yorkshire and Cumbria form a circular tour from York (roughly speaking). All the castles can be seen at http://www.richard111.com/Lord%20of%20the%20North.htm, with information, so websites below are included for their added information, photographs, and visiting details.

About 13 miles northeast of York, on a minor road to the left off the A64, lies **Sheriff Hutton**, whose church contains an alabaster monument to a Prince of Wales, generally thought to be that of Richard's son by Anne Neville. See http://www.richardiii.net/sites_hutton.htm for a photograph of the church and information. At time of writing, websites are promised for Sheriff Hutton and its church.

Back to the A64 and onwards toward the coast to **Scarborough Castle**, which came into Richard's possession in 1474. From it, he supervised the outfitting of his ships. See http://www.castlexplorer.co.uk/england/scarborough/scarborough.php and http://www.theheritagetrail.co.uk/castles/scarborough%20castle.htm for detailed histories and visiting details. Also in Scarborough, there is an ancient house dating from about 1350 where Richard is reputed to have stayed. You can see a photograph of this house at http://www.interludeshotel.co.uk/history.htm.

Inland again, and westward, you cross the A1 to plunge into the Yorkshire Dales to view the imposing remnants of **Middleham Castle**, a favorite residence of Richard's. His son Edward is said to have been born in the southwest, or Prince's, Tower, in 1473. You can take a virtual tour of the castle at http://205.243.96.180/ricardian_britain/middleham/photoplan.html, with plenty of images at http://205.243.96.180/ricardian_britain/middleham/image1.html, including a 20th century interpretation of images of Richard. Visiting details and a local map may be seen at http://www.castleuk.net/castle_lists_north/99/middlehamcastle.htm.

On your way back to the A1 and also in the Dales is **Richmond Castle**, acquired by Richard in 1478 and now owned by English Heritage. Visiting and other details appear at http://www.english-heritage.org.uk/server/show/conProperty.376 and http://www.richmond.org.uk/guide/castle/castle.html. The latter site also covers the market town of Richmond.

Our next stop is **Barnard Castle**, in the attractive town of the same name. Acquired by Richard in 1475, the castle is strikingly positioned on cliffs above the river Tees. It's now in the hands of English Heritage, who present it at http://www.english-heritage.org.uk/server.php?show=ConProperty.115.

Photographs of the town and river can be viewed at http://www.freefoto.com/regional/europe/united_kingdom/england/county_durham/barnard_castle/index.asp.

Barnard Castle lies off the A66, which leads to our next destination, **Penrith Castle**, dating from the 1390s. In 1471, it came into Richard's possession as part of the Warwick inheritance of his wife. His most notable addition was the banqueting hall. The sandstone remains of the castle can be viewed at http://www.visitcumbria.com/pen/penrithc.htm and http://www.castleuk.net/castle_lists_north/90/penrithcastle.htm (including visiting details). Penrith, a market town of 12,000 inhabitants, is situated at the junction of the M6 and the A66, on the edge of the beautiful Lake District.

Back near York again, and tucked on the eastern edge of the conurbation of Bradford and Leeds, is **Pontefract Castle**. This was one of Richard's official residences, in his position as Steward of the Duchy of Lancaster. For details regarding the castle, see *Richard II*.

Only thirteen miles away is **Sandal Castle**, in Sandal, part of the city of **Wakefield**. See *Henry VI* for information about Wakefield and the castle.

Further south again, the **Angel Hotel**, where Richard III signed the death-warrant of the Duke of Buckingham in 1483, lies in the heart of **Grantham**. Now known as the Angel and Royal Hotel, it is still a flourishing hostelry, one of the oldest inns in Britain. You can see a photograph of its 15th century façade and click on a street map showing its location at http://www.nottspubs.co.uk/lincolnshire/pubs/granthampubs.htm. Grantham, a town of 31,000 inhabitants, is centrally located for touring, lying on the A52, just off the A1 between Stamford and Newark-on-Trent; the town website appears at http://www.grantham-online.co.uk/.

Sir John Crosby rented his property, **Crosby Place**, to Richard in 1483 as the latter's London base. At that time, Crosby Place was a mansion in Bishopsgate, London, built in 1466. occupying most of Crosby Square, right beside the major street called Bishopsgate (nearest tube is Liverpool Street). Sir Thomas More bought the house in 1523, and his son-in-law Will Roper lived there. The house burned in the 17th century, but the great hall was spared. In 1910, this was moved to Cheyne Walk, Chelsea, in London, and became known as **Crosby Hall**. At present, it is in private ownership and cannot be viewed by the public. However, it may be visited in the virtual manner at http://www.richardiii.net/sites_crosby.htm. An engraving of the former house can be seen at www.londonancestor.com/views/vb-crosby.htm, and a more detailed history can be read at www.britannia.com/history/londonhistory/lon-pal2.html.

At **Stony Stratford**, Richard intercepted Edward V and the Woodvilles. See details above at *Edward V.*

The site of the Battle of **Bosworth**, where Richard III died, lies west of Leicester, of the A447. There is a visitor center, and a walking tour of the battlefield takes about 45 minutes. An account of the battle and details for visiting, including a local map, appear at http://www.richardiii.net/sites_bosworth.htm.

After the battle, Richard's naked body was tethered to a horse and taken to the town hall in **Leicester**—not the present one, which dates from the late 19th century. According to tradition, his body was then interred in the monastery of Grey Friars, but at Henry VIII's Dissolution of the Monasteries was cast into the river Soar. No trace of the monastery exists. At the Bow bridge over the river, a plaque commemorates his supposed resting place. The bridge is no. 7 on a medieval plan of Leicester at http://www.leicester.gov.uk/index.asp?pgid=803.

Anne is buried in Westminster Abbey, on the southern side near the altar, with nothing marking the spot. In 1960 a brass plate and coat of arms was placed in the south ambulatory; see this at http://westminster-abbey.org/library/monarchs/anne_neville.htm.

Tudors:

Plantagenets "Reconciled"

Catherine of Valois and Tudor Origins

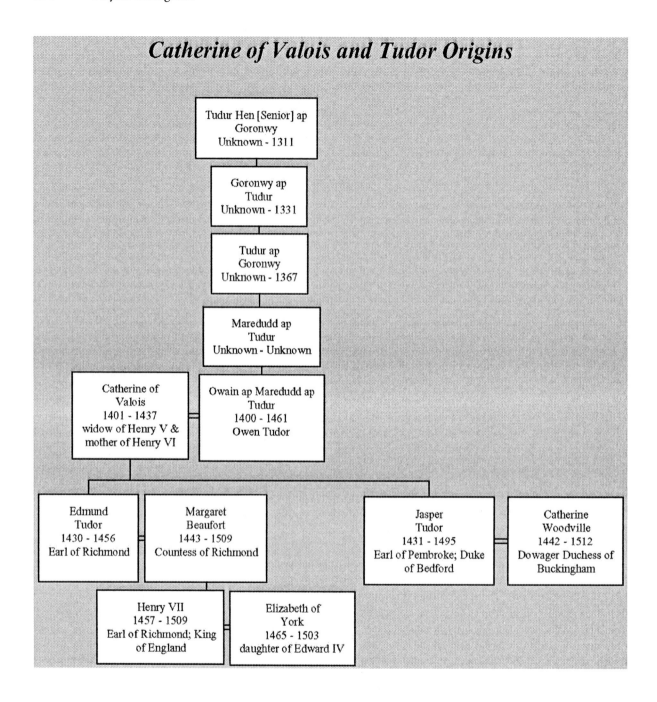

Catherine of Valois and Tudor Origins (1401–1437; reigned as Queen Consort to Henry V, 1420–1422)

The members of the celebrated Tudor dynasty begun by Henry VII and Elizabeth of York descended from a number of misalliances. Henry VII's mother, Margaret Beaufort, belonged to the Beaufort line begotten by John of Gaunt upon his mistress, Catherine Swynford or Catherine de Roët. After Gaunt's wife, Constance of Castile, died, he married Catherine, and the Pope and two English Kings subsequently legitimized the Beauforts. Elizabeth of York herself was born from Edward IV's marriage to the "unsuitable" Elizabeth Woodville. In addition, Edward IV may have precontracted himself to Eleanor Talbot, thereby invalidating the Woodville marriage. Elizabeth Woodville came from the notorious brood borne by her mother, Jacquetta of Luxembourg—daughter of Pierre, Count of St Pol and widow of John, Duke of Bedford—who had forgotten her station and wed Richard Woodville. Jacquetta's sister-in-law, Catherine of Valois—the widow of Bedford's brother Henry V—also married beneath her social level for love. Catherine of Valois's second husband, Owen Tudor, begat Edmund Tudor, Henry VII's father. But for a dowager Queen's fancy for a fine Welshman, we might never have heard of Henry VIII or Elizabeth I.

After Henry V's unexpected death in 1422, his 21-year-old widow took their baby son, Henry VI, with her to her manor at Waltham or her castle at Hertford. Because Edmund Beaufort, later 2nd Duke of Somerset, courted Catherine in the 1420s, her brother-in-law, Humphrey, Duke of Gloucester, grew alarmed at the prospect of a marriage between the Queen Dowager and the nephew of his antagonist, Henry Beaufort. Thus, in 1427–28, an edict prohibited Catherine from remarrying without the approval of her son (only six years old at the time) and his council.

Nevertheless, Catherine apparently married Owen Tudor in 1429 and proceeded to bear him four children, among them Edmund Tudor (1430) and Jasper Tudor (1431). Because Catherine lived in retirement, she successfully concealed both their marriage and her pregnancies. In the 1420s, the squire Owen Tudor seems to have served in the Queen's household; before then, he may have belonged to a group associated with Henry V's steward that went to France in 1421. Born Owain ap Maredudd ap Tudur, he went by several names over the years: Owen ap Meredith ap Tudur, Owen Meredith, Owen ap Meredith, Owen ap Tuder. Naturalized as Owen fitz Maredudd in 1432, he received an annuity from the crown as Owen Tudor, Esquire in 1459. The surname that evolved out of his patronymic stemmed from the given name of his grandfather, Tudur ap Goronwy.

Catherine herself died in 1437 at the Abbey of Bermondsey. (For over 300 years, visitors to her tomb in Westminster Abbey could ask to see her corpse, and Samuel Pepys kissed her during his 1669 visit to celebrate his 36th birthday: "[I] had her upper part of her body in my hands. And I did kiss her mouth, reflecting…that this was my birthday, 36 years old, that I did first kiss a Queen.") Owen Tudor soon faced charges and imprisonment, from which he twice escaped. Finally released from prison in 1439, Owen then received a pardon and became part of his stepson Henry VI's household until the mid-1450s. In 1460, he became Parker of the King's Parks near Denbigh but did not enjoy this dignity for very long. After the 1461 Yorkist victory at Mortimer's Cross, the future Edward IV had the captured 61-year-old Owen executed at Hereford. As a chronicler related, "He thought and trusted all along that he would not be beheaded until he saw the axe and block, and when he was in his doublet he trusted on pardon and grace until the collar of his red velvet doublet was ripped off. Then he said, 'That head shall lie upon the stock that was wont to lie on Queen Katherine's lap', and put his heart and mind wholly on God, and very meekly took his death."

When Catherine herself had died in 1437, her boys Edmund and Jasper came under the care of Catherine de la Pole, Abbess of Barking and sister to potentate William de la Pole, Earl of Suffolk. There they stayed until about 1442, when their elder half-brother, Henry VI, now in his twenties, took an interest in them. Knighted in 1449, Edmund and Jasper became the first Welshmen elevated to the English peerage in 1452, with Edmund being named Earl of Richmond and Jasper Earl of Pembroke. Then, in 1455, Edmund married Margaret Beaufort. With tensions rising between Lancaster and York, Edmund left his pregnant, 13-year-old wife to bolster Lancastrian strength in Wales. (Richard, Duke of York, controlled east Wales, in contrast to Lancastrian west Wales.) Sir William Herbert and Sir Walter Devereux, both tenants of the Duke of York, attacked Edmund in west Wales, captured him, and imprisoned him at Carmarthen Castle. Edmund died there in November 1456. Almost three months after Edmund's death, Margaret Beaufort gave birth at Pembroke Castle to the new Earl of Richmond—their son, Henry Tudor.

Edmund and Jasper Tudor, despite their kinship to Henry VI, actually had supported Richard, Duke of York, during his first Protectorate in 1454–1455. By 1457, the intrepid Jasper had broken with York and begun a lifetime's service to the House of Lancaster through which he demonstrated amazing resourcefulness and deep loyalty—first to his half-brother, Henry VI and later to his nephew, who would become Henry VII.

After the Lancastrian defeat at Northampton in 1460, Henry VI's Queen, Margaret of Anjou, fled to Pembroke Castle. She then left for Scotland, while Jasper prepared for the next struggle against the Duke of York, who died in late 1460 after the Battle of Wakefield. Intending to weld his forces to Margaret's, in early 1461, Jasper encountered York's son, the future Edward IV, at Mortimer's Cross. Sir William Herbert, Sir Richard Herbert, and Sir Walter Devereux all fought for the victorious Yorkists; Jasper escaped; his captured father, Owen, died at Edward's command. Following the Lancastrian disaster of Towton, Sir William Herbert captured Pembroke Castle in late 1461, and Parliament attainted Jasper Tudor, a fugitive in north Wales, Ireland, and Scotland.

Sir William Herbert, once a friend of Edmund Tudor, had changed to the Yorkist side after the Lancastrian defeat at Northampton. When Pembroke Castle fell, Herbert found Edmund's widow and their son there. After Herbert became his guardian, Henry Tudor remained at Pembroke Castle and at Herbert's Raglan Castle, under the care of Ann Devereux, Sir Walter's sister and Herbert's wife. In the new court of Edward IV, Herbert rose to prominence as a counterweight to Richard Neville, Earl of Warwick. Not only did Herbert's son marry Queen Elizabeth Woodville's sister Mary and become Lord Dunster, but the older Herbert himself assumed Jasper's title, Earl of Pembroke, in 1468. Warwick soon rebelled against Edward IV and exacted retribution against Herbert by executing him after the Battle of Edgecote.

Throughout the 1460s, Jasper had labored for the restoration of his half-brother and the House of Lancaster by intriguing in Wales, Scotland, Brittany, and France. He had followed Henry VI and Margaret of Anjou from France to Northumberland in 1462 and held Bamburgh Castle after Margaret withdrew to Scotland. Following Warwick's strange alliance of convenience with Margaret against Edward IV in 1470–1471, Jasper met with Warwick in France and tried to secure Wales once the attack on Edward began. During the brief restoration of Henry VI by Warwick, Jasper regained his title of Earl of Pembroke. Once Margaret of Anjou had landed in April, 1471, she had planned to join her forces with Jasper's. On 4 May, Tewkesbury blasted forever the Lancastrian tree. Earlier reunited with his young nephew, Henry of Richmond, Jasper then fled with Henry to Brittany.

Jasper had waited ten years for the restoration of Henry VI. After the murder of his half-brother in the Tower followed the Yorkist triumph at Tewkesbury, more than another decade passed before a second Lancastrian restoration became possible. Just as Yorkist discontent in the person of Warwick had revived otherwise hopeless Lancastrian aspirations in 1470–71, so would Yorkist infighting after the death of Edward IV in 1483. The flight of Henry of Richmond with Jasper Tudor to the Continent had preserved a potential Lancastrian champion.

Edward IV died; the Prince of Wales briefly ruled as Edward V; alleging the bastardy of Edward IV's heirs because of Edward IV's precontract to Eleanor Talbot, his brother Richard, Duke of Gloucester, became

Richard III; Edward V and his brother, Richard, Duke of York, disappeared. Their mother, Elizabeth Woodville, conspired against Richard III with Henry Tudor's mother, Margaret Beaufort. They revived an old proposal that Margaret Beaufort had discussed with Edward IV: that her son, the Earl of Richmond, marry his daughter, Elizabeth of York.

At the same time, Henry Stafford, 2nd Duke of Buckingham, an ally of Richard III despite his marriage to Catherine Woodville, himself planned another uprising against Richard. (Buckingham, Richard III, and Henry Tudor were the only adult males left to the Plantagenet dynasty.) Supporting the Woodville-Beaufort conspiracy, Buckingham wrote to Henry, Earl of Richmond, in Brittany to ask him to lead a force against Richard III. Buckingham's rebellion collapsed, Richard executed him, and bad weather aborted Henry's invasion, but the consequent flood of conspirators to Brittany strengthened Henry's position. In their presence at Christmas 1483, Henry vowed to marry Elizabeth of York after his accession as King.

Just as Edward IV had done before him, Richard III pressured François II, Duke of Brittany, to turn over Jasper Tudor and Henry Tudor. The last such attempt, in 1484, caused Henry to flee into France, followed later by his supporters, at a time when France saw helping Henry Tudor as a way to dilute the strength of an Anglo-Breton alliance. Thus, when Henry Tudor made for Wales in 1485, French aid made possible his invasion with French, Scottish, and Welsh troops.

Henry's stepfather, Thomas, Lord Stanley, nominally a partisan of the King, refused to state clearly whether he would support Henry's army with his own forces as the final confrontation approached. At Bosworth, as Richard III attacked Henry Tudor in mortal combat, Sir William Stanley (Thomas's brother) sent his men to help Henry. Fighting bravely and alone, Richard died among his enemies. Lord Stanley crowned his stepson on the battlefield.

Far more devoted than Henry VII's equivocal stepfather, his uncle Jasper Tudor had protected him in exile, advocated his claim, and—before that—demonstrated remarkable loyalty to Henry VII's uncle, Henry VI. Earl of Pembroke yet again, Jasper also became Duke of Bedford in October, 1485. That same autumn, Jasper married Catherine Woodville, Buckingham's widow. With her, Jasper acquired the Stafford lands, which added to his power in Wales and the March and his holdings in Pembroke and Glamorgan. Perhaps all of this glory served as a partial recompense for the more than 20 years sacrificed for Lancaster.

Catherine of Valois and Tudor Family Sites

Catherine was born in the **Hôtel de St Pol, Paris**, a home belonging to her mother's family, in 1401. She married Henry V in the cathedral of **Troyes**, France (see *Henry V*).

After Henry's premature death, Catherine took their baby son with her to **Waltham Manor** and **Hertford Castle** (see *John of Gaunt*). The former may have been the manor at **White Waltham**, west of Windsor. The manor was called Walthamsland or Windsors, the latter because it belonged to the Windsor family at one time. The house is now called Waltham Place and dates from the 18th century; it's privately owned, but the grounds are open to the public: see its website at http://walthamplace.com. White Waltham is just off the B3024 after the latter passes over the M4.

Sources disagree about whether she ever married Owen Tudor. The Tudor family home for centuries was at **Penmynydd**. Two miles to the northwest, the present building dates from 1576; it is privately owned and not open to the public. Penmynydd is on the B5420, a few miles inland from the Menai Strait on the Isle of Anglesey. Read about the history of the Tudor family and Plas Penmynydd at http://www.anglesey-history.co.uk/places/penmynydd/.

Of Catherine's children by Owen Tudor, Thomas became a monk at **Westminster Abbey**, where he died and is buried. The monastic life of the Abbey belonged to the Benedictine Order, and the life of a monk at the Abbey is described at http://www.westminster-abbey.org/library/monastery.htm, with a sketch depicting the Abbey in Norman times. Edmund was born at a summer residence of the Bishop of London, the Bishops' Palace at **Much Hadham**, Hertfordshire, and Jasper at **Hatfield** (see *Six Queens of Henry VIII*). Much Hadham, which is small to this day, lies on the B1004 between Hertford and Bishop's Stortford, north of London.

Catherine died, possibly in childbirth, at **Bermondsey Abbey** in 1437 (Edward IV's Queen Elizabeth Woodville also died there). Her tomb is in the Henry V Chantry Chapel in **Westminster Abbey**; read about both Henry's and her tombs at http://www.westminster-abbey.org/library/monarchs/henry_v.htm. After her death, her sons Edmund and Jasper were cared for in **Barking Abbey**. Almost all that remains of the once-great abbey is the Curfew Tower, although excavations of the site have unearthed rich artifacts. Read about Barking Abbey at http://www.barking-dagenham.gov.uk/4-heritage/abbey/abbey-menu.html. Barking is within eastern Greater London, north of Dagenham.

Owen Tudor became Parker of the King's Parks near **Denbigh** in 1460, the castle his headquarters. See the website for Denbigh Castle at http://www.castlewales.com/denbigh.html for the usual clear photographs and detailed information. Denbigh is located in north Wales, between St. Asaph and Ruthin, on the A543 near its intersection with the A525. On a hill, it overlooks the pretty Vale of Clwyd. Visit the town of Denbigh at http://www.denbigh.com/index.html.

Owen fought in the Wars of the Roses, was captured at Mortimer's Cross, and was executed at Hereford in 1461. For the battle of **Mortimer's Cross**, see *Edward IV*; for **Hereford Castle**, see *Henry III*.

Catherine and Owen's son Edmund married Lady Margaret Beaufort and died while imprisoned in **Carmarthen Castle** in 1465. Read about and visit the castle at http://www.castlewales.com/carmarth.html. Carmarthen is in southern Wales on the intersection of the north-south A484 with the A40/48. After his death, his son, Henry Tudor, Earl of Richmond, was born in **Pembroke Castle**—see *Lady Margaret Beaufort*.

Edmund is interred in **St. David's Cathedral**, the largest church in Wales. The see was traditionally founded by St. David about 550. The present building was begun in 1180 and mostly finished 200 years later, the Lady Chapel being added in the early 1500s. The situation is rather bleak, almost at the furthest point west on a bare plateau above the river Alun, swept by weather off the Atlantic Ocean. The town of St. David's is very small, just above the size of a village, although called a city because of the presence of the cathedral. Visit the cathedral at http://www.stdavidscathedral.org.uk/.

Jasper Tudor, Earl of Pembroke, fought in the Wars of the Roses on the Lancastrian side. He held **Denbigh Castle** (see above) for the Lancastrians, and also raised his nephew Henry Tudor, whom he took with him into exile in Brittany. On their return from France, Jasper and Henry won the day on **Bosworth Field** (see *Henry VII*). He followed Margaret of Anjou and held Bamburgh Castle for her—for this striking castle on the Northumberland coast, see *Henry VI*.

Jasper became the first in the long line of Dukes of Bedford. In 1488 he was given **Cardiff Castle**. The castle is, unusually, situated right near the city center of busy Cardiff, the capital of Wales with a population of over 300,000. Visit Cardiff Castle at http://www.castlewales.com/cardiff.html.

He was buried in **Keynsham Abbey**, near Bristol. In the 1960s, the abbey's demolition (begun in 1776) was completed when a bypass was made through the former site.

Margaret Beaufort

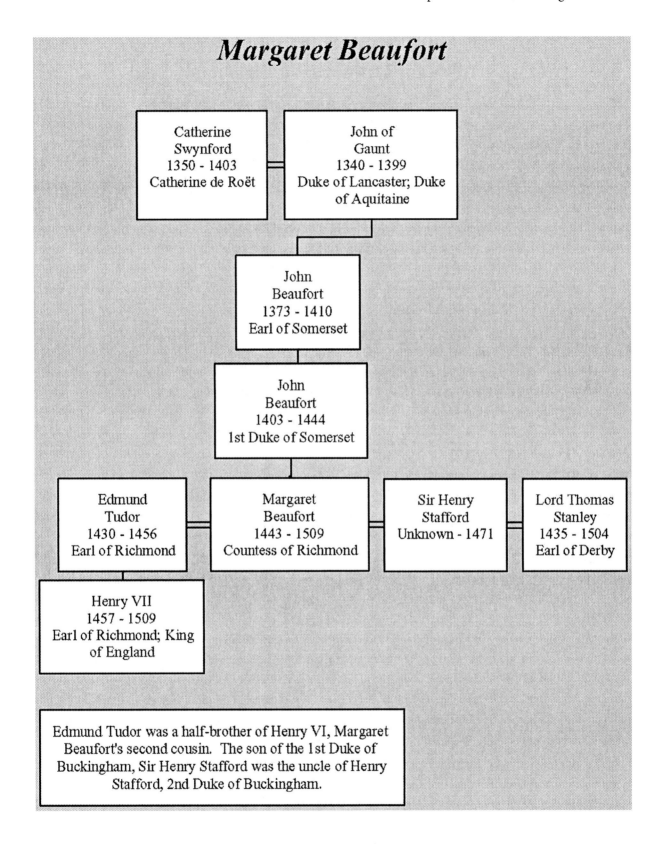

Catherine
Swynford
1350 - 1403
Catherine de Roët

John of
Gaunt
1340 - 1399
Duke of Lancaster; Duke
of Aquitaine

John
Beaufort
1373 - 1410
Earl of Somerset

John
Beaufort
1403 - 1444
1st Duke of Somerset

Edmund
Tudor
1430 - 1456
Earl of Richmond

Margaret
Beaufort
1443 - 1509
Countess of Richmond

Sir Henry
Stafford
Unknown - 1471

Lord Thomas
Stanley
1435 - 1504
Earl of Derby

Henry VII
1457 - 1509
Earl of Richmond; King
of England

Edmund Tudor was a half-brother of Henry VI, Margaret
Beaufort's second cousin. The son of the 1st Duke of
Buckingham, Sir Henry Stafford was the uncle of Henry
Stafford, 2nd Duke of Buckingham.

Lady Margaret Beaufort, Countess of Richmond (1443–1509)

"For the children of this world are wiser in their generation than are the children of light."

Were it not for the devotion of Margaret Beaufort and Jasper Tudor to the ambitions of the Earl of Richmond, Henry Tudor, he would never have become Henry VII, and neither Henry VIII nor Elizabeth I would have fascinated the ages. The barely pubescent Margaret Beaufort, already a widow to Edmund Tudor in 1456, gave birth to her only child, Henry, in 1457. Later, as the wife of Sir Henry Stafford and then of Thomas, Lord Stanley, the Lancastrian Margaret apparently made peace with her Yorkist kin. The death of Edward IV, the deposition and disappearance of his heir Edward V, and the usurpation of his brother Richard III activated Margaret's energetic support of Henry Tudor's regal ambitions. After his accession in 1485, the King's mother exercised an unique influence over him until his death, shortly before her own. Besides her political activities, Margaret Beaufort translated and patronized literature, financed printing, founded chantries as well as Christ's and St. John's Colleges at Cambridge, and as a great landowner shrewdly managed vast estates. Her tiny but powerful figure united many apparent polarities. Most striking of the polarities she lived out in her 66 years were her intense involvement with her religion and, always intertwined with this, her perennial presence in the thick of the murderous dynastic struggles of her relatives.

Studded with saints, her life could serve as a précis of the Christian faith of the 15th century. Margaret Beaufort was given to many acts of piety, to regular devotions, and to charitable beneficence. The circumstances of her life also exposed her—from nearby or at a distance—to figures currently and later revered for sanctity. After her father's death in 1444, Henry VI made Margaret the ward of William de la Pole, Earl of Suffolk, the implacable antagonist of St. Joan of Arc. Margaret as a young widow with a posthumous child born in 1457 would later name her baby Henry after the same Henry VI—whose reputation for sanctity almost rivaled his renown for political fatuity. Much later in life, Margaret would take as her confessor John Fisher, whom she urged her grandson, the young Henry VIII, to obey in all things. Henry VIII would instead propel Fisher towards canonization by executing this courageous defender of Queen Catherine of Aragon and denigrator of the royal supremacy over the Church in England.

Margaret's closeness to Fisher, in particular, underscored her deep concern with the unworldly. Yet her family heritage, her marriages, and her advocacy of her child, Henry Tudor, Earl of Richmond, could serve as a veritable index to the vagaries of the Lancastrian/York conflict and to its eventual resolution in the establishment of the Tudor dynasty. A daughter of the Beaufort house born on the wrong side of the blanket during John of Gaunt's prolonged affair with Catherine Swynford, Margaret was naturally a Lancastrian by blood. Her 1455 marriage to Edmund Tudor, Earl of Richmond, half-brother to Henry VI, bonded her even more to the Lancastrian side. Henry VI, her brother-in-law as well as her second cousin, in urging Edmund to marry Margaret, may even have intended to make his half-brother his heir in the right of Margaret Beaufort.

The eventual birth of the Prince of Wales, Edward of Lancaster, to Henry VI's Queen Margaret of Anjou, in 1453 made all such shifts to create a Lancastrian succession seemingly unnecessary. Moreover, Henry VI's saintly incompetence and the ambitions of Richard, Duke of York, to supplant Edward of Lancaster as the heir ended in the political maelstrom of the Wars of the Roses. The accession of Edward IV in 1461 and the dominance of the York dynasty necessitated Margaret's coming to terms with her Yorkist relatives through her next husband, Sir Henry Stafford. Her father-in-law, Humphrey Stafford, the first Duke of Buckingham, was another antagonist of Joan of Arc; her husband's nephew and namesake, Henry Stafford, the second Duke, was a protégé of Edward IV, as well as the ally of Richard III. Margaret became a widow for the second time when Sir Henry Stafford died from wounds suffered from fighting for Edward IV at Barnet.

As the young widow of Edmund Tudor, she had proposed the 1459 marriage to Henry Stafford, which turned out to be a close and happy union. As the widow of Henry Stafford, she again made terms with her Yorkist relatives by marrying in 1482 an ally of Edward IV and the steward of his household, Thomas, Lord Stanley, the Earl of Derby. When Richard III came to power, Stanley played an equivocal role. Stanley, who became steward of Richard's household, carried Richard's mace at the coronation, and Margaret carried Queen Anne Neville's train. Yet Margaret's involvement in her nephew Buckingham's failed rebellion caused Richard to attaint her and to jail her in the keeping of her husband. Undeterred, Margaret conspired with Bishop John Morton to supplant Richard III with her son, Henry Tudor, and Stanley won the battle of Bosworth Field in 1485 for his stepson Henry by delaying his participation until he could effectively betray Richard by turning the tide.

Not only a conspirator and financier of a rebellion and invasion, Margaret was also a dynasty-maker. Years before the accession of Richard III, Margaret had discussed with Edward IV the possibility of uniting the Lancaster and York strains by marrying Princess Elizabeth of York to Henry Tudor. Now, with Richard III in power, she resumed those negotiations with Edward IV's widow, Elizabeth Woodville.

With Henry VII married to Elizabeth, Margaret's influence on both made her a formidable figure at court and in the land. Tragically for her, she outlived both her son and her daughter-in-law, being named as the chief executor of Henry VII's will and seeing her grandson begin his gaudy career as Henry VIII.

How do we reconcile the unworldly and devout Lady Margaret with this portrait of a mover and shaker whose designs had crucial impact on the death throes of the House of York and the birth pangs of the Tudor dynasty? Perhaps we could say that Lady Margaret Beaufort both enjoyed and was fit for the exercise of power, both spiritual and political, and that she saw no such contradictions between spirituality and clout. The undoubted goodness and piety of her kinsman Henry VI had undermined his political acumen. The effective and ferocious political leadership of his Queen, Margaret of Anjou, had seemed to dismiss the spiritual realm. In contrast, Margaret Beaufort comfortably united religiosity with an appetite for power.

The historians and biographers admire her as a formidable woman, who even gained the right to hold property and to sue, giving her an unique legal status. Their questions center upon what reading to give the ambiguous evidence about certain matters: (1) how valid did the Beaufort claim to the throne seem to contemporaries?; (2) did Henry VII base his claim upon his Beaufort descent or not?; (3) what was the exact nature and extent of Margaret Beaufort's influence upon Henry VII?

Cicely Neville, the mother of Edward IV and Richard III, came from an older generation of Beauforts. The granddaughter of John of Gaunt, Cicely was Margaret's father's first cousin and thus Margaret's first cousin once removed. Both were mothers and grandmothers of Kings. Moreover, these blood cousins were further related by the marriage of Henry Tudor to Elizabeth of York, for Margaret was Elizabeth's mother-in-law and Cicely Elizabeth's grandmother. Thus Henry VIII had Margaret Beaufort as a grandmother and Cicely Neville as a great-grandmother. When this matriarch of the York dynasty died in 1495, her will left to Margaret a breviary bound in cloth of gold. Was this elegant gift in itself emblematic of the contradictions Margaret Beaufort embodied?

Lady Margaret Beaufort Sites

The castle at **Bletsoe**, a village seven miles north of Bedford and just off the A6, is considered to be Lady Margaret's birthplace. Her mother was the daughter of Sir John Beauchamp of Bletsoe, whose first husband, Sir Oliver St. John, from whom she was widowed, was also of Bletsoe. The only remains of the castle belong to the house built on the site. Further details about Bletsoe can be found at http://www.dawson98.freeserve.co.uk/NewFiles/Bletsoe.html.

Margaret may have spent much of her early childhood in the villages called **the Deepings:** East and West Deeping, Deeping Gate, and Deeping St James. Among the many estates inherited from her maternal grandmother, Margaret Holland, were land and property in the Deepings, thus earning her the right to an ancient title, Lady of Deeping. She took a particular interest in the priory at Deeping St. James, allowing, for example, the monks to use her own mill when theirs was out of action. When she founded the preachership at Cambridge University, the church at Deeping St. James was one of those listed to receive six sermons per year by the holder of the preachership.

The villages with Deeping in their names are clustered north of Peterborough, around the intersection of the A15 and A16. The website for Deeping St. James is http://www.users.zetnet.co.uk/mwarrick/history/, which gives a detailed history and illustrated tour of the Priory Church at Deeping St. James. For further information regarding the Deepings, see *Edward the Black Prince*.

Margaret's son, Henry VII, was born at **Pembroke Castle**, at the time owned by her brother-in-law, Jasper Tudor, Earl of Pembroke. Margaret's first husband, Edmund Tudor, had sent her there for protection. A room in the Henry VII Tower claims to be where she gave birth, although one website (http://www. castlewales.com/pembroke.html) casts doubt on this, calling it a "most unlikely birthplace, and [it] is to be hoped that his mother…was given more consideration." The same site gives a good description, with photographs, and history of the castle. Surrounded on three sides by river, the castle is strategically located in southwest Wales to overlook not only local traffic but also that from Ireland. Its massive structure dates from Norman times. Of special note are the huge Keep and Gatehouse, and the Wogan, a natural cave over which the castle was constructed. The cave overlooks the river, and there is a spiral staircase leading from it up into the castle.

Lady Margaret inherited estates too numerous to be mentioned here. One of them is **Corfe Castle** (see *John*). Nearby is **Wimborne,** an ancient town centered on its fine Minster, established about 1043. The greater part of the church we see today was built between 1120 and 1180. Margaret's parents are buried at Wimborne Minster, her father having died in 1444 and her mother in 1482. Along with the monuments to her parents in the presbytery, attractions of the Minster are the chained library and the 16th century clock in the west tower. In 1496, Margaret endowed a chantry in Wimborne Minster, with a priest who was to pray for herself and her parents and to "teach grammar to all comers." This formed the basis of what became a grammar school, taking the name Queen Elizabeth from Elizabeth I, bestowed in 1562. More information on the school can be found at http://www.qe.dorset.sch.uk/qe500/school.htm and http://www.qe.dorset.sch.uk/qe500/tradition.htm, in which there is a school song where she is referred to as "the good Lady Meg."

Torrington (or **Great Torrington**) is near the attractive west coast towns of Appledore and Clovelly, a few miles inland from Bideford. Its manor and church were properties of Margaret's, and the subject of an anecdote illustrating her thoughtfulness and generosity, when she bestowed her manor house on the parish priest. There is a 19th century carved stone head of Lady Margaret by the west door of the chuch (the other is of Cardinal Wolsey). The present vicarage, dating from the 19th century, occupies the site of her manor house. A detailed description of the old church, which dates from the 13th century, with photographs, can be found at http://www.great-torrington.com/.

The village of **Collyweston** also saw a palace owned by Margaret. Today's Collyweston is still a stone-built village, known more for its stone roofing slates, manufactured from medieval times, than for its architectural distinction. The remnants of the palace comprise terraces, fishponds, a barn with a dovecote, and a sundial which dates from the 18th century. Collyweston is 5 miles southwest of Stamford, extending on each side on the A43.

The two sites most notably associated with Margaret are, of course, Christ's College and St. John's College at **Cambridge University**. A visit to this great university, with its many beautiful buildings attractively set in town, river, and gardens, is essential. Visitors should not miss King's College Chapel, one of the most exquisite buildings in England, and should make sure that their walking tour includes the Backs, the tree-shaded grounds along the river Cam and on other side of the river, providing fine views of the buildings themselves. Several bridges from the colleges provide access, notably the Bridge of Sighs at St. John's College (see below).

Christ's College was established in 1505 when Margaret refounded the college of God's House (first established in the mid-15th century), naming it Christ's College. Her figure stands in a niche in the entrance gate. The oldest part of the college is the chapel, dating back to the foundation of God's House, rebuilt under Margaret and consecrated in 1510. It contains some of the oldest stained glass in Cambridge. Monuments relating to Margaret include a portrait above the arch, and, in the east window, her figure appears with those of Bishop John Fisher and Henry VI below the figure of Christ. High on the south wall is an oriel window, originally the window of Lady Margaret's oratory; supposedly she used this in order to join in services.

The home page for Christ's College is http://www.christs.cam.ac.uk, with links to much useful information, although a tad short on illustration. Both it and St. John's have fine chapels and choirs, and music lovers should try to attend a chapel service where the choir is to take part.

St. John's College is a handsomer college than Christ's. St. John's College was founded in 1511, replacing the 13th century Hospital of St. John. The hospital survived until the 16th century in a much dilapidated state, when it came to the attention of John Fisher, who persuaded Margaret to refound the Hospital as a College. Unfortunately she died in 1509 before any progress had been made on this new plan; the Charter of the College of St John the Evangelist was finally granted in 1511. The Front Gate is richly carved with yales (mythical beasts) supporting Margaret's coat of arms. The Second Court contains beautiful Elizabethan brickwork. Otherwise, the Hall and the Combination Room both contain fine paneling. One of the most attractive sights is the so-called Bridge of Sighs across the river Cam, named for its supposed resemblance to the Bridge of Sighs in Venice. Regardless, it is a pretty sight. It links the Third Court to the New Court, and is a picturesque way not only to get from the one to the other, but also to access the "Backs." Visit the college at http://www.joh.cam.ac.uk/; see http://www.cambridge2000.com/cambridge2000/html/0007/P7281904.html for photographs of the college.

Visitors have to be mindful that the colleges are places of study and work, and can be closed during examinations, for example, or at other times.

Lady Margaret's Readerships were established in 1502 at both Oxford and Cambridge. At Cambridge, John Fisher was the first holder; traditionally, he was followed by Erasmus of Rotterdam, but this is now thought not to be the case. Continuing to the present day, the readerships are now known as **Lady Margaret's Professorships in Divinity**. A list containing most of the holders of the Cambridge professorship can be found at http://www.divinity.cam.ac.uk/LM500/lmprofs_prominent.html.

Lady Margaret Hall, Oxford University, the first women's college at Oxford, was founded in 1878 and named after Margaret Beaufort. Neo-Georgian and elegant, the college is set in 14 acres of garden extending down to the river. It has been coeducational since 1979. Visit Lady Margaret Hall at http://www.lmh.ox.ac.uk.

Margaret died either at **Baynard's Castle** or the Deans' House at Westminster Abbey. For basic information about the castle, see *William the Conqueror*. She is buried at **Westminster Abbey**, in the Henry VII chapel. Her finely modelled tomb by Pietro Torrigiano shows a recumbent figure in gilt-bronze, with especially delicate modelling of the hands.

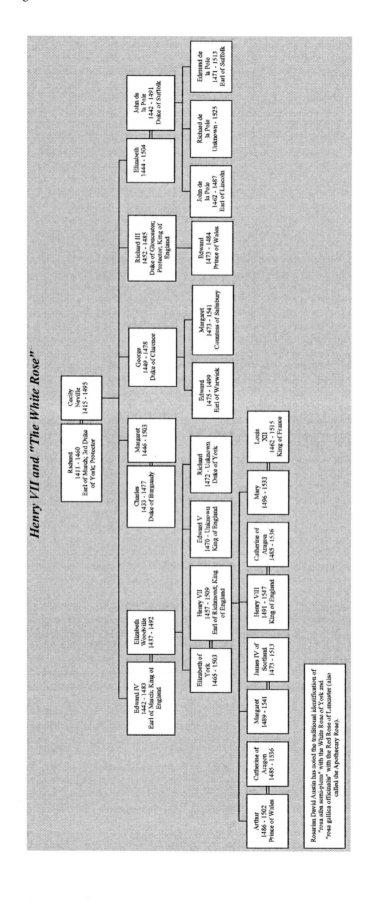

Henry VII and "The White Rose"

Rosarian David Austin has noted the traditional identification of "rosa alba semi-plena" with the White Rose of York and "rosa gallica officinalis" with the Red Rose of Lancaster (also called the Apothecary Rose).

Henry VII (1457–1509; King of England and Lord of Ireland, 1485–1509)

One of the most remarkable sovereigns ever to rule in England, Henry VII built the Tudor dynasty in the rubble of civil war, succeeding as King of England despite his sparse knowledge of the country and no experience or training for his role. The success he achieved required that he ruthlessly put down any domestic opposition, raise his status among the other princes of Europe with alliances and diplomatic marriages, and restore solvency to royal finances. His first steps in gaining acceptance for his reign involved claiming the throne by right of conquest at Bosworth Field over the slain Richard III in 1485 and, as the Lancastrian conqueror, marrying Edward IV's daughter and Richard III's niece Elizabeth of York shortly afterwards. Despite this reward to those Yorkists who had conspired against Richard III, Henry VII had reconciled York and Lancaster only on the surface. "The White Rose" would resprout again and again in his reign—threatening the survival of the dynasty begun with the 1486 birth of his heir, Arthur.

Henry VII had claimed the throne as a conqueror, probably because he had only the starved shadow of a claim by lineage through his Lancastrian ancestry. His father's being half-brother to the last Lancastrian King, Henry VI, brought Henry Tudor no right to the throne, and his mother's descent from John of Gaunt, Duke of Lancaster, provided only a questionable claim. In any case, other Lancastrian descendants could boast superior credentials by pedigree. While Queen Elizabeth of York, as daughter to Edward IV, possessed a claim, Richard III had bastardized her and all her siblings on the grounds of the purported invalidity of Edward IV's marriage to Elizabeth Woodville. Henry quietly had that Act nullified by Parliament but also avoided basing his own right to the crown on hers.

As a conquering usurper, Henry VII remained quite vulnerable to challenge by other aspirants seeking to imitate his success. Yorkists resentful of his de facto assumption of kingship strove to replant "The White Rose" several times. After the death of Richard III's son, Edward, Prince of Wales, in 1484, Richard III had named his nephew John de la Pole, Earl of Lincoln, his heir presumptive. Another name to rally disaffected Yorkists belonged to Edward, Earl of Warwick, another nephew and possible heir presumptive to Richard III, taken into custody after Bosworth and imprisoned in the Tower of London. John de la Pole, his brother Edmund, and Warwick would all figure in Yorkist insurrections against Henry VII—either as inspiring figures or as actual participants.

So would Elizabeth of York's brothers, the "Princes in the Tower," Edward V and Richard, Duke of York. Although they had disappeared from sight during the reign of Richard III, no one really knows what happened to them. Rumors had alleged that Richard III murdered them; other rumors reported that the Princes had survived to live abroad. Once Henry VII had nullified the Act bastardizing the Princes and his own wife, any news of the continued existence of her brothers threatened his own hold on the crown. His mother-in-law, Elizabeth Woodville, apparently supported the insurrection of the Yorkist pretender Lambert Simnel. The Princes' paternal aunt, Margaret, Duchess of Burgundy, vigorously supported both Simnel and the later Yorkist pretender Perkin Warbeck. In light of this, some have identified these pretenders as the Princes themselves, fighting to secure their rights and then being defeated and discredited by Henry VII as imposters.

Whether the Yorkist insurrections supported Warwick, the de la Poles, Edward V, or Richard, Duke of York, they attracted relatively few supporters in England and Wales but much foreign interest and financing. In 1487, Lambert Simnel allegedly claimed the crown as Edward, Earl of Warwick, and was crowned as "Edward VI" in Christ Church Cathedral in Dublin. John de la Pole, Earl of Lincoln, conspired to promote Simnel's invasion of England. After defeat at Stoke, where John de la Pole died, Simnel fell into Henry VII's custody. The King imprisoned Simnel but then pardoned him and afterwards promoted him from work in the royal kitchens to falconry. Both Elizabeth Woodville and Margaret of Burgundy had supported Simnel's conspiracy; some think that the original Simnel truly was the elder Prince, Edward V, and that Henry VII substituted a person of baser origins to serve him as an exposed imposter.

A decade later, in 1497, a second Yorkist pretender, Perkin Warbeck, invaded Cornwall. For several years, Warbeck had claimed to be Richard, Duke of York, the younger Prince—a claim considered by the Holy Roman Emperor Maximilian I, the husband of Mary of Burgundy, stepdaughter to the Princes' paternal aunt Margaret of Burgundy. Not only did Margaret and Maximilian support Warbeck, but so did Maximilian's son Archduke Philip of the Netherlands, as well as Charles VIII of France. In 1495, Henry VII executed Sir William Stanley for his conspiracy in support of Warbeck. Warbeck eventually took refuge in Scotland, where, befriended by James IV, he married James IV's cousin Catherine Gordon, sister of the Earl of Huntly. In 1496, James IV of Scotland actually invaded England, but in 1497 he expelled Warbeck from Scotland. During Warbeck's subsequent invasion of Cornwall (as "Richard IV"), he landed near Land's End. Proclaimed King at Bodmin but defeated at Exeter, Warbeck moved to Taunton and then to Beaulieu in Hampshire. The captured Warbeck allegedly confessed himself an imposter. After some months in loose custody at Henry VII's court, Warbeck was arrested after an escape attempt and imprisoned in the Tower of London. He and his fellow prisoner, the mentally retarded Edward, Earl of Warwick, supposedly plotted there against Henry VII, which led to their 1499 execution. So far from his being another fraud, some believe that Perkin Warbeck really was Richard, Duke of York.

Having disposed of Warwick, John de la Pole, Lambert Simnel, and Perkin Warbeck, Henry VII still had to contend with other members of the de la Pole family as well as unhelpful foreign monarchs eager to destabilize his rule and weaken England. From 1501, Edmund de la Pole, Earl of Suffolk, conspired against Henry VII at the court of the Holy Roman Emperor Maximilian. (Louis XII of France would recognize Richard de la Pole as "Richard IV" of England.) When Maximilian's son Archduke Philip of the Netherlands (Philip I of Castile by virtue of his marriage to Joanna of Castile) visited England, Henry persuaded Philip to turn Edmund de la Pole over to him. After this 1506 surrender into Henry VII's custody, Edmund de la Pole remained in the Tower of London until his 1513 execution by Henry VIII. (Henry VIII would also rid himself of Warwick's sister Margaret, the elderly Countess of Salisbury, by having her executed on trumped up charges in 1541.) Because of supposed treasonous activity involving Edmund de la Pole and the Emperor Maximilian, Henry VII also imprisoned Sir James Tyrell in the Tower in 1502; before Tyrell's execution, he confessed to murdering the Princes in 1483 at the direction of Richard III. Some find the timing and content of this belated and dubious confession highly convenient for a King recently threatened by insurrections in the Princes' names.

Henry VII himself had won his throne as an usurper aided by France and Brittany. In one way or another, he fought off all of these challengers encouraged and financed by foreign monarchs. In addition, he negotiated his way to a respected place among European rulers. His diplomacy tried to arrange several advantageous marriages for Henry's children and for the King himself once Elizabeth of York had died after childbirth in 1503 on her 37th birthday. In that same year, Margaret Tudor—the King's elder surviving daughter—married James IV of Scotland in Holyroodhouse. Two years before, Arthur, Prince of Wales, had wed a daughter of Ferdinand and Isabella of Spain, Catherine of Aragon, after Henry, Duke of York, walked the bride up the aisle of St. Paul's. This marriage, first negotiated in 1489, soon withered with Arthur's death in 1502 in Ludlow Castle. Catherine of Aragon's subsequent betrothal to the new Prince of Wales, Arthur's younger brother Henry, endured many uncertainties until their eventual marriage in 1509 after Henry VII's death. Mary Tudor—the King's younger surviving daughter—became the focus of diplomacy designed to marry her to the son of Philip and Joanna of Castile, the Archduke Charles, later the Holy Roman Emperor Charles V. Although betrothed to Charles in 1507, Mary never actually married him. (Pressured by her brother Henry VIII to marry Louis XII of France, the soon-widowed Mary Tudor then married for love Charles Brandon,

Duke of Suffolk, a son of William Brandon, Henry Tudor's standard bearer slain at Bosworth by Richard III.)

Henry VII considered several potential second wives for himself, but he never remarried. (After Philip I of Castile died in 1506, Henry proposed that he marry Philip's widow, Joanna of Castile—Catherine of Aragon's sister.) The King sank into noticeable decline after Arthur, Prince of Wales, and Elizabeth of York died. Always careful with money, as well as highly successful in returning the Crown to the rare state of solvency it had enjoyed under his father-in-law Edward IV, he became in his last years avaricious and grasping. Although the Venetian envoy in 1509 described the late King as "a very great miser but a man of vast ability," miserliness characterized his failing years only.

He died at Richmond, a palace he erected on the site of a favorite residence, Sheen, after its destruction by fire. The former Earl of Richmond also rebuilt Baynard's Castle and Greenwich (his Queen's favorite) and enjoyed both Eltham (where his children received their education) and Woodstock. Besides finishing the St. George's Chapel begun by Edward IV at Windsor, Henry VII envisioned a shrine to his uncle Henry VI that eventually became the Chapel of Henry VII at Westminster Abbey. His efforts to have Henry VI canonized sank in the mud of Roman inaction.

Henry VII prevailed over tremendous odds and deserves recognition as one of England's most successful Kings. In digging a deep foundation for his insecure dynasty, he crushed Yorkist challengers without pity and may have sent his brothers-in-law, among other bearers of "The White Rose," to their graves.

Henry VII Sites

Henry was born in **Pembroke Castle**. For details regarding the castle, see *Lady Margaret Beaufort*. He spent a large portion of his childhood in **Harlech Castle**; see *Edward I*. Henry also spent time in **Raglan Castle**; go to http://www.castlewales.com/raglan.html for a history and virtual tour. Raglan is a few miles southwest of Monmouth, off the A40 just after its junction with the A449. Raglan Castle retains an impressive amount of stonework and is strikingly situated; architecturally, it dates mainly from the 15th and 16th centuries, which lends it a combination of medieval fortified strength and later palatial accommodations.

Henry sailed from **Harfleur** on August 1, 1485 after 13 years in exile in France. For basic information about Harfleur, see *Henry V*. He landed at **Milford Haven**, south Wales (see *Henry II*).

On his way to Bosworth, Henry lodged in a large, three-story half-timbered house, dating from about 1430, in **Shrewsbury**. The house, named Henry Tudor House, is at 72 Wyle Cop, below the old Lion Hotel. At http://www.pbase.com/bmcmorrow/shrewsbury, you will see photographs of the house, along with those of other old buildings in Shrewsbury.

For Shrewsbury generally, see *Edward I*.

At **Bosworth Field**, Henry became Henry VII by defeating and killing Richard III. For Bosworth, see *Edward V/Richard III*. Henry's standard, depicting the dragon of Wales, fulfilled a longstanding Welsh legend that a Welshman would occupy the British throne, based on Merlin's prophecy regarding the two sleeping dragons, one red and one white, who, when awakened, fought, the red dragon prevailing.

In gratitude for the support of the Welsh, Henry is traditionally supposed to have presented the 14th century Church of St. Peter at **Ruthin** with the beautiful oak roof in the north aisle (at that time the nave), containing over 400 carved panels, no two of them the same. Ruthin, an attractive town with several interesting old buildings, stands on a hill overlooking the river Clwyd, south of Denbigh on the A525. Its personable website, at http://www.ruthin-wales.co.uk/ruthintc2/vtour3.htm, contains many photographs; the church is "toured" on the second page of the virtual tour.

After Bosworth, trouble arose in the form of a rebellion around the pretender Lambert Simnel, crowned in Dublin by his followers as "Edward VI." The two armies met near the village of **Stoke** in 1487 for the last battle in the War of the Roses. For online information and a plan of the battle (especially the latter because the former is extremely difficult to read), see http://www.tudorplace.com.ar/Documents/the_battle_of_stoke.htm; the written information at http://www.fari.org/sites/eaststoke/stokefields/stokefield.htm is not only readable but more detailed. Simnel had a relatively merciful end: he was captured, and, Henry deeming him a harmless boy, put him to work in the royal kitchens. The site of the battlefield, Stoke Fields, is on the south side of the A46 from **East Stoke**, which stands astride the A46 a few miles south of Newark-on-Trent.

The hapless Perkin Warbeck, the other pretender, was evidently not deemed harmless by Henry. He met Henry at **Taunton** Castle in 1497 and was imprisoned in the Tower of London, to be executed at **Tyburn**. Tyburn, or Tyburnia, was where so many were hanged, the gallows standing on the site of Marble Arch. The restored Taunton Castle now houses the Somerset County Museum and a hotel. See photographs of the castle at http://www.ecastles.co.uk/taunton.html and read historical information, with a diagram of the original, at http://www.britannia.com/history/somerset/castles/tauntoncast.html, and visit the hotel at http://www.the-castle-hotel.com. Taunton is the county town of Somerset, with about 60,000 inhabitants; it lies to the south of the Bristol Channel and is easily reached off the M5.

Elizabeth of York was born in **Westminster Palace** (see *William the Conqueror*) in 1466. Henry and she were married in 1486 at **Westminster Abbey**. Later, Henry was to add significantly to the abbey with his beautiful Henry VII Chapel in the east end, where they are both buried (see below).

Henry established the world's first dry dock at **Portsmouth** by 1490, and declared the port a royal dockyard and garrison. This was the beginning of the importance of Portsmouth, previously a small town, and it became the chief naval base, which it remains today. Today's Portsmouth is a city of 180,000 population on the peninsula of Portsea Island, at the mouth of the Portsmouth harbor, where this meets Spithead; the city includes the resort of Southsea and Gosport, across the mouth of the harbor. The Tudor fortifications are still a feature of Portsmouth. See http://www.historicdockyard.co.uk/welcome.html, the website for Portsmouth Historic Dockyard, with links for attractions and tours; http://www.flagship.org.uk/short_history.htm for a history of the docks; and http://www.portsmouthand.co.uk/ for visiting Portsmouth itself. The old *Mary Rose* and Nelson's HMS *Victory* are to be seen refitted as they were when actively used, among other attractions.

Henry often stayed at **Eltham Palace**, and carried out extensive renovations. For details regarding the palace and a virtual tour, see *Edward II*. The palace at **Greenwich** had been Bella Court, which Margaret of Anjou had improved. After the Wars of the Roses, the palace became royal property, and it became known as Placentia (or Pleasance). Henry changed the name to Greenwich Palace and refaced the building in red brick. For more about Greenwich Palace, see *Henry VIII*. His main residence in London was **Baynard's Castle** (see *William I*).

At Richmond, **Sheen Palace** burned down in 1499. Henry then built another palace on the site and called it **Richmond Palace**, after his previous title as Earl of Richmond. Sheen had been essentially a manor house; now Henry, normally so careful with money, wanted a palace. Richmond Palace was a huge, beautiful place of numerous turrets, pinnacles, domes, and many windows, with galleries and loggias extending into the gardens and orchards. It boasted spring water piped into the palace, and its chapel contained pews, an innovation at the time. See http://tudorhistory.org/castles/richmond/ for the building or Richmond with links to illustrations at Richmond Palace Gallery, and http://www.plus44.com/royal/richmond/richmopal.html for a more general history of Sheen and Richmond, along with more images. More information follows at *Henry VIII*.

At the **Tower of London**, Henry added a new private chamber, library, long gallery, and garden, centered on the **Lanthorn Tower**, part of the complex called the Medieval Palace. See the Lanthorn Tower at http://www.camelotintl.com/tower_site/tower/twrlanth.html, and read about Henry's additions in the context of the development of the Tower as a whole at http://www.castles.org/castles/Europe/Western_Europe/United_Kingdom/England/england12.htm. At **Hampton Court**, the surrounding land was leased from the owners, the Knights Hospitallers, by Sir Giles Daubeney, Henry's Lord Chamberlain. He then enclosed 300 acres as a deer park. The present Home Park at Hampton Court may also have been deer parkland for Sir Giles. For Hampton Court, see *Henry VIII*.

At **Windsor Castle**, Henry rebuilt the old chapel (now the **Albert Memorial Chapel**) behind St. George's Chapel and added a new range of buildings west of the state apartments. The intricate vault of the nave in **St. George's Chapel** was probably completed during the last years of Henry's reign; a major contributor to the work was Sir Reginald Bray, one of Henry's supporters. For detail regarding St. George's Chapel, see *Edward IV*. Under Henry's patronage, the stone fabric of **King's College Chapel**, **Cambridge**, left unfinished when Henry VI died, was completed. See *Henry VI*.

Henry's masterpiece, his lasting contribution, is the **Henry VII Chapel** in **Westminster Abbey**, sometimes called the Lady Chapel, in the east end of the abbey. Henry originally intended it as a burial place for Henry VI, whom he hoped would be canonised. That never taking place, Henry then decided that his chapel would make a suitable resting place for himself and his family. The result is a chapel with the size and proportions of a large church, and one that is exceptionally beautiful, with exquisite fan-vaulting, fine carving, and statuary, let alone the bronze gates and splendid tombs. The first person buried there was Elizabeth of York, Henry joining her six years later. Many royals have taken their places in the chapel since, and a small chapel at the east end is dedicated to the memory of members of the Royal Air Force killed in the 1940 Battle of Britain. Since 1725, the chapel has played host to the Order of the Bath, a chivalric order going back to the Middle Ages. The present Grand Master of the Order is Charles, Prince of Wales. The baptismal font for the abbey is housed in the chapel. View the chapel at http://www.westminster-abbey.org/tour/lady_chapel/.

Elizabeth of York died in the **Tower of London**, and her body lay in state in the Chapel of St. John the Evangelist in the White Tower, before burial in the Henry VII Chapel. Henry died at his creation, **Richmond Palace**, and is buried with Elizabeth in Westminster Abbey.

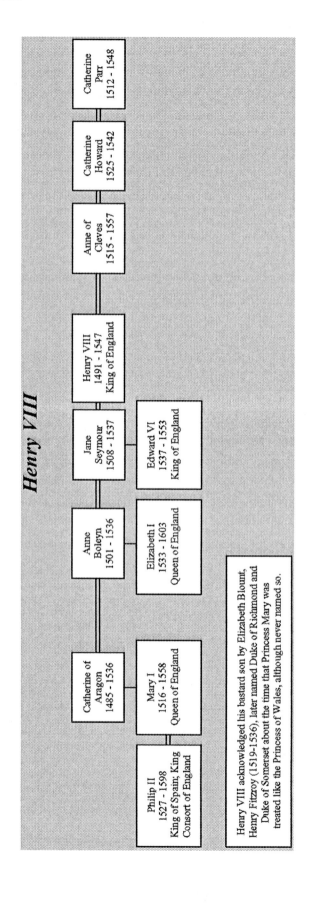

Henry VIII acknowledged his bastard son by Elizabeth Blount, Henry Fitzroy (1519-1536), later named Duke of Richmond and Duke of Somerset about the time that Princess Mary was treated like the Princess of Wales, although never named so.

Henry VIII (1491–1547; King of England and Lord, then King of Ireland, 1509–1547)

When the Victorian novelist Anthony Trollope portrayed a husband so obsessed with unjust suspicion about his wife's fidelity that he destroys his marriage, his family life, and his own sanity, Trollope called this novel *He Knew He Was Right*. Rather than admit any doubt of his own perceptions and judgments, the husband obstinately clings to them regardless of consequences. Henry VIII likewise exalted his own perceptions and judgments to an extreme degree. King by divine right, he also exhibited a personality prone to self-exaltation and avoidant of self-questioning. His role and his personality in total, fatal conjunction, *he knew he was right*.

His identity as a royal personage signified to him a special closeness to his God denied to less favored mortals. To Henry, it seemed that God invariably approved of Henry's decisions. As Henry noted to the ambassador of the Holy Roman Emperor, Charles V, "God and my conscience are on perfectly good terms." The fact that his conscience predictably justified Henry's appetites for women, revenge, loot, and power, although obvious to others, did not trouble the King. He identified his self-will with his conscience and his conscience with the divine will. In a sense, Henry had too much conscience rather than too little. Lacey Baldwin Smith explained "his compulsive need to wall out doubt by keeping conscience clear and placing blame on others" and depicted him as a "man of conscience…set upon convincing himself of his innocence."

God expected much of Henry as a King and would punish Henry more severely than lesser mortals if he failed. Therefore, he did not fail. The failures were always those of others who had misled or tricked him into marrying his brother's widow, refusing to see the damnable sin he had innocently committed, or advising him wrongly about other matters. Because God's disapproval terrified Henry, the King always maintained a belief in his own goodness and moral superiority, in his unique knowledge of God's will that prevented him from wrongdoing except when misled by others. After he executed Thomas Cromwell in 1540, for example, the King complained that "by false accusations, they made me put to death the most faithful servant I ever had!" If Henry were wrong, he might incur damnation; therefore, Henry was never wrong.

Francis Hackett's witty summation noted, "To touch Henry on any point of his conduct was like turning the simplest of door-handles and setting off all the burglar alarms." Why could not others understand that he had innocently committed incest in agreeing to a diplomatic marriage with Catherine of Aragon, the widow of his brother Arthur? If in disagreeing about his need to annul this marriage, they deliberately left his soul in peril of hellfire, surely they—John Fisher, Bishop of Rochester; Sir Thomas More, former Lord Chancellor of England—must be evil and worthy only of death. Never mind, as Smith noted, that "the execution of More, Fisher, and the Carthusian monks was regarded as an act of barbarism which placed Henry beyond the pale of Christian civilization." Henry's second cousin Reginald Cardinal Pole commented, "[he has] torn like a wild beast the men who were the greatest honor to his kingdom."

Having rid himself of Catherine and bastardized their daughter Mary to solace his conscience, Henry then pursued a notorious marital career that further murdered his reputation. Like Catherine, Anne Boleyn failed to produce a living son. Henry again annulled his marriage, bastardized his daughter Elizabeth, and this time executed his Queen. A third try, with Jane Seymour, ended with a boy baby, Edward, but a dead mother. Next, Anne of Cleves, like Catherine the spouse in a diplomatic marriage, displeased Henry's amorous expectations. Never consummating their union, he again annulled his marriage, for a total of three annulments out of four weddings. The very young Catherine Howard unluckily attracted the King into wedlock, soon ruptured by evidence of her lively premarital sexual life and possible adultery. She lost her head at the block. Lastly, the already twice-widowed Catherine Parr made a good stepmother for Henry's three motherless children, as well as a good helpmeet to the King. She survived at least one vicious plot against her in which her husband had connived, and she outlived him, though not for long. Henry characteristically noted "his ill-luck in meeting with such ill-conditioned wives." Such was not the interpretation voiced by others.

Wooed for the King in the late 1530s after the death of Jane Seymour, Christina of Denmark, the widowed Duchess of Milan, allegedly evaded, "If I had two heads, one should be at his Grace's service." Asking the French ambassador if several potential French wives could be sent "on approval" for Henry's inspection, the King turned red at the reply, "Perhaps you would like to try them one after the other, and keep the one you found the most agreeable."

Henry pursued matrimony largely to secure the Tudor succession. Perhaps his conscience's ready approval of his drastic methods resulted from a secret awareness of the essential flimsiness of the Tudor claim to the English throne: thus the need for a son to rule after him, regardless of the price paid by Henry's wives and daughters, not to mention his subjects; thus the judicial murders of Plantagenet relatives who hardly posed a credible threat, such as the aged Margaret Pole, Countess of Salisbury, hacked to death at her 1541 execution.

The golden boy who had succeeded Henry VII became a much-feared tyrant; Smith described "a singular lack of proportion to Henry's intellectual and emotional approach to life which might have been acceptable in an adolescent or understandable in an undergraduate but was terrifying in royalty." If Henry possessed too much conscience rather than too little, his conscience nevertheless remained a shrunken thing, confused with his self-will and the divine will, made defensive and dishonest by his fear of divine anger. His conscience made him a judicial murderer. As Bernard Shaw wrote in another context, "The tragedy of such murders is that they are not committed by murderers. They are judicial murders, pious murders; and this contradiction at once brings an element of comedy into the tragedy: the angels may weep at the murder, but the gods laugh at the murderers." Henry was not simply a bad man but a good man made bad because of his fear of his own badness. *Corruptio optimi est pessima: The corruption of the best is the worst.*

Henry VIII Sites

Henry was born in **Greenwich Palace**, then known as the Palace of Placentia, in 1491. Greenwich, on the south bank of the Thames river, has been a royal domain since the times of Alfred. There was a manor house on this site in the 14th century. Henry V's brother, Humphrey, Duke of Gloucester, enclosed the park and developed it into a castle, which he named Bella Court. Henry VI's widow, Margaret of Anjou, annexed Bella Court after Duke Humphrey's death and dubbed it Placentia, or Pleasaunce, and under this name it became a favorite residence of the Tudors. (Henry's daughters Mary and Elizabeth were also born here, and his son Edward VI died here.) Here the papal legate dubbed Henry "Defender of the Faith," and it was here, ironically, that Henry's liaison with Anne Boleyn began, eventually leading to Henry's breach with Rome. Henry enlarged the castle, adding a tiltyard and an armory where craftsmen produced armor. The palace was ruined during the Commonwealth, its collections removed. The remains were incorporated into the Naval Hospital, which later became the Royal Naval College, now part of the Maritime Campus of the University of Greenwich. A history of Greenwich Palace, in two parts, can be read at http://www.britannia.com/history/londonhistory/grw-pal1.html. An image showing the Tudor palace is available at http://tudorhistory.org/castles/greenwich/gallery.html.

He was baptized in the church of **St. Alfege** at Greenwich. The earliest church on this site dated from 1012, with a newer church being constructed in 1290. This collapsed in 1710 and was replaced by the present church, created by Nicholas Hawksmoor. The church of St. Alfege's home page is at http://www.st-alfege.org/page1.htm. As a child, Henry lived at **Eltham Palace**. See *Edward II* for the Palace, and *Edward IV* for the Great Hall.

Henry's marriages to both Catherine of Aragon and Anne Boleyn took place in the **Tower of London**. For Anne's coronation, **St. Thomas's Tower** was largely rebuilt in order to accommodate high-ranking officials, and the **White Tower** saw renovations. Henry also built a large range of timber-framed lodgings against the wall of the Inmost Ward; these were demolished in 1846. Anne was tried in the Great Hall of the Tower and beheaded on Tower Green in 1536, her cousin and successor Catherine Howard following her a mere six years later.

Henry went from Windsor to **Woodstock**, to hunt with Anne Boleyn on the day Queen Catherine of Aragon was removed from his daily life. For basic information about Woodstock, see *Henry II*.

Whitehall Palace originated in a mansion purchased by Walter de Grey, Archbishop of York in 1240, which for nearly 300 years became the London residence, known as York Place, of his successors. When Wolsey succeeded to the Archbishopric in 1514, he enlarged and enriched it, adding to its grounds. When Henry seized the property in 1529, he renamed it Whitehall, a name then generally applied to any center of festivities, and acquired more land towards St. James's Park, on which he erected a bowling green, tiltyard, cockpit, and tennis courts. Whitehall sprawled over 23 acres, the buildings crammed with 2,000 rooms, many of them small and irregularly shaped; see a plan dating from the reign of Charles II at http://www.londonancestor.com/maps/whitehall-palace.htm. Whitehall became the chief residence of the court in London. Anne Boleyn was brought here on the day of her marriage to Henry in 1533; in 1536, Henry married Jane Seymour here, and it saw his own death in 1547. In the Privy Chamber stood Holbein's huge painting of the Tudor monarchs, Henry VII and Henry VIII, with their Queens.

Only the rebuilt **Banqueting House** remains of this great palace after it was burned to the ground in 1698. A detailed history and description of the palace can be read at http://www.solutions.co.uk/clients/hrp/bh/hista.htm. There is a model of the palace as it was in 1649 in the Museum of London. The latter is situated just south of the Barbican Center, off Aldersgate and the London Wall.

Henry is said to have met Wolsey at **Waltham Abbey**. Little remains of what was once a great and rich foundation, owning most of the land around: the 12th century nave survived to become the parish church and materials from the rest were used to construct the church tower. King Harold, who founded the abbey, is thought to have been buried there, and a stone memorializes this. Waltham Abbey, a market town, is in Essex and north of London, with, however, a country atmosphere because it's between Epping Forest and Lee Valley. See Waltham Abbey Church and the town at http://www.leevalley-online.co.uk/towns/wabbey/wabbeyhist1.htm; there's a town website at http://www.walthamabbey.org.uk/, but as of time of writing, almost everything is "coming."

Hampton Court Palace was begun in 1514 by Wolsey, who bought the manor of Hampton from the Knights of St. John of Jerusalem. Although he succeeded in building a splendid and richly-furnished mansion, when, in 1529, he was obliged to surrender the palace to Henry, the latter substantially enlarged and rebuilt it. He added the moat and drawbridge and wings decorated with 16th century diapered brickwork to each side of the Wolsey's gatehouse; his arms appear in a panel below the central oriel. He added the exquisite **Astronomical Clock**, made for him by Nicholas Oursian, to the **Clock Court**, the second court through Anne Boleyn's Gateway, which he had embellished. From the Clock Court, Henry's state apartments are entered by the staircase under the clock. There, he rebuilt the earlier, smaller hall into the **Great Hall**, the largest room in the palace. The intricate hammerbeam roof designed by James Nedeham is richly decorated. No less rich are the Flemish tapestries lining the walls, commissioned by Henry probably for the Great Hall. The big stained glass window contains the arms, mottoes, and badges of both Wolsey and Henry, and the names and pedigrees of the six wives. The **Horn Room** was originally a waiting place for servants conveying food to the **Great Hall** and **Great Watching Chamber**. It takes its name from the antlers and horns which used to decorate the galleries and were taken down by William III and stored here: the present arrangement on the walls of the Horn Room was accomplished in 1993.

In the **Great Watching Chamber**, Yeomen of the Guard were stationed to watch over the King's rooms: it was originally the first of Henry's state apartments. This is the only watching chamber of Henry's time that has remained in the form it would have taken when he lived there, in spite of William III's changes. The **Pages' Chamber** is off the watching chamber; then the **Haunted Gallery** leads to the **Chapel Royal**. The Haunted Gallery takes its name from the ghost of Catherine Howard (see *Six Queens of Henry VIII*). More Flemish tapestries line both the Great Watching Chamber and the Haunted Gallery. The **Chapel Royal** has seen changes over the centuries from the time Wolsey first built it. It's divided into two sections, the Royal Pew and the rest, basically. In Henry's time, the Royal Pew consisted of two parts, one for the King and one for the Queen: now, the Pew is unitary, with bay windows overlooking the rest of the chapel. Henry's vaulted ceiling remains; the windows have undergone several changes, especially a huge stained-glass window at the east end, now hidden by Grinling Gibbons's oak reredos, constructed and installed by Sir Christopher Wren when the chapel was refitted for Queen Anne. The pews and panelling were also constructed for Anne, and not part of Henry's chapel. Services are held every Sunday in the chapel, and visitors are welcome to attend them.

Henry also enlarged Wolsey's **kitchens** to suit his household, double the size of Wolsey's at 1200 people. The kitchens were later changed to suit smaller households and changing needs, but were restored in 1991 to the Tudor model, although Henry's **Great Wine Cellar** remains. Outside in the **gardens**, Henry's layout remains today, the privy (private) garden and the public, with parkland beyond; the pleasure ground; and the **Tiltyard** built for Henry late in his reign but never actually used by him. All of Henry's wives lived here from time to time, and also the royal children. Take a virtual tour at http://www.the-eye.com/hc3.htm. An actual tour needs at least half a day; there is so much to be seen, inside and out. Travelling and visiting details can be found at http://www.hrp.org.uk/webcode/content.asp?ID=7 under Planning Your Visit and How To Find Us. Aspects of the palace that are particularly pertinent to Henry appear at http://tudorhistory.org/castles/hcp/gallery/html.

St. James's Palace stands on the site of a hospital for fourteen "maidens that were leprous" dedicated to St. James the Less and mentioned at least as early as 1100. Henry acquired the hospital and grounds in 1531, and between 1532 and 1540, he built a palace here, of which only the Gatehouse (bearing his arms), parts of the **Chapel Royal**, and the Old Presence Chamber (Tapestry Room) remain. Because the palace is a royal residence, the London home of the Princess Royal (Princess Anne) and the Queen's cousin Princess Alexandra, it is not open to the public, except for Sunday services in the Chapel Royal—check at http://www.royal.gov.uk/output/Page590.asp. The latter is also a venue for fine music. A more detailed history is presented at http://www.princeofwales.gov.uk/about/bio_stjames_palace.html.

In 1536, Henry acquired the manor of **Chelsea** and built a two-story brick mansion, occupying the area generally of 19 to 26 Cheyne Walk. It was known as the New Manorhouse to distinguish it from the Old Manorhouse. Prince Edward and Princess Elizabeth lived here, and, after Henry's death, both Catherine Parr and Anne of Cleves, who died here in 1557. The house was demolished in 1753. At **Chelsea Old Church**, also on Cheyne Walk, Henry is said to have secretly married Jane Seymour some days before their official marriage. The church was almost completely destroyed during the Second World War, then rebuilt in a style faithful to the original. Among the memorials in the church is one to Henry James, and there is a statue of Sir Thomas More outside the church, seated and overlooking the Thames. The church's website is http://www.chelseaoldchurch.org.uk/.

Bridewell Palace was built by Henry on the site of an existing castle. Edward VI granted the palace to the City of London, and it first became an orphanage, then a notorious prison for vagrants. Nothing remains of it; the vast Unilever House, built in 1931, stands partly on the site, at New Bridge Street, just off Blackfriars Bridge.

Henry lived at **Richmond Palace** with Catherine of Aragon; the palace later became one of the many houses granted to Anne of Cleves after the annulment of her marriage to Henry. Later, the house fell into disrepair, the remnants being used to construct private houses. See *Henry VII*. Henry acquired the land which would become **Hyde Park/Kensington Gardens** from the Westminster Abbey monks. He enclosed the land, stocked it with deer, and kept it as a royal chase. The website for Hyde Park is http://www. royalparks.gov.uk/parks/hyde_park/. Henry also acquired Marylebone Fields, which formed another enclosed hunting preserve; this was to become present-day **Regent's Park**.

Henry took over the manor of **Oatlands** and built a palace there for the reception of Anne of Cleves. He may have married Catherine Howard in the chapel. Oatlands later underwent two more rebuildings, eventually to become in 1856 the Oatlands Park Hotel, which it remains today. See http://www.oatlandsparkhotel.com/; a detailed history is available through the link Country House.

Nonsuch Palace was almost complete by the time Henry died. Built in the Italian Renaissance style in imitation of the châteaux of the Loire region in France, it was unique in its octagonal towers at each end of the south front. In 1556, Mary I sold it to the 12th Earl of Arundel, who left the palace to his son-in-law, Lord Lumley. Elizabeth I then bought it from him, to settle a debt. Nonsuch then moved down the line of monarchs until Barbara Villiers, Countess of Castlemaine, received it as a gift from Charles II. She sold it to pay her debts, and it was demolished. A history of Nonsuch can be read at http://www.sutton.gov.uk/leisure/ heritage/n.+palace.htm, along with a drawing by George Hoefnagel. It stood on the west side of Nonsuch Park in Ewell (southwest of London, between Sutton and Epsom); Nonsuch Mansion, on the east side of this park, is another building dating from the late 18th and early 19th centuries.

Christ Church, Oxford is the largest college in Oxford. "Cardinal College" was founded in 1525 by Wolsey on the site of St. Frideswide's priory and refounded in 1532 by Henry VIII. It was suppressed in 1546 and Christ Church founded in its place. The Great Quadrangle, or Tom Quad, is the largest in Oxford. From it, a staircase with a fan-tracery roof leads to the large, fine Hall, its walls lined with portraits including one of Henry by Sommans. Another notable feature is Tom Tower, built by Wren in 1681 over Wolsey's Gateway, containing "Great Tom," a huge bell from Osney Abbey on which 101 strokes are sounded every evening at five minutes past nine o'clock, formerly giving the signal for the closing of all college gates. The home page for Christ Church College is http://www.chch.ox.ac. uk/modules/standard/viewpage.asp?id=1. The college chapel is also the cathedral church for the Diocese of Oxford; information can be reached through the same website.

Trinity College, Cambridge was established in 1546 by Henry, who incorporated the earlier foundations of King's Hall and Michaelhouse. The Great Gateway contains statues of Henry on its east face. This leads into the large Great Court, with a fountain dating from early Tudor times. Notable is the college library, built by Wren and known as the Wren Library (http://rabbit.trin.cam.ac.uk/~stewart/wrentour.html for description and photo of interior)—this is best seen from the Backs, the riverside. See http:// www.trin.cam.ac.uk/index.php?pageid=2 for Henry outside Trinity College Cambridge, brandishing a chair leg instead of a scepter: this began as an undergraduate prank, and has continued. This is also the home page for Trinity College.

Also, out of London, **Hurst Castle** was built by Henry VIII at the end of a long pebble spit from Keyhaven, to guard the west entrance to the Solent, looking over to the Isle of Wight. The castle was modernized in the 19th and 20th centuries. The visitor can walk the spit or take a ferry from Keyhaven. The nearest larger town is Lymington, south of Southampton. See Hurst Castle at http://www.hants.gov.uk/discover/places/ hurst.html. For Lymington, see *Henry II*.

Henry built the main gateway, known by his name, into **Windsor Castle**, and **St. George's Chapel** was completed during his reign. The gateway is shown in two photographs at http://www.heritage.me.uk/castles/

windsor.htm, along with a tour of the exterior of the castle which includes some amusing remarks. For St. George's Chapel, see **Edward IV**.

Henry is buried, along with Jane Seymour and Charles I, in a vault in the choir of the chapel; see the plaque marking the vault at http://www.royal.gov.uk/output/Page2770.asp.

Descent from John of Gaunt of Catherine of Aragon and Philip II of Spain

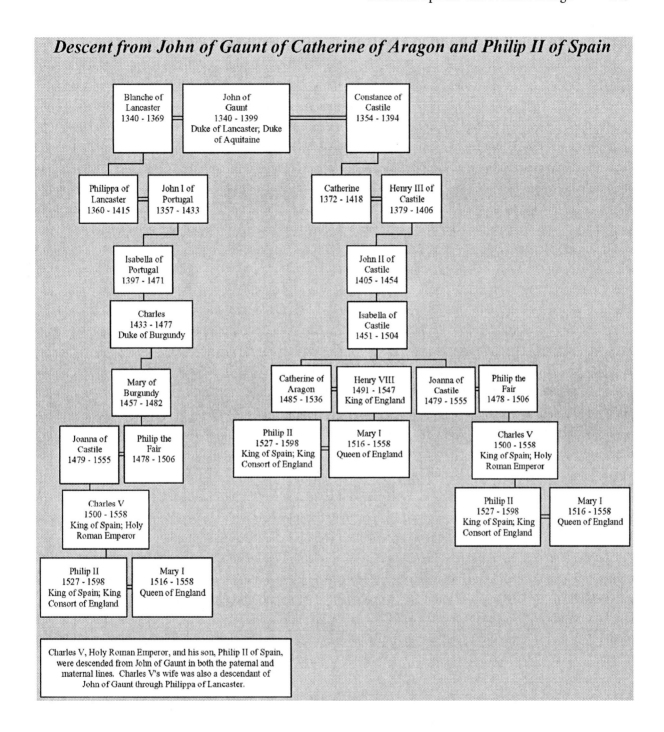

Charles V, Holy Roman Emperor, and his son, Philip II of Spain, were descended from John of Gaunt in both the paternal and maternal lines. Charles V's wife was also a descendant of John of Gaunt through Philippa of Lancaster.

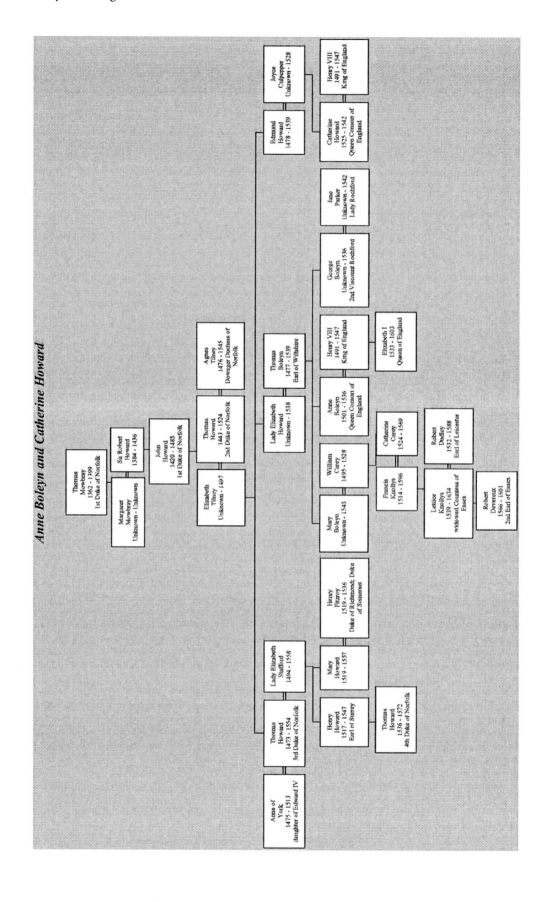

Anne Boleyn and Catherine Howard

Jane Seymour and Catherine Parr

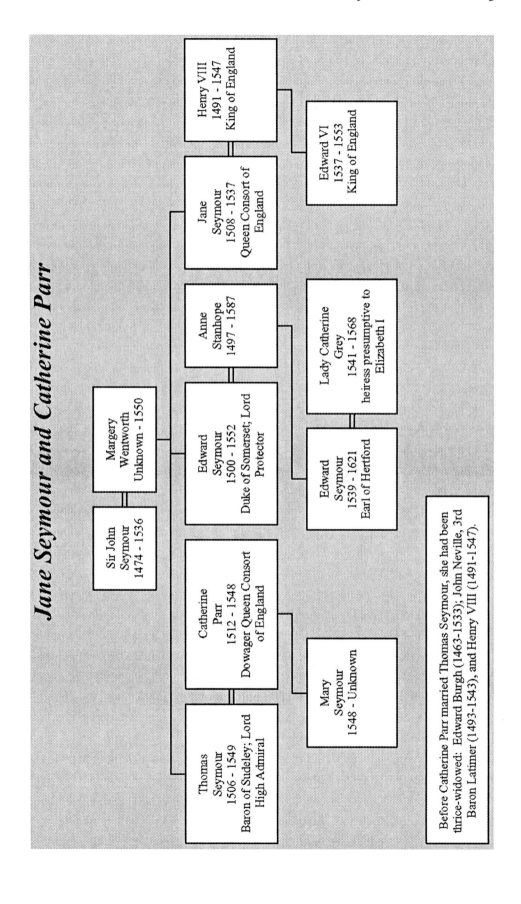

Before Catherine Parr married Thomas Seymour, she had been thrice-widowed: Edward Burgh (1463-1533); John Neville, 3rd Baron Latimer (1493-1543), and Henry VIII (1491-1547).

Anne of Cleves

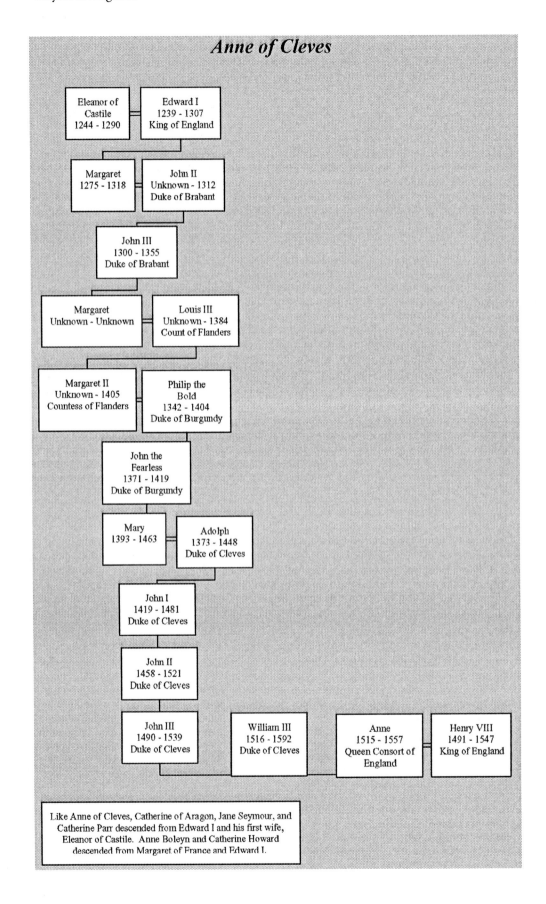

Like Anne of Cleves, Catherine of Aragon, Jane Seymour, and
Catherine Parr descended from Edward I and his first wife,
Eleanor of Castile. Anne Boleyn and Catherine Howard
descended from Margaret of France and Edward I.

The Six Queens of Henry VIII

Notoriously much-married, Henry VIII displayed some quirky recurring patterns in his courting and decoupling. Although he twice made state marriages, he also wed four of his subjects, an altogether unusual habit for a reigning sovereign. When straying because of a wife's pregnancy or his disillusion with their marriage, Henry quarried his love interests from his Queens' or his sister Mary's maids of honor. Anne Boleyn, Jane Seymour, and Catherine Howard all stepped up from being maids of honor to their predecessors as Queen. Problems with Henry's sexual performance, including impotence, led Anne Boleyn to divulge to her sister-in-law that the King had neither the skill nor the virility to make love satisfactorily, and he later found himself completely impotent with Anne of Cleves. His sexual incapacity provided part of the grounds of the precipitate annulment of their marriage. Henry's penchant for divesting himself of unwanted wives by invalidating his marriages (rather than divorcing) resulted in three annulments and might have caused a fourth annulment if his fifth bride had cooperated. Besides annulling three marriages, Henry executed two wives. Though these tried-and-true methods effectively rid him of the women, they made him increasingly less desirable as a husband, to either a foreign or an English bride. After a mostly happy union with Catherine of Aragon that had endured for nearly a quarter-century, Henry married five other women in the last decade of his life. Of these brief marriages, his second and his sixth lasted for three-and-a-half years, his third and his fifth for one-and-a-half years, and his fourth for six months. His first and fourth marriages occurred for reasons of state, his second and fifth resulted from sexual passion, and his third and sixth at last contented the King with a cozy spouse. Henry's first three marriages constitute one story, and his second batch another, as the King reacted to disenchantment in each cycle by remarrying and then remarrying again. The first cycle ended with Jane Seymour's death in childbed, the second with Henry's own death.

Catherine of Aragon, 1485–1536

Born near Madrid to Isabella of Castile and Ferdinand of Aragon, Catherine bore the name of Isabella's English grandmother, the daughter of Edward III's son John of Gaunt. Catherine of Aragon's auburn hair, fair skin, and blue eyes revealed some northern ancestry. Very close to her remarkable mother, Catherine left Spain in 1501 knowing that she would most likely never see Isabella again. She departed for England in order to marry Henry VII's eldest son Arthur, born in Winchester a year after Catherine. The English people immediately took her to their hearts, an affection that never wavered through all her troubles.

Her new family also took a strong liking to Catherine, as did her husband, Arthur, with whom she lived in Ludlow Castle in Shropshire, a former fortress of the Mortimers as Earls of March. Catherine formed a close friendship as well with Margaret Plantagenet, daughter to Edward IV's brother, George, Duke of Clarence, and sister to Edward, Earl of Warwick, executed by Henry VII in 1499 to calm any anxieties Ferdinand and Isabella might feel about potential challenges to Tudor rule. (In 1513, Margaret Plantagenet became Countess of Salisbury. She would become governess to Catherine's daughter Mary, and her son Reginald Pole would champion the cause of both Catherine and Mary.) The long-negotiated marriage between Catherine and Arthur ended abruptly with Arthur's sudden death in 1502. His passing stranded Catherine in England, with her status and her future remaining uncertain for many years.

Negotiations between Spain and England after Arthur's death concerned Catherine as a bride for his younger brother Henry, resulting in marriage treaties eventually signed in 1503. Pope Julius II provided the requested papal dispensation for this sister-in-law and brother-in-law to marry. (Canon law required a dispensation before marriage if previous sexual union with another partner had occurred, whether in marriage or out of it. If the previous marriage was unconsummated, canon law mandated another kind of dispensation on the grounds of "public honesty.") However, the death of Queen Isabella in 1504 called into question the advisability of the union, meant to buttress alliance with her domain of Castile. Then Henry VII opposed the match because Ferdinand had not paid all of Catherine's marriage portion. All of this diplomatic bickering amounted to a very long wait by Catherine, who spent much of her time in Durham House on the Strand. It also overstrained her personal finances.

Just after Catherine finally had lost all hope, Henry VII's death in 1509 spun her wheel of fortune. The new King, Henry VIII, decided for the match, partly because he wanted Ferdinand as an ally against France, partly because he admired Catherine herself, for "it is she…that we would choose for our wife before all other." From 1509 until the middle 1520s, for about 15 years, the marriage surmounted many failed pregnancies (1509–1518) and Henry's infidelities, as well as a temporarily ruptured alliance with Ferdinand, with the Queen and King respecting and supporting each other. Although Catherine, serving as Regent in 1513 while Henry warred on France, repelled an invasion by their brother-in-law, Scotland's James IV, and reported to Henry the English victory over the Scots at Flodden, her influence declined with the rise of Thomas Wolsey to the position of Lord Chancellor. Catherine invested her attention in their surviving child, Mary, who adored both of her parents.

Welcoming the 1516 birth of Mary, Henry's commented, "We are both young. If it was a daughter this time, by the grace of God the sons will follow." When no living sons did follow, Henry focused on ensuring the succession by marrying Mary to a foreign potentate, envisioning that Mary would give way as ruler of England to her husband and then to their eldest son. Among many marriage schemes proposed by diplomats, two concerned Mary's first cousins: her maternal first cousin Charles V—heir to Burgundy, the Netherlands, Spain, and much of Germany and elected Holy Roman Emperor, and her paternal first cousin James V of Scotland. The failure of both of these projects frustrated the King.

He then turned to enobling his recognized bastard by Elizabeth Blount, one of Catherine's ladies. Henry VIII in 1525 named Henry Fitzroy a Knight of the Garter, as well as Earl of Nottingham, Duke of Richmond, and Duke of Somerset. Fitzroy also received his own household. Catherine protested these honors as a threat to Mary's position. (As the daughter of Isabella of Castile and the sister of Joanna of Castile, Catherine viewed Queens Regnant as normal phenomena.) However, Henry also treated Mary as Princess of Wales (although she never formally assumed the title), with a household at Ludlow.

These moves towards recognizing Fitzroy or Mary as his successor fell by the way after Henry VIII fell in love with Catherine's maid of honor Anne Boleyn, to whom he secretly betrothed himself on New Year's Day, 1527. The King's desire to jettison his middle-aged wife and to beget sons upon Anne instead caused him to challenge the 1503 papal dispensation that had legitimized his marriage to Catherine in 1509. He now believed that the papal dispensation authorizing the marriage of a woman to the brother of her late husband violated a Biblical prohibition. At the same time, however, Henry in 1527 sought a second papal dispensation to allow him to marry Anne despite the fact that her sister Mary had been his mistress in the early 1520s—a papal dispensation authorizing the marriage of a man to the sister of his former mistress. Pope Clement VII did grant this second dispensation in 1527 but only if Henry's marriage to Catherine was indeed invalid. Simultaneously, Henry asserted in public that no one would feel more pleased than he if his marriage with Catherine turned out to be valid after all.

An extremely complicated judicial process then consumed much diplomatic energy as well as several years, during which Henry tried to persuade Clement VII to invalidate the dispensation of Julius II. Despite the poverty of his argument (another Biblical verse called for the surviving brother to beget issue for his dead sibling upon the widow), Henry might have secured his annulment if Charles V, Catherine's nephew, had not intimidated Clement VII after Imperial troops sacked Rome and imprisoned the Pope in the Castel Sant'Angelo. If Henry had not alienated Catherine with an approach that reduced her to the status of a concubine and their daughter to the status of a bastard, she might have cooperated. Instead, Catherine adamantly insisted that Arthur had left her a virgin and that her marriage to Henry was valid. Egged on by Anne, Henry so angered and offended Catherine that she also refused to countenance the Pope's sensible suggestion that she retire into a convent. This solution possessed the considerable advantages that it did not invalidate the marriage or bastardize Mary but still allowed the King to remarry and beget male children. Adopting it would have saved much suffering.

One victim of the King's failure to win his annulment from the Pope, Cardinal Wolsey fell from power, dying just after his 1530 arrest for high treason. Having given Hampton Court to Henry, Wolsey also lost York Place. Renaming it Whitehall, Henry used the palace to lodge Anne near him, with Catherine being excluded. Catherine herself loved Greenwich the best of all her residences as Henry's acknowledged Queen. During this protracted consideration of their annulment (1527–1531), Catherine for a long time clung to the delusion that Henry's conscience would eventually cause him to abandon the campaign for severance of their marriage. For his part, Henry felt concern that Catherine might emulate her militant mother Isabella and make war on him. Catherine would never consider leading an armed rebellion against her husband, despite much encouragement, nor would Henry ever give up Anne Boleyn.

Anne Boleyn (1501–1536)

Daughter to the diplomat Thomas Boleyn and sister to Henry VIII's mistress Mary Boleyn (later Mary Carey), Anne fascinated Henry with her strength and willfulness as well as her refusal to succumb to seduction as her sister had done. On the Continent for much of her earlier life, Anne served in three households: that of the Archduchess Margaret of the Netherlands, Regent for Charles V; that of Henry's sister Mary Tudor, briefly Queen Consort to Louis XII of France; and, after the death of Louis XII, that of his daughter Claude, wife to François I. Anne returned to England in the early 1520s and became a lady-in-waiting to Queen Catherine. A love affair with Henry Percy, son of Earl of Northumberland, led to their betrothal. At the King's behest, Wolsey in 1525 broke off the match by trying to intimidate Percy and then by summoning his father to hector him.

No one knows if Henry's opposition to the marriage with Percy derived from an attraction to Anne, but by 1526 his interest in Anne certainly existed. She withdrew from the court that year to live at Hever, her parents' house. As the long struggle to persuade Clement VII to annul Henry's marriage to Catherine led nowhere, Anne's evangelical and reforming opinions influenced Henry to reformulate his approach. No longer would he petition the Pope for relief. Instead, at the suggestion of Boleyn protégé Thomas Cranmer, Henry in 1529 solicited the opinions of learned faculties of theology and faculties of canon law at English and Continental universities. This approach allowed the King to argue that no Pope could dispense with Biblical teaching, that the Church in England could resolve the question without reference to the Pope, and, eventually, that he as King—not the Pope—governed the Church of England. Displacement of the papal supremacy by the royal supremacy would always remain central to Henry's religious beliefs. Distrustful of much in the reformist agenda that he considered heretical, Henry would prove to be a schismatic Catholic rather than a heretic.

With this assertion of jurisdiction over the annulment question came the decline of Catherine's fortunes and the rise of Anne Boleyn. Henry in 1531 ordered Catherine to move from Windsor to The More, a manor near the Abbey of St. Albans in Hertfordshire, and their daughter Mary to move to Richmond. Except for one visit by Catherine to Mary during a 1534 illness, Henry never allowed this mother and daughter to see each other again. Catherine and Mary continued to correspond as Catherine's residence changed to Bishop's Hatfield, then Hertford Castle, then Ampthill in Bedfordshire, then Buckden, and finally Kimbolton in Huntingdonshire. In the meantime, Anne received Hanworth as her country seat and became Marquess of Pembroke, the first peeress created in her own right.

Conferring honors and property upon his prospective bride proved easier than winning acceptance for her. During a royal progress in the North of England, "Wherever he went accompanied by the Lady, the people on the road so earnestly requested him to recall the Queen, his wife, and the woman so especially insulted the Royal mistress, hooting and hissing on her passage, that he was actually obliged to retrace his steps." Although Continental royalty displayed a similar reluctance, Anne accompanied Henry to a meeting with François I at Calais that she attended as Henry's future Queen. At this point, Anne may finally have allowed Henry full sexual intimacy. They secretly married after their return from France, and Anne became pregnant in December 1532. They repeated their vows in 1533 at York Place. Cranmer, now Archbishop of Canterbury, tried the marriage of Henry to Catherine at Dunstable Priory in Bedfordshire and annulled it. After appearing for the first time as Queen at Easter, Anne was crowned, while Henry stripped Catherine of her title and emphasized her new status as Princess Dowager of Wales, the widow of his brother Arthur. Neither the Pope nor Charles V acted decisively to protect Catherine, although Rome, irritated by Henry's claim of jurisdiction over the annulment, finally in 1534 affirmed the validity of their marriage.

The degradation of Mary's status accompanied that of her mother. The 1534 Act of Succession settled the crown upon Henry's heirs male by Anne or any subsequent wife and did not even mention Mary. After the 1533 birth of Elizabeth, the baby girl became Henry's heir by default, until he begat a son who would displace her. Not only was Mary no longer the heiress presumptive, a Princess, or a legitimate child, but Henry and Anne also demanded that she serve as a lady in Elizabeth's household. Moved from Beaulieu or New Hall in Essex to Hatfield to serve her sister and bereft of her beloved Countess of Salisbury, Mary resisted both blandishments and threats calculated to manipulate her into acknowledging Anne as Queen. Henry indignantly avoided seeing Mary during his visits to Elizabeth at Hatfield.

Anne's status as Queen Consort brought her little security or joy so long as she bore no living male heir to Henry. The King's dalliances with other women provoked Anne's jealousy and fierce reproaches, to which Henry retorted "that she must shut her eyes and endure as her betters had done." Henry reminded Anne "that it was in his power to humble her again in a moment more than he had exalted her." Her unpopularity worsened with the executions of those who resisted the recent turn of events—the Carthusian monks, John Cardinal Fisher, Sir Thomas More—but Anne pushed for the execution of Catherine and Mary because they had not signed the Oath of Succession that named Elizabeth as the heiress presumptive until the Boleyn marriage produced sons. Then Catherine's mortal illness in 1536 precipitated Anne's downfall.

So long as Catherine lived, Henry could not repudiate Anne without incurring pressure to return to his first wife. Her death freed the King from both of his wives. On the very day of Catherine's internment as Princess Dowager at Peterborough Abbey, Anne miscarried. Already affronted by Anne's assertiveness, tired of the widespread disapproval of their actions in England and on the Continent, Henry felt enraged by what he termed her failure to give him a son. In addition, the desired reconciliation with Charles V depended on the removal of Anne. Considering himself "seduced and forced into this marriage by means of sortileges and charms," Henry now viewed Anne as a witch. If the miscarriage had involved a deformed fetus, this might have suggested to the King's mind divine punishment to the mother for adultery or incest.

If so, this would explain Henry's readiness to believe the absurd charges concocted to drag Anne down. Accused of adultery with five men, one of them her brother, George, Anne also stood trial on charges of poisoning Catherine, trying to poison Mary, and designing Henry's own death. A guilty verdict inevitably followed. In addition, Cranmer dissolved the marriage, probably on the grounds of Henry's affair with her sister Mary or of Anne's precontract with Percy. (A precontract could invalidate a subsequent marriage to another party.) Henry now bastardized Elizabeth just as he had bastardized Mary. Swearing that she was innocent but reportedly remorseful about her treatment of Mary, Anne went to her death on Tower Green before the Great White Tower. After a swordsman from Calais swiftly beheaded her, Anne was buried in the Chapel of St. Peter ad Vincula.

Jane Seymour (1508–1537)

Lady-in-waiting to both Catherine of Aragon and Anne Boleyn, Jane Seymour attracted Henry's interest during his tumultuous marriage to Anne Boleyn, whose enemies pushed Jane forward as a means of ending Anne's influence, restoring Mary, and reversing Henry's other reforms to the Church in England. During the King's progress in the North in 1535, Henry and Anne had stayed for five days at the Seymours' house, Wolf Hall, near Marlborough. However, Henry had already known Jane for several years. By 1536, he had established some sort of special relationship with Jane, although she resisted his advances in imitation of Anne. Betrothed on the day after Anne's execution, they married 10 days later at York Place, and Henry proclaimed Jane Queen a few days after that.

Jane tried to persuade Henry to restore Mary to favor. However, Henry would do so only if he forced Mary to submit to his will. She must acknowledge the royal supremacy over the Church in England, repudiate the Pope, and affirm the invalidity of her parents' marriage and her own bastardy. Broken in her defiance by a fear of fatal consequences, Mary signed the required documents, and then Henry saw her for the first time in five years. He might have restored his elder daughter to favor, but Henry now concentrated on fathering a son by Jane. The 1536 Second Act of Succession named as his successors his heirs male by Jane; then his heirs male by any other wife; then his female heirs by Jane; then his female heirs by any future wife. Henry's three living children all suffered from their bastard status. In 1536, his illegitimate son, Henry Fitzroy, who had married the Duke of Norfolk's daughter Mary Howard, died.

Conservative in her own religious beliefs, Jane protested to Henry against the Dissolution of the Monasteries (1535–1540) urged upon Henry by Anne. At Canterbury, Henry would also desecrate the tomb of Thomas Becket, as well as put Becket's bones on trial and burn them. The royal attack on the monasteries, disliked religious changes, and economic discontent motivated the rising in the North called the Pilgrimage of Grace, which also reflected disapproval of the King's matrimonial career. However, neither Jane's influence nor the aborted risings deflected Henry from his purpose.

After enduring labor for more than two days, Jane delivered the long-anticipated male heir, Edward, in late 1537, but Jane herself soon succumbed to puerperal fever. Mary, who adored her baby brother and felt maternal affection for her little sister, felt distraught after the death of her beloved stepmother. Henry so cherished Jane's memory that his will directed that he be buried with her at Windsor. Had this good-natured, generous woman lived, notoriety might not now discolor Henry's memory. As it was, he had lost three Queens in 1536–1537, and he would always yearn to replace Jane.

Anne of Cleves (1515–1557)

The diplomatic marriage to Anne of Cleves strived to protect England's interests when France and the Empire seemed about to set aside their enmity to each other and the Pope appeared to threaten Henry's hold on his throne. After Jane Seymour died, Henry at first had tried to woo a bride who would ally England with either France or Spain. This motivated the King's interest in Christina of Denmark, Duchess of Milan, and in Mary of Guise. Besides creating for Henry portraits of various French candidates, Hans Holbein also painted a fetching portrait of Christina that now hangs in the National Gallery in London. These ambitions foundered, however, after the Franco-Imperial alliance of 1539. In addition, Pope Paul III's bull of excommunication deposed Henry and released his subjects from their allegiance to him.

Henry feared that Paul III might instigate an invasion of England by France or the Empire in the name of pulling down Henry as a schismatic ruler. An advocate of the Franco-Imperial friendship, Paul III also had made Reginald Pole a cardinal. Son of the Countess of Salisbury, Reginald Pole had inherited the claim to the throne of his maternal grandfather, George, Duke of Clarence, and Henry suspected that Paul III would seek to displace him as King with Reginald Pole. Paul III already had sent Cardinal Pole to Charles V to solicit assistance to the rebels in the Pilgrimage of Grace. These anxieties precipitated the 1538 crackdown on the Pole and Courtenay families. (The Courtenay claim to the crown derived from Henry's maternal aunt, Catherine of York.) Various arrests and executions, including the detention of Cardinal Pole's aged mother, would end with her horrific execution in 1541—the year in which Henry attainted Cardinal Pole himself as a traitor.

Foiled in his attempts to ally himself by marriage with France or the Empire, alarmed by the Franco-Imperial alliance and Paul III's hostility, Henry sought antipapal and anti-Imperial friendship with William, Duke of Cleves. Like Henry a schismatic—not a heretical—ruler, a self-styled reforming Catholic, Duke William ruled in northern Germany in the lower Rhine river valley, with his capital at Düsseldorf. Thomas Cromwell had pushed for this alliance and the marriage that would secure it.

With the marriage already settled upon, Holbein journeyed to Cleves to paint two sisters of Duke William. The Holbein portrait of Anne of Cleves now in the Louvre decided Henry in Anne's favor. The bride embarked for England, where she would first encounter Henry in a formal ceremony at Blackheath. All these careful arrangements collapsed, however, when Henry followed a chivalric or courtly tradition observed by rulers towards foreign brides. During an informal visit by the ruler to his bride, the lady was supposed to pretend not to know her masked visitor but then to feel the pull of his immense attraction. Anne did not recognize the King in disguise; she did not know English and may not have understood the situation. Furious, Henry announced to Cromwell that Anne repelled him and that he wanted to back out of the situation. Only fear of alienating Duke William kept the King a surly captive in his fourth wedding: "If it were not to satisfy the world and my realm, I would not do that I must do this day for none earthly thing."

Besides disappointing Henry's romantic and erotic expectations, Anne had arrived in England without papers substantiating the dissolution of her precontract to François of Lorraine (who actually would marry Christina, Duchess of Milan, in 1541). Henry's anxiety rose as he contemplated making yet another marriage defective in title. In addition, their marital intimacy fostered his irrational conviction that Anne had already lost her virginity to another because she had droopy breasts and a slack belly. His consequent impotence prevented any consummation of their marriage. Henry hid his dissatisfaction from most everyone for a while, while Anne may not have known that they had fallen short: "When he comes to bed, he kisses me and taketh me by the hand and biddeth me, 'Goodnight, sweetheart'; and in the morning [he] kisses me and biddeth me, 'Farewell, darling'. Is this not enough?"

Though understandably enough for Anne, it was certainly not enough for Henry. The King's broodings convinced him that his impotence resulted from papist witchcraft trapping him in an infertile marriage—a wicked interference with his plan to beget more sons for England. Because Henry thought that Cromwell wanted to preserve this unlawful marriage, he turned against his minister with his customary ferocity. Newly created Earl of Essex and Lord Great Chamberlain, Cromwell fell from power with his arrest for heresy and treason. Before his execution in July 1540, Cromwell cooperated in the effort to invalidate the marriage he had arranged.

As Henry fell out of love with his fantasy about Anne of Cleves, he became besotted with his Queen's lady-in-waiting Catherine Howard. Anne herself complained about the King's infatuation with Catherine. The marriage that began in January 1540 was annulled in July, mainly on the grounds of nonconsummation but also because of Anne's precontract to François of Lorraine. Ordered in June to remove to Richmond Palace, Anne eventually accepted Henry's offer to be her brother and to give her a financial settlement plus the residences of Richmond and Bletchingley. He later gave her Kemsing, Seal, and Hever in Kent, and Anne of Cleves would mostly live in Hever, associated with Anne Boleyn. During Edward VI's reign, Somerset and Dudley confiscated Richmond and Bletchingley from Anne in 1547, replacing them with the Kent residences of Penshurst (another former Boleyn property) and Dartford Priory.

During the brief reign of Anne of Cleves as Queen Consort of England, she had won some popularity, and Henry's repudiation of her created popular regret. Hoping to regain her place after the fall of her successor, Catherine Howard, Anne of Cleves felt crushed when Henry instead married Catherine Parr in 1543 as his sixth bride. Anne had reached out to Henry's daughter seven-year-old Elizabeth; in 1553, Anne and Elizabeth rode together during Queen Mary's entrance into London, and Anne ate with Mary at her coronation banquet. Four years later, Anne of Cleves died at Chelsea Manor, a residence also associated with both Sir Thomas More and Catherine Parr.

Catherine Howard, 1525–1542

Catherine Howard—first cousin to Anne Boleyn through Catherine's father, Edmund Howard—lost her mother, Joyce Culpepper, in 1528. After that, young Catherine grew up in the household of her father's stepmother, Agnes Tilney Howard, the Dowager Duchess of Norfolk—both at Chesworth near Horsham in Sussex and at Lambeth near Whitehall. Under the Dowager Duchess's erratic supervision, Catherine lived in the household with many other young women and young men. A Howard cousin, Francis Dereham, persuaded Catherine to grant him sexual intimacy, and they seem to have made a precontract of marriage. All this fell by the way after Catherine in 1539 became a lady-in-waiting to Anne of Cleves. Now at court, she met Thomas Culpepper, Gentleman of the Privy Chamber and her maternal sixth cousin. Catherine may have fallen in love with Culpepper then. Promoted by her paternal uncle, Thomas Howard, 3rd Duke of Norfolk, in order to restore Norfolk's influence over the King and to destroy that of Cromwell, Catherine served as a sexual lure to attract Henry VIII from his unloved fourth Queen. Marriage to the King swiftly followed in August 1540, not long after the execution of Thomas Cromwell.

Henry adored his very young bride, who enjoyed her regal status if not her intimacy with her sovereign, 34 years her senior. Mary's being older than her newest stepmother and disliking the renewed tie to the Boleyn family created some discord between them, but Catherine made some efforts to be a good stepmother to Henry's three children. At the same time, she secretly met with Culpepper, about whom she developed an obsessive passion. Jane, Lady Rochford, widow of George Boleyn and Catherine's intimate, acted as their pander. (Lady Rochford had provided the "evidence" that her husband had committed incest with his sister Queen Anne Boleyn.) In addition, Catherine gave Dereham a position in her household. Gossip about the Queen's former intimacy with Dereham reached the notice of Cranmer, who left a letter for the King to read after he arrived for All Souls Day Mass. Henry refused to believe its charge that Catherine had already lost her virginity to Dereham before her royal marriage, but the unwarranted suspicion that she had later committed adultery with Dereham led to torture during which Dereham pointed out that Catherine actually had strayed with Culpepper.

Dereham's revelations devastated the King. While Cranmer had hoped to save Catherine's life by annulling her marriage on the grounds of a precontract to Dereham, Catherine denied that she had precontracted herself. No one admitted guilt to the charges of adultery. While being investigated, Catherine lived in the palace of Syon (a former convent). The inevitable executions followed, Dereham enduring the full rigors of a traitor's death but Culpepper only being beheaded. Catherine even rehearsed her own execution. Her fellow culprit, Lady Rochford, lay her own neck on a block slimed with Catherine's blood.

Catherine Parr, 1512–1548

Catherine Howard's betrayal gravely injured Henry, who—according to a witness—demonstrated "greater sorrow and regret at her loss than at the faults, loss or divorce of his preceding wives." Norfolk and his stepmother, the Dowager Duchess of Norfolk, tasted of royal resentment that they had not informed the King of whatever they knew about his prospective bride's past; henceforth, anyone who did not step forward with such information would be guilty of high treason. Naturally, this did not enlarge the pool of domestic candidates for the King's hand. Fortunately, his last wife's being already twice-widowed erased the question of her virginity from consideration.

Born Catherine Parr, she had married Sir Edward Burgh, 2nd Baron Borough of Gainsborough, in 1529 and lost him in 1533. Catherine Burgh's subsequent marriage to John Neville, 3rd Baron Latimer, ended with his March 1543 death. By then, Catherine Neville, Lady Latimer, had fallen passionately in love with Thomas Seymour, brother to Jane and Edward Seymour, and hoped to marry him, but Henry VIII began courting Lady Latimer as soon as (or even before) Lord Latimer's dead body cooled. Naturally reluctant either to wed or to offend her sovereign, Lady Latimer married Henry VIII in July 1543—motivated mostly by her fervently evangelical hope that she could support England's deliverer from papist misrule.

Despite Catherine Parr's devout evangelicalism as an adult, she had come from a family closely tied to Catherine of Aragon. Her father had served as Vice-Chamberlain of Catherine of Aragon's household; her mother, one of Catherine of Aragon's ladies, had named this daughter for the Queen, who stood as the baby's godmother. This background eased Queen Catherine Parr's relationship with her stepdaughter and age peer, Mary, but the new Queen also displayed truly maternal care to all of her stepchildren. As an intelligent woman interested in religious reform and capable of acting as Regent during Henry VIII's absence in France, Catherine influenced her stepdaughter Elizabeth, and Prince Edward's letters addressed her as "my dearest mother" who possessed "the chief place in my heart." The 1544 Act of Succession that reinstated the still-bastardized daughters in the line of succession probably resulted from Catherine's persuasion.

All of Catherine Parr's many virtues and abilities did not prevent a crisis that endangered her life, for the King, who had always fancied himself as a theologian, resented his wife's daring to express her evangelical opinions. She had published in 1545 her *Prayers Stirring the Mind unto Heavenly Meditations* (which went through seven editions in three years) and had started a project of translating Erasmus's *Paraphrases* of the Gospels. Catherine's friendship with Cranmer allied them as antipapal and evangelical believers. Her more openly Lutheran *Lamentation of a Sinner* dared to appear only after Henry's death. In the meantime, Henry groused, "a good hearing it is when women become such clerks, and much comfort to come in mine old age, to be taught by my wife!" He allowed Catherine's enemies in 1546 to assemble evidence against her and plot her arrest. Learning of the imminent danger to her life, she persuaded the King that she had not presumed to instruct him but merely had wanted to learn from him. This adroit manipulation and display of feminine submissiveness predictably charmed her vain husband: "Is it even so, sweetheart? And tended your arguments to no worse end? Then perfect friends we are now again, as ever at any time heretofore." The next day, the King aborted her arrest in his presence.

After Henry VIII finally passed away in January 1547, Catherine Parr, Dowager Queen Consort of England, secretly wed Thomas Seymour in May. Sadly, this estimable woman, pregnant at long last, died at Sudeley in September 1548 after the birth of her daughter Mary Seymour, named for Mary Tudor. The puerperal fever that killed Thomas Seymour's wife had also caused his sister Jane Seymour to die a decade earlier.

Sites for the Six Queens of Henry VIII

Catherine of Aragon

Catherine was born in **Alcalá de Henares**, Spain, a distinction shared by the writer Cervantes. Alcalá de Henares is 31 km northeast of Madrid, with about 170,000 population. It is a Unesco World Heritage site, the first planned university city, dating from the early 16th century. The university, once a premier university in Europe, was moved to Madrid in 1836. Badly damaged during the Spanish Civil War, the town has since grown into an industrial suburb of Madrid and is home to a new university, established in 1977. See its website at http://www.ayto-alcaladehenares.es/homeenglish.asp?site_language=4, with links to photographs and detail. See also http://www.softdoc.es/madrid_guide/daytrips/alcala_henares.html for more description and instructions for making a day trip from Madrid.

Catherine landed in **Plymouth** in 1501. She married Prince Arthur in **St. Paul's**, London; see *John of Gaunt*.

Arthur died at **Ludlow Castle**. For Ludlow, see *Edward V.*

Catherine married Henry in the **Tower of London**. They lived at **Richmond Palace** (see *Henry VII*).

In **St. George's Chapel, Windsor**, Henry had the wooden Royal Closet built, with an oriel window overlooking the choir so that Catherine could watch the Garter ceremony. It can be seen at http://www.stgeorges-windsor.org/tour/tour_choir.asp.

After their estrangement, Catherine was taken to **The More**, near Rickmansworth, one of Cardinal Wolsey's former residences. Rickmansworth is in northwestern Greater London, just south of Watford; a history of The More can be read at http://homepage.mac.com/philipdavis/English%20sites/1558.html. From there, she went to **Hatfield House** (see *Elizabeth I*). She also stayed at **Hertford Castle** (see *John of Gaunt*). Then she was taken to **Ampthill Castle**, to await the fate of her marriage being deliberated in Dunstable; a memorial cross with an inscription by Horace Walpole marking the site of the castle is in Ampthill Park. Here she spent two years in an impressive castle in the attractive surroundings of a well-treed park. A memorial cross with an inscription by Horace Walpole marking the site of the castle, and Catherine's sojourn within it, is in Ampthill Park. Ampthill is located between Dunstable and Bedford. See Katherine's Cross at http://www.ampthill.org.uk/history.htm, then click on Katherine of Aragon.

At the Priory church of St. Peter, **Dunstable**, Thomas Cranmer annulled the marriage of Catherine to Henry VIII. The priory dates back to its establishment by Henry I in 1131; the priory church survived the Dissolution of the Monasteries by becoming the parish church, with the nave and west front surviving today. Visit Dunstable at http://www.dunstable.towntalk.co.uk/about.shtml#top.

Catherine then lived in **Buckden**, in the 15th century brick palace of the Bishops of Lincoln. Buckden is located off the A1, a few miles south of Huntingdon. The palace was moated; only part of the wall, the Great Tower, and the Inner Gatehouse survive, but these have been renovated and adapted to modern uses, such as apartments within the Gatehouse and a center for conferences and spiritual retreats, among others. Buckden Towers, as it's called, belongs to Claretian Missionaries. For several pages of the history of Buckden, inluding Catherine's sojourn at Buckden Palace, see http://www.buckden-village.co.uk/history/index.htm; the Friends of Buckden Towers' website appears at http://www.fobt.fsnet.co.uk/aboutthetowers.htm.

Kimbolton Castle is only a few miles west of Buckden. There, Catherine lived for the rest of her life. Originally a castle, the house was rebuilt during the 18th century by John Vanbrugh into a grand country home. Visit the school at http://www.kimbolton.cambs.sch.uk/castle_visits.htm for a history, visiting details, and photographs of the home.

Catherine was buried in **Peterborough Abbey**. Her tomb was demolished by Puritans, but there is a memorial to her in the north choir aisle, near the high altar. A photograph appears at http://tudorhistory.org/aragon/gallery.html. The website for Peterborough Cathedral is at http://www.peterborough-cathedral.org.uk/.

Anne Boleyn

Anne is generally considered to have been born at **Blickling Hall**, Norfolk, in the earlier medieval manor house on the same site, and spent her childhood there. The house standing there now is one of the finest Jacobean houses in the country. See Blicking and check visiting details at http://www.nationaltrust.org.uk/historicproperties/index.cfm?fuseaction=property&property_id=125, Blickling being a National Trust property. Blickling is located on the B1354, off the A140 north from Norwick.

Hever Castle, the 15th century castellated mansion of the Boleyn family and her rumored birthplace, is interesting as the traditional meeting place of Anne Boleyn and Henry, who afterwards granted Hever to Anne of Cleves. The evidence that Anne was born there is lacking, but after she had spent time at the French court, she lived at Hever until becoming a lady of Catherine of Aragon's court.

Two Books of Hours inscribed by Anne Boleyn are on display. Restored in 1903 by William Waldorf Astor, its owner at the time, Hever offers magnificent gardens as well as a medieval moated mansion and a neo-Tudor village built for Astor. http://www.hevercastle.co.uk/ is Hever's home page, for history, photographs, and visiting details. The other traditional meeting place is **Greenwich Palace**.

Anne and Henry were married in the **Tower of London**. For her coronation, **St. Thomas's Tower** was largely rebuilt in order to accommodate high-ranking officials, and the **White Tower** saw renovations. For more, see *Henry VIII*.

At Hampton Court Palace, Anne Boleyn's Gate memorializes her. The intricate carvings within the gate incorporate her and Henry's intertwined initials and the Boleyn falcon. See these at http://tudorhistory.org/castles/hcp/gallery.html.

The Tower also saw Anne's end. She was tried in the **Great Hall**, beheaded on **Tower Green**, and buried in the **Chapel Royal of St. Peter ad Vincula**. See Tower Green and the church at http://www.hrp.org.uk/webcode/content.asp?ID=213; the block, complete with ax, appears at http://www.toweroflondontour.com/chapblok.html. Her grave can be seen at http://tudorhistory.org/castles/tower/gallery.html. There is a rumor that she was buried in the church of St. Peter and St. Paul in **Salle**. Salle is in Norfolk, tucked away on a country road off the B1145 north of Norwich, and a few miles west of Blickling Hall. Regardless, the church is splendid, richly decorated inside.

Jane Seymour

Jane was born at **Wolf Hall**, near **Burbage**. Were she and Henry married there? It has been thought so, but London is a much more likely venue. See http://www.burbage-wiltshire.co.uk/historic/wolfhall.html for photographs and an account of Wolf Hall. Burbage is a village on the B3087 in Wiltshire, to the south of Marlborough. The hall is the traditional home of the wardens of Savernake Forest, now to the northeast of Burbage on the A346. What can be seen today is a largely Victorian building.

They were betrothed at **Hampton Court** a mere 24 hours after Anne Boleyn's execution, and were married quickly and quietly after that. It has been thought that Henry and Jane were married at her parental home, Wolf Hall, but it was much more likely to have been **Whitehall Palace**. For details regarding both places, see *Henry VIII*. It had also been rumored that at **Chelsea Old Church**, near Henry's manorhouse in Chelsea, he secretly married Jane some days before their official marriage.

Jane died of puerperal fever at Hampton Court following the birth and christening of her son Edward. Her body was then conveyed in procession to **Windsor Castle**, to be buried. Along the way, the poor were given alms, and the Provost and students of **Eton College** saluted with caps and tapers in hands. The coffin was lowered into a vault beneath the center of the choir of **St. George's Chapel** the next day. She shares the space with Henry and Charles I.

Anne of Cleves

Anne's family home was the **Schwanenburg** at **Cleves**, the castle of the Dukes of Cleves. Cleves (Kleve) is located in the western extremity of Germany, only a few miles from the border with the Netherlands and the Dutch city of Nijmegen. See photographs with descriptions at http://www.kleve.de/kommunen/kleve/english/www.nsf/pages/0index.htm. It straddles the Rhine and is popular with tourists as a resort destination.

Anne travelled to England via Antwerp and Calais, meeting the English in each place. She then landed in Deal, after the Channel crossing, spending a night at **St. Augustine's Abbey, Canterbury**. Suppressed as an abbey in 1538, it was now used as a royal lodging place; view it at http://www.canterbury.co.uk/cgi-bin/ buildpage.pl?mysql=304.

At **Rochester**, she was conducted to the Bishop's Palace, and this was where she had her fateful meeting with Henry. Nevertheless, they were married at **Greenwich**.

Henry had built **Oatlands Palace** at Weybridge, Surrey, for her reception (she was never to live there). For more details, see *Henry VIII*.

Anne received a considerable amount of property as part of her settlement after agreeing to the annulment. She received **Richmond Palace** and **Bletchingley Manor**, but was persuaded after Henry's death to relinquish them for **Penshurst Palace** and **Dartford manor**, constructed by Henry on the site of Dartford Priory after the Dissolution of the Monasteries.

The manor at **Bletchingley** survives, although rebuilt and restored so that the current house dates mostly from the 18th century. Bletchingley lies south of Croydon, London, on the A25 just south of the junction of the M23 and M25. Only the gatehouse of **Dartford** manor still exists, to the east of London and just north of the A2, as a well-preserved, charming house with rooms available for ceremonial occasions, including the Anne of Cleves Room. A detailed history of the manor appears at http://www.dartfordarchive.org.uk/ early_modern/buildings_mgh.shtml, along with a photograph of the gatehouses.

Penshurst Place is situated south of Sevenoaks, off the B2176. The seat of the Sidney family since Edward VI gave it to his steward and tutor, Sir William Sidney, it is a beautiful, well-preserved house in magnificent gardens. See Penshurst's attractive and informative website at http://www.penshurstplace.com/. Anne of Cleves ended up living permanently at **Hever Castle** (see *Anne Boleyn* above), where she spent most of her life. She was also allowed the use of **Chelsea Manor**, where she died.

The **Anne of Cleves House**, at Lewes, Sussex, is rumored to be part of her settlement after the annulment; whether or not Anne ever lived there, the house is set up as a quasi-museum containing items relevant to Sussex and period furniture, and can be viewed at http://www.sussexpast.co.uk/property/ site.php?site_id=14, along with visiting details.

Anne is buried in **Westminster Abbey**. See http://www.westminster-abbey.org/library/monarchs/ anne_cleves.htm for details regarding her tomb in the south transept of the abbey.

Catherine Howard

Catherine was raised poor, in spite of her noble family. She was taken into the household of her step-grandmother, the Duchess of Norfolk, at her homes in **Chesworth** (near Horsham) and in London, at **Lambeth**. Chesworth was the setting for her romance with Henry Mannox, and the Duchess's splendid Lambeth house for that with Francis Dereham.

Henry married Catherine at **Oatlands Palace**. For more information, see *Henry VIII*.

Catherine's ghost supposedly haunts **Hampton Court Palace**, in the aptly named **Haunted Gallery**. The legend goes that when under house arrest in the palace, one day she managed to escape and ran along the gallery to the door of the **Chapel Royal** where Henry was at Mass. She was dragged back to her rooms, screaming.

Like her cousin Anne Boleyn, Catherine was beheaded on **Tower Green**, and both are interred in the **Chapel Royal of St. Peter ad Vincula**, in the Tower of London. For the Chapel Royal, see *Anne Boleyn* above.

Catherine Parr

Tradition has it that Catherine was born at the family home, **Kendal Castle**, in Westmoreland, but it seems more likely that it was the family's London home. Visit http://www.visitcumbria.com/sl/kencas.htm to view the remnants of Kendal Castle.

As Lady Latimer, wife of John Neville, Lord Latimer, Catherine lived in **Snape Castle,** Yorkshire. The first manor house at Snape was built c.1250. The house Catherine would have known was built 1426–50, a plain, stone manor house, later transformed into an Elizabethan "castle," with a Gothic exterior and crenellations, by Thomas Cecil. Cecils owned the house until a son-in-law sold it to the Milbank family. Today, half the house is owned privately, and the other half remains with the Milbanks' Thorp Perrow estate. See and read about Snape Castle at http://www.communigate.co.uk/ne/slhg/page2.phtml. Snape lies on a country road off the B6268, north of Ripon.

The Latimers' London home was in **Charterhouse Yard**. The Charterhouse was founded in 1370 as a Carthusian monastery. The monks having been killed for their opposition to the Reformation, the Charterhouse was used by Tudor monarchs and aristocrats. It later became a famous school, which has now moved to Surrey. The Charterhouse today is part of an interesting grouping including the old monastery buildings themselves, along with the old Church of St. Bartholomew the Great, the Cloth Fair, and St. Bartholomew's Hospital, the oldest charitable institution still on its original London site. Look for Charterhouse near the Barbican Underground station. See the Charterhouse at http://www.english-heritage.org.uk/server/show/nav.001003005005004001.

She and Henry were married in the Queen's Closet adjoining the **Chapel Royal** at **Hampton Court**. The chapel was built by Wolsey, with improvements by Henry like the richly colored and starred vaulted ceiling. You can see this on the virtual tour at http://www.the-eye.com/hc3.htm.

Catherine watched Henry's funeral in **St. George's Chapel**, Windsor Castle, from the oriel-windowed Royal Closet Henry had had constructed for Catherine of Aragon; see *Catherine of Aragon* above.

She lived in the manor house Henry had built in **Chelsea** (see *Henry VIII*) until she married Lord Seymour of Sudeley. **Sudeley Castle** is featured at http://tudorhistory.org/castles/sudeley/, with a link to photographs at Sudeley Gallery, including a couple of Catherine's tomb in St. Mary's Church, Sudeley. Sudeley Castle is located near Winchcombe, Gloucestershire, a few miles northeast of Cheltenham, on the B4637; its own website can be seen at http://www.english-heritage.org.uk/server/show/nav.001003005005004001.

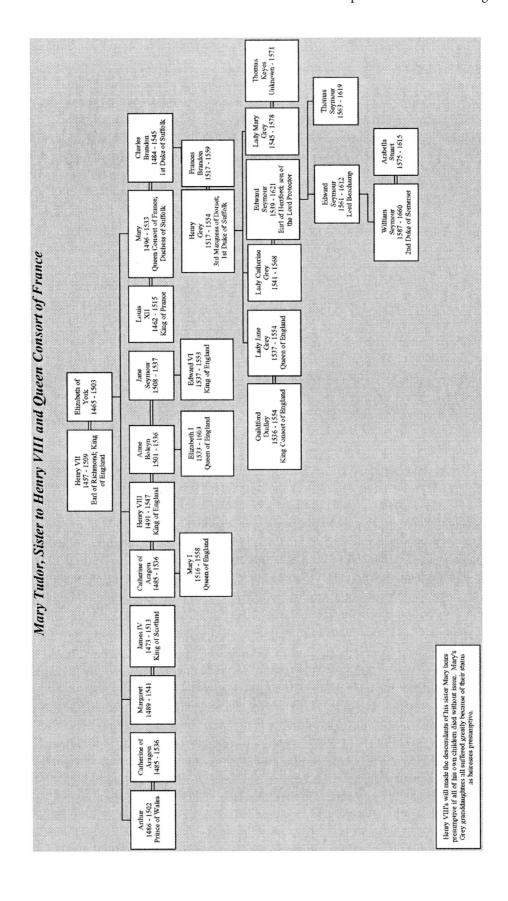

Mary Tudor, Sister to Henry VIII and Queen Consort of France

Henry VIII's will made the descendants of his sister Mary heirs presumptive if all of his own children died without issue. Mary's Grey granddaughters all suffered greatly because of their status as heiresses presumptive.

Edward VI (1537–1553; King of England and Ireland, 1547–1553)
Jane (1537–1554; Queen of England and Ireland, 1553)

Their births intertwined; so did their deaths. Lady Jane Grey was born to Frances Brandon, niece to Henry VIII, and to her husband Henry Grey, Marquess of Dorset, in October 1537, around the time that Jane Seymour gave to Henry VIII his long-deferred living male heir, Prince Edward. Grey and his wife actually named their baby daughter after Queen Jane Seymour. When Henry VIII's son and successor Edward VI died in 1553, his premature passing set in motion a sequence of events that culminated in Jane Grey's own death by execution in the following year. Fervent reformers both, these two intelligent, well-educated, and strongminded youths yet were too young to escape being controlled by powerful elders who used them as pawns in elaborate political moves. Although the reformed religion both cherished seemed eradicated by the restoration of Roman Catholicism by Edward's successor, his much older sister, Mary, it eventually prevailed during the reign of their age peer Elizabeth.

Edward's and Elizabeth's religious policy forsook the conservative settlement of Henry VIII in favor of a more radical reform. During Edward's short reign and during Elizabeth's earlier years as Queen, most English people preferred the traditional religion but also did not want restoration of papal supremacy over the Church. Therefore, the changes imposed by Edward VI's ministers in his name went beyond the popular will and even provoked unrest. These included vernacular services, repeal of heresy laws and of restrictions on preaching and on the reading of the Scriptures in private, and the acceptance of married clergy. Edward's reforms destroyed traditional relics, images, and symbols as idolatrous, as well as dissolved chantries and shrines, the revenues from which enriched the royal coffers as well as the purses of private individuals. With little support from the religious and political establishments, the 1549 Act of Uniformity mandated the use of the first Book of Common Prayer, repudiated the doctrine of transubstantiation, and outlawed the Mass. (Edward's sister Mary Tudor resolutely refused to conform to the 1549 Book of Common Prayer.) Three years later, a second Act of Uniformity and second Book of Common Prayer incorporated more explicitly evangelical views. Although fervently anti-papist, Edward remained too young to have any very great role in this religious revolution, propelled instead by his Archbishop of Canterbury, Thomas Cranmer, and his ministers—first Edward Seymour, the Lord Protector, and later John Dudley. Seymour, although firmly evangelical and influenced by a highly radical wife, opposed religious persecution. Dudley assumed the coloring of a reformer to gain the King's trust but probably did so merely out of expediency.

Because of the King's youth and his untimely death, the story of his reign mostly concerns these two magnates. While they controlled his government, Edward celebrated Christmas and New Year at Hampton Court or Whitehall, then, after Epiphany, went to Whitehall or Greenwich, observed Easter at Greenwich, spent the summer at Hampton Court or Oatlands, and finally enjoyed the autumn at Windsor or Hampton Court. (He fancied Oatlands the most.) The 1536 Succession Act had authorized Henry VIII to name guardians for a minor heir in his will. A decade later, Henry VIII's will appointed a regency council made up of 16 executors intended to rule jointly during his son's minority. These executors included Seymour, Dudley, and Cranmer. After Henry VIII's death in 1547, the executors chose as Lord Protector Edward Seymour, the King's maternal uncle. Named Earl of Hertford at Prince Edward's 1537 christening, Seymour now in 1547 became Duke of Somerset; at the same time, Dudley became Earl of Warwick.

Conflict with Scotland and France characterized Seymour's rule over the next two years, as did domestic upheaval. The Scots had declined to abide by the betrothal of their child Queen Mary to Edward that Henry VIII had arranged in 1543, and Seymour had in 1544 invaded Scotland, captured Edinburgh, and then burned it. Now, as Lord Protector, he won in 1547 a victory over the Scots at Pinkie. However, this feat of arms did not secure Mary for Edward. Instead, with her marriage to the French Dauphin arranged in 1548, she was taken to France. (Forsaken by Mary Queen of Scots, in 1551 Edward contracted to marry Elizabeth of France, daughter to Henry II.) In addition, English aggression stiffened the traditional Scots-French alliance. Then, in 1549, England went to war with France over Boulogne, taken by Henry VIII five years earlier. Besides these conflicts on foreign fields, Seymour's government experienced peasant rebellions inspired by economic and religious discontent. Sympathetic to the poor, who perhaps naively called him "The Good Duke," Seymour had advocated fixed rents and an end to the enclosure of common lands. This conciliatory stance won Seymour no friends among the wealthy, but Dudley impressed them as he crushed the rebellion led by Robert Kett.

Revolt against Seymour's domination included that of his brother Thomas Seymour, Baron of Sudeley and Lord High Admiral, who resented his brother's greater glory and power. When Catherine Parr had married Henry VIII as his sixth bride, she had to forsake her attachment to Thomas Seymour. A few months after Henry VIII died in 1547, Catherine Parr followed her heart and wed Thomas Seymour secretly—much to the eventual displeasure of the Lord Protector. Living at Catherine's properties of Chelsea Old Place, Wimbledon, and Hanworth, as well as at Sudeley, Catherine and the Lord High Admiral took on the care of Edward's sister Elizabeth, as well as of Lady Jane Grey. Thomas Seymour planned to persuade Edward VI to marry his ward, Lady Jane; he also fanned Edward's dislike of the strict Lord Protector, who limited the boy's pocket money. Besides his designs concerning Edward and Jane, the Lord High Admiral contemplated seducing and (after Catherine Parr's death in childbed) marrying the Lady Elizabeth. His busy but foolish mind also conceived an attempt to kidnap the King, which led to his attainder as a traitor and his execution. Although the Lord Protector resisted sending his brother to his death, some criticized him for not preventing it.

Members of the regency council also resented Edward Seymour's arrogance and highhandedness, and they supported a coup d'état led in 1549 by their fellow executor John Dudley, Earl of Warwick (who in 1551 made himself Duke of Northumberland). After confinement in the Tower and house arrest, Seymour gained the King's pardon and then rejoined the council. He probably had allied himself with Dudley, but they soon fell out again. Seymour's inevitable arrest in 1551 preceded a trial by his peers in which they acquitted him of treason but convicted him of the felony of inciting a riot. The populace expressed discontent at his execution in 1552, but his fellow executors and the King himself preferred Dudley to Seymour. More competent than the Lord Protector, Dudley pointedly consulted the council and flattered the King by including him in council meetings. These differences in personal style and ability masked the facts that Dudley's avarice and corruption resembled Seymour's, as did the policies he followed.

The prospect of the King's early death threatened Dudley's hold on power, and he settled on Lady Jane Grey as his means of holding on to it. Not a frail boy but instead one who delighted in sports, hunting, tournaments, and feats of war, Edward nevertheless succumbed to an insidious pulmonary infection that he could not throw off and that eventually created fatal septicaemia and kidney failure. Dudley would not be able to control Edward's presumptive successors, the strongminded Mary and Elizabeth, and Edward dreaded turning over his reformed Church to Mary, as fervently Roman Catholic as he was evangelical. Unmarried and thus susceptible to domination by a foreign and possibly Roman Catholic husband, Elizabeth also presented difficulties. Dudley persuaded Edward to disinherit both Mary and Elizabeth and name as his successor Lady Jane Grey, as evangelical as Edward and now married to an Englishman, Guildford Dudley, not coincidentally Dudley's own son.

All of this remained quite illegal, despite the King's passionate insistence on implementing it. The 1544 Act of Succession that had authorized Henry VIII to bequeath the crown in his will had also specified that Mary and her issue would succeed Edward, followed by Elizabeth and her issue. Two years later, Henry VIII's will added the provision that if none of his children had issue, the crown would go to the descendants of Henry VIII's sister Mary Tudor. By rerouting the line of succession to the younger of his two sisters, Henry VIII deliberately ignored the descendants of his other sister Margaret Tudor, including her granddaughter Mary Queen of Scots. Margaret's progeny would gain the English throne only if the line of descent from Mary Tudor dried up.

As the granddaughter of Henry VIII's sister Mary Tudor and his crony Charles Brandon, whom Henry VIII had named Duke of Suffolk, Lady Jane Grey indeed possessed a claim to the throne but only after the succession of both of Edward VI's sisters. In fact, Lady Jane's mother, Frances Brandon, had a close friendship with Edward VI's sister Mary Tudor, her first cousin, and the Greys frequently visited her. Born at Bradgate Manor in Leicestershire, Jane Grey also lived at her parents' London residence at Westminster, Dorset House. From the age of four years, Jane had received a superb education by John Aylmer (later Bishop of London under Queen Elizabeth). A sensitive and highly intelligent child continually tormented by both of her parents for the slightest imperfection, Jane found Aylmer's kindly presence a very heaven of emotional and intellectual sustenance. Jane had lived for a time in the care of Thomas Seymour and his wife Catherine Parr, another benevolent and stimulating adult, for whom in 1548 Jane acted in the ceremonial role of chief mourner. In 1551, Jane's father Henry Grey, Marquess of Dorset, became Duke of Suffolk in right of his wife, and two years later, the Greys and the Dudleys forced Jane to marry Guildford Dudley.

Although Dudley may have persuaded Edward VI to disinherit Mary and Elizabeth, the King made the project his own because of his anxiety to protect his religious reformation. His 1553 Device for the Succession willed the throne to Lady Jane Grey and her male heirs. In law, this could not stand. Not only could a minor not make a valid will, no one—minor or not—could thus negate an unrepealed Act of Parliament like the 1544 Act of Succession. However, the King's obstinacy and Dudley's power intimidated those who sought to resist this second coup d'état. After Edward's death, Jane Grey herself would resist becoming England's first Queen Regnant and utterly refused to make her husband Guildford King Regnant, but the pressure from the Greys and the Dudleys overpowered her resistance to being named Queen Jane.

Comforted by his Device for the Succession, Edward did not linger for long. A student doctor in attendance at his deathbed described the King's revolting symptoms: "He does not sleep except when he is stuffed with drugs. The sputum which he brings up is livid black, foetid and full of carbon; it smells beyond measure. His feet are swollen all over. To the doctors, all these things portend death." Frantic attempts to keep him a live may have tormented him further with the symptoms of arsenical poisoning. Dudley needed time to build support for his coup d'état. Therefore, he needed to delay Edward's death and afterwards to keep the King's death secret. The corrupted state of Edward's body may have motivated its secret burial and the substitution of a fresher, murdered, corpse for official display.

French support for the substitution of Queen Jane for Queen Mary left the Lady Mary in an apparently weak position, and the Holy Roman Emperor, Mary's first cousin and supporter Charles V, actually told his ambassadors to persuade Mary to accept Jane as Queen. However, Dudley failed in his attempts to secure the persons of both Mary and Elizabeth, and Mary showed unexpected fight. Sentiment for her as the rightful heir partly derived from the affection with which the English people had long regarded both her and her mother. Queen Jane's reign therefore lasted a mere nine days, perishing with the collapse of Dudley's hold on power. Mary imprisoned Dudley in the Garden Tower at the Tower of London, the Dudley sons in Beauchamp Tower, and Jane herself in the Gentleman Gaoler's house next door. At Dudley's trial, he stressed that he had coerced Jane "by enticement and force." His last-minute conversion to Roman Catholicism failed to avert his execution.

After being tried and convicted with her husband Guildford, his brothers Ambrose and Henry, and Archbishop Cranmer, Jane may have found that imprisonment in the Tower actually provided a welcome escape from both her family and her husband's family. She now possessed ample leisure for intensive study and devotions, as well as the comfort of her probable release. Queen Mary resolutely resisted intense pressure to execute Jane, whom she recognized as an innocent pawn. However, Henry Grey repaid Mary's mercy to him by participating in Wyatt's 1554 rebellion. Her father's treason underlined Jane's value to malcontents as a focus for conspiracy; thus it precipitated her and Guildford's executions just before Grey's own. Guildford died first, on Tower Hill, and Jane glimpsed his decapitated corpse and severed head in the cart that bore them to the Tower chapel. After writing in her prayerbook "the day of death is better than the day of our birth," Jane died on Tower Green. Her body then was buried between those of Henry VIII's executed wives Anne Boleyn and Catherine Howard in St. Peter ad Vincula.

Queen Mary's brief reign gave way to her sister Elizabeth's very long one, but neither of them bore an heir. Thus, Lady Jane Grey's younger sisters, as granddaughters of Henry VIII's sister Mary Tudor, themselves suffered the penalties of being heiresses presumptive to Queen Elizabeth. Both Lady Catherine Grey and Lady Mary Grey drew upon themselves the Queen's wrath by marrying without her permission. In 1560, Lady Catherine secretly became the wife of Edward Seymour, Earl of Hertford, son of Edward VI's Lord Protector. She compounded her errors by bearing him two healthy sons. Then, in 1565, Lady Mary Grey wed a gatekeeper, Thomas Keyes. The death in 1568 of Lady Catherine left Lady Mary for a decade in the precarious position of heiress presumptive to Queen Elizabeth, but her death a decade later released her from its anxieties and discomfort. No serious advocacy favored the succession of any other descendant of Mary Tudor, and thus the progeny of Margaret Tudor regained prominence. These, of course, included Mary Queen of Scots, dreaded as a Roman Catholic candidate, and her resolutely Protestant son, James VI, King of Scotland. Henry VIII's designs to prevent the accession of the descendants of his sister Margaret had failed utterly.

Edward VI and Jane Sites

Edward was born at **Hampton Court Palace** (see *Henry VIII*) and christened in its **Chapel Royal**. As a child, he spent time in the homes of his older sisters, but was given his own establishment at **Hunsdon**. Hunsdon House was built in the 15th century and restructured by Henry VIII from 1525–34. The luxurious royal apartments were in a range off a great gallery, and the house was moated. Edward gave it to his sister Mary for life in 1548, and it became one of her favorite residences. Read about Hunsdon at http://www. britannia.com/history/chouses/hunsdon.html, and see a photograph of the present house, along with a portrait of Edward with Hunsdon in the background. The town of Hunsdon is in Hertfordshire, on the B180, north of Harlow.

Christ's Hospital is a school, founded by Edward VI in 1552 for poor children, which became known as "Blue Coat School" for its uniform of blue gowns, knee breeches, and yellow stockings. Over the centuries, it moved out to Hertfordshire and then to Horsham, Surrey, and is now located at Horsham. A history appears at http://www.hertford.net/history/bluecoats.asp, and the school's home page is at http://www.christs-hospital.org.uk/. Horsham, with about 25,000 inhabitants, is a market town on the A24 south of Dorking. Christ's Hospital School is about two miles southwest of Horsham. It is an independent, co-educational boarding school of about 850 students.

Sherborne School dates back to the 8th century, when St. Aldhelm began to teach at the Benedictine abbey. Edward refounded the school in 1550, and it has remained a school for boys. It stands on abbey land, and some of the original abbey buildings are now incorporated, although modified, within the school. Read its history at http://www.sherborne.org/history_general_info.htm, and directions for getting there at http://www.sherborne.org/location_maps.htm. The Abbey Church next door to the school is a very fine example of perpendicular architecture. Considered one of the most beautiful towns in England, stone-built Sherborne has 7600 population, and is situated on the A30 a few miles east of Yeovil. Read about the town of Sherborne at its website, http://www.sherbornetown.co.uk/. Its 16th century castle, built by Sir Walter Raleigh, can be seen at http://www.sherbornecastle.com/entry.htm.

Another well-known school founded by Edward, of younger age, is **Shrewsbury School**, in 1552. The school was originally in the old town; it moved to its present site on the hill across the river Severn from the Dingle, overlooking the old town of Shrewsbury. Visit Shrewsbury School at http://www.shrewsbury.org.uk/.

Among grammar schools founded by Edward is **King Edward's Grammar School** (or just King Edward's School) in Birmingham. Originally, its name was the Free Grammar School, and it stood on the south side of New Street. It was later moved south to the suburb of Edgbaston.

Lady Jane Grey was born at Bradgate House, within **Bradgate Park**. The house is now in ruins, but the large park is well-treed with oaks and is home to herds of red and fallow deer; it is considered the best place to see the natural appearance of the nearby and much larger **Charnwood Forest**. Bradgate House was built by Sir Thomas Grey, a son of Elizabeth Woodville, one of the first in the new fashion of comfortable country houses, with the coming of peace and less need for fortified home. The Grey family lived in it until 1750, when it fell into ruin, and sold it in 1928 to a new owner who donated the park for use as a public park, a refreshing retreat from the busy industrialism of Leicester. The house is open twice a week; it's to the northwest of Leicester, out of **Groby**, once the home of Queen Elizabeth Woodville. See and read about Bradgate Park and house at http://members.lycos.co.uk/bradgate/bradgate.htm.

Her parents' London homes were **Dorset House**, Westminster, and **Suffolk Place**, in Southwark; neither place has survived. In her youth, Jane joined the household of Catherine Parr at **Chelsea Manor** and **Sudeley Castle**; for both these places, see *Six Queens of Henry VIII*.

Guildford Dudley's family home was **Dudley Castle**, now in ruins in the town of Dudley, a suburb of Wolverhampton. His father, John Dudley, rebuilt the residential part into a grand home in the Renaissance style. However, barely 100 years later, each side in the Civil War took a hand in wrecking the castle, the Royalists the church and the Parliamentarians the walls, turrets, and gate. In 1750, a fire got rid of what was left. Some reconstruction was done, but the castle was never inhabited again; it's now a recreational site with a zoo, introduced in 1937. See and read about Dudley Castle at http://www.dudleymall.co.uk/loclhist/olddudley/dudleycastle.htm. The Dudley London home was **Ely Place**, in Holborn, where their lifestyle was equally magnificent. No trace of the house exists.

Jane and Guildford were married at **Durham House**, in the Strand, London, which belonged to Edward; the house was richly refurbished for the occasion. Today's Durham House Street runs parallel with the Strand, and just south of it, between Charing Cross and Lancaster Place.

On her accession to the throne, Jane was taken by water to **Syon House**, home of John Dudley (now Duke of Northumberland) at Isleworth on the Thomas, where she was proclaimed Queen in the Chamber of State. For Syon House, see *Henry V*. She was then conveyed to the **Tower of London**, where she was offered the keys in the Presence Chamber of the **White Tower**. The party then moved to the **Chapel of St. John the Evangelist** for divine service. The chapel is on the first floor (second floor to North Americans) of the White Tower; it's the oldest church in London, totally Norman in design, although unique for chapels within keeps in having aisles and a tribune. Its monotoned simplicity and the warmth of its yellow stone are much admired, but it was probably painted in bright colors in its early years. See the chapel at http://www.toweroflondontour.com/stjohn.html.

Later, after Jane had relinquished the throne at the Tower, she was moved from the royal apartments to the **Queen's House**, where important prisoners lived. This is the half-timbered, black and white residence overlooking the Tower Green. See the Queen's House at http://www.toweroflondontour.com/kids/queen.html. From there, she saw her husband being escorted from the **Beauchamp Tower** (where the Dudley family were lodged) to **Tower Hill**, where he was executed, and his headless corpse returning to the **Chapel of St. Peter ad Vincula** for burial (see *Six Queens of Henry VIII*).

Jane was tried at the **Guildhall**. The Guildhall was built in the 15th century, and has been rearranged over the centuries; it suffered a lot from the bombing of London during the Second World War but has survived well. It is the headquarters of the City Corporation, and stands on Guildhall Yard, north of Gresham Street. Today, it's used for various meetings, but also for ceremonies and State banquets, and it hosts a library and bookshop, and the Guildhall Art Gallery, housing the City's art collection. Being of royal blood, Jane was executed more privately than Guildford, on **Tower Green**. See the site of the scaffold, in front of **St. Peter ad Vincula**, at http://www.hrp.org.uk/webcode/content.asp?ID=213.

Edward VI died at **Greenwich** (see *Henry VIII*) at the age of 16, his alleged remains interred in the **Henry VII Chapel at Westminster Abbey**, beneath the painting on the altar (by Vivarini)—see *Henry VII*. Both Jane and Guildford are buried in the **Chapel of St. Peter ad Vincula**: Jane lies between Anne Boleyn and Catherine Howard.

Mary I, the Courtenays, and the Poles

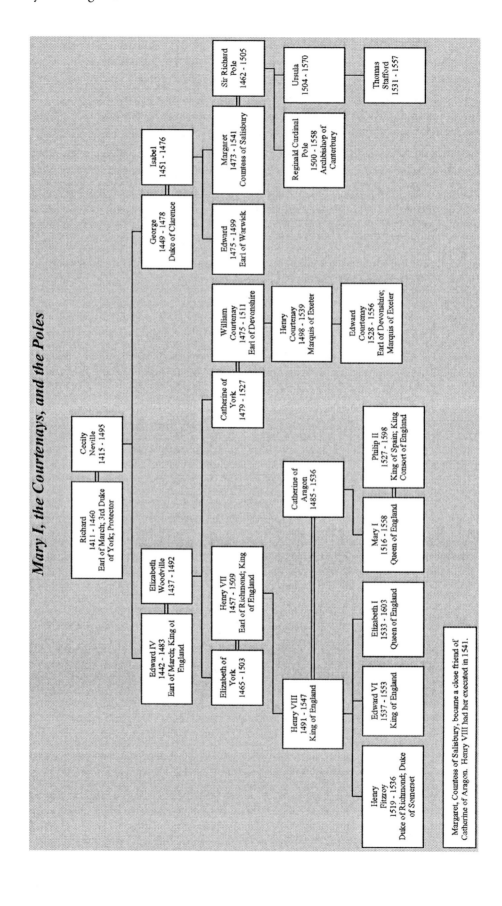

Margaret, Countess of Salisbury, became a close friend of Catherine of Aragon. Henry VIII had her executed in 1541.

Mary I (1516–1558; Queen of England and Ireland, 1553–1558)

Suffering persistently disfigured Mary Tudor's tragic life—both the pain she endured as Henry VIII's displaced daughter as well as Philip of Spain's disregarded wife, and the pain she inflicted as the persecutor of England's evangelical minority. From 1527, when Mary's father began annulment proceedings against her mother, until 1553, when Mary herself acceded to the throne, frustration and uncertainty characterized her life, and, at times, she feared imprisonment, trial, and even execution. In ridding himself of Catherine of Aragon, Henry bastardized their daughter Mary, who lost her title of Princess and, for a time, her place in the succession. Uncertainty about her status led to the suspension of the plans to marry her that had proliferated in her girlhood. Mary's joyful release from all these anxieties came with her assumption of the crown at the age of 37 and the marriage to Philip that followed. Unfortunately, Mary interpreted these happy events as part of God's plan that she should restore the papal supremacy over the Church in England. Her strategy for accomplishing the complete restoration of Roman Catholicism included the burning of heretics, which failed to suppress evangelical belief but also bred a pervasive detestation of Roman Catholicism among the English that lasted for centuries. So far from restoring Roman Catholic orthodoxy, the utterly devout Mary had made it anathema.

Her own gender had jeopardized her parents' marriage, for England had never had a Queen Regnant, and Henry VIII eventually convinced himself that God had punished him for marrying his brother Arthur's widow by denying to him and Catherine a male heir. The widespread conviction of female inferiority questioned a woman's fitness to rule. In addition, the customary authority of a husband over his wife might result in Mary's husband's ruling England in her name. If she married a foreign Prince, this could mean that England would lose her independence. Before Henry decided to repudiate his marriage to Catherine, he did give their daughter in 1525 a separate household as Princess of Wales (though he never actually conferred the title), with residences at Ludlow, Thornbury near Bristol, Tickenhill in Shropshire, and Hartlebury in Worcestershire. However, at the same time, he gave his acknowledged bastard Henry Fitzroy a larger household than Mary's and several titles to shore up his status. Perhaps, in his uncertainty about the safest course to take, the King was keeping his options open. But then, in 1527, his passion for Anne Boleyn precipitated his move towards the severance of his marriage.

From 1527 until Anne Boleyn's execution in 1536, Mary endured the pain of the King's rejection of herself and her mother, as well as the devastation of losing her status as Princess and her place in the succession. The unofficial Princess of Wales became the Lady Mary serving her baby half-sister Elizabeth in Elizabeth's household. Anne Boleyn neglected no threat or insult calculated to humiliate or intimidate Mary, and the King pointedly avoided seeing Mary when he visited Elizabeth. Separation from Catherine, even at the point of death, also broke Mary's heart. The shock of all of this ill-treatment and degradation permanently harmed Mary.

She remained loyal to her beloved mother, upholding the validity of her parents' marriage and her own legitimacy. The English people resented the King's actions against Catherine and Mary, whom they cherished, and this resentment motivated pressure on both Catherine and Mary to authorize uprisings on their behalf or active intervention by foreign powers, who also schemed to facilitate Mary's escape abroad. However, Catherine's death, the fall of Anne Boleyn, and Henry's immediate marriage to Jane Seymour altered Mary's situation. Jane advocated that Henry restore Mary to her proper place. Angered by Mary's resolute resistance, the King (who had gone so far as to contemplate trying his daughter for treason) offered reconciliation but only in wounding terms. Mary acknowledged her own illegitimacy and the King's sovereignty over the Church in England. Tormented by her submission, Mary asked for but did not receive a secret dispensation from the Pope, though eventually she received papal absolution in the year of her accession. She now had the King's and Jane's affection, as well as the support and protection of the King's minister Thomas Cromwell, and the King restored Mary's household while he reduced Elizabeth's. At the 1537 birth of Henry's son by Jane, Mary became baby Edward's godmother and soon afterward the chief official mourner for his mother. Despite Mary's detestation of Anne Boleyn, her deep love of children had attracted her to baby Elizabeth; now, she formed a lasting affection for her infant half-brother. After he became Edward VI, in 1548 he granted Hunsdon House in Hertfordshire to Mary for life, as well as her beloved New Hall or Beaulieu in Essex, purchased from Boleyn family by Henry VIII in 1516.

Henry VIII's 1547 will did not mention the legitimacy issue but named Edward, Mary, and Elizabeth as his successors. When Edward VI himself died in 1553, John Dudley, the Duke of Northumberland, engineered a seizure of the throne that crowned his daughter-in-law, Lady Jane Grey. With her headquarters at Kenninghall and then at Framlingham, Mary led a rising in support of her own accession, and with widespread public support, she soon secured the throne. Others deplored the mercy Mary showed to the conspirators, especially to the innocent Lady Jane Grey, but the Queen persisted in her clemency. It did not survive repeated batterings by subsequent conspiracies, which also heightened anxiety about heretics, perceived by her government as seditious as well as religiously deviant.

The hoped-for accession of Elizabeth served as a focus for these plots as religious persecution and the fear of Spanish domination alienated the Queen's subjects. Mary's affection for the child Elizabeth had waned as the presence of the older Elizabeth continually reminded Mary of Anne Boleyn, and Mary even deluded herself that Mark Smeaton, not Henry VIII, had fathered Elizabeth. Thomas Wyatt's rebellion in 1554 in protest of Mary's marriage to Philip of Spain preceded Henry Dudley's 1556 plot to displace Mary with Elizabeth and marry Elizabeth to Edward Courtenay, their Plantagenet kinsman and the so-called "last sprig of the White Rose." Mary fantasized about ridding herself of her half-sister, but her own failure to produce an heir made this an impractical option. Attracted to his sister-in-law Elizabeth, Philip protected her as well as urged Mary to name Elizabeth as her successor and marry her to his Catholic ally Emmanuel Philibert, Duke of Savoy. Despite Philip's pressure, Mary resisted and finally named Elizabeth as her successor in 1558 only at the urging of her council as she was dying.

Just as Mary had suffered continual uncertainty about her own accession during the reigns of Henry VIII and Edward VI, as Queen she constantly worried about conspiracies and assassination attempts as her hold on the English people weakened. The Lady Mary's uncertain status as Henry VIII's bastard had dimmed her worth in the marriage market. Once she made her own choice as Queen, her rapture soon changed to sorrow and desolation because Philip neglected her. In addition, she never bore the much-longed-for child.

Before Henry VIII's 1527 decision for an annulment, the King at various times had considered marrying Mary to François I of France, to two of François's sons, to Catherine's nephew the Holy Roman Emperor Charles V, and to Henry's nephew James V of Scotland. With the rise of Anne Boleyn, Mary's marriage prospects withered. However, after Anne's death and Mary's submission to her father in 1536, her potential bridegrooms included Charles V's brother-in-law Dom Luiz (a younger brother of the King of Portugal), the Duke of Angoulême, Philip of Bavaria, Charles V's nephew the Archduke Ferdinand, and the Duke of Savoy later proposed for Elizabeth. However, Mary remained unmarried and therefore childless. A companion noted her pessimistic words in 1542: "it was folly to think that they would marry her out of England, or even in England, as long as her father lived…. she would be, while her father lived, only Lady Mary, the most unhappy lady in Christendom."

Despite her advanced age upon her accession, Mary as a maiden Queen of 37 years came under intense pressure to marry and bear a child. Those who advocated English candidates for her hand favored Edward Courtenay and Reginald Pole, whose mother, Margaret, Countess of Salisbury, had long before discussed this union with her close friend Catherine of Aragon. Although a Cardinal since 1536, Pole had never been ordained a priest, and his deacon's orders would not prevent his marrying Queen Mary. However, Pole bowed out of this contention, and Charles V urged Mary to consider his son Philip, whom he soon made King of Naples and Jerusalem. Entranced by a portrait of Philip painted by Titian in 1551 that now hangs in the Prado in Madrid, Mary consented to the match. Philip's 1554 wedding to Mary in Winchester Cathedral secured an alliance of England with Spain and the Holy Roman Empire. If Mary bore a son, he would inherit England, Burgundy, and the Netherlands, but Philip had no claim on England if Mary died childless. (Parliament later established that Philip would serve as Regent for an infant successor to Mary.) With Mary being 11 years older than her spouse, her unlucky marriage replicated that of her mother Catherine, who was six years older than Henry VIII, as did Mary's failure to bear an heir. Twice she thought herself pregnant, but this hope (persisted in for months) proved delusional and heartbreaking. (During the 1558 "pregnancy," Elizabeth made a layette of baby clothes and brought it to court. It still exists at Hever Castle in Kent.) Mary's prayerbook preserves the marks of her tears on the page on which appears a prayer for a woman with child.

Opposition to this deeply unpopular marriage included Wyatt's rebellion in 1554. Although anti-Spanish English Catholics like Wyatt made up most of the conspirators, Jane Grey's father joined the rebellion, and his involvement doomed Lady Jane. Mary faltered under pressure to execute Jane to safeguard her own marriage to Philip. Edward Courtenay, although involved in the plot, had betrayed it. No firm evidence implicated Elizabeth, who also had known of the conspiracy, but Mary's suspicion sent Elizabeth to imprisonment in rooms in the Bell Tower at the Tower of London that had housed John Fisher, Bishop of Rochester, in 1535 and then to custody at Woodstock in Oxfordshire.

Besides fears for her own safety and grief over the lack of a child, Mary suffered because she loved Philip far more than he loved her. Although Philip influenced his wife and wielded real power in her name as his father Charles V had envisioned, he felt highly dissatisfied with and insulted by his role as King Consort without revenue or patronage or formal authority. When he left England in 1555 for the Netherlands, the Queen's distress at his prolonged absence gave him leverage over the Queen that he used to demand a coronation.

The abdicating Charles turned over to Philip the Netherlands, Spain, and Sicily, and these extensive responsibilities left Philip with less time for England. After sustained pleading by Mary, Philip finally returned in 1557, motivated by his desire to have England as his ally in his war against France. He brought with him his first cousin, Christina of Denmark, Duchess of Milan and Lorraine, who had attracted Henry VIII as a potential bride in 1539. Despite her jealousy of Christina as Philip's probable mistress, Mary insisted that England involve herself in the war against France. A French-supported raid on Scarborough by Thomas Stafford, a member of the Pole family who had conspired with Thomas Wyatt and Henry Dudley, angered Mary's reluctant council into supporting Philip's war with France. This participation would cost England her last remaining French possession, Calais.

Mary's sorrows mounted as events demonstrated her weak hold on her people's affection and on Philip's loyalty. In addition, her fervent campaign to restore Roman Catholicism in England actually caused her subjects to hate both their Queen and her religion. Her relentless pressure on her sister Elizabeth to turn Catholic led only to Elizabeth's dissembling and Mary's suspecting her sincerity. The Queen hated the thought of turning over her Kingdom to one who would undo all her efforts.

Their brother Edward VI, a firm Reformer, himself had pressured the Lady Mary to adopt evangelical beliefs and abandon the Mass he had outlawed, but she resolutely argued that he should accord her the tolerance granted her by Henry VIII after she acknowledged the King as the head of the Church in England. Mary's devotion to the Mass did not differ from Henry's, and she advocated that Edward VI leave in place the Henrician religious settlement. This difference over religion strained her affectionate relationship to her half-brother, for "the king's conscience would receive a stain if he allowed her to live in error." Although

Edward threatened to punish her disobedience as heresy, Mary courageously defied him, and the threat of war by Charles V caused the King to retreat. Then renewed pressure ended Mary's attendance at public Masses, but she continued her observances in secret. Some schemed to spirit Mary out of England to safety, but the King's death and her own accession ended that danger.

Her memories of being persecuted because of her faith did not prevent Mary from persecuting her half-sister Elizabeth, who pretended to attend Mass with devotion and to interest herself in Catholic doctrines. Despite Elizabeth's apparent conformity, Mary did not trust her. Just as she failed to convert Elizabeth, Mary failed to effect a lasting restoration of Roman Catholicism in England. With evangelicals still a tiny minority in England, she would have done better to respect the wishes of the majority to restore the Henrician religious settlement but not the papal supremacy. Instead, against the advice of Charles V and indeed of Pope Julius III, Mary insisted on restoring papal authority. Reginald Cardinal Pole, returning as a papal envoy, absolved Parliament and England. Parliament repealed Henry VIII's antipapal laws and Edward VI's religious legislation, restored ecclesiastical courts and laws against heresy but did not restore Church property, and outlawed the Book of Common Prayer, just as Edward VI had outlawed the Mass.

The conservative majority turned against the Marian restoration after the Spanish marriage associated it with the Inquisition, a dread immeasurably heightened by Mary's relentless burning of heretics. The almost 300 people burned in four years included Hugh Latimer and the former Archbishop of Canterbury Thomas Cranmer. (In contrast, Henry VIII had burned 81 heretics in 38 years, and Elizabeth would burn five in 45 years.) Latimer's heroic defiance—"We shall this day light such a candle, by God's grace, in England, as I trust shall never be put out"—and Cranmer's repudiation of his recantation of his evangelical beliefs (he burned his own right hand and arm for having signed it) inspired others to emulate their example. The steadfast resistance of so many martyrs bred more heresy, not less.

Pole replaced Cranmer as Archbishop of Canterbury in 1556 and underwent ordination as a priest at that time. A leading reformer of the Roman Catholic Church during the Council of Trent who had almost become Pope himself in 1549, Pole was shocked when Pope Paul IV attempted to recall him in 1557 and the Roman Inquisition investigated him as a heretic, along with Pole's friend Giovanni Cardinal Morone, whom the Inquisition arrested in Rome. Apparently, Paul IV suspected Morone and Pole of being secret Lutherans. Paul IV, bitterly antagonistic toward both Charles V and Philip, who had tried to prevent his election in 1555, eventually excommunicated Philip. Mary felt deep distress at the Pope's condemning her husband and her Archbishop of Canterbury. It seemed a poor reward to all of them for their labors in the cause of Roman Catholicism.

Domestic sedition and heresy, a disappointing marriage, two fruitless pregnancies, an untrustworthy heir, the failure of the Marian restoration, the loss of Calais—all these sorrows crowded one another at Mary's 1558 deathbed. (Pole died a few hours later.) Perhaps revealing her poignant longing to bear a child, the dying Queen told her ladies "what good dreams she had, seeing many little children, like angels, play before her, singing pleasing notes, giving her more than earthly comfort." Earthly comfort there was none. Despite high intelligence, loyalty, courage, and manifold other virtues—her very real habits of clemency and generosity, her extreme industry and sense of dedication, Mary had gone wrong by evaluating policies not by their political effect but by their moral rightness, as she rigidly defined it. Hers was not the story of monstrous sadism delighting in cruelty but the far more terrifying story of human goodness deluding itself that its evil means were just.

Mary I Sites

Mary was born at **Greenwich Palace** (see *Henry   VIII)*. Of the residences Henry gave Mary, for **Ludlow Castle**, see *Edward   V*. **Thornbury Castle** was built in Tudor times. Henry visited it with Anne Boleyn, and

Mary spent several years there. It's now a luxury hotel. Visit it yourself at http://www.celticcastles.com/castles/thornbury/. Thornbury is located in south Gloucestershire, near the river Severn and just north of the M4 and the Severn bridges, on the B4461. **Tickenhill House** (also called palace and manor) is located over the town of **Bewdley**, on the upper reaches of the river Severn, and a few miles west of Kidderminster, near the A 456. Bewdley is an attractive old town with about 8500 population. Tickenhill House, once Tudor, now has a Georgian façade. At time of writing, the only satisfactory website for Bewdley appears at http://www.bewdley.com/, but the information is short and no image of Tickenhill House could be located online.

One of Mary's favorite residences was **Hunsdon**, which her brother Edward had granted her for life in 1548. For further information, see *Edward VI*. Another was **New Hall**, which was also her most splendid. Henry VIII bought it from the Boleyn family and carried out extensive renovations. Located near Chelmsford, Essex, it was large, with all the accoutrements of a royal residence, many windows and courtyards, a great hall, grand staircase, and royal apartments in their own wing, three stories tall. The Tudor house was largely demolished in the 19th century, and replaced by other buildings; all that remains from the Tudor era are the Elizabethan wing and Henry VIII's coat of arms in the chapel. Newhall today is owned by Community of the Canonesses of the Holy Sepulchre, and is the oldest independent Catholic girls' school in England, 350 years old, of which over 200 have been spent at Newhall. Visit the Community at http://www.newhall.org.uk/home/community.

Henry VIII had seized **Framlingham Castle** from the Howard family. Subsequently, Edward VI gave the castle to Mary, who restored it to the Howards and often stayed there at crucial times in her life: there, she took refuge during the attempt to place Lady Jane Grey on the throne, and there she was told of her accession to the throne. Later, the castle was taken again by Elizabeth I and used as a prison for Catholic priests. Over the centuries, the castle has been poorhouse, courthouse, drill hall, meeting hall, and even a fire station! It's now maintained by English Heritage. Framlingham is different from most castles of the 12th century in having no keep: rather, it consists of a curtain wall punctuated by 13 circular towers (12 remain). It's possible to walk the castle walls. Visit Framlingham and its castle at http://www.framlingham.com/visit/castle/castle.html. Framlingham is in Suffolk, west of Saxmundham, on the B1119.

The castle at **Kenninghall** was another of Mary's homes in East Anglia. The Duke of Norfolk had built a brick manor house near the ancient castle, which passed to the Crown and then to Mary. It was demolished in 1650. The village of Kenninghall stands in the middle of a web of country roads between the A11 and the A143; the nearest towns are Diss and Thetford. Kenninghall's website is at http://www.kenninghall.org.uk/.

Copped Hall, or Copt Hall, was another residence. On the northern edge of Epping Forest, just to the east of Waltham Abbey, the original hall was given to Henry VIII to save Waltham Abbey from his Dissolution of the Monasteries, a vain attempt. Henry visited the hall but never lived there; Edward VI allowed Mary to live there. Elizabeth I gave the hall to Sir Thomas Heneage, where he built a mansion. Including Heneage's building, Copped Hall was rebuilt twice and then burned in 1917, although the gardens and what was left of the house were maintained. The Copped Hall Trust took it over in the 1990s, intent on saving the property from development, and has a splendidly informative website at http://www.coppedhalltrust.org.uk/index.html.

Mary sold **Nonsuch Palace** to the Earl of Arundel. For Nonsuch, see *Henry VIII*.

When she was staying with Sir John Huddlestone at **Sawston Hall**, the place was burned by Protestants. Mary promised to rebuild the house, which was completed in 1584. Her ghost is said to inhabit the house, appearing from time to time in the hall. Sawston Hall stands in the center of the village of Sawston, a few miles to the southeast of Cambridge, and on the A11; the Huddlestone family continued to live there until the 1970s, and the house is now a language school. See Sawston Hall at http://huddleston.bravepages.com/history/sawston.html.

When the shrine of Edward the Confessor in **Westminster Abbey** was despoiled after Dissolution and his body buried in another part of the abbey, Mary restored the coffin to its proper place in 1557 and gave new jewels to replace those stolen. For details and views, see ***Henry III.***

At **Windsor Castle**, Mary built houses for the Military Knights on the south side of the Lower Ward. The two ranges, with the **Mary Tudor Tower** in the center, are next to the Henry VIII Gate. Read about the Military Knights at http://www.stgeorges-windsor.org/today/tod_knights.asp.

On her way to marry Philip II of Spain, awaiting his arrival in Winchester, Mary stayed at **Farnham Castle**. Built during the 12th century, the castle was ordered demolished by Henry II, but was rebuilt shortly afterwards. It formed a residence for the Bishops of Winchester until the early 20th century. Most of the castle is occupied by the Farnham Castle International Briefing and Conference Center and can be seen only sometimes, but the keep, maintained by English Heritage, is open to the public. Farnham, an attractive town with 36,000 inhabitants, is midpoint between London and Winchester; visit it and see a photograph of the keep at http://www.castlexplorer.co.uk/england/farnham/farnham.php, and aerial photograph at http://www. information-britain.co.uk/showPlace.cfm?Place_ID=1813.

Mary and Philip were married in **Winchester Cathedral**; the chair she used is in the Lady Chapel of the cathedral. For basic information regarding the cathedral, see ***William   Rufus***. After the wedding, the nuptial banquet was served at **Wolvesey Palace**, the residence of the Bishops of Winchester. The palace we see today is the one remaining wing of the 1680s house, with the ruins of the 12th century palace Mary and Philip knew. The earlier palace, built in the 12th century, was stripped of most of its stone for the construction of the 1680s house. It's known as Wolvesey Castle, or Old Wolvesey; see it at http://britannia.com/tours/winchester/wolvesey.html, making sure you click on the link to Old Wolvesey for an aerial view of the size and bulk of the old palace. For the current palace, see http://britannia.com/tours/winchester/palace.html.

Mary died in **St. James's Palace** in 1558 (see ***Henry VIII)***. She is buried in the **Henry VII Chapel**, **Westminster Abbey**, sharing a monument with her estranged sister, Elizabeth. The inscription reads: "Consorts both in throne and grave, here rest we two sisters, Elizabeth and Mary, in the hope of one Resurrection." Apparently this was due to some wishful thinking on the part of their successor James I.

Philip II survived Mary by 40 years, dying in 1598 at **El Escorial**, near Madrid, where he is also buried. He had married Elizabeth of Valois in 1559, the year following Mary's death. El Escorial (the full name is El Real Sitio de S. Lorenzo el Real del Escorial) was built by Philip as a royal burial place, and to fulfil a vow made at the battle of St. Quentin, fought in 1557 on St. Lawrence's Day. West of Madrid, in the foothills of the Sierra de Guadarrama, the site was chosen for its water and air and a nearby quarry.

While the palace was being built, Philip lived at the clergy-house at nearby Galapagar, the last intermediate halt of royal funerals. El Escorial, huge and austere, is a small city in itself, with a monastery, church, library, as well as royal palace and mausoleum. The statistics regarding its architecture are mind-boggling: the place is 400,000 square feet, with 16 courtyards, 86 staircases, 1200 doors, and twice as many windows. Read about it in English at http://www.madrid-on-line.com/eng/turisme/alrededores_escorial.htm. In Spanish, see http://www.patrimonionacional.es/escorial/escorial.htm; there are photographs of the various parts of the building on subsequent screens, along with good information for those who read Spanish.

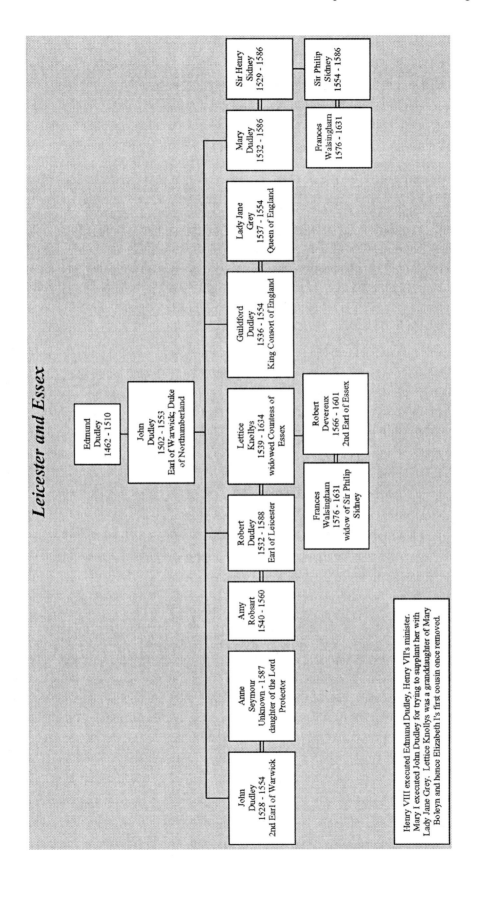

Leicester and Essex

Henry VIII executed Edmund Dudley, Henry VII's minister.
Mary I executed John Dudley for trying to supplant her with
Lady Jane Grey. Lettice Knollys was a granddaughter of Mary
Boleyn and hence Elizabeth I's first cousin once removed.

Elizabeth I (1533–1603; Queen of England and Ireland, 1558–1603)

Elizabeth Tudor rewrote the script set out for her as a Queen Regnant. If by ill chance a woman should succeed to the throne, as a fallible and inferior female she must seek the wiser counsel of a husband and bear him sons to return the crown to a fit wearer. Loving power and majesty, Elizabeth felt no need or desire to share them. Hating marriage, Elizabeth often proclaimed her preference for spinsterhood. Fearing popular disaffection, Elizabeth refused to breed for the succession or even to name a preferred successor. In her rejection of the conventional expectations of a Queen Regnant, Elizabeth saw before her the examples of her more conventional predecessor, her sister Mary I, and of her rival, Mary Queen of Scots. Marriage had brought misery and vulnerability to each of them, as it had to her own mother and stepmothers; the obligatory pregnancy had tortured Mary Tudor as well as killed Jane Seymour and Catherine Parr. Responding to pressures to marry from Parliament, her advisors, and foreign suitors, Elizabeth procrastinated, prevaricated, dissembled, and changed her mind, seeming to consider various matches even as she exalted her virgin state. A master of doubletalk, she fostered ambiguity. A highly skilled political strategist hid behind her mask of feminine indecisiveness. Far from alone in his exasperation, a Spanish ambassador complained, "what a pretty business it is to deal with her.... she must have a thousand devils in her body, notwithstanding that she is forever telling me that she longs to be a nun and to pass her time in a cell praying." Others perceived her real intentions through the cobwebs she spun. Very early in her reign, the Scottish ambassador commented to her, "Your Majesty thinks that if you were married you would be but Queen of England, and now you are both Queen and King." As she improvised this strategy for holding power and succeeded in resisting her prescripted role, the accomplished actress Elizabeth grew in her mastery of her part, until she had completely revised the play to suit herself.

Before her accession, Elizabeth had survived a quarter-century of insecurity, humiliation, and danger. Demoted from legitimacy and the status of Princess after the fall of Anne Boleyn, her three-year-old daughter questioned the governor of her household, "How haps it, Governor: yesterday My Lady Princess, and today but My Lady Elizabeth?" She had learned to keep her own counsel, to act a part, to keep others unsure of her meaning or motive. Her advisers sometimes coped by deceiving her in their turn. Elizabeth's penchant for ambiguity and delay constituted her strategy for maintaining control of her government, of foreign affairs, and of the religious controversies of her day.

Despite Mary Tudor's compliance with the conventional expectations of a Queen Regnant, her reign had left one positive legacy for her sister. Considering the question of whether the husband of a Queen Regnant owned and ruled the realm as his wife's property, automatically handed over to him after marriage, Parliament established by statute that the Queen ruled just as her male predecessors had done. Marital traditions did not limit a Queen Regnant's right to the crown or constrain her regal authority. Elizabeth's love of power as well as aptitude for governing caused her to reject the advice of her brother-in-law Philip II of Spain to "take a consort who might relieve her of those labours which are only fit for men." Even those who recognized her intelligence, ability, and hard work, however, wanted her to marry to ensure the succession and to secure an alliance with a foreign power. Instead, she waved aside concerns about her successor and, instead of allying England with one power by a marriage of state, encouraged many allies to expect her eventual favor.

At the same time that she seemingly considered foreign suitors, Elizabeth openly expressed her strong aversion to marriage: "Beggarwoman and single, far rather than Queen and married." Instead of wedding a mere mortal man, she as Queen had united herself with her realm: as she told her first Parliament in 1559, "I am already bound unto a husband which is the Kingdom of England." As the Virgin Queen of this husband, the Kingdom of England, Elizabeth expected homage paid to her as Gloriana in many celebrations and courtly compliments. Thus, she maintained control of her male courtiers and advisers, who competed for her favor as their Lady.

Of all of the handsome men whose careers she fostered, she loved best Robert Dudley. Although Dudley sometimes hoped (and many others feared) that Elizabeth might eventually wed him, their old intimacy had taught him better: "I really believe that the Queen will never marry. I have known her since she was eight years of age, better than any man in the world. From that time she has always invariably declared that she would remain unmarried." As a new Queen, Elizabeth appointed Dudley Master of the Horse. Two years later, the mysterious death of Amy Robsart, Dudley's wife of ten years, at Cumnor House in Oxfordshire, bred scandalous interpretations that spoke of marriage profiting from murder. At that time, Elizabeth promised her closest adviser and Secretary of State, William Cecil (later Lord Burghley) that she would never marry Dudley. This did not keep her from showing Dudley what others considered undue favor. Very ill from smallpox in 1562, Elizabeth asked that Dudley become Protector and later added him to her council. William Cecil persuaded her also to name to the council Thomas Howard, 4th Duke of Norfolk, Dudley's antagonist. Then, in 1563, William Cecil urged a proposal that Mary Queen of Scots should marry Dudley in return for recognition as Elizabeth's successor. To make Dudley a more eligible match for the Queen of Scots, Elizabeth made him Earl of Leicester. However, neither Dudley nor Mary fancied each other, and Dudley, who preferred to marry Elizabeth, persuaded her to allow Henry Stuart, Lord Darnley, to visit Mary in Scotland. Darnley married Mary in 1565, uniting two Catholic claims to the English throne and increasing potential danger to Elizabeth. Dudley himself secretly married the Queen's cousin Lettice Knollys, the widow of the Earl of Essex. United with Norfolk in a ploy to topple William Cecil in 1569 that the Queen defeated, Dudley also supported attempts to marry Norfolk to Mary Queen of Scots after her imprisonment in England. His relationship with Elizabeth survived many rifts, and she sent Dudley as commander to the English armies fighting the Spanish in the Netherlands, where his nephew, the poet and soldier Sir Philip Sidney, made a famous heroic death. Lieutenant General for the defence of the realm during England's defeat of the Spanish Armada in 1588, Dudley himself died soon afterward. He left to Elizabeth his indelible memory, as well as his stepson, Robert Devereux, Earl of Essex. With Essex, the ambiguously erotic favoritism of the Queen continued, until his arrogance, insubordination, and treason forced Elizabeth to execute him in 1601. The fall of Essex increased the power and influence of his enemy Robert Cecil (later Earl of Salisbury).

Elizabeth's apparent and real infatuations with goodlooking courtiers did not sway the Queen from her underlying determination never to marry. Nor did the many negotiations, protracted over years, for a diplomatic marriage with one or another foreign candidate. The Queen spun silken webs of ambiguity that kept many royal suitors in her net. The Austrian Emperor Maximilian complained about English responses to a proposal to marry her to his brother the Archduke Charles: "This answer is most obscure, ambiguous, involved and of such a nature that we cannot learn from it whether the Queen is serious and sincere or whether she wishes to befool us." In 1579, François, Duke of Alençon and Anjou, son of Henry II of France and Catherine de'Medici, became the first wooer to press his suit in person. Responding to her "Frog's" ardor and to his emissary's romantic theft of her nightcap and garter for his master's delectation, Elizabeth actually seemed to favor this proposal and to storm against the popular opposition that killed it. No one knows if she meant what she said or simply engaged in yet more obfuscation and contradiction. Perhaps Alençon's suit exposed her to the pain of a deep ambivalence.

Ambiguity hoarded her power and safeguarded her person from sexual violation and from pregnancy. She also tried to use it to avoid religious violence. Impatient with theologians, Elizabeth called their arguments "ropes of sand or sea-slime leading to the moon." She often shouted at impertinent preachers during their sermons. No religious fanatic (unlike her brother and sister), the Queen had no interest whatever in the inner thoughts of her subjects. She had had her own inner thoughts during Mary's reign but conformed outwardly to the State's expectations of Catholic observance, and outward conformity was all she asked of her subjects.

Her reimposing the religious settlement of Edward VI at the beginning of her reign went beyond the preferences of the conservative majority, but the Church of England that she established became synonymous with English patriotism by the end of her reign. The tolerance she had tried to foster changed into her government's active repression of English Catholics. Both the identification of the reformed Church of England and the persecution of English Catholics resulted from the intertwining of religious preference with sedition against her rule or loyalty to her.

The 1568 flight from Scotland to England of the deposed Mary Queen of Scots, Catholic claimant to the English crown, precipitated efforts to displace the bastard heretic Elizabeth with Mary. After a failed Northern Rebellion in 1569 by the Earls of Northumberland and Westmorland, Pope Pius V issued the 1570 papal bull *Regnans in Excelsis*. Pius V excommunicated Elizabeth and released her subjects from their allegiance to her; the papal Secretary of State later clarified that assassinating Elizabeth would be a holy act. Although earlier schemes to marry Mary had caused the imprisonment of Norfolk, he nevertheless involved himself in the 1571 Ridolfi conspiracy to gather papal and Spanish support for a rising by English Catholics to enthrone Mary and marry her to Norfolk. Norfolk's treason led Elizabeth reluctantly to sign his 1572 death warrant. Undeterred by these failures, later plots on behalf of Mary Queen of Scots included the 1583 Throckmorton plot and the 1586 Babington plot, after which the trial of Mary for conspiracy to assassinate Elizabeth ended in her condemnation. Although Elizabeth finally signed Mary's death warrant in 1587, the Queen denied responsibility after Mary's beheading. The 1588 invasion attempt by Philip II of Spain, who took up the Catholic cause against Elizabeth as her potential successor, further united the English against the Catholic menace threatening their autonomy and their sovereign.

Contrary to the Queen's previous intentions and preferences, all of this caused Elizabeth's government to crack down on those who absented themselves from reformed services or continued to hear Mass, who now became possible traitors, even though most observant English Catholics actually remained loyal to the Queen. After the expression of papal support for her assassination or overthrow, most faithful English Catholics suffered some financial and social penalties, with the harshest measures being directed against priests and missionaries. The union of sedition with religious choice created the persecution of Catholics in England, as well as their civil disabilities, and it identified membership in the reformed Church of England with patriotism.

Despite papal hostility to the English Queen, a papal admirer applauded her courage and leadership during the crisis of the 1588 invasion attempted by the Spanish Armada. "What a valiant woman," reacted her fellow professional celibate, Sixtus V, "It is a pity that Elizabeth and I cannot marry; our children would have ruled the whole world." Her improbably successful reign stretched from 1558 to 1603—for 45 years after she had learned of her accession at Hatfield Old Place and exclaimed, "This is the Lord's doing, and it is marvelous in our eyes." From the residences she had inherited from Henry VIII—Hatfield, Ashridge House, and Enfield Palace, the bastard child that no one had expected to reign for almost 50 years came to live in Hampton Court, Whitehall, Greenwich—a favorite palace, where she had been born, Eltham, and Windsor. At her most cherished home, Richmond, she finally in 1603 met Death, the one antagonist she could not evade or put off, lamenting "I am tied with a chain of iron around my neck. I am tied, I am tied, and the case is altered with me." Deeply depressed, for four days the dying Elizabeth sat on cushions on the floor of her Privy Chamber, staring at the ground, refusing to eat, still not naming a successor until her final moments, if she did so even then.

Elizabeth I Sites

Elizabeth, like her father and half-sister, was born at **Greenwich Palace**. Her white christening robe is on display at **Sudeley Castle**, Catherine Parr's later home (see *Six Queens of Henry VIII*). After her father's death,

Elizabeth went to live with Catherine Parr at her dower house, **Chelsea manorhouse**, built by Elizabeth's father. See *Henry VIII* for background information regarding Chelsea.

Elizabeth was not to spend much time at the places she lived as a child: Hatfield, Enfield Place, Elsynge, Ashridge. Newhall and Hunsdon were leased, as was Ashridge. For Newhall, see *Mary I*. Elizabeth stayed with her sister Mary at **Hunsdon**, where, it is rumored, the latter taught her how to play cards for stakes. For details regarding Hunsdon, see *Edward VI*.

Elizabeth's household had first been established at **Hatfield House**, a red brick palace built around a quadrangle by Cardinal John Morton between 1480 and 1497, which she had been given in 1550 and became her chief residence in 1555. Only the western range, including the great hall, survives today, because after her death Robert Cecil demolished the old house to make way for a splendid Jacobean mansion, leaving only remnants of the old house, called the Old Palace, in the grounds. Even in Elizabeth's time the gardens at Hatfield were beautiful, and they have since become legendary: the present Jacobean layout was the work of John Tradescant, and the gardens continue to be maintained in the style and plantings of that period by the Marchioness of Salisbury, wife of the owner and a gardening expert. The style may be different, but in spirit the gardens Elizabeth knew have continued. More concretely, remnants of the oak tree under which Elizabeth learned of her accession to the throne can be seen in the palace shop. Portraits of Elizabeth are included in Hatfield's collection of paintings. Visit Hatfield House at http://www.hatfield-house.co.uk/. This is a clear, attractive, and informative site, including a map and visiting details. See also http://tudorhistory.org/castles/hatfield/ for Tudor History's account of Hatfield, including a Gallery of photographs.

Ashridge is a Gothic mansion standing on the site of a monastery of Bonhommes, where Elizabeth was arrested in 1554 by Mary. The house stands about 3 miles north of Berkhamsted, and is now Ashridge Management College; see it at http://www.conference-hotels.com/london-2/ashridge.htm.

Elizabeth was given **Enfield Palace** in 1550; all three children had stayed there. Enfield Chase, now within Greater London, was a favorite hunting place for Henry VIII. The Lancasters had inherited the manor at the end of the 14th century; the palace was probably constructed on the site of the medieval manor house. See the house at http://www.heritagesites.eu.com/england/enfield.htm.

Nearby, and much larger, was **Elsynge Place**, also at Enfield, which Henry VIII enlarged and refurbished. The moated house was entered over a drawbridge; two fine gatehouses led to two courtyards. As well as the hunting available in the park and surrounding woodland, the royal family enjoyed bowling and archery. During the Civil War, Elsynge was demolished, and a Jacobean house, **Forty Hall**, built on the other side of the lake. This was bought by the Enfield Borough Council in 1951 and opened as a museum in 1955. Fine gardens still surround the house. For photographs and an account of Forty Hall, see http://www.enfield.gov.uk/fortyhall/; click on Forty Hall Trail for a history of Elsynge and Forty Hall.

When Elizabeth grew up, she tended to avoid the places where she had been confined. Thus, she avoided **Woodstock**, where she had been confined in the gatehouse, and she never used the state apartments in the **Tower of London** after the pre-coronation obligatory stay. The Bell Tower, where Mary had had her confined, can be seen at http://www.toweroflondontour.com/belltow.html. She arrived by boat at Traitor's Gate; see several photographs at http://tudorhistory.org/castles/tower/gallery.html. Elizabeth inherited many castles and houses, selling or leasing most of them. She ran those she kept and lived in with strict economy, and she spent little on rebuilding or extending her houses, in contrast to her father.

Westminster Palace had burned down in 1512. **Whitehall Palace** opposite was therefore Elizabeth's chief residence, and the place she stayed in more than any other. It was a vast, sprawling range of buildings occupying 23 acres, and with 2,000 rooms, most of them small and poky, it was probably the largest palace in Europe. For more information, see *Henry VIII*.

Elizabeth was not as fond of **St. James's Palace** as Mary had been, using it only when **Whitehall** was being cleaned. Her coat of arms is above the door to the Chapel Royal, supported by a carved lion and red dragon. See *Henry VIII* for background on St. James's Palace.

Elizabeth also favored **Windsor** as a residence, although only in the summer months; it was too cold for her otherwise. In 1583, she built a 90-foot long gallery where she could exercise indoors, when necessary, which now houses the Royal Library; she was fond of hunting in Windsor Great Park. On the northern side of the Upper Ward, she extended and widened the stone North Terrace. Other constructions outdoors—a bridge, chapel, and banqueting pavilion—no longer exist. Early in her reign, she planned a tomb for Henry in St. George's Chapel, but she never built it.

She used **Greenwich Palace** for conducting ceremonies on state occasions and for receiving foreign envoys at the riverside gatehouse. See *Henry VIII* for background information on Greenwich. Having had a near-fatal experience with smallpox in 1562 in **Hampton Court**, she tended to avoid this palace, too, but later came to appreciate it for holidays like Easter, Whitsun, and Christmas, and, like Greenwich, for state occasions and entertainment, like plays performed in the Great Hall, although continuing to think of it as uncomfortable and unhealthy. As usual, she didn't spend time and money on further construction and refurbishment but had the stables extended and barns and a coach house built; she also took an interest in the gardens, ordering the new plants recently discovered in the New World, potatoes and tobacco, planted there. For background information on Hampton Court, see *Henry VIII*.

Also later in her reign, she spent more time at **Richmond Palace**. Its modern construction made it warm—a change from the draughts of other residences. Elizabeth called it "a warm nest for my old age," and she was to die there. See *Henry VII* for Richmond Palace.

Mary I had leased **Nonsuch** to the Earl of Arundel, and Elizabeth could not take possession of it until he died in 1592. Nevertheless, she visited frequently and cited it as the one "of all places she likes best." There, she rode and hunted in the park, and received ambassadors, although the house was too small to accommodate everyone (tents had to be set up in the grounds), and there was no great hall. For background information concerning Nonsuch, see *Henry VIII*.

Elizabeth used **Eltham Palace** (see *Edward II*) as a hunting lodge and visited **Oatlands** (see *Six Queens of Henry VIII*) frequently for the hunting. Another hunting lodge she inherited from her father is preserved in **Epping Forest**. Epping Forest is an ancient woodland northeast of London. At 6,000 acres, 12 miles long and 2 ½ miles wide, it's the largest open public space near London. As such, royalty had hunted in it since Norman times, and commoners had the right to graze livestock and collect wood for building and fires. It is now owned by the Corporation of London, preserved for the "recreation and enjoyment of the people." The half-timbered hunting lodge is relatively humble, three-storied and painted white, on Ranger's Road, **Chingford**. See http://www.cityoflondon.gov.uk/Corporation/leisure_heritage/architectural_heritagehunting_lodge.htm for some background information and visiting details. There's a legend that she raced her horse up the stairs of the lodge on hearing that the Spanish Armada had been defeated.

At **Tilbury Fort**, Elizabeth made the best-known speech of her reign to the soldiers assembled in a camp in anticipation of the Armada in 1588: "I know that I have the body of a weak, feeble woman, but I have the heart and stomach of a king, and of a king of England too." Tilbury, on the north bank of the Thames where the river narrows, and opposite Gravesend on the south, is a container port which, in the past, was strategically important. Henry VIII built the fort, which is a little west of the town of Tilbury and is open all year. Its present appearance is mostly due to Charles II, who had Henry's fort replaced by the most up-do-date in military engineering. For a photograph and brief description, see http://www.riverthames.co.uk/thingstodo/places/_tilbury.htm. Tilbury fort is now maintained by English Heritage; see an aerial view and read its history at http://www.english-heritage.org.uk/server/show/

conProperty.48 and more at http://www.castlexplorer.co.uk/england/tilbury/tilbury.php. Read Elizabeth's speech at http://www.luminarium.org/renlit/tilbury.htm.

Elizabeth made frequent trips to the great houses of England, usually putting her hosts to considerable expense as many of them pulled out all the stops for her visit. There are too many to mention here, but notable among them was **Kenilworth Castle**, which Elizabeth had granted to Robert Dudley, Earl of Leicester, in 1563. At this time, Kenilworth was a splendid house, unusual in that it was developed in medieval style, in conformity with its 12th century structure, and not in the new Renaissance style, with gardens and a lake with a fountain surrounded by statues of nude nymphs. Leicester's entertainments were mind-bogglingly extravagant and imaginative, and after her last visit in 1575, his household economy never recovered. Kenilworth today presents only a splendid ruin; for basic information, see *John of Gaunt*.

It's often said that Elizabeth founded **Jesus College, Oxford University**, in 1571. However, it was Hugh Price, the treasurer of St. David's Cathedral in Wales, who persuaded Elizabeth to lend her prestige to the initiative, as is reflected in its charter: "Jesus College…of Queen Elizabeth's Foundation." Intended for the education of future clergymen, it has maintained a strong connection with Wales over the centuries. About 15% of undergraduates are Welsh, and the college houses Celtic Studies and is a leader in the area. St. David's Day is an important celebration at the college. See Hugh Price, and read about the founding of the college at http://www.jesus.ox.ac.uk/history/founders.php. For the college's history, go to http://www.jesus.ox.ac.uk/history/beginning.php, and http://www.jesus.ox.ac.uk/tour/ takes you on a comprehensive tour.

Elizabeth died at **Richmond Palace** (see *Henry VIII*). She is buried in the tomb she shares with her estranged sister, Mary I, in the **Henry VII Chapel**, **Westminster Abbey**. See the tomb and her face on her effigy at http://www.westminster-abbey.org/tour/lady_chapel/elizabeth1.htm.

Stuarts:

Scottish Royals and Tudor Offshoots

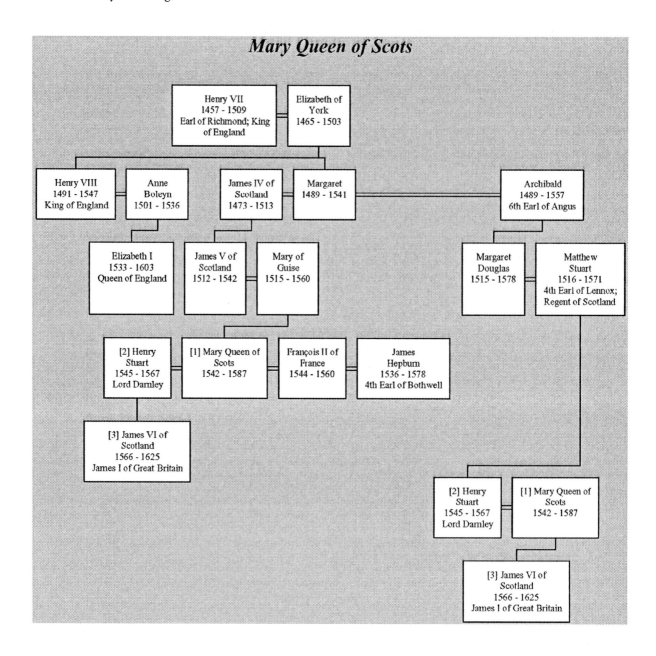

Mary Queen of Scots

Mary Queen of Scots (1542–1587; reigned in France as Queen Consort, 1559–1560, in Scotland as Queen Regnant, 1542–1567)

Is Mary Queen of Scots more famous for marrying badly or dying well? Her life was fraught with drama from its very beginning, as her father, James V of Scotland, died the very week in which Mary was born, and his six-day-old daughter became Scotland's Queen. Brought up in France and married there to the Dauphin (later François II), the soon-widowed Queen of Scots then returned to her native land, where she twice wed disastrously, suffered forced abdication, imprudently fled to England, spent 20 years there in illegal imprisonment, incessantly plotted against her jailer Elizabeth I, and died for her conspiracies. Arguably, by putting Mary on trial and executing her at Fotheringhay, Elizabeth transformed Mary's notoriety into glamorous victimhood and actually ensured Mary's immortal fame.

When the condemned Queen of Scots partially disrobed as she prepared herself for her beheading, she cast off a black satin dress to stand in a red satin bodice, long red sleeves, and a red petticoat. Thus she died robed in the liturgical color of Roman Catholic martyrdom. Martyr for her faith as she seemed to many, to others Mary Stuart's red clothing might well have signified her status as a scarlet woman. She seemed to them both an evil, designing whore and an advocate of an evil religion, the Whore of Babylon. In truth, Mary Queen of Scots was neither a Roman Catholic martyr nor *la belle dame sans merci*. Instead, an expendable victim, she repeatedly fell into the power of the unscrupulous. A charming, accomplished, and brave woman with a genius for personal relations and a fine sense of personal loyalty, she lacked any political sense and in crucial moments lacked sound judgment.

Such a character, bound up with her pedigree, doomed her. A sovereign with her bloodlines and in her precarious position could not afford to prefer personal affections to political realities. Born the granddaughter of Henry VIII's sister Margaret Tudor, Mary stood to inherit the throne of England if her first cousin once removed, the Protestant Elizabeth I, died without issue. Indeed, many Catholics considered Elizabeth Tudor Henry VIII's bastard rather than the child of a legitimate marriage. They therefore believed that Mary Stuart should reign, not after Elizabeth, but in Elizabeth's place. In addition, the 1570 papal bull *Regnans in Excelsis* excommunicated Elizabeth and released her English Catholic subjects from their bond of loyalty to her. Even to her loyal Protestant subjects, Elizabeth's continuing childlessness perpetuated Mary's status as her potential heir until the growth to manhood of Mary's son James VI of Scotland provided an alternative and Protestant descendant of Margaret Tudor to sit on the English throne.

Thus, Mary naively hoped that her personal relationship with her cousin Elizabeth could develop into a trusting friendship. Elizabeth more accurately perceived Mary as a dagger pointed at her own heart. Always remembering that "I have found treason in trust," Elizabeth possessed a sounder political sense than Mary did.

The trouble between them began in the very year of Elizabeth's accession, 1558. Henry II of France claimed for his new daughter-in-law Mary Queen of Scots the throne of England. After her husband, François II, died a few years later, Mary in 1561 returned to Scotland. Seeking to rule a now-Protestant realm from which she had been absent for thirteen years, she began well, charming the people and deciding not to disturb the Protestant character of her country. Instead, she simply asked for the freedom to practice her Roman Catholic faith in private.

Mary's religious tolerance and personal charm, however appealing, did not equip her to deal with contentious and ruthless Scottish nobles intent upon preserving and expanding their power. Out of her depth in power politics, she made several crucial errors of judgment that allowed them to depose her and to justify that deposition by vilifying her.

In 1565, an infatuated Queen of Scots married her first cousin, Henry Lord Darnley, an English subject with his own claims to Elizabeth's throne derived from his and Mary's grandmother, Margaret Tudor. In short order, Darnley (now King Henry of Scotland) alienated his bride as well as the Scottish nobles, who felt jealous of his ascendancy in any case. In early 1566, some of these nobles inflamed Darnley's own jealousy of his now-pregnant wife's affection for her servant David Rizzio. This ruffian band invaded the Queen's rooms in Holyroodhouse to murder Rizzio before her eyes by stabbing him between fifty and sixty times. Darnley then betrayed his co-conspirators by helping Mary escape. His own unsurprising murder at Kirk o'Field, at the hands of Scottish nobles, followed less than a year later.

Mary then made her second crucial mistake. Just as she had blindly married Darnley, three months after Darnley's death in 1567, she weakly married his murderer the Earl of Bothwell after colluding with him in staging her own kidnapping. The Scottish nobles yet again conspired to enhance their own power at her expense. They imprisoned Mary, forced her to abdicate in favor of her baby son James, and defeated her in battle after her escape from Loch Leven Castle. Her marriage to Bothwell allowed them to implicate her in Darnley's murder, of which she was most probably innocent. She had lost the affection of the Scots, who now commonly regarded Mary as a scarlet woman and a murderess.

Her reputation and throne lost, Mary made a third crucial error based on her tendency to view decisions in personal rather than political terms. She fled to England to throw herself under Elizabeth's protection. Mary brought with her not only an unsavory repute, but also danger. She also constituted a powerful Catholic threat to Elizabeth's hold on her own throne, whether she remained in England or went abroad to seek allies among the enemies of England.

Elizabeth would neither release Mary from her illegal imprisonment nor execute her, despite many plots discovered over the next twenty years and much pressure. Mary remained in dolorous captivity at many prisons—among them Carlisle, Bolton, Tutbury, Wingfield, Chatsworth, Tixall, Chartley, and Fotheringhay. Finally, double agents hired by Elizabeth's spymaster Sir Francis Walsingham infiltrated and encouraged the Babington Plot to assassinate Elizabeth and replace her with Mary. In a final crucial error of judgment, Mary had assented to the plot.

Mary's enemies prevailed, blackening her reputation by unearthing all of the old imputations of harlotry and murder. After Mary's trial, Elizabeth dithered about signing the death warrant. Elizabeth even suggested a secret murder by Mary's jailer, a Puritan who detested Mary but indignantly refused to salve the English Queen's conscience at the expense of his own. Finally, in February 1587, Mary knelt to put her head on the block to wait for the stroke of death. She had forgiven the executioners, "for now I hope you shall make an end of all my troubles." Betrayed as an expendable victim even by her own son, Mary had reason to feel weary of her earthly destiny. She also exulted at the thought of release into the eternity of blessedness she so confidently anticipated.

Mary Queen of Scots Sites

Mary's fan club is the Marie Stuart Society, home page http://www.marie-stuart.co.uk/index.htm. This is well worth exploring, as there are many links to the places associated with her, with mostly good photographs and descriptions; take special note of the reconstructions provided. Click on the Places to Visit link to the left—first click for sites within each country, each given with some detail, then click on each in turn for much more detail. All the following sites are covered very well at this major website, so only other websites are included below, this one being taken for granted as having the information.

Mary was born in **Linlithgow Palace**, as her father, James V of Scotland, had been and baptized in the chapel. She lived there for the first seven months of her life but as an adult returned to the palace to visit. Originally a castle, it became a palace when James I of Scotland built the east range and adjacent parts of the north and south, making it into a C shape. James IV of Scotland then closed off the open side, extending the building into a quadrangle and including suites of royal apartments along with renovations to the rest. When he went off to fight the English in Flodden Field, his wife, Margaret Tudor (sister of Henry VIII and Mary's grandmother) reputedly waited for his return in the tower now called Queen Margaret's Bower. During James V's reign, the magnificent fountain in the courtyard was built; it supposedly flowed with wine instead of water when he married Mary of Guise, Mary's mother. He also carried out a number of improvements and enhancements. Although the palace burned down in 1746, it is still a splendid sight above the attractive stone town of Linlithgow, especially when viewed from the other side of Linlithgow Loch. Visiting details appear at http://www.historicscotland.gov.uk/properties_sites_detail?propertyID=PL_199, and the town's website, http://www.linlithgow.com/.

At the tender age of nine months, Mary was crowned Queen of Scots in the Old Chapel of **Stirling Castle**. For background information on Stirling, see *Edward I*. Mary's father James V built the royal palace, and it became one of Scotland's most magnificent. Her son James VI (James I of Great Britain) remodeled the Chapel Royal for the baptism of his son Henry in 1594; he had been baptized himself in the same chapel in 1566. The heart of the castle is the buildings around the Outer and Inner Closes: the plain King's Old Building and the imposing, ornate palace, the Great Hall with its hammerbeam roof, the Chapel Royal, and the kitchens, which contain a display of their use during the 16th century, including lifesize models and foodstuffs.

In France

Mary's childhood and early adulthood in France made her a familiar at several legendary châteaux of the Loire region, including exquisite **Chenonceau** (sometimes spelled in the plural, Chenonceaux, which is the spelling for the nearby town), with its gallery spanning the river Cher (a tributary of the Loire), and stunning **Chambord** with its roof sprouting a forest of gables, cupolas, domes, and chimneys. Chambord is also noted for its novel central, double-spiral staircase, the flights corkscrewing around one another and never meeting. Other Loire châteaux are **Amboise** and **Blois**, with its stunning octagonal François I staircase in the courtyard. Geographically, they are situated between Orléans and Tours, on the Loire except for Chenonceau, which is a little further east, on the Cher. The best English websites are to be found at the castles.org websites: Chenonceau at http://www.castles.org/castles/Europe/Western_Europe/France/france13.htm; Chambord at http://www.castles.org/castles/Europe/Western_Europe/France/france5.htm; Blois at http://www.castles.org/castles/Europe/Western_Europe/France/france110.htm; and Amboise at http://www.castles.org/castles/Europe/Western_Europe/France/france12.htm.

Another château known to Mary was **Anet**, the newly built home of Diane de Poitiers after she was banished there by Catherine de'Medici, and a favorite of the French royal children. Anet is situated directly west of Paris, on the river Avre, a good, safe distance away from the glittering galaxy on the Loire. The château was sold after the Revolution to an owner who then pulled down the central apartments and right wing, leaving the west wing, chapel, and imposing gateway. For a photograph, along with visiting details and a guide to other activities in the area, see http://www.chateaux-france.com/~anet.en. The previous splendor of the gardens qualifies it for a garden tour; see http://www.gardenvisit.com/ge/anet.htm for a brief description of the gardens.

Fontainebleau was used by the Kings of France as a hunting lodge until François I constructed the palace. The palace stands in a large park, itself surrounded by forest, and can be visited on a day trip from Paris. See http://www.castles.org/castles/Europe/Western_Europe/France/france20.htm, but also http://www.musee-chateau-fontainebleau.fr/visite.html (in French) for sumptuous photographs and a plan of the château.

Mary married the future François II at **Notre-Dame Cathedral in Paris**. For details regarding the cathedral, see *Henry VI*.

Back in Scotland

Once Mary had returned to rule Scotland, her home was the **Palace of Holyroodhouse** in Edinburgh at the foot of the Royal Mile, today the official residence in Scotland of the British monarch. An Augustinian abbey was founded here in 1128. Its surrounding woods and hills attracted royal hunters, who began building near the abbey for this purpose and spending time there rather than at the less-felicitously located Edinburgh Castle. Gradually, palace eclipsed abbey. However, Holyrood's main association is certainly with Mary's residence there, and the dramatic events that took place during her reign, like the murder of her secretary Rizzio in her private apartments in Holyrood. At www.lancs.ac.uk/users/history/studpages/maryqofs/sophie/holyroodpalace.htm you will find a detailed and comprehensive account, with plans and drawings, of Holyrood at the time of Mary's occupancy, a description of the rooms and the life of the court there. Complete visiting details are available at http://www.royal.gov.uk/output/page559.asp.

Holyroodhouse is at one end of the Royal Mile and Edinburgh Castle at the other, a walk visitors should make. See the features of this walk at http://www.aboutscotland.com/edin/royal.html.

Edinburgh Castle is the most-often visited monument in Britain after the Tower of London. Spectacularly situated on a crag within the city, the site has been inhabited since the Bronze Age. The castle is, in fact, recommended as a first destination in Edinburgh, not only for its history, but also for the view of the city it gives.

Within the castle, the room in which Mary gave birth to her son (later James VI of Scotland and James I of Great Britain) is on view in the Royal Palace. The regalia of Scotland—the crown, scepter, and sword of state—are in the Crown Room, along with the Stone of Destiny, the granite of the latter looking rather incongruous beside the sparkling jewels and gleaming gold. The Great Hall should also be seen, with its hammerbeam roof—the stone corbels on the walls supporting the trusses of the roof are carved with small Renaissance motifs. As well as royal mementoes, Edinburgh Castle is home to a number of other past and present uses to do with the military and law and order within Edinburgh. Visiting details can be found at http://www.historic-scotland.gov.uk/index/properties_sites_detail?propertyID=PL_121, but the best site, particularly for photographs, seems to be http://www.undiscoveredscotland.co.uk/edinburgh/edinburghcastle/.

Mary met Darnley at **Traquair House**. White Traquair, situated on the banks of the Tweed river, has had a long and tranquil history, memorialized by the wealth of objects and relics seen in the house. Visiting details can be found at http://www.aboutscotland.com/traquair/house.html.

Mary was fond of golf, falconry, and hunting, and **Falkland Palace** was the hunting lodge of the Stuarts; see http://www.rampantscotland.com/visit/blvisitfalkland.htm. Falkland was built in the early 1500s in the style of the French Renaissance and was a favorite place of relaxation for the family. The fine gardens were developed in the 1950s. Unusually, it stands on the High Street of Falkland, set off from other buildings only by the gates and the low iron railings, and otherwise in the heart of the town.

Mary was imprisoned in **Loch Leven Castle**, on an island in that loch, from June 1567 until her escape in May 1568. Again, the best site appears to be from rampantscotland at http://www.rampantscotland.com/visit/blvisitlochleven.htm. Loch Leven is easily reached from the M90 between the Forth Road Bridge and Perth. To visit the castle or even to get a good view of it, you need to take a boat out onto the loch and to the island; Historic Scotland runs a ferry. See details at http://www.historic-scotland.gov.uk/properties_sites_detail.htm?propertyID=PL_202.

Mary Queen of Scots House (officially Mary Queen of Scots Visitor Center) at **Jedburgh** is a museum dedicated to Mary. This was the house where Mary supposedly recuperated after a riding accident on her way back from her visit to Bothwell in Hermitage Castle. The house belonged to the Kerr family at the time, and the Kerrs were friends of Mary's. Visiting details at http://www.rampantscotland.1com/visit/blvisitmqoshouse.htm.

Hermitage Castle, home of the Bothwell family, was the scene of Mary's dramatic dash. It's reached down the long, winding B6399 south from Hawick through varied scenery, from high hills and sweeping views to the intimacy of glens and rivers. Although small and low in a glen, the squat and sturdy castle possesses considerable drama, its huge, high arches being darkly compelling. Visit it at http://www.aboutscotland.com/hermitage.html.

Borthwick Castle now offers bed-and-breakfast accommodation, with an additional price for overnight stays in the Mary Queen of Scots' Four Poster Room. Borthwick is reached from the A7 south from Dalkeith. Visit the castle at http://www.rampantscotland.com/stay/bldev_castles_borthwick.htm.

In England

Workington was where Mary landed in England. She spent her first night at Workington Hall, as the guest of Sir Henry Curwen's servants. Workington is on the west coast, off the A596 southwest from Carlisle. Visit the substantial ruins of Workington Hall at http://www.allerdale.gov.uk/main.asp?page=15, including visiting details: at time of writing, the Hall was closed to visitors. The town of Workington has a useful website at http://www.visitcumbria.com/wc/workton.htm.

From Workington, Mary was escorted to **Carlisle Castle,** founded in 1092. She stayed here for nearly two months, perhaps in the 14th century part later called Queen Mary's Tower. Like many castles, it contains two wards. The striking Norman keep, in the inner ward, houses the museum of two regiments. (See *William Rufus*.)

Bolton Castle contains rooms furnished as they would have been when Mary was detained here as a guest of the Scrope family. The castle was built in 1399 by Richard le Scrope, 1st Lord Scrope of Bolton, and is still inhabited by his descendants. Bolton Castle is located at the southeastern edge of the Yorkshire Dales National Park, and is reached off the A684; the nearest town is Leyburn. For visiting details and lots of other information, see http://www.boltoncastle.co.uk/.

From Bolton, Mary was taken to **Tutbury**. She was to spend three periods in this, the most hated of her prisons. Even at the time Mary was there, the castle was falling into ruin, and it was damp and malodorous, due to a marsh underneath it. Perhaps her only consolation was her friendship with her jailors, George Talbot, Earl of Shrewsbury, and his redoubtable wife, Bess of Hardwick, with whom Mary chatted and engaged in joint embroidery projects, seen today notably at Oxburgh Hall.

Not much remains of this formerly vast castle, dating from Norman times and with Plantagenet associations; a brief history with photographs and visiting information is provided at http://www.castlexplorer.co.uk/england/tutbury/tutbury.php. The village and castle of Tutbury are located off the A511 northwest from Burton-upon-Trent.

Much more felicitous for Mary was **Wingfield Manor**, in Derbyshire, out of Matlock, which she called a palace. It was a place of considerable grandeur, rising high above the river Amber. Here she stayed in cheerful surroundings, with relative freedom, and the company of her amiable jailors, Shrewsbury and Bess.

It's now administered by English Heritage, whose website for the manor is http://www.english-heritage.org.uk/server/show/conProperty.74. A detailed historical account can be found at http://www.britannia.com/history/chouses/wingfield.html, along with visiting details and a link to a detailed description of the interior.

Near Wingfield lies the splendid, excellently preserved **Chatsworth House**, which belonged to Bess of Hardwick as the widow of Sir William Cavendish of Chatsworth. Chatsworth has belonged to the Cavendish family since the first half of the 1500s, and is still lived in by their descendant, the Duke of Devonshire. Mary was to visit Chatsworth several times. Queen Mary's Bower, in the gardens, was named for her: the story goes that she was permitted to walk outside so long as the Earl of Shrewsbury accompanied her, and the Bower marks what was deemed the safest place. There's disappointingly little substantiation for this romantic story, and the Bower was heavily restored by Wyatville in the 1820s.

This is one of the great houses of Britain, with beautiful rooms, splendid art, and fine gardens. Full visiting information appears at Chatsworth's own website, http://www.chatsworth-house.co.uk/. The about-britain site, at http://www.aboutbritain.com/Chatsworth.htm, adds information and some small but attractive photographs.

Tixall Hall was one of Mary's last places of confinement. Built in 1555, it was taken down and rebuilt two centuries later, and finally demolished in 1928 and 1929. However, the imposing gatehouse, built c.1580, remains. Mary stayed here only two weeks, between visits to Chartley Hall. Tixall Hall is located 1 ½ miles north of Milford, just east of Stafford on the A513. A lively website at http://pages.britishlibrary.net/tixandrews/tixall/tixhall.html provides illustrations and description.

Only ruins remain of **Chartley Hall,** once an Elizabethan mansion and home of the first female highwayman, Kathleen, Lady Ferrers. Originally a castle, Chartley Hall stands on the A518 between Stafford and Uttoxeter. See the remnants at http://www.bramhall.org.uk/chartley.htm.

And so Mary finally arrived at the place of her trial and execution, the castle of **Fotheringhay**. Alas, nothing but a mound of the once mighty keep remains of the castle, first built in the time of William the Conqueror and then rebuilt in the reign of Edward III—let alone of the Great Hall where Mary was tried and so splendidly defended herself. When Mary arrived, Fotheringhay was used as a state prison; it was a huge grim place, moated around three sides with the river Nene as a watery defense on the fourth side. It began falling into disrepair after her execution, a process completed in the following century. See *Richard III* for more information.

A commemorative plaque in the south aisle of **Peterborough Cathedral** marks the supposed burial-place of Mary. In 1612, her son, now James I of Great Britain, transferred her remains to a more stately tomb in Westminster Abbey. For Peterborough Cathedral, see *Six Queens of Henry VIII*.

Visit Mary's tomb in **Westminster Abbey** at http://www.westminster-abbey.org/tour/lady_chapel/mary_scots.htm. This lies in the south aisle of the Lady Chapel (also known as Henry VII's Chapel). The work of Cornelius and William Cure over 1605–1610, her tomb was the last royal one erected in the Abbey. Next to Mary's tomb is that of her mother-in-law, Margaret, Countess of Lennox, with the kneeling figure of Margaret's son, Mary's husband Lord Darnley, atop it.

James I

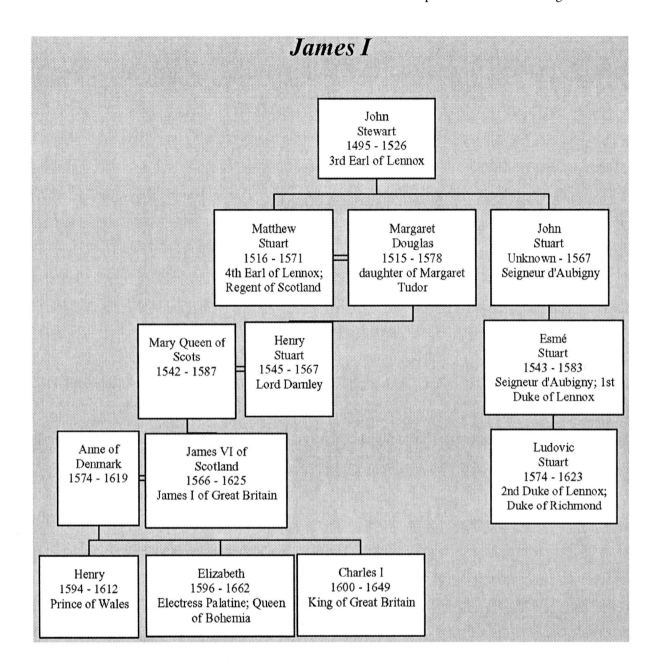

James I (1566–1625; reigned as James VI, King of Scotland, 1567–1625; as James I, King of Great Britain and Ireland, 1603–1625)

Until recent years, historians and biographers have tended to disparage James I, who styled himself King of Great Britain in 1603 when, as King of Scots, he inherited the throne of England. Perhaps comparing James to his predecessor Elizabeth I, blaming James for the disasters of his son Charles I's reign, and reacting disapprovingly towards James's homosexuality have distorted traditional evaluations of his rule. If we compare James neither to Elizabeth I nor to Charles I and avoid assessing his erotic preferences, a more just judgment of James does indeed emerge. Though far from faultless, James Stuart survived a tumultuous and danger-filled youth to become an excellent King of Scotland and sought to rule England as a farseeing and pacific statesman. James I also fostered many masterpieces of English literature, including Shakespeare's Jacobean plays, the poetry of Ben Jonson and John Donne, and the English translation of the Bible that justly bears his name. Few sovereigns have accomplished or sought to accomplish so much.

The infant James became King of Scotland in 1567 after the forced abdication of his mother, Mary Queen of Scots. Her supporters actively challenged James's rule until 1573, and even from her English prisons Mary remained a threat to James until her 1587 execution. In the previous year, James and Mary's jailer, Elizabeth I, had reached an understanding: James's Scotland would follow England's lead in foreign affairs, and Elizabeth would refrain from repeating her earlier pattern of meddling in Scotland. An alliance with Elizabeth solidified James's position as a sentimental advocacy of his mother would not have done. Just as Mary threatened James's hold on his Scottish crown, she also blocked his grip on a prospective English throne. With her gone, he came that much closer to his dream. "How fond [foolish] and inconstant I were," he noted in 1586, "if I should prefer my mother to the title."

Danger to James's rule of Scotland came, not from Mary alone, but also from his Scottish nobles. Born in Edinburgh Castle in 1566 and baptized as a Catholic in Stirling Castle that same year, the young James lived at Stirling with his guardian, John Erskine, 1st Earl of Mar. His uncle, Mary's half-brother, James Stewart, 1st Earl of Moray, ruled Scotland as Regent until his 1570 assassination. The second Regent, Matthew Stuart, 4th Earl of Lennox, James's loved paternal grandfather, died by violence in James's presence in 1571. The third Regent, James's guardian, the Earl of Mar, died a natural death in 1572. Then, James Douglas, 4th Earl of Morton, took over as Regent until 1581.

In the next year, James himself became a target when William Ruthven, 1st Earl of Gowrie, in the "Raid of Ruthven," kidnapped fifteen-year-old James to counteract the influence of Esmé Stuart, 1st Duke of Lennox, and James Stewart, Earl of Arran. James had become infatuated with Esmé, his father's dazzling first cousin, now forced from Scotland. (Esmé's son Ludovic would become James's lifelong friend and be buried next to him in Westminster Abbey.) From 1591 to 1595, Francis Hepburn, 5th Earl of Bothwell, would periodically attack James's safety and liberty. In 1600, John Ruthven, 3rd Earl of Gowrie, and his brother, the Master of Ruthven, apparently engaged in the "Gowrie Conspiracy" to kidnap James.

This record of notable and recurrent instability makes James's eventual establishment of peace and order in Scotland all the more impressive. After he added England to his Kingdoms and lived there permanently, returning to Scotland only once, he ruled Scotland through Scots, not Englishmen. Partly to protect Scottish interests, James envisioned and promoted the union of his two Kingdoms in one Great Britain, and, as a Scot, he resented the ignorant hostility with which the English Parliament rejected this proposal. Calling him "a skillful and tenacious King of Scotland," his biographer Antonia Fraser named him "in many ways the most successful King Scotland ever had."

James did not succeed nearly as well in England—partly because he failed to adapt sufficiently his personal style of kingship and his political tactics. In addition, James's openhanded generosity, combined with his poor grasp of financial limits, led him into extravagances that overstrained his resources. Some have criticized him for a dogmatic insistence on ruling by divine right as well as inattention to his kingly responsibilities. Others point out that, in practice, James ruled far more flexibly than he theorized and that he worked far harder and more efficiently than some have believed. In addition, James's health and energy may have suffered from attacks by the disease porphyria that reputedly maddened his descendant George III.

James's passionate attachments to his male favorites have drawn severe criticism persuasively questioned by scholar Maurice Lee, Jr. Homophobic discomfort and disapproval of his erotic preferences have twisted portrayals of James. An evaluation purged of homophobia and based more neutrally on mere common sense might still fault him for unwise partiality but acquit him of any very great dereliction of kingly responsibility. As a young King of Scotland, James had loved his first cousin once removed, Esmé Stuart, who died in 1583, soon after leaving Scotland. His 1589 marriage to Anne of Denmark produced three children who survived to adulthood: Henry, the adored Prince of Wales who died tragically young; Elizabeth, the future Electress Palatine and Queen of Bohemia; and Charles, later parted by execution from the crown he wore as Charles I. James indulged in some heterosexual affairs but tended to feel more attracted to men. Of a number of younger men favored by James over many years, two were significant: Robert Ker (Anglicized to Carr) and George Villiers.

The first Scot in the English House of Lords, Robert Carr became Viscount Rochester in 1611, a member of the Privy Council in 1612, Earl of Somerset in 1613, as well as Lord Chamberlain and Keeper of the Privy Seal in 1614. Carr openly resented his rival Villiers, who at this point had attracted James's affection. Carr's unconcealed anger at Villiers's rise, coupled with Carr's involvement in the sensational poisoning of his friend Sir Thomas Overbury by Carr's wife, precipitated his downfall. Villiers became a Knight of the Garter in 1616, Earl of Buckingham and member of the Privy Council in 1617, Lord High Admiral in 1618, and Duke of Buckingham in 1623. Acquiring control of the patronage in the King's gift, Villiers became a very powerful and resented figure. The erotic element in James's regard for Villiers added to the venom with which some regarded him. Guiltless of any knowledge of the Overbury murder, James nevertheless became tainted by his association with Carr and his wife, whom he did not punish severely enough for her crime. Although Villiers was corrupt, he also worked very hard, but others simply perceived him as a favored sexual plaything and ignored his industriousness.

By the end of James's reign, Villiers and Charles, Prince of Wales, were advocating war with Spain, a policy that the pacific James blocked with all his might. He also had resisted pressure to go to war after his daughter Elizabeth and her husband had lost both Bohemia and the Palatinate. King James had consistently worked for peace, fostered reconciliation, shown clemency. Hating religious persecution, he wanted to show tolerance of both his Catholic and Puritan subjects, provided that they refrained from political intrigue. He dreamed of presiding over an ecumenical council to resolve the disputes fracturing Christendom. In vain, he depicted his vision of an united Great Britain. If others failed to help him to realize these goals, at least he had the nobility and openmindedness to conceive of them.

James I Sites

James was born in 1566 in **Edinburgh Castle**, in the room in the Royal Palace designated as the birth chamber. The room is shown on the Marie-Stuart Society website, http://www.marie-stuart.co.uk/index.htm, as you pay your virtual visit to Edinburgh Castle. James made his next and last visit to his birthplace in 1617 for the celebration of his Golden Jubilee, which led to the complete remodeling of the Royal Palace. For basic information about Edinburgh Castle, see *Mary Queen of Scots*.

At the age of one year, James became King and was crowned five days later at a hastily arranged service in the parish church of Stirling, the **Holy Rude**, John Knox preaching the sermon. The church is on the hill leading up to the castle, so it also commands views of the town and surrounding countryside. Although it is altogether an attractive church, a unique feature, apart from its being the only still-active church in Britain (apart from Westminster Abbey) to have hosted a coronation, is the original wooden roof of the nave, still held together with wooden pegs. Visit the church, and see many views of it, at http://www.undiscoveredscotland.co.uk/stirling/holyrude/.

James spent his childhood at **Stirling Castle**, under the tutelage of George Buchanan. For background information about the castle, see *Edward I* and *Mary Queen of Scots*. There were attacks on the castle in 1571 and 1578, and after the Ruthven Raid, James was taken there as a virtual prisoner. The castle was again under siege in 1585. In 1594, James had the **Chapel Royal** rebuilt for the baptism of his first son, Prince Henry. After the Union of the Crowns of Scotland and England and James's consequent move to London, the castle lost its role as a palace. He revisited it only once, in 1617, prompting renovations; Charles I was there before his Scottish coronation in 1633, but royal visits became rare.

Huntingtower Castle, site of the Ruthven Raid, used to be known as Ruthven Castle. It consists of two three-story tower houses, perhaps built to accommodate the two families after a division between them, joined by a later façade. The gap between the two houses, up the spiral staircase to the battlements, was the site of the Maiden's Leap, when a daughter of the house supposedly leaped from one building to the other to escape her mother's discovery that she had been in her lover's chamber: the gap was roofed in the late 17th century. Visitors today may look at the gap and estimate their own chances of making the jump. The well-preserved castle is home to a colony of pipistrelle bats. The great hall contains the traces of 16th century paintings of hunting scenes. Visit the castle at http://www.undiscoveredscotland.co.uk/perth/huntingtower/. Huntingtower is situated just north of Perth, where the A9 meets the A85.

James's Queen Anne was born at **Skanderborg Castle**, Jutland (Jylland), Denmark. A history and illustration of the castle appear at http://www.ecomuseum.dk/english/skan/permanent_exhibitions.htm. Skanderborg is situated just south of Arhus, across the Kattegat from Copenhagen; the town's website, with tourist information, is http://www.visitskanderborg.dk/show.asp?id=72.

James was married to Anne by proxy in **Kronborg** Castle. Kronborg, site of Shakespeare's Elsinore in *Hamlet*, was known as Krogen, a medieval castle until Frederik II transformed it into a Renaissance-style palace in 1585. Pay a visit to Kronborg at http://www.ses.dk/157000c.

James gave the Royal Palace of **Dunfermline** to Anne, who commissioned William Schaw to remodel it. An addition was a chamber at the east end with a view of the river Forth, where the future Charles I may have been born to Anne, but the main work was the conversion of the abbey guesthouse into a palace for Anne. For the foundation of the abbey and palace, see *Henry I*. Today, Dunfermline is the main center for the "Kingdom" of Fife, separated from Edinburgh and environs by the Firth of Forth and access over the elegant Forth Road Bridge.

After acquiring the Kingdom of England, James went south. The oft-beleaguered town of **Berwick-upon-Tweed** finally experienced peace after having gone back and forth many times between Scotland and England over the previous centuries, and at great cost. From 2003–2004, the town of Berwick-upon-Tweed celebrated the Union of the Crowns, which brought peace to the townspeople and their neighbors 400 years ago. Read about it at http://www.union-of-the-crowns.co.uk/index2004.htm; background information regarding Berwick can be found at *Edward I*.

In **Ireland**, James established the Plantation program to broaden Protestantism there, which gave land to Protestant settlers from Scotland, and not coincidentally displaced Irish from that land. Read about the program at http://www.tartans.com/articles/plantation1.html.

In London, James's great architectural achievement was the **Banqueting House** at **Whitehall Palace**, built for him by Inigo Jones from 1619 to 1622. Today, the Banqueting House is one of the few remnants of Whitehall Palace. An elegant building today, it was extraordinary for its time, introducing Classical architecture to London; Jones had already begun the Queen's House at Greenwich, but at that time, Greenwich was out of London. The Banqueting House was designed for state occasions, plays, and masques, not for banquets as we know them, and opened with a masque performed on Twelfth Night in 1622. Visitors to the Banqueting House enter a humble door and proceed to the basement, where a video is shown on the building's history. Upstairs, the hall is impressive after the plainness of the rest, opening out into a great, lighted space with white Ionic columns leading to scrolled brackets supporting the balcony above. After James's death, his son Charles I commissioned the magnificent painted ceiling from Peter Paul Rubens; it's difficult to imagine the hall without it, but so it was in James's day. See the interior of the hall at http://www.theheritagetrail.co.uk/royal%20palaces/banqueting%20house.htm, and the exterior of the Banqueting House at http://www.greatbuildings.com/buildings/Banqueting_House.html; see Rubens's vision of the Union of Crowns at http://www.hrp.org.uk/history/default.asp?sectID=2&id=2.

The **Queen's House** at **Greenwich** was begun for Anne by Jones in 1616, and later finished for Charles I's wife, Henrietta Maria, in 1637. Conceived by Jones as a country villa, based on those in Italy, it represented the gestation of Classical architecture in Britain, having been begun before, and then interrupted by, the Banqueting House; the style took another generation and then was widely reproduced. Highlights are the 40-foot cube hall with a beautiful black-and-white marble floor of Italian craftsmanship, the cantilevered, spiral Tulip Staircase, and the painted ceilings and panels. In the 1660s, John Webb added the wings, extending from each side, to the original elegant box. Later, the colonnades were added. See many views of the exterior at http://www.greatbuildings.com/buildings/The_Queens_House.html, with more views and history at http://www.greenwich-guide.org.uk/queens.htm. Today, the house belongs to the National Maritime Museum, and part of the Museum's splendid collection of paintings hangs on its walls. The house is said to be haunted.

As the palace at Dunfermline had been Anne's Scottish home, **Somerset House** became her London home, the couple mostly living apart in spite of having seven children. During her regimen there, the name changed to **Denmark House**; the name Somerset had come from Edward Seymour, Earl of Somerset (brother of Jane Seymour and Lord Protector during part of the reign of her son Edward VI), who came into the property after the Dissolution of the Monasteries. He built the house in 1547, on the north side of the river Thames (on the Strand today) as a Tudor palace but with an innovative Renaissance-style façade. Somerset was beheaded in 1552, and his house became a royal palace, lived in by Edward VI's sister Princess Elizabeth, and then by her as Queen Elizabeth I for some state occasions.

In Anne's hands, Inigo Jones carried out a program of construction and reconstruction, and Anne used it as a center of entertainment, especially the performance of masques, and it continued to be renovated and refurbished until her death, at ruinous cost to James. Today, Somerset House houses government offices along with three art collections, the famous **Courtauld Institute and Gallery** (http://www.courtauld.ac.uk/); the **Hermitage Rooms** containing exhibitions from the vast State Hermitage Museum in St. Petersburg (http://www.hermitagerooms.com/); and the **Gilbert Collection** of objects in gold and silver, hardstone and what Gilbert called micro-mosaics (http://www.gilbert-collection.org.uk/). Quite apart from the lovely galleries, the courtyards beyond the Strand provide a restful oasis for the footweary visitor: fountains, restaurants, cafés, concerts, and an ice-skating rink in winter. The official website for Somerset House is http://www.somerset-house.org.uk/, and although short on historical illustrations, it provides evidence of the astonishing variety of events for the visitor.

Otherwise, in London, James held court at **St. James's Palace**. One of his achievements was opening up **Hyde Park** to the public. Originally a hunting ground for Henry VIII and Elizabeth I, over the centuries, and with the help of other royals, it has become the park it is today: plenty of space for any number of people sunbathing (deckchairs are available) and picnicking (or eating at hot-dog stands), or, more energetically, strolling, swimming and rowing boats (on the **Serpentine**), and rollerblading or riding horses, along with attending various events from time to time. It's contiguous with **Kensington Gardens**, which lead to **Kensington Palace**, at the southwestern end. Each space has its own character, but both form green oases for visitors. It's also the site of the **Diana Memorial Fountain**, commemorating the life of Diana, late Princess of Wales. And, on Sundays, you can visit **Speaker's Corner**, at the top northeast extremity, in the corner formed by Cumberland Gate and Park Lane, opposite Marble Arch, to hear the views of anyone wanting to take the soapbox on any subject. See Hyde Park and what it offers at http://www.royalparks.gov.uk/parks/hyde_park/.

Outside of London, James managed to coerce Robert Cecil into exchanging **Hatfield House** for Cecil's nearby old moated manor house of **Theobalds**. At Theobalds, James enclosed the park and stocked it with deer, and he was to die here. From the present viewpoint, it wasn't one of James's best moves: Hatfield House is flourishing today, and Theobalds was soon in ruins. For an image of the Tudor mansion of Theobalds, see http://www.heritagesites.eu.com/england/theobol.htm. Another house was built slightly to the west, which is now a hotel under the name Theobalds Park—visit it at http://www.hotelsandguesthouses.net/218682. Some of the remains of the original Theobalds were incorporated into other houses, including one called The Cedars, and ruins are today to be seen within **Cedar Park**, a municipal park with gardens, a lake, and an arboretum. Both are in Cheshunt, Hertfordshire, just north of Enfield and near Waltham Cross. For Hatfield House, see *Elizabeth I*.

James visited **Newmarket** in 1605 and constructed a palace there between 1606 and 1610, with a three-story, Italianate lodge added by Inigo Jones in 1619 for Prince Charles. This palace stood on an area of ground between the present Palmer's Department Store and the Jockey Club. After Charles I's death, the house fell into disrepair, to be replaced by another, built by his son Charles II (see *Charles II*). Newmarket, the center of flat (thoroughbred) racing in England, is located in Suffolk, east of Cambridge.

On the site of today's **Buckingham Palace**, James established a mulberry garden for the cultivation of silkworms, and ultimately the production of silk, one of many mulberry plantations he developed in England. For the ongoing story of Buckingham Palace, see *George III*.

Visitors may wish to note **Prince Henry's Room**, at 17 Fleet Street, London. Henry, elder son of James I, used this as an office from which to run the Duchy of Cornwall. He never succeeded his father because he died of typhoid at the age of 19. A history and visiting details may be read at http://www.touruk.co.uk/london_museums/princehenry_rooms1.htm.

Anne died at **Hampton Court Palace** in 1619, lay in state at Denmark House, and is buried in Westminster Abbey. James died at **Theobalds** in 1625. He is interred in the **Henry VII Chapel** of Westminster Abbey, in the same vault as his ancestors Henry VII and Elizabeth of York. Read more about their deaths and funerals at http://westminster-abbey.org/library/monarchs/james_i.htm.

The settlement of **Jamestown** in the North American colony of Virginia was named after James I.

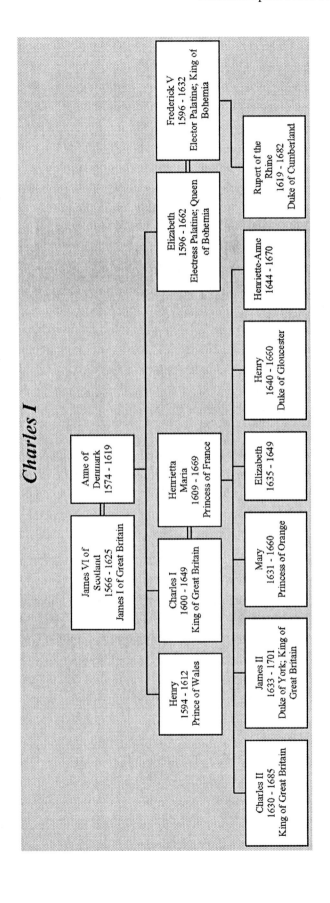

Charles I

James VI of Scotland 1566 - 1625 James I of Great Britain — **Anne of Denmark** 1574 - 1619

Frederick V 1596 - 1632 Elector Palatine; King of Bohemia — **Elizabeth** 1596 - 1662 Electress Palatine; Queen of Bohemia

Rupert of the Rhine 1619 - 1682 Duke of Cumberland

Henry 1594 - 1612 Prince of Wales

Charles I 1600 - 1649 King of Great Britain — **Henrietta Maria** 1609 - 1669 Princess of France

Charles II 1630 - 1685 King of Great Britain

James II 1633 - 1701 Duke of York; King of Great Britain

Mary 1631 - 1660 Princess of Orange

Elizabeth 1635 - 1649

Henry 1640 - 1660 Duke of Gloucester

Henriette-Anne 1644 - 1670

Charles I (1600–1649; reigned as King of Great Britain and Ireland, 1625–1649)

Charles I's successful predecessors and successor—Elizabeth I, James I, and Charles II—may have believed that they ruled by divine right, but they acted as though they knew their authority rested on persuasion and consent of those whom they governed. In contrast, Charles I—like his grandmother Mary Queen of Scots and his son James II—lacked their sound political sense. In his own mind accountable to God alone, the King had but a theoretical understanding of his role, and he never became the canny negotiators both Elizabeth and his father had been. Instead, Charles I asserted his royal authority as though such assertion in itself warranted his subjects' unquestioning compliance with his controversial domestic, foreign, and religious policies. Any opposition to his policies quickened his anxiety that his opponents sought to emasculate the King of England into a Doge of Venice—an obsessive image for both Charles I and his similarly inept son James II. Both saw conceding ground as exhibiting fatal weakness. An indecisive ruler, Charles I would grudgingly make concessions (usually conceding too little, too late), then end his high anxiety by cutting off any possibility of further negotiations by dissolving Parliament or declaring war. While his vacillations produced inadequate concessions, in his moments of decision Charles I overreacted into war or destructive intrigue. Believing that his opponents always acted from base motives, he felt no obligation to keep his word to such vermin as these. Naturally, after a while, no one trusted him as a negotiator. Charles I's unrealistic attempts to smother conflict and avoid compromise guaranteed a reign of endless conflict and finally convinced his opponents of the necessity of executing him as a dishonorable and untrustworthy tyrant.

His own father, James I, had worried about Charles's poor political judgment. Upset that Charles, Prince of Wales, had sought to rouse Parliament against his father's pacific Spanish policy, James I warned him that "he would have his bellyful of Parliaments." Born at Dunfermline Castle in 1600 to James VI of Scotland and Anne of Denmark, their second son to survive childhood, the sickly Charles had remained in Scotland for months after the rest of his family moved to England in 1603 as James acquired a second Kingdom. Brought up in England in the household of Sir Robert Carey (a grandson of Elizabeth I's aunt Mary Boleyn who had galloped 400 miles in 60 hours to tell James of Elizabeth's death), Charles flourished under the care of Lady Carey. The unexpected death in 1612 of his dynamic older brother, Henry, pushed Charles to the forefront. Charles became Prince of Wales four years later.

Charles went from resenting James I's closeness to George Villiers, 1st Duke of Buckingham, to forming as close a friendship with Buckingham as his father's. Eager to revive the prospect of a marriage between the Spanish Infanta and the Prince of Wales that diplomats had pondered since 1608, Buckingham and Charles in 1623 journeyed in disguise to Madrid to woo the Infanta in person. Neither Philip IV of Spain nor his sister Donna Maria, the Infanta, truly desired the match, so the Spanish delayed consummation of the deal by suggesting ever-more-stringent conditions. Besides being infatuated with the Infanta, Charles wanted to secure the support of the Spanish Hapsburgs against the Austrian Hapsburgs who had deposed his brother-in-law Frederick and sister Elizabeth, rulers of the Palatinate and of Bohemia. Enraged by the failure to come to terms, Charles and Buckingham returned from Spain to England, determined to pressure James to attack Spain in support of Elizabeth and Frederick. James resisted, but after his 1625 death, Charles and Buckingham prevailed.

The same desire to secure help for Elizabeth and Frederick motivated Charles's 1625 marriage to Henrietta Maria, sister of Louis XIII of France. The Queen's London residence was Denmark House or Somerset House, where Anne of Denmark had lived. Tensions with France, however, soon led to war, with Charles and Buckingham entangled in two unsuccessful wars at once. Tensions in the royal marriage fed by Buckingham and the Queen's French attendants soon estranged the newlyweds. When Charles told Henrietta Maria that he was expelling her French attendants from England, the Queen in her rage punched out a window.

Military failures and unhappiness with Buckingham's influence led Parliament to express ever more vocal dissent from the royal will. Besides their anger at Buckingham, some members of Parliament objected to the growing power of Buckingham's protégé William Laud, who rose from 1626 to 1633 to the successive posts of Bishop of Bath and Wells, Bishop of London, and Archbishop of Canterbury. Charles supported Laud's "Arminian" attempts to impose uniformity upon Church of England rituals—attempts that many deplored as Catholic corruptions. Parliament then sought to employ its power of the purse over the King. This began a cycle in which successive Parliaments would irritate Charles with their grievances and refusals to grant him much-needed funds, and Charles would then dissolve Parliament and seek money elsewhere, such as by a forced loan—a request that his subjects could not refuse with safety.

When the 1626 Parliament began to impeach Buckingham, Charles dissolved it. In 1628, a mob lynched the Duke's physician. Ten weeks later, an assassin deprived Buckingham of further influence, causing both popular exultation and Charles's stunned grief. Buckingham's funeral featured an empty coffin, the corpse having been already interred privately for fear that mobs might attack it. Unexpectedly, Charles's troubled marriage recovered as a result of Buckingham's death, with Henrietta Maria comforting the distraught King. The affection born of this reconciliation endured throughout the 1630s.

Charles also achieved peace with Parliament after 1629 by the simple expedient of ruling without it. During the 11 years of Charles's "personal rule," his government gathered revenue by many clever if bitterly resented means—among them reviving the enforcement of long-dormant laws that imposed unexpected fines on violators. Laud's attempts to impose uniformity of belief and worship sent many Puritans and Catholics to North America. Besides assembling a peerless art collection (mostly sold after his death) and enjoying his royal residences, Charles governed distantly by delegating and issuing orders. If Charles ruled more or less successfully during the 1630s, he still had not learned to rule by persuasion and negotiation.

The King and Laud wanted uniformity of Scottish worship with English. Consulting with the Scottish bishops in revising the prayerbook, they imposed it in 1637 upon the Scots, sparking a riot at St. Giles Cathedral in Edinburgh. The action seemed to many Scots to disregard their objections to religious and political domination. Not only did numerous Scots sign a Covenant against these policies, but their church assembly in 1638 replaced its episcopal governance with a presbyterian structure. The First and Second Bishops' Wars of 1639 and 1640 ended in Charles's defeat.

Recognizing that the King needed funds to prosecute these wars, Thomas Wentworth, Earl of Strafford, a close friend of Laud's, advised Charles to summon Parliament into session. True to precedent, Charles reacted to the Short Parliament's insistence on discussing its grievances before it would grant funds by dissolving it. The Long Parliament summoned later in 1640 outlawed many of Charles's hated means of extorting revenue, arranged to meet regularly, and agreed that the King could no longer dissolve Parliament without its consent. Laud was imprisoned, and Strafford executed. Committing a betrayal that forever haunted him, Charles reluctantly and weakly consented to Strafford's death.

Mutual misperceptions poisoned the relationship between the King and Parliament. Ever sensitive to encroachments on royal supremacy over Church and State, Charles suspected republican intentions that actually did not exist until just before the end of the 1640s. For their part, many Puritans misread into Arminianism designs to return Britain to Catholicism by force. (Laud died by execution in 1645.) The massacre of British Protestants in Ulster during a Catholic uprising in 1641 heightened the dread of Popery. Like all the Stuart Queens Consort, Henrietta Maria was Catholic, and her influence seemed sinister.

Outraged by Parliament's challenge to his authority, Charles sought to arrest five leaders of the House of Commons in 1642 and soon raised his standard at Nottingham against his foes, starting the First Civil War. After defeats at Marston Moor (1644) and Naseby (1645), Charles surrendered to the Scots, who eventually turned him over to his Parliamentary enemies. Although seeming to negotiate with Parliament, Charles contemplated and perpetrated his escape from Hampton Court to the Isle of Wight and a secret alliance with the Scots. The Second Civil War that followed again ended in Charles's defeat.

The New Model Army that had won both civil wars had possession of the King's person and soon rid Parliament of all members who would object to his trial and execution for high treason. Charles's secret alliance with the Scots had convinced the Army that "he had no intention to the people's good but to proceed by our factions to regain by art what he lost in fight." Oliver Cromwell spoke for many in the Army when he called Charles "this man against whom the Lord had witnessed" and "the hardest hearted man on earth."

When charged in Westminster Hall in 1649 as "Tyrant, Traitor, and Murderer," Charles laughed. His captors had moved him from Hurst Castle to Windsor Castle; he also stayed at Cotton House, Whitehall, and St. James's, being moved for greater security against attempts at rescue. Because Charles rejected the authority of the court to try an anointed King, he refused to plead: "I have a trust committed to me by God, by old and lawful descent; I will not betray it, to answer a new unlawful authority." His refusal to plead at all amounted to a plea of guilty. Whitehall had become Army headquarters, and Charles's beheading took place there, outside Inigo Jones's Royal Banqueting House. Charles died believing himself guiltless of any wrong except having consented to Strafford's execution: "An unjust sentence that I suffered to take effect, is punished now by an unjust sentence on me." The same executioner, Richard Brandon, dispatched them both.

Long separated from her husband by flight into exile, Henrietta Maria finally learned of his fate in the Louvre. On the day before his death, Charles had parted from his two captured children, Elizabeth and Henry, in a heartbreaking meeting. He told Elizabeth that he would die to uphold law and liberty, and for the Church of England, both of which he identified with royal supremacy. He told Henry not to agree to be made a puppet King instead of his older brothers Charles and James. Eight-year-old Henry, staring at his father, promised, "I will be torn in pieces first." In speaking to Elizabeth, Charles termed himself a martyr. He died without fear and with great courage and resolution. Nevertheless, by a long series of ill-judged decisions, Charles I had precipitated his own needless death and the deaths of many others.

Charles I Sites

Charles was born in the Royal Palace in **Dunfermline**, Scotland; see *Henry I* and *James I* for basic information. He was crowned King of England in 1626 and King of Scotland in 1633.

Henrietta Maria was born at the **Louvre Palace**, Paris. The Louvre had its origins in a 12th century medieval fortress. In 1528, François I had the keep demolished and began the transformation of the fortress into a Renaissance-style palace in 1546. Catherine de' Medici had the Tuileries Palace built, and Henry VI, in 1594, had the Louvre joined to the Tuileries to form one huge palace: the "Grand Dessein" or "Grand Design," of which only the first stage, the Grande Galerie, was completed. Louis XIII and Louis XIV then built the Cour Carrée, of apartments, colonnades, and galleries, work that broke off when Louis XIV chose Versailles. Subsequent developments have culminated recently in the "Grand Louvre," modernizing and renovating, and the construction of I.M. Pei's 1989 Glass Pyramid, which forms the main entrance and illuminates the underground visitors' center. An important recent development is the excavated area showing the base of the twin towers and drawbridge support of the medieval fortress. At its website, http://www.louvre.fr/llv/commun/home_flash.jsp?bmLocale=en, you can read the history and take a virtual tour.

As a child, she lived a great deal at the château of **St-Germain-en-Laye**, strategically and scenically located 12 miles northwest of Paris, and 300 feet above the river Seine. The first château was built in the 12th century and destroyed by the Black Prince in 1346. Charles V demolished the ruins and rebuilt the château within the early wall, incorporating the chapel, which had been spared earlier. Building was then continued in the 16th century, Philibert d'Orme beginning the Château-Neuf, below the earlier structure (the Château-

Vieux). The terraced gardens that sloped down to the Seine contained not only flowers and fruit trees but fountains and grottoes with sophisticated mechanical elements: mechanical nightingales and lizards, water organs, and the figure of Neptune in his chariot, which rose from the center of a pool, turned around, and vanished once more beneath the waves.

Later, Louis XIV was to be born in the Château-Neuf, only to abandon it with his removal of his court to Versailles in 1682. Nevertheless, extensive and expensive improvements were carried out from 1664–80, and at about the same time, Le Nôtre created the amazing terrace, 1 ½ miles long and 100 feet wide, surveying the valley of Seine, Paris, and the surrounding hills. The Château-Neuf was demolished in 1776 with the exception of the Pavillon Henri IV, which is now a hotel, and the Pavillon Sully. The old castle was used as a military prison for about 30 years until restored by Napoléon III, who then made it the home of the Museum of Celtic and Gallo-Roman Antiquities in 1862. One hundred years later, the Musée des Antiquités Nationales was opened here. See the château at http://www.jacobite.ca/gazetteer/France/SaintGermain.htm. The town of St-Germain-en-Laye, on the edge of the Forest of St-Germain, is a worthwhile destination in itself, an attractive town with splendid mansions and a beautiful setting. Its website, http://www.ville-st-germain-en-laye.fr/en/cto/de/mu.html, provides information and details for getting there. At http://www.gardenvisit.com/ ge/saintgermain.htm, you will see another view of the château and a brief description of the gardens.

Her marriage to Charles was celebrated first by proxy, outside the west door of **Notre-Dame Cathedral** in Paris (see *Henry VI*). In England, she was married again to Charles in person, in the Great Hall of **St Augustine's Abbey, Canterbury** (see *Six Queens of Henry VIII*). They then set out for Gravesend, where they embarked on royal barges, arriving at **Denmark House** (see *James I*), now to be Henrietta Maria's London home.

Henrietta Maria was to live at **Denmark House** (formerly Somerset House, and now known by that name again) twice, the second time after the Restoration in 1660 of her son Charles II. In 1626, she commissioned Inigo Jones to make her a new private chamber, remodeling an existing room and transforming it with white, gold, and blue, a marble floor, and fine iron balcony overlooking the river. She also ordered a chapel built, which she shared with English Catholics, and, for secular pleasures, she provided for masques to be performed in the hall, often appearing in them herself. After the Restoration, the house was suffering from 20 years of neglect: she had it substantially rebuilt in the style of a Venetian palace. After Henrietta Maria's death, her daughter-in-law, Charles II's Queen, Catherine of Braganza, lived there.

The **Queen's House, Greenwich** was finished for Henrietta Maria in 1635 by Inigo Jones; see *James I*. At **St. James's Palace**, while Charles was riding to Spain in his vain attempt to court the Infanta, ongoing, extensive preparations were made to greet the Spanish princess: along with the renovation and refurbishment, Inigo Jones designed a chapel for the princess's personal use. For Henrietta Maria, he had Inigo Jones create a new withdrawing chamber and a sculpture gallery in the garden. See *Henry VIII* for background about the Palace.

Charles's principal residence was **Whitehall Palace**. He commissioned the beautiful painted ceiling in the Banqueting House from Rubens in memory of his father. For more details, see *James I*. It was a grim irony that he was to be executed outside this very building.

Charles was the last sovereign to sleep in the Royal Palace at **Edinburgh Castle**. For information about Edinburgh Castle, see *Mary Queen of Scots*.

Civil War

During the Civil War, **Oxford and Shrewsbury** were headquarters for Charles and his nephew Prince Rupert. Shrewsbury fell to Cromwell's troops in 1645. For information about Shrewsbury, see *Edward I*. Oxford was transformed into a garrison town, the various colleges housing personnel, armaments, and supplies. Rupert moved into St. John's College, and Charles made the deanery of **Oxford Cathedral** his home—see its website at http://www.chch.ox.ac.uk/modules/standard/viewpage.asp?id=231. **St. John's College** had been founded in 1555 on the site of the old College of St. Bernard, and was staunchly Jacobite in loyalties and connections: its president from 1611–21 was William Laud, later Archbishop of Canterbury and one of Charles's chief advisers, and his successor as president, William Juxon, as Bishop of London was to minister to Charles when he faced the scaffold. Canterbury Quad was built by Laud; it contains Hubert Le Sueur statues of Charles and Henrietta Maria. The website for the college is http://www.sjc.ox.ac.uk/.

In 1642 Charles stayed at **Aston Hall**, Birmingham. Aston Hall is a red-brick Jacobean house, with gables and chimneystacks in Aston Park, with a room named after Charles. Visit the hall at http://www.bmag.org.uk/aston_hall/. It's situated in Trinity Road, Aston, between the A38M and A34, in the northern suburbs of Birmingham.

Charles passed through **Broadway** several times during the Civil War, staying at the manor house, now the Lygon Arms, a hotel. There are several Broadways in Britain; this is the village in the Cotswolds, a few miles to the west of Chipping Campden, and southeast of Evesham; it's a pretty place, popular with tourists. The Lygon Arms is one of several 16th–18th century houses on the stone-built High Street; it has a bedroom named after Charles, with a secret passage leading downstairs. Visit the hotel at http://www.the-lygon-arms.com/default.htm, and Broadway at http://www.cotswolds-calling.com/central-cotswolds/broadway.htm.

Hull, officially Kingston upon Hull, was storing arms and ammunition needed by Charles. He came from York in 1642, requested entrance to the city, and was refused. Hull, founded by Edward I, has always been an important port, and today it is a large and busy city of 252,000 situated on the Humber river, which divides Yorkshire from Lincolnshire. The first panel of a tapestry begun during the 1990s, depicting the history of Hull, shows Charles at the Beverley Gate, Hull. See the tapestry at http://www.hullcc.gov.uk/hulltapestry/index.php; it is on show in the Guildhall.

Charles opened the Civil War in 1642 by raising his standard north of the castle walls of **Nottingham** on the hill now called Standard Hill. The castle was soon seized by Parliament troops and demolished in 1651. See *Edward III* for more information about the castle.

In **Stafford**, Greengate Street contains, among a number of fine old buildings, the half-timbered High House, dating from 1555, where Charles I and Prince Rupert of the Rhine, a nephew who came to his uncle's defense, were lodged in 1642. It now houses the Staffordshire Yeomanry Museum, with a commemoration of Charles's and Rupert's visit in the Civil War Room. A photograph of the house, with an account of its history and museum, can be seen at http://www.aboutbritain.com/AncientHighHouse.htm.

Rupert's first victory occurred at **Powick Bridge**, a short distance southwest of Worcester. Information and pictures can be seen at http://www.thevickerage.worldonline.co.uk/ecivil/powick.htm and http://www.battlefieldstrust.com/resource-centre/civil-war/battleview.asp?BattleFieldId=35.

At **Edgehill**, the two armies met in battle on October 23, 1642. The battlefield of Edgehill is a short distance from Kineton, on the B4086 and about 10 miles east of Stratford-Upon-Avon. The village of Kineton's home page is located at http://www.kineton.org.uk/; by clicking on Picture Galleries, you can take a virtual tour of Kineton.

After Edgehill, and close to London, Rupert launched a surprise attack on Parliament's outpost at **Brentford**, under cover of mist. After their victory, Rupert's Cavaliers sacked Brentford. However, the Parliament forces rallied to bar their way at **Turnham Green**. Brentford and Turnham Green are in the western area of Greater London: Turnham Green between Chiswick High Road and Chiswick Common, and Brentford further west, beyond Kew.

In 1644 Charles's army defeated the Parliament forces at **Cropredy Bridge**. Cropredy is a village on the river Cherwell, 2 miles east of Mollington and directly north of Banbury, in Oxfordshire; see its website at http://www.cropredyvillage.info/. A plaque commemorates the battle.

Charles came to **Chester** in September 1645, spending the night at Gamul House, in Lower Bridge Street, before the battle of Rowton Moor the next day. King Charles's Tower (at that time Phoenix Tower) stands on the northeast corner of Chester's city walls, later named after Charles because he is said to have watched the battle from here. The tower contains a small exhibition on the Civil War. Chester, a city of 59,000, on the river Dee, is deservedly popular with its circuit of old walls and half-timbered "rows," galleries forming passages along the upper floors of the houses and shops. Although some are medieval in origin, more owe their existence to 19th century construction, but the later blends well with the earlier. Gamul House was a Jacobean half-timbered house, now covered with a brick façade. See it on Lower Bridge Street at http://www.dudleymall.co.uk/loclhist/rayner/chesterlbs.htm. See King Charles's Tower at http://www.chestertourist.com/charles.htm. For tourism in Chester, see http://www.chestercc.gov.uk/tourism/index.html#tourism. **Rowton Moor** is three miles southeast of Chester, off the A55; see it at http://www.geograph.co.uk/photo/11194.

Before the Battle of Naseby, Charles spent six nights at the Wheatsheaf Inn, in **Daventry**. The Wheatsheaf, on The Green, is today a popular pub and inn. Daventry, a town of 17,000 inhabitants, is located in a loop of the A361 and the A45, south of Leicester; see its website at http://www.daventrydc.gov.uk/tourism/.

He is said to have spent the night before the battle in a house in **Market Harborough**, then known as Harborough. Market Harborough is an old town still laid out on its 12th century plan, has 17,000 inhabitants, and is on the river Welland, in a corner formed by the junction of the A4304 and the A508. Read about the town at its informative website, http://www.marketharboroughonline.co.uk/tourism/historicharborough.htm.

A column erected in 1936 marks the site of the Battle of **Naseby**, where Charles and Prince Rupert were decisively defeated in 1645. This is reached off the A14, just to the east of the A5199 to Leicester. An account of the battle appears at http://www.britainexpress.com/History/battles/naseby.htm and http://www.british-civil-wars.co.uk/military/1645-leicester-naseby.htm, with Naseby itself, its history and information for visitors, covered at http://www.hillyer.demon.co.uk/.

Rupert had taken **Bristol** in 1643, which then became the chief Royalist stronghold in the West until it was stormed in 1645. This marked the downfall of Rupert: he was disgraced in his uncle's eyes and retreated to Europe until the Restoration. See *Stephen and Maud* for information about Bristol.

Rupert relieved **Newark** in February 1644, and stayed in the half-timbered Governor's House in Stodman Street, where he and Charles I quarreled. See the house, along with other buildings of Newark-on-Trent, at http://homepages.nildram.co.uk/~jimella/nwrkpub.htm. Information about Newark Castle appears at *John of Gaunt*.

On his way to relieve the city of York, Rupert was met by the Parliamentarians at **Marston Moor** and was decisively defeated in a surprise attack by vastly superior numbers. See http://www.british-civil-wars.co.uk/military/1644-york-march-marston-moor.htm and http://www.battlefieldstrust.com/resource-centre/civil-war/battleview.asp?BattleFieldId=24 for accounts of the Battle of Marston Moor. The village of **Long Marston** is your destination for a visit to the battlefield, directly west of York on the B1224.

Charles surrendered himself to the Scots Commissioners in the King's Arms Hotel, **Southwell**, a half-timbered coaching inn on Old Market Place, near Southwell Minster. The hotel is now known as the Saracen's Head; visit Southwell at http://www.southwell.org.uk/southwell.htm. Southwell is directly west of Newark-on-Trent, northeast of Leicester, on the A612.

In 1647 Charles was held prisoner at **Holdenby House**. Built by Sir Christopher Hatton to entertain Elizabeth I, it then became one of James I's houses. Originally large, it was reduced by the Parliamentarians to a single wing. Bought by the Duke of Marlborough in 1709 and passed down or sold through descendants, it finally became the property of the Lowther family, who own it today. The gardens and falconry center are open to visitors, but the house is open to tour groups only by appointment, and for British Bank

Holiday Mondays. The website for Holdenby House is http://www.holdenby.com/. Holdenby is located northwest of Northampton, on a country road between the A428 and the A5199.

The **Red Hall** is near the junction of Albion Street and The Headrow, **Leeds**, and reputedly the first brick-built house in Leeds. Here, Charles was confined for a few days on his way to London in captivity. See and read about the Red Hall at http://dnausers.d-n-a.net/leodis-leeds/redhall.html. Leeds is a large industrial city with 449,000 inhabitants. An old textile center, there's not a lot left of its past prior to the 19th century. The city Council website is http://www.leeds.gov.uk/

Charles was a prisoner in **Hampton Court Palace** for three months, before he escaped. See *Henry VIII* for basic information about Hampton Court.

He was arrested at **Titchfield Abbey** in 1647, before being imprisoned on the Isle of Wight. For basic information about the abbey, see *Henry VI*. On the **Isle of Wight** he stayed in the Jacobean grammar school in **Newport,** and in **Carisbrooke Castle**. The grammar school, in St. James Street, was built from 1610 to 1614, and is no longer in use as a school. Newport forms a hub in the center of the Isle of Wight; a town of about 24,000 inhabitants, it's located on the river Medina and is a lively and attractive place. For tourist information, see http://isleofwightnewport.ukontheweb.net/.

Carisbrooke Castle is situated on a hill about ½ mile south of Newport. Its origins go back to Roman and Anglo-Saxon times; after the Norman invasion, a castle was built on the site, using the existing defenses, and was then developed from a motte and bailey into a large, strong stone castle with walls, towers, and keep. Edward I bought it, and it remained Crown property. Charles tried to escape twice from the castle, but was essentially a prisoner there for 10 months, from November 1647. Visit the castle at http://www.castlexplorer.co.uk/england/carisbrooke/carisbrooke.php. It's now the home of the Carisbrooke Castle Museum, and to a team of donkeys used to demonstrate the workings of the treadwheel in the 16th century well house. For good photographs of the castle, see http://www.wightonline.co.uk/islandinfo/castle.html. For visiting the museum, see http://www.carisbrookecastlemuseum.org.uk/#. Charles was then confined in **Hurst Castle** for 18 days. For basic information regarding this castle at the end of a pebble finger pointing to the Isle of Wight, see *Henry VIII*.

Charles was tried in **Westminster Hall** in 1649. For basic information regarding the Hall, see *William Rufus*. Before his execution, he received Holy Communion in the **Chapel Royal**, at **St. James's Palace** (see *Henry VIII*). He walked to his execution across **St. James's Park**, which took place outside the **Banqueting House** (see *James I*). The place is marked with a plaque. He lies in the Royal Vault in the center of the floor of **St. George's Chapel, Windsor Castle**.

Henrietta Maria died at **Colombe**, near Paris, in 1669, and was buried in St-Denis. In 1670, her daughter Henrietta (Minette) was buried there too, in her mother's tomb. For the **Basilica of St.-Denis**, see *Henry V*.

The State of **Maryland** in the United States was named after Queen Henrietta Maria, as a condition of the charter granted by Charles I and conveyed to Lord Baltimore. The States of **North Carolina** and **South Carolina** are named after Charles I.

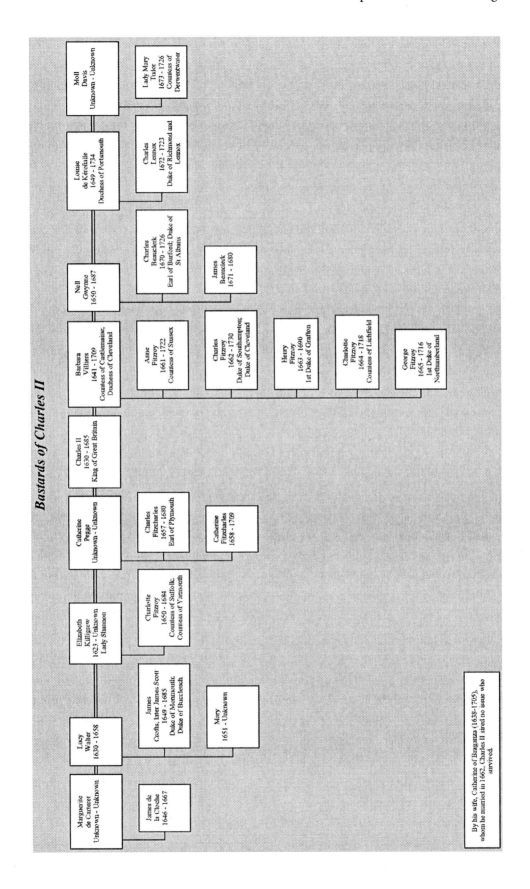

Bastards of Charles II

Marguerite de Carteret
Unknown - Unknown

James de la Cloche
1646 - 1667

Lucy Walter
1630 - 1658

James
Crofts, later James Scott
1649 - 1685
Duke of Monmouth;
Duke of Buccleuch

Mary
1651 - Unknown

Elizabeth Killigrew
1623 - Unknown
Lady Shannon

Charlotte Fitzroy
1650 - 1684
Countess of Suffolk;
Countess of Yarmouth

Catherine Pegge
Unknown - Unknown

Charles Fitzcharles
1657 - 1680
Earl of Plymouth

Catherine Fitzcharles
1658 - 1709

Charles II
1630 - 1685
King of Great Britain

Barbara Villiers
1641 - 1709
Countess of Castlemaine;
Duchess of Cleveland

Anne Fitzroy
1661 - 1722
Countess of Sussex

Charles Fitzroy
1662 - 1730
Duke of Southampton;
Duke of Cleveland

Henry Fitzroy
1663 - 1690
1st Duke of Grafton

Charlotte Fitzroy
1664 - 1718
Countess of Lichfield

George Fitzroy
1665 - 1716
1st Duke of Northumberland

Nell Gwynne
1650 - 1687

Charles Beauclerk
1670 - 1726
Earl of Burford; Duke of St Albans

James Beauclerk
1671 - 1680

Louise de Kéroüalle
1649 - 1734
Duchess of Portsmouth

Charles Lennox
1672 - 1723
Duke of Richmond and Lennox

Moll Davis
Unknown - Unknown

Lady Mary Tudor
1673 - 1726
Countess of Derwentwater

By his wife, Catherine of Braganza (1638-1705), whom he married in 1662, Charles II sired no issue who survived.

Charles II (1630–1685; King of Great Britain and Ireland, 1660–1685)

Many people, enjoying vicariously the privileged lives of famous royals, in effect identify with the sorrows and the joys of the privileged. Far more rarely, the royal person can identify with the plight of commoners. Bernard Shaw wrote of Charles II: "Kings are not born: they are made by artificial hallucination. When the process is interrupted by adversity at a critical age…, the subject becomes sane and never completely recovers his kingliness." Unlike other restored monarchs who "had learned nothing and forgotten nothing," Charles did not vindictively remember those who had kept him in exile for a decade. Moreover, Charles never forgot either the plight of the common people who had hidden him and fostered his escape from these enemies or his own decade-long poverty and ignominy as a discarded royal. Experiencing and remembering great and prolonged adversity, this already courageous, intelligent, generous, and sensitive man evolved into a shrewd and cynical ruler whose memories reminded him that "Sceptre and crown must tumble down / And in the dust be equal made / With the poor crooked scythe and spade."

Two-and-a-half years after the 1649 execution of his father, Charles I, in 1651 Charles II lost the Battle of Worcester to Cromwell's army. The young King, who—as a contemporary noted—had "hazarded his person much more than any officer of his army, riding from regiment to regiment," spent the next 40 days on the run and in hiding from his enemies. Hungry, dirty, extremely uncomfortable, and greatly endangered, Charles—as Antonia Fraser has commented—"had been stripped of the last vestiges of his kingly prerogatives. His character, not his office, was tested in the crucible."

That character was not only tested but also developed by his experiences as a royal refugee hidden by many courageous people who ignored the financial rewards offered for betraying Charles's whereabouts. As his yacht sailed to England for his 1660 Restoration and for the rest of his reign, Charles enjoyed recounting the tale of the 40 days following his defeat at Worcester, until he had escaped to France. Just as he was to be restored to kingly glory, he narrated the tale of his inglorious suffering. Charles defined himself by what he chose to remember.

He remembered the living conditions of the commoners who hid him. Always after his Restoration, he remained friendly and available to the poorest of his subjects. Charles showed great concern during the Great Fire of London (1666), encouraging those fighting the fire, himself distributing water, as well as helping to douse the flames until he retired, sooty, soaked, and muddy. He ordered food for those left homeless and collected funds for their relief.

He remembered the Roman Catholics among those who had hidden him after Worcester. Charles advocated but failed to secure religious tolerance for Roman Catholics, as well as Protestant Dissenters from the Church of England. He himself would assent to a secret deathbed conversion to Roman Catholicism.

He remembered how precarious his royal position had become after the execution of Charles I and his own defeat at Worcester. Sceptre and crown might tumble down yet again. Not only had his own subjects executed his father and driven him into exile, but during Charles's prolonged exile his relatives in other royal dynasties declined to risk much on his behalf, including money for his support, much less armies for his Restoration. After his unlooked-for and seemingly improbable Restoration at the request of his subjects, Charles dryly commented that clearly he himself had been remiss in not returning earlier, because all the English assured him that they had always advocated his return. In addition, the regard of his royal relatives in Europe dramatically increased after he resumed his place. Obviously, these reactions would not build in him any great belief in the reliability of most people with whom he would have to deal. While he respected goodness, he did not expect to find it.

He reacted with cynical humor but also with wisdom. Despite his deep love for his father and his indignation about the late King's execution, Charles II showed a remarkable lack of vindictiveness toward his former political enemies. Rather than instigate a bloodbath, he executed only a few of those who had murdered Charles I. Nevertheless, he maintained a wariness about the political factions that surrounded him. He never lost a sense of potential danger.

In addition to an awareness of the precariousness of his position, Charles had to contend with perennially inadequate financing and struggled with Parliaments that often held him in check. He answered these challenges with cunning, being far more tactful and politically skilled than his father. As a French contemporary noted, "His conduct is so secret and impenetrable, that even the most skilful observers are misled. The King has secret dealings and contacts with all the factions and those who are most opposed to his interests flatter themselves that they will win him over to their side." Secretly accepting money from Louis XIV offered one way around the King's financial problems. Besides this pragmatic deceitfulness, Charles tended to defer decision if possible, rivalling another masterly procrastinator, Elizabeth I, who herself had experienced the prolonged danger that may have taught each of them that inaction has its virtues and benefits.

Yet, when a situation cried for action, Charles could show courage in his defense of the innocent, as when those who created anti-Catholic hysteria by testifying about a fictional Popish Plot attacked his Catholic Queen, Catherine of Braganza. In 1678, they alleged conspiracy to poison Charles, false charges that roused the King to vigorous protection of his wife, whom he greatly respected as a good woman. He also refused to countenance divorcing Catherine, despite her inability to present him with a living heir. In this refusal, and in his gentle empathy with his Queen's distress over her failed pregnancies, Charles showed himself temperamentally the very opposite of his predecessor Henry VIII. His spectacular record of siring bastards by several mistresses did not prevent Charles from simultaneously enjoying a very happy marriage.

The contentment of his personal life aside, the King continually dealt with danger in his political role. Charles seems to have played whatever cards seemed least likely to cost him the game—being forthright in his advocacy of the innocent when it seemed best, delaying action if that appeared less dangerous, never for a moment forgetting the lessons he had learned after Worcester and in exile: "Those people who take upon themselves to censure whatever I do…. had need of a less difficult game to play than mine is."

Charles II Sites

For **St. James's Palace**, Charles's birthplace, see *Henry VIII*.

Charles was baptized (and Nell Gwynne is interred) in the church of **St-Martin-in-the-Fields**. The present church was built from 1722 to 1726, its much older predecessor having been torn down. You can read about the history at the church's website, http://www.stmartin-in-the-fields.org/jserv/home/index.jsp, along with links to its present-day activities as an active church and site for concerts. The church stands on Trafalgar Square, across St. Martin's Place from the National Gallery (and National Portrait Gallery).

Charles was crowned King of the Scots at **Scone** (see *Edward I*) in 1651, and King of England at **Westminster Abbey** (see below) in 1661.

Forced into exile during the English Civil War, Charles went first to the **Isles of Scilly** and then to Jersey. The Scillies are located off the southwest tip of Cornwall. You can learn about them and visit them at http://www.scillyonline.co.uk/scilly.html, and, for more specific travel information, http://www.simplyscilly.co.uk/.

Charles paid two visits to **Jersey**. His first, during the summer months of 1646, was much the happier. Staying in Elizabeth Castle at St. Helier, he developed an affection for the place and people, which they reciprocated. Jersey, which had always been royalist in its sympathies, was the first place to proclaim Charles King after his father's execution in 1649. Later that year, Charles paid his second visit to Jersey, but he was almost penniless during his exile, and his stay was a considerable burden on his hosts.

Jersey is one of the Channel Islands, belonging to the United Kingdom but domestically independent. Situated between Brittany and Normandy, they are noted for their mild climate and attractive appearance—gardens of the sea, Victor Hugo called them. You can read Jersey's history at http://www.islandlife.org/history_jsy.htm. Take a virtual tour of the Virtual Villages of Jersey at http://jerseyisland.com/, and a walking tour of St. Helier at http://www.walkingbritain.co.uk/jersey/walks/j06.shtml. Elizabeth Castle can be viewed at http://www.jerseyheritagetrust.org/venue/elizabeth.html, where you can also discover how to hire this magnificently situated castle for your wedding or other celebration.

Charles, always grateful and generous to his supporters, granted the North American territory that became **New Jersey** in 1664 to Lord Berkeley of Stratton and Sir George Carteret, of Jersey. A silver-gilt mace, presented by Charles to Jersey, is still carried before the Bailiff in the Court and States.

In 1651, Charles returned from exile in Europe to be crowned on Moot Hill, in **Scone**, Scotland. For further information about Moot Hill and Scone, see *James I.*

Worcester was the first city to declare for Charles I in the Civil War, and it turned out to be the last stand by the Royalist troops supporting Charles II in his 1653 attempt to take England, marking their defeat by Cromwell's Parliamentarians and sending Charles into flight for his life. Its situation at the confluence of the Severn and Teme rivers, along with surrounding hills, made it a defensive location where Charles felt he could rest with his troops, but which also allowed Cromwell to deploy his numerically much stronger army in a semicircle around the city. A map at http://members.bellatlantic.net/~vze2c48q/BattleWorcester.htm shows movements of the Royalist and Parliamentarian troops, along with a clear description of the battle.

Visiting details for the attractive city of Worcester and its beautiful cathedral can be found under *John.*

Charles was then in flight, or "escape," for six weeks before he managed to leave England. Read an account of it at http://www.sealedknot.org/knowbase/docs/0071_EscapeKing.htm. The strong-legged can retrace Charles's "escape route," with many scenic and historic diversions, by taking the **Monarch's Way**, a long-distance footpath (LDF) covering some 600 miles—read about this, and the guidebooks for the walk, at http://www.monarchsway.50megs.com/.

From the north gate of Worcester, he made his way north to **White Ladies Priory** on the Boscobel estate. What remains can be seen and read about at http://www.theheritagetrail.co.uk/priories/white%20ladies%20priory.htm, and http://www.virtual-shropshire.co.uk/gallery/white_ladies_priory (pictures only). White Ladies and Boscobel are situated northwest of Woverhampton, just to the north of the M54 before the intersection with the A41.

From there, Charles stole to **Madeley**, where Francis Wolfe gave him refuge in the barn at the Upper House. Read the history of the Upper House at http://www.localhistory.madeley.org.uk/buildings/upperh.html. It is now government offices. Madeley is west of White Ladies, a few miles south of Telford. From Madeley, they hoped to cross the Severn river into Wales, but discovered that the river was closely guarded, so they had to retreat to the White Ladies area.

There, he spent that famous day in the branches of an oak tree in the forest of Brewood surrounding **Boscobel House,** and a night in a hiding-hole beneath the floor of the house. The existing "royal oak," now standing in a field without its former forest cover, is almost certainly not the original. Please note that just as you can't climb into royal beds, you can't replicate Charles's experience of spending a day in a tree: it's protected by a barrier! Although the original 17th century house was added to during the 19th century, Boscobel is not a grand house; it's described as "modest." Fully restored, it presents more charms for visitors than its Caroline past alone. The origin of the name is the Italian *bosco bello*, or "beautiful wood." Read about it at http://www.theheritagetrail.co.uk/notable%20houses/boscobel.htm, and for Boscobel House and the Royal Oak, see http://www.bbc.co.uk/stoke/360/boscobelhouse/index.shtml.

In almost a straight line east (and the present-day visitor would take the M54 east to it) lies **Moseley Old Hall**, built in 1600 and the home of the Whitgreave family until 1925. Charles was given hospitality here for two days.

The timberwork of the house was covered in brick in the 1870s and was later used as a farmhouse, the family preferring a more modern residence. However, it is now fully restored, with a 17th century-style garden, a formal box parterre. In the barn, an exhibition recounts Charles's escape after the Battle of Worcester. Moseley is on the north side of Wolverhampton, south of the M54. See http://www.theheritagetrail.co.uk/notable%20houses/moseley%20old%20hall.htm for more details plus photograph of house and knot garden. Now on the outskirts of Wolverhampton, Moseley belongs to the National Trust. See http://www.nationaltrust.org.uk/scripts/nthandbook.dll?ACTION=PROPERTY&PROPERTYID=130.

A cairn marks the site of **Bentley Hall**, from where Charles set off on horseback with Jane Lane, daughter of John Lane, the owner, and her cousin Henry Lascelles. Like Moseley, Bentley lies on the outskirts of Wolverhampton, but to the east of Moseley, near Walsall; see and read about the cairn at http://www.lhi.org.uk/projects_directory/projects_by_region/west_midlands/walsall/bentley_hall_cairn/. From Bentley, they rode to **Abbot's Leigh**, 4 miles west of Bristol, the home of Jane Lane's friends. On the way, the Crown Inn in **Cirencester** is rumored to have played host to the party for a night. Now named the Kings Head Hotel, the inn depicts Charles's head on the sign; however, evidence is indecisive either that Charles stayed there or that the head of the King alluded to in the sign is that of Charles. Cirencester, an attractive old market town of 16,000 dwellers, is beautifully situated in the Cotswolds; see http://www.cirencester.org.

In Abbot's Leigh they hoped to learn of a ship to take Charles to France. This being unavailing, they moved on down to the **Trent Manor House**, near Sherborne, in Dorset. Jane Lane and Henry Lascelles returned home, and Charles lay hidden here for two weeks.

In **Charmouth**, the party went to the Queen's Arms Inn to await the captain of the ship to take them to France. Charmouth is located on the Dorset coast, just east of the larger, well-known resort Lyme Regis. Read about it at http://freepages.genealogy.rootsweb.com/~villages/dorset/charmout.htm.

Frustrated by the captain's wife having locked her husband in his chamber, Charles went on to **Bridport** (http://freepages.genealogy.rootsweb.com/~villages/dorset/bridport.htm) and then on to **Broadwindsor** (http://freepages.genealogy.rootsweb.com/~villages/dorset/broadwin.htm), from where he was forced to escape, returning to Trent House. He then spent the next few weeks there while friends attempted to secure his passage to France.

They then spent five days at **Heale House** near Amesbury, in Sussex, home of Mrs. Amphillis Hyde. From there he visited Stonehenge. Heale House stands between Amesbury and Salisbury, between the villages of Middle and Upper Woodford. The house is not open to the public, but its eight acres of varied, beautiful gardens are open daily throughout the year. There is also a plant center. Photographs are available at www.armin-grewe.com/holiday/wiltshire/heale-garden.htm.

The royal party then made for the village of Brighthelmstone, today the large, flourishing seaside resort of **Brighton**, where he may or may not have spent his last night at the King's Head Inn before sailing to France. On the other hand, it is also said that he spent his last night in England at Bramber, a little village just to the north of **Shoreham-by-Sea**. From Shoreham's harbor, he escaped to Fécamp, Normandy. A description of Bramber can be found at http://www.aboutbritain.com/towns/Bramber.asp, and Shoreham at http://www.allaboutsussex.co.uk/default.asp?id=townsandcities4 (with links to visiting details and postcards). For Brighton, see *George IV*, and for Fécamp, see *William the Conqueror*.

Charles was now away from Britain for over eight years, in exile in France and present-day Belgium, Netherlands, and Germany.

Return to England

In 1660 Charles landed in **Dover**. Dover, a town of about 35,000, has for centuries beeen an important link in the chain of England's defence, and a major point of departure for Europe, as well as being famous for its white (chalk) cliffs. A comprehensive website at http://www.dover-web.co.uk/ supplies pictures and information through links. For information about Dover Castle, see *Henry II*. He went on to **Canterbury**, where he spent his first night back in England and attended Sunday service in the cathedral; for details regarding Canterbury Cathedral, see *Henry II* also.

In **Rochester,** he is rumored to have stayed overnight in the Tudor Mansion called Restoration House. The ancient city of Rochester is associated with several of Charles Dickens's works; for example, Restoration House served as the model for Miss Havisham's Satis House in *Great Expectations* (http://www.lang.nagoya-u.ac.jp/~matsuoka/CD-Kent-Rochester.html for description and photographs).

For an account of his reception at the **Banqueting Hall,** and a painting of this, see http://www.solutions.co.uk/clients/hrp/bh/histh.htm. For information about the Banqueting Hall, see *James I.*

Charles was crowned in **Westminster Abbey**. On the eve of his coronation he was the last monarch to take part in the procession from the Tower of London to Whitehall, a tradition begun by Richard II.

In Government House **Portsmouth**, the residence of the governor, Charles married Catherine of Braganza in 1662. Government House was demolished in 1826, but the church, of which it had formed a part following Henry VIII's Dissolution of the Monasteries, was restored later in the century and can be seen today. Read about it at http://www.portsmouth-guide.co.uk/local/rgchurch.htm. Catherine had been born at **Vila Viçosa**, Portugal. Vila Viçosa is a town in eastern Portugal, east of Lisbon and near the Spanish border. It's a town of marble quarries and the ducal palace of the Dukes of Braganza. See Vila Viçosa at http://www.portugalvirtual.pt/_tourism/plains/vila.vicosa; more about the royal associations can be read at http://www.chivalricorders.org/orders/portugal/vilavic.htm. The ducal palace now houses part of Portugal's National Coach Museum; visit it at http://www.museudoscoches-ipmuseus.pt/en/museu_vicosa.htm.

Charles laid the foundation stone for the **Royal Hospital Chelsea**, following an idea by Sir Stephen Fox of emulating Kilmainham Hospital, Dublin, for veteran soldiers or those incapacitated by wounds. The hospital did not open until 1692, seven years after his death. Designed by Wren, it is still in use, the original buildings still providing housing and care for "the succour and relief of veterans broken by age and war." There are currently about 350 In-Pensioners living there. Its website is http://www.chelsea-pensioners.co.uk/index.asp. The gardens of the hospital are host to the famous Chelsea Flower Show in May each year (http://www.rhs.org.uk/chelsea/index.asp).

The oldest theater in London, **Theatre Royal, Drury Lane**, Catherine Street, was erected through letters patent granted by Charles II in 1663, and used by Killigrew's "King's Company," who for some years were the only players allowed to perform in London. Nell Gwynne was an actress here, having progressed from being an orange seller to performing on the stage. The present building dates from 1812, remodelled in 1922. Visit the theater at http://www.touruk.co.uk/london_theatres_halls/durylaneroyal_theatre1.htm.

Nell Gwynne may have been born in **Hereford**. A plaque on the side of the Bishop's Palace, in the cathedral complex, marks the supposed place of her birth.

Charles augmented the Royal Armories collection in the **Tower of London**. It's rumored that Charles decreed the practice of having six ravens at the Tower at all times—see http://www.historic-uk.com/DestinationsUK/TowerRavens.htm for an account. During Charles's reign, the supposed bones of the two Princes in the Tower (Edward V and his brother Richard, Duke of York) were found. At his command, they were transferred to Westminster Abbey and placed in an urn designed by Wren. The Royal Warrant referred to a "white Marble Coffin for the supposed bodies of the two Princes…," indicating doubt; however, the inscription asserts that the bones "were deposited here by command of King Charles II, in the firm belief that they were the Bones of King Edward V and Richard Duke of York."

Charles became the Fundator (founder) of the **Royal Society,** granting it a Royal Charter in 1662. Begun as a group of scholars meeting informally in Oxford or London, this important scientific body occupies nos. 6–9 of Carlton House Terrace, the Mall; its home page is at http://www.royalsoc.ac.uk, with the graceful Carlton House Terrace at http://www.royalsoc.ac.uk/publication.asp?id=1842. For more information about Carlton House Terrace, see *George IV.*

His interest in science led him to be responsible for the foundation of the Mathematical School at **Christ's Hospital** in 1673, to instruct boys in navigation. Christ's Hospital was and is a school, founded by Edward VI in 1552 for poor children, and termed the "Blue Coat School." Over the centuries, it moved out to Hertfordshire and then to Horsham, Surrey, where it is still located. A history appears at http://www.hertford.net/history/bluecoats.asp, and the school's home page is at http://www.christs-hospital.org.uk/.

At **Greenwich**, Charles disliked the derelict Tudor palace and found the Queen's House too small for his court. In 1665 he commissioned a King's House to be built by John Webb, a student of Inigo Jones, which resulted in what is now known as the King Charles Block of the Old Naval College, now the University of Greenwich. However, construction had to cease for lack of funds before the house was finished. Charles's major accomplishment at Greenwich was the **Royal Observatory**. In 1675, he directed Wren to "build a small observatory within our part at Greenwich, upon the highest ground, at or near the place where the castle stood." Wren was a former astronomer; he designed a house of red brick with stone dressing, named Flamsteed House after the first Astronomer Royal, John Flamsteed. Flamsteed House is a museum devoted to the foundation and purpose of the observatory, and also to astronomy generally.

Of note is the beautiful Octagon Room, restored to its original 17th century appearance. The Meridian Building was added in the mid-18th century to house the collection of instruments. During the past decades, the Royal Observatory has moved to Hurstmonceux Castle, and then to Cambridge University. The URL for the Greenwich Observatory is http://www.rog.nmm.ac.uk/. For background and visiting information, see http://www.greenwich-guide.org.uk/observ.htm. Finally, Charles's interest in gardening and parks benefited Greenwich, which he forested with chestnuts and elms, among other trees and shrubs. For background information regarding Greenwich generally, see *Henry VIII.*

At **Windsor Castle**, Charles's contribution was the renovation of the **state apartments** into a baroque palace, work which has largely survived to the present day. Hugh May, as architect, gave the exterior a more uniform and regular appearance; inside, the walls were panelled in oak and richly decorated with carving by Grinling Gibbons, and the ceilings were painted by Antonio Verrio: the latter can still be seen in the **King's Dining Room**, and the **Queen's Audience** and **Presence Chambers**.

During the period of the Commonwealth, **Hampton Court** was reserved for Cromwell and thus was preserved with its contents. Charles preferred Windsor Castle, but he added an apartment at the southeast corner for his mistress Barbara Villiers, Lady Castlemaine: in style, these rooms diverge dramatically from Henry VIII's Tudor palace, having more in common with the building that was to come from William III and Mary II. Outside, the modern garden layout owes its origins to Charles; he also had the **Long Water** dug in the Home Park, a canal lined by lime trees (*Tilia*) as a welcome for his bride, Catherine. For information about Hampton Court Palace, see *Henry VIII*; an annual flower show is held at Hampton Court—details can be seen at http://www.rhs.org.uk/hamptoncourt/2005/index.asp.

St. James's Park benefited from Charles's interest. He threw the park open to the public, and he introduced a lake (or canal), various species of birds both within a specially built aviary and on Duck Island in the lake, and games—croquet, bowls, pall-mall, and wrestling, as well as ice skating, when the lake froze. He often strolled in the park himself, with his many dogs. His love of birds is reflected in the name Birdcage Walk, beside Buckingham Palace. See the park at http://www.royalparks.gov.uk/parks/st_james_park/.

Charles never returned to Scotland, but took a strong interest, from England, in the restoration of **Holyroodhouse**. Repairs were needed after Commonwealth troops occupied the palace, and Charles had a royal apartment constructed for himself and the old royal apartment in James V's Tower renovated for Catherine. Under the supervision of Charles's Secretary of State for Scotland, James Maitland, Duke of Lauderdale, and architect Sir William Bruce and master mason Robert Mylne, the new rooms were arranged around a courtyard: although constructed in Classical style, their height and style are in graceful and tranquil harmony with the original. The three-story range consists of an arcaded ground floor, with Doric pillars, topped by two floors of royal apartments, their ascending order of grandeur exemplified in the use of first Ionic, then Corinthian pillars. Charles also had the Abbey Church made into the Chapel Royal. In 1768, the roof of the chapel collapsed, and the building itself was permitted to decline into the graceful ruin seen today. Read about Charles's improvements at http://www.royal.gov.uk/output/Page580.asp.

In England as a whole, **New Forest** and **Sherwood Forest** were restocked under Charles. King's House at **Lyndhurst** in Hampshire, built by his father in 1635, was completed by Charles, and was used as a hunting lodge for the New Forest—it's now known as the Queen's House. Charles spent £4,000 enlarging it and building new stables. An edict of 1662 concerning Sherwood Forest forbade anyone there to kill a deer without a warrant from the King, unless Charles himself or the Master of the Buckhounds was actually present. The Duke of Oldenburg sent over a freight of stags from Europe to help replenish the forest. The King's deer were kept in Windsor Forest, Waltham Forest, Enfield Chase, and Hunsdon Part.

Horse racing at **Newmarket** began under James I and has been a regular activity since the time of Charles I. Charles II would move his court up from London for the racing season. The Rutland Arms Hotel stands on the site of his home there. The town of Newmarket (16,000 inhabitants) is situated northeast of Cambridge on the A1304. See Newmarket's website (noisy) at http://www.newmarket.org.uk/, and http://www.newmarketracecourses.co.uk/ for more about the horse racing.

Charles began renting, and then he bought **Audley End**, at Saffron Walden, a palatial Jacobean mansion begun in 1603 for use when racing at Newmarket. Visiting details for Audley End can be seen at http://www.english-heritage.org.uk/filestore/visitsevents/asp/visits/Details.asp?Property_Id=1. Among other charms, there's an organic kitchen garden (http://www.hdra.org.uk/audley.htm) and a miniature railway (http://www.audley-end-railway.co.uk/) that takes guests through the woods. Saffron Walden, a pretty town of about 12,000, has a website at http://www.saffronwalden.gov.uk/. More photographs can be viewed at http://www.eppingforest.co.uk/Saffron_Walden.html.

Winchester Palace was Charles's last project, never finished. Designed by Wren, it was to be surrounded by a park, including ornamental water and a river navigable by small vessels. One hundred and sixty rooms were planned. There was to be a central portico and two wings, as well as a raised terrace. The park itself, an eight-mile circuit, would open into the forest, suitable for stag-hunting. Only the outside walls and roof of the palace had been built when Charles died. The shell lingered, vague plans being made for it from time to time, until it burned down at the end of the 19th century. The only part of Wren's building left, now occupied by the Peninsula Barracks, can be seen at http://www.britannia.com/tours/winchester/peninsula.html.

Charles died at Whitehall Palace and is buried in the Henry VII Chapel in **Westminster Abbey**, in a vault under the monument to General Monk, Duke of Albemarle, along with the remains of his niece Mary II, his nephew William III, and his niece Anne and her spouse, Prince George of Denmark. Within **Westminster Abbey Museum**, in the Norman undercroft, among the 11 wax effigies is the contemporary figure of Charles in his Garter robes. Read about the Museum of the Abbey at http://www.westminster-abbey.org/tour/museum.htm, which incorporates the collection of royal and other effigies and see that of Charles (on the left). More about the making of the wax effigies, along with visiting details for the museum, appears at www.britannia.com/hiddenlondon/abbeyt.html.

Seven years after Charles's death, Catherine returned to Portugal and lived in the Bemposta Palace, **Lisbon**. She is buried in the Pantheon of the House of Braganza, in the cathedral of São Vicente de Fora. Her tomb can be seen online at http://homepage.mac.com/crowns/gb/avgal.html, along with the Italianate exterior of the cathedral. Lisbon, the capital of Portugal, is also its largest city with about 675,000 population. Its setting on the Tagus river and near a thriving coastal area is magnificent, and the harbor is beautiful. As well, there is much to see among its old quarters and buildings. Visit Lisbon at http://lisboa.kpnqwest.pt/i/lisboa.html, and take a virtual tour at http://www.virtourist.com/europe/lisbon/. The coastal area of Lisbon, pleasant and historical in itself, can be visited at http://www.portugalvirtual.pt/_tourism/costadelisboa/.

The borough of Queens, in New York City, is named after Catherine. The King's borough was named for Charles; this is today's Brooklyn.

James II

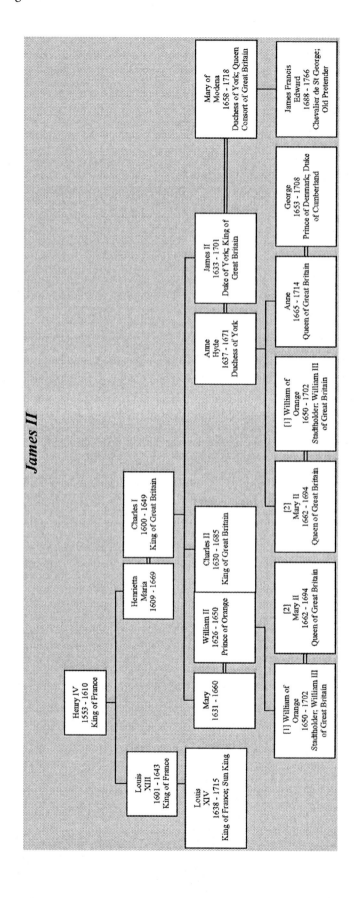

James II (1633–1701; reigned as King of Great Britain and Ireland, 1685–1688)

After the death of Charles II, his younger brother, James, Duke of York, succeeded him on the thrones of England and Scotland as James II. While Charles had reigned from his Restoration in 1660 to his death in 1685, James quickly alienated even his supporters and lost the throne in 1688 to his invading nephew and son-in-law, William of Orange. Charles II, in fact, had predicted to their nephew William in 1681 that his brother James would not retain power for more than four years. Determined to destroy the penalties and barriers suffered by Catholics and by Protestant Dissenters from the Church of England, James II alarmed many by his heavyhanded tactics. Although his deposition cleared the way for a more competent King, James's betrayal by his daughters Mary and Anne, his son-in-law William, and his servants constituted a moving personal tragedy of profound loss. He had obtusely insisted upon a laudable goal of instituting religious toleration for non-Anglicans while employing hamfisted means that ignored Anglican sensitivities and heightened Anglican fears. James thereby defeated his own goal and made his betrayal inevitable.

Charles II had foreseen that James's political ineptitude would abort his reign. James II was nowhere as clearsighted in his judgments of his older brother or, indeed, of their father, the martyred Charles I. In James's view, both Charles I and Charles II had often failed to crush opposition with strength; both had conceded too much to their opponents. This opinion confirmed James in his confusion of strength with obstinacy and with force. While Charles II had learned from their father's defeat and execution both flexibility and cunning, James II refused to emulate these successful means and instead failed by wielding an iron fist. James identified opposition with the republicanism that had murdered his father. His fear and demonization of all opposition to his kingly will actually augmented it and then precipitated the very deposition he dreaded.

As a boy, James had lived at Oxford when it served as Charles I's Royalist capital during his struggles with Parliament. When Oxford fell, James (as well as his sister Elizabeth and brother Henry) became a prisoner of Parliament. Algernon Percy, the Earl of Northumberland, kept James a prisoner at St James's Palace, from which he escaped to Holland in 1648. Having as a mere helpless boy seen his father in captivity and been a captive of those who later murdered his father, James learned to dread political opposition. He rigidly defended against his dread with an exaggerated emphasis on kingly power.

In Continental exile, the Duke of York fought bravely in the armies of France and Spain. The surprising Restoration of his exiled brother as Charles II of course returned James to England as well. During Charles II's reign, James served his brother in many capacities, among them being Lord High Admiral as well as the Proprietor of New York Colony (1664–1672, 1674–1689), so named in his honor. The Duke of York lived in St. James's Palace and Hampton Court, at Whitehall in the winter, and at Richmond in the country. Just as James and Charles in their boyhood had lived apart from their parents at Richmond, James's children had their own establishment there.

Their mother and James's first wife, Anne Hyde, an intelligent and strongminded woman, dominated James. As Samuel Pepys noted, "The Duke of York is in all things but his codpiece, led by the nose by his wife." Anne's conversion to Catholicism probably led to James's. Converted in 1668–1669, James stopped taking Anglican communion by 1671 and avoided Anglican services after 1676. Himself secretly inclined toward Catholicism, Charles II discouraged any public display of James's conversion and insisted that James's daughters Mary and Anne receive Anglican instruction and marry Protestant princes. Growing awareness of James's fervent Catholicism created attempts to deprive him of office and to exclude him from the succession. Charles II fought to protect his brother but also exiled him to Flanders and Scotland to calm deep anxieties that James aroused.

As Charles lay dying, he asked James to bring a Catholic priest in secret to accept Charles's conversion. After James's accession, he gathered much support to crush rebellion but soon lost the allegiance of even the most loyal. James wanted both to relieve Catholics of penalties attached to their practicing their religion and to restore to them full political rights such as those to serve in office or sit in Parliament. Many who might have assented to religious toleration balked at the prospect of greater political power for Catholics. Although they amounted to only about five percent of the general population, some members of the more prominent and powerful classes were Catholics. In addition, many feared that James might seek by force to return Britain to Catholicism. James seems genuinely to have believed in religious toleration, and he apparently thought that Britons exposed to unfettered Catholicism would not help but see it as embodied truth. In other words, he did not aim at disestablishing the Church of England and establishing the Catholic Church in its stead. Instead, he hoped to convert by persuasion. Nevertheless, his unsubtle methods of seeking an end to penalties and barriers convinced many that he would also eventually resort to forced conversion. Even some of the Protestant Dissenters whose burdens he sought to lift suspected that although he needed them as allies, James would discard them in the end.

In this atmosphere of cascading suspicions, James discerned republicans and would-be regicides in all opponents to his measures. His second wife, Mary Beatrice of Modena, after many failed pregnancies and lost children, became pregnant again. This excited rumors that the King and Queen were faking a pregnancy in order to foist a "suppostitious" Catholic male heir upon Britain to rule instead of James's resolutely Protestant daughters, Mary (married to William of Orange) and Anne (married to George of Denmark). Princess Anne herself convinced her sister that their half-brother James, born in 1688, was not their kin. To protect Mary's claim as heiress presumptive and to serve Dutch interests, William of Orange prepared to invade England, supposedly to restore violated liberties and the rule of law but actually to take power if he could. Faced with betrayal by his daughters and sons-in-law, as well as by such servants as John Churchill (later Duke of Marlborough)—whose career James had promoted, James collapsed psychologically. The advocate of stern kingly rule and the brave commander offered no serious resistance to William. Indeed, James allowed William to succeed beyond his wildest hopes by escaping to the France of James's first cousin Louis XIV, who housed his cousins in St-Germain-en-Laye, twelve miles west of Paris and not far from Versailles. James II's later attempt to challenge William in Ireland ended with the disastrous Battle of the Boyne in 1690.

James II fell because he had learned the wrong lessons from the overthrow of his father, Charles I. He misjudged both his father and his brother, Charles II, as weakly conceding ground to their opponents. Wisely understanding the need for negotiation and flexibility and well as the complicated motives of his opposition leaders, Charles II had succeeded in ruling for a quarter-century. Although a failed King who (like his son James) could never credit dissidents with any worthy motive, Charles I had sat through his trial and later died with immense dignity and calmness. James II, in contrast, had fled in undignified panic from the deposition and death he feared, invoking the memory of England's deposed and murdered Kings. In defense of James II, however, one must remember that Charles I had never doubted the love and loyalty of his children. Their betrayal had never pierced his heart.

James II Sites

James was born in 1633 at **St. James's Palace** (see *Henry VIII*) and was baptized at the chapel there. The royal children passed their time between St. James's and the palaces outside London, **Hampton Court**, **Richmond**, and **Greenwich**, until the Civil War, when the family was forced to retreat to the Royalist stronghold of **Oxford** until the city surrendered in 1646. Back in London, he was made a prisoner in St. James's Palace for 20 months until he managed to escape through a back door in the garden. Disguised as a girl, he was taken by barge from Billingsgate to Tilbury, where a Dutch merchantman was cleared and ready to sail. When he stepped ashore in **Middelburg**, Holland, in April 1648, he was still wearing his girl's clothing. The old town of Middelburg is on the island of Zeeland. German bombing took out most of the old buildings in 1940, but these have been reconstructed along their original lines. Gardens and walks line the surrounding moat, the Vest. A pictorial tour (rondvaart) can be taken at http://www.rondvaartmiddelburg.nl/ (in Dutch or German), with some attractive photographs from the Vest. A website in English but with fewer attractions is http://www2.world66.com/europe/netherlands/middelburg.

James married Anne Hyde in 1659 at **Worcester House**, The Strand, London; Worcester House was the home of Anne's father, Edward Hyde. Anne had been born at **Cranbourne Lodge**, in Windsor Great Park. Cranbourne Chase, a hunting ground in Windsor Forest, dated from the 13th century, the Keeper residing in the lodge. Only the octagonal tower now stands of what was once a grand home—see it at http://www.berkshirehistory.com/castles/cranbourne_lodge.html). Detailed information can be read at (http://www.georgianindex.net/Cranbourne/cranbourne_lodge.html.

Anne Hyde died at **St. James's Palace** in 1671, and is interred in **Westminster Abbey**. James later married Mary of Modena. Mary had been born in the Ducal Palace of **Modena**, Italy, home of the Este family. The palace is now the home of the Italian Military Academy, and can be visited only once each year, when there is a festival. Visit the palace at http://turismo.comune.modena.it/h3/h3/a2000t2/d?NRECORD=MO50-AAAABOES;LNG.x=ENG. Located almost directly north of Florence and about 23 miles northwest of Bologna, Modena is an industrial city of about 177,000 population with an old center containing some interesting buildings, including the Ducal Palace. Visit Modena at http://www.emmeti.it/Welcome/Emilia/Modena/index.uk.html.

The year before, James had been in command of the English fleet in its war with Holland. Notable was the battle of **Sole Bay (Southwold)** on the Suffolk coast. Southwold, located about 10 miles south of Lowestoft, is a town of about 1800 inhabitants, noted as a seaside resort and fishing port, with colorful houses. Its website can be found at http://www.southwold.ws/index.php.

James II fled into exile in 1688, from **Rochester**. His previous attempt to leave from **Sheerness** had been thwarted by the ship's running aground, and his subsequent detention in **Faversham** (see *Stephen and Maud*). **Sheerness**, on the Isle of Sheppey—east of London and lying between the Medway and Thames rivers, and The Swale—is known primarily as a busy port and for the remnants of the Royal Navy dockyard, established by Samuel Pepys in the 17th century and finally abandoned abandoned in 1960; see http://www.kenttourism.co.uk/en/what_to_see_and_do/shopping_sheerness.asp. **Rochester** is an ancient city in a strategic position on the Medway; see *Charles II*.

In 1690, he met William III, his nephew and son-in-law, in Ireland, at the Battle of the **Boyne**, where he was defeated and then forced to retreat to France. For details, see *William III and Mary II*.

His place of exile was the family residence at **St-Germain-en-Laye**. For details, see *Charles I*. George IV erected tablets in the parish church to the memory of James, Mary, and their daughter, succeeded in 1855 by another ordered by Queen Victoria. In 1855, Princess Albrecht of Saxe-Coburg and Gotha visited the church and later raised a monument to James, which stands in the first chapel right as one enters the church: this may be viewed at http://www.jacobite.ca/gazetteer/France/SaintGermain.htm. Mary of Modena is buried in the Abbey of Visitation of St. Mary, **Chaillot**; see http://www.jacobite.ca/gazetteer/France/Paris.htm, La Colline de Chaillot. Her coffin was lost during the French Revolution, but her coffin plate is in the British Museum.

New York is named after James, the name being changed from New Amsterdam after his defeat of the Dutch.

William and Mary

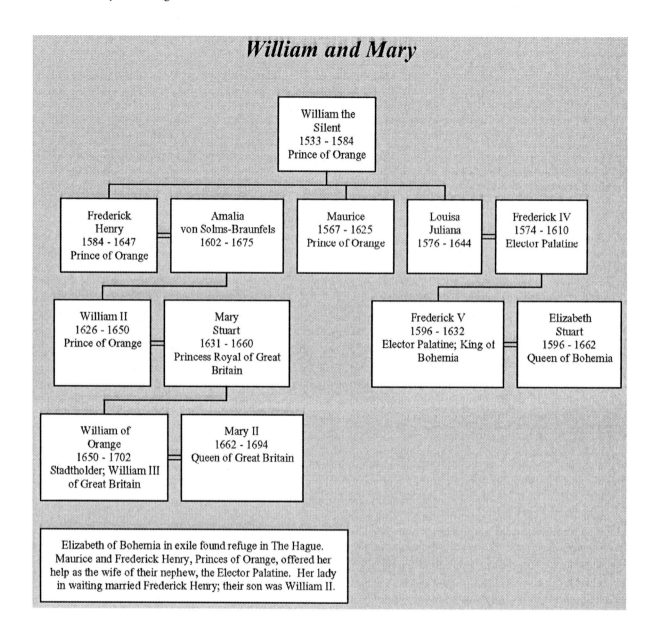

Elizabeth of Bohemia in exile found refuge in The Hague.
Maurice and Frederick Henry, Princes of Orange, offered her
help as the wife of their nephew, the Elector Palatine. Her lady
in waiting married Frederick Henry; their son was William II.

Mary II (1662–1694; reigned as Queen of Great Britain and Ireland, 1689–1694)
William III (William of Orange) (1650–1702; Stadtholder of the United Provinces of the Netherlands, 1672–1702; King of Great Britain and Ireland, 1689–1702)

James II's ill-conceived policies destroyed his reign because they seemingly justified apprehensions about James II that others had felt for many years before his accession. Protestant resistance to James culminated in the "Glorious Revolution" that drove James II from the throne of Great Britain in 1688. In turn, it fostered the counter-revolutionary attempts of the Jacobites to restore James II and, after his death, to supplant the usurpers with James's heir, James Francis Edward. A ring of William of Orange's first cousins peoples this story. William's mother, Mary Stuart—later Princess of Orange—was the sister of James II and his elder brother Charles II. William's cousins included his wife, Mary and her sister, Anne—both daughters of James II; James, Duke of Monmouth—a bastard son of Charles II; James II's bastard by Arabella Churchill—James, Duke of Berwick; and James II's Prince of Wales, the so-called "Old Pretender." Although much more than a family tragedy, this drama of usurpation and failed restoration repeatedly sounds the themes of estrangement, betrayal, guilt, and loyalty.

Prefiguring the later successful revolt of James II's Protestant daughter, Mary, and his nephew and son-in-law, William of Orange, William and Mary's cousin, James, Duke of Monmouth, rose against James II in the early months of his reign. Unsupported by most Britons and defeated by James's forces, Monmonth died by execution. Not long afterward, William of Orange and Mary succeeded where he had failed, and the crown eventually passed to Mary's sister Anne. James II's bastard by Arabella Churchill, James, Duke of Berwick, supported his father and, later, his brother, James Francis Edward, in their attempts to regain their Kingdom. Although all of these Jacobite plots and risings ultimately failed, they engendered an atmosphere of intrigue, suspicion, fear, and hatred that lingered for decades.

As the son of Mary Stuart, Princess of Great Britain, and William II of Orange, William III in his own right possessed a claim to the throne of Great Britain that some considered superior to his wife's. (James II's first wife, Mary's and Anne's mother Anne Hyde, had been a commoner, which degraded her offspring in some eyes.) Besides promoting his own claim and protecting his wife's from the encroachment of an infant half-brother, William challenged James II because he and Mary opposed James's policies that seemed to threaten the supremacy of the Church of England. William's passionate hatred of French aggression on the Continent, however, probably most strongly influenced his decision to invade England, for British resources would strengthen the European alliance against Louis XIV.

His resourceful and heroic defiance of Louis XIV had led to William's becoming Stadtholder of the United Provinces of the Netherlands in 1672. He had resented Charles II's support of Louis XIV and aggression against the Netherlands. Peace came after marriage to Charles II's 15-year-old niece Mary in 1677, on William's 27th birthday. Intelligent and industrious but ill-educated, the beautiful and gregarious Mary wept at the thought of marrying her physically unattractive and taciturn cousin and wept even more at the prospect of leaving England. Her aunt, mother-in-law, and namesake, William's mother Mary Stuart, as Princess of Orange had not hidden her snobbish preference for things English and detestation of the Dutch. William's wife Mary, despite her girlish despair, did not take his mother's path. Instead, she quickly fell deeply in love with her groom, as well as with his country. She would grieve over leaving the Netherlands for England: "self-love made me shed a flood of tears at the thought of leaving a country where…I had all earthly content."

Mary termed her love for William, "a passion that cannot end but with my life." She enjoyed directing architectural renovations and gardening designs at one of his palaces, Het Loo, as she would later enjoy overseeing the expansion of Hampton Court and the newly purchased Kensington House. William loved hunting at Bushy Park, near Hampton Court, but as a widower, William would avoid Hampton Court and stay in Windsor Castle.

As Mary's affection for William ascended, so did her gradual disaffection from her father and his second wife, Mary Beatrice of Modena. A loving father, James had favored Mary above all his other children, and Mary Beatrice teasingly addressed her beloved stepdaughter as "Lemon." (They had played together at Blind Man's Bluff and Hide and Seek when the 15-year-old bride Mary Beatrice first became Duchess of York.) Now, political and personal differences strained these relationships. Among other resentments, William deplored James's unwillingness to protest French aggression (for example, against his Principality of Orange in southern France), and William and Mary's friendly reception of his detested nephew Monmouth angered James. James seems to have tried through his agents in Mary's household to destroy her trust in William by alleging infidelity with her childhood companion Elizabeth Villiers, a grand-niece of James I's favorite George Villiers. (Remembering that Elizabeth "squinted like a dragon," Jonathan Swift, her friend in later life, seemed to regard her relationship with William as mostly intellectual: "Her advice hath many years been asked and followed in the most important affairs of state.") Most importantly, James's pursuit of policies calculated to diminish the penalties and exclusions attached to Roman Catholics and Dissenters alienated both Mary and William. They supported freedom of conscience but insisted that only members of the Church of England who took Anglican communion should serve in Parliament or in civil, ecclesiastical, or military posts.

James did not improve matters by trying to convert both of his daughters to Roman Catholicism. The 1688 birth of a Roman Catholic Prince of Wales heightened widespread fear that a Catholic dynasty would now succeed to the throne. The new Prince's half-sister Anne spread false suspicions that James and Mary Beatrice were feigning her pregnancy in order to foist upon Britain a Catholic male heir who would take precedence over his Protestant sisters in the line of succession. In her bigotry suspecting them as Catholics who "will stick at nothing, be it never so wicked, if it will promote their interests," Anne persuaded her sister Mary that the Prince of Wales was not their father's true son. Herself horrified by Roman Catholicism and dismayed by both her parents' conversion to it, Mary truly believed this calumny until her death. Despite Anne's industrious malice, she herself later seems to have doubted its truth. William never believed it but never challenged Mary's belief either, for her illusion suited his purposes.

Invited by some to invade Britain in order to restore liberty and the rule of law, William could not have anticipated how easy James would make the usurpation he intended. William had no desire to confront, fight, harm, or imprison his father-in-law and uncle, and indeed he encouraged James's flight to France, where Louis XIV, Mary Beatrice, and the infant Prince of Wales waited. With the throne vacant, however, William soon clarified for the British that he intended to rule as King Regnant, not merely as Mary's consort. Feeling herself unqualified to reign, Mary agreed to their joint rule as King and Queen Regnant, which actually meant that she relinquished all power to William. During his periodic absences on the Continent or in Ireland, Mary served as as a capable and conscientious Regent with limited powers. Because she loved William devotedly and disliked the role of Queen, William knew he could trust her implicitly.

His trust in Mary stood William in good stead, for he could trust few others. Dangers loomed everywhere for them both—of French aggression towards the Netherlands or Britain in William's absence, of assassination, of Jacobite intrigues involving those who desired James II's forgiveness or his good will, in case the tide should turn. Among those suspected of Jacobite loyalties were the heir of the childless William and Mary, Anne, and her close friends, John and Sarah Churchill. Pressed by Mary to give up her association with Sarah, Anne adamantly refused, ultimately causing a complete severence of affection between them. "I did what I could towards a reconciliation without effect," Mary remembered, "it made me change quite and grow (at least, endeavor to grow) as indifferent as she."

They had not reconciled when Mary, Queen for only six years, died suddenly of the smallpox that had killed both of her husband's parents—his father a few days before William's birth, his mother in his childhood. Mary's death devastated her supposedly unemotional husband. The death in 1700 of Anne's sole living child, William, Duke of Gloucester (beloved of both William and Mary), forced the solution embodied in the 1701 Act of Settlement: Sophia, Electress of Hanover—the granddaughter of James I through his daughter Elizabeth Stuart, later Queen of Bohemia—and Sophia's descendants would succeed Anne. Earlier, William had considered making James Francis Edward his own heir and proposed this to James II and Mary of Modena, who indignantly refused to countenance the necessary conversion of their son to Protestantism. The Prince of Wales's half-brother, James, Duke of Berwick, considered their refusal a colossal error.

After Gloucester's death, William himself did not have long to live. Always suffering from poor health, especially from respiratory problems that included asthma, he did not recover from a fall from his horse, who may have stumbled on a molehill. (Exultant Jacobites toasted "the little gentleman in black velvet.") William left behind the results of his powerful actions and influence: a monarchy sharing power with Parliament; a Protestant succession; the eventual union of England and Scotland unto a single political entity called Great Britain; greater freedom for the press and for the judiciary; and greater religious liberty for Dissenters. Above all, he left behind the inspiration and the results of his steadfast defiance of the aggression of the France of Louis XIV. He had built and sustained an alliance through diplomacy, and he had advocated checking the power of domineering states, not only through wartime alliances, but also through compulsory obedience to arbitration.

While Mary had become a popular Queen, the British never cared much for William, who returned the sentiment. Dismissing the importance of their esteem, he commented, "Hosanna today, and perhaps tomorrow crucify." Daniel Defoe thought the King's scepticism justified: "We blame the King that he relies too much on [foreigners].... He has so often been betrayed by us, he must have been a madman to rely on English gentlemen's fidelity." A reserved and detached attitude towards most other people seems to have characterized William, as well as a dry humor—traits that rarely create popularity. Not popular among the many, he was yet loved deeply by the few, and he loved them ardently in return: his wife, as well as his friends—Hans Willem Bentinck, whom he made Earl of Portland, and Bentinck's hated rival, Arnout van Keppel, created Earl of Albemarle. Even his more discerning enemies esteemed his worth. Noting "he had extraordinary intelligence, was an astute politician, and no matter the obstacles in the way, never turned aside from his object," William's cousin and antagonist Berwick acknowledged William as "a great man" and, even though an usurper, "a great King."

William III and Mary II Sites

William was born in **The Hague** in 1650. Mary was born at **St. James's Palace**. Their marriage took place in the **Chapel Royal, St. James's Palace**, in 1677.

Their first married home was at **Honselersdijk**, between Delft and the coast; the palace no longer exists. The Dutch royal palaces we know today were known to them: William built two of them. The foundation stone of **Huis Ten Bosch** palace, on the northeast side of The Hague, was laid by Elizabeth of Bohemia on September 2, 1645. It came into William's possession in 1686, when he needed a summer home near the seat of government. Lately, it has been the home of Queen Beatrix of the Netherlands. **Paleis Soestdijk**, just outside Baarn, built in 1674 as a place for William to hunt, has remained a royal home, lately that of Queen Juliana (who died there in March 2004). Baarn and its environs is known today for its fine, large homes, the summer residences of wealthy merchants during Holland's golden age as the greatest trading nation in the world. William and Mary acquired Het Oude Loo, near Apeldoorn, and built **Paleis Het Loo**, a royal residence until 1975, and now open to the public after restoration of the palace and its gardens to their 17th century appearance. The beautiful and varied gardens were already famous in the 17th and 18th centuries. Today, there are both King's and Queen's gardens, and flowers and fountains on several levels. For opening times at Het Loo, see http://www.paleishetloo.nl/ (in Dutch; the link to English is for visiting details only.)

The Dutch royal palaces can be toured at http://www.koninklijkhuis.nl/english/content.jsp?objectid=5682, with many fine photographs and 360-degree views, along with information about the royal family generally.

The castle (kasteel) in **Breda** was reconstructed by William in 1696; a castle has been on the same site since 1198. William's reconstruction was of the 1536 building. In 1826, it became a military academy, resulting in fairly dramatic changes to William's building, and is still one today: there is no admittance. There is a 1921 equestrian statue of William in the Kasteelplein and copies of the Willem Wissing portraits of William and Mary II in the Breda Town Hall. See the statue and the portrait of William at http://stadsarchief.breda.nl/actueel/Breda_750/Februari/gebouw_E.htm in the middle of successive screens of information and photographs of the castle.

In 1688, William departed from **Hellevoetsluis**, for England. This center for pleasure boating faces the Haringvliet, southwest of Rotterdam. Tour Hellevoetsluis on its website, at http://www.hellevoetsluis.nl/ (there's optional English), with attractive photographs, history, and tourist information.

William landed in **Brixham**, Devonshire. Brixham is one of three towns on Tor Bay ("the English Riviera," the others, Torquay and Paignton, being larger and better-known). Visit the English Riviera at http://www.theenglishriviera.co.uk/home/home.asp?area=HOME. At the southern end of Tor Bay, Brixham is a busy fishing port and family resort, with a statue commemorating William's arrival. He is said to have been first proclaimed King at the nearby St. Leonard's Tower, **Newton Abbot**. The tower, in the center of pleasant Newton Abbot, is all that remains of the 14th century church. Then, it is claimed, he sought refreshment and accommodation at Forde House. See Forde House at http://www.teignbridge.gov.uk/index.cfm?articleid=1592; click on History of Old Forde House for a detailed account.

A special coronation chair was constructed for Mary's joint coronation with her husband. The chair is now in the **Westminster Abbey Museum**. Visiting details for the museum can be read at http://www.westminster-abbey.org/tour/museum.htm/.

William, especially, and Mary disliked **Whitehall Palace**. The only remnant of their occupancy (the palace burned in 1698) is **Queen Mary's Steps**, what's left of a terrace overlooking the river, built for Mary by Sir Christopher Wren. This can be seen from the Victoria Embankment, in the garden behind the Banqueting House and Ministry of Defence building.

William purchased **Nottingham House** in Kensington village from Daniel Finch, 2nd Earl of Nottingham, for £18,000. Asthmatic, he hoped for alleviation by having a London home outside the center of the city. This was to become **Kensington Palace**, although William and Mary saw it more as a retreat than a palace—**Hampton Court** (see below) was, for them, the latter. Ordered to enlarge Nottingham House, which was left intact, Wren added four pavilions to the four corners and a two-story courtyard, the **Great Court**, on the west side, along with some smaller additions. William was impatient to have the house ready for occupation by himself and Mary on his return from the war in Ireland; in 1689, Mary moved in.

Because William and Mary were joint sovereigns, the house had to have an entrance and staircase for each, at the west and north ends, the staircases leading to their respective apartments. Wren's **King's Grand Staircase** was originally simpler than it became later; it was remodelled 1692–3, and then considerably more embellished under George I (see *George I*). The **King's Apartments** consist of the Presence Chamber, the Privy Chamber, the Cupola Room, and the King's Drawing Room and Gallery. Their present appearance owes more to George I and George II's tastes than to William's.

However, the **Queen's Staircase** leads to the series of rooms built and furnished for Mary, and they are to be seen as such today: Gallery, Closet, Dining Room, and Bedroom. The **Gallery**, which was a recreation place for Mary, where she and her ladies embroidered whilst being read to, is hung with portraits of herself and her family (including Wissing's portraits of Mary and William), along with a full-length portrait of Peter the Great, Tsar of Russia, in armor, painted by Godfrey Kneller during the Tsar's visit to London in 1698. During her reign, the room housed her extensive collection of oriental porcelain. There is some splendid carving by Grinling Gibbons. It's likely that she died in the Bedchamber.

William's last addition was the **south front**, in 1695. Externally, this now became the architectural focus of the house. Internally, the south front provided him with a new picture gallery, the long **King's Gallery**, still used today to house some of the finest pictures in the Royal Collection. Apart from the pictures, a feature is the wind-dial above the chimneypiece, made for William by Robert Morden in 1694. The wind-dial is linked to a weathervane on the roof, to indicate the direction of the wind. The marble chimneypiece and carved overmantel around it were added by William Kent at the behest of George I.

A bronze statue of William by German sculptor Heinrich Baucke, presented to Edward VII in 1907 by his nephew, Kaiser Wilhelm II, stands outside the south front. The **gates** were installed in the late 1980s, having been moved here from the north side of the palace. In the days following her death, they became the repository of the many tributes to Diana, Princess of Wales, who had occupied apartments in the northwest part of palace from 1981 to 1997.

William and Mary were both keen gardeners, extending and improving the already fine **gardens**. Under their aegis, George London laid out the **south garden** in a combination of parterre and wilderness. Work on the north side of the palace came to an end with William's death. Later monarchs added substantially to the gardens. Read about Kensington Palace at http://www.hrp.org.uk/webcode/kensington_home.asp, and at http://www.royal.gov.uk/output/Page563.asp.

William and Mary lived in **Holland House**, Kensington, at the edge of Holland Park, while Kensington House was being built. Holland House is a beautiful and historic Tudor mansion famous in the time of the 3rd Baron Holland as a gathering place of all that was witty, artistic, intellectual, and fashionable. Today, Holland House is a youth hostel: see and read about it at http://www.yha.org.uk/hostel/hostelpages/141.html.

At **Hampton Court**, William's and Mary's contributions were substantial. They decided to establish their palace there, employing Wren to replace the whole Tudor building. Due to financial constraints and Mary's death in 1694, only Henry VIII's and his Queen's apartments were destroyed, although Wren modernized some of the remaining Tudor palace. Additions made were the King's and Queen's Apartments, each side of the new Fountain Court, and the Trophy Gates at the entrance to the estate, along with the replanning of the gardens.

Entrance to Hampton Court is made through the **Trophy Gates**, constructed for William. Wren's **King's** and **Queen's Apartments** for William and Mary, which transformed the south and east sides of the palace, are at the furthest end from the gates, and arranged around the **Fountain Court**. Entry to the King's Apartments is made under the colonnade in the **Clock Court** (the middle of the three courts).

The **King's Staircase** was planned to be grand. It was decorated by Antonio Verrio around 1700 in an allegory glorifying William as Alexander the Great, alluding to William's defeat of James II and triumph over the Jacobites. The **King's Guard Chamber** displays a collection of more than 3,000 weapons brought from the Tower of London in 1699 by William's gunsmith, John Harris. Grinling Gibbons's carving is to be seen on the centerpieces on each wall; he was appointed Master Carver to the Crown in 1693, and his work is often in evidence in royal homes of that time. Both the **King's Presence** and **Privy Chambers** saw audiences with William. Prominent on a wall of the Presence Chamber is Kneller's huge painting *William III on Horseback*, depicting William in a Roman soldier's dress.

The rest of the many rooms in the King's State Apartments are also hung with art, tapestries as well as paintings, and many display porcelain from Mary's collection. Another painting by Jan van Orley of William, this time as King Solomon, hangs in the **King's Backstairs**, smaller, more intimate rooms forming the **King's Private Apartments**. The walls of the **King's Private Dining Room**, the last in the sequence, are hung with portraits commissioned by Mary from Kneller depicting the principal ladies of her household, the *Hampton Court Beauties*. William's red velvet bed with its matching furniture can still be seen in the magnificent **Great Bedchamber**; however, he usually slept in the **Little Bedchamber**, which contains a reproduction of the original bed there. His desk still stands in the **King's Closet** (not to be confused with the series of small closets downstairs in the King's Private Apartments), with documents showing his signature. In the **King's Private Drawing Room**, a painting by Adam-François van der Meulen, *William and Mary on Horseback*, hangs over the fireplace.

In 1986 the apartments were badly damaged by a disastrous fire in an apartment on the third floor, but they have since been restored to the way they would have been when William occupied them and rebuilt by using Wren's materials and techniques. During the restoration process, much was learned about how the apartments were originally created, and significant evidence of Henry VIII's apartments beneath William's was uncovered.

The **Queen's State Apartments** were begun but not completed before Mary's death in 1694. The **Queen's Staircase** leads to a suite of rooms: the Guard Chamber, Presence Chamber, Public Dining Room, Audience Chamber, Drawing Room, State Bedchamber, Queen's Gallery, and Queen's Closet. The staircase was originally plain, whitewashed, and panelled; William took over the Gallery and the Closet, which adjoined his own, after Mary's death. Eight panels of needlework hang in the Closet; they came to Hampton Court in 1700, and must have been intended for Mary. The **Queen's Gallery** displays porcelain that belonged to Mary, Delftware and Chinese jardinières. Otherwise, these rooms reflect the taste and use of Queen Caroline, wife of George II.

Outside, in the gardens, the **Privy Garden** was made for William, and has been restored to the appearance it would have had at that time. The **Lower Orangery** was constructed to house Mary's collection of botanical specimens, some imported from Virginia. Also on the south side of the palace is the **Banqueting House**, built in 1700 for informal parties after dinner at the palace. Verrio also decorated the main room, known as the Painted Room. The Banqueting House is open in summer only. The gardens on the east side of the palace consisted of parkland in Henry VIII's time; the area was gradually enclosed by the Stuarts and then laid out under William as a huge semicircular parterre with 12 marble fountains. Also on the east side is the **Home Park**, where William suffered his fatal riding accident; William also enjoyed hunting in the adjacent **Bushy Park** (for more details about Bushy, see *William IV*).

Henry VIII's **Great Orchard** comprised the land on the north side of the palace and became known as the **Wilderness**. William planted the area with tall clipped hedges in geometric patterns; in spring, flowering bulbs carpet the ground. The famous **Maze**, planted in 1702, consists of half a mile of paths and continues to puzzle and entertain visitors. Read about Hampton Court and see images at http://www.hrp.org.uk/webcode/hampton_home.asp and at http://www.hamptoncourt.org.uk/.

William preferred Kensington and Hampton Court to **Greenwich**. However, Mary wished to build a naval almshouse, like the Royal Hospital Chelsea, on the site of the old palace, incorporating the King Charles Block. Wren was surveyor, assisted by Nicholas Hawksmoor; construction took place between 1696 and 1712 but wasn't finished until 1752. Four blocks of buildings, each with a central courtyard, eventuated—the **King Charles Block** and **Queen Anne Block** along the river, and the **King William Block** and **Queen Mary Block** behind them. The first seamen came to live in the Royal Naval Hospital in 1705. During the Napoleonic wars, the numbers rose to 2710, but then fell to such a low point by 1869 that the hospital closed. In 1873, the Royal Naval College was transferred from Portsmouth to Greenwich. With the merging of the staff colleges of the Army, Navy, and Air Force in the 1990s, the Greenwich buildings were no longer to be used by the Navy, which moved out at the end of 1998. The Greenwich Foundation for the Old Royal Naval College, set up in 1996, now assumed responsibility for letting the buildings. The Maritime Greenwich University Campus, of the University of Greenwich, now occupies most of three buildings; the King Charles Block is occupied by the Trinity School of Music.

King William Block and **Queen Mary Block** have become known as among Wren's finest work. The **Painted Hall**, a spectacular dining hall in the King William Block, is especially noteworthy. The painting is the creation of Sir James Thornhill, who was paid £3 per square yard for the ceiling and £1 for the walls. In the ceiling of the dining room, Thornhill shows Peace and Liberty triumphing over Tyranny. William and Mary are depicted, enthroned, with the Virtues behind them. Through the arch in one end of the room is the Upper Hall, where Thornhill depicted the powerful and successful Britain, Queen Anne and Prince George of Denmark central, surrounded by the four known corners of the world. See the Painted Hall at http://www.greenwichfoundation.org.uk/newpage2.htm. The **Chapel** of St. Peter and St. Paul in the Queen Mary Block was completed 20 years after Wren's death but then gutted by fire in 1779. The resulting restoration changed the style from the original Baroque to the new Rococo; contrast its style with the Baroque of the Painted Hall by viewing and reading about the chapel at http://www.greenwichfoundation.org.uk/newpage3.htm. The organ of the chapel is of historical significance to organ connoisseurs.

Read about the **Old Royal Naval College** at http://www.greenwich-guide.org.uk/rnc.htm. Numerous links take the visitor to the various attractions of Greenwich and its immediate surroundings, with instructions and maps.

In 1690, William embarked from **Hoylake** for the Battle of the Boyne against James II. Hoylake is a resort at the mouth of the river Dee, Liverpool Bay, and home of the Royal Liverpool Golf Club. Originally known as Hoyle Lake, it used to be the deep-water anchorage for vessels going on to Liverpool or down the Dee to Chester. Several websites provide bits of information and pictures of the area: http://64.33.116.68/hoylake-history.html (Wirral Sand Yacht Club),

http://www.deeestuary.co.uk/nwirral.htm (bird watching), and http://www.royal-liverpool-golf.com/ (Royal Liverpool Golf Club).

Before the Battle of the Boyne, William stayed in **Carrickfergus Castle**, in now-northern Ireland. Carrickfergus is on the east coast, northeast of Belfast. Photographs of the castle and visiting details appear at http://www.ehsni.gov.uk/places/monuments/carrick.shtml; a detailed history of the castle can be read at http://www.carrickfergus.org/template1.asp?pid=75&parent=74&area=3.

The **Battle of the Boyne** marked the completion of English conquest of Ireland. Read about the battle, with photographs and a diagram of the battlefield, at http://www.orangenet.org/jlol130/boyne.htm. Tourist information for the area is set out in http://www.drogheda-tourism.com/. The fertile Boyne Valley was home to society in Neolithic times, with monuments to be seen today at Newgrange, Dowth, and Knowth. Tours must be arranged through Brú na Bóinne Interpretive Center near Newgrange. In the **Bank of Ireland building** (originally built as the Irish parliament building) in Dublin, there is a huge tapestry representing the Battle. It hangs on a wall in the chamber of the old House of Lords; read and see more at http://encyclopedia.laborlawtalk.com/Irish_Houses_of_Parliament. An equestrian statue of William was erected in College Green, Dublin, in 1701 but was destroyed in 1928. See it at http://firstlight_2.tripod.com/Dublin.htm.

William used the nearby **Mellifont Abbey** as his headquarters. Mellifont was the first Cistercian monastery built in Ireland. The monastery, founded in 1142, became the model for other Cistercian centers in Ireland. The most interesting feature is the remains of a 13th century octagonal lavabo, where the monks washed their hands. Tourist information resides at http://www.heritageireland.ie/en/HistoricSites/East/OldMellifontAbbeyLouth/, with a photograph of the lavabo.

The Throne Room at **Dublin Castle** contains a throne reputedly presented by William after victory at the Boyne. See this among other photographs of the castle at http://irelandforvisitors.com/articles/castles_of_ireland2.htm.

The Charles Fort just outside **Kinsale**, built by the English in the 1670s, was taken by William's army in 1690 and then remained a garrison until the British left in 1922. Kinsale itself consists of an attractive town and harbor, matched by its website at http://www.kinsale.ie/.

Limerick's strategic position has involved it in Ireland's relationship with England, and not least under William. After the Battle of the Boyne, James II's Jacobite army withdrew to Limerick. William's siege of Limerick and the consequent defeat of the Jacobites resulted in the Treaty of Limerick, and longlasting bitterness. The website for Limerick is http://www.limerick.ie/.

On his journeys to and from Holland, William used **Quex House** as a stage. The present house was built in 1813, thus replacing the one William knew; it is open to the public, housing the Powell-Cotton Museum of natural history and ethnography, including 500 stuffed African animals among a vast collection of animal remains and artifacts. It stands half a mile outside Birchington, a resort joined to the much larger Margate. Photographs and visiting details, including those for the surrounding area, may be viewed at http://www.aboutbritain.com/powellcottonquexhse.htm.

William's death, in 1702, occurred five days after a fall from his horse in the Home Park of **Hampton Court Palace**. Both William and Mary died at **Kensington Palace**, and both are buried in the Henry VII Chapel, **Westminster Abbey**, in the same vault with Charles II and Mary's estranged sister, Queen Anne and her husband Prince George of Denmark, under the monument to General Monk, Duke of Albemarle. Their effigies are included among those in the Museum, in the undercroft of the Abbey. Details for visiting can be found at http://www.westminster-abbey.org/tour/museum.htm. See the effigies and read about their deaths and burials at http://westminster-abbey.org/library/monarchs/william_iii.htm and http://westminster-abbey.org/library/monarchs/mary_ii.htm.

In historic **Williamsburg, Virginia** (named for William), the **College of William and Mary**, founded in 1693, is named for both of them.

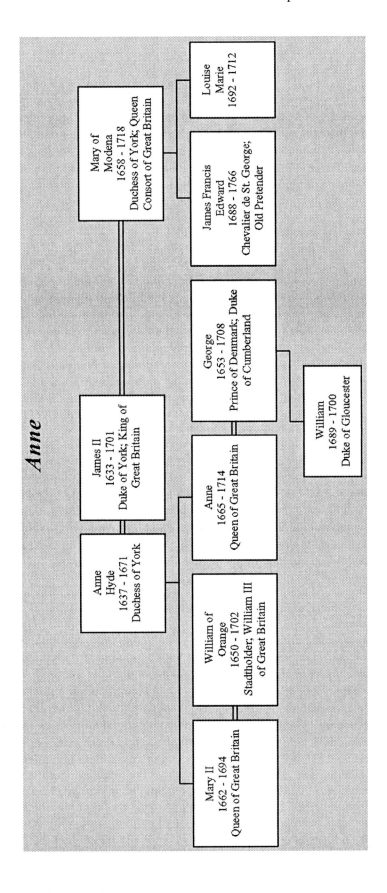

Anne

Anne (1665–1714; reigned as Queen of Great Britain and Ireland, 1702–1714)

During Anne's life of passionate attachments and aversions, she suffered from many seismic ruptures caused by estrangement or death. Loss and betrayal characterized so many of her closest relationships that she endured (and caused) great pain. The question of ensuring the Protestant succession dominated her life, as did her fealty to the Church of England, which Anne sought to protect and from which she gained much solace during her tragic life. When she came to die, as her physician, John Arbuthnot, confided to his friend Jonathan Swift, "sleep was never more welcome to a weary traveller than death was to her."

The estrangements and betrayals that Anne experienced and perpetrated largely resulted from political and religious differences with her blood relations and her friends. Anne's determination to secure the Protestant succession and the Church of England led to her breaking with her father, James II, while her political positions later alienated her as well from her brother-in-law and sister, William and Mary, and still later from her friend and ally, Sarah Churchill, Duchess of Marlborough. Concurrently, as the happy wife of Prince George of Denmark (brother to Christian V), Anne (pregnant 18 times) grieved many failed pregnancies or early deaths, the passing of her surviving child, and, finally, the loss of her beloved husband.

In Anne's girlhood, her uncle, Charles II, had insisted on her being instructed in the Anglican faith, and he had arranged for her 1683 marriage with a Protestant prince. In the following year, Charles gave Anne the Tudor apartments in Whitehall as her residence, called "the Cockpit." As the unmarried daughter of James, Duke of York (later James II) and Anne Hyde, Princess Anne had lived in Richmond Palace while her parents lived at St. James's Palace and Windsor Castle. Besides this physical separation, two years before Anne Hyde's death in 1671, both parents had converted to Roman Catholicism. In 1676, James stopped attending services of the Church of England. Princess Anne had learned to feel distrust and horror towards papists. While Charles II himself privately leaned towards Roman Catholicism, he sought to improve the position of Catholics in England but not to declare his own private beliefs or to impose them on others. Charles's respect for the political and religious realities led him to have James's daughters raised as Anglicans and married to Protestants, much to the dismay of their father.

James accentuated his Catholic loyalties by marrying a Catholic second wife, the Italian Mary Beatrice of Modena. Although gentle and devout, Mary Beatrice aroused only distrust in her stepdaughter Anne, who described her as "the most hated woman in the world of all sorts of people." Like Anne, Mary Beatrice suffered from many failed pregnancies and the early deaths of children. After James's accession as James II in 1685, Queen Mary Beatrice again became pregnant in 1687. Not only did Anne (like some other Protestants) react with suspicion to this news because of dread of a Catholic male heir who would supplant James's Protestant daughters, but she may have reacted negatively also because she herself had lost two daughters and had two miscarriages in less than a year. If a half-brother was born, he would displace Anne and her older sister Mary.

Anne fostered false rumors that Mary Beatrice was not really pregnant at all but instead was feigning pregnancy in order to push aside her stepdaughters with a borrowed male child who would rule as a Catholic King. She convinced her sister Mary of this deception by their father and stepmother. Anne also arranged her absence so as not to be one of the eyewitnesses validating the birth. Fears of the birth of a Catholic Prince of Wales and of James's intentions regarding the Church of England led Anne to support the invasion of England by her brother-in-law, William of Orange, and his deposition of her father, James II—the "Glorious Revolution" of 1688. In its aftermath, Anne gained apartments in Whitehall that had belonged to Charles II's mistress the Duchess of Portsmouth, and George became Duke of Cumberland.

Although Anne had allied herself with William and Mary against James, her relationship with her older sister and brother-in-law did not long survive James's reign. By 1690, Anne had become the focus of political opposition to William and Mary, who also felt antagonized by Anne's friendship with Sarah Churchill. Relations worsened into a complete break between the sisters two years before Mary's death in 1694. The childless widower William III, now that Anne was his heiress presumptive, gave her St. James's Palace as her residence, but they liked each other no better than before. While Anne had long referred to William as "Caliban" and "the Dutch abortion" when discussing him with Sarah, William resented the fact that Anne held a better claim to inherit the throne than he himself did, even though he reigned in her stead.

Anne's relationship with William and Mary, bolstered by their rebellion against James II, did not long survive James's reign. So, too, her long friendship with Sarah, solidified by their shared antagonism to James and then to William and Mary, did not long survive William's reign and Anne's accession in 1702. Again, political differences frayed the bond. Sarah, Duchess of Marlborough, a passionate Whig, fervently attacked Anne's Tory sympathies—sympathies bound up with her lifelong loyalty to the Church of England.

Although Sarah's persistence in her tactless aggression upon political themes annoyed Anne, her presumptuous familiarity alienated Anne just as much. As Duchess of York, Mary Beatrice had fostered the match between Sarah Jennings and John Churchill. A maid of honor to the Duchess of York, Sarah, Lady Churchill, became part of Anne's household upon Anne's marriage. Two years later, Sarah became Anne's first lady of the bedchamber and groom of the stole. Anne stood by the Churchills after William and Mary turned against them, and after her 1702 accession, she elevated Sarah to the posts of the Queen's groom of the stole, keeper of the privy purse, and mistress of the robes and Churchill to his dukedom. Whenever separated, Sarah and Anne, from 1691, had corresponded on equal terms as "Mrs. Freeman" and "Mrs. Morley," but Sarah absented herself more and more from Kensington Palace and Windsor Castle, being more interested in family life and the classics, and "Mrs. Freeman" presumed to be more than familiar—indeed, to be positively insulting. The Queen complained to Marlborough, "no body [sic] was ever so used by a friend as I have been by her ever since my coming to ye crown." Wrecked upon personal and political shoals, the friendship foundered. Strained by 1704, affection had died by 1706, but Anne's fears of Sarah protracted their unpleasant disengagement through 1707. In possession of Anne's letters, Sarah threatened publicity and even blackmail. Enraged by Anne's growing closeness to Abigail Hill (later Masham), Sarah's first cousin and Anne's bedchamber woman or maid, Sarah hinted that Anne enjoyed a lesbian passion for Abigail. Finally, Anne paid off the Duchess.

In the meantime, less complicated but precious relationships had ended by death. Of Anne's 18 pregnancies, her only child to survive long, William, Duke of Gloucester, had become ill on his eleventh birthday in 1700 and died within the week. Always abnormal, Gloucester had not talked until he was three years old, nor had he walked until he was five. Apparently, he suffered from hydrocephalus. His father, Anne's beloved George of Denmark, himself died in 1708.

Anne sought consolation for her manifold losses in the Church of England, and in order to protect her Church, intrigued to ensure a Protestant succession. After Gloucester's death ended all hope of direct descent from Anne herself, the childless widower William III devised through the 1701 Act of Settlement that Anne's successors would be Hanoverians: Sophia—the granddaughter of James I through his daughter Elizabeth Stuart, later Queen of Bohemia—and Sophia's descendants. While Anne disliked thinking about her own passing and the Hanoverians' succeeding, her devotion to the Protestant succession mandated her acceptance of this arrangement. At the same time, from 1691 onward, she misled her exiled father and his wife and, eventually, their son and her half-brother, James Francis Edward, into believing that she favored a Jacobite restoration upon her death. She had always deceived James and Mary Beatrice about her true feelings towards them, stunning James by her betrayal during his deposition. As Swift commented, "there was not, perhaps in all England, a person who understood more artificially how to disguise her passions." Her loyalty to her

Church (and therefore to the Protestant succession) superseded her loyalty as a daughter and a subject. It cost her her health, ruined by many pregnancies, as well as her family, and her closest friend.

Anne Sites

Anne was born at **St. James's Palace**, and married Prince George of Denmark in the **Chapel Royal** in 1683. For basic information regarding St. James's Palace, see *Henry VIII*; for the Chapel Royal, see *Charles I*.

George had been born in **Copenhagen**. The capital of Denmark, Copenhagen, with a population of 465,000, is situated on the east of Sjælland and the north of Amager islands, and on the Øresund river. As well as being a major port and manufacturing center, it's the seat of various universities and colleges and a cultural center of some charm. Several royal palaces dotted about the city include four around Amalienborg Square, with the Amalienborg Palace being the home of the present Queen of Denmark. Visit it at http://www. copenhagen.com/start.asp?Menu=Home, and the royal palaces at http://www.copenhagen. com/tourism/royalpalaces/amalienborg.asp?Menu=Tourism.

Anne lived in **Whitehall Palace** and **St. James's Palace** (see *Henry VIII* for both) but bought **Campden House** in Kensington, London for her son, and she also inhabited it before her accession. This house no longer stands. When she succeeded to the throne, and moved into **Kensington Palace**, Anne added only a few small rooms to the Queen's Apartments, within the small courtyard between the old Nottingham House and William's new King's Gallery. However, she commissioned new furniture and, in general, maintained a palace that visitors admired. **Queen Mary's Closet**, in the Queen's Apartments, saw her last meeting with her former intimate Sarah, Duchess of Marlborough. It is hung with portraits of herself and Prince George, including the famous Kneller portrait of Anne in profile. Next to it is Michael Dahl's oval portrait of Prince George. Her real contribution was to the **gardens**.

Although she otherwise detested him, Anne shared with her brother-in-law William III a love of gardening, reflected at both Kensington Palace and Hampton Court Palace. At Kensington Palace, her gardener, Henry Wise, transformed the garden William had created. In the summer of 1702, she undertook the development of the northern part of the estate, the wilderness. The incorporation of this area more than doubled the size of the gardens. It was thickly planted in trees and shrubs, crossed by intersecting walks. Sir Christopher Wren designed a summer house for her, called **Queen Anne's Alcove**, in Kensington Gardens. Originally in the south garden, it was moved to its present position at the north end of the Serpentine, near Marlborough Gate, in the late 19th century. An important addition during her reign was the **Orangery**. Attributed to Nicholas Hawksmoor with modifications by Sir John Vanbrugh, the Orange House—or Green House, as it was called during the late 18th and early 19th centuries—was designed to house plants during the winter and for court entertainments in the summer. The interior features Corinthian columns, statues of female deities by Pietro Francavilla, copies of Roman busts, and large vases, and Grinling Gibbons's exquisite carving in pine and pearwood. The Orangery now houses an all-day restaurant. See the Orangery at http:// www.hrp.org.uk/webcode/content.asp?ID=407, and at http://www.hrp.org. uk/webcode/content.asp?ID=331, you can see a photograph of the white, pretty restaurant inside. For basic information regarding Kensington Palace, see *William III/Mary II*.

At **Windsor**, Wise planned and created for Anne a new formal garden on the south side of the Castle, while in the park new walks and avenues were laid out, with care taken to level the rides through the park where Anne hunted in her chaise.

Anne also hunted from her chaise at **Hampton Court**. When she stayed at the Palace, she occupied the King's Apartments because the Queen's Apartments were unfinished, and she continued some of the works begun by William III. She commissioned the decoration of the **Queen's Drawing Room**, where Antonio Verrio depicted her receiving homage from the world; on the ceiling, she is portrayed as Justice, attended by

Neptune, Britannia, Peace, and Plenty. The large overmantel shows Prince George as Lord Admiral, with the fleet. In the **Chapel**, Wren installed a royal pew and gallery structure for Anne, along with a vast oak reredos carved by Grinling Gibbons, which hid the great double, stained-glass east window. In the **east gardens**, she surrounded William III's great semicircular parterre with semicircular canals in 1710. See *Henry VIII* and *William III/Mary II* for more information about Hampton Court.

Blenheim Palace, which Anne called "the castle of Blenheim," was constructed at her expense as a reward to John Churchill, Duke of Marlborough for his great victory. In 1704, she gave him the manor of Woodstock. Sir John Vanbrugh was chosen as architect, and the foundation stone was laid in 1705. However, he fell out with Sarah, Duchess of Marlborough in 1716, over the remains of the old Woodstock Palace: Vanbrugh wanted to preserve them, but he was overruled by Sarah. After that, James Moore and Nicholas Hawksmoor completed the palace. Blenheim Palace became the only building in Britain not intended for royal occupation to bear that title, and is one of the great houses of Britain today, the home of the Duke of Marlborough. Its website is at http://www.blenheimpalace.com/, with links to photographs, history, special events, and visiting details.

In addition, Anne granted a royal plot in Pall Mall to Sarah, Duchess of Marlborough, who erected **Marlborough House** there. Constructed by Sir Christopher Wren from 1709 to 1711, it is the last in the row of splendid houses along the Mall from Buckingham Palace. During the last century, two widowed Queens lived there—Edward VII's Queen Alexandra, then George V's Queen Mary. In the late 1950s, Elizabeth II gave the house to the government, and since the 1960s it has been the home of the Commonwealth Secretariat. See http://www.thecommonwealth.org/Templates/Internal.asp?NodeID=34467&int1stParentNodeID=20596&int2ndParentNodeID=20635. Because of its nature, the house can be visited only at certain periods, like Open Days.

At **Greenwich**, the **Queen Anne Block** was begun in 1699. View it at http://www.greenwich-guide.org.uk/rnc.htm, and, from another angle, http://www.greenwich-guide.org.uk/rncpresent.htm. Also, Anne and Prince George are depicted in Sir James Thornhill's work in the Painted Hall, **King William Block**, appearing in the ceiling of the Upper Hall. For information regarding the Wren construction at Greenwich, see *William III/Mary II*.

Anne inherited her uncle Charles II's interest in horse racing, keeping several horses and running them under her own name. In August 1711, she held the first race meeting at **Ascot**.

Ascot racecourse is closed for redevelopment until the next Royal Ascot, June 2006. Visit Ascot at http://www.ascot.co.uk/index1.php, with a link to its Photo Gallery; historical photographs can be seen at http://www.royalascot.co.uk/. Royal Ascot, each June, is when members of the royal family, aristocrats, and celebrities turn out in style.

Both Anne and Prince George died at **Kensington Palace** and are buried in the Henry VII Chapel of **Westminster Abbey**, in a vault along with her uncle Charles II, her estranged sister Mary II and Mary's husband William III, under the monument to General Monk, Duke of Albemarle. Her effigy, carried at her funeral, is in the **Museum** of the Abbey, in the Norman Undercroft. Details for visiting can be found at http://www.westminster-abbey.org/tour/museum.htm. See Anne's wax effigy and read details of her death and burial at http://westminster-abbey.org/library/monarchs/anne.htm.

Hanoverians
(Protestant Stuarts)

and

Pretenders
(Catholic Stuarts)

George I

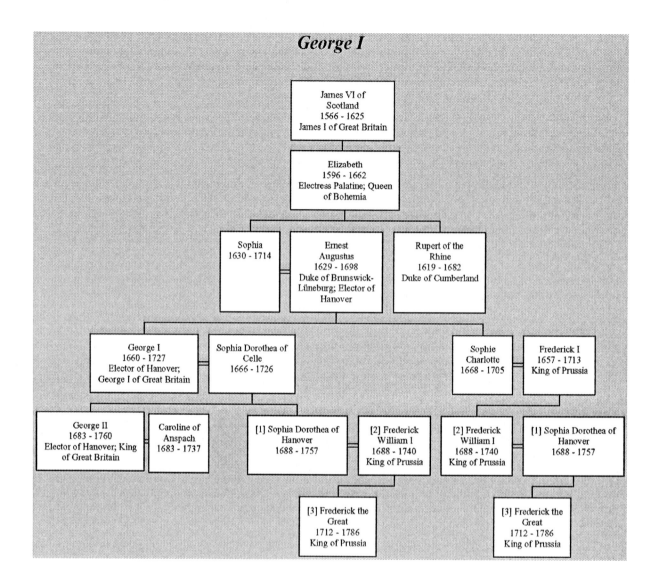

George I (1660–1727; reigned as King of Great Britain and Ireland, 1714–1727 and as Elector of Hanover, 1698–1727)

The 1701 Act of Settlement grafted onto the British succession a Germanic branch. It displaced some familiar British figures with some decidedly foreign ones. The first beneficiary of the Act of Settlement, George Louis, Elector of Hanover—who, upon the death of Queen Anne, became George I of Great Britain—remained distinctly foreign. So did (to some extent) his son and successor, the Hanoverian Prince George Augustus (later George II). As the years wore on and Jacobite rebellions failed to supplant George I and George II with the descendants of James II, the Protestant Hanoverians seemed ever more British and the Catholic Jacobite Pretenders ever more foreign. In the later 18th century, the contrast between the robustly British George III and the Italian-bred Jacobite Henry Cardinal York could not have been more stark. Yet, at the beginning of the Hanoverian dynasty, Britain and George III's great-grandfather, George I, displayed a mutual lack of enthusiasm for their union.

As the successors of Anne, the Act of Settlement had named Sophia, the widow of Ernest Augustus, Elector of Hanover, and Sophia's descendants. (The Dukes of Brunswick-Lüneburg ruled as Electors of Hanover from 1692 onward.) The grandaughter of James I of Great Britain through his daughter Elizabeth Stuart, later Electress Palatine and Queen of Bohemia, Sophia actually sympathized with the deposed James II and his displaced son, the so-called "Old Pretender." She went so far as to display the Old Pretender's portrait in her room. Nevertheless, the prospect of becoming Queen of Great Britain excited Sophia. Unfortunately for her, she died shortly before the passing of Queen Anne, and her right passed to her son, George Louis.

Even before the 1701 Act of Settlement, George Louis had had prospects of being allied to the British royal house. In the early 1680s, William of Orange and Sophia's brother Prince Rupert of the Rhine had advocated the marriage of George Louis and Anne herself. George Louis spent four months in England in 1680–81 but never made a formal proposal. Such a marriage did not suit the designs of Anne's father, James, Duke of York, and her uncle, Charles II. Instead, Anne married George of Denmark in 1683, while George Louis had married Sophia Dorothea of Celle the previous year.

Anne deeply loved her husband, and her marriage succeeded, but first cousins George Louis and Sophia Dorothea had always detested each other. Marriage did not soften their mutual dislike. While George Louis indulged in extramarital liaisons, by 1692 Sophia Dorothea had become attracted by and attached to Count Philip von Königsmarck, a Swedish noble and Colonel in the Hanoverian army. In 1694, Königsmarck disappeared after a visit to Sophia Dorothea. (Ernest Augustus may have ordered his murder. The absent George Louis probably bore no direct responsibility for it.) That same year, George Louis divorced Sophia Dorothea. Imprisoned for the rest of her life—for more than 30 years—in the Castle of Ahlden, she never saw her two children again. George Louis's treatment of Sophia Dorothea alienated their son, George Augustus, who always carried her image hidden on his person. Upon her death in 1726, George Louis forbade their son to wear mourning. When George Augustus succeeded as George II in 1727, as one of his first acts, he openly displayed two portraits of his long-lost mother. Never good, relations between father and son worsened with the years.

While George Louis enjoyed being Elector of Hanover, he felt no great enthusiasm in 1714 for uprooting himself from a place and people whom he loved to reign in a foreign land notorious for deposing its sovereigns. In Hanover, he ruled absolutely and paternalistically; in Britain, Ministers and Parliament would check his power. At 54 a middle-aged transplant from the Continent, George I relied upon French and German to communicate in England, and he never gained much proficiency in English. (Because his Minister Robert Walpole spoke no German and little French, George I conversed with Walpole in Latin.) In addition to George I's suspicion of the British and his limited grasp of the English language, he had a shy and reserved temperament and hated being the center of attention. Consequently, his new subjects had little access to him.

Instead, he preferred the company of his familiars. His Hanoverian favorites lost no time in extorting riches as their reward for influencing the King to grant requests. Besides the natives' resentment of the successful rapacity of these foreigners, many ridiculed the oddly contrasting appearance of two of the King's female favorites. They nicknamed the obese Sophie Charlotte von Kielmansegge—who became Countess of Darlington—the Elephant, and the cavernous Melusine von der Schulenburg—who became Duchess of Kendal—the Maypole. As Horace Walpole later noted, "the mob of London were highly diverted by the importation of so uncommon a seraglio!" George I's half-sister, the Elephant probably was not his mistress, although he may have eventually married the Maypole as a morganatic wife. The two women hated each other, and each assidously created trouble between George I and his son George Augustus, the Prince of Wales.

Although George I (who lived unostentatiously in two rooms at St. James's Palace) spent most of his evenings cutting out paper patterns in the Duchess of Kendal's apartments, the presence of Hanoverian favorites did not suffice, and he yearned for Hanover. In 1716, he began returning to Hanover for extended periods and eventually made seven summer visits there. In addition, he always felt more concerned about Hanover's interests than about those of Great Britain. Despite his prolonged absences, George I refused to give to the Prince of Wales any significant role in governing Great Britain. For example, in preparing for his first absence, George I avoided making George Augustus Regent and instead named him Guardian of the Realm, a post with highly restricted powers.

Resentful of his father's treatment, George Augustus simmered with hate. Their relationship crashed and burned after a family baptism at which George Augustus made a hostile remark to a favorite of the King, who of course hastened to repeat and distort it. George I reacted by evicting George Augustus and his wife, Caroline of Anspach, from St. James's Palace and forbidding them to visit their children without royal permission. Even after Walpole patched things up, their children remained with the King.

George I's treatment of his wife and son tells against him, yet it does not relay the full truth about him. While he reacted with cold cruelty to Sophia Dorothea and George Augustus (probably because he perceived them both as insulting and threatening), he expressed great love for his daughter, Sophia Dorothea, and his granddaughters by George Augustus became fond of him. George Augustus's elder son, Frederick, had remained behind in Hanover in 1714, and the grandfather visited him there during George I's periodic escapes from Great Britain. Frederick, too, developed feelings of warm affection for George I.

In addition to his more successful family relationships, George I enjoyed the esteem of the people of Hanover, where he felt happy, secure, and understood. When he died during his last visit to Hanover in 1727, the British did not bring his body back for burial, and instead he was buried at Osnabrück in Hanover. His remains now lie in the Mausoleum at the Herrenhaüsen Berggarten. At his death, broadsheets in England exulted, "The Devil has caught him by the throat at last." George I's unpopularity—indeed, notoriety—among the British and his contrasting good repute in Hanover would recur in another generation during the life of his descendant Ernest, Duke of Cumberland, King of Hanover from 1837, detested by many Britons but deeply mourned by Hanoverians in 1851.

George I Sites

Hanover (Hannover in German), George's childhood home, is the capital of Lower Saxony. With just over half a million population, it is a busy, commercial, mostly modern city, hosting an important industrial trade show each year in addition to Expo 2000. Prosperous commercialism has been its forte over the centuries, although there was a cultural flowering under George's father, the Elector Ernest Augustus and especially his wife, Sophia, daughter of Elizabeth Stuart, Princess of Great Britain, Electress Palatine, and Queen of Bohemia. Over half the city and most of the center was destroyed in the Second World War, including the **Schloss Herrenhaüsen**, summer home of the Hanoverian monarchs, only the gallery building (Galeriengebaüde) remaining. Although there are some attractive old buildings in Hanover, some reconstructed after the War, the remaining baroque gardens of Herrenhaüsen are probably the chief attraction of Hanover. And what gardens!—not only beautiful but historically unique, being the only surviving example of its kind, Low German baroque. Begun by Duke Johann Friedrich, they were brought to fruition by George's mother, Sophia. They consist of two parts, the Grosser Garten and the Berggarten. The former, surrounded by a moat, comprises walks and trees, flower and rose beds, high fountains and waterworks of various kinds, statues and sculptures, and an orangery, all structured formally by its many hedges. Performances of plays, ballet, and concerts take place within a hedge theater. The Berggarten, north of the Grosser Garten and across Herrenhaüser Square from it, was originally the kitchen or herb garden and is now a botanical garden with a collection of rare and exotic plants. Visit the garden at http://www.hannover.de/english/tourist/erlebens/freizeit/gaerten/herrenha.htm, and http://www.hannover.de/english/hgstart/koe_gart.htm. There is a mausoleum devoted to George in the garden.

Hanover is easy to visit by air, train, or bus, and the city has an extensive local public-transport system. Pay a virtual visit at http://www.hannover.de/deutsch/start.php.

In 1682, George's father arranged his marriage to Princess Sophia Dorothea of Celle, born and raised at the white, moated castle of **Celle**, about 44 km northeast of Hanover. The chapel and the Italian-style theater in the schloss are both noteworthy; the latter, lavishly decorated, is the oldest surviving in Germany. Celle escaped destruction during the Second World War, so the many buildings belonging to its prosperous past can still be seen. See http://www.region-celle.com/american.html, where Celle is called "Rothenburg of the North," and www.celle.de—click on English at top left. To take a tour of the city, click on Sightseeing Tour; then, to see the castle, click on Royal Seat, with a number of thumbnail photographs of the castle and its gardens, along with details regarding visiting. Although the marriage produced two children (separated by eight years in age), the couple disliked each other intensely. Both took lovers, but the headstrong young woman made the mistake of flaunting her affair with Count Philip von Königsmark, which led to George's divorcing her in 1694. She was separated from her children and confined, all visitors prohibited, in the castle at **Ahlden** for the rest of her life.

Already 54 years old when he became King of Great Britain, George I continued to live at least half the time in Hanover, so his impact on English royal sites was slight. However, his arrival in England must have been quite a sight: accompanying him on September 29, 1714, in Greenwich, amongst his entourage of German advisors, friends, and servants, were two Muslim servants, captured during a Turkish campaign, and two mistresses in place of the wife already imprisoned for 20 years.

His accession was celebrated at **Kensington Palace** with a celebratory bonfire in the gardens, this becoming a regular event each August 1, the anniversary of his accession. He pronounced himself satisfied with the house and gardens, but when a 1716 survey showed that extensive repairs were needed, designs for alterations included a grandiose scheme by Sir John Vanbrugh to rival Blenheim Palace. However, much more modestly, and under William Benson rather than Vanbrugh, the core of Nottingham House was replaced in 1718–22 by three new state rooms, the **Privy Chamber**, the **Cupola Room**, and the **Withdrawing Room**. The most extraordinary feature of the renovations was the ceiling paintings. Sir James Thornhill was considered too expensive, so William Kent did the job at under half the fee, and, although his work was controversial at the time, Kent ended up painting the ceilings of nearly all the royal apartments in the palace. His final statement was the **King's Staircase**, where he removed most of the wooden panelling and painted the walls and ceilings in the Italian illusionist manner: on the walls, he painted a marble balustrade and gallery behind, crowded with members of George's court. These included the picturesque representatives who had accompanied him from Germany: his Turkish servants, his Polish page, and Peter, a "wild boy" found in the woods near Hanover, living in trees. All these characters, along with Kent and his mistress among others, who are painted on the ceiling, look down upon visitors ascending the staircase.

For the next room, the **Presence Chamber**, Kent decorated the ceiling in the 16th century Italian "grotesque" style: a central roundel shows the sun god, Apollo, in his chariot, supported by four red diagonal bands. An overmantel decorated with limewood carvings of drapery, birds, fruit, flowers, and cherubs' heads by Grinling Gibbons was originally in the King's Gallery, being moved to the King's Drawing Room in 1721 and then to Presence Chamber in 1724. The **King's Gallery** was decorated for George in 1725; the present furnishings and decorations faithfully reflect those of 1725, following restoration in 1993–4. Kent incorporated decorative features designed for William III, including the design of a new marble chimneypiece and carved overmantel around the wind-dial (see *William III and Mary II*). Read more about George's renovations at Kensington Palace at http://www.hrp.org.uk/webcode/content.asp?ID=402, and view the decorations mentioned, along with the Cupola Room and other work of Kent's at the Palace. George introduced exotic animals, including three tigers and two civet cats, moved after his death to the menagerie at the Tower of London. Otherwise, he commanded the gardener Henry Wise to prepare plans for the gardens, but these were carried out in the reign of his successor, George II; in the meantime, Wise continued to maintain the gardens. For detail regarding Kensington Palace generally, see *William III and Mary II*.

George spent little time in Kensington, both because of the rebuilding and because of his preference for spending time in his private apartments, usually his two rooms at **St. James's Palace**, where he lived most unregally, eating and sleeping in one and receiving guests and holding audiences in the other. For St. James's Palace, see *Henry VIII*.

Sophia Dorothea died at **Ahlden** in November, 1726, after over 30 years' imprisonment there. She was interred beside her parents in the crypt of the Stadtkirche at **Celle**, mausoleum of the Dukes of Brunswick-Lüneburg.

George died in **Osnabrück** on his way to **Hanover** in June, 1727. He was buried in the chapel of the **Leineschloss**, Hanover, but after severe bomb damage during the Second World War, his coffin was reinterred in the Mausoleum in the **Berggarten** across the street from **Herrenhaüsen** in 1957. Leineschloss, which dates from 1637, overlooks the river Leine and is now the seat of the parliament of Lower Saxony; see http://www.ltsich.niedersachsen.de/englisch/default_englisch.htm.

James Francis Edward, Prince of Wales

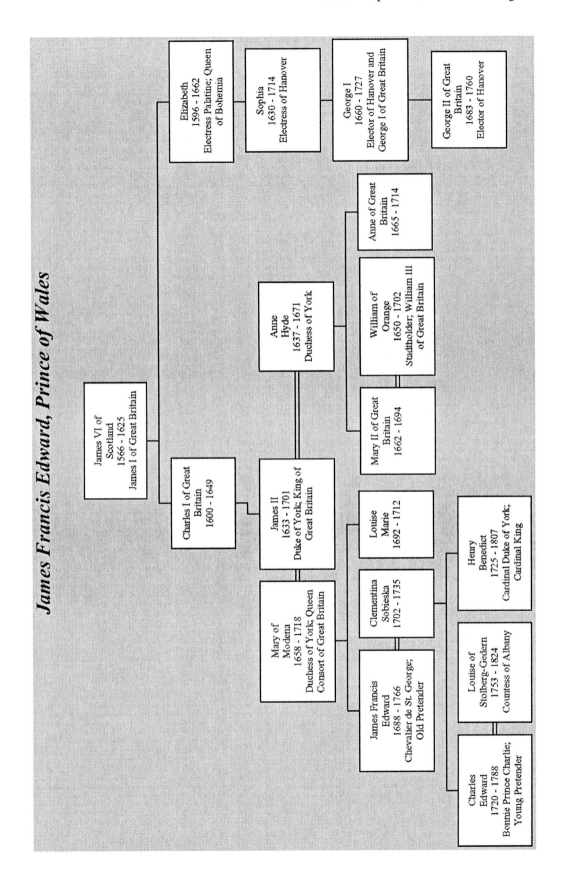

James Francis Edward, Prince of Wales: The "Old Pretender" (1688–1766; "reigned" in exile as "James III" of Great Britain, 1701–1766)

Call your companions,
Launch your vessel,
And crowd your canvas,
And, ere it vanishes
Over the margin,
After it, follow it,
Follow The Gleam.

—Alfred Lord Tennyson

Shortly after the 1688 birth of James Francis Edward to James II of Great Britain and Queen Mary Beatrice, James II lost his crown to his daughter and her husband. The birth of a Catholic Prince of Wales precipitated the expulsion of his Catholic parents by the "Glorious Revolution" that enthroned the Protestants William III and Mary II. Resisting his overthrow, in 1689–1690 the expelled James II challenged William in Ireland and Scotland, but his challenges failed. After the death of James II in 1701, his son James Francis Edward and, later, his grandsons Charles Edward and Henry all in turn inherited and proclaimed their right to rule Great Britain. For a century, "Jacobites" argued, schemed, conspired, fought, and died on their behalf. Each of these three very different men struggled with his entangling legacy of denied kingship, either allowing the dream of restoration to dominate his life or making another life quite immune from its seductive pull, for the dream could become very nightmarish indeed.

James Francis Edward both felt and resisted the pull of the dream. An introverted and conscientious man, James Francis Edward agreed to three attempts at his restoration: two aborted efforts in 1708 and 1719 that bookended his all-out Scottish campaign in 1715 (called "the Fifteen"). Thirty years later, his more dynamic son Charles Edward ("Bonnie Prince Charlie") enthralled the Scottish clans in "the Forty-five." All of these major Jacobite rebellions depended for their success on Continental support and British discontent holding steady just when competent generalship was available and the weather agreed with their purpose. Such a happy conjunction of forces, however, never held long enough to effect a Jacobite restoration.

James Francis Edward felt compelled to assert his right as Prince of Wales to the British throne stolen from his father and made many plans that finally culminated in his three campaigns of 1708, 1715, and 1719. His own withdrawn personality and frequent malarial illnesses proved detrimental to military success. Nicknamed "Old Mr. Melancholy" or "Old Mr. Misfortune" by English satirists, James Francis Edward seemed lethargic, depressed, and uninspiring to his followers in Scotland. As one Jacobite Scot recorded, "we found ourselves not at all animated by his presence; if he was disappointed in us, we were tenfold more so in him. We saw nothing in him that looked like spirit.... Some said the circumstances he found us in dejected him; I am sure the figure he made dejected us." In 1745, the far more athletic and extroverted Bonnie Prince Charlie would spark a very different reaction.

Yet, while Charles Edward proved himself the better leader of men at arms, James Francis Edward would have made the better King and was the better man. The conscientiousness that drove James Francis Edward to assert his father's right would have driven him also to rule well. In addition, he had none of the religious bigotry that had hardened James II's subjects against him. In fact, the dying James II advised James Francis

Edward to establish liberty of conscience upon his restoration. James Francis Edward himself wrote, "I am a Catholic, but I am a King, and subjects, of whatever religion they may be, have an equal right to be protected. I am a King, but as the Pope himself told me, I am not an Apostle." Yet, at the same time, James Francis Edward utterly refused to listen to any persuasion that he should change his own religion in order to become King more easily. (In 1701, the Act of Settlement sought to ensure a Protestant succession and to exclude his claim. Heirs to the throne must themselves be Protestants, and they must not marry Catholics.) In contrast, Charles Edward eventually became an Anglican for such opportunistic reasons. Surely, James Francis Edward revealed himself as the more principled man of the two.

His greater strength of character showed, too, in his reaction to the failure of the Jacobite risings in which he himself took part. While after 1746 Bonnie Prince Charlie brooded over defeat and drank himself into a stupefied and miserable middle age, James Francis Edward after 1719 for the most part shelved any ideas about active campaigning and lived a new life in Italy. Born in St. James's Palace in London, he had lived but a few weeks on his native soil before his parents' 1688 exile led them to seek refuge with James II's first cousin, Louis XIV of France. Louis had housed his cousins in St-Germain-en-Laye, twelve miles west of Paris and not far from Versailles. Although Louis recognized James Francis Edward as the rightful King of Great Britain in 1701, the Treaty of Utrecht (1713–1714) forced Louis to expel James Francis Edward from French soil. After the subsequent failure of the Fifteen, James Francis Edward wandered—to Lorraine, to Avignon (then papal territory), to various places in Italy, then finally to Rome and Urbino. A sympathetic Pope Clement XI gave the exile a pension and allowed him to live in Palazzo Muti in Rome, near Santi Apostoli. Clement also lent Palazzo Savelli at Albano as a summer home. By accepting refuge in Rome, James Francis Edward effectively surrendered any hope of gaining the Protestant support vital to his restoration. After 1719, he still claimed to rule as "James III" and indulged in some intrigue but essentially made another life for himself for the next 45 years. The scene had shifted to Rome internally as well as externally.

His marriage in 1719 to Princess Clementina of Poland, granddaughter of John III Sobieski and goddaughter of Clement XI, produced two sons: Charles Edward, born in 1720, and Henry Benedict, born in 1725. So uninterested was James Francis Edward in further Jacobite risings that Charles Edward told him of the Forty-five in a letter written on the day Charles Edward sailed for Scotland. James Francis Edward reacted with dismay, "Heaven forbid that all the crowns of the world should rob me of my son."

After the disaster of the Forty-five, James Francis Edward showed again how little he thought of Jacobite aspirations when in 1747 he supported his son Henry's being made a Cardinal of the Catholic Church. Alive to the political consequences of this event, enraged by what he saw as his father's and brother's betrayal of the Jacobite cause, Charles Edward never saw James Francis Edward again. While Charles Edward wrote to his father from time to time, he maintained a total estrangement from his brother Henry for 18 years. Henry reestablished contact with Charles Edward as their aging father declined, but Charles Edward refused to visit until Pope Clement XIII recognized his rights to the throne as James Francis Edward's heir. James Francis Edward died in 1766 as Charles Edward preserved a stubborn absence that had lasted 22 years.

After honorably asserting his claim, James Francis Edward sensibly recognized the futility of further assertion. And yet, sensible as his turning away from Jacobitism seems, the romance of his being the "Chevalier de Saint George" or "the King over the Water" still lingers. The rising of 1708 acted against James Francis Edward's half-sister Queen Anne, who had succeeded William and Mary. Angered by his action into terming James Francis Edward "the Pretender," Anne nevertheless sought to give the impression at times that she preferred her half-brother to any other successor, especially the detested Hanoverians specified by the 1701 Act of Settlement. As Anne's health declined a few years later, the Jacobite James Douglas, 4th Duke of Hamilton, wanted James Francis Edward in Scotland to await the Queen's death. James Fitzjames, 1st Duke of Berwick (a bastard of James II by Arabella Churchill), planned to have James Francis Edward meet their half-sister Queen Anne in London. Hamilton's suspicious death in a duel aborted such plans, and the throne passed to the Hanoverian descendants of Elizabeth of Bohemia. The risings of 1715 and 1719 (against George I), and of 1745 (against George II) failed to dislodge them. With Hamilton's death in 1712 and Anne's death in 1714, the opportunity for reconciliation and restoration had died as well. A brilliant rendering of Jacobite intrigue complete with an unflattering, unfair, and unforgettable view of James Francis Edward, Thackeray's historical novel *Henry Esmond* portrays this lost moment—and all the Jacobite strivings—in all their comedy, tragedy, romance, and futility.

James Francis Edward, Prince of Wales Sites

James Francis Edward Stuart was born at **St. James's Palace** (see *Henry VIII*) in 1688, in a four-poster bed belonging to Mary of Modena. Because a rumor circulated that he was not the Queen's own child but an infant smuggled into the bed in a warming pan, the bed has become known as the "warming-pan bed." The bed is certainly not wholly of James's time, being composed of beds of several periods, but because crowns and cyphers on the principal bed hangings are those of James II and Mary of Modena, it's likely these were made for the couple. This bed can be seen in Queen Mary's Bedchamber, **Kensington Palace**. For information about Kensington Palace, see *William III and Mary II*.

Early in his life, he was exiled with his mother to France, before his father left England. The family sought refuge with James II's first cousin Louis XIV, who housed them in the **château of St-Germain-en-Laye** (see under *James II*).

The first Jacobite uprising in support of James ended at the Battle of **Sheriffmuir** in 1715. The battlefield lies about two miles east of the old cathedral town of Dunblane, which, in its turn, is about five miles north of Stirling. View military maps held in the National Library of Scotland at http://www.nls.uk/digitallibrary/map/military/placename.cfm?keyword=Sheriffmuir, and read about the battle at http://www.clan-cameron.org/battles/1715.html. There is a short row of standing stones nearby; see http://www.megalith.ukf.net/NN832022.htm. Read about the Bouzy Rouge restaurant at the Sheriffmuir Inn, followed by a description of the countryside, at http://www.rampantscotland.com/stay/bldev_stay_sheriffmuir.htm.

After this fiasco, James remained in Europe. For a while he resided in **Avignon** at the Hôtel de Villefranche in the Passage des Boucheries from 1716–1717 (and again in 1727). This building was destroyed in 1743. Of 90,000 population, today's Avignon retains its character as quintessentially Mediterranean and also of historical, religious significance as the center of the Great Schism and the native or chosen home of many cultured personages. The walls enclosing the medieval city are very well-preserved, and visitors are able to walk the full circuit. Visit Avignon at http://www.avignon.fr/en/.

When James had to leave France, Pope Clement XI made the Ducal Palace (Palazzo Ducale) in **Urbino** available as a home from James, from July 1717 to October 1718. This splendid building, among the architectural treasures of Italy, is open every day in a quiet, old town known for its humanist scholars and artists during the Renaissance. Visit Urbino at http://www.cti.hull.ac.uk/~lcm0kjc/, including a link to the Ducal Palace under Places to Visit. More photographs of the Palace, along with architectural detail, can be seen at http://www.bluffton.edu/~sullivanm/laurana/laurana.html. Urbino is a Unesco World Heritage Center.

An emissary for James, Charles Wogan, sought out Clementina Sobieska to be his master's wife. Wogan travelled to Prince James Sobieski's home, the Palace of **Ohlau**, in Silesia. Now Oława, this is a town of about 32,000 inhabitants, between the rivers Odra (Oder) and Oława (Ohle) in Poland, southeast of Wrocław.

On her way to marry James, Clementina was imprisoned in **Innsbruck**, in **Schloss Ambras** in 1718. Today the castle houses part of the Kunsthistorisches Museum Wien. The Schloss may be viewed at http://www.jacobite.ca/gazetteer/Austria/Ambras.htm; visiting hours are also provided here.

Immediately before his wedding, in 1718, James came to **Viterbo**, taking up residence in the episcopal palace. And here he first met Clementina, after his proxy marriage to her in Bologna and before their wedding in Montefiascone. Later, he again visited Viterbo, once with Clementina. Viterbo is located about 50 miles northwest of Rome; it is one of those many smaller Italian cities that have retained their old walls and medieval center. Unfortunately, websites providing photographs of them are scarce. The most useful website in English appears to be http://www.viterboonline.com/, which also provides a reference to Montefiascone and Lake Bolsena (see below).

After their proxy wedding in **Bologna** (see below), James and Clementina renewed their marriage vows in person in the episcopal palace at **Montefiascone**, about 10 miles (13 km) north of Viterbo and 60 miles (100 km) north of Rome on September 3, 1719. The ceremony took place in what is now the second room of the Cancelleria of the Curia Vescovile (episcopal offices) on the second floor. There is a Latin inscription recording this, with another recording that the Bishop baptized their son Charles (Bonnie Prince Charlie) in Rome the following year—read these at http://www.jacobite.ca/gazetteer/Lazio/Montefiascone.htm, and more details. Montefiascone is located on the edge of a crater facing Lake Bolsena. It is well-known for its vineyards covering the surrounding countryside and delicious wine. Read the story behind the wine's becoming known as Est! Est! Est! at http://utenti.lycos.it/montefiascone/eindex.htm. The same site also presents pictures of Montefiascone and its environs. Old monuments, along with an account, can be seen at http://www.romeartlover.it/Francige3.html.

Pope Clement XI gave James a pension and allowed him to live in **Palazzo Muti** in Rome, near Santi Apostoli. His sons, Charles (Bonnie Prince Charlie) and Henry (Duke and later Cardinal of York) were born at the Muti. The Muti is now known as **Palazzo Balestra**, and is located at the north end of Piazza dei Santi Apostoli, at no. 49. Inscriptions to Henry can be seen on the left wall of the corridor through the door from the piazza. Photographs and a description of the palazzo can be seen at www.jacobite.ca/gazetteer/Rome/PalazzoBalestra.htm.

Palazzo Savelli, a summer home also lent him by Pope Clement, is situated at **Albano Laziale**, on the shores of Lake Albano, a short distance from Castel Gandolfo, about 25 km south of Rome. James's annual routine became to move to Albano in May, with his son Henry. They would return to Rome every St. Peter's Day (June 29) and remain there until September, when they would then spend another six weeks or so in Albano. Today, the palace serves as the town hall, the Palazzo Municipale, Albano Laziale. Pay a virtual visit at www.jacobite.ca/gazetteer/Lazio/Albano.htm.

James visited **Bologna** on numerous occasions, using the **Palazzo Belloni** or Casa Cantelli, at Via de' Gombruti 13, at corner of Via Barberia. He first stayed here in March 1717, a marble tablet on the staircase wall commemorating this event. In 1718, he returned here, awaiting the arrival of Clementina, delayed owing to her arrest by the Holy Roman Emperor. It is possible that the Casa Belloni was the site of her marriage by proxy to James on May 9 (or 19), 1719. View the house and the inscription at www.jacobite.ca/gazetteer/Bologna/CasaBelloni.htm.

James returned to Bologna alone in October 1726, staying again in Casa Belloni. However, he was joined by his two sons and found more appropriate lodging in **Palazzo Fantuzzi** at Via San Vitale 23 and stayed there afterwards. View the palazzo at http://www.jacobite.ca/gazetteer/Bologna/PalazzoFantuzzi.htm. He also used a country residence outside Bologna at **Villa Pallavicini** (www.jacobite.ca/gazetteer/Bologna/VillaPallavicini.htm), known in the 18th century as Villa Alamandina. It's located at Via Tommasso Martelli, 22/24, and today houses various departments of the University of Bologna, about four km east of city walls.

The **Convent of Santa Cecilia in Trastevere**, Rome, whence Clementina fled from James in 1725, remaining until 1727, is probably not the restored building seen today. The church to which the convent is attached was first established in the 3rd or 5th century, and, by tradition, was built over the house in which St. Cecilia lived: excavations have revealed early houses, along with the baptistery from the earliest church building. The present church dates from the 18th century, with some older elements preserved, like the Romanesque campanile and columns. Read about, and view, the convent at http://www.jacobite.ca/gazetteer/Rome/SCeciliaTrastevere.htm. For more information about the church, see http://roma.katolsk.no/cecilia.htm.

Clementina Sobieska died at the **Palazzo Muti** at the age of 32, in 1735. Her body lay in state for three days in the **Church of the Holy Apostles (Basilica dei Santi XII Apostoli**, or, simply, **Santi Apostoli)**, and was then carried to **St. Peter's Basilica**. Her heart is preserved in Santi Apostoli within a monument by Filippo della Valle against the second pillar of the right (south) aisle. Santi Apostoli stands on the Piazza dei Santi Apostoli, beside the Palazzo Balestra; the church stands beside the huge Palazzo Colonna. Visit it at http://www.jacobite.ca/gazetteer/Rome/SSXIIApostoli.htm.

The Old Pretender died at the **Palazzo Muti** on January 1, 1766. In his will, he had expressed his wish to be buried in Santi Apostoli, which had been his parish church when he resided at Palazzo Muti, but Pope Clement XIII determined that he should lie beside his wife. Like Clementina's, his body lay in state for three days at the Church of the Holy Apostles, and his requiem Mass was said here. Then his body was taken in procession to **St. Peter's Basilica**, where a second requiem Mass was said.

Tombs and monuments for both James and Clementina are to be found in **St. Peter's Basilica, Rome**. James reposes with his sons, Charles and Henry, the bodies brought together in 1807, and the Stuart monument installed in 1819. A work by Antonio Canova, the latter is to be found against the first pier of the left aisle. Of white marble, it consists of two mourning angels standing at the foot, at each side of the entrance to a tomb. Above are portraits, in relief, of James and his sons, Henry and Charles, in that order. The tomb of the Stuart "Kings" is in the crypt, in a simple travertine sarcophagus. View both, respectively, at http://www.jacobite.ca/gazetteer/Vatican/Stuart_monument.htm, and http://www.jacobite.ca/gazetteer/Vatican/Stuart_tomb.htm.

The original tombstones, which stood over their graves until 1939, can be seen at the **Pontifical Scots College** (Pontificio Collegio Scozzese), Rome, at http://www.jacobite.ca/gazetteer/Rome/ScotsCollege.htm.

A monument to Clementina is in the left aisle of **St. Peter's Basilica**, above the doorway from which visitors exit after having descended from the dome and roof. Dominant is the figure of Charity, who bears a mosaic portrait of Clementina along with a putto, above a porphyry sarcophagus. Below the sarcophagus, two putti play. Her tomb is in a niche in the spiral staircase leading to the roof and the dome. Although it is located behind the monument, it isn't accessible from the nave; the visitor must purchase a ticket for the dome, climb to the roof either by stairs or elevator, and then descend the long spiral ramp. The monument and tomb can be viewed virtually at, respectively, www.jacobite.ca/gazetteer/Vatican/Clementina_monument.htm and www.jacobite.ca/gazetteer/Vatican/Clementina_tomb.htm.

Charles Edward Stuart and Henry Benedict Stuart

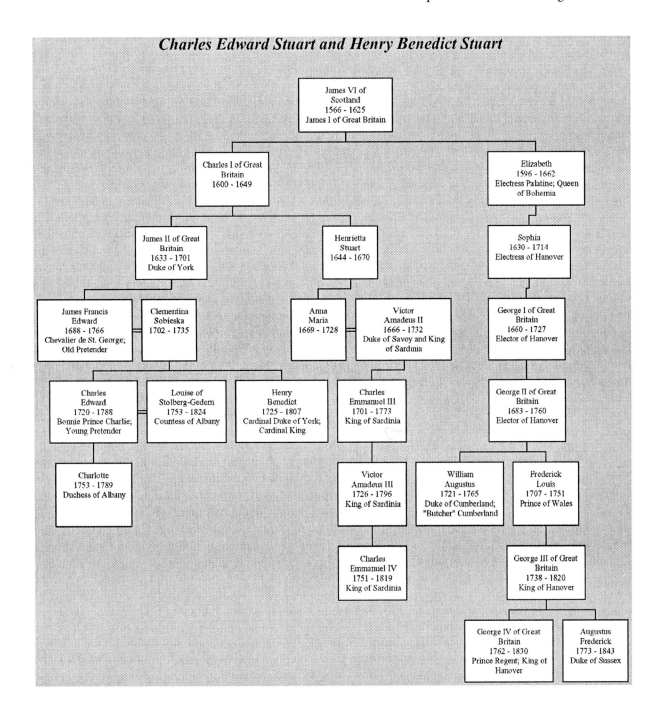

Charles Edward, "The Young Pretender" (1720–1788) and Henry, Cardinal Duke of York (1725–1807) ("reigned" in exile as "Charles III," 1766–1788 and "Henry IX," 1788–1807)

> *For who better may*
> *Our high scepter sway,*
> *Than he whose right it is to reign:*
> *Then look for no peace,*
> *For the wars will never cease*
> *Till the King shall enjoy his own again.*

So sang Bonnie Prince Charlie to Flora Macdonald during their flight together after the disastrous Jacobite defeat at Culloden in 1746. First sung in reference to the imprisoned and executed Charles I and his successor in exile, Charles II, "The King Shall Enjoy His Own Again" later became a Jacobite song. It heartened the supporters of the expelled James II, his son James Francis Edward, "the Old Pretender" or "the Chevalier de Saint George," and his grandson Charles Edward, "the Young Pretender" or "the Young Chevalier." In 1746, Charles Edward defiantly sang it after the final defeat of Jacobite hopes.

Those hopes had always depended on the lucky conjunction of foreign diplomatic, military, and financial support with British discontent and competent generalship. In 1689–90, 1708, 1715, and 1719, James II and then James Francis Edward had found that conjunction unstable. In the third phase of Jacobite rebellion, this time led in 1745–46 by Charles Edward, equivocal foreign aid, unreliable English support, and questionable military decisions doomed Bonnie Prince Charlie's attempt to gain Britain for his father and to rule there himself as Regent. Though smashed by the Hanoverians at Culloden and disillusioned about European recognition of his claim, Charles Edward never accepted the defeat of Jacobite hopes. His father and his younger brother, Henry Benedict, more realistically knew that Culloden had rung the death knell. Charles's obstinately clinging to the dream of a Jacobite restoration, and Henry's realizing its inherent impracticality set the brothers on very different—indeed, diametrically opposed—paths. While Charles insisted on being a Prince of Great Britain, Henry settled for being a Prince of the Church—by choosing in 1747 the path that led to his becoming a Roman Catholic Cardinal.

Divided in life by these choices, the brothers are buried together with their father James Francis Edward in the crypt of St. Peter's Basilica in the Vatican beneath the Monument to the Stuart Kings commissioned by Pope Pius VII, sculpted by Canova, and paid for by George IV. (George VI and his Queen Elizabeth in 1939 had a sarcophagus built over the three tombs.) The grave of the mother of Charles and Henry, James Francis Edward's wife Clementina, also lies in St. Peter's, behind the Monument to Queen Clementina. Finally united in death, the members of this fractious family seldom were united during their lives.

Granddaughter of the Polish King John III Sobieski and goddaughter of Pope Clement XI, the 17-year-old Clementina married James Francis Edward in 1719. Doing a favor for George I, the Holy Roman Emperor Charles VI had sought to prevent the marriage by arresting Clementina at Innsbruck; from there, she made a daring escape with the help of James Francis Edward's supporters and then married him by proxy in Bologna. She gave birth to Charles Edward in 1720 and to Henry Benedict in 1725. During these early years of the family's long sojourn in Palazzo Muti in Rome, husband's and wife's initial delight in each other soured with familiarity.

A power struggle evolved over the Protestant members of James Francis Edward's household. Although the Pope scolded Clementina for her intolerance, she feared their influence over her sons. Failing to sway her husband, Clementina ran away to the Ursuline convent at Santa Cecilia in Trastevere. James Francis Edward lost financial and political support because his alleged but unlikely adultery supposedly provoked her flight. Clementina stubbornly stayed in her convent for many months until the Pope told her she might be forbidden the sacraments unless she returned to her husband. In 1727, she finally complied, but a much-changed woman now lived in Palazzo Muti. She had become extremely devout, compulsive in her religious observances, and so stringent in her fasting that she ate alongside the family at a small table holding scanty portions of specially prepared meals. An emaciated 33-year-old Clementina died in 1735. Perhaps anorexia served as a defiant, if self-destructive, response to her perceived powerlessness in her household and contributed largely to her death.

Charles supposedly resembled his mother in temperament, while Henry resembled their father. As the boys grew to manhood without their mother, the athletic Charles trained himself to lead a Jacobite rebellion by hunting, shooting, hiking in bare feet, and reading military manuals. Early in his own life, Henry became extremely observant of his religion, just as their father became after Clementina's death.

The European political situation seemed to offer Charles an opening. France sought a way to hamper George II from helping Austria during the War of the Austrian Succession (1740–48). A Jacobite rising in Scotland might serve as an effective means. Promises of French support proved equivocal, however, and James Francis Edward distrusted them out of long experience. Determined to go ahead even without French support, Charles announced his embarking for Scotland in a letter written to his father on the very day Charles left.

He gallantly landed with a tiny force in the Hebrides, on the island of Eriskay, at a place later called "the Prince's Strand." With charm, courage, gallantry, and persuasiveness—by sheer force of personality—he stirred the reluctant Highlanders not only to recognize his claim but also to fight for it. Later the Jacobite Lord Balmerino at his own execution testified about Charles: "the incomparable sweetness of his nature, his affability, his compassion, his justice, his temperance, his patience, and his courage are virtues, seldom to be found in one person." Resentful of the 1707 Union with England that had ended Scotland's status as a discrete nation with its own Parliament, the clan chiefs sought to restore the Stuarts to a Scottish throne and to achieve Scottish independence. Charles succeeded with the Highlanders' help in mastering Scotland, but his desire to invade England met with Highlander misgivings and resistance. Eventually, his officers argued for a retreat to Scotland, where William Augustus, the Duke of Cumberland and the son of George II, routed Charles's troops at Culloden Moor in April, 1746. A hunted fugitive until he escaped to France in September, 1746, Charles received much help from such supporters as Flora Macdonald during his perilous journey to safety.

In France, Charles found that defeat increased equivocation exponentially. Henry (and their father) understood that Jacobite hopes had died at Culloden, but Charles obstinately insisted on living as though those hopes were realizable. He refused to leave France after the 1748 Treaty of Aix-la-Chapelle specified that Pretenders to the British throne could not reside in Britain, France, Holland, Germany, Spain, or Genoa; Louis XV had to expel Charles by force. After a stay in papal Avignon, Charles went underground for almost 20 years. Wandering through Europe in disguise, he even made secret visits to England in 1750 and later. In London in 1750, he became an Anglican, probably out of political calculation.

Henry heard nothing from Charles and James Francis Edward very little, because Charles had felt enraged by Henry's becoming a Cardinal in 1747. Although at that time Cardinals need not be priests, Henry chose ordination in 1748. His ecclesiastical career proceeded as he became a Cardinal-Priest in 1752; the Camerlengo in charge of the papal conclave in 1758; Cardinal-Bishop with a see in Frascati in 1761; and Vice-

Chancellor of the Church in 1763. Before abolishing the Jesuit order in 1773, Pope Clement XIV put Henry in charge of the Jesuit seminary at Frascati and made him an investigator of the Jesuit seminary in Rome.

Addressed as "Your Royal Highness and Eminence," the Cardinal Duke of York made his home at the Palace of LaRocca in Frascati, with a summer home at Villa Muti outside Frascati. After he became Vice-Chancellor, he lived at Palazzo Cancelleria when in Rome. His large income derived from ecclesiastical offices in Flanders, Spain, Naples, France, and Spanish America, especially Mexico, where he owned land. Henry supported many Jacobites and eased the plight of Frascati's poor. Nicholas Cardinal Wiseman, Archbishop of Westminster, later remarked of Henry, "to a royal heart he was no pretender. His charities were without bounds: poverty and distress were unknown in his see."

Realizing the impracticality of a Jacobite restoration, Henry had entered upon a notably successful ecclesiastical career, while his brother, a determined Jacobite to the end, wandered through Europe in disguise. Their aging father, to whom Charles wrote occasionally, served as a tenuous link between the severed brothers. In 1765, Henry notified Charles of James Francis Edward's decline and approaching death, but Charles refused to visit until the Pope recognized Charles's royal claims. The father died without seeing again his prodigal son, and Charles returned in 1766 to live in Palazzo Muti in Rome. Although he now assumed the name of "Charles III," he received little official recognition of his title and reluctantly accepted being called "Count of Albany." ("Albany" was the traditional title of the second son of the King of Scotland.) Henry gave Charles Henry's rights to their father's papal pension.

Although their father's death had reunited the brothers, many crises strained their relationship. During his wandering years, Charles had lived with Clementina Walkinshaw, who had given birth to his daughter Charlotte. In 1760, Clementina ran away from Charles and took their daughter with her. "You pushed me to the greatest extremity, and even despair" she wrote to him, "as I was always in perpetual dread of my life from your violent passions." James Francis Edward, and later Henry, supported mother and daughter because Charles would not do so. In 1772, Charles married Louise of Stolberg-Gedern, granddaughter of a Prince of the Holy Roman Empire. The marriage quickly deteriorated while they lived in Palazzo Guadigni in Florence; as an English observer commented in 1779, "she has paid dearly for the dregs of royalty." As jealous of Louise as he had been of Clementina, Charles reverted to his pattern of physical abuse in a drunken rage on St. Andrew's Day in 1780. He apparently also raped his wife because he suspected her of adultery with the Italian poet Count Vittorio Alfieri, whose muse Louise had become.

In a reprise of the events of 55 years before, Louise ran away to the Convent of the White Nuns in Florence, and she turned the Pope and Henry against Charles. Henry even arranged for her to stay in Rome in the same Ursuline convent where his mother had sought refuge, but Louise eventually preferred to live in Palazzo Cancelleria.

Henry did not become fully reconciled to Charles until after Charles in 1784 legitimized his daughter Charlotte, named her Duchess of Albany, and asked her to care for him in his decrepit middle age. Having developed a habit of drinking six bottles of Cyprus wine after dinner, Charles obviously needed a caretaker. To her credit, Charlotte took good care of her previously neglectful father, though he tried her patience. She exasperatedly noted that he resembled a fifteen-year-old boy. Charlotte also effected a reconciliation of Charles with Henry. Charles returned to Rome in 1785 to live once again in Palazzo Muti, this time with Charlotte. When he had lived there with Louise before they moved to Florence, the Romans had called her their "Queen of Hearts."

Three years later, after Charles died, Henry, tears streaming down his face, conducted a private royal burial in Frascati. (The public royal funeral held for James Francis Edward was not permitted for Charles.) He sent a Memorial to foreign courts asserting his claim to be Henry IX and the right of his named successor Charles Emmanuel IV, King of Sardinia (a descendant of Henrietta Stuart, sister of James II). Other than honorably keeping faith with his dead by asserting their and his claim, Henry made no move to effect a Jacobite restoration after forty years' realization of its futility.

The 1796 Napoleonic invasion of Italy, with its threat to the Papacy, caused the Cardinal King to donate much of his fortune to preserve the Holy See. Two years later, the fortunes of war caused Henry to flee from his beloved Frascati to Naples, then to Sicily, then to Venice in order to hold a conclave to elect a successor to Pope Pius VI. In the meantime, Henry's wealth had vanished. His friends sent an appeal to Prime Minister William Pitt, who informed George III. Henry's Hanoverian cousin sent immediate financial relief and instituted a pension for life in 1800. (Pitt probably never told George III that the British government actually owed over £1 million to this heir of James II's Queen Mary of Modena.) The Cardinal King appreciated this kindness (as well as the friendly and gracious encounters he had had with George III's son, Augustus Frederick, Duke of Sussex, who insisted on addressing the Cardinal as "Your Royal Highness," a courtesy reciprocated by Henry). In his will, he left to the Prince of Wales (later George IV) the British crown jewels carried by James II and Queen Mary Beatrice in their 1688 flight from England.

Henry's 1802 will also left his claim to the King of Sardinia (of the House of Savoy), the claim eventually by a tangled chain being passed to the Dukes of Bavaria. In 1803, as the most senior Cardinal, the Cardinal King became Dean of the College of Cardinals. Four years later, he died on the 46th anniversary of his being made Bishop of Frascati. While Charles had spoiled more than 40 years by making undignified attempts to preserve his royal dignity, Henry merely called himself King *non desideriis hominum sed voluntate Dei—"not by the desire of man but by the will of God."* Endearingly, Henry did insist, however, that the stray King Charles spaniel that glued itself to him one day at St. Peter's had instinctively recognized him as a royal Stuart.

> *Will ye no come back again?*
> *Will ye no come back again?*
> *Better loed ye canna be;*
> *Will ye no come back again?*
>
> *Ye trusted in your Hielan men,*
> *They trusted you dear Charlie!*
> *They kent your hiding in the glen,*
> *Death and exile braving.*
>
> *English bribes were a in vain*
> *Tho puir and puirer we mun be;*
> *Siller canna buy the heart*
> *That aye beats warm for thine an thee.*

Charles Edward Stuart and Henry Cardinal Duke of York Sites

Charles Edward was born and brought up at the **Palazzo Muti** (see *James Francis Edward*). He was baptized in the palace (a plaque in the old episcopal palace at Montefiascone records this—also see *James Francis Edward*).

Henry Benedict was also born at the **Palazzo Muti** and baptized there. He was a supporter of his brother's efforts to restore their father on his British thrones.

Charles's first attempt to muster a force and go to Britain failed in 1743. In 1745, aboard the *Du Teillay*, he and his followers experienced their first glimpse of Scotland, **Bernera**, a small island at southern tip of the Outer Hebrides. Charles disembarked on the island of **Eriskay**, on that stretch of shore known ever since as the Prince's Strand, or Beach; a rare convolvulus (bindweed) that grows there has become associated with him, the theory being that a seed must have fallen from one of his pockets. Eriskay is one of the smallest of the Western Isles of Scotland. Its population is small, about 200. A newly constructed causeway to the island of South Uist is expected to generate more communication with its neighbors and perhaps reverse its declining population. See a description of Eriskay along with beautiful photographs, including one of the Prince's Beach, at http://www.undiscoveredscotland.co.uk/eriskay/eriskay/index.html.

Unable to muster support in the islands, Charles moved on to the mainland, arriving in **Loch nan Uamh** and going ashore at **Arisaig**. A small resort at the head of the Loch nan Ceall, Arisaig looks out over the sea toward the Inner Hebrides, Rum and Eigg, and northwest to the mighty **Skye**. Read about Arisaig, and the activities that can be enjoyed from there, at http://www.road-to-the-isles.org.uk/arisaig.html. Visit Loch nan Uamh at http://www.road-to-the-isles.org.uk/lochailort.html.

Charles's next move was inland to **Glenfinnan**, at the head of Loch Shiel. Here, he raised his standard. Macdonald of Glenaladale, a descendant of Charles's supporters, erected the Glenfinnan Monument in 1815. The website for Glenfinnan, http://www.glenfinnan.org/whattodo.htm, is a rich guide to walking, cycling, cruising, and taking the Jacobite steam train in the area. At http://www.undiscoveredscotland.co.uk/glenfinnan/glenfinnan/, you will read more history and also see further photographs of the rugged and strikingly beautiful scenery in this spot. The Glenfinnan Gathering and Games are held on the Saturday in August nearest the anniversary.

Charles's next move was to march further east, through the lonely, bleak **Corrieyairack Pass** (over 2900 feet high), where the Jacobites almost encountered the Hanoverians, to **Dalwhinnie**. Corrieyairack is featured at http://www.corrieyairack.org/, with details of traversing the pass in the Corrieyairack Challenge for charity. Dalwhinnie is a small, isolated village of only a few houses and one hotel at the head of **Loch Ericht** (no roads), which is part of a hydroelectric scheme; to the east, the bare hills around close off the Spey valley. Visit Dalwhinnie at http://www.undiscoveredscotland.co.uk/dalwhinnie/dalwhinnie/. Highland whisky connoisseurs will recognise the home of the Dalwhinnie Distillery! It's the highest distillery in Scotland and, given its isolated position, has to be completely self-supporting when storms blow in. Read about the Dalwhinnie whisky, and how to visit, at http://www.scotchwhisky.com/english/about/malts/dalwhinb.htm.

With the Hanoverians gone in the opposite direction, Charles marched south to Blair Atholl, where he took possession of **Blair Castle** when the Duke of Atholl left for the south. The castle dates from at least 1269 and has been owned by the Earls, then Dukes, of Atholl since. The white mansion seen today is owing to the 2nd Duke, who remodelled the original castle into a Georgian mansion: he removed obvious signs of a castle, like the castellations and turrets, but in 1870, when Highland romantic baronial style was fashionable, the 7th Duke put them back, as well as adding an entrance hall and ballroom. Within the castle, the Tullibardine Room is devoted to the family's Jacobite connections, with portraits of Charles.

Blair Castle is the center of the only remaining private army in Britain, the Atholl Highlanders. Every May, they gather in the grounds of the castle for inspection from the Duke of Atholl, their commander-in-chief. Visit white Blair Castle at http://www.blair-castle.co.uk/. The nearby town of **Blair Atholl** is located along the Garry river, at the southern end of the strategic Glen Garry; visit Blair Atholl at http://www.blairatholl.org.uk/.

Charles's march southward took in **Dunkeld** and **Perth**, with a visit to **Scone**, where his ancestors had been crowned (see *Edward I*), and south to **Stirling Castle** (see *Mary Queen of Scots*), **Bannockburn House**, later his headquarters before the Battle of Falkirk (see below), and **Callendar House**. See http://www.falkirk.gov.uk/cultural/museums/call-ho.htm for a photograph and visiting details regarding Callendar

House. Today, Callendar House has modern, interactive displays and exhibitions on the 18th and 19th centuries, with reconstructions of a kitchen, printers' and clockmakers' shops, and a general store. It's situated in Callendar Park, Falkirk.

Charles took possession of **Linlithgow**; a visit to **Linlithgow Castle** caused the fountain in the courtyard to flow with wine (see *Mary Queen of Scots*). **Edinburgh** fell to his troops, although **Edinburgh Castle** held out successfully (see *Mary Queen of Scots*). He rode in triumph to **Holyrood Palace** (see *Mary Queen of Scots*) and, after the Battle of Prestonpans, held brilliant court at the palace for several weeks, including, it is said, giving a ball in the Great Gallery. Read about the battle at http://www.clan-cameron.org/battles/1745.html; see the monument commemorating the battle at http://www.geo.ed.ac.uk/scotgaz/features/featurefirst285.html.

On his way south, one of the places Charles stayed in was **Traquair House**. The Bear Gates, at the end of the tree-lined avenue, were erected in 1737–38: iron gates flanked by brick pillars with menacing, standing bears atop each pillar. The Jacobite Traquair family, after seeing Charles off, decreed that the gates would be closed, not to be reopened until the Stuarts were restored to the throne. To this day, the gates remain closed, and visitors to this attractive house proceed down the "temporary" drive parallel to the avenue! For more information about Traquair House, see *Mary Queen of Scots*.

Carlisle (see *William Rufus*) then fell to the Jacobites, and Charles and his army went down through England. At **Penrith**, he stayed at the George Hotel on both the advance and the later retreat. See the George at its website, http://www.georgehotelpenrith.co.uk/. Penrith is situated at the junction of several roads, including the A66 leading west to the Lake District and east over the Pennines to Yorkshire, and is very near the M6. It's one of those many British medium-sized market towns, cheerful and lively with shops and pubs, attracting too much traffic for the older, winding streets; see the town at http://www.visitcumbria.com/pen/penrith.htm.

In **Derby**, Charles took up residence at Exeter House, which no longer stands. That night, the Jacobites seized **Swarkestone Bridge**, 4 miles south of the city, but this was to mark their furthest point south: from now on, they were in retreat back to Scotland. Every year, Derby holds the Bonnie Prince Charlie Parade; see it at http://www.derbyphotos.co.uk/special/bonnieprince.htm. Derby has 216,000 population and isn't the most interesting of cities; read about it on its comprehensive website at http://www.derbycity.com/home.htm. **Swarkestone Bridge** has interest apart from its Jacobite connections, being a half-mile long, medieval bridge over the river Trent, the longest stone bridge in Britain. See the bridge at http://www.derbycity.com/derby2/swarkest.html. A monument, erected by the Prince Charles Edward Stuart Society and Marston's Brewery, in the adjacent picnic ground, tells the story. The bridge is located off the A514 and A5132 and is tucked almost under the east-west A50.

Retreating, Charles spent Christmas at **Drumlanrig Castle**, near Thornhill along the valley of the Nith north of Dumfries. Drumlanrig, the seat of the Dukes of Buccleuch and Queensberry, was built between 1679 and 1690 for the 1st Duke of Queensberry. Set in formal gardens with beautiful woodland beyond, the castle houses a rich art collection and fine furnishings. Its welcoming and richly informative website is http://www.buccleuch.com/, where you can find details of how to make an actual visit, and can take a virtual tour. See the bedroom occupied by Charles at http://www.buccleuch.com/pages/content.asp?PageID=59.

Hearing that his Hanoverian adversary, George II's son William, Duke of Cumberland, had taken Carlisle, Charles moved to **Bannockburn House**, where he was to meet Clementina Walkinshaw, one of the many nieces of the owner. Read about Bannockburn House as described by the Royal Commission on the Ancient Monuments of Scotland at http://web.ukonline.co.uk/Members/tom.paterson/places/AMS295.htm, with an elevation and plan of the house.

The stage was set for the disaster that was **Culloden**. Five miles east of Inverness, the battlefield extends for 1 ½ miles each side of the B9006. The Culloden Visitor Center provides displays, artefacts, and an audiovisual presentation. The National Trust for Scotland maintains the site of the battlefield, which it is seeking to restore to the moorland of 1746. Read about Culloden, and tour the battlefield at http://www. undiscoveredscotland.co.uk/inverness/culloden/.

Charles, in full retreat, went back to **Arisaig** and set sail from **Loch nan Uamh**, wishing to reach Eriskay again. Instead, a storm caused him to land on the island of **Benbecula**, in the middle of the southern islands of the Outer Hebrides, tucked in between North and South Uist, to each of which it is joined by causeways. Benbecula, a flat island of many small lochs, five miles long by five wide, is noted for its golden beaches. The small population is concentrated in Balivanich, near the airport, which hosts the Royal Artillery Rocket Range. From Market Stanch, a four-mile track follows the route of Charles to the eastern peninsula of Rossinish, where he and Flora Macdonald took a boat. See photographs and description of Benbecula at http://www.undiscoveredscotland.co.uk/benbecula/benbecula/index.html.

Charles and Flora's legendary trip to **Skye**, with him disguised as a woman called Betty Burke, is well-known. He landed on the **Trotternish peninsula**, the long middle finger of Skye pointing north, and was sheltered at a house in **Kingsburgh**, which Flora later owned. Visit Trotternish at http://www.trotternish.co.uk/. At Mac-Nab's Inn (now the Royal Hotel) in **Portree**, Charles bade Flora farewell. Visit the colorful town of Portree, capital of Skye, at http://www.undiscoveredscotland.co.uk/skye/portree/.

The island of Skye is the most visited of the islands off the west coast of Scotland. It's also the largest and contains the most spectacular scenery. Its home page is http://www.skye.co.uk/, with links to descriptions and dramatic photographs, as well as much useful tourist information. In the Kilmuir churchyard, there is a tall Celtic cross monument to Flora. See the monument silhouetted against one of Skye's memorable sunsets at http://www.flodigarry.co.uk/flora_history.htm.

Charles now set off the island of **Raasay**, small, long and thin, off the east coast of Trotternish. See Raasay at http://www.calmac.co.uk/Raasay. From there, he managed to get back to **Loch nan Uamh**, where French ships were waiting to take him back to France. There, he landed at **Roscoff**, in Brittany. Roscoff, a port and ferry terminal, perches on the northwest coast of Brittany. It's home to a marine biological station (http://www.sb-roscoff.fr/index_eng.php), old buildings, and a lighthouse on the Ile de Batz.

Charles found a home with his brother Henry in **Paris** in the **Quai Malaquais**, on the Left Bank of the Seine. His first mistress there, Louise, Duchess of Montbazon, Princess of Rohan, lived with her mother-in-law at the house that is now the **Maison Victor Hugo**, in no. 6 Place Royale (now **Place des Vosges**—see http://www.hugo-online.org/090200.htm). He was imprisoned in **Vincennes** while attempting to visit his next mistress, Marie Anne Louise Jablonowska, the Princess of Talmond and a leading courtesan, at the opera. For Vincennes, see *Henry V*. The present, splendid **Opéra** was constructed in 1861–75, so it isn't the building Charles attempted to reach.

Henry moved to **Rome** in 1747 to become ordained, to his brother's dismay. He was first given the **Church of Santa Maria in Campitelli**, or in Portico. The church building dates from its rebuilding by Carlo Rainaldi from 1659–67 in late Baroque style. Visit this church at http://www.jacobite.ca/gazetteer/Rome/SMariaCampitelli.htm. He was then transferred to the **Church of the Santi XII Apostoli** (see *James Francis Edward*), and was ordained to the episcopate here.

Appointed Bishop of **Frascati**, Henry spent most of the rest of his life in this town about 15 km south of Rome, on the northwest slope of the Alban Hills. Frascati was the most fashionable and most frequented country resort of the *Castelli Romani*, attracting huge, splendid villas in the 16th and 17th centuries built by leading families, each trying to outdo the others, and hosting popes and clergy from the most elevated offices of the Church; see tourist information at http://www.italyheaven.co.uk/frascati.html, and also at http://www.jacobite.ca/gazetteer/Frascati/index.htm, with links to the various relevant sites there. At Frascati, the episcopal palace was **La Rocca**. This is a somewhat severe-looking medieval structure in the town, between the Piazzas Paolo III and San Rocco. Although Henry was to take up a more senior office in 1803, the new bishop allowed him to continue to reside in La Rocca, and he died here in 1807. Today's La Rocca is home to various church offices, including that of the Bishop of Frascati. Limited visits can be made. Pay a virtual visit, and read about actual visits at http://www.jacobite.ca/gazetteer/Frascati/LaRocca.htm. Henry also used as a country residence the **Villa Muti** at **Grottaferrata**, owned by a close associate of his. Like Frascati, Grottaferrata is one of the Castelli Romani, or Roman castles, the name given to the area formed by the Alban Hills and the Roman Campagna, attractive to Romans with its elevated, cooler position in the hills and the views of the sea. The Villa Muti is situated at the intersection of the Viale di Conti di Tuscolo and Via dei Sale; it's not open to the public. Instructions for the best ways to see it at a distance, and other details can be read at http://www.jacobite.ca/gazetteer/Lazio/Grottaferrata.htm.

Henry also retained a home in **Rome**, the **Palazzo della Cancelleria** (or Chancellery). Located on the south side of the Corso Vittorio Emanuele, it became his official residence when he became Vice-Chancellor of the Church. He also allowed Charles's estranged wife Louise and Charles's illegitimate daughter, Charlotte, Duchess of Albany, to live here. The palace was built by Bregno, under orders from Cardinal Riario and the della Rovere popes from 1483–1511; the courtyard and Church of San Lorenzo have been attributed to Bramante. Henry's chasuble can be seen in the church; view it online at http://www.jacobite.ca/gazetteer/Rome/SLorenzoDamaso.htm. The palace still belongs to the Vatican and houses the three tribunals of the Vatican. Excavations from 1988–91 uncovered the 4th–5th century remains of the basilica of San Lorenzo in Damaso, one of the most important early Roman churches. Visit the Cancelleria at http://www.jacobite.ca/gazetteer/Rome/PalazzoCancelleria.htm.

Alienated from his father and brother, Charles now lived in various places, among them **Avignon**, where his father had resided (see *James Francis Edward*). From 1755 to about 1760, Charles lived in the castle of **Bouillon** and moved Clementina Walkinshaw and their child there. The town of Bouillon and its château, perched on the bluff above the town, are located in Belgium, just inside the French border, on the edge of the Ardennes. The first castle was built in the 8th century, and the estate was granted to Louis XIV in 1678, and was then in the hands of the Dukes of Bouillon, a son allowing Charles the use of the castle. See Bouillon at http://stronghold.heavengames.com/history/cw/cw30.

There, Charles degenerated into a heavy drinker, and his tyrannical ways drove Clementina and their child back to Paris. Some time after leaving him, Clementina and Charlotte took refuge in the Abbey of **Meaux**, France, remaining there several years. For Meaux, see *Henry V*.

Returned to **Rome** after James Francis Edward's death, Charles established himself in his father's house, the **Muti Palace**, also using his father's summer residence, the **Savelli Palace** at **Albano Laziale**. For both, see *James Francis Edward*. Invited back to **Paris**, Charles met Louise, whom he married, first by proxy in Paris, and then in the **Marefoschi Palace**, in **Macerata**, Italy. Macerata, a walled town of about 43,000, is situated in the Marche area of east-central Italy and home to a university dating from 1290. See Macerata at http://www.maceratagallery.it/macerata.html. Read about the wedding and see the Marefoschi Palace at http://www.jacobite.ca/gazetteer/Italy/Macerata.htm.

Charles and Louise moved to **Florence** in 1774, living in the **Palazzo Corsini sul Prato**, among several Corsini palaces in Florence the one lent to them by Prince Corsini. Today, members of the Corsini family live there, and the gardens are open to the public. Visit the palace at http://www.jacobite.ca/gazetteer/Florence/PalazzoCorsini.htm.

In 1777, Charles bought from the Guadagni family the **Palazzo Guadagni** (now called the **Palazzo San Clemente**), today located at Via Pier Antonio Micheli 2, at the corner of Via Gino-Capponi, just to the north of the Chiesa della Santissima Annunziata. Louise lived here until 1790, when she retired to the **Convent of the White Nuns** (the Bianchette) in Via Guisi. Charles continued living here until 1785, when he left for Rome. After his death in 1788, Louise inherited it and sold it the following year. See the Palazzo

Guadagni at www.jacobite.ca/gazetteer/Florence/PalazzoSanClemente.htm. At the present time, the palace is home to the offices of the Faculty of Architecture of the Università degli Studi di Firenze.

According to the Jacobite Gazetteer, the exact location of the **Convent of White Nuns** isn't known. "There was formerly in Via del Mandorlo a convent of 'suore del Conservatorio della Pietà'; this building is now a technical institute. The two convents may be one and the same." See http://www.jacobite.ca/gazetteer/Florence/ViaGuistiConvent.htm for more details.

Charles drank heavily again, and Louise fell in love with Count Vittorio Alfieri, with whom she fled to **Rome**. Later, she retired to the countryside and ended up living with the French artist Fabre. According to the Jacobite Gazetteer, Louise spent five months in 1784 at **Palazzo Vizzani Sanguinetti**, in **Bologna**, on the southwest side of Via Santo Stefano, 43, at the intersection with Via Castellata: it's sometimes called the **Palazzo Ranuzzi**. Visit it at http://www.jacobite.ca/gazetteer/Bologna/PalazzoVizzani.htm, and see another view at http://www.comune.bologna.it/iperbole/q_sstef/gal2.htm.

Charles's daughter by Clementina Walkinshaw, Charlotte, came to live with her father in Florence, where he made her Duchess of Albany. He suffered a stroke and died on December 31, 1788 at the **Muti Palace**. Initially, he was buried in the cathedral at **Frascati** (see http://www.jacobite.ca/gazetteer/Frascati/Cattedrale.htm for the cathedral), then transferred to **St. Peter's Basilica, Rome**, and is interred with his father and brother Henry in the monument created by Antonio Canova. See it at http://www.jacobite.ca/gazetteer/Vatican/Stuart_monument.htm.

In 1824, Louise died at the **Palazzo Gianfigliazzi**, in Florence, which she had acquired in 1793. Today the consulate of the United Kingdom, it stands at Lungarno Corsini 2 near the Ponte Santa Trinita, along the Arno. It is open from April to October. See it at www.jacobite.ca/gazetteer/Florence/PalazzoGianfigliazzi.htm. Her tomb is in the Cappella del Santissimo of the **Basilica di Santa Croce** in Florence, the first monument on the left wall. Four meters tall and 2.45 wide, it's big, of white marble. Two mourning angels stand each side of a funerary stele. Above is a relief depicting Faith, Hope, and Charity, and above that, Louise's arms, the royal arms of Great Britain and the princely arms of Stolberg-Gedern. View it at http://www.jacobite.ca/gazetteer/Florence/SCroce.htm.

George II

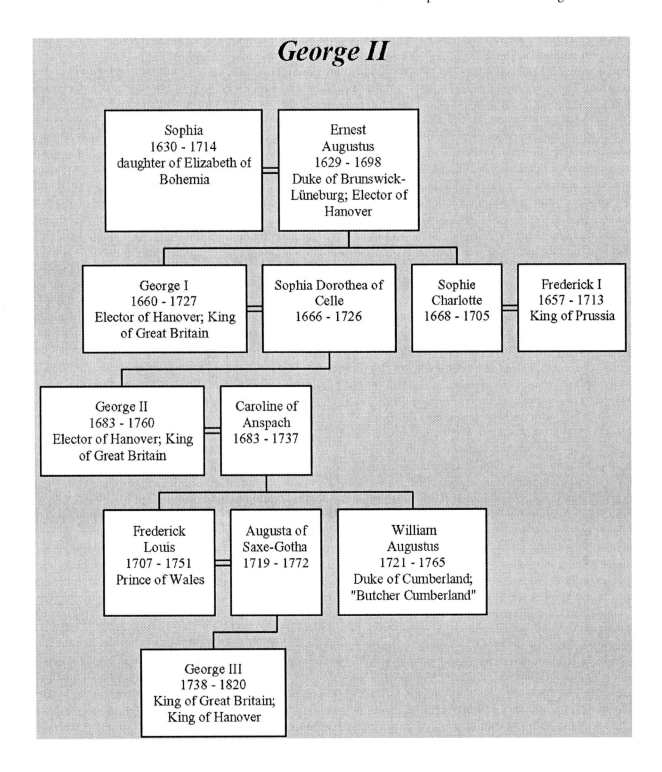

George II (1683–1760; reigned as King of Great Britain and Ireland and as Elector of Hanover, 1727–1760)

A British sovereign has an adored spouse. While the sovereign possesses a remarkable knowledge of European royal and noble genealogy and works conscientiously, the spouse far surpasses the sovereign in an innate grasp of statesmanship and ability to govern. In effect, the spouse rules in the name of the sovereign. Devastated by the spouse's early death, the sovereign carries on as well as one can expect for many years afterwards and does not remarry. While this narrates the story of Queen Victoria and Prince Albert, it also describes the remarkable love story of Victoria's ancestor George II and his consort, Caroline of Anspach. Their marriage began as a love affair and remained one, even though George II took mistresses. In fact, while Caroline waited to die, George II declared that "if she had not been his wife he would rather have had her for his mistress than any woman he had ever been acquainted with."

The detested son of George Louis, Elector of Hanover (later George I of Great Britain) and his detested, divorced, and imprisoned wife, George Augustus (later George II) had married Caroline of Anspach in 1705. An orphan, Caroline had been brought up by George Louis's sister, Sophie Charlotte, Electress of Brandenburg and later Queen of Prussia. The highly liberal and intellectual Sophie Charlotte had fostered in the gifted Caroline a love of learning, a respect for intellect, and liberal sympathies. Despite Caroline's tie to his sister, George Louis reacted coolly to his daughter-in-law. The bond between the newly married Caroline and George Augustus deepened in 1707 when George Augustus refused to leave her bedside after smallpox sickened her. He himself then came down with the disease, but both of them recovered.

Seven years later, when George Louis became George I of Great Britain upon the death of Queen Anne, George Augustus and Caroline went with George I to Britain. They left behind, not only Hanover, but also their seven-year-old son Frederick. As Elector of Hanover, the King insisted (against their objections) that Frederick remain there as a representative of the family. They would not see their son again for 14 years. This prolonged separation broke the bond between Frederick and his parents and siblings, and their eventual reunion never really repaired it.

After a quarrel with George I in 1717, the King ordered George Augustus and Caroline to leave St. James's Palace and forcibly separated them from their other children, one of whom died. Eventually, the Prince and Princess of Wales lived in Leicester House and spent the summers at Richmond Lodge. Both residences drew elements of the political opposition, which did not sweeten George I's relations with his son. In addition, the King perceived and resented Caroline's domination of George Augustus. Robert Walpole patched together this fractious family in 1720, but the nominal reconciliation left the Prince and Princess of Wales still living apart from the King and from their children.

After George I's death in 1727, George II and Queen Caroline moved back to St. James's Palace. Walpole had acquired so much power during the later years of George I's reign that he had become Britain's first "Prime Minister," and Caroline persuaded George II (against his initial inclinations) to retain Walpole. For the next decade, until Caroline died in 1737, Walpole and Caroline would make decisions together, and then Caroline would introduce them to George II in such a way as to make him believe that he had originated them. Retaining the intellectual and liberal tendencies of her youth, Caroline advocated for better prison conditions, penal reform, and other compassionate measures. As her biographer Peter Quennell noted, "Caroline exercised an authority more real, more solid and more continuous than that of any other Queen Consort or most other Kings Regnant…. She shared her power with Walpole and with Walpole alone."

George II confided in Caroline about his mistresses and miscellaneous lusts. Henrietta Howard (later Countess of Suffolk), the Queen's dresser, served as George II's mistress for many years. Eventually, George

II fell in love with Madame von Walmoden (later Lady Yarmouth) and wrote from Hanover voluminous letters detailing her charms. When she apparently took a secret lover, the King turned to his Queen for advice and consolation. His affair with "the Walmoden" did not dampen George II's ardor for his Queen, who still attracted his passion even into obese middle age.

Besides their physical tie, George II remained bound to Caroline by their dislike, intermittently fanned into hatred, of their elder son Frederick, Prince of Wales, whom they eventually summoned from Hanover to live in England. George II referred to Frederick as "my half-witted coxcomb," while Caroline exploded, "My dear first-born is the greatest ass, and the greatest liar, and the greatest *canaille*, and the greatest beast in the whole world, and I heartily wish he was out of it." Despite this expression of extreme dislike, Caroline struggled to improve their relationship, to George II's disgust: "I have scolded the Queen oftener for taking the rascal's part and have had more quarrels with her when she has been making silly excuses for his silly conduct than ever I had with her on all other subjects." Among many other irritants, George II resented what he considered Frederick's disrespectful attitude toward Caroline. Shut out from all authority (just as George Augustus had been), Frederick grew angry when George II named Caroline Regent during his frequent prolonged absences in Hanover. Again, like George Augustus and Caroline in the days of George I, Frederick attracted the support of the political opposition. In addition, in a strange replay of George I's eviction of George Augustus and Caroline, they themselves in 1737 evicted Frederick and his wife Augusta of Saxe-Gotha from St. James's Palace.

Frederick had bought Kew House (near Richmond Lodge) as a country residence; he and Augusta began the work that culminated in the present-day Kew Gardens. While in the country, they also lived at Cliveden (where he died suddenly in 1751, nine years before his father); Carlton House and Leicester House served them as town houses. Because George II hated Windsor Castle but Caroline loved it, she stayed there during her Regencies when George visited Hanover. Caroline conducted her duties as Regent mostly at her favorite residence, Kensington Palace, and made summer trips to Hampton Court and Richmond Lodge, where she built Merlin's Cave and the Hermitage.

No last meeting with Frederick occurred as Caroline lay dying in 1737. She acquiesced in George II's refusal: "He wants to come and insult his poor dying mother but she shall not see him." The King already felt thoroughly devastated by the certainty of losing his beloved wife. When she recommended that he marry again, he brokenheartedly declared his intention never to remarry but only to take mistresses. The sight of a Queen on a playing card upset the widowed King so greatly that a daughter removed all the Queens from decks of cards that he might use.

Surviving Caroline by many years, George II reigned as best he could without her far superior ability, just as Victoria did after losing Albert. Although an obsessive-compulsive and peppery man who reputedly kicked his wig around the room when enraged, George II had his own abilities and virtues. Always conscientious in fulfilling his duties, he possessed a good memory and developed an extensive knowledge of history, European dynastic intricacies, and foreign affairs. Like his father, he fought bravely in battle. As a young man, George Augustus had served under Marlborough in 1708 at Oudenarde; George II, in his capacity as Elector of Hanover, led his troops at Dettingen in 1743—the last British sovereign to do so. With him fought his younger son, William, Duke of Cumberland, later nicknamed "Butcher Cumberland" because of the atrocities perpetuated upon the Jacobites after his 1746 victory at Culloden. Associated as well with the 1753 founding of the British Museum, George II donated the Old Royal Library to it. Nevertheless, as the kingly consort to the Queen Consort who reigned in his name, he remained perpetually bound to her and directed that, when he came to die, his survivors would remove a side panel from each of their coffins to mingle their dust forever.

George II Sites

Born in **Schloss Herrenhaüsen, Hanover**, 1683, George II died at **Kensington Palace** in 1760. Like his father, he preferred being in Hanover to ruling in England. For information about both Herrenhaüsen and Hanover, see *George I.*

Daughter of the Margrave of Anspach, Caroline was born in **Anspach**, now called **Ansbach**, a Bavarian town of about 40,000 population, about 38 km southwest of Nuremburg, on the Rezat river. The town developed out of an 8th century Benedictine monastery and became the home of the Hohenzollern family in 1331, then the seat of the Margraves of Brandenburg-Anspach in 1460. The present castle (Markgrafen-schloss) was built between 1704 and 1738 for Margrave Carl Wilhelm Friedrich, incorporating the Renaissance palace Caroline would have known as a child, with an exterior in Italian Baroque style and an interior including French rococo features such as a hall of mirrors and great hall with painted ceiling, and rooms tiled with the famous 18th century Anspach porcelain. The garden Caroline would have known as a child was laid out in the 16th century, then remodeled in the 18th century, with an orangery. The schloss now contains the offices of the administration of Middle Franconia, of which Ansbach is the capital; see http://uk.ansbach.de/cda/showpage.php?SiteID=40&lang=uk for visiting details and some photographs, and a larger photograph at http://www.cityalbum.de/germany/rundgaenge/ansbach0007.htm. Ansbach is also home to a U.S. military base. See photographs of Ansbach at http://www.meinestadt.de/ansbach/tourismus/pix/. Generally, it's an attractive town, fortunate in that its old town was spared the ravages of war.

After George Augustus and Caroline were expelled from St. James's Palace by his father, George I, they went to live in **Leicester House**, Leicester Square. At one time, Leicester House, the London residence of the Earl of Leicester, consumed the south side of Leicester Square. Leicester Square was a fashionable place to live in the 18th century but declined during the 19th, and nothing remains of the house. There is still a garden there, but it's difficult to imagine it in its heyday. Read about Leicester Square at http://www.touruk.co.uk/london_squares/leicester_square1.htm. George and Caroline's first country home, **Richmond Lodge**, also no longer exists. It was rebuilt for them, in 1721, from a keeper's lodge, in the Old Deer Park, in the grounds of **Richmond Palace**. Here they found refuge from George I, and William Kent designed Merlin's Cave and The Hermitage for Caroline. **Maids of Honour Row**, in Richmond Green, was built in 1724 to house Caroline's ladies when she was Princess of Wales, living in the nearby Richmond Lodge. This is a row of houses along the southwestern side of Richmond Green, and just short of the old gateway leading to Old Palace Yard; see the houses at http://www.artandarchitecture.org.uk/images/conway/81fd0d01.html.

White Lodge, Richmond Park, was built 1727–29 for George Augustus. Originally called Stone Lodge, then New Lodge, it became a favorite resort of Caroline's. In 1751, their daughter Amelia became Ranger of Richmond Park and occupied the Lodge for 10 years, in which the two wings were added. White Lodge was later the residence of the Duke and Duchess of Teck, the parents of May of Teck, later George V's Queen Mary. Occupied since 1955 by the junior section of the Royal Ballet School, it is sometimes open to the public. See a photograph at http://www.artandarchitecture.org.uk/images/conway/e164c883.html.

In the Hanoverian tradition begun with his father and continued to his descendant Victoria, George Augustus couldn't abide his own son and Prince of Wales, Frederick ("poor Fred"), who set up a rival establishment nearby, at **Kew House**, also known, confusingly, as the White Lodge or White House. Kew House no longer stands, but you can read about it at http://www.royalcollection.org.uk/eGallery/object.asp?category=DBTHE+ROYAL+RESIDENCES%3A+INTERIOR+VIEWS&object=702947a&row=1&detail=about. There, his wife, Augusta, a keen gardener, laid out the first botanic garden. After Frederick's death in 1751, Augusta continued to live in Kew House, and, in her turn, she set a fashion for Gothic fantasies by having Sir William Chambers construct a Turkish mosque, Roman arch, and Gothic cathedral in the gardens.

The great Kew Gardens, officially the **Royal Botanic Gardens, Kew**, began from the gardening efforts of the royals at this time. Under the guidance of Charles Bridgeman and William Kent, George Augustus and Caroline had begun to develop a garden in the grounds of Richmond Lodge, which now forms the south part of Kew Gardens. Their daughter-in-law Augusta carried the process much further with her commissioning of garden buildings from Sir William Chambers, and, most important, her establishing a botanic garden. Under the renowned botanist Sir Joseph Banks from 1772 to 1819, gardeners sent to South Africa, Australasia, and the Pacific collected plants. Augusta was instrumental in the design and construction of several buildings in the grounds: the 10-story Pagoda, the Orangery, and some small temples still survive. The Pagoda is not open to the public; the **Orangery** is now a restaurant. See the Orangery at http://www.rbgkew.org.uk/collections/orangery.html. The **Pagoda** can be seen towering above the trees from many parts of the gardens; see it online at http://www.rbgkew.org.uk/heritage/places/pagoda.html.

From these beginnings, Kew has become world-famous, a leader in botanical science, plant collection, and landscape design as well as a very pleasant visitor destination. The URL for the Royal Botanic Gardens is http://www.rbgkew.org.uk/index.html. Visitor information is listed in a useful table of links at http://www.rbgkew.org.uk/visitor/visitkew.html, with an interactive map to be clicked on to plan your visit, at http://www.rbgkew.org.uk/visitor/KewMap.html. There's a lot of information, with much detail, but this is doled out somewhat piecemeal, so persistence is needed.

George Augustus's only contribution to **Kensington Palace** was a stable block built in 1740 for his younger son, William Augustus, Duke of Cumberland (the "Butcher" of Culloden); William had a detached home nearby, originally built by William III for the Earl of Albemarle—this house no longer exists. Terra-cotta busts of George and Caroline by Michael Rysbrack can be seen in the **King's Presence Chamber**. In the Presence Chamber, George, seated on the throne under a great damask canopy, received a party of Cherokee Indian chiefs in 1734. **Kensington Gardens** largely owe their layout to Caroline. After George I died, his tigers and civet cats were moved to the menagerie at the Tower of London, leaving the paddock free. In this, Caroline conceived of her garden, executed by Henry Wise and Charles Bridgeman. Out of this came the Broad Walk, running north-south along the old gardens and wilderness; the Round Pond, with tree-lined avenues radiating out from it; and a flooded series of ponds that formed the Long Water and the Serpentine, effectively dividing Kensington Gardens from **Hyde Park** (Buck Hill Walk, on the eastern side of the Long Water, was Caroline's intended boundary). Visit Kensington Gardens at http://www.royalparks.gov.uk/parks/kensington_gardens/, and Hyde Park at http://www.royalparks.gov.uk/parks/hyde_park/. For background information on Hyde Park, see *Henry VIII* and *James I*.

Caroline also had William III and Mary II's elaborate 17th century gardens removed: their design had made for very expensive maintenance, and fashions had changed toward the more sweeping simplicity of parterres of grass and gravel. During George's reign, the gardens were opened to the public on Sundays, when the court was out at Richmond. It was only later in the 18th century that the gardens and park were open every day. For their leisurely observation of their gardens, William Kent designed two summer houses: a revolving one was placed on the summit of an earth mount on the southeastern corner, and the Queen's Temple, which still survives, was placed in an area of naturalistic planting. View Kensington Palace and plan your visit at http://www.hrp.org.uk/webcode/kensington_home.asp. After George II died in 1760, the palace was never again the seat of a reigning monarch, although various members of the royal family have lived in the palace, or portions of it, to the present day, including the late Diana, Princess of Wales.

Queen Caroline's mark is also very much felt at **Hampton Court Palace**. The **Queen's State Apartments** were built at the end of the 17th century for Mary II, but were never completed because of her premature death in 1694. They lay empty until work resumed on them, and then were finished for Caroline. She used them from 1716 to 1737, both as Princess of Wales and as Queen, for meetings and entertainments, and the apartments are set up today in the style of her time, with portraits of herself and George. The **Queen's Stair-**

case had been painted in white and panelled: George Augustus and Caroline commissioned William Kent to decorate the stairs. In the Queen's Audience Chamber, her original throne canopy survives but not the throne. In the **Queen's Drawing Room**, George Augustus had the Verrio painted walls covered with silk damask in 1737; they were uncovered again only in 1899. The **Queen's State Bedchamber** contains the original state bed made for Caroline and George in 1715, complete with 18th century mattresses. Sir James Thornhill's painted ceiling includes, on the cove, medallion portraits of George I, George Augustus and Caroline, and their son Frederick. The **Queen's Private Bedchamber** contains an overmantel by Grinling Gibbons which surrounds a portrait of Caroline by Joseph Highmore. In the **Queen's Gallery**, George Augustus replaced Mantegna's *Triumphs of Caesar*, which William III had hung there, with tapestries depicting the story of Alexander the Great (which remain there today); he then rehung the Mantegna paintings in the **Queen's Drawing Room**, over the silk he had had installed on the walls (see above). View the Queen's State Apartments at www.hrp.org.uk/webcode/content.asp?ID=413.

The **Georgian Rooms** were those used by George Augustus, Caroline, and their family, displayed today as they may well have appeared in 1737, the last visit of the full court to the Palace—this visit also marked an explosive quarrel with their son Frederick. Caroline's death followed later that year, and George Augustus was never to live there again. The **Cumberland Suite** was built for their second son, the Duke of Cumberland. The **Duke's Presence Chamber** stands out among these rooms in being the only one that is painted and gilded; family and court portraits line its walls. Although the bed in the **Duke's Bedchamber** is not the original, it is a rare period survival: it was intended for field purposes, readily dismantled for travelling. In the gallery outside the **Wolsey Closet**, are portraits of George Augustus and Caroline.

As with the Queen's State Apartments, the **Queen's Private Apartments**, although originally intended for Mary II, were completed for Caroline as Princess of Wales. The **Queen's Private Drawing Room** is set up for tea and cards; a large book open on a table shows engravings of Houghton Hall in Norfolk, the home of Sir Robert Walpole, Prime Minister during the reigns of George I and II, a book Caroline is known to have possessed. The bed in the **Queen's Private Bedchamber** is not the original, although it belonged to the 2nd Viscount Townshend, Secretary of State to George, so it has a connection; however, the silver warming pan on the bed did belong to Caroline. Her portrait in profile hangs over the mantel, within carving by Grinling Gibbons. A painting of George and Caroline's daughters Anne, Amelia, and Caroline hangs in the **Queen's Bathroom**. In the **Oratory**, the prayer book on the reading stand was dedicated to Caroline, and its binding displays the royal arms. See the Georgian Rooms at http://www.hrp.org. uk/webcode/content.asp?ID=414. George's and Caroline's last visit to Hampton Court in 1737 also marked the last time that the entire palace was used by the royal family. No monarch after that took up any residence of any length there.

Marble Hill House, built for George II's mistress Henrietta Howard, Countess of Suffolk, stands in over 60 acres of parkland near the river Thames at Twickenham, across the river from Ham House (a ferry runs from Marble Hill Park over to Ham House). A beautifully symmetrical Palladian house, exhibiting a gleaming white simplicity against its green background, it can be visited today, one of the many royal attractions in the Richmond-Kew-Twickenham area. Within, the house presents collections of furniture, paintings, and chinoiserie. Read the history of the house, and see photographs at http://www.twickenham-museum.org.uk/ detail.asp?ContentID=16. The house belongs to the National Trust; visiting details at http://www. nationaltrust.org.uk/main/w-vh/w-visits/w-findaplace/w-hamhouse.htm.

George's participation in the Battle of Dettingen was the last time an English sovereign led his troops in person. Read about the battle at http://www.britishbattles.com/battle_of_dettingen.htm. **Dettingen**, a village and part of the municipality of Karlstein, lies on the north bank of the river Main and the railway line between Frankfurt Am Main and Aschaffenburg. A painting of the battle by F. Daremberg can be viewed at http://www.bridgeman.co.uk/search/view_image.asp?button=add&image_id=70133.

George's death at Kensington Palace marked the end of an era; he was the last reigning monarch to live there. Not only that: he was the last monarch to be buried in the **Henry VII Chapel, Westminster Abbey**, where he lies alongside his beloved Caroline. They are interred in the floor in front of the altar. The bed in which he died is in the State Bedroom at **Chatsworth**, the great home of the Dukes of Devonshire, out of Bakewell, Derbyshire; for Chatsworth, see *Mary Queen of Scots*.

The North American colony of **Georgia,** now part of the United States, is named after George II.

George III

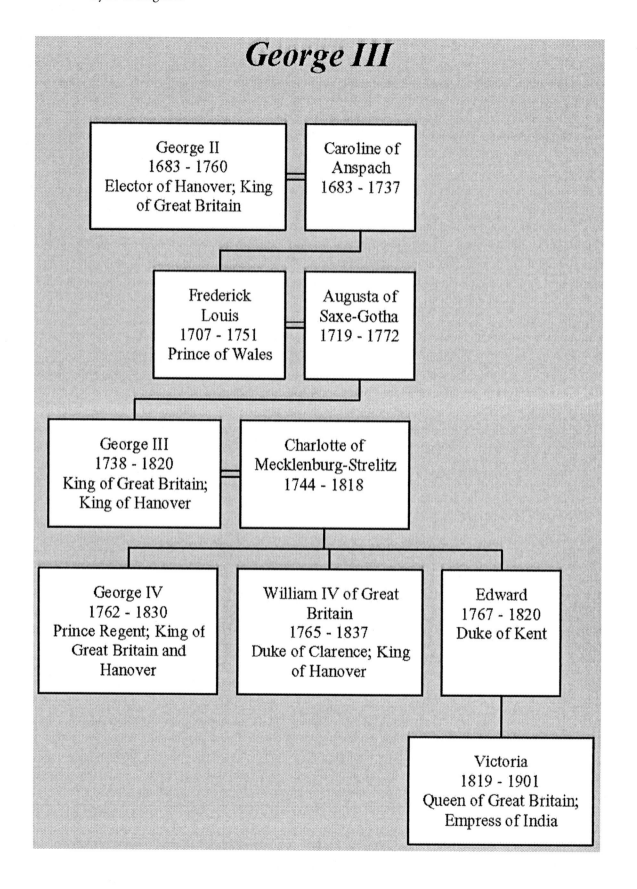

George III (1738–1820; reigned as King of Great Britain and Ireland and as Elector and later King of Hanover, 1760–1820; son George reigned as Prince Regent, 1811–1820)

During the very long reign of George III, the King endured much conflict with some of his American colonists and British subjects, as well as with his own sons. The fame of these conflicts has obscured the fact that he eventually reconciled with most of these opponents. In addition, George III suffered periodically from episodes of madness, the last of which plunged him into a permanent state of delusion during which his eldest son reigned as Prince Regent in his name for the last decade of his life. However, for most of his over 80 years of life, George III was sane. In 1819, Shelley heartlessly described George III as "An old, mad, blind, despised, and dying King." In fact, most of his people had long respected his great probity, conscientiousness, courage, and honor. Although never the despot whom his critics denounced, George III exhibited as his major failings an excessive reliance on his own fallible and reactionary opinions and a stance of regarding any compromise with dissent from these opinions as a betrayal of his sacred duty. This closeminded, self-righteous, inflexible attitude guaranteed an unimaginative and failed approach to conflict—and created much heartache for George III himself.

His rigidity probably resulted from his very insecure beginnings as the eldest son of Frederick, Prince of Wales (the son of George II and Caroline of Anspach) and Augusta of Saxe-Gotha. Never on good terms with Frederick, George II had followed a family falling-out with an eviction notice that ordered Frederick and Augusta to leave St. James's Palace. Not long afterward, Queen Caroline died in 1737, and Augusta bore Prince George in 1738. After Frederick himself passed on in 1751, George II nominally reconciled with his daughter-in-law Augusta, but she retained for herself Frederick's old role as a magnet for the political opposition. An overwhelming presence to her son George, Augusta persistently sought to control him and, later, his bride. George learned from her a deep sense of his personal inadequacy as well as an immense awe of the royal duties that he assumed in 1760.

This sense of being overawed by both his sacred responsibilities and his own unworthiness at first led George III to be rather subservient to his Ministers, especially Augusta's favorite, John Stuart, Earl of Bute. As the King gained a better knowledge of his role and became a more skilled political player, he developed rigid views on governmental policy. Coupled with his always profound sense of honor, this rigidity led him to identify any compromise with those who might dissent from his opinions with his betrayal of a sacred trust. Although George III held his views with seeming certainty, their very rigidity actually testified to his underlying insecurity about his own worthiness. In effect, he had resolved the conflict between his sense of inadequacy and his sense of reverence, first by feeling excessively unsure of himself and then by feeling too sure of himself. This unfortunate resolution of his inner conflict left him with few effective options when he faced determined opposition.

John Wilkes and other British radicals charged George III with tyranny, as did the rebelling American colonists. The King responded to these domestic and colonial rebellions with a serene certainty of the rightness of his own views that did little to temper the conflicts he faced. Nevertheless, he eventually accepted the necessity to work with such formerly detested opponents as Charles James Fox, as well as the necessity to recognize the new United States of America. His remarks to John Adams, in 1785 the American Minister to the Court of St. James and later the second President of the United States, displayed George III's stubborn identification of his views on policy with his moral duty as well as revealed his desire for reconciliation. "I have done nothing in the late contest," George III noted to Adams, "but what I thought myself indispensably bound to do by the duty which I owed my people. I was the last to consent to the separation, but the separation having been made and having become inevitable, I have always said I would be the first to meet the friendship of the United States as an independent power."

He approached conflicts with his many sons in a similar way, with similar results: prolonged conflict and eventual reconciliation, painfully achieved. In trying to prepare his sons, especially the Prince of Wales, for their destined roles, the King veered from the warm affection he had shown them as small children to growing severity and incessant criticism about their numerous faults. "If I did not state these things," George III noted to his eldest son, "I should not fulfil my duty either to my God or to my country" and called himself "an affectionate father trying to save his son from perdition." A younger son, William (later William IV) questioned the wisdom of this approach even as he recognized the King's good intentions. "Does he imagine he will make his sons his friends by this mode of conduct?" William asked his elder brother George in the mid-1780s. "If he does he is sadly mistaken. He certainly wishes us all well and thinks he is doing his best.... [I] would do anything to please him, but it is so difficult to satisfy." After many trials of affection, the aged King reconciled with his sons, even with the Prince of Wales.

Among other things, his madness bound his family to him. George III temporarily succumbed to delusions in 1788–89, with further attacks in 1801 and 1804; in 1810, the death of his beloved youngest child, Amelia, precipitated a permanent separation from rationality. During the earlier outbreaks, the King had suffered hideously under the care of his physicians. After the 1810 breakdown made the Prince of Wales Regent, the blind, deaf, and mad King at times wore mourning for himself and played tunes of which he had been fond, he said, when he was alive. In contrast to the earlier episodes, in this period he seemed happy. Former royal attendant Fanny Burney noted, "The beloved King is in the best state possible for his present melancholy situation; that is, wholly free from real bodily suffering, or imaginary mental misery, for he is persuaded he is always conversing with angels." Byron commented to a friend that George III's insanity might well have left him a happier man than any of his subjects.

George III's madness and his other misfortunes, especially his conflicts with his sons, endeared him to the British people, who respected his manifest goodness and his many virtues. Among other things a generous philanthropist, George III had given away out of his own income never less than £850,000 a year (by today's reckoning). John Wesley admired him, "When will England ever have a better prince?" His inflexible notion of his sacred duty, although so damaging to his ability to resolve conflicts, was but the shadow side of his honorable dedication of himself to his role.

George III Sites

Norfolk House, St. James's Square, London, George's birthplace, was rebuilt in 1939 and is now no. 31. It was the property of the Dukes of Norfolk from 1722 to 1937, and was leased by George's father, Frederick, Prince of Wales, from 1737 to 1741. A plaque on the house shows that here Eisenhower formed the 1st Allied Force headquarters and planned the North African 1942 campaign and the 1944 invasion of northwest Europe. There is nothing, however, to indicate that this is the birthplace of George III.

The family moved to **Leicester House**, Leicester Square when he was four years old (see *George II*). Nine years later, he and his brother, Prince Edward, moved next door to **Savile House**. Neither house still stands. He attended **Eton College** (see *Henry VI*).

Charlotte was born in **Mirow**, a small town in Mecklenburg-Strelitz, northeast of Berlin and near the Müritz See and the Müritz National Park, an area of lakes, marshes, and woodland; see its website at http://www.nationalpark-mueritz.de/?id=85&file=sommer&lang=en. The nearest main town is **Neustrelitz**, capital of Mecklenburg-Strelitz and seat of the ducal residence; visit it at http://www.neustrelitz.de/ (click on Welcome for English). She and George were married in the **Chapel Royal, St. James's Palace** (see *Henry VIII*).

In 1762, George purchased **Buckingham House** from the Duke of Buckingham for £28,000 as a family home in preference to St. James's Palace, Buckingham House having extensive gardens. James I had originally established a mulberry garden on the site for the production of silk by silkworms. Later, Lord Goring, as Keeper of the Mulberry Gardens, erected a house to the south, then known, unsurprisingly, as **Goring House** until it burned down in 1674 and **Arlington House** took its place. In 1702, it was bought by the Duke of Buckingham, who pulled down Arlington House and had Buckingham House built. At the time, the house was regarded as exemplary, much imitated for country houses of the period. This house later became Buckingham Palace. During George's tenure, the south wing, the octagon library, was added to contain his books. In 1823, 65,000 of these, transferred by George IV to the British Museum, formed the nucleus of the national museum. **St. James's Palace** remained the center for ceremonial occasions: balls, levees, and drawing rooms, and for marriages and christenings solemnized in its Chapel Royal, but Buckingham House was now the center of the family's London life. Later, the house was assigned to Charlotte as a dower house, instead of **Somerset House**, which had served this purpose, and it then became known as the **Queen's House**. It was only during George IV's reign that it was called Buckingham Palace, when Nash's substantial alterations were in progress; see *George IV*.

Like his father and grandfather, George valued the homes at Richmond and Kew. The family lived in **Richmond Lodge**, which became too small for their rapidly expanding family (and which was later demolished). After Princess Augusta's death, they moved into the **White House** (Kew House), which, too, the family outgrew, so they leased the nearby **Dutch House** for the Prince of Wales (the future George IV) and his brother Frederick, and bought it in 1781. The four-story, red-brick Dutch House was built in 1631 by Samuel Fortrey, a merchant of Dutch descent, in an essentially Dutch and simple style after Jacobean and Tudor exuberance.

George and Charlotte wanted to expand the **White House** but, after being frustrated by the reluctance of local people to sell, decided to build their own enormous palace beside the Thames in Kew, taking up residence in the Dutch House in the meantime. The White House was pulled down to make way for the projected Gothic enterprise, nicknamed the Castellated House. Alas, George became ill before any more than the shell was completed, and the project was not to the Prince Regent's taste. Some of the vast amount of money spent on the building to this point was recouped by selling the materials and otherwise using them at other royal residences, like **Buckingham Palace**.

So, alone of the royal residences of the area, the Dutch House, later named **Kew Palace**, remains today, the smallest of all the present palaces. Visit Kew Palace at http://www.hrp.org.uk/webcode/timeline.asp?ID=17, and read about its history. Kew Palace has been closed to the public since 1996 for extensive interior renovation, which you can read about at http://www.hrp.org.uk/webcode/content.asp?ID=18. Included is a scheme for an interpretation of the palace during George's reign, when he and Queen Charlotte and their children stayed there so often.

Queen Charlotte's Cottage (1772) was designed for and possibly by Charlotte as a summer- and teahouse. The first floor contains decorations by her daughter Princess Elizabeth. Picturesque, and quintessentially "cottagey," the small home, at the opposite end of Kew Gardens from Kew Palace, is open to the public. Pay your virtual visit at http://www.rbgkew.org.uk/places/kew/queenscottage.html; visiting details, along with a couple of rather romantic images, can be read and seen at http://www.hrp.org.uk/history/default.asp?sectID=6&id=6 by clicking on Queen Charlotte's Cottage on the left of the screen. The surrounding areas of woodland and meadow are being preserved as a natural area, the grass left unmown so that wildflowers and grasses are allowed to develop. For basic information regarding Kew Gardens, see *George II*.

George III bought **Frogmore House**, in Windsor Great Park, for Charlotte and their daughters, as a quiet retreat, and had it modernized. Charlotte used it much during the years her husband became so ill that he was largely confined to **Windsor Castle**. After her death, her daughter Princess Augusta lived there in the house and farm Charlotte had bequeathed to her. Visit Frogmore at http://www.royal.gov.uk/output/page558.asp, which may be the only opportunity: although the house is not inhabited permanently, it is used for various royal occasions and is open only on a limited basis.

George had no desire to visit, let alone live in, **Hampton Court Palace**; his father had once boxed his ears there, and the palace held only unpleasant memories for him. During his reign, however, a grape vine was planted by Capability Brown in a greenhouse in the gardens; known as the **Great Vine**, it's now 248 years old, producing several hundred pounds of grapes each year, which can be bought when they ripen in the autumn. Read about the Great Vine at http://www.hrp.org.uk/webcode/content.asp?ID=492. See how much it's spread since at http://www.twickenhammuseum.org.uk/detail.asp?ContentID=183.

George was interested in astronomy and was a generous patron to the **Royal Society** (see *Charles II*); he persuaded William Herschel to give up his career as a musician to become his private astronomer. The George III Collection in London's **Science Museum** houses objects either owned by George or constructed under his patronage. The Science Museum is behind the Natural History Museum, on Exhibition Road, part of the agglomeration of museums that include the Victoria and Albert Museum. Visiting details are provided at http://www.sciencemuseum.org.uk/visitors/location.asp: the Museum is open every day from 10 a.m. to 6 p.m., except for the period December 24 to 26. Admission is free, but charges do apply to certain parts (simulators, mostly) and some exhibitions. The George III collection is on the Third Floor and labelled "Science in the 18th Century." For the virtual visitor, enter the museum via http://www.sciencemuseum.org.uk/galleryguide/EG.asp. Click on the circle on the left marked 3, which leads you to colored photographs of some of the beautiful objects in this collection. Of course you may visit the rest of the museum at the same time, right down to the washrooms in the Basement!

George was also patron of the **Royal Academy of Arts**, founded in 1768 with Sir Joshua Reynolds as its first president. In 1775, Sir William Chambers, probably due to his association with royalty, managed to acquire space for the Academy in the then-neglected **Somerset House** and set about the restoration of the building. For background information, see *James I*. The Royal Academy now occupies **Burlington House**, along with various learned societies. Burlington House was built in 1665 by the 3rd Earl of Burlington. Read about tours of Burlington House at http://www.royalacademy.org.uk/?lid=15, and about the collections at http://www.royalacademy.org.uk/?lid=29.

George enjoyed summers in **Weymouth**, benefiting from the newly fashionable sea-bathing and, in turn, making Weymouth fashionable although it was already known as a port and military base: from there, John Endicott sailed to North America in 1628 to found Salem, Massachusetts. In Weymouth, the family stayed at **Gloucester House**, now a hotel. The surprisingly humble hotel, one of a long row of Georgian buildings, can be found on the Esplanade, facing the sand beach and sea; and especially striking is the tall painted and gilded statue of George at one end of the Esplanade. Pay a virtual visit to Weymouth at http://www.weymouth.here-on-the.net/.

On his way to Weymouth, George and his entourage stayed at **Lyndhurst**, at the edge of the New Forest, at Charles II's hunting lodge (see *Charles II*.) Another time, he visited **Cuffnells Park** before proceeding to Weymouth. Cuffnells Park is perhaps most famous for being the home of the model for Lewis Carroll's Alice, Alice Liddell, after she married Reginald Hargreaves. She is buried in Lyndhurst churchyard. Lyndhurst lies southwest of Southampton on the A35; visit it at http://www.new-forest-tourism.com/lyndhurst.htm.

George's 1788 visit with **Cheltenham** to take the waters helped spur a fashion for what had been a small market town. Subsequently, other noted people followed, and later, Cheltenham became popular as a retirement town for colonial officers, who built villas amidst gardens they stocked with plants brought back from exotic places. Today's Cheltenham is a flourishing and charming small city, popular today with visitors for its handsome Regency architecture, attractive gardens, and several well-known schools. Visit Cheltenham at http://www.cheltenham.gov.uk/libraries/templates/index.asp.

George is buried beneath **Albert Memorial Chapel** at **Windsor Castle**, along with Queen Charlotte and six of their sons, including George IV and William IV.

Among other places named for Charlotte are **Charlottetown, Prince Edward Island**, Canada as well as **Charlotte**, North Carolina (the "Queen City") and its county, **Mecklenburg**.

George IV and William IV

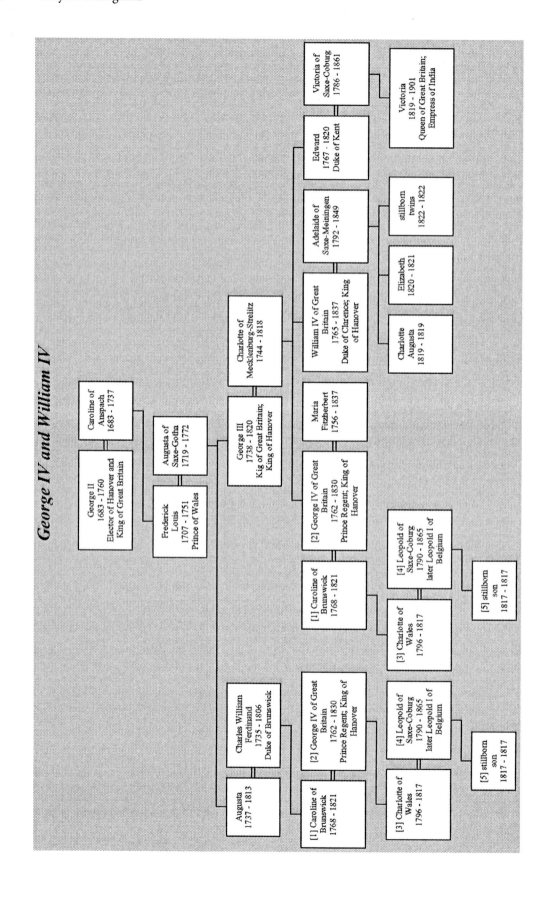

George IV (1762–1830; reigned 1811–1820 as Prince Regent, 1820–1830 as King of Great Britain and Ireland and as King of Hanover)

A perennial weed of great hardiness, George IV's bad repute sprouted in his early youth. For decades, his extraordinary extravagance infuriated British public opinion almost as much as it maddened his father, the spartan and beloved George III. In addition to his torrential spending, George IV hardened the public's and posterity's dislike because of his spectacularly troubled relationships with his father; his daughter, Charlotte of Wales; and his wives, Maria Fitzherbert and Caroline of Brunswick. He conducted himself in the roles of son, father, and husband in a highly emotional, self-indulgent, narcissistic, and destructive fashion. After George IV's funeral, *The Times* pronounced a common verdict: "There never was an individual less regretted by his fellow-creatures than this deceased King." Although much of George IV's behavior warranted this crushing dismissal, it scants his close relationships with many of his 14 siblings, especially his eight sisters, and with his mother. In addition, it ignores his very substantial contributions to British culture, which earned for George IV the Duke of Wellington's eulogistic praise in the House of Lords as "the most accomplished man of his age."

So, which is the true portrait of George IV: wastrel or aesthete? The emotionalism and self-absorption that wrecked his relationships to his father, his daughter, and both his wives also drove him in happier, less conflicted relationships and energized his devotion to culture and beauty as exemplified in the arts and in architecture. One cannot tease apart the positives and the negatives in his character, for they have the same root. Keeping this in mind, one can enjoy Thackeray's demolition of George IV in *The Four Georges* while knowing that Thackeray did not spell out the whole truth: "[he] never resisted any temptation; never had a desire but he coddled and pampered it; if ever he had any nerve, frittered it away among cooks, and tailors, and barbers, and furniture-mongers, and opera-dancers."

As the eldest son born in 1762 to George III and Queen Charlotte, George as Prince of Wales had little to do but wait for his father to die. George III did not oblige his heir presumptive until 1820, when George III was over 80 years old and his heir was almost 60. In addition, George III chronically underestimated how much money his son needed. The Prince responded to his father's stinginess by mounding debt upon debt, reasoning that his father *ought* to give him more and that debts would force the paternal hand. Their tug-of-war over the Prince's finances greatly embittered their relationship.

It did not help matters that the Prince had no sense at all of how to manage money. By his middle thirties, in the middle 1790s, he owed to creditors about £639,890. In modern terms, that amounted to between £18 million and £33 million. Thackeray commented acidly, "If he had been a manufacturing town, or a populous rural district, or an army of five thousand men, he would not have cost more. " Twenty-five years later, by the time of his Coronation in 1820, his sense of entitlement had not dwindled. George IV hired 12,532 diamonds for the setting of his crown. Provisions for the state banquet for the royal family and 312 other guests included 7,742 pounds of beef, 7,133 pounds of veal, 2,474 pounds of mutton, 75 quarters and five saddles of lamb, 160 geese, 720 pullets and capons, 1,610 chickens, and 1,730 pounds of bacon.

George III's parsimony and lectures about financial responsibility produced only extravagance in his contrary son. The undeniably virtuous father's unimaginative, unsympathetic, and contemptuous approach to guiding his heir, and the sensitive and intelligent prodigal son's stubborn defiance, locked them into years of mutual disdain and frustration. George III refused to give his son more money or any responsibility and then lectured him on waste and idleness. The Prince then became more wasteful and more idle. He espoused radical politicians as another way of needling his father, a strategy adopted early in life when the Prince as a boy yelled "Wilkes and Liberty" through the keyhole of his father's study door. An apparent supporter of the

Whigs, he dropped their views as soon as he acquired real power, and he never showed much interest in the daily round of governing.

Complicating this already torturous struggle between father and son, George III suffered periodically from delusions that incapacitated him. One hypothesis holds that porphyria, an inherited metabolic disorder traced back to James I, created toxins in George III's nervous system that affected his brain and created his delusions. One delusional episode that began in 1788 stretched into 1789. The Whig opposition championed the Prince's hopes for an unfettered regency during his father's period of madness. A bill authorizing a restricted regency never came to a final vote because the King recovered his reason. The Prince's desire for a regency seemed disloyal to his father and the public.

Further, time-limited outbreaks recurred in 1801 and 1804. The 1810 recurrence, however, plunged George III into a permanent state of delusion, and on 5 February 1811 a Regency Bill finally passed. After a year's restricted Regency, the Prince Regent assumed the full powers of a sovereign in 1812. George III was now beyond all hope of recovery. Long before this, their relationship had passed beyond all hope of full repair. Years earlier, the Prince had shown letters from the King to James Harris, 1st Earl Malmesbury, who characterized them as "harsh and severe…void of every expression of parental kindness or affection." The Prince stressed to Malmesbury, "The King hates me…he always did, from seven years old."

The Prince interpreted as hate George III's unceasing attempts to control him. Yet, in his own behavior as a father to his daughter by Caroline of Brunswick, Princess Charlotte of Wales, the Prince faithfully replicated George III's severity. Loving Charlotte, the British public condemned the Prince's harshness toward her. He isolated her, just as he himself had been isolated as a youth, and he quarrelled with her about her lovers and marital prospects. Eventually, Charlotte found a brief happiness after marrying Leopold of Saxe-Coburg-Saalfeld and in living with Leopold at Warwick House, next door to her father's longtime residence, Carlton House. Unfortunately, in 1817, Charlotte died suddenly after giving birth to a stillborn son. "It really was as if every household in Great Britain had lost a favorite child," remembered opposition politician Henry Brougham. The devastation that swept the Kingdom also afflicted the Prince, prostrated by his daughter's death.

Before Charlotte had engaged herself to Leopold, the Prince, in pressuring her to agree to another, more disagreeable match, reminded her, "We cannot marry like the rest of the world." He had reason to feel this sentiment. Long before, the Prince had secretly married Maria Fitzherbert, whom he loved but could not openly acknowledge, and a decade later married Caroline of Brunswick, whom he loathed. Like his extravagance, like his tempestuous relationships to George III and to Charlotte of Wales, his two marriages gravely damaged George IV's contemporary and posthumous reputation.

For one thing, both marriages suffered from an ambiguous status. His marriage in 1785 to the Catholic widow Maria Fitzherbert was canonically valid in both Anglican and Catholic terms but illegal. His marriage in 1795 to his paternal first cousin Caroline of Brunswick was impeccably legal but bigamous because he had a wife still living. Caroline herself commented about Maria, "That is the Prince's true wife. She is an excellent woman: it is a great pity he ever broke with her."

Passionately in love with Maria Fitzherbert in the early 1780s, the Prince relentlessly pursued her, but she would not agree to be a royal mistress. Eventually, George talked Maria into agreeing to a secret wedding in 1785. Their marriage violated several laws. The 1689 Bill of Rights and the 1701 Act of Settlement excluded from the throne any heirs presumptive married to Catholics. Advocated by George III, the Royal Marriages Act of 1772 mandated that most of the descendants of George II needed the sovereign's permission to marry. Any marriage contracted without this permission remained legally null and void, and an ecclesiastical court would formally annul it. After the age of 25, a royal person could marry without the sovereign's consent but only after giving a year's notice to the Privy Council and encountering no significant opposition in either House of Parliament. But Maria knew her marriage was religiously valid, and that satisfied her conscience.

Their marriage—an open secret among their intimates and an open marriage on the Prince's side—continued until 1794. He then broke off with Maria by sending her a note when she was dining at Bushy Park with his brother the Duke of Clarence and the Duke's mistress, Dora Jordan. Frances, Lady Jersey, the Prince's newer conquest, had engineered the break. She had also chosen Maria's replacement as the Prince's wife, fixing on an woman Lady Jersey knew the Prince would find unattractive. Getting rid of Maria Fitzherbert and marrying the Prince to Caroline of Brunswick would enhance Lady Jersey's own position and power.

Besides, the Prince needed money from Parliament to appease the creditors to whom he owed those £639,890. A royal marriage as advocated by his father presumably would secure funds that would ease the Prince's financial cramp. He did not care whom he married, for "any damn'd German frau would do." As it turned out, not only would any damn'd German frau not do, but this particular German frau definitely would not do.

Caroline stank. As Malmesbury (her escort from Brunswick) urbanely noted, "She neglected her *toilette* to such an extent that she offended the nostrils by this negligence." The Prince aborted his first meeting with Caroline in 1795 after sniffing her. He retreated, asked Malmesbury for brandy, and hurriedly left the room. Further encounters with his future bride deepened the fastidious Prince's repugnance into, in Herman Melville's phrase, "an antipathy spontaneous and profound." After the wedding, a dead-drunk bridegroom eventually impregnated the bride. Telling Malmesbury later about his three attempts, the Prince complained, "it required no small [effort] to conquer my aversion and overcome the disgust of her person." Considering the infrequency of marital congress, Caroline herself felt astonished by her subsequent pregnancy with Princess Charlotte.

His daughter's birth in 1796 did nothing to soften the Prince's hatred for his wife. A few months later, Caroline suggested, and the Prince agreed, that even if Charlotte should die, they would never again indulge, as he put it, in "a connection of a more particular nature." They essentially led separate lives and, by 1798, had unofficially separated. Moving from Carlton House, Caroline lived at Blackheath, mostly in Montague House, and eventually had apartments in Kensington Palace. Their emotional separation was complete as well. The Prince told his mother that Caroline was "a very monster of iniquity." For her part, Caroline stuck pins into wax models of her husband, then burned them. The Duke of Clarence sensibly commented, "My brother has behaved very foolishly…. he should not have treated her as he has done, but have made the best of a bad bargain."

George's affections had returned to Maria. Indeed, in spite of all appearances, she had never lost his heart. On the morning of his wedding to Caroline, George told the Duke of Clarence, "tell Mrs. Fitzherbert she is the only woman I shall ever love." On the way to his wedding, George commented to the Earl of Moira, "It's no use, Moira. I shall never love any woman but Fitzherbert." Now he fervently pursued Maria yet again. Before agreeing to resume their marriage in 1800, Maria confidentially sought and received recognition of the 1785 wedding by Pope Pius VII. For the next eight years, she lived very happily with George, much of the time at Brighton, where he had built a house for her near his Pavilion. With the ascendancy of George's new favorite—Isabella, Lady Hertford—and the 1811 advent of the Regency, however, Maria's hold on George broke yet again, and they separated forever.

For her part, Caroline left England for the Continent in 1814, earning her husband's toast, "To the Princess of Wales's damnation, and may she never return to England." When their daughter Charlotte died in 1817, Caroline received no official notification but instead learned of the death by accident. In 1820, Caroline and George, now King, jousted about divorce terms but could not agree. When he cut her name from the prayers for members of the royal family, an enraged Caroline decided to return to England and fight for the status of Queen.

On the Continent, Caroline had behaved with great indiscretion, impropriety, and recklessness. While she had been cavorting abroad, George had his agents gather much evidence that he hoped would support a case for divorce on the grounds of her adultery. His ministers opposed proceeding against Caroline, largely because the British public loved her as much as it hated the King. George insisted on a trial before the House of Lords that lasted for 80 days and mesmerized the country. Despite much scandalous evidence, public opinion remained with Caroline, its attitude embodied in Thackeray's remark, "If wrong there be, let it lie at his door who wickedly thrust her from it." The government finally withdrew the bill, and the public exulted.

Cheated of his divorce, George banned Caroline from his coronation, and she died suddenly not long afterward. When George himself lay dying, in 1830, Maria wrote him a concerned and loving letter, which he put under his pillow. She felt comforted to learn that George IV was buried with a locket containing her portrait placed on his heart. The Duke of Clarence, now William IV, returned to Maria all of her husband's keepsakes of her, invited her to Brighton Pavilion, and presented her to the royal family as his brother's widow. Already a close friend of William's wife, Adelaide, Maria remained part of the family.

She also remained part of Brighton, where she had lived for many years and where she is buried, in St. John the Baptist Church. The architecture that George commissioned in Brighton is, of course, part of his immense aesthetic legacy. As biographer Saul David has listed, George IV's cultural contributions include Regency architecture, patronage of individual artists, the purchase of the Elgin marbles, the founding of the Royal Society of Literature, the donation of George III's library to the British Museum, and the restoration of the Royal Collection. Another biographer, E.A. Smith, devoted two chapters to George's achievements as a royal builder, a patron, and a collector. Some have compared the aesthete King George IV to the aesthete Emperor Nero, an interesting conjunction of personalities and outrages. One easily can imagine Nero's last words being George's: "What an artist dies with me!"

George IV Sites

Five days after his birth at **St. James's Palace**, George was created Prince of Wales, and then baptized as George Augustus Frederick. He was created Knight of the Garter at the age of three and a half. Much of his childhood was spent in rural **Kew** or the privacy of **Buckingham House**, which George III had purchased in the year of his son's birth.

Carlton House was given to George by his father, for his London residence. Standing on the site of the present Waterloo Place and Duke of York's Column, it was built in 1709 and had been a home of George's grandmother, Princess Augusta, only to become neglected during the 11 years after her death. The economical George III remarked that all Carlton House needed was "a touch of paint and handsome furniture where necessary," which didn't suit his son's tastes. Henry Holland transformed Carlton House from a modest Queen Anne house to a palace, sprouting Corinthian porticoes as well as an Ionic colonnade, and balustraded wings overlooking a garden containing a cascade and an Italian marble temple. Chinese decoration and a Gothic dining room, drawing room, library, and conservatory followed as George's debts skyrocketed and architects left. See photographs and plans, and read a history at http://www.georgianindex.net/carlton/carlton.html.

Carlton House served him as a true home for some years; it was where he retreated when bereaved or upset, where he forbade entry to his hated second wife Caroline of Brunswick, and where their daughter, Princess Charlotte of Wales, lived until she was nine, and where he lived when he was in London. But, as he was wont to do, George lost interest in Carlton House over time, and after he became King and needed a grander home. It was damaged by fire in 1825. When John Nash reported that the house needed extensive renovations, it was pulled down and replaced by his magnificent terraces, **Carlton House Terrace**. It is now home to the **Royal Society** (see *Charles II*).

George, as Regent, lent his name to **Regent Street**, running from Portland Place in the north to Pall Mall and the rear of Carlton House Terrace. George, previously involved in the development of **Regent's Park** to the north of Portland Place, saw the street as a processional way from the park down to Carlton House. The beautiful part of Regent Street is its elegant curve, lined with elegant Georgian buildings housing fine shops, from Oxford Street to Piccadilly Circus. A guide to the shops is provided at http://www.streetsensation.co.uk/regent/rs_intro.htm.

Regent's Park was initially a royal chase, the land appropriated by Henry VIII. Nash landscaped it into the park we know today and was the architect for the grand terraces along part of it. Queen Victoria opened it up to the public, and today it's a 487-acre expanse, with many activities and events. Visit Regent's Park at http://www.royalparks.gov.uk/parks/regents_park/.

George had discovered **Brighton**, a cobblestoned, modest fishing port still called Brighthelmstone, on a trip to accompany his uncle, the Duke of Cumberland, for the recuperative sea-bathing. After several annual visits thereafter, during which he made Brighton fashionable, he employed Holland to transform his leased farmhouse on the Old Steine (or Steyne), the center of Brighton, into his pavilion by the sea in 1787. Originally, this was done in a neo-classical style, but from 1815–22 Nash pulled out all the stops in Oriental splendor, happily mixing Indian, Chinese, and Gothic, inside and out, to produce the lush and beautiful **Royal Pavilion** of today. The Pavilion is the centerpiece of the Old Steine. You can pay a virtual visit to the Royal Pavilion at its website, at http://www.royalpavilion.org.uk/.

At the same time, you can see Maria Fitzherbert's Brighton home at 54 The Steine. A tall house with deep windows and a balcony running the width of the second floor, it has a surprisingly modern look, and one more Mediterranean than English. The house was bought by the YMCA in 1884 and is still used by them. See http://www.womenofbrighton.co.uk/mariafitzherbert.htm for photographs. It's easier to identify the house by the YMCA sign than to try and find the number. Brighton's website is http://www.brighton.co.uk/ (noisy); also read about the annual, month-long Brighton Festival at http://www.brighton-festival.org.uk/.

In the meantime, after considering the merits of a new residence in Green Park, George commissioned Nash to convert **Buckingham House** into a palace in 1826. Unfortunately, George was short of funds and then died in 1830. However, Nash managed to double the size of the main block with the addition of rooms on the garden side of the palace, and he extended and enlarged the wings to form a solid U-shape around a central courtyard. The open fourth side was finished with iron railings on each side of a triumphal arch, the Marble Arch, moved to its present position during Victoria's reign when that fourth side was built. Nash finished the exterior in the warm Bath stone we see today and added French neoclassical detailing, with large bow windows on the garden side. The interior of the main block was remodelled to allow for access to, and suitability for, both state occasions and social events. George had the interiors enriched under Sir Charles Long, giving a more opulent and grand appearance. He died before the rooms could be finished, leaving his brother and successor, William IV, with the completion on a much more economical scale. See *William IV* for more information, and visiting details.

George's principal interest was in modernizing **Windsor Castle**, to continue the Gothicization and to make the apartments more comfortable and splendid. Sir Charles Long's plans heightened the **Round Tower** and added extra towers and battlements. He built the **Grand Corridor** around the Upper Ward and created the **Waterloo Chamber**, after the victory over Napoleon at Waterloo in 1815 (see http://www.windsorfestival.com/venues/castle/waterloo.shtml).

Charles II's **Long Walk** was continued up to the castle, and the **George IV Gateway** was added. New rooms showcased George's art collection, and the old hall and chapel were combined to make the large **St. George's Hall**. Jeffry Wyatt carried out Long's plans in all this work, changing his name to Wyatville and receiving a knighthood for his pains. George took up residence in 1828. See the Hall being cleaned at http://www.royal.gov.uk/output/Page3007.asp.

Outside, in **Windsor Great Park**, George had the old Deputy Ranger's Lodge renovated and extended to form a home, which became known as **Royal Lodge**. Nash drew up the plans, and much of the work was carried out from 1813–22. A verandah was added around the south and east sides; the south façade was extended, including a conservatory; on the north side, a new entrance was added, with rooms to each side. George first used the house in 1815, to host a party during Ascot week. In 1823, Jeffry Wyatt replaced the thatched roof with a slate one, and changes continued up to the end of George's life. Although William IV had most of it torn down, the house was then rebuilt and added to in a mishmash of styles over the years. Nevertheless, it has remained a loved royal residence, being the home of George VI and his Queen Consort Elizabeth when they were still Duke and Duchess of York, and their elder daughter (later Elizabeth II) spent the early years of her childhood there. More recently, it was one of the homes of George VI's widowed consort, then known as Queen Elizabeth, the Queen Mother, and, since her death in 2002, it has become the home of her grandson Prince Andrew, Duke of York. Being a royal residence, it's not open to the public; pay a virtual visit to George IV's home at http://www.georgianindex.net/HMR-Lodge/royal-lodge.html. In keeping, perhaps, with the informality and privacy of this home, websites providing today's appearance don't seem to be available.

At **Kensington Palace**, where he, Caroline of Brunswick, and Charlotte of Wales were allocated adjoining apartments, George doubled the area of the kitchen gardens, including new greenhouses for the cultivation of peaches and pineapples. For background information about the palace, see *William III and Mary II.*

George visited **Holyroodhouse** in 1822. He didn't stay there, the palace being in a state of some dilapidation, but he did host some occasions, wearing Highland dress. He inspected the royal apartments and recommended repairs but advised keeping Mary Queen of Scots's rooms from alterations. For Holyroodhouse, see *Mary Queen of Scots.*

George paid one visit to **Hanover** in 1821 to visit his subjects there. For Hanover, see *George I.* He left from **Ramsgate**, where an obelisk by the harbor records his departure, and a King George IV memorial park was created along the sea front. Ramsgate, which is on the east shore of Kent, extends over two cliffs, East Cliff and West Cliff, with the "gate," or valley between them. With a population of 38,500, Ramsgate is a popular resort and marina, close to two others, Broadstairs and Margate, on the Isle of Thanet. Visit Ramsgate at http://www.aboutbritain.com/towns/Ramsgate.asp.

In 1823, he presented many of the books in his father's splendid library to the **British Museum**, which then formed the impetus for the creation of a national museum. Since 1759, exhibits had been collected in Montague House, Bloomsbury; work on the new King's Library began in 1823, developing into the vast complex we see today, occupying a large square between Montague Place and Great Russell Street, to north and south, and Gower Street and Montague Street, to west and east. The **British Library** moved into its own building near St. Pancras Station in 1998, leaving the magnificent Reading Room. In 2000, the central court was covered by a glass canopy. Visit the museum at http://www.thebritishmuseum.ac.uk/, and the British Library at http://www.bl.uk/.

Queen Caroline was raised in the ducal castle at **Wolfenbüttel**, Brunswick, Germany. A small city with a good supply of beautiful, well-preserved old buildings, it was the home of the Dukes of Brunswick from 1432 to 1753, who left a notable library now preserved as the Herzog AugustBibliothek (Leibniz and Lessing were ducal librarians at different times). Wolfenbüttel is a mere 10 km south of its big sister city, **Braunschweig** (Brunswick). Visit Wolfenbüttel at http://www.wolfenbuettel-tourismus.de/ (in German).

Her arrival in England took place at **Greenwich**, where she was met by dignitaries, including George. They were married in the **Chapel Royal, St. James's**, then went to **Buckingham House** for supper. Their wedding night, the only night they were to spend together, took place in **Carlton House**. They then lived their lives as separately as they could, Caroline living in a succession of houses for the rest of her life. Among them were **Montague House**, in Blackheath, after George III made her Ranger of Blackheath—the house was demolished in 1815. and she, George, and Charlotte were allocated apartments in **Kensington Palace**, where she lived, dividing her time between Montague House and the palace, until she left for Europe in 1814. Remnants of Montague House can be seen in **Greenwich Park**, along with Queen Caroline's Bath House; see a photograph and read details of the latter at http://knowledgeoflondon.com/odds.html. Greenwich Park is one of the Royal Parks; see http://www.royalparks.gov.uk/parks/greenwich_park/. Blackheath Gate is at the opposite end of the Park from the royal complex of buildings at Greenwich; the map on the Royal Parks website shows it, and Queen Caroline's Bath to the south of the gate.

In the course of her wanderings in Europe, she lived for a while on Lake Como, at the **Villa d'Este**. The name has nothing to do with the Este family; Caroline bought it as Villa del Garrovo and renamed it Villa d'Este herself. Nevertheless, her name for it has stuck. She left it when George III died, to return to London, and the house then passed through the hands of several owners until being renovated in 1873 to become the luxurious hotel it is today. Pay a visit and read its history (and a lot about Caroline's habitation there) at http://www.georgianindex.net/como/Villad.html.

On her return, she lived at **Marlborough House** (see *Anne*) and **Brandenburg House**, in Hammersmith, where she died. This house no longer exists. Her coffin was taken to **Braunschweig** (Brunswick), for interment among other members of the ducal family in the crypt of the cathedral. It bore the inscription "Caroline of Brunswick—the injured Queen of England."

Princess Charlotte lived at **Carlton House** or at **Windsor** with her father, celebrating her 20th birthday at the **Royal Pavilion**, Brighton. **Warwick House**, where she met with Prince Frederick of Prussia, was in London—see a postcard of the house at http://www.georgianindex.net/Prn_Charlotte/P_Charlotte.html). Upon discovering this liaison, George made her a virtual prisoner in **Cranbourne Tower** (see *James II*). After Caroline married Prince Leopold of Saxe-Coburg, her uncle and aunt, the Duke and Duchess of York, lent the young couple **Oatlands** http://www.georgianindex.net/Oatlands/Oatlands.html) for their honeymoon—Charlotte complained that it was like inhabiting a dog kennel—and then the newlyweds moved to **Camelford House**, at the intersection of Park Lane and Oxford Street, opposite Hyde Park (see http://www.georgianindex.net/camelford_house/camelford_house.html) and, in the country, **Claremont Park**, the house near Esher, Surrey, which her father had bought for them. Visit Claremont at http://www.georgianindex.net/Prn_Charlotte/Claremont.html. She died there, tragically, of complications following a long and arduous labor in which her son was stillborn, and the country was plunged into mourning.

Her tomb, by Matthew Cotes Wyatt, fills **Urswick Chantry**, in **St. George's Chapel**, Windsor Castle. In the sculpture, she is rising to heaven, flanked by angels, one of which is carrying her dead child. Outside the chantry is a statue of her husband, Prince Leopold, later King Leopold I of the Belgians, placed there by Queen Victoria. (Charlotte was Victoria's paternal first cousin, while Uncle Leopold was Victoria's mother's brother.) See Charlotte's tomb at http://www.georgianindex.net/Prn_Charlotte/P_Charlotte.html/.

Maria Fitzherbert was born Mary Ann Smythe, in 1756, into a prosperous Shropshire family, whose seat was **Acton Burnell Hall**, 8 miles south of Shrewsbury. It is thought that she was born at **Tong Castle**, of which only the gates are left; see them and other illustrations at http://www.localhistory.scit.wlv.ac.uk/listed/tong.htm. When she was six, her family moved to **Brambridge House**, just outside the village of Twyford, about 6 miles south of Winchester. The house no longer exists, but Brambridge Park Garden Center boasts that it is the childhood home of Maria Smythe.

Her first marriage was to Edward Weld of **Lulworth Castle**. Lulworth, which stands today in good condition and may be visited (http://www.touruk.co.uk/houses/housedor_lulw.htm), was built by Thomas Howard, the third Lord Bindon between 1608 and 1610. An exact cube, it has a basic harmony carried on by the matching round towers on each corner. Edward Weld contributed a grand, circular staircase and extensions to the terrace and gardens, along with modernization. In 1929, the castle was gutted by fire, but the Weld family, who still live nearby, were able to save the shell and rebuilt the walls and roof.

Maria's second husband, Thomas Fitzherbert, became Lord of the Manor of Swynnerton on the death of his father. **Swynnerton Hall** had been built in 1725, an impressive building on a rise with splendid views from its windows. Still the home of Fitzherberts, it survives almost as it was built; view it at http:// www.swynnerton.8m.com/hallpic.htm. Swynnerton is located in Staffordshire, directly south of Newcastle-under-Lyme, near the intersection of the M6 and A51.

As a widow courted by George, then Prince of Wales, Maria fled to Europe but returned to marry him secretly, illegally, but canonically at her home in Park Street. In London, she lived in various houses; just before George's marriage to Caroline of Brunswick, she left London to stay at **Marble Hill House**, the beautiful mansion at Twickenham, built for George II's mistress Henrietta Howard, Duchess of Suffolk (see *George II*). A woman of dignity, Maria is said to have left instructions to illuminate her London house on the Prince and Caroline's wedding night, to conceal her flight.

Maria outlasted both George and Caroline, dying at her home in **Brighton** (see above), and is buried in the 1835 Roman Catholic church of St. John the Baptist, Bristol Road, Kemp Town (do not confuse this with the other church of St. John the Baptist in Brighton), with a monument to her. Kemp Town is reached by following the Marine Parade along the shore from the old town.

George is buried beneath the **Albert Memorial Chapel**, Windsor Castle, in the royal vault that also holds his father and many of his siblings.

William IV (1765–1837; reigned 1830–1837 as King of Great Britain and Ireland and as King of Hanover)

The third of George III's seven sons, Prince William went to sea in 1779 as a midshipman in the Royal Navy. William's ten years of active duty included stints in the American colonies that were fighting for their independence as well as in the West Indies. His father gave him the title of Duke of Clarence in 1789, as well as an apartment at St. James's Palace. Many amorous escapades and social gaffes during his youth made William's gaucherie notorious. Reading about his flighty bachelor years is highly amusing. His numerous but mostly unsuccessful love affairs rapidly succeeded one another, as the quicksilver Prince found himself in love yet again. More a romantic than a Regency rake, he never seduced a virgin but pursued more experienced women. However, he lacked the polish to retain what conquests he made. The courtesan Polly Finch, whom William kept in 1789, endured only so much of his reading aloud from *The Lives of the Admirals* before she left him.

However, once the Duke had finally found the right woman, his inconstancy collapsed with his bachelorhood. This happened twice: when he met the actress Dora (sometimes called Dorothy or Dorothea) Jordan in 1791, and when he married Princess Adelaide of Saxe-Meiningen in 1818. William's successful record of two 20-year monogamous and devoted relationships with Dora and Adelaide, and his outstanding record of paternal devotion, both argue against the conventional portrait of William IV simply as a buffoon and a clown. His husbandly and fatherly virtues complemented a lifelong pattern of liking and being concerned about other people and especially about women, of intervening to help them when he could, of being honorable about his financial obligations, of failing in vindictiveness toward former enemies. He was tactless but true. Giving him a backhanded compliment, his *Spectator* obituary sniffed, "His late Majesty, though at times a jovial and, for a King, an honest man, was a weak, ignorant, commonplace sort of person." The *Times* more charitably stressed, "he was not a man of talent or much refinement…. But he had a warm heart, and it was an English heart."

A few years after losing Polly Finch, in 1791, the Duke of Clarence, frequenting the Theatre Royal in Drury Lane, fell madly in love with the greatest comic actress on the English stage of her day, Dora Jordan. Over the next 20 years, this notably harmonious and monogamous liaison produced 10 children. Even though the Duke had sired his 10 Fitzclarence bastards by Dora outside of wedlock, in all other respects he exemplified devotion both to her and to their children. He repeated this pattern after he married Adelaide. In 1797, as the new Ranger of Bushy Park, William acquired its accompanying house and estate, where he and Dora brought up the Fitzclarences. Bushy was a happy home. As Dora wrote to a friend in 1809, "We shall have a full and merry house at Christmas…. A happier set, when altogether *[sic]* I believe never existed."

Alas, the Duke eventually separated from Dora in 1811. Dora herself thought that money pressures drove him to seek an heiress to marry him into solvency. In fact, she even counseled her former lover about how to woo his heiress: "*be cautious* for fear of a *disappointment*. All women are not to be taken by an open attack, and a *premeditated* one stands a *worse chance* than any *other*." Others have speculated about increased pressure from his mother to marry a suitable German princess. William also realized that he was third in line to succeed his father as King of Hanover and fourth in line to become King of Great Britain.

Twenty years of Dora Jordan did not make the Duke any more successful with other women in 1811. Although Dora had advised him in his campaign, William failed to secure his heiress. William scrupulously paid a generous financial settlement made to Dora. However, she died abroad in 1816, alone and greatly distressed by illness and debts. Then, the unexpected death of his niece Charlotte of Wales in 1817 drew William even closer to the British throne of the mad George III. If the now-childless Prince Regent (later George IV) and the childless Duke of York both died, William would become King of Great Britain.

This prospect gave new urgency to the tasks of marrying and begetting. However, several subsequent proposals also wilted on the vine. Fortunately, William successfully proposed to Adelaide in 1818, beginning 12 years of contentment together as Duke and Duchess and then seven years together as King and Queen Consort. The Duke of Clarence, although madly in love with another woman, had reluctantly bowed to his dynastic duty and finally wed a German princess whom he had never met before. Luckily, William and Adelaide took to each other immediately and lived in notable harmony until his death almost 20 years later.

Interestingly enough, both Dora Jordan and Queen Adelaide behaved admirably in many respects. Devoted to her Duke, Dora worked incessantly for him and all of her children as well as displayed great constancy and love. For her part, Adelaide strove to love her husband and the children tragically torn from her by death between 1819 and 1822: the premature Charlotte, three-months-old Elizabeth, and stillborn twins. Adelaide also cared for his Fitzclarence bastards and his grandchildren. Many of them repaid her kindness with ingratitude and discourtesy.

Indeed, Adelaide's sterling qualities appear most clearly in her attitude towards Dora Jordan herself. Before William eventually took Adelaide home to Bushy, where he and Dora had lived for so long, he had ordered Dora's portraits taken down. Adelaide explained to him why she had a portrait of Dora restored to its proper place over the mantelpiece: "the picture had long hung there; it was the picture of the mother of your children and it was not fit it should be displaced. You must gratify me, and let it remain." After William's death, Adelaide, finding hundreds of letters from Dora to the Duke, preserved them to pass on to a Fitzclarence son.

Adelaide, Dora, and William all exemplified homely but difficult-to-practice virtues. So far from simply being a buffoon, William was a good man, fallible but honorable and also lucky in the two women who loved him and whom he loved. Setting aside the conventional contempt of William, it seems as if the feeling of the common people about him was more accurate. He was popular, as royal historian Roger Fulford commented, "for there is no surer way to popularity in England than to be a character—to be the kind of person of whom anecdotes are told. Especially is this true of a crowned character."

The anecdotes abound. Awakened to hear the news of his accession after the death of George IV, he returned to his bed "in order to enjoy the novelty of sleeping with a Queen." Mobbed by well-wishers when walking unattended, as well as kissed by an Irish whore, he couldn't see why he should restrict his movements now that he was King: "Oh, never mind all this: when I have walked about a few times they will get used to it, and will take no notice." William's Coronation struck him as "a useless and ill-timed expense," and he agreed only to a much-scaled-down version. His daily life was as unpretentious. Disregarding Court etiquette, William issued impromptu invitations to naval friends: "do not bother about clothes. The Queen does nothing but embroider flowers after dinner." Although unpretentious, he held strong, quirky opinions, such as "all pictures of sacred subjects are improper and ought to be destroyed" and "I know no person so perfectly disagreeable and even dangerous as an author." He could be equally downright in his approach to people. Although William was very fond of his niece and heiress presumptive Victoria, he loathed her mother, the Duchess of Kent. After much arrogant and silly provocation from the Duchess, the King dressed her down in a ferocious public scolding. No wonder Victoria remembered him fondly as "very odd and singular."

However rough his manners, William had a nobler heart than many a smoother character. He referred to Adelaide as "this beloved and superior woman" and commented after his separation from Dora, "I cannot help thinking her one of the most perfect women in the world." In 1830, almost 20 years after leaving her, in one of his first acts as King, the 64-year-old William IV commissioned Sir Francis Chantrey to create a lovely marble sculpture of Dora Jordan, tenderly mothering two of their children. Denied for many decades the place of honor that he wanted for it, the sculpture now sits in Buckingham Palace near portraits of William and Adelaide.

William IV Sites

William was born in **Buckingham House**. His childhood, like that of his siblings, was divided between Buckingham House, Richmond Lodge, and Kew Palace.

On his creation as Duke of Clarence, William was provided with an apartment at **St. James's Palace** (see *Henry VIII*). It's a large, rather sprawling and irregularly shaped building between the end of St. James's Street and the Mall, next door to Clarence House (below). St. James's Palace was built by Henry VIII. After Queen Anne brought the court to the Palace following the fire at Whitehall Palace, it remained an official royal residence until the death of William IV, when his successor Queen Victoria chose to live in Buckingham Palace. A history and description of the functions of St. James's Palace can be read at http://www.royal.gov.uk/output/Page562.asp. Because it comprises the private residences of members of the royal family and offices, it is not open to the public. The buildings can be seen from the nearby Green Park.

The **Theatre Royal, Drury Lane**, in Catherine Street, is the oldest theater in London. For over 25 years, Dorothy or Dorothea (Dora) Jordan was a very popular actress there, and it's likely that that's where William first saw her. The present building dates from 1812 (remodelled in 1922), so it would have been quite new when Dora gave her last performance in 1815. See *Charles II* for more information.

Bushy House, the home that went with William's job as Ranger of Bushy Park, and which he shared with Dora and their children, stands in the park, near Hampton Court Palace. It is now used by the National Physical Laboratory. According to its website, the NPL, in "its role as the UK's national standards laboratory maintains the nation's standards for most physical measurements, including time, length, mass, density and force." The NPL includes a history of the house at http://www.npl.co.uk/about/bushy_house_history/, which is well worth reading: the history is detailed, and there are some fine photographs. During the Second World War, the Supreme Headquarters Allied Expeditionary Force under Major General Dwight D. Eisenhower was located in Bushy House; Operation Overlord was planned from there. Bushy Park is noted for its fine, old trees, particularly a mile-long triple avenue of chestnuts and limes leading to the Diana Fountain (not to be confused with the Diana Memorial Fountain in Hyde Park), near the gates to Hampton Court Palace. Instructions for getting to Bushy House and Park can be found at http://www.npl.co.uk/location/, with links to detailed maps. Visits can be usefully combined with those to Hampton Court.

William married Princess Adelaide of Saxe-Meiningen in **Kew Palace** in 1818. Adelaide was born in **Meiningen** in 1792. Meiningen, a city of about 25,000 population, is situated in Thuringia, in the middle of Germany, northeast of Frankfurt and southwest of Gotha, on the Werra river. It was first mentioned in the 10th century and became the capital of the Duchy of Saxe-Meiningen. The city is otherwise famous for its theatrical performances, the Meiningen Players, which began in the late 19th century in the ducal theater; also, its ducal orchestra became famous. See the theater at its website, http://www.meiningen.de/, and the city itself at http://meiningen-online.de/ (both in German).

Clarence House was built in 1825 by Nash for William and Adelaide. A white stucco house, Clarence House stands along the Mall between Lancaster House and St. James's Palace, in Stable Yard. In the middle of the 20th century, it was restored for the newly married Princess Elizabeth (later Elizabeth II) and Prince Philip of Greece and Denmark, who became the Duke of Edinburgh, and it was their London home until her accession to the throne in 1952. From 1953 until her death, it was the London residence of Elizabeth II's mother, Queen Elizabeth, the Queen Mother. When she was in residence, a piper played in the garden every morning at 9 a.m. Since her death, it has undergone extensive refurbishment and redecoration to become the new London residence of her grandson Charles, Prince of Wales, and his sons, Princes William and Harry. Visiting details, with a map, can be seen at http://www.royal.gov.uk/output/page2262.asp.

George III's son William always enjoyed visits to the **Brighton Pavilion**, joining his brother George, as Prince of Wales and later George IV, in drinking bouts, and, both having strong heads, drinking other guests under the table. After William became King, he and Adelaide enjoyed entertaining at the Pavilion. William would invite between 30 and 100 guests to dinner every day, choosing their names from lists the hotels sent him. Although he was generous with his hospitality, the food was very plain. He and Adelaide had suffered from indigestion following George IV's rich, lavish meals, so he replaced the latter's many French chefs with English ones, a move largely unappreciated by guests who had known both regimens. For the Pavilion, see *George IV*.

On his accession to the throne, William inherited the work-in-progress that was the transformation of **Buckingham House** into **Buckingham Palace**. For background information, see *George III*; for George IV's improvement, see *George IV*. Unfortunately, the expense was extraordinary. He sacked John Nash and had the work completed under Edward Blore. Ironically, he was never to live in the palace himself. The state rooms of Buckingham Palace are open to the public during August and September. See http://www.royalcollection.org.uk/default.asp?action=article&ID=30 for visiting details including public transport and a link to a map. A history and a description of some of the state rooms can be read at http://www.royal.gov.uk/output/Page568.asp.

Dora Jordan died in **St-Cloud**, France, in 1816. St-Cloud is a western suburb of Paris, on the river Seine. Its main features are its famous racetrack and the park, the Domaine National de Saint-Cloud. The latter forms the major remnant of the former château, destroyed during the German occupation of 1870–71: the park is notable for its waterworks, the Grande Cascade (in operation on Sundays in June) and the Grand Jet, along with other waterjets, fountains, and ponds.

William is buried beneath the **Albert Memorial Chapel** at Windsor Castle, along with his father, George III; his mother, Queen Charlotte; and five of his brothers, including George IV. For information about the Chapel, see *Victoria*.

After William's death, Queen Adelaide lived at **Marlborough House** (see *Anne*). She died in 1847, in Stanmore at **Bentley Priory**, at that time the home of the Marquesses of Abercorn. Bentley Priory was founded around 1170, housing Augustinian friars. After the Dissolution of the Monasteries under Henry VIII, nothing is known of the priory until 1766, when the estate was sold to James Duberly. He pulled down the original priory building and had Sir John Soane build him a contemporary house, at some distance from the original priory. He sold the house in 1788 to the Marquess of Abercorn. Queen Adelaide then leased the priory from April 1846 until her death in December 1849, at the priory. Bentley Priory later passed through other hands, being a hotel and a girls' school at different times. During the Second World War, it housed the headquarters of Fighter Command, based at the priory until disbanding in 1968. The D-Day landings were planned at the house. Today, the house remains in the hands of the Royal Air Force, and the latter has provided a history of the house, with photographs, at http://www.raf.mod.uk/stations/bentley.html.

The city of **Adelaide, Australia**, was named after Queen Adelaide at William's request. The main street in Adelaide is King William Street, one of many in cities developed during his reign.

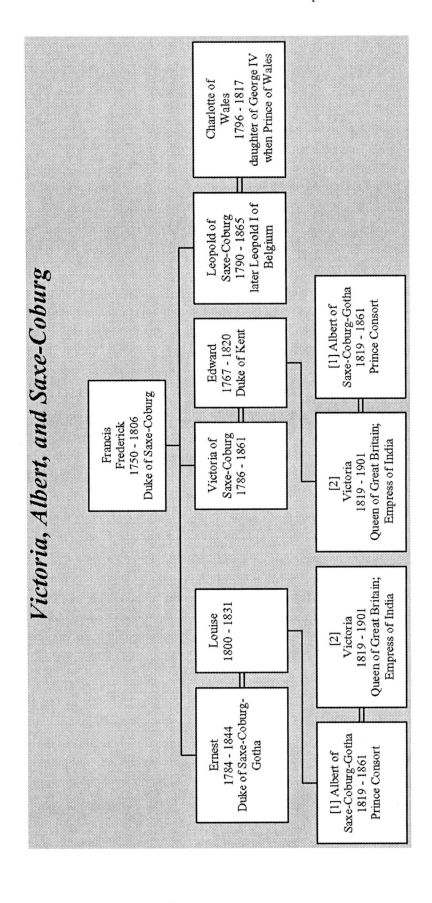

Victoria, Albert, and Saxe-Coburg

Victoria (1819–1901; reigned as Queen of Great Britain and Ireland, 1837–1901, and as Empress of India, 1877–1901)

Oscar Wilde—that celebrated victim of Victorian mores—actually admired Queen Victoria, calling her one of the three great personalities of their era. Anyone addicted to anecdotes and biographies about Victoria feels the same fascination as Wilde did. We do not remember Victoria for her accomplishments and her deeds so much as for her personality—for its perennial egotism and the imperiousness conceded to one who was, after all, imperial. In enjoying her life, we view her egotism at a safe distance, and we experience vicariously the pleasures of acting exactly as we please—out of the best motivations, of course. No one can doubt Victoria's impeccable honesty, virtuous intentions, and essential goodness; these, bundled up with her passionate nature, unselfconsciousness, and lack of emotional inhibition, made her a memorable "character." Hers was indeed a passionate life, largely spent in dominating others or in seeking to be dominated and protected. The irritation, alienation, and aversion with which others often reacted to her egotism softened—as she reached a great age and the end of the longest reign—into a reverence that did not quite forget her intensely human faults. Her mother, her husband, their children and grandchildren, her Ministers, her servants—all experienced the full flood of Victoria's extraordinary personality.

Most often remembered as an obese and elderly matriarch of a far-flung royal line, Victoria had begun her reign more than 60 years earlier as a tiny young girl who, on the evening of her coronation day, ran up the stairs at Buckingham Palace to bathe her spaniel, Dash. Still earlier, as the fatherless Princess Victoria, heiress presumptive to her paternal uncle William IV, she had been caught between "Uncle King" and her mother, the Duchess of Kent, as they strove in mutual deep disdain. The Duchess's ambitions to be Regent after the death of William IV caused her to combine with her adviser, Sir John Conroy, in attempts to bully and manipulate Victoria into submission. With the support of her beloved governess, Louise Lehzen, Victoria resisted these controlling maneuvers, and William IV even announced in public his determination to live past Victoria's 18th birthday in order to frustrate his sister-in-law. Upon becoming Queen in 1837, Victoria politely broke with the mother whom she now thoroughly distrusted and disliked. Her fervent attachment to her faithful servant Lehzen presaged other such relationships in her future. While she addressed Lehzen as "Mother," Victoria coolly kept the Duchess at a distance; at her 1840 wedding, the bride Victoria kissed her aunt Queen Adelaide, but she merely shook hands with the Duchess.

Victoria's passionate advocacy of Lehzen and denigration of the Duchess and Conroy led to the Flora Hastings scandal that considerably decreased the newly crowned Queen's popularity. Victoria and Lehzen, among others, gossiped that Conroy's friend, Lady Flora (a lady-in-waiting to the Duchess of Kent), had become pregnant by him. Although Victoria eventually apologized for her groundless slander, the press seized the matter, and then Lady Flora died of liver cancer, which increased public disapproval of the Queen's behavior. This unpleasantness (and her consciousness of being in the wrong) further soured the Queen's feelings about the Duchess.

In 1839, however, Victoria fell madly in love with the person who would supersede both her mother and Lehzen in her affections: Albert of Saxe-Coburg-Gotha, her maternal first cousin. Their older relatives had long planned the match, but Victoria resisted, until Albert's physical attractiveness turned her head and ignited a passion that lasted for 60 years, long after Albert's own early death.

Not content merely to breed for the succession, conscious of his considerable gifts as a statesman, Albert resented his ornamental status and strove to exert greater political influence. He conceived of the monarchy as a dispassionate and disinterested but potent and influential force in British affairs, and he honorably sought to meet that ideal. Distrusted and excluded by many as a meddling foreigner, Albert gained some recognition for his organization of the 1851 Great Exhibition at the Crystal Palace, and he became Prince Consort in 1857. More and more obsessed with his responsibilities, Albert worked himself into a state of exhaustion, and his health failed. His last bit of meddling, during his deathbed illness, averted armed conflict between the United States (then embroiled in its Civil War) and Great Britain over the *Trent* affair. After he died of typhoid fever in 1861, when he and Victoria were both 42 years old, Benjamin Disraeli commented, "With Prince Albert we have buried our sovereign. This German Prince has governed England for twenty-one years with a wisdom and energy such as none of our Kings have ever shown."

Albert's untimely death crushed Victoria. For two decades, the Queen had relied on her husband's guidance in discharging her duties as sovereign and mother of their nine children—the first born in 1840, the last in 1857. She had regarded their marital relationship as far more important than her relationship with her sons and daughters. Now severed from Albert by death, Victoria entered a dark tunnel of mourning from which she would not really begin to emerge for over a decade. For the 40 years of life that remained to her, she would have Albert's room preserved as he left it—with his clothes laid out every evening and hot water ready on his washstand. During a visit to Florence in 1888, Victoria showed the Duomo to Albert's visage portrayed on a locket she carried, so that Albert could view the improvements wrought by repairs.

In her boundless grief, Victoria assumed his responsibilities of state. Much less suited to this task than he, the Queen insisted on continuing his work—the immense burden of which, she said, prevented her from exercising her more ceremonial duties as a sovereign. Her consequent isolation and her neglect of her subjects' expectations—prolonged over many years—would bring increasing criticism, which the Queen usually ignored. Her behavior provoked worry about her emotional stability.

Albert's death also caused Victoria to treat their oldest son, Bertie (later Edward VII), with extreme aversion, because she blamed Bertie for worrying his father with sexual misbehavior and thereby causing Albert's death. Her irrational and abusive attitude continued a pattern begun by both Victoria and Albert in Bertie's early childhood of punishing his perceived inferiority of character with ever-increasing severity and guilt. The widowed Victoria would always seek to control and direct Bertie, as well as her other eight children. Like many other parents, the Queen indulged her 40 grandchildren far more than she had her own offspring.

Victoria indulged her Ministers no more than she did her children. She expected them to travel 600 miles to Balmoral in Scotland to attend on her there. (After spending her years as a Princess in Kensington Palace, Victoria during her marriage established a cycle during which she spent the earlier months of the year at Buckingham Palace and Windsor Castle, spring and early summer at Osborne, later summer back at Buckingham Palace, August at Balmoral, early winter at Osborne, and Christmas at Windsor. Other migratory patterns developed in later years.) In addition, her emotionality often intensified her highly partial relationships to her Ministers.

As a young, unmarried Queen, she enjoyed an infatuation with William Lamb, 2nd Viscount Melbourne, her first Prime Minister. Grieved by the prospect of losing the urbane Melbourne, she refused to replace some of the Whig ladies of her Household with Tories, as requested by the prospective Prime Minister, Sir Robert Peel—thus precipitating the Bedchamber Crisis. Later, both Victoria and Albert repeatedly tangled with Henry Temple, 3rd Viscount Palmerston, when Palmerston served as Foreign Secretary and as Home Secretary, although their relationship calmed down when he became Prime Minister. Notorious for her steady dislike of William Gladstone, four times her Prime Minister ("this half crazy & really in many ways ridiculous old man"), Victoria warmed to Gladstone's great antagonist, Benjamin Disraeli, with whom she established as intense a relationship as she had had with the beloved Melbourne.

Just as intense were her relationships with her servants and courtiers, who shivered with her Ministers in her frigid palaces because of Victoria's insensitivity to the cold. Albert had detested her adored Lehzen and finally gotten rid of her. After Albert's death, Victoria became greatly attached to Albert's ghillie, the Scotsman John Brown. She seemed to feel protected by him, as well as comforted by his fervent, if domineering, loyalty and devotion. After Brown's 1883 death, Victoria mourned "my best and truest friend," "the truest heart that ever beat," crying "all, all is gone in this world, and all seems unhinged again in thousands of ways." Four years later, Abdul Karim (the Munshi) became her *munshi* (secretary), and she became his partisan, as she had been Brown's, against her outraged Household and family.

Obstinate and willful from her girlhood, Victoria stood her ground against all opposition to her preferences and favorites. She had directed her servants to conceal in her coffin John Brown's photograph and a lock of his hair, hidden from her family's gaze in her left hand under flowers. From her childhood, too, others had noted her regal bearing—remarkable in one so tiny and, later, so dumpy and ill-dressed. Rather than wear at her Golden Jubilee in 1887 the crown and robes of state cast off since Albert's death in 1861, the Queen ignored her Ministers and her family and kept on her widow's bonnet. She needed no crown to seem royal.

Victoria Sites

Victoria was born in **Kensington Palace**, and baptized in its **Cupola Room** (see *George I*). Her father died when she was very small, at **Woolbrook Glen**, or **Cottage**, in **Sidmouth**. This small white house is now the Royal Glen Hotel. Read the history of the house at http://freespace.virgin.net/sidmouthroyalglen.hotel/Pages/history.html; and about royal visits to Sidmouth, with photographs, at http://www.visitsidmouth.co.uk/guide/royal.htm. From Sidmouth, his coffin was transported to Windsor Castle. Its great length caused it to get stuck as it was being lowered into the entrance of the royal vault.

After Edward's death, his widow, the Duchess of Kent, along with her son and daughter from her previous marriage, and their infant daughter Victoria, continued to live at **Kensington Palace**. They converted the **King's State Bedchamber** into a bedroom for Princess Victoria; the wall between the **Great** and **Little Closet** was removed to make the **Duchess of Kent's Dressing Room**; and they partitioned the **King's Gallery** into three rooms for themselves, along with other takeovers, without permission—to William IV's fury. Princess Victoria's bedroom, now called **Queen Victoria's Bedroom,** remains to this day, as does the **Duchess of Kent's Dressing Room**, but the **King's Gallery** was restored as such in 1993–94. For more regarding the Victoria Rooms, see *Victoria*.

However, Victoria spent some holidays at the seaside, as at **Norris Castle, East Cowes**, and **Pierremont Hall** in **Broadstairs**. Norris Castle, designed by Wyatt in the late 18th century, remains a private home; see it at http://www.iwight.com/just_visiting/towns/eastcowes.asp. Broadstairs lies between Margate and Ramsgate on the eastern shore of Kent, and is smaller than they, although developing a residential population. Like them, it's a seaside resort; Pierremont Hall today houses various council offices. Visit Broadstairs at http://www.broadstairs.gov.uk/. She also visited **Cheltenham** (see *George III*) and stayed in **Bognor**, on the West Sussex coast, between Portsmouth and Brighton; Bognor added the word Regis to its name after George V convalesced nearby in 1929 and has about 40,000 population. The best website for our purposes is http://www.bognor-local-history.co.uk/.

Heir apparent to William IV in 1837, Princess Victoria was asleep in the room in **Kensington Palace** in her bedroom, previously the **King's State Bedchamber** and still known as **Queen Victoria's Bedroom**, when she was awakened early with the news of her accession to the throne. Although she moved to **Buckingham Palace** very soon, she took a keen interest in the 1898 restoration of the **State Apartments**, opened to the public on her 80th birthday, May 24, 1899. The rooms she and her mother had occupied had been lived in by other royals throughout her reign, but the State Apartments had been left to languish. Their restoration was triggered by a newspaper article, and her interest persuaded Parliament to pay, with the condition that they be made accessible to public visitors. Much cleaning needed to be done to uncover the paint and giltwork, and the rooms were then hung with portraits and other paintings and furnishings to reflect past inhabitants, work which continued after her death. Queen Mary, consort of Victoria's grandson George V, in 1932–33 arranged the old Queen's previous bedroom, **Queen Victoria's Bedroom**, to include some of the furniture used by Victoria, including her bed and portable writing desk. The **Duchess of Kent's Dressing Room** was furnished to reflect her mother's earlier life there. See the Victorian Rooms at http://www.hrp.org.uk/webcode/content.asp?ID=404.

Buckingham Palace was now her home, freshly completed during William IV's reign. But it was only after Victoria married Prince Albert and began having their children that the need for further development became clear.

Albert was born in the castle of **Rosenau**, a country residence for the Dukes of Coburg tucked into the forested halls around. Here he had been raised quietly in a rural setting. Information about and photographs of Schloss Rosenau appear at http://www.sgvcoburg.de/ (more photographs and in German) and http://www.schloesser.bayern.de/englisch/palace/objects/co_rosen.htm (in English, but only two views).

A painting of Rosenau by J.M.W. Turner is in the Liverpool Art Gallery, England—view it at http://www.liverpoolmuseums.org.uk/sudley/collections/turner-coburg.asp; William Callow's *Souvenirs of Rosenau* can be seen in the Bridgeman Art Library online at Image IDs 25712-25716. To access these images, go to http://www.bridgeman.co.uk/search/quick_search.asp, and enter the Image IDs.

The home of the Dukes of Coburg was **Veste Coburg**, dating from 1075. Situated on a rocky outcrop overlooking the valley of the Itz and dominating Coburg, Veste Coburg is enclosed by three walls, parts of which form the oldest extant structures of the castle. The various buildings of this massive complex were added over the centuries so there is no one style; the castle was falling into neglect until 1838, when Albert's father, Duke Ernest I, began its restoration. Martin Luther had taken refuge here for several months during 1530, and Luther memorabilia are displayed within the fortress. Otherwise, there are displays of arms and armor, sleighs and carriages, and significant paintings by Lucas Cranach. Coburg is a city of 46,000 population, tucked into the middle of Germany, to the east of Frankfurt, on the river Itz. The webpage for **Coburg** is http://www.coburg-tourist.com/com/englisch/index_1.html.

Victoria and Albert were married in the **Chapel Royal, St. James's Palace** in 1840. Their main contribution to **Buckingham Palace** was to remove the iron railings and Marble Arch from the opened fourth side, enclosing this with buildings to form a quadrangle. Apartments for visitors occupied the ground floor, and the much-needed nurseries were above. They also extended the State Apartments with new galleries, the **Ballroom** and **Ball Supper Room**. Albert involved himself in the redecoration of many of the rooms in the palace. In her widowhood, Victoria was to live for most of the time at Windsor Castle and her other homes; her eldest son, Edward VII, was to restore the palace to splendor when he came to the throne. For visiting details, see *William IV*.

Victoria and Albert bought **Osborne House** in 1845, as a home with the privacy they needed for themselves and their growing family. Seeing the house as too small, they had it pulled down, and then Albert worked with Thomas Cubitt on the design of a new home, in a style based on Italian villas. The work went quickly, and the house was ready in 1846 for their occupation. Albert also supervised the landscaping of the grounds, creating a park. Half a mile east of the house, the Swiss Cottage was built for their children. After Albert's death in 1861, Victoria decreed that nothing be changed in the house; she spent a lot of time in Osborne House, eventually dying there in 1901.

After her death, her successor Edward VII presented Osborne to the nation as a memorial to his mother. Part of it was then made into a convalescent home for officers and civil servants; for a while the Swiss Cottage was used as the Royal Naval Training College, but this closed in 1921, and the Cottage now contains a small museum. Visitors today can see both Osborne House and the Swiss Cottage; it's open to the public all year, at varying times depending on the season. The best site for visiting details is http://www.tourist-information-uk.com/osborne-house.htm. or http://www.islandbreaks.co.uk/what_to_see_and_do/attractions/detailed.

asp?id=40. Osborne House still preserves the royal family's way of life; objects include Victoria's bathing-machine.

At Osborne, the family worshiped at **St. Mildred's Church, Whippingham**. The church, built from 1854–62, is said to have been designed by Albert. See the Royal Pew at http://www.iow.uk.com/whippingham-church/royalpew.htm, although in Victoria's day they sat on chairs—the pews were ordered by Edward VII. In the Royal Pew area of the church are memorial windows to Victoria's children Princess Alice and Prince Leopold, along with the Queen's grandsons, the Princess Royal's two sons who died as children. The Royal Pew and the Battenberg Chapel are at either side of the chancel in St. Mildred's. Victoria's daughter Princess Beatrice married Prince Henry of Battenberg in the church.

Victoria had fallen in love with the **Scottish Highlands** during visits in the Royal yacht; to Albert, the landscape was reminiscent of his childhood home. On one of their trips, they visited **Blair Castle**, where Victoria conferred on its owners, the Dukes of Atholl, the distinction of being allowed to maintain a private army. For more information, see *Charles Edward Stuart*.

In 1848, they rented **Balmoral House**, near **Braemar**, and bought the estate in 1852. Three years later, **Balmoral Castle** was ready for the family, a curious blend of idealized baronial and Scottish country house styles. Balmoral was unlike Osborne in that it was less isolated from a local community. As does the royal family today, Victoria and Albert's family members participated in the life of **Braemar**, attending the annual Braemar gathering, and they enjoyed walking, travelling, and visiting in the area. Balmoral today is a working estate and a favorite home of the present royal family, present during August and September. Consequently, it may be visited only from the beginning of April to the end of July each year during the usual hours of 10 a.m. to 5 p.m., with the last visitors admitted at 4 p.m. If you're into horseback riding, you may be interested in pony trekking, which must be booked in advance. For details, see http://www.royal.gov.uk/output/Page585.asp, and http://www.balmoralcastle.com/, the latter providing details of all the activities available.

In 1893, Victoria had **Crathie Kirk** built near the gates of the castle. From the outside, it looks like a simple Highland church, but the interior was built along the lines of the grandest of Victorian churches. The present royal family, when in residence at Balmoral, attends Sunday morning services there, and Princess Anne, daughter to Elizabeth II and herself the Princess Royal, chose it for her second wedding. See the church at http://www.ballaterscotland.com/tourism/b&c.htm and http://www.luxuryscotland.co.uk/directory_associates/scotlandmag/queenvictoria.html.

The **Braemar Gathering and Highland Games**, the ne plus ultra of Highland games, are held in the village of Braemar on the first Saturday in September. Pipe bands, Highland dancers, and macho events like tossing the caber, putting the stone, and throwing the hammer, let alone the tug of war contest, are all featured. Read about it at http://www.royal-deeside.org.uk/RDnews/gathering.htm. Note the warning that tickets and accommodation should be booked in advance, due to the popularity of the event.

In 1842, Victoria paid her first state visit to Scotland. Like George IV, she didn't stay at **Holyroodhouse**; but after she and Albert had established themselves in Balmoral Castle, the palace in Edinburgh made for a convenient stop. Under Robert Matheson, Holyrood Palace was restored, Albert taking his usual interest in the project. Not only was the interior spruced up, but the grounds also, and new entrances were made to avoid the nearby slums, breweries, and gasworks. Matheson modelled a new fountain on the one in **Linlithgow Palace** (see *Mary Queen of Scots*), and rooms in the palace were opened to the public.

In England, Albert was a prime mover behind the Great Exhibition of 1851 and the construction of the huge glass and iron **Crystal Palace**, designed by Sir Joseph Paxton, to house it. **Hyde Park** was the venue; it was only after the exhibition that the Crystal Palace was moved to Sydenham Hill. Over 6 million visitors viewed 13,000 exhibits from all over the world, the profits later fueling public works like the Albert Hall, the Science and Natural History Museums, and the Victoria & Albert Museum; the latter, for example, grew from a collection of applied art bought from the exhibition. After the exhibition closed, and the Crystal

Palace was reconstructed at Sydenham Hill, a 200-acre theme park developed around it featured fountains, statues, animal and geological displays, and even fireworks. Later, it was used for the development of television, but burned to the ground in 1936. The last remnants were removed in 1941 because they provided a guide for enemy bombers. See the **Crystal Palace** and read all about it at http://www.victorianstation.com/palace.html.

The museums complex in south Kensington drew on the exhibition, with Albert's strong encouragement and interest in the arts and sciences. Thus grew the **Natural History Museum** (http://www.nhm.ac.uk/), the **Science Museum** (see *George III*), and the **Victoria and Albert Museum** (http://www.vam.ac.uk/index.html).

After Albert's early death in 1861, Sir George Gilbert Scott was engaged to create the **Albert Memorial**, which stands on the south side of Hyde Park, between Queen's and Alexandra Gates. The execution comprised 175 lifesize figures surrounding the central figure of Albert, over four meters high, within a soaring Gothic cage. It's glorious and hideous at the same time; see it and judge for yourself at http://www.victorianweb.org/sculpture/albertmem/, with a closer view at http://www.travellondon.com/templates/attractions/gallery_albertmemorial.html. Opposite it, the **Royal Albert Hall**, opened in 1871, makes a definite contrast, architecturally: the Hall is classical, restrained, and even bare. It hosts musical events of all kinds and is famous for the summer promenade concerts, or Proms, which make serious music fun and popular from July to September. Visit the Hall at http://www.royalalberthall.com/.

The rebuilding of the **Houses of Parliament**, after the 1834 fire, also had absorbed Albert's interest. He chaired the Select Committee which worked on the decoration of the interior. Work began in 1837 under Charles Barry for the planning and construction, and A.W.N. Pugin for the decoration and ornament. The House of Lords was completed in 1847, and the House of Commons in 1852. During 1941–41, the House of Commons was largely destroyed in the bombing of London but later rebuilt by Sir Giles Gilbert Scott, a grandson of Sir George Gilbert Scott. The Victorian detailing was not restored. The Houses of Parliament (Palace of Westminster) website is http://www.parliament.uk/, where visiting and other details can be read; tours are somewhat restricted, so times need to be heeded. Overseas visitors are permitted to take tours only during the summer opening.

George IV had left **Windsor Castle** in good order. Victoria carried out some minor work, reconstructing the **Grand Staircase** and, in the Lower Ward, restoring the **Curfew Tower** and the **Horseshoe Cloisters**. She created a new private chapel, which burned in 1992; but her major work was remodelling the disused chapel east of St. George's Chapel into the **Albert Memorial Chapel**. Sir George Gilbert Scott was the architect. Richly decorated, it contains a marble effigy of Albert, by Henri de Triqueti, and the dominating tomb of the eldest son of Edward VII, Victoria's grandson, the Duke of Clarence. Visit the Albert Memorial Chapel at http://www.stgeorges-windsor.org/tour/tour_albert.asp.

In 1841 Victoria gave **Frogmore House** to her mother, the Duchess of Kent, who died there in 1861. The **Frogmore** estate has been in royal ownership since the reign of Henry VIII. The original house, built between 1680 and 1684, has been added to since. George III bought the house for Queen Charlotte in 1792, and she used it as a country retreat. After Albert's death (also in 1861), Victoria chose Frogmore for the site of the **Royal Mausoleum**, where he was buried, and where she visited frequently. Every December 14, the anniversary of his death, a service was held there. When she herself died in January 1901, her body was placed beside his. For more information about Frogmore, see *George III*.

The latest of the royal residences is **Sandringham House**, in Norfolk, near the village of Dersingham. Victoria bought the estate for the Prince of Wales, who commissioned A.J. Humbert to design the current house. It became a beloved home for later monarchs also; the current royal family members gather there at Christmas. Visit Sandringham at http://www.royal.gov.uk/output/page561.asp.

Suggested Reading for <u>Royals of England</u>

Allmand, Christopher. *Henry V*. Berkeley: University of California Press, 1992.

Ashdown-Hill, John. "The Lancastrian claim to the throne." *Ricardian*, <u>XIII</u>(2003), 27-38.

Ashley, Maurice. *James II*. London: Dent, 1977.

_____. *The life and times of William I*. New York: Cross River Press, 1992.

_____. *The Stuarts*. Berkeley: University of California Press, 2000.

Auchincloss, Louis. *Persons of consequence: Queen Victoria and her circle*. New York: Random House, 1979.

Baldwin, James. *Elizabeth Woodville*. Gloucestershire: Sutton, 2002.

Barber, Richard. *The Devil's crown: a history of Henry II and his sons*. Conshohocken, PA: Combined Books, 1996.

_____. *Edward, Prince of Wales and Aquitaine: a biography of the Black Prince*. New York: Charles Scribner's Sons, 1978.

_____. *Henry Plantagenet* (new ed.). Woodbridge, Suffolk, UK and Rochester, NY: Boydell Press, 2001.

Barlow, Frank. *William Rufus*. Berkeley: University of California Press, 1983.

Bates, David. *William the Conqueror*. London: George Philip, 1989.

Beeson, Trevor. *Westminster Abbey*. [No Place Given]: FISA, no date.

Bennett, Daphne. *Queen Victoria's children*. London: Victor Gollancz, 1980.

Bevan, Bryan. *Henry IV*. New York: St. Martin's Press, 1994.

_____. *Henry VII : the first Tudor King*. London: Rubicon Press, 2000.

_____. *King Richard II.* London: Rubicon Press, 1990.

_____. *King William III: Prince of Orange, the first European.* London: Rubicon Press, 1997.

Blanchard, Laura. "Dramatic history of the first Queen Elizabeth." *Ricardian Register*, Winter 1997, 10-12. [available online at www.r3.org]

Bingham, Caroline. *James I of England.* London: Weidenfeld and Nicolson, 1981.

_____. *The life and times of Edward II.* London, Weidenfeld and Nicolson, 1973.

Bradbury, Jim. *Stephen and Matilda : the civil war of 1139-53.* Far Thrupp, Stroud, Gloucestershire: A. Sutton Pub., 1996.

Callow, John. *The making of King James II: the formative years of a fallen King.* Stroud, Gloucestershire: Sutton, 2000.

Cannon, John, and Griffiths, Ralph. *The Oxford illustrated history of the British monarchy.* Oxford and New York: Oxford University Press, 1988 & 1998.

Carlton, Charles. *Charles I, the personal monarch* (2nd ed.). London and New York: Routledge, 1995.

Carpenter, D.A. *The minority of Henry III.* Berkeley: University of California Press, 1990.

_____. *The reign of Henry III.* London and Rio Grande, Ohio: Hambledon Press, 1996.

Chancellor, John. *The life and times of Edward I.* London: Weidenfeld and Nicolson, 1981.

Chapman, Hester W. *Mary II, Queen of England.* London: Jonathan Cape, 1953.

Les Châteaux forts. [No City Given}: Éditions du Rocher, 1989.

Chibnall, Marjorie. *The Empress Matilda : Queen Consort, Queen Mother, and Lady of the English.* Oxford and Cambridge, Mass.: Blackwell, 1991.

Chrimes, S.B. *Henry VII.* Berkeley and Los Angeles: University of California Press, 1972.

Clanchy, M.T. *England and its rulers, 1066-1272, with an epilogue on Edward I (1272-1307)* (2nd ed.). Oxford and Malden, Mass.: Blackwell, 1998.

Clarke, John. *The life and times of George III.* London: Weidenfeld and Nicolson, 1972.

_____, and Ridley, Jasper. *The Houses of Hanover and Saxe-Coburg-Gotha.* Berkeley and Los Angeles: University of California Press, 2000.

Claydon, Tony. *William III and the godly revolution.* Cambridge and New York: Cambridge University Press, 1996.

Clive, Mary. *This sun of York.* New York: Knopf, 1974.

Corns, Thomas N. (Ed.). *The royal image: representations of Charles I.* Cambridge and New York: Cambridge University Press, 1999.

Corp, Edward. *The King over the water: portraits of the Stuarts in exile after 1689.* Edinburgh: Scottish National Portrait Gallery, 2001.

Croft, Pauline. *King James.* Houndmills, Basingstoke, Hampshire and New York: Palgrave Macmillan, 2003.

Cruickshanks, Eveline, and Corp, Edward (Eds.). *The Stuart court in exile and the Jacobites.* Rio Grande, OH: The Hambledon Press, 1995.

Curtis, Gila. *Life and times of Queen Anne.* London: Weidenfeld and Nicolson, 1972.

Daiches, David. *The last Stuart: the life and times of Bonnie Prince Charlie.* New York: G.P. Putnam's Sons, 1973.

David, Saul. *Prince of pleasure: the Prince of Wales and the making of the Regency.* New York: Atlantic Monthly Press, 1998.

Davis, R.H.C. *King Stephen, 1135-1154* (3rd ed.). London and New York: Longman, 1990.

Doherty, Paul. *Isabella and the strange death of Edward II.* New York: Carroll & Graf Publishers, 2003.

Dunn, Jane. *Elizabeth and Mary: cousins, rivals, Queens.* New York: Alfred A. Knopf, 2004.

Durston, Christopher. *Charles I.* London and New York: Routledge, 1998.

Earle, Peter. *The life and times of James II.* London: Weidenfeld and Nicolson, 1972.

Erickson, Carolly. *Bloody Mary.* New York: St. Martin's Griffin, 1998.

_____. *Mistress Anne.* New York: St. Martin's Griffin, 1998.

Falkus, Gila. *The life and times of Edward IV.* London: Weidenfeld and Nicolson, 1981.

Fields, Bertram. *Royal blood: Richard III and the mystery of the Princes.* New York: Regan Books, 1998.

Fothergill, Brian. *The Cardinal King.* London: Faber and Faber, 1958.

Fraser, Antonia. *King James VI of Scotland, I of England.* New York: Knopf, 1975.

_____. *Mary Queen of Scots*. New York: Dell, 1971.

_____. *Royal Charles*. New York: Alfred A. Knopf, 1980.

_____. *The warrior Queens*. New York: Viking, 1989.

_____. *The wives of Henry VIII*. New York: Vintage Books, 1994.

_____ (Ed.). *The lives of the Kings & Queens of England* (rev. and updated). Berkeley: University of California Press, 1998.

Fraser, Flora. *Princesses: the sx daughters of George III*. New York: Knopf, 2005.

_____. *The unruly Queen: the life of Queen Caroline*. New York: Knopf, 1996.

Fulford, Roger. *Hanover to Windsor*. London: B. T. Batsford, 1960.

_____. *Royal Dukes* (rev. ed.). London: Collins, 1973.

_____. *The wicked uncles* (reprint of 1933 edition). Freeport, NY: Books for Libraries, 1968.

Furtado, Peter, et al. (Ed.). *The Ordnance Survey guide to historic houses in Britain*. New York: W.W. Norton, 1987.

Gillingham, John. *The Angevin empire* (2nd ed.). London: Arnold; New York: Oxford University Press, 2001.

_____. *Richard I*. New Haven: Yale University Press, 1999.

Gillingham, John and Earle, Peter. *The Middle Ages*. Berkeley: University of California Press, 2000.

Goodman, Anthony. *John of Gaunt: the exercise of princely power in 14th-century Europe*. New York: St. Martin's Press, 1992.

Gregg, Edward. *Queen Anne* (rev. ed.). New Haven: Yale University Press, 2001.

Gregg, Pauline. *King Charles I*. Berkeley: University of California Press, 1984.

Griffiths, Ralph A. *The reign of King Henry VI* (2nd ed.). Gloucestershire: Sutton, 1998.

_____, and Thomas, Roger S. *The making of the Tudor dynasty*. Gloucestershire: Sutton, 1985.

Gross, Pamela M. *Jane, the Quene: third consort of King Henry VIII*. Lewiston, N.Y.: Edwin Mellen Press, 1999.

Hackett, Francis. *The personal history of Henry VIII*. New York: Modern Library, 1945.

Hamilton, Elizabeth. *William's Mary: a biography of Mary II*. New York: Taplinger, 1972.

Harriss, G.L. (Ed.). *Henry V : the practice of Kingship*. Oxford and New York: Oxford University Press, 1985.

Harvey, John. *The Plantagenets* (rev. ed.). London and Glasgow: Fontana/Collins, 1967.

Hatton, Ragnhild. *George I: Elector and King*. Cambridge, Mass.: Harvard University Press, 1978.

Hedley, Olwen. *Royal palaces: an account of the homes of British sovereigns from Saxon to modern times*. London: R.Hale, 1972.

Hibbert, Christopher. *Charles I*. New York: Harper and Row, 1968.

_____. *George III: a personal history*. New York: Basic Books, 1998.

_____. *George IV*. Harmondsworth: Penguin, 1976.

_____. *Queen Victoria: a personal history*. New York: Basic Books, 2000.

_____. *The Virgin Queen: Elizabeth I, genius of the Golden Age*. Reading, Mass.: Addison-Wesley, 1991.

Hicks, Michael. *Warwick the Kingmaker*. Oxford and Malden, Mass.: Blackwell Publishers, 1998.

Hollister, C. Warren. *Henry I*. edited and completed by Amanda Clark Frost. New Haven : Yale University Press, 2001.

Holme, Thea. *Caroline of Brunswick*. London: Hamish Hamilton, 1979.

Howarth, David. *1066 : the year of the Conquest*. Harmondsworth, Middlesex and New York: Viking, 1978.

Hutchison, Harold F. *Edward II*. New York: Stein and Day, 1971.

Iremonger, Lucille. *Love and the Princesses*. New York: Thomas Y. Crowell, 1958.

Ives, Eric. *The life and death of Anne Boleyn: "the most happy."* Malden, Mass.: Blackwell, 2004.

James, Susan E. *Kateryn Parr : the making of a Queen*. Aldershot, Hants and Brookfield, Vermont: Ashgate, 1999.

Johnson, P.A. *Duke Richard of York, 1411-1460*. Oxford and New York: Oxford University Press, 1988.

Johnson, Paul. *The life and times of Edward III*. London: Weidenfeld and Nicolson, 1973.

Jones, George Hilton. *Convergent forces: immediate causes of the Revolution of 1688 in England*. Ames: Iowa State University Press, 1990.

Jones, M.K., and Underwood, M.G. *The King's mother*. Cambridge and New York: Cambridge University Press, 1992.

Kenyon, J.P. *The Stuarts: a study in English kingship*. London and Glasgow: Fontana/Collins, 1958.

Kirby, J.L. *Henry IV of England*. London: Constable, 1970.

Lee, Maurice, Jr. *Great Britain's Solomon: James VI and I in his three Kingdoms*. Urbana: University of Illinois Press, 1990.

Lees-Milne, James. *The last Stuarts: British royalty in exile*. New York: Charles Scribner's Sons, 1984.

Levine, Mortimer. *Tudor dynastic problems, 1460-1571*. London, Allen and Unwin; New York, Barnes and Noble, 1973.

Lindsey, Karen. *Divorced, beheaded, survived: a feminist reinterpretation of the wives of Henry VIII*. Reading, Mass.: Addison-Wesley, 1995.

Linklater, Eric. *The royal house of Scotland*. London: Sphere, 1972.

Lloyd, Alan. *The maligned monarch: a life of King John of England*. Garden City, N.Y.: Doubleday, 1972.

Loach, Jennifer. *Edward VI*. Edited by George Bernard and Penry Williams. New Haven: Yale University Press, 1999.

Loades, David. *Chronicles of the Tudor Queens*. Gloucestershire: Sutton, 2002.

_____. *Elizabeth I*. London and New York: Hambledon and London, 2003.

_____. *Henry VIII and his Queens* (paperback edition of *Politics of marriage)*. Gloucestershire: A. Sutton, 1996.

_____. *Mary Tudor : a life*. Oxford and Cambridge, Mass.: Basil Blackwell, 1989.

Longford, Elizabeth (Ed.). *The Oxford book of royal anecdotes*. Oxford and New York: Oxford University Press, 1989.

Luke, Mary. *The nine days Queen : a portrait of Lady Jane Grey*. New York: W. Morrow, 1986.

MacCulloch, Diarmaid. *The boy King: Edward VI and the Protestant Reformation*. New York: Palgrave, 2001.

Marlow, Joyce. *The life and times of George I*. London: Weidenfeld and Nicolson, 1973.

Marples, Morris. *Poor Fred and the Butcher: sons of George II*. London: Michael Joseph, 1970.

_____. *Six royal sisters*. London: Michael Joseph, 1969.

_____. *Wicked uncles in love*. London: Michael Joseph, 1972.

Marshall, Rosalind K. *Bonnie Prince Charlie*. Edinburgh: Her Majesty's Stationery Office, 1988.

_____. *Henrietta Maria: the intrepid Queen*. Owings Mills, MD: Stemmer House, 1991.

_____. *The Winter Queen: the life of Elizabeth of Bohemia, 1596-1662*. Edinburgh: Scottish National Portrait Gallery, 1998.

Maurer, Helen. "Margaret of Anjou." *Ricardian Register*, Winter 1997, 4-5.
[available online at www.r3.org]

_____. "Whodunit: the suspects in the case." *Ricardian Register*, Summer 1983, 4-27. [available online at www.r3.org]

Merten, Klaus. *German castles and palaces*. [No Place Given]: Vendome Press, 1999.

Miller, John. *James II: a study in kingship* (rev. ed.). New Haven: Yale University Press, 2000.

Miller, Peggy. *James*. New York: St. Martin's Press, 1971.

Morris, Christopher. *The Tudors*. London and Glasgow: Fontana/Collins, 1973.

Mosley, Charles. *Blood royal*. Bournemouth: Smith's Peerage, 2002.

Munson, James. *Maria Fitzherbert: the secret wife of George IV*. New York: Carroll and Graf, 2001.

Nicholson, Robin. *Bonnie Prince Charlie and the making of a myth: a study in portraiture, 1720-1892*. Lewisburg: Bucknell University Press, 2002.

Oman, Carola. *Mary of Modena*. London: Hodder and Stoughton, 1962.

_____. *The Winter Queen: Elizabeth of Bohemia*. London: Phoenix Press, 2000.

Ormrod, W.M. *The reign of Edward III: crown and political society in England, 1327-1377*. New Haven: Yale University Press, 1990.

Owen, D.D.R. *Eleanor of Aquitaine: Queen and legend*. Oxford and Cambridge, Mass.: Blackwell, 1993.

Packe, Michael. *King Edward III*. (edited by L.C.B. Seaman). London and Boston: Routledge & Kegan Paul, 1983.

Pain, Nesta. *Empress Matilda: uncrowned Queen of England*. London: Weidenfeld & Nicolson, 1978.

_____. *George III at home*. London: Eyre Methuen, 1975.

_____. *The King and Becket*. New York: Barnes and Noble, 1966.

Patterson, Benton Rain. *Harold and William : the battle for England, A.D. 1064-1066*. New York, N.Y.: Cooper Square Press, 2001.

Plowden, Alison. *Lady Jane Grey: nine days Queen*. Stroud: Sutton, 2003.

Plumb, J. H. *The first four Georges* (reprint of 1956 edition). Boston: Little, Brown, 1975.

Pollard, A.J. *Richard III and the Princes in the Tower*. New York: St. Martin's Press, 1991.

Prestwich, Michael. *Edward I* (new ed.). New Haven: Yale University Press, 1997.

_____. *The three Edwards: war and state in England, 1272-1377*. New York: St. Martin's Press, 1980.

Public Record Office. *Royal portraits from the plea rolls: Henry VIII to Charles II*. London: Her Majesty's Stationery Office, 1974.

Quennell, Peter. *Caroline of England: an Augustan portrait*. New York: Viking Press, 1940.

Rees, David. *The son of prophecy : Henry Tudor's road to Bosworth* (2nd, rev. ed.). London: J. Jones, 1997.

Richardson, Geoffrey. *The popinjays: a history of the Woodville family*. Shipley, England: Baildon Books, 2000.

Reston, James, Jr. *Warriors of God: Richard the Lionheart and Saladin in the Third Crusade*. New York: Anchor Books, 2002.

Roberts, Jane. *The King's head: Charles I, King and martyr*. London: Royal Collection Enterprises, 1999.

Roll, Winifred. *The pomegranate and the rose: the story of Katharine of Aragon*. Englewood Cliffs, N.J.: Prentice-Hall, 1970.

Ross, Charles. *Edward IV* (new ed.). NewHaven: Yale University Press, 1997.

Saaler, Mary. *Edward II: 1307-1327*. London: Rubicon Press, 1997.

Saul, Nigel. *Richard II*. New Haven: Yale University Press, 1997.

Senior, Michael. *The life and times of Richard II*. London: Weidenfeld and Nicolson, 1981.

Seward, Desmond. *Henry V: the scourge of God*. New York: Viking, 1987.

_____. *The Wars of the Roses.* New York: Viking, 1995.

Simon, L. *Of virtue rare: matriarch of the House of Tudor.* Boston: Houghton Mifflin, 1982.

Sinclair-Stevenson, Christopher. *Inglorious rebellion: the Jacobite risings of 1708, 1715, and 1719.* New York: St. Martin's Press, 1971.

Smailes, Helen (Ed.). *The concise catalogue of the Scottish National Portrait Gallery.* Edinburgh: Trustees of the National Galleries of Scotland, 1990.

_____, and Thomson, Duncan. *The Queen's image: a celebration of Mary, Queen of Scots.* Edinburgh: Scottish National Portrait Gallery, 1987.

Smith, Alan G.R. (Ed.) *The reign of James VI and I.* New York: St. Martin's Press, 1973.

Smith, E.A. *George IV.* New Haven and London: Yale University Press, 1999.

Smith, Lacey Baldwin. *Henry VIII: the mask of royalty.* Chicago: Academy Chicago, 1982.

_____. *A Tudor tragedy: the life and times of Catherine Howard.* New York: Pantheon Books, 1961.

Smurthwaite, David. *The complete guide to the battlefields of Britain.* London: Michael Joseph, 1984.

Somerset, Anne. *The life and times of William IV.* London: Weidenfeld and Nicolson, 1980.

Speck, W.A. *Reluctant revolutionaries: Englishmen and the revolution of 1688.* Oxford and New York: Oxford University Press, 1988.

St. Aubyn, Giles. *The year of three Kings, 1483.* New York: Atheneum, 1983.

Starkey, David. *Elizabeth: the struggle for the throne.* New York: HarperCollins, 2001.

_____. *Six wives: the Queens of Henry VIII.* London: Chatto & Windus, 2003.

Strachey, Lytton. *Queen Victoria.* New York: Harcourt, Brace, and World, 1949.

Strickland, Agnes. *Lives of the Queens of England.* Boston: Brown and Taggard, 1860.

_____. *Lives of the Queens of Scotland and English Princesses connected with the regal succession of Great Britain.* New York: Harper and Brothers, n.d.

Strong, Roy C. *The cult of Elizabeth: Elizabethan portraiture and pageantry.* Berkeley: University of California Press, 1986.

_____. *Gloriana: the portraits of Queen Elizabeth I.* New York: Thames and Hudson, 1987.

Stuart, Dorothy Margaret. *Daughters of George III*. London: Macmillan, 1939.

Thackeray, William Makepeace. *The four Georges*. In *Roundabout papers*. New York: F.M. Lupton, n.d.

Tomalin, Claire. *Mrs. Jordan's profession: the actress and the Prince*. New York: Alfred A. Knopf, 1995.

Turner, Ralph V., and Heiser, Richard R. *The reign of Richard Lionheart: ruler of the Angevin empire, 1189-99*. New York: Longman, 2000.

Turton, Godfrey Edmund. *The dragon's breed: the story of the Tudors from earliest times to 1603*. London: Peter Davies, 1970.

Van der Kiste, John. *George III's children*. Far Thrupp, Stroud, Gloucestershire: A. Sutton, 1992.

_____. *King George II and Queen Caroline*. Stroud, Gloucester: Sutton, 1997.

_____. *Queen Victoria's children*. Stroud, Gloucester: Alan Sutton, 1986.

Van der Zee, Henri and van der Zee, Barbara. *William and Mary*. New York, Knopf, 1973.

Waller, Maureen. *Ungrateful daughters: the Stuart princesses who stole their father's crown*. New York: St. Martin's Press, 2002.

Warnicke, Retha M. *The marrying of Anne of Cleves: royal protocol in early modern England*. New York: Cambridge University Press, 2000.

Warren, W.L. *Henry II*. Berkeley: University of California Press, 1973.

_____. *King John*. Berkeley: University of California Press, 1978.

Watts, John Lovett. *Henry VI and the politics of Kingship*. Cambridge: Cambridge University Press, 1996.

Waugh, Scott L. *England in the reign of Edward III*. Cambridge and New York: Cambridge University Press, 1991.

Wedgwood, C.V. *A coffin for King Charles: the trial and execution of Charles I*. New York: Time Incorporated, 1966.

_____. *The sense of the past* [originally titled *Truth and opinion*]. New York: Collier Books, 1967.

Weir, Alison. *Britain's royal families: the complete genealogy* (new edition). London: Pimlico of Random House, 2002.

_____. *The children of Henry VIII*. New York: Ballantine Books, 1996.

_____. *Eleanor of Aquitaine: a life*. New York: Ballantine Books, 2000.

_____. *Elizabeth the Queen*. London: Jonathan Cape, 1998.

_____. *The Princes in the Tower*. New York: Ballantine, 1994.

_____. *The six wives of Henry VIII*. New York: Grove Weidenfeld, 1991.

Wigram, Isolde. "Were the 'Princes in the Tower' murdered?" [available online at http://www.r3.org/bookcase/misc/wigram01.html]

Williams, Neville. *The life and times of Elizabeth I*. New York: Cross River Press, 1992.

_____. *The life and times of Henry VII*. London: Weidenfeld and Nicolson, 1973.

_____. *Royal homes of Great Britain from medieval to modern times*. London: Lutterworth Press, 1971.

Wilson, Derek. *The King and the gentleman: Charles Stuart and Oliver Cromwell, 1599-1649*. New York: St. Martin's Press, 1999.

Wolffe, Bertram. *Henry VI* (new ed.). New Haven: Yale University Press, 2001.

Ziegler, Philip. *King William IV*. New York: Harper & Row, 1973.

Zvereva, Alexandra. *Les clouet de Catherine de Médicis: chefs-d'oeuvre graphiques du Musée Condé*. Paris: Somogy Éditions d'Art, 2002.

Indexes

Index of Place Names

Index of Personal Names

978-0-595-37312-

0-595-37312-7

Printed in the United States
40402LVS00001B/147-152